Peasant and Nation

A CENTENNIAL BOOK

One hundred books
published between 1990 and 1995
bear this special imprint of
the University of California Press.
We have chosen each Centennial Book
as an example of the Press's finest
publishing and bookmaking traditions
as we celebrate the beginning of
our second century.

UNIVERSITY OF CALIFORNIA PRESS

Founded in 1893

Peasant and Nation

The Making of Postcolonial Mexico and Peru

FLORENCIA E. MALLON

University of California Press

BERKELEY   LOS ANGELES   LONDON

University of California Press
Berkeley and Los Angeles, California

University of California Press, Ltd.
London, England

A different version of the materials contained in chapter 3 appears in
Heather Fowler Salamini and Mary Kay Vaughan, eds., *Creating Spaces,
Shaping Transition: Women of the Mexican Countryside, 1850–1990*
(Tucson: University of Arizona Press, 1994).

The materials on Cajamarca contained in chapter 7 appeared earlier in
Steve J. Stern, ed., *Resistance, Rebellion, and Consciousness in the
Andean Peasant World, Eighteenth to Twentieth Centuries* (Madison:
University of Wisconsin Press, 1987).

Sections of the arguments in chapters 1, 3, 4, and 9 appear in a different
formulation in Gilbert Joseph and Daniel Nugent, *Everyday Forms of
State Formation: Revolution and the Negotiation of Rule in Modern
Mexico* (Durham: Duke University Press, 1994).

Library of Congress Cataloging-in-Publication Data

Mallon, Florencia E., 1951–
  Peasant and nation : the making of postcolonial Mexico and Peru /
Florencia E. Mallon
    p.   cm.
  "A Centennial Book"—P.
  Includes bibliographical references and index.
  ISBN 0-520-08504-3 (alk. paper). — ISBN 0-520-08505-1
(alk. paper ; pbk.)
  1. Mexico—Politics and government—19th century.
  2. Peru—Politics and government—1829–1919.
  3. Peasantry—Mexico—History—19th century.
  4. Peasantry—Peru—History—19th century.   5. Political
culture—Mexico—History—19th century.   6. Political
culture—Peru—History—19th century.
  7. Nationalism—Mexico—History—19th century.
  8. Nationalism—Peru—History—19th century.   I. Title.
F1231.5.M34   1995
972'.04—dc20   93-34677
                                                          CIP

Printed in the United States of America
9 8 7 6 5 4 3 2 1

For Steve, enduring source of inspiration;
and
for Ramón and Ralph, who root me to each unfolding day.

When you play the fiddle at the top of the state, what else
is to be expected but that those down below dance?

Karl Marx

There are many stories,
Both old and new;
What is true?

Ziggy Marley and the Melody Makers

The publisher gratefully acknowledges the contribution provided by the General Endowment Fund of the Associates of the University of California Press.

Contents

Maps

Preface

This book attempts the comparative archaeology of popular political cultures in Mexico and Peru (see maps 1 and 2), and the reinsertion of those cultures into so-called national political history. Having worked on this project for the past twelve years, I have learned through experience how difficult and daunting such a task can be. Had I known at the outset what I know now, I might well have decided to work on something different. I'm glad I did not know.

To bring this book to fruition, I had to accomplish four large tasks beyond the actual comparative archival research. First, I had to learn enough about the historiography of Mexico, a new region for me, to allow me to make a coherent contribution to existing debates. Second, I found I needed to learn enough about postmodernism and poststructuralism—and their use in the fields of anthropology and literary criticism—so that I might do a credible job of analyzing popular political cultures and discourses. Third, I needed to rethink existing historical and theoretical categories on nationalism and state formation. And fourth, I found it necessary to rethink the art and method of comparison so that it became possible to compare widely differing case studies and types of data.

I have accomplished none of these tasks to my own satisfaction. When first engaging the historiography on nineteenth-century Mexico, I felt like a bibliographical extraterrestrial. I often made mistakes because I was not familiar with the region's most elementary historiographical rules. Sometimes, though, I found that my lack of knowledge could also be a strength. I asked new questions because I was operating from a different set of assumptions, because I had not yet learned the ways of the nineteenth-century Mexicanist. This was not always the best historian's etiquette, and it has made it more difficult for me to engage effectively or intelligently the work of specialists much more knowledgeable than myself. But it may be easier for neophytes to ask fresh questions. With all the attendant costs and benefits, then, switching research specializations has extended my tenure as a neophyte.

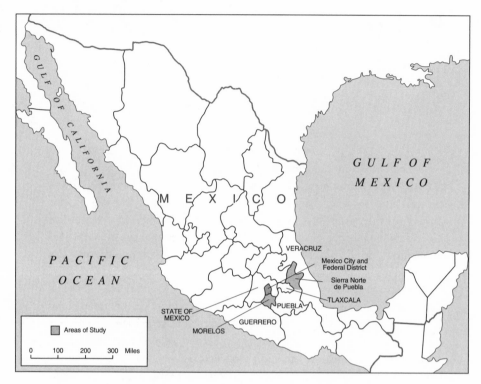

Map 1. Mexico and the general area of study

Engaging postmodernism and poststructuralism, too, produced mixed results. Selective reading has made my understanding of social movements, political structures, and popular culture much more flexible, contingent, and dynamic. Yet two characteristics of the postmodern literature have also proved significant stumbling blocks. First, I have found the language and jargon prohibitive, not only in the reading but, more important, in the writing. Second, much postmodernism is distressingly ahistorical. Language and discourse seem to exist outside time and outside the people and the sociopolitical struggles that used, transformed, and produced them.

My readings on nationalism and state formation yielded contradictions as well. I found that the most theoretically and conceptually engaging works were not by historians and did not deal with Latin America. How easily or legitimately could I transfer their frameworks or perceptions? How effectively could I institute dialogues across disciplinary and regional boundaries? And, especially since my main audience consisted of historians of Latin America, how much space could I give to a discussion of other works without seeming to engage in academic name-dropping?

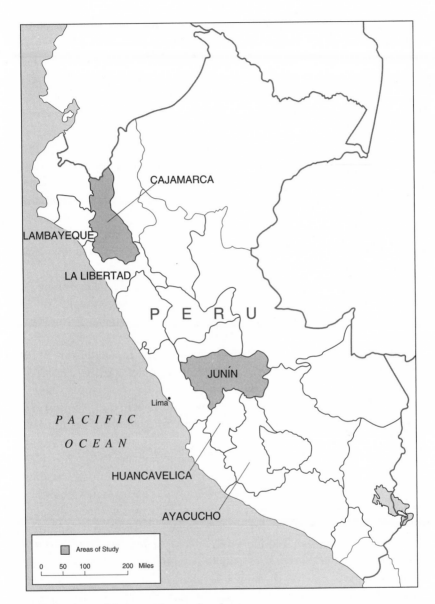

Map 2. Peru and the general area of study

A final question that emerged during the writing had to do with the nature of my comparisons. At first I struggled mightily to make the comparison equal: for every chapter on Mexico, one on Peru; for every treatment of one region, equal time for the other three. It simply did not work. The book that has emerged is the one I needed to write to make sense of my data, rather than the ideal book into which I tried to cram my materials. Thus, Peru is treated more lightly than Mexico, and Morelos more lightly than the Sierra Norte de Puebla. By the time I finished I did not consider this apparent imbalance a liability. In fact, I had decided that perfectly symmetrical comparisons were either impossible or were an illusion created by their author. This reflection is meant to prepare the reader for the asymmetries that follow.

One of my most important goals in this book is to communicate to the reader some of the excitement I experienced through theoretical and methodological engagement while at the same time producing a readable and historically sensitive text. I am not sure I have always negotiated the pitfalls successfully. But I console myself with the knowledge that my struggles with language, theory, and methodology have improved the substance and depth of my work. I offer it with clear knowledge of its imperfections but also with excitement about its accomplishments.

My analysis starts from a relatively simple premise. At the beginning of Latin America's postcolonial history, Mexico and Peru were roughly comparable. They had been the great centers of pre-Columbian indigenous civilizations and of Spanish imperial rule. They had the richest silver mines, the wealthiest colonial elites, and the largest indigenous populations in all of Spanish America. Both countries entered the so-called national period in political disarray, and each faced a good half-century of civil war before efforts at political stabilization began to take hold. In both cases, too, foreign intervention and occupation interrupted these first promising attempts at state formation.

Despite these broad similarities, however, Mexico's and Peru's paths had diverged dramatically by the first decades of the twentieth century, certainly by the 1930s. What happened? This book provides a partial answer to this question by analyzing popular movements and discourses during the second half of the nineteenth century. Even as these movements and discourses were repressed, defeated, and submerged by elite statemakers, they marked each country's political structures and future potential. In effect, the differential outcome of nineteenth-century struggles in Mexico and Peru limited twentieth-century options. I aim to demonstrate that present-day citizens in both countries still live with the consequences of nineteenth-century events.

I hasten to emphasize, however, that my book only partially explains the differences between Mexico and Peru. If the structures that limit options for historical actors are themselves the embedded results of previous human agency, of contingent choices among earlier options, then nineteenth-century actors were just as bound by earlier events as are people in the twentieth century. Indeed, the interaction between structure and human agency, between contingent choice and bounded alternatives, occurs in an ongoing, unending chain in which the outcomes of previous struggles and dynamics are constantly affecting present and future conflicts and contingencies.[1] In Mexico and Peru, this chain also stretches backward from the nineteenth century into the colonial period. I provide some of the relevant colonial background in chapter 1.

The organization of the book reflects my struggles with theoretical, methodological, and empirical concerns. After an initial theoretical chapter in which I lay out my new approach to nationalism and popular political culture and provide some general historical context for Mexico and Peru, the rest is divided into three parts. The first part treats only the Sierra de Puebla, in central Mexico, because this is the case for which I discovered the richest archival materials. I therefore develop my perspectives on popular nationalism, community politics, and alternative nationalist discourses in initial dialogue with the Sierra de Puebla materials.

Part 2 expands to include my other three case studies. First I test the hypotheses developed for Puebla against the materials available for Morelos, Mexico, and Junín, Peru. In the seventh chapter I bring together all four cases, including Cajamarca, Peru, to examine the limits as well as the dynamics of popular nationalism.

Part 3 takes a broad comparative view of Mexico and Peru, exploring the differences in historical and political processes in both countries. Chapter 8 examines the distinct legacies of repression, while chapter 9 analyzes local intellectuals in both countries. Chapter 10 summarizes my findings and reaches some general conclusions.

In the context of politics and military struggle, all the way from the community to the evolving "national" level, women do not play a visibly central role in the drama that unfolds in this book. Sometimes gaining access to what women did, thought, or argued was a feat of historical imagination. Sometimes it was either impossible or the result of blind luck. Yet the category of gender—understood as the social construction of sexual difference and its use in the organization of power relations—is crucial to the story. It organizes hierarchies among men, and between young and old, as much as between women and men. Especially in periods of rapid social and political change, it is a reliable if contentious script to which all can turn.

Finally, a few words about the painting reproduced on the cover of this book. I saw the original of Diego Rivera's *Paisaje Guerrillero—El Zapatista* (1915) in Mexico City in 1985, at an exhibition of his cubist paintings sponsored by the Museo Nacional de Arte. Painted while he lived in Paris, before his muralist period, *Paisaje Guerrillero* is one of the only cubist canvases Rivera painted on a Mexican theme. It was the first painting I saw as I walked into the exhibition, and I knew immediately that it had to be the illustration for my cover. Though clearly a Mexican figure, the stylized quality of the cubist guerrilla suggested the commonalities among peasant rebels who, throughout Latin America, struggled for justice and political inclusion during the nineteenth century. Specifically for Mexico, although I was only halfway through my research at that time, I already suspected that the communitarian and popular Liberalisms whose origins I was tracing had been a direct inspiration for the popular strands of revolutionary ideology that had emerged after 1910. Reproducing a Zapatista guerrilla on the cover seemed the most direct statement I could make regarding these various connections and reverberations.

Recent events have only increased the painting's relevance to my book's subject matter. By taking Zapata as their symbol of popular justice, the indigenous guerrillas in Chiapas have extended the relevance and resonance of the communitarian and radical strands in Mexican popular culture. My argument in this book provides, I think, some historical background on where those strands came from, and why they still matter.

Acknowledgments

This book has been a long time in the making, and I have incurred numerous debts to people and institutions for the support that made it possible. You all know who you are; please accept my heartfelt thanks. Limitations of space make it impossible to thank you all individually.

I have been fortunate to receive support from a wide variety of sources, not only to do the research contained herein but to take the time off in order to organize and write up the results. My original Peruvian research was funded by a postdoctoral research grant under the auspices of the Latin American and Caribbean Program, Social Science Research Council, and American Council of Learned Societies. The Fulbright Faculty Research Abroad Program, Department of Education, funded my stay in Mexico in 1984–1985. I organized and sorted my materials with the help of a fellowship at the Institute for Research in the Humanities, University of Wisconsin–Madison. I began writing with the help of an H. I. Romnes Fellowship from the Research Committee of the Graduate School at the University of Wisconsin–Madison. The bulk of the book was written while I was a fellow at the Center for Advanced Study in the Behavioral Sciences (1990–1991). I am grateful to the staff at the Center, as well as to the National Endowment for the Humanities, for providing me with material and moral support during that crucial year.

The staffs at all the archives and libraries I have used—in Peru, Mexico, and the United States—have been encouraging and helpful. They took the extra time to find an obscure reference or expended the extra energy to reach the especially heavy box and bring it down from the second floor. In some cases, such as in the municipalities of the Sierra de Puebla or other business offices, staff shared their desks and answered seemingly pointless questions. Sometimes they stayed past closing hours because I was trying to finish an especially important document. Limitations of space prevent me from thanking each person separately. The following is a partial list of the archives and collections used.

For Peru, I list only the repositories I visited again in 1981: Archivo Departamental de Cajamarca; Archivo Histórico-Militar (Lima); Biblioteca Nacional del Perú, Sala de Investigaciones and Archivo Piérola. In Mexico: Archivo de la Secretaría de la Defensa Nacional; Archivo de la Secretaría de Relaciones Exteriores; Archivo del Congreso del Estado de Puebla; Archivo del Instituto Nacional de Antropología e Historia; Archivo General de la Nación; Archivo General de Notarías del Estado de Puebla; Archivos Históricos Municipales de Chignahuapan, Zacapoaxtla, Tetela de Ocampo (Sierra de Puebla); Biblioteca Nacional (Mexico City); Centro de Estudios para la Historia de México–Condumex. In the United States: the Bancroft Library at the University of California–Berkeley; the Library at the Center for Advanced Study in the Behavioral Sciences; and the Rare Documents Collection at Memorial Library, University of Wisconsin–Madison.

To list the networks of friends and colleagues who have helped and encouraged me over the past ten years would require a separate volume. In Peru, ongoing friendships and relationships have motivated me to continue confronting that country's painful reality: Alberto Flores Galindo, whose premature death from brain cancer was a crushing loss for many of us; Nelson Manrique; my goddaughter Claudia Mateo Ortega; and Willy Rochabrún and Teresa Oré. In Mexico, friends eased my transition toward a partial understanding of that country's complex culture and history: Roger Bartra and Josefina Alcazar; Leticia Reina; Donna Rivera Moreno; María Dolores Huerta Jaramillo. Colleagues and audiences across the United States—at Harvard, Princeton, Middlebury, Yale, Chicago, Marquette, Illinois, Iowa, San Diego, Irvine, and Stanford; and at numerous panels at American Historical Association meetings since 1987—have listened to parts of the argument I was developing in this book. Their praise and criticisms have motivated me to continue and to make my analysis stronger. And last but not least, I thank the graduate students in Latin American history at the University of Wisconsin–Madison. I never tire of saying that their questions keep me honest and keep me growing. Their comments on chapters and ideas in the manuscript, both in seminar and outside of it, have been consistently the most challenging and thought-provoking. I also wish to thank my project assistants Sarah Chambers, Andy Daitsman, and Patrick McNamara for their help with transcriptions, bibliography, and editing.

People providing help on each end of this project also deserve special mention. I wrote the first draft of my introductory chapter in fall 1989 in the context of my graduate seminar on state and society in the Third World. The students in that seminar, both in the general discussions of readings and in their specific comments on my chapter draft, proved a real inspiration to me. I hope finally to have lived up to their challenge to find my own voice.

The three people handling my book at the University of California Press have made up an exemplary production team. My editor, Eileen McWilliam, has been a model of support and sensitivity. The project's director, Tony Hicks, has been patient and efficient throughout. And Dan Gunter, my copyeditor, has been truly inspiring; at times he accomplished gravity-defying acts by rescuing my metaphors from terminal dangling! Finally, for drawing the maps and generously funding the work involved therein, I thank the Cartographic Lab at the University of Wisconsin, and especially Onno Brouwer.

For reading specific chapters and for providing me with general support and stimulating intellectual conversation, I would like to thank Jeanne Boydston, Suzanne Desan, Steven Feierman, Ramón Gutiérrez, Allen Hunter, Stanlie James, Mary Layoun, Gerda Lerner, Nellie McKay, Kathleen Much, and Francisco Scarano. For friendships that started even before this book was born: Marjorie Becker, Marisol de la Cadena, Steven Hahn, Gilbert Joseph, Brooke Larson, Linda Newman, Karen Spalding, and Barbara Weinstein. For caring above and beyond the call of duty in recent years: Jane Hemeon, Dorothy Watson, and Rosemary Zurlo-Cuva. At the Center for Advanced Study in 1990–1991, reading and lunching groups of historians and social scientists were my anchor during that very creative and emotionally choppy year: Jeanne Altman, Jane Burbank, Fred Cooper, John D'Emilio, Larry Griffin, Wendy Griswold, Jacquelyne Hall, Carol Heim, Don Herzog, Jaromir Janousek, Bob Korstadt, Chuck Lawrence, Gaea Leinhardt, Larry Levine, Jim Oakes, John Padgett, Bill Sewell, and Steve Stern. For helpful, supportive, and challenging readings of an earlier draft of the manuscript: Charles Hale, Peter Klarén, John Tutino, and Arnold Bauer. Finally, to those additional people who wish to remain anonymous: thank you.

Obtaining the permission to reproduce Diego Rivera's painting on the cover, as well as a slide of the painting that was appropriate for reproduction, proved an arduous task. I am grateful to many people for their help. Thomas Gombar, Curator of the Slide and Photo Collection in the Department of Art History at the University of Wisconsin, provided the names and telephone numbers that made my first contacts possible. At the Museo Nacional de Arte, the Director, Maestra Graciela de Reyes Retana, and Licenciada Blanca H. Olivares, Subjefe de Difusión, did the necessary paperwork to provide me with the permission and the slide. Licenciada Norma Rojas Delgadillo,

Director of Asuntos Jurídicos at the Instituto Nacional de Bellas Artes, expedited the legal side of the permission. At the most general level, of course, I am grateful to the Instituto Nacional de Bellas Artes and to the Museo Nacional de Historia for granting permission. But my deepest and most heartfelt thanks go to Licenciada Leticia Juárez González, Dirección General de Planeación, Oficina de la Presidencia de la República, Asesoría Técnica. At various points toward the end of the process, when I nearly had given up hope of success, Leticia Juárez provided the support, help and dedication that kept me going. I am convinced that without her the cover would not have been the same.

This book is dedicated to my husband, Steve J. Stern. Over a decade ago, when I was applying for a job at the University of Wisconsin, he took me out to lunch. He had just read a book on Mexico during the nineteenth century and was impressed by the similarities between what was described there and my forthcoming book on the Peruvian central highlands. He thought a comparison might be interesting: perhaps in the form of an article? This book is my answer to his initial question. Not only was he present at the original creation, but he has nurtured it—and me—all along the way.

My book is also dedicated to my sons, Ramón Joseph and Ralph Isaiah Mallon Stern. It is customary for an academic parent to praise her or his children for their patience, to ask their forgiveness for extended absences, and to promise that things will settle down once the book is out. I can do none of the above. My children have demanded their due in my life throughout and have (usually) received it. My absences have always been short, simply because I can't bear to be away any longer. Things will not settle down once the book is out, because both boys have already demanded that we spend more time in Latin America. What I can say is this: Letting go of this project is made especially momentous by the fact that I researched the Peruvian materials while carrying my first son and the Mexican data while carrying my second. They, too, were present at the creation.

1 Political History from Below

Hegemony, the State, and Nationalist Discourses

On a clear and frigid morning fifteen years ago, in the second-floor archive of the Prefectura of Junín, Nelson Manrique, Ludy Ugarte, and I uncovered the first in a group of striking documents. For the past several months we had been ordering the dusty and disorganized papers of the prefect's archive, located in the city of Huancayo in Peru's central sierra. As this series of letters and official reports emerged from the mass of paper, dirt, and animal excrement we worked with every day, we saw that they dealt with an ongoing peasant mobilization in the community of Comas both during and after the War of the Pacific (1879–1884). According to these documents, the residents of Comas had formed a guerrilla force to defend their region from protracted Chilean occupation. After the end of the war, they had expected to be rewarded for their service to the nation. Instead, they were accused of stealing cattle from neighboring haciendas and treated like common criminals. They consequently rebelled against the newly reconstituted central government, creating an "independent federation" that survived for nearly twenty years. Only in the first few years of the twentieth century did they finally surrender, victims of a bloody counterinsurgency campaign.[1]

Six months after our discovery, at a conference in the city of Ayacucho, Nelson Manrique and I began to understand its potential explosiveness. Listening to a presentation by Heraclio Bonilla in which he argued that Peru had lost the war with Chile precisely because the population had no interest in defending national territory and no notion of what that meant, we both had the same reaction. Incensed at Bonilla's lack of attention to and respect for existing forms of popular resistance and consciousness, we felt we had to use the materials discovered in the central highlands to challenge his conclusions. Manrique stood and summarized our findings in the central highlands archive. There began a debate that continued for many years, informing and shaping the work of the three historians involved in those initial confrontations.

The theoretical framework within which Bonilla placed his argument was, and among many scholars still is, the dominant vision of nationalism as an ideology created by the bourgeoisie, along with the internal market, in a society undergoing a successful transition to capitalism. In societies such as nineteenth-century Peru, where there was no consolidated bourgeoisie or internal market and certainly no successful transition to capitalism, there could be no developed nationalism. This was especially true among subordinate classes and ethnic groups, to whom nationalist ideology came only secondarily after having been elaborated by the bourgeoisie as one of its "historic tasks." Thus Bonilla explained Peru's easy defeat by Chile in the War of the Pacific: while Chilean soldiers were fighting for their country, which they understood in nationalist terms, Peruvians at best fought for a personalistic patron, and at worst allied themselves with the invaders against their class or ethnic enemies.[2]

For Manrique and myself, this perspective simply did not explain the documents we had been finding in the central sierra. The more we became involved in the data, the more supporting evidence we began to find, and the more we became convinced that the indigenous peasantry itself formed the backbone of the resistance to the Chileans in that region. Contrary to what Bonilla would have predicted, the landowners and merchants ultimately allied with the Chileans, wishing to end the invasion and the consequent raiding and destruction of their properties. So the subaltern classes of the region led the nationalist struggle, quite against the interests of the local dominant classes. But how to explain this seeming contradiction? Was it possible to theorize nationalism to take this eventuality into account?

We began, perhaps inevitably, by romanticizing the central sierra peasantry and its nationalism. In my earlier work I saw nationalist consciousness emerging out of the resistance itself, through specific confrontations with a foreign invader, and I narrated the development of this consciousness from a perspective sympathetic to the peasants themselves. Manrique proposed that the very intensity of events as experienced in the central sierra allowed for the rapid acceleration of historical time, permitting the peasants to formulate a nationalist ideology and consciousness that they would not have developed under "normal" circumstances. Neither of us was clear, however, on how broadly one could generalize from this case to understanding nationalism in the context of state consolidation. Unable to go beyond presenting the data and arguing for the reality of the nationalist feeling involved, we had used a case study to question a paradigm, but we could neither explode it nor theorize a new perspective.[3]

Two stumbling blocks stood in our path. The first was that a single example could not bear the weight of an entire new approach. If the case of Peru's central highlands was exceptional, it might prove the rule that peasants were generally incapable of formulating broader national projects. The second problem was that, even if the central sierra were not an exception, existing approaches to and definitions of nationalism were not adequate for explaining what we had found. Manrique and I began, quite independently, to explore comparative angles and to rethink our approaches to popular politics and nation-state formation.[4]

My comparative research carried me first into northern Peru and then to Morelos and Puebla in central Mexico. By the time the archival dust had cleared, I was convinced that the Peruvian central sierra was not a unique case. Of the four regions I had studied, three developed a form of peasant nationalism out of the national and international struggles affecting their countries in the second half of the nineteenth century. No longer was it possible, then, to reconstruct the more orthodox approaches to nationalism by pronouncing the Peruvian central sierra an exception. Instead, an entirely new formulation was necessary, one that accounted for the active participation and intellectual creativity of subaltern classes in processes of nation-state formation.

The challenge, in my view, was to conceptualize nationalism and nationalist consciousness as analytically separate from—though historically connected to—the politics of the triumphant nation-state. That such an analytical separation proved so difficult is a tribute to the massive power of European capitalism and colonialism. But it does not change the fact that, in much of the literature on nationalism, the nationalist story told by the winners of the eighteenth- and nineteenth-century scramble for world power has been served up as objective truth. In this version, nationalism was an integrated ideology whose proponents or believers put the interests of the nation—an already defined, integrated community with a territory, language, and accepted set of historical traditions—before the more divisive loyalties of region, class, family, or ethnic group.[5] And this was the yardstick held up to (or straitjacket forced on) any social group that ostensibly might or might not "have" nationalism or "be" nationalist: could such a loyalty be demonstrated to exist?

I have become convinced that few nineteenth-century social groups, whether in Latin America or elsewhere, could have passed this particular test. As an ex post facto construction of a much more complex history, this version of nationalism was offered precisely by the political factions that won the battles to control the nation-state. As such, it does little to help us understand the struggles themselves, since its very purpose was to enshroud and bury the various and multitudinous debates and confrontations that had gone on before. And this is indeed the second challenge that Nelson Manrique and I faced in our work on the central highlands: the need to reformulate our conceptions of nationalism so that we could understand the complex politics of rural nineteenth-century Latin America without subjecting political actors to ineffective or useless tests that obscured more than they explained.

My new formulation of nationalism, then, began from the realization that nationalism as such cannot be demonstrated to exist, precisely because there is no single "real" version. Instead, I began to see nationalism as a broad vision for organizing society, a project for collective identity based on the premise of citizenship—available to all, with individual membership beginning from the assumption of legal equality. Within such a broad vision there was much room for disagreement; thus, in any particular case, nationalism would become a series of competing discourses in constant formation and negotiation, bounded by particular regional histories of power relations. For Mexico and Peru, my entry was through the specific questions that emerged from comparative study, not only in the types of documents and events that needed analysis but also in the historiographical debates existing in each case. In both countries the form in which questions were asked about peasant participation depended on the very political histories of state formation I was investigating.

In Peru the lack of a successful national-bourgeois revolution was articulated to the perception that the Indian majority had been unable to comprehend, much less creatively engage, concepts of nation and nationalism. Some radical thinkers, influenced by *indigenista* currents in the 1920s, suggested that an Indian-based socialism could resuscitate indigenous collective traditions and connect them to European Marxism, thus solving Peru's national problem. Conservatives, often in tandem with a sector of indigenista thinkers and politicians, argued instead that the only solution was the triumph of European culture. The failure of the Peruvian nation could be traced back to the Conquest, they suggested, and to the legacy of Inca despotism and authoritarianism that made Indian society and culture impervious to individual creativity, innovation, and market forces.[6]

In Mexico the existence of a revolutionary liberal tradition framed the discussion. While campesinos or Indian peasants had clearly participated in the three great conflagrations of modern Mexican history—independence, the 1855 Liberal Revolution, and the 1910 Revolution—had they done so as more than cannon fodder? Could they actually build, or participate in, popular liberalism? Liberal historians and intellectuals associated with the official revolutionary party (Partido Revolucionario Institucional, or PRI) answered both questions with a resounding "yes." In fact, they argued that the aspirations of peasants for land and social justice had fueled all three revolutions and had been answered and realized by the postrevolutionary Mexican state. Starting in the 1970s, however, revisionist scholars in the post-Tlatelolco generation began to suggest a different reading of the same events, in which Indians and peasants were constantly repressed and expropriated by an ever more centralized state.[7]

What connected my four cases, in two such distinct national settings, was my common quest to excavate political history from below. Such a history, however, could no longer be a simple celebration of subaltern agency. While peasants and other rural folk actively struggled and thought in national terms, they never emerged as influential members of the political coalitions that took control of the state. Why did peasants and other subordinate groups participate so dramatically in the political and ideological formulation of national projects, consciously making alliances across classes, ethnic groups, even regions, yet at the same time never form part of the alliance in power? Answering this question forced me to rethink my whole approach to politics, including my understandings of class, gender, race, ethnicity, and the state. This book constitutes my reworking of what I have learned, with the purpose of theorizing a new approach that will, I hope, have implications beyond the cases for which it has been developed.

The common theoretical image throughout is that of decentering. To take seriously the intellectual and cultural history of indigenous peasants, we must decenter the concepts of intellectual and community. To understand the role of subaltern people in history, we must decenter our vision of the historical process. To comprehend political history from below, we must decenter our concepts of politics. To incorporate local complexity and contentiousness into our understanding of state formation, we must decenter our concept of the state. And to understand ideas of nation and nationalism from below, we must decenter theories of nationalism by deconstructing the twin myths of bourgeois and Western exceptionalism.

To decenter our analysis of nationalism, we might fruitfully begin with Benedict Anderson's image of the nation as an "imagined community."[8] "Imagining" means to create by using one's mind; it involves cultural, political, and intellectual construction. At least theoretically, anyone with an imagination can do it. Nationalism is, in this sense, a form of discourse—defined as the combination of intellectual and political practices that makes sense of events, objects, and relationships.

My use of the term *discourse* shares more with post-Marxist attempts to reformulate the work of Antonio Gramsci than with a poststructural emphasis on language. A discourse is a political as well as an intellectual process, because human struggles over power and meaning are intimately interconnected. Even if meanings are multiple and relational, hence always changing, people struggle with uneven access to power and knowledge in order to construct and tell their stories. Thus, the contingency and creativity of human imagining is conditioned by preexisting inequalities as well as by previous patterns of discursive practice. In making sense of these complex patterns of openness and closure, of agency and domination, I have found the concept of hegemony especially useful.[9]

Originally conceptualized by Antonio Gramsci as rule through a combination of coercion and consent, *hegemony* has since been defined in a variety of ways. I have found it necessary to go beyond equating hegemony with a belief in, or incorporation of, the dominant ideology. Instead, I will define hegemony in two distinct, though sometimes related, ways. First, hegemony is a set of nested, continuous processes through which power and meaning are contested, legitimated, and redefined at all levels of society. According to this definition, hegemony is hegemonic process: it can and does exist everywhere at all times. Second, hegemony is an actual end point, the result of hegemonic processes. An always dynamic or precarious balance, a contract or agreement, is reached among contesting forces. Because hegemonic processes have contributed to the emergence of a common social and moral project that includes popular as well as elite notions of political culture, those in power are then able to rule through a combination of coercion and consent.[10]

Using the first definition of hegemony, it is possible to analyze politics at all levels as nested arenas of contestation, where hegemonic processes are at work. In families, communities, political organizations, regions, and state structures, power is always being contested, legitimated, and redefined. Some projects, stories, or interpretations are winning out over others; some factions are defeating others. The interaction among different levels, locations, or organizations in a given society—say, between families and communities, communities and political parties, or regions and a central state—redefines not only each one of these political arenas internally but also the balance of forces among them.

In this constant, complex interaction among spaces of conflict and alliance, there are moments of greater change or transformation. These moments can be explained by analyzing the historical articulation of different hegemonic processes into a broader coalition or political movement. And it is here that the second definition of hegemony enters. The leaders of a particular movement or coalition achieve hegemony as an endpoint only when they effectively garner to themselves ongoing legitimacy and support. They are successful in doing so if they partially incorporate the political aspirations or discourses of the movement's supporters. Only then can they rule through a combination of coercion and consent and effectively bring about a "cultural revolution."[11]

The first definition of hegemony, therefore, is always useful in the analysis of processes of political conflict and alliance. The second, however, becomes useful only when a coalition achieves broader influence. Thus, a hegemonic process becomes a hegemonic outcome only when leaders partially deliver on their promises and control the terms of political discourse through incorporation as well as repression. Yet any outcome is precarious and unstable, subject once again to challenge and contestation.

Confusing process with outcome is doubly dangerous. In cases where a hegemonic outcome has been achieved, the contributions and struggles of subaltern groups will be reorganized and redefined, obfuscated and partially buried. In cases where hegemonic process has resulted in repression and violence, subaltern discourses and actions will simply disappear from the official story. In all cases the dynamic contributions of subaltern groups to the history of politics will be submerged and rearranged.

It seems particularly useful to apply these concepts of discourse and hegemony to our analysis of nationalism. If nationalism, as a form of imagining community, is an open-ended discourse, then why, according to most theories, does the imagining occur first and foremost in Europe? If the hegemonic practices around nationalism can involve a broad variety of social actors in an expanded discursive field, then why is nationalist ideology associated preferentially with the bourgeoisie? Answering these questions involves undoing what I have come to see as a triple knot: the historical tying together of democracy, nationalism, and colonialism.

Between the seventeenth century and the French Revolution, a new discourse of liberty and equality began to emerge in the world. This discourse arose, according to both Marxist and non-Marxist scholars, from a series of revolutions: the creation of a market economy; the rise of nation-states; the development of technology; and the formation of a world system—economic and political—through exploration and colonialism. Yet for most the stage for the "democratic revolution" was Western Europe.[12]

To transform our perspective on this democratic revolution, I wish to start from precisely the opposite assumption: to understand the play's central plot we need to place on center stage what has been relegated to the scenery and the wings. Recent work has made clear that a world system—with markets, technological and financial innovation, and widespread and sophisticated cultural experimentation—existed already in the thirteenth and fourteenth centuries, when Europe was still very much on the periphery. As relative newcomers to world commercial relations, Europeans competed fiercely in a system that was geographically and socially stacked against them. During the fifteenth and sixteenth centuries a series of historical events combined to give Europe—especially what Janet Abu-Lughod calls the "Atlantic rim" of Spain, Portugal, and Genoa—the edge over declining commercial powers in Africa, Asia, and the Middle East.[13]

Thus, the capitalist world system, central to the transformations that underwrote the democratic revolution, was itself the product of competition and restructuring within an already widespread system of cultural and economic exchange. The victory of Europe in this process was a contingent one, resting on the colonization of America and the emergence of the Atlantic trade system as dominant within the new world system. The concept of Western exceptionalism, resting partially on the idea that Europe built the first world system, must be seen as an official story, constructed by the people who won the commercial wars of the fifteenth and sixteenth centuries.

Further, what happened in Western Europe between the seventeenth and nineteenth centuries can be fully understood only with reference to the rest of the world. World trade, exploration, and conquest helped to buttress and extend the free-market system by facilitating the accumulations necessary for capitalist transition. The development of colonial mining and plantation economies in the Americas contributed to further innovations in technology and the organization of the labor process. Competition among European powers for broader markets and colonies, increased warfare, and the need to manage colonial struggles of various kinds fostered the development of the state. The concept of freedom was partially recast in dialectic with the concepts and relationships of "New World" slavery. The idea of nation, as an "imagined community," grew in relation to its opposite: colony.[14]

But that is not the way the story usually gets told. In the official story, markets, capitalism, democracy, nationalism, and all other inventions originated in Europe and thus legitimated and explained European hegemony in the world as a whole. A crucial piece in this transformation was orientalism, defined by Edward Said as the set of discursive practices that made non-Western peoples into simple and unchanging "others" and then academically defined their essence. According to Said, orientalism became a systematic school of thought during the second colonial expansion of the nineteenth century, operating as the discursive mirror image of Western exceptionalism. Through the construction of colonized peoples as unchanging "others," Europeans also constructed discourses about themselves that privileged Europe as the original location of all innovation.[15] The democratic revolution was thus constructed as a European creation, and the development of democratic nation-states as the "historic task" of capitalism and the bourgeoisie.

In the story I wish to tell, the democratic revolution is the very process of tying together the triple knot of democracy, nationalism, and colonialism. Within this narrative the contradictory universality of capitalist, nationalist, and democratic discourses—of the "new" ideas of equality, nationality, and free market that supposedly applied to all—makes a great deal more sense. From the very beginning, the historical combination of democracy and nationalism with colonialism created a basic contradiction within national-democratic discourse. On the one hand, the universal promise of the discourse identified the potential autonomy, dignity, and equality of all peoples, and people, in the world. In practice, on the other hand, entire groups of people were barred from access to citizenship and liberty according to Eurocentric, class-, and gender-exclusionary criteria.[16]

This contradiction between promise and practice became a central tension in the historically dynamic construction of national-democratic discourses and movements, providing the space for struggles over their practice and meaning. Throughout the world between the eighteenth and twentieth centuries, the discourse of universal promise inspired struggles to break open the notion of citizenship. My book is precisely about such a moment, when Mexican and Peruvian peasants and other rural folk took up the challenge of national-democratic discourse and attempted to create their own version of a more egalitarian practice.[17]

Struggles over citizenship and liberty, attempts to expand and make real the universal promises of nationalism and democracy, can be understood as hegemonic processes. When subalterns engaged in conflict over power and meaning, they helped define the contours of what was possible in the making of nation-states. This approach helps us understand the contributions of popular politics and popular culture to the broad metanarratives of political history. Yet at the same time we must be careful not to focus excessively on hegemonic process. For if we lose track of power relations and their condensation in state structures, we will be unable to transcend the uncritical celebration of popular resistance.

The state, in this context, can best be understood as a series of decentralized sites of struggle through which hegemony is both contested and reproduced. State institutions are locations or spaces where conflicts over power are constantly being resolved and hierarchically reordered. Since these conflicts are never equal for all groups, in the long run they tend to reorder, reproduce, and represent relations as inequality and domination. Yet at the same time, because conflict is at the very core of the state, subaltern struggles are woven throughout the fabric of state institutions.[18]

Subaltern struggles themselves are not unified, transparent representations of popular culture. People give meaning to their experiences through the social and historical construction of multiple, crosscutting identities and power relations. Class relations—differences in wealth, work experience, and location in systems of production—help define and limit the contours of community and consciousness. Women and men give social meaning to sexual difference through gender relations, both between and within groups. Differences in power between the generations crosscut and help organize gender hierarchy. Ethnicity is the social construction of differences in color, culture, language, and dress; and in the context of specific class and gender systems, people historically define ethnic boundaries and identities in a three-way struggle: within and between ethnicities, and between the state and ethnic groups.[19]

In societies and in states, class, gender, and ethnic hierarchies are equally important in structuring and reproducing systems of domination. State structures combine these enduring hierarchies and power differences, through daily conflict and contingency, to construct and reconstruct a "pact of domination." The state can and does take different roles vis-à-vis inter- or intragroup ethnic, class, and gender conflicts, depending on its own interests in social control, reproduction, and security. And this complexity of overlapping conflicts, identities, and hierarchies contributes to the reproduction of a pact of domination, conceptualized best as a network of interlocking forms of power.[20]

Viewed from below, the historical construction of a pact of domination involves subalterns as conscious actors rather than simply as those acted upon. Such a perspective, however, works only if we also rethink our view of rural communities and of peasant intellectual history. Too often peasants and other rural folk have been seen as acting only on the urging of their stomachs. A political history from a subaltern perspective must also take seriously the intellectual history of peasant action. This means, on the one hand, breaking down the artificial division between analyst as intellectual and peasant as subject—understanding analysis as a dialogue among intellectuals. And it means, on the other hand, rethinking our concepts of the rural community so that it is no longer "a given society- or culture-outside-of-history but . . . a political association formed through processes of political and cultural creation and imagination."[21] Let us begin with an exploration of the concept of the rural community.

Many analysts of rural history and peasant politics have shared an undifferentiated view of the rural community. Identities were stable and given, and communities were endowed with a primordial unity and collective legitimacy that did not need to be explained. In this context, political action was simply the representation, in the political sphere, of this unproblematic collective identity. Once such an approach was found wanting, however, the tendency was to discard the concept of community politics altogether. Political action became the province of village elites, who did not represent the interests of their fellow villagers; community institutions were seen as disciplining individuals to obey the rules established by elites.[22]

Neither approach to communal politics, or to counterhegemonic politics more broadly, is sufficient. While romantic notions of "the community" are not helpful in explaining the complexity and contradiction of rural conflict, it is still true that counterhegemonic collective identities do sometimes emerge from and contribute to social movements. While it is no longer possible to celebrate the unblemished heroism of popular struggle, smaller and even more impressive heroisms do stand out in the historical record as subaltern people have overcome divisions among themselves to take a collective political stand. Under such conditions the challenge for those of us wanting to understand popular political culture and action is to develop approaches that make visible both the hierarchy and the heroism, the solidarity and the surveillance. My starting point in meeting this challenge has been the concept of *communal hegemony*.

The idea of communal hegemony begins from the complexity and hierarchy of communal social and political relations. Even without identifiable social classes, the supposedly primordial unity of the community was based on kinship and its legitimacy on the figure of the father. Indeed, both gender and ethnic conflicts and hierarchies were worked out and reordered on the terrain of kinship and generational authority. Differences in wealth, too, were perceived within categories that emphasized lineage, ethnic identity, and generational status.[23]

Rural communities were never undifferentiated wholes but historically dynamic entities whose identities and lines of unity or division were constantly being negotiated. The discourses of gender and ethnicity combined and wove together a series of struggles and transformations. While there were periods of greater change or continuity, the creation and transformation of the sociopolitical identities associated with the community were part of an open-ended process that never achieved closure.

If these apparently unchanging communal entities were historically contingent constructions, neither the colonial encounter nor the transition to capitalism transformed a tabula rasa. Instead, colonialism, nationalism, and capitalism added new possibilities to an already dynamic and complex discursive field. Our challenge is to understand how the multiple discourses of gender, race, ethnicity, and, increasingly, class interacted and were transformed and rebuilt historically, in the context of particular social formations, conditioned by the particular practices of the people involved.

The people who led the process of discursive transformation were local intellectuals. In the villages, local intellectuals were those who labored to reproduce and rearticulate local history and memory, to connect community discourses about local identity to constantly shifting patterns of power, solidarity, and consensus. Political officials, teachers, elders, and healers— these were the ones who "knew," the ones to whom the community would turn in times of change or crisis, the ones who provided mediation with the outside. They supervised communal hegemonic processes, organizing and molding the different levels of communal dialogue and conflict into a credible consensus. As with any process of hegemony, of course, conflict and dialogue did not occur under conditions of equal access to power and knowledge; in fact, local intellectuals had greater access to both than did most villagers. But at the same time, community leaders and elites needed to demonstrate a commitment to the good of the collectivity and to formulate a discourse about local history, politics, and needs that would convince a broad sector of the village to give them their support. Local notables and village intellectuals spoke for the villages, then, not because they represented them or took advantage of them in some pure way but because a local political coalition had been built through processes of inclusion and exclusion.[24]

The period of the national-democratic revolution provided an unusually challenging opportunity for local intellectuals. During a moment of deep rupture and transition between more hierarchically structured social, cultural, and political orders, struggles between old and new, high and low, powerful and powerless became particularly intense and fluid. Indeed, this historical opening greatly facilitated and made more flexible the interplay between power structures and human agency, between hegemony and counterhegemony, between the accumulated discursive practices of the past and the constant new possibilities afforded by shifting fields of discourse. In the context of a new world system, the construction of a universalistic democratic ideal was imbued with deep contradictions in its exclusionary practice. New discursive elements were fixed and others set free. People throughout the world struggled, with changing degrees of consciousness and uneven effectiveness, to hegemonize diverse combinations of the discursive elements and practices available to them.[25]

The tensions and contradictions in national-democratic discourse were worked out historically and politically in three broad stages. The first was the moment in which the possibility of a national-democratic project emerged for a particular society; Partha Chatterjee calls this the "moment of departure."[26] New conjunctures of struggle and rebellion opened the way for potentially new hegemonic coalitions. In such a political opening, different possible projects or discourses emerged to compete for influence in the emerging balance of power.

The process of competition, which often—but not necessarily—took the form of violent conflict, constituted the second period. Chatterjee calls this the "moment of manoeuvre," during which new elites emerged as dominant in a national alliance through the "mobilization of the popular elements in the cause of [a democratic] struggle and, at the same time, a distancing of those elements from the structure of the state." Harnessing popular energy and creativity was central to the success of this maneuver, because only by utilizing the strength and dynamism of popular politics and culture could something new be created. Once used, however, subaltern movements would be politically excluded from the coalition in power and partially marginalized from the official version constructed about the struggle that had just ended.[27]

This repression, exclusion, and marginalization constituted the third period, which Chatterjee calls the "moment of arrival." At this point a national-democratic discourse deemphasized radical rupture. It became "a discourse of order, of the rational organization of power . . . not only conducted in a single, consistent, unambiguous voice, [but also] . . . glossing over all earlier contradictions, divergences and differences."[28] At this point, in fact, the earlier conflicts were constructed as a process of natural evolution, supervised by the dominant groups whose "historic task" it was to bring about national unity.

A satisfactory historical analysis of nationalist movements all over the world must therefore come to grips with how the struggle between a universal national-democratic promise and a Eurocentric, patriarchal, and exclusionary practice worked itself out in each particular case. If we apply this perspective to the original debate among Bonilla, Manrique, and me about Peruvian peasants and the War of the Pacific, it becomes clear that the search for evidence of a predefined nationalist ideology in the behavior of different classes and social groups will always be fruitless. Instead, within an open discursive field and with a constant eye for the interaction of structures and human action, we need to ask the following questions: What mobilizing effect does the universal promise of a national-democratic project have on different subaltern groups within a particular society or social formation? When and how do the colonial, patriarchal, and hierarchical underpinnings of nationalist discourse end up justifying the repression of the more radical forms of the national-popular? Finally, how are "the marks of disjuncture . . . suppressed" to create a unitary, rational, and linear account of historical development? At every point in the analysis we also need to ask how structures, as the embedded results of previous human action and struggles over meaning, condition and limit the possible outcomes of new action; and how new actions, struggles, and alliances modify and condition the reproduction of structures.[29] This, in short, is the kind of historical "archaeology" to which all nationalist movements must be subjected; and this, with all inevitable contradictions and limitations, is what I propose to do for nineteenth-century Mexico and Peru.

In Latin America the "long nineteenth century" between 1780 and 1930 was the period of the "democratic revolution," during which Latin Americans experienced and struggled with the twin processes of transition to capitalism and nation-state creation. Two massive upheavals in the Andes and Saint Domingue, in the 1780s and 1790s respectively, initiated deep crises of hegemony in the mature colonial empires. Alliances of colonized peoples rose up to question the colonial order and actively imagine alternative utopias. This initial challenge continued through the upheavals associated with independence between 1810 and 1825. Autonomy gave way to generalized civil war through midcentury and renewed efforts at state consolidation and economic development between 1850 and 1900. The general strengthening of states and national economies between 1910 and 1940 brought the period of nation-state formation to an end; for better or worse, the contemporary Latin American countries existed in recognizable form.[30]

Mexico and Peru started the "long nineteenth century" as privileged centers of Spanish colonial rule. They were home to the largest indigenous populations and the most enduring indigenous cultures in the Americas. By 1940, however, they inhabited diametrically opposed sides of the spectrum, at least in terms of the hegemonic construction of a nation-state.

In Mexico a popular revolution beginning in 1910 resulted in a stable one-party state, where the ruling revolutionary party had institutionalized the incorporation of the popular sectors, carried out a massive agrarian reform, and set the basis for the participation of the state in the economy and in negotiations between capital and labor. That this political system was not a democracy would become increasingly clear in the 1960s and 1970s; but the struggles within and outside the Mexican state had, between 1910 and 1940, successfully created and reproduced a national-populist discourse around which to articulate a hegemonic political alliance.[31]

In Peru, by contrast, in 1940 the state was still precariously perched on a series of negotiated convergences between a coastal bourgeoisie and various highland regional elites. A variety of opportunities had presented themselves, between 1910 and 1940, for a new political alliance to hegemonize state power around a more national-populist, inclusive core. The two most notable of these occurred in the early 1920s with Augusto Leguía and the indigenista movement and again in the 1930s and early 1940s with the rise of populist and working-class parties. Yet these openings had generally ended in repression. With the exception of occasional attempts by presidential candidates to court the Lima working classes, no political alliance or effort to hegemonize a national-popular discourse had reached successfully into the diverse and rich popular traditions and practices of the country's subaltern classes. Thus, in Peru, despite elections that were contests between competing political parties, popular political cultures had less presence in the formal political arena than they did in Mexico.[32]

A close analysis of the period between 1850 and 1910, during which the first serious efforts were made in both countries to construct nation-states around hegemonic national-democratic discourses, is absolutely central to understanding the divergent paths taken by the two countries in the twentieth century. Yet at the same time the two countries' colonial legacies, combined with different independence processes, conditioned what was possible between 1850 and 1910. Specifically for the late colonial transitions, we can contrast a colonial crisis in Mexico that led to an independence movement rooted in popular struggle with a Peruvian crisis that set off an early civil war in the 1780s, the repression of which doomed popular participation during independence itself.[33]

A broad popular movement in central Mexico, with a strong base in the Bajío mining region and in the villages of the center-south, initiated and backed the push for independence. Even though this movement was heavily repressed, some negotiation occurred with its major surviving leaders after 1821. In the first decades after independence, moreover, an emerging federalist faction inherited a connection to this surviving popular movement, and local or regional mediators found a place within the federalist movement. This faction did gain national power briefly in the late 1820s, facilitating the development of an alternative political culture at the local and regional levels. But it was only after 1855, when the Liberal Revolution brought the federalists to power once again, that it was possible to give a more consistent place to local issues, movements, and intellectuals in national politics. Indeed, the struggles around the Liberal Revolution and the French Intervention provided important new alternatives for local intellectuals, both in their local communities and in larger regional or even national coalitions.[34]

In Peru the great Andean civil war, under the leadership of Túpac Amaru, constituted an early and unsuccessful popular protonational movement. The intense repression that followed decimated the local indigenous intelligentsia and instilled deep caution among surviving village leaders and political factions. When independence occurred in Peru, it was essentially a top-down affair, orchestrated from outside by the armies of José de San Martín and Simón Bolívar. Guerrilla participation was the exception rather than the rule. In the postindependence period, struggles over state power were centered in Lima and surrounding coastal regions, deepening the rift between highlands and coast that had been a part of the colonial system of rule. The War of the Pacific dramatized the political fragmentation of Peruvian territory and the failure of national or regional leaders to connect to local intellectuals.[35]

Within these distinct contexts Mexican and Peruvian politicians and intellectuals faced a common quandary during the nineteenth century. Would it be possible to construct a nation, a community whose members were legally equal citizens, out of a society based on colonial regional divisions and ethnic hierarchies? In both cases liberals and conservatives debated the legal status and potential citizenship rights of the indigenous population. If under colonialism Indians had enjoyed a separate and protected status, as second-class citizens of an "Indian Republic," what would be appropriate for them in a postcolonial society?[36]

In both countries during much of the nineteenth century, despite a common belief among most elite politicians that Indians were backward, uneducated, and degenerate, indigenous peoples did have the formal right to vote. What suffrage meant in practice, however, varied greatly depending on local relations and coalitions. In some areas, as those opposed to universal manhood suffrage argued, Indian votes were bandied about as so much political currency by landowners or other regional power brokers. When village leaders, local intellectuals, and other mediators had greater success in constructing broadly popular or populist alliances, however, suffrage could become a more effective exercise of citizenship rights.

Under such conditions it is perhaps not surprising that liberalism, as a revolutionary ideology, gained more influence in Mexico. The 1855 Revolution built on the popular and federalist legacies of the 1810–1850 period and connected to surviving regional popular movements throughout the center-south. This broad articulation of the notions and practice of citizenship gave Mexican liberalism, itself an internally variable and contradictory discourse, a greater strength and potential for growth. In Peru, by contrast, the legacy of Túpac Amaru and of independence lived on in the fragmentation of political space and in the inability of local and village intellectuals to articulate broader coalitions. Suffrage, under these conditions, did not serve to broaden the exercise of citizenship rights but generally to reinforce the more powerful regional brokers in relation to the central state. Beyond the ideas and writings of a few educated individuals, then, liberalism as a revolutionary ideology would gain little influence in nineteenth-century Peru.

In Mexico and Peru after 1850, broadly similar national questions would thus be raised and answered in very different ways. These conflicts over nation-state formation form the main empirical focus of my book. In both countries international war interrupted internal processes of negotiation, mobilization, and conflict. In Mexico the Conservative party countered their defeat in the 1858–1861 civil war by inviting the French Intervention and the creation of a new monarchy with the Austrian archduke Maximilian as emperor. In Peru geopolitical and economic conflict over nitrate deposits resulted in the War of the Pacific and the military occupation of Peru by the Chilean army between 1881 and 1884. It was in these moments of national emergency, when international struggles intersected with internal processes of attempted unification, that the richest, most varied and open possibilities for maneuver and discursive practice occurred. And the actual unfolding of the conflicts, with their shifting discourses and alliances, also helped define the possibilities for success in the incorporation or neutralization of the more radical or popular alternatives.

In both countries the universal promise of a national-democratic project had intense mobilizing effects on rural subaltern classes, effects that were further deepened by the actual physical presence of a foreign army. The message was clear: it was necessary for all, regardless of class or ethnic background, to mobilize in defense of national territory. In so doing, people would become part of the nation-in-the-making and be granted the rewards of effective citizenship—participation, inclusion, and a portion of the spoils of victory. In all four regions that form the empirical base for my study—Cajamarca and Junín in Peru, Morelos and Puebla in Mexico—people responded to the call. In Junín, Morelos, and Puebla they organized irregular military forces on a village and communal basis and waged guerrilla war on the invaders. Called *montoneras* in Peru and national guards in Mexico, these irregular forces formed a sociopolitical space connecting local communal hegemonic practice to broader state apparatuses, especially the regular army.[37] And it was in this intermediate space, composed of discourse, structure, and action, that rural subalterns in all three areas constructed alternative national-democratic projects. In Cajamarca, where the intermediate space constructed by the montoneras was inhabited by an alliance of landowners, peasants, and merchants, control was in the hands of the landowners and merchants, and no alternative national-democratic discourse emerged.

Within the montoneras and national guards, subalterns struggled to create their own national-democratic vision. They used the notions of reciprocity, communal responsibility and accountability, and solidarity present in communal political culture to reinforce the universal promise of national-democratic discourse. Yet communal consensus was itself precarious, achieved through hegemonic process and coalition among a series of factions organized by lineage, generation, ethnicity, gender, and class. Not surprisingly, the possible outcomes in each case were varied and complex, offering a constantly changing panorama for articulation with other discourses and struggles in the society as a whole.

As communal discursive practices connected to the universality of the national-democratic promise, stretching the very edges of national-democratic discourse as a whole, the exclusionary practices within the national-democratic project began to come to the fore. In both countries the deepening fissures within the national-democratic alliance were papered over until the retreat of foreign troops was complete; but then the cracks opened violently. In the resulting civil wars the repression of the independent montoneras and national guards became the first priority. Indeed, the distancing of the popular elements from the reconstituting Mexican and Peruvian states was achieved, in the immediate postwar years, through blood and fire. Yet even in repression the different legacies and processes in Peru and Mexico would continue to construct distinct systems of rule.

In Mexico popular movements continued to ally with oppositional coalitions—most notably those led by Porfirio Díaz—through the 1870s. Even in the increasing authoritarianism and repression of the later Porfiriato, local intellectuals would guard village documents and memories and facilitate the survival of popular political cultures through 1910. The crisis of elite rule and ensuing civil war made possible, between 1910 and 1920, the reemergence of these broad popular movements. In the 1920s and 1930s the postrevolutionary state became hegemonic through the incorporation of a part of the popular agenda constructed from the 1850s.[38]

In Peru, by contrast, the Pierolista state of the 1890s repressed the popular project by recreating the colonial ethnic fragmentation of "divide and rule." For the first time since 1836 limitations on suffrage effectively barred indigenous peoples from voting. The maintenance of a system of representation by provinces, moreover, underwrote the preponderant influence of highland and rural elites within the central state. The Peruvian attempt to construct a national-democratic state was thus abandoned by 1900, with the re-creation of a system of ethnically and regionally fragmented dominance that rested on contingent alliances with distinct regional elites. The 1969 military revolution would be a final and tardy attempt to hegemonize a national-democratic discourse and rebuild the state. It, too, had failed by the mid-1970s.[39]

I do not wish to fall into a common error among historians, which is to argue that the period I study is *the* crucial juncture in understanding the entire process of the national-democratic revolutions. A decade of heavy archival work and theoretical reading pushes me precisely in that direction. But even as I resist the pressure, I must still insist that the popular democratic discourses constructed during the mid-nineteenth century, partially or completely repressed as they were in the following years, today still form a part of embedded memory and practice within popular political cultures. Recovering these discourses involves digging them out from under the dominant discourses that suppressed them, whether through the neocolonial "divide and rule" as in Peru or the successful construction of a hegemonic state as in Mexico. In both cases this recovery allows us to imagine more clearly how subaltern peoples might, after conquering the space to do so, create their own alternative polities.

A close examination of these popular democratic discourses will also help us to understand the Janus-faced, internally contradictory traditions and practices they represent. As the result of complex internal processes of struggle along gender, ethnic, and class lines, popular political cultures are both democratic and authoritarian, hegemonic and counterhegemonic. A central concern of my book is the understanding of popular politics as coalition, as a combination of domination and resistance, and as a powerful force in political change more generally.

And so a quest that began fifteen years ago, in a dusty archive, ends and begins again in the attempt to decenter our analysis of political history, rural communities, and national-democratic revolutions. The final layer of decentering must be, for me, the application of the concept of dialogue to my own relationship to the historical actors who inhabit my narrative. I recognize openly the many layers of the dialogue. As the one constructing the narrative, I have power over its form and over the images of the actors it contains. In a way I am tearing down official stories only to build up a new one. Yet my efforts will bear fruit only if I am willing to listen, to open my narrative to contending voices and interpretations, to struggle to avoid the role of the omniscient or positivistic narrator.[40]

I take some comfort in Raymond Williams's statement that "a lived hegemony is always a process. It is not, except analytically, a system or structure." In this sense we all contribute to and are complicit with a process over which we cannot establish control. The struggle to identify the discourses, actions, and relationships I excavate will itself become part of a hegemonic process. In this way I too am a link in the ongoing chain of human agency and structure I am analyzing. For, to quote Williams once again, "it is significant that much of the most accessible and influential work of the counter-hegemony is historical: the recovery of discarded areas, or the redress of selective and reductive interpretations." But as Williams also points out, the recovery of submerged or discarded discourses and debates makes little difference "unless the lines to the present . . . are clearly and actively traced."[41] This process of tracing connections—between myself and local intellectuals, between submerged and unsubmerged discourses, between what happened then and what happens now and in the future—places me squarely inside the struggles over power and meaning. I cannot stand outside or above them, and in any case I would not want to.

1

INDIGENOUS COMMUNITIES, NATIONAL GUARDS, AND THE LIBERAL REVOLUTION IN THE SIERRA NORTE DE PUEBLA

2 Contested Citizenship (1)

Liberals, Conservatives, and Indigenous
National Guards, 1850–1867

In March 1865 Simón Cravioto and his son Rafael, both prestigious leaders of the Liberal resistance against the French Intervention along the western side of the Puebla highlands, rode into Tulancingo to surrender to imperial officials (see map 3). Flanked by an honor guard of *plateados*, their allied bandit cavalry, and accompanied by the plateado leader Antonio Pérez, the Craviotos came to work out the final details of their agreement to end hostilities in the district and villages under their command. This agreement was the product of many months of negotiation during which Simón Cravioto had tried hard to preserve the family fortune, demanding from the emperor reparations of 132,000 pesos. In its final form it did nothing to compensate the family for their losses—which included, beyond properties and investments, the death of Rafael's brother Agustín—but it did preserve their dignity and honor, relegating them to exile, under house arrest, in Puebla city. Until the tide had turned noticeably against the empire a year and a half later, that is where the Craviotos would remain.[1]

Nearly a year later, in February 1866, another important resistance force in the central to eastern highlands also surrendered to the empire. Sitting among the charred ruins of what used to be the village of Xochiapulco, officers and soldiers together signed a collective document that reflected the communal decision-making process by which the local indigenous national guard unit had been run. For nearly two years, armed with little more than what they could strip from their fallen enemies, they had confronted the Interventionist forces. They had burned their own village to the ground rather than let it fall into enemy hands. But finally, facing exhaustion and a total lack of resources and ammunition, they had no alternative but to end the fighting. Tersely, with no expectation but a blood-soaked break in the war and no recognition of the legitimacy of the imperial government, all literate guerrillas signed; a mere six months later they would be back in the struggle.[2]

The variations in form and content of these two surrenders reflect deep differences in the organization, composition, and purpose of the Liberal movements based in the west and center-east of the Sierra de Puebla.

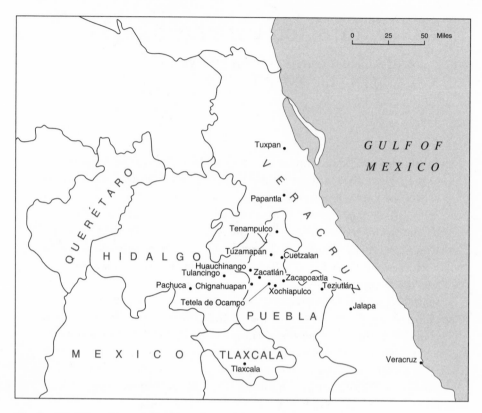

Map 3. The Sierra Norte de Puebla and environs

Although usually allies fighting on the same side, the two forces had distinct histories, ideologies, and practices. Built up over the previous decade and a half of Liberal-Conservative conflict, these came to define for each a unique vision of the Liberal national project.

For the western Liberals, predominantly merchants, landowners, and entrepreneurs, Liberalism meant the free market—the right to accumulate and invest capital without the restrictions represented by such neocolonial institutions as the Catholic church or the Indian community. The political practice of their movement was generally exclusionary, in the sense that leaders defined ideologies and imparted them in a top-down way to their followers, educating the masses—inevitably poorer and more indigenous— in the ways of modern politics. These particular meanings and practices were reflected in the process of negotiation by the Craviotos: their main purpose was to get their personal losses covered, and they assumed that if they themselves surrendered, so would their followers.

For the central and eastern Liberals, by contrast, Liberalism represented the right of all individuals to citizenship—defined broadly as the just exercise of property rights, equitable access to resources and revenues, and the right to elect representatives and hold them accountable for their actions. This more collective definition of Liberalism was reflected in and nurtured by the communal political practices of the region's national guards, where the responsiveness of leaders to followers generated an ideology informed by dialogue rather than imposition. And this practice was in turn reflected in Xochiapulco's surrender, where no individual stood apart to gain personal benefit and where all had to agree formally before the surrender could take effect.

Even a superficial analysis of these differences makes clear the potential diversity of Liberal ideology and practice in Mexico between 1850 and 1867. It suggests as well that, even if the conflict between Liberals and Conservatives was foremost during these years, the sometimes violent disagreements among Liberals over the definition of their own national project were equally important in defining what would happen on the other end. Indeed, as Liberal fighters and leaders refined and rethought their goals and methods across nearly two decades, the various strands that emerged, interacted, or competed had mutual effects on one another. And it was these various dynamics internal to Liberalism, until 1867 usually hidden within a broader alliance against Mexican Conservatives and French and Austrian Interventionists, that would quickly take center stage after the defeat of the empire.[3]

The case of the Puebla highlands is particularly well suited for exploring these internal dynamics. A tapestry of ethnicities and economic subregions, the Sierra de Puebla generated the greatest variety of both Liberals and Conservatives. A center of confrontation during the Liberal Revolution of 1855–1858 with the Conservative Plan of Zacapoaxtla (1856), it was also an important arena of conflict during the 1858–1861 civil war and a key area of guerrilla resistance to the French Intervention and Second Empire (1862–1867). Throughout these years, even while allied to each other, western and central eastern Liberalisms evolved and were practiced in different ways. In 1867 adherents of both stood ready to claim the national inheritance each felt was justly theirs. To understand the depth and drama of that moment of confrontation, one must first understand the complexities and conflicts that preceded it.

The Definition of Sides

Between 1850 and 1855 the Nahua Indians living in some of the western barrios of Zacapoaxtla town joined with the laborers resident on the

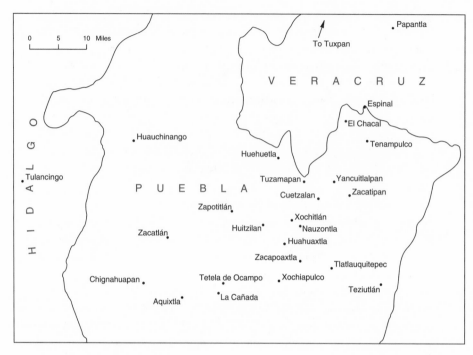

Map 4. The Sierra Norte de Puebla

haciendas Xochiapulco and La Manzanilla (see map 4) in a movement against the owners of these properties. In the context of the Sierra de Puebla's complex colonial heritage of economic reorganization, ethnic conflict, and political struggle, a postindependence process of commercialization had, by 1850, deepened social and ethnic tensions in the western, central, and eastern subregions of the sierra. As Xochiapulco and La Manzanilla haciendas were equidistant from the main towns that organized economic and political relations in the center and east, the movement on them can thus be best understood by placing it on the more general social, economic, and ethnic map of the region as a whole.

The movement's original motivations came from conflicts with Zacapoaxtla, the main *cabecera* (district capital) that, since the seventeenth century, had organized ethnic politics and marketing for the whole eastern, Nahua-dominated region of the Puebla highlands. After independence from Spain, changing and broadening forms of economic activity in the eastern region as a whole intensified existing tensions within the municipality of Zacapoaxtla as Indian, mestizo, and white merchants vied for success in the increasing trade between the area and Veracruz. Starting in 1845, moreover, the Salgado family—residents of Zacapoaxtla town and owners of Xochiapulco, La Manzanilla, and other properties to the west of the cabecera—had been expanding sugar cane production on their land. When they attempted to intensify work rhythms and expand the land devoted to cane on Xochiapulco, the resident laborers or *colonos* faced new labor obligations and a money tax for grazing their animals on the estate. By 1850 they were tired of the situation.[4]

When they rebelled, the colonos from Xochiapulco and La Manzanilla found a good leader in Manuel Lucas, a Nahua merchant from the barrio of Comaltepec in Zacapoaxtla district who had also worked on the haciendas. For quite some time Lucas had been involved in selling wool between Puebla and the Veracruz coast, but he had become increasingly frustrated by the lack of opportunities he faced in his home village. Several years earlier he had migrated to Veracruz in search of new opportunities, taking his family with him and providing additional education to his son Juan Francisco. On his return, however, he once again confronted the fact that his Nahua heritage prevented him from gaining effective power in his district, where markets, municipal rents, and political office were manipulated by a few white families and where indigenous commerce was still considered separate from and inferior to that in the hands of whites and mestizos. Other indigenous inhabitants of Zacapoaxtla's barrios must have shared his frustration.[5]

Between 1850 and 1855 the rebel coalition in Xochiapulco managed to establish military control of the western part of Zacapoaxtla district, repelling all efforts to repress them made by the Salgados and their allies from the district capital. In effect, Xochiapulco became a "liberated zone," its defenders known as Cuatecomacos, named after the area of the forest where they had dug their first line of defense. Then, with the Liberal Revolution of 1855, and especially when Manuel Lucas's son Juan Francisco joined the Liberal army to escape local persecution, the stage was set for a broader political alliance.[6]

As the inhabitants of the haciendas Xochiapulco and La Manzanilla reached beyond the rebellious *sujetos*, or dependent villages, of their own district, they built their closest alliance with the mestizo Liberals in neighboring Tetela. Located in the center of the sierra and known initially as Tetela del Oro because of its mines in nearby Santa Rosa canyon, Tetela district had long been a heavily multiethnic district combining highland Nahua and mestizo populations with the Totonac villages of the north central and northeastern lowlands. Although Tetela had been the site of early and repeated disputes between the cabecera and its dependent barrios or sujetos, not only over ethnic questions but also over land, labor services, and electoral disputes, the district nevertheless remained an area where land was worked in small or medium plots, mainly with family labor. Except on the mining haciendas, the local merchant class—mostly mestizo, with some migrant families from neighboring Tlaxcala—tended not to exploit directly the labor power of the indigenous population. Only during the mid-nineteenth century, with the generally increasing level of trade and commercial production and the establishment of some local *trapiches* for the preparation of *aguardiente*, did the more egalitarian if conflictual style of socioeconomic and ethnic relations in Tetela potentially begin to change.[7]

Xochiapulco's alliance with Tetela also made possible a mediated coalition with some Totonac and Nahua communities to the north, east, and south. Concerns about political autonomy and access to land had intensified in this area with postindependence processes of reorganization and commercialization. In the 1830s and 1840s, for example, indigenous villages in the Nahua and Totonac areas north and east of Tetela—particularly those that held land in the lowland expanses east and north of Teziutlán—began to feel the pressure from expanding Hispanic enterprises in cattle ranching and tropical crop cultivation. By the early to mid-1840s three villages had entered into litigation over these issues: Atempan, a predominantly Nahua community; and Ecatlan and Tenampulco, both mainly Totonaco. As we shall see, the issue had not been solved by the late 1850s and would emerge as a central bone of contention during the 1858–1861 civil war.[8]

The third major subregion to become involved in the conflicts of the 1850s was the western sierra, particularly the area between the highland towns of Huauchinango and Zacatlán, both of which had boasted substantial Spanish and mestizo populations since the colonial period. A part of the exchange networks that provided the nearby Pachuca mines with products and labor, Huauchinango's commercial and agricultural elites had, since the seventeenth century, pressed surrounding Indian villages with the *repartimiento*, or labor draft, for the mines of Pachuca and the haciendas of Tulancingo. Indian communities had also lost substantial land to Spanish and mestizo pressure. Especially after 1840 white merchants collaborated with recent immigrants to Huauchinango in the development of a local aguardiente industry, raising new and old struggles over labor power, municipal revenues, and boundaries between properties.

In Zacatlán the development of nearby Tetela's mining economy, when combined with the exploitation of local sulfur deposits, had early led to conflict with the indigenous population in surrounding villages over the conditions of the labor draft, most likely leading to the separation of sujetos Chignahuapan and Aquixtla during the eighteenth century. Political reorganization after independence frustrated newly independent municipal authorities in Chignahuapan and Aquixtla by reestablishing political cabeceras in Zacatlán and Tetela. During the same years, moreover, sugar and fruit production, as well as commerce with Huauchinango and the mine region of Tetela, provided new opportunities for local merchant and landowner families and resuscitated old conflicts over labor and revenue.[9]

With the outbreak of the Liberal Revolution of 1855, political party conflicts intermingled with these localized socioeconomic, ethnic, and political relations. Innovative white landowners and merchants in Huauchinango and Zacatlán, interested in gaining broader support for their investments and activities and in competition with the more traditionally Spanish and Conservative city of Tulancingo, allied with the Liberals. Some indigenous communities, connected to the Liberal elites by patron-client ties, fought with them. But given the rising tensions between pueblos, other villages in the western region allied themselves against their local Liberal enemies by fighting on the Conservative side. Chignahuapan, for example, backed by an eighty-year history of struggle for independence from Zacatlán, not only fought with the Conservatives but ultimately organized a famous battalion integrated into Maximilian's Interventionist army. Aquixtla also, given its long-standing disputes with Zacatlán and Tetela over labor power and revenue, allied with Chignahuapan.[10]

To the east the dominant white landowners and merchants from Zacapoaxtla town opposed the Xochiapulco rebellion by allying with the Conservative, and later the Interventionist, forces. A strong allegiance to the Catholic church, not only among elites but also in many indigenous neighborhoods, further predisposed Zacapoaxtla's villages to the Conservative side. To this was added the rivalry existing among indigenous barrios located on the Xochiapulco and Manzanilla boundaries, where the claims of Xochiapulquenses to land and municipal autonomy were sometimes viewed with distrust, and loyalty to Zacapoaxtla's cabecera seen as protection against expansionary neighbors. Such was the case in 1849, for example, when the Nahua *alcaldes* (local mayors) of Zongozotla, Nanacatlán, and Tuxtla granted power of attorney to the Zacapoaxteco law student Pascual Angeles Lobato, who presented a petition to the state congress in Puebla city asking for the reversal of an earlier decision to separate them from Zacapoaxtla. In the end, therefore, the possibilities for a multiethnic and multiclass conservative alliance were strong in Zacapoaxtla, and nothing would prove that better than the success of the Conservative rebellion of 1856, organized by Antonio Haro y Tamariz, a *poblano* with commercial and patron-client ties in the sierra.[11]

Between the whiter Liberalisms of the west and the potential for populist Conservatisms in the east stood Xochiapulco. Local tradition, confirmed by Conservative documents, recounts that after repelling several invasions from Zacapoaxtla, a delegation of Xochiapulquenses traveled to meet Juan Alvarez, the radical leader of the 1855 Revolution. Representatives from both sides agreed that Xochiapulco would fight on the Liberal side. In exchange the government would recognize their claims to the land of Xochiapulco and La Manzanilla and would declare them an independent municipality. Until 1861, when the Liberal party won the three-year civil war, Manuel and Juan Francisco Lucas maintained around a thousand men on the battlefield, armed mainly with garrotes, against the Conservative forces headquartered in Zacapoaxtla. The "rebellious Indian"—as the Conservatives in Zacapoaxtla referred to Manuel Lucas—became known, along with his son Juan Francisco, as the most important sierra supporter of the Liberal cause. Then in 1862, at the invitation of the defeated Conservatives, the French army intervened in Mexico.[12]

For the Xochiapulquenses, the French Intervention and the so-called Second Empire brought the cruelest and most violent struggles they had yet faced. With their allies from the neighboring village of Tetela de Ocampo, they formed the majority of the Sixth Battalion of the Puebla National Guard, leading the first charge of the Mexican army in the city of Puebla on 5 May 1862. The only Mexican victory before the French invasion was completed, this battle postponed the taking of Mexico City by an entire year. Between 1863 and 1864 Xochiapulco was at the center of the highland resistance to the empire, and Maximilian considered the town important enough to send the Austro-Belgian Legion, his crack volunteer force, into the area in a counterinsurgency campaign. As a reward for the sacrifices of the Xochiapulquenses, the Liberal governor Fernando María Ortega signed a decree in 1864 confirming their claim to independent municipal status. By 1867, with a new Liberal victory, Xochiapulco had suffered repeated invasions. Its inhabitants had preferred to burn their own houses to the ground rather than allow them to fall into the hands of the Austro-Belgian invaders. Thus, the village played such a central role in the resistance that it literally disappeared during the war.[13]

Xochiapulco's determined Liberalism was grounded, then, in a historically constructed and contingent process of ethnic, social, and political alliance that emerged in the highlands between 1855 and 1872. The founding moment for this alliance was the agreement with the Liberal leader Juan Alvarez, in which Xochiapulquenses exchanged loyalty to Liberalism for a promise of land and political autonomy. Its reproduction in the 1858–1870 period was grounded in Xochiapulco's mediation between prominent Tetela Liberals and the Totonac and Nahua communities to the north and east. Over the whole period the intersection of national statemaking and foreign invasion made possible the construction of a new, more inclusive, more participatory concept of citizen, challenging peasants and rural communities to become involved in the fashioning of a new nation-state. But this challenge was not an easy one to meet, for it involved internal debate and conflicts between peasants and other sociopolitical groups over how best to negotiate local needs while building a national coalition.

The construction of Liberalism in the Sierra de Puebla was thus defined by the varied intersections of the Liberal struggle to consolidate national power, with regional struggles for ethnic and social justice. From the standpoint of the Liberals, a national policy that would carry them to power was composed of two parts. The first was to eliminate colonial forms of power, such as the corporate privileges of church, army, and indigenous communities, in order to create new socioeconomic groups that would become an ongoing Liberal constituency. The second involved building and maintaining an army that could assure military victory over Conservatives and Interventionists and then reproduce control over national territory. On both counts, of course, the Liberals needed to build regional alliances; and it was here that local constituencies and needs could play a determining role.[14]

In the Puebla highlands the local struggles for ethnic and social justice that provided the connection for involvement in Liberal nation-building were themselves composed of two broad strands. The first concerned access to land and other resources; the second reflected the desire for political, social, and economic equality regardless of ethnic origin. Given the intricate map of ethnic, economic, and political relations in the region, however, these issues did not mean the same thing to all inhabitants. Land hunger, for example, could unite people across ethnic lines; yet the questions of landownership and ethnicity were connected by three centuries of colonial domination. In some cases a community's desire to revindicate ownership of their lands could fly in the face of the Liberal commitment to abolish colonial monopolies, including corporate Indian landholdings. In other cases a village's struggle to reestablish claim to lost lands, even by privatizing them, might conflict with the claims of a Liberal landowner. Thus, the intersection between local demands and national Liberal priorities was constantly defined and redefined in the process of struggle.

There were clear social, ideological, and territorial limits on the forms of broader Liberal coalition possible in the Sierra. As we shall see, the whiter, more entrepreneurial Liberalisms of Zacatlán, Huauchinango, and Teziutlán, as well as the populist-Conservative movements in Chignahuapan and Aquixtla to the west and Zacapoaxtla to the east, raised painful questions about the inevitability of Liberalism's commitment to a popular agenda. But in Xochiapulco and Tetela, spreading north, east, and south to constellations of indigenous villages in Tetela and Zacapoaxtla districts, popular Liberalism remained strong. This was because, at its best, the popular Liberalism developing in the sierra's central region provided the sociopolitical space for peasant cultivators and village merchants, both indigenous and mestizo, to join in fashioning a regionally oriented, multiethnic concept of citizenship. The Liberal nation was perceived through the lens of local concepts of justice and equality and built through daily struggle in confrontation with Conservative and foreign enemies.

As they fought shoulder to shoulder between 1855 and 1868, the guerrillas from Tetela and Xochiapulco formulated a vision of political and economic democracy with regional and national implications. Although they did not expect a society without classes, they did think about a nation in which labor and tax obligations, as well as revenue, could be distributed evenly and where everyone had the right to citizenship and to be heard by their government. The revolutionary implications of such a vision, as well as the inability of most white Liberals to accept it, can be understood only through a closer examination of how it was built.

Ethnic Conflict and Civil War, 1858–1861

In January 1858, when the Conservatives successfully took Mexico City and forced the exile of the Liberal government led by Benito Juárez, the Liberal forces in the Sierra de Puebla could be divided into three broad groups. In the western sierra, innovative white landowners and merchants from Huauchinango and Zacatlán—led in the former city by Italian immigrant Simón Cravioto and his sons Rafael and Agustín and in the latter by the Márquez Galindo brothers Ramón and Vicente—dominated the Liberal coalition. In the central district of Tetela del Oro, mestizo merchants and Liberal schoolteachers, such as Juan Nepomuceno Méndez and Juan Crisóstomo Bonilla, enthusiastically organized in support of the Liberal cause. And in Xochiapulco, indigenous peasants led by the Nahua merchant Manuel Lucas and his schoolteacher son Juan Francisco had been fighting to defend their Liberal "liberated zone" for at least five years.[15]

On one level these diverse Liberal forces were united in their common support for the Liberal party and its reformist national project. From 1858 forward they could all agree that the first priority was to strengthen the regional coalitions that could return their party to national power. On another level, however, we have seen that the reasons for supporting the Liberals varied a great deal from one sector to another. For the white Liberals in Huauchinango, the goal was simply to connect to an emerging national power bloc that could facilitate expanded investments and influence in their home territory and help them consolidate broader regional, economic, and political power. In Xochiapulco and Tetela, by contrast, the vision included as well a need for ethnic and social justice—the redistribution of land and revenue and the accountability of political officials. Among the mestizo and Indian leaders, especially Juan Nepomuceno Méndez and Juan Crisóstomo Bonilla of Tetela and Juan Francisco Lucas of Xochiapulco, this radical Liberal vision was nurtured and reproduced in their common training as schoolteachers in Veracruz and in their roles as local intellectuals and political mediators. In the end, therefore, even as the Liberal forces from Huauchinango, Zacatlán, Tetela, and Xochiapulco stood ready to collaborate in the face of a common Conservative threat, potential ethnic, social, and ideological divisions were close to the surface. And they would emerge, for the first time, in the conflicts of the 1858–1861 civil war.[16]

During the first four months of 1858, villages and towns in the Puebla highlands scrambled to line themselves up in the violent national conflict between Liberals and Conservatives. Since shortages of funds and men made it impossible for national forces to combat all the Liberal bands existing in the country, the Conservative government in Mexico City used and deepened local tensions between rival cabeceras and between cabeceras and their sujetos. In the western sierra, for example, soldiers from the rebellious *anexos* Chignahuapan and Aquixtla actively combated and pressured Liberal troops. In return for such loyalty, the new government usually promised a reorganization of political districts so that villages or towns defending the Conservative cause could have greater political autonomy and independent access to tax revenue. Yet at least in some cases, such manipulations could open a Pandora's box of tensions and conflict, causing disagreements among Conservative officials about the wisdom of using age-old angers in the consolidation of local power.[17]

Despite Conservative takeovers in Huauchinango and Teziutlán, Liberal forces continued to hold the bulk of the central sierra through 1858. The area between Zacatlán and Tetela became the headquarters for the Liberal forces, giving protection to the Craviotos from Huauchinango and providing refuge and additional ammunition to the indigenous forces from Xochiapulco. With the moral and material support of the Tetela commander Juan Nepomuceno Méndez, Manuel and Juan Francisco Lucas organized repeated forays into Zacapoaxtla town, forcing Conservative troops there to be constantly on the alert. Slightly to the southeast, regular troops led by Miguel Cástulo de Alatriste, the Liberal former governor of Puebla, engaged the Conservative forces occupying Teziutlán.[18]

By early 1859 the situation had become critical for the Conservatives, as a combination of Liberal forces encircled Zacapoaxtla from the south and west. In the first few days of February, the military commander Agustín Roldán reported increased attacks and the concentration of forces to the north and northeast of the district capital. With his lines of communication to Puebla cut, he requested reinforcements from General Miguel Negrete, in charge of the military fortress in Perote, Veracruz. The Sierra de Puebla, he argued, was becoming a center of Liberal resistance for the entire area of Puebla and Tlaxcala. Unfortunately for Roldán, the mere one hundred men in Perote could barely defend the fortress, much less rescue his beleaguered forces.[19]

When the successful attack on Zacapoaxtla occurred on 15 February, the main pressure came from Tetela and Xochiapulco. Supported by forces from Zacatlán and Huauchinango under the command of Ramón Márquez Galindo, Tetela's national guard battalion successfully dislodged Conservative soldiers from their trenches the night of the fourteenth. While pursuing them toward the heights of Apulco, to the north of the town, the Liberals were joined by the Cuatecomacos from Xochiapulco. Only the next morning did the bulk of the regular Liberal forces, led by Alatriste, arrive in Zacapoaxtla from the south. Many of the national guard soldiers must have thought it odd that their top Liberal general arrived only after the victory was all but assured. This impression of sluggishness was confirmed by the fact that, in the violent hand-to-hand combat that secured the plaza by early afternoon, the only dead on the Liberal side were Xochiapulquenses.

Colonel Juan N. Méndez, commander of the Tetela forces, was certainly impressed by the commitment and strength of the national guard soldiers. "The proud fanaticism . . . of the Zacapoaxtecos," he wrote in his report to Alatriste, "has been defeated by the soldiers of the people, who with admirable will and discipline defended the just cause of that same people." On 13 March this victory of the people was further buttressed when Méndez, as new principal commander of Zacapoaxtla district, supervised the swearing in of the new municipal council: few members of the local white elite signed the document, while several Nahua names, including Lucas, were represented.[20]

Alatriste, himself a white urban Liberal from Puebla city, seemed unable to take seriously these mestizo and Indian forces in charge of the central and eastern sierra. Focusing on southern Puebla and Tlaxcala, he planned preferentially to arm and support the white Liberal elite in Teziutlán, transforming the town into a *prefectura* and de facto center of his administration. Indeed, he retired immediately to Teziutlán after the Zacapoaxtla victory and filed his first and final battle reports from there on 16 and 18 February.[21]

Alatriste ignored the sierra at his peril. Scarcely a week after the Liberals took Zacapoaxtla, displaced Conservatives were already reorganizing at the Perote fortress. Conservative advances along the western sierra challenged Liberal control in Huauchinango and Zacatlán and competed for vital trade routes to the port of Tuxpan. A lifelong resident of the region, Méndez understood these matters quite well. His concern about Alatriste's neglect, combined with a healthy dose of personal ambition, prompted him to begin direct and independent communication with Benito Juárez's government in Veracruz. By mid-May 1859 a personal visit from Méndez had convinced the Liberal government to provide weapons and other support and to pressure Alatriste to back Méndez in raising and training two new sierra battalions.[22]

Alatriste perceived Méndez's actions as manipulation and insubordination. When renewed Conservative pressure near Zacatlán forced Méndez to campaign in the western sierra, Alatriste moved into Zacapoaxtla; on 1 June he signed a decree that made Zacapoaxtla the Liberal capital of the state. He also prohibited independent contact with the government in Veracruz, threatening any person who communicated directly with Veracruz with internal exile. Four days later he continued to solidify his power, signing a proclamation to the Zacapoaxtecos in which he reaffirmed his role as leader of the state and the irrevocability of the state's alliance with Liberal principles.[23]

The brewing conflict between Méndez and Alatriste represented and helped reorganize existing divisions among sierra Liberals and between the sierra and the southern part of the state. In about equal parts, this conflict involved competing personal ambitions and differences over political principles. Between mid-1859 and January 1861, when the general Liberal victory in the civil war reinstalled Alatriste as governor in Puebla city, competition and confrontation divided Liberals in Puebla and helped define and deepen the rift between popular and elite conceptions of the Liberal

national project. Defined through specific military and political battles, this
controversy concerned three basic issues: the impact of racism on military
strategy and organization; Liberal definitions of land and property rights;
and the definition of the Liberal political community. As we shall see, popular Liberalism in the sierra would answer all three questions in opposition
and confrontation with Miguel Cástulo de Alatriste.

Between June and October 1859 the soldiers of the sierra national guards
experienced directly the intense impact that racism could have on military
strategy and organization. When Alatriste reestablished control of Zacapoaxtla in the first days of June, he issued a proclamation announcing that
Zacapoaxtla had fought for the Conservative cause because a few bad leaders
had manipulated the "candor, patriarchal customs, and pure innocence" of
the population, making the inhabitants, as he told them, "victims of your
warlike spirit, your passionate, burning souls, and of the same natural pro-
pensities of the primitive races to which you belong." In the mid–
nineteenth century, of course, when Conservatives and Liberals alike
routinely granted broad explanatory power to racial characteristics, Alatriste was not alone in his opinion that indigenous people were politically
innocent and inferior.[24] The problem was that he translated this belief into
disdain for the sierra's political and military importance, a disdain that
would cost him dearly in the months to come.

Not only did indigenous people constitute some of Liberalism's most
enduring political allies in the sierra, but Conservative loyalties in Zacapoaxtla were a great deal deeper and more potent than Alatriste was willing to accept. Already on 7 June town notables had signed a secret agreement
with representatives of some of the outlying barrios committing them to
the Conservative government and promising to kill off the main Liberal
leaders. Alatriste, however, seemed to have no knowledge of the conspiracies
taking place under his very nose. With Méndez in the western sierra
through July, Conservative conspiracies in Zacapoaxtla had free reign
through the end of August.[25]

On the evening of 29 August 1859, Tetela del Oro's national guard commander wrote to Méndez in Zacatlán. He had just received a letter from
Alatriste, who was northwest of Zacapoaxtla in Xochitlán, informing him
that a concentration of five hundred men from the fortress of Perote was
about to attack Zacapoaxtla. All the forces from Tetela and Zacatlán, as well
as Huauchinango, were required to mobilize immediately to defend the
town. Only a few hours later, at three o'clock on the morning of 30 August,
a Conservative force succeeded in taking the Liberal command post in the
town. When the commander of the dispersed forces encountered Alatriste

in Huahuaxtla, south of Xochitlán, they continued south toward Xo-chiapulco to join the Cuatecomaco national guard and attack the Conserva-tives. Together, with an estimated total of sixty men, they led a first charge into Zacapoaxtla at 8:30 A.M. and tried again several hours later with about two hundred. But it would only be in the mid-afternoon, reinforced by two hundred national guard troops from Tetela, that the Liberals finally routed the Conservative forces, sending them in disorganized retreat toward the Perote fortress.[26]

On the face of it, the Conservatives' inability to hold the town spoke well for the Liberal forces, yet the events surrounding the battle, and most im-portant the behavior of Alatriste himself, showed a combination of racism and military incompetence that deeply angered the indigenous national guards under his command. Alatriste's unwillingness to risk himself in battle was clearly represented in the overwhelming preponderance of na-tional guard casualties, while his total lack of military foresight put the troops at risk unnecessarily. Why had he chosen to travel to Xochitlán, well to the northwest of Zacapoaxtla and outside the range of all potential troop movements, when Conservative troops were gathering at Perote? The Lib-erals in Méndez's faction simply did not believe that Alatriste had acted innocently. As it turned out, they were right: on 5 August Alatriste had already reported to the Veracruz government an attempted conspiracy from Perote to retake Zacapoaxtla.[27]

Alatriste thus went north to get out of the line of fire and to force others to enter it ahead of him. In so doing, moreover, he left the Liberal garrison in Zacapoaxtla without leadership, probably facilitating the Conservative takeover. The Liberal command post in Zacapoaxtla, defended by a total of approximately twelve men and four artillery pieces, fell to a surprise am-bush of twenty men, all from the same town, of whom only three had functioning firearms. In fact, the Liberal officer in charge reported that only one shot was fired at him, the rest of the attack consisting of blows from his assailants. The majority of the Liberal soldiers never saw action, simply dispersing into the night.[28]

But Alatriste's behavior went beyond mere cowardice to dishonesty and manipulation. In his version of events, there were five hundred men in Perote ready to take Zacapoaxtla. As soon as he heard about the action, he quickly marched south from Xochitlán and, at the head of a few na-tional guards from Xochiapulco, fought outnumbered five to one to retake the city. If we read carefully both the Conservative and Liberal versions of events, however, a very different picture emerges. According to the Conservative report, although initially about two hundred men were raised in the barrios of the town, little more than sixty remained at the time of battle because the rest of the improvised troops dispersed in the face of danger; thus, the numbers during the first attack were about even. Reinforcements from Tetela as well as Xochiapulco—the former confirmed by Liberal reports from Papantla, but never mentioned by Alatriste—would have given the Liberals at least a two-to-one advantage over the Conservatives and closer to five or six to one if we believe the Conservative report. The truth about Alatriste's role, then, turned out to be quite different from the image he wished to present to the Veracruz government.[29]

From the point of view of the indigenous and mestizo national guards in Tetela and Xochiapulco, Alatriste's actions in the region provided support to the Conservatives. To add insult to injury, the soldiers complained that he did not provide their daily rations in a dependable fashion. Clearly, Alatriste's main interests were elsewhere, and by mid-October 1859 the national guard soldiers had reached the end of their patience.

On 10 October 1859 the national guards from Zacapoaxtla district—including, of course, the Cuatecomacos—joined with forces from Tetela to invade Zacapoaxtla town and violently demand that the governor step down. In a report to Veracruz two days later, Juan N. Méndez claimed that he had initially considered coming to Alatriste's aid. He thought better of it, however, when he understood the extent of the villagers' antipathy toward the governor. According to Méndez, Alatriste deserved the hostility of the area's communities because he

> with the courage and bravery of their national guards pretends to achieve, not the glory of the state and the Constitutional cause, but his own personal glory, after which he thirsts more each day: [the villages] are outraged by the complete neglect [the governor] has shown toward these same national guards on the many occasions they fought under him, leaving them demoralized and disorganized because of the nakedness and hunger to which he has submitted them. These villages, I repeat, . . . anxiously desire his removal from the post of governor, where undeserving of the confidence they put in him [he] has become an obstacle to the progress of Liberal troops in the state, and to the cause in general.[30]

The October rebellion in Zacapoaxtla must be seen in the context of earlier actions by Méndez. Méndez had very deep personal ambitions, wishing to ingratiate himself with Veracruz and to discredit Alatriste whenever possible. He was encouraged in these ambitions by the fact that, from the start, Alatriste had not taken Méndez's actions and talents seriously. By late July, in fact, Méndez had already renewed independent communication with Veracruz, and in September he had encouraged public declarations by the national guard units of Zacatlán and Tetela de Ocampo against Alatriste.[31]

Yet aside from personal ambition and a deep sense of having been snubbed, Méndez was also motivated by a sense of obligation to the people of his region. While the actions of the Liberal governor helped buttress Méndez's position as the trusted, populist, radical leader of the indigenous-mestizo sierra Liberals, it is also clear that the villagers of the central region felt they could rely on Méndez. Their reliance emerges distinctly in the 21 September declaration of Zacatlán against Alatriste, in which—after detailing all the abuses of power committed by the governor, which had resulted in their district's total lack of arms and ammunition in the face of a major Conservative threat—the citizens of the town voted to give Méndez their approval and help in staffing a commission to travel directly to Veracruz to petition the Juárez government.[32]

In and of themselves, Alatriste's abuses must have fired Méndez's indignation, further inspiring him in his emerging role as popular hero of the central sierra's national guards. The extent of the injustices was especially clear in a declaration signed in Tetela del Oro. After approving in all its parts the earlier declaration in Zacatlán, the citizen-soldiers of Tetela added that it was necessary for the Liberal government to investigate the aberrations and mistakes committed by Alatriste,

> for the confusion that exists between [Alatriste] and the villages of this department is a grave problem for our general cause, and especially for this important military front [i.e., the sierra]: and even more, that the militiamen of the battalion from our cabecera, who on several occasions have fought under his orders, express their discontent with these simple words: we will not fight under Alatriste's orders ever again, because he is capricious [*desarreglado*] and starves us to death.[33]

Alatriste did not discern the social and ethnic undertones of his struggle with Méndez and the sierra national guards. For him the issue was plainly one of power politics: Ramón Márquez Galindo, a deputy to the congress and subordinate to Méndez, was leading a move in Zacatlán and environs to replace Alatriste as governor, pushing Méndez into the position. Alatriste's response was to send a circular to the towns under his command, instructing the inhabitants to sign proclamations supporting him. He then forwarded a copy of his circular to the government in Veracruz.[34]

After the Zacapoaxtla rebellion, however, the Liberal government required more than circulars and, on 19 October, ordered Alatriste to travel to

Veracruz and answer charges. A state of siege was declared in the area under Alatriste's command, and Méndez was left in charge until the investigation was completed. When Alatriste received the orders, however, he chose to disobey them, instead sending his secretary to Veracruz. He then evacuated Zacapoaxtla, leaving it without Liberal protection, and moved the capital of the state back to Teziutlán.[35]

By the end of 1859 the effect of racism on military strategy and organization was painfully clear. The two Liberal factions would not help each other, each demanding prior obedience to their side. On 1 December Alatriste printed a decree in which he retracted his recognition of the government in Veracruz, retook control of Puebla state on his own initiative, and declared all his opponents traitors. In the following days Méndez decided to travel personally to Veracruz to clear up the situation. As animosities intensified, differences between the two factions over the definition of land and property rights also came to the fore.[36]

Since the beginning of 1859, to maintain their troops Alatriste and his allies had been receiving loans from wealthy individuals in Teziutlán, especially Juan N. Flandes, to be paid back through the redemption of ecclesiastical capital according to the Liberal Law of 1857. As later became clear, Flandes intended to charge the loans against an ecclesiastical mortgage on his estate of San Juan de Puchingo, located in San Juan de los Llanos, which had a border in conflict with the Indian village of Tlatlauqui. In addition, several of Alatriste's closest friends in Teziutlán, and especially those who served as officials in his state government, had been claiming municipal and ecclesiastical properties in Teziutlán district, using the disamortization decree Alatriste issued in Zacapoaxtla on 25 June 1859. Although most of the properties claimed were houses, the broad definition of properties affected, as well as the large size of the district itself, meant that several indigenous communities disputed the status of municipal lands claimed by erstwhile Liberals from Teziutlán town.[37]

In the early months of 1860 the disputes over land and property that underlay the conflict between Alatriste and Méndez finally boiled to the surface. Ramón Márquez Galindo, Méndez's Liberal ally from Zacatlán, offered weapons and support to the indigenous communities of Tenampulco and El Chacal, both in Teziutlán district. He promised to return the municipal lands they claimed in exchange for their participation in the invasion of Teziutlán town. On 13 March Márquez's forces occupied Teziutlán, violently entering the houses of two local officials who were key supporters of Alatriste: Rafael Avila, secretary of the local government and the main opponent in the land disputes; and Mariano E. Ramos, as treasurer the person responsible for carrying out property adjudications. As Avila described it, the invasion was intended to overcome the opposition he offered to "their attempt to take by force, as they have now done, the municipal lands in this district and private property belonging to me and other individuals, which have now been invaded by the Indians from Tenanpulco [*sic*]." But neither he nor any other member of the Alatriste faction ever considered the possible legitimacy of indigenous claims to municipal or communal lands in their district.[38]

The issues of property and ethnicity were intimately intertwined in the dispute, feeding the deep hatred each side felt for the other. From the standpoint of Alatriste and his supporters, Méndez and Márquez Galindo were fomenting caste war, manipulating credulous and violent Indians in their struggle for personal power. As a result, the local enemy became defined in racial terms. Only in this way can we understand the behavior of Antonio Carvajal, Alatriste's most prominent military ally. He and his troops entered the town of Tlatlauqui, one of the contenders in the land privatizations, on 2 and 13 April, preferentially sacking, burning, robbing, and raping in the indigenous neighborhoods.[39]

Ethnicity also divided Liberals over definitions of land and property rights. Should these rights derive simply from private ownership, and whoever first laid claim to the land, whether through legal manipulation or other methods, would be recognized as the owner? Apparently this was how Alatriste's group interpreted the 1857 Law. Or should private property have a social component and be legitimized by the community? If so, then the privatization of municipal land was a collective affair in which all interested parties had a say. This second position more closely approximated the vision of the Méndez faction and in particular of the indigenous national guards and soldiers who made a clear connection between service to the Liberal cause and their own right to property and political autonomy. Indigenous people in the highlands had constructed this connection over decades of postindependence struggle involving boundaries and property rights. At the same time, however, political and ethnic definitions of property had been at war with economic expansion and market mechanisms since the colonial period.[40]

Yet another deep disagreement emerged in the struggle between Alatriste and Méndez: what was the nature of the Liberal political community? For Alatriste's faction, the Liberal political community was relatively exclusive, involving mainly the white and prosperous. White Teziutlán Liberals, in this context, saw their role as a version of the "white man's burden": to bring civilization and education to the indigenous masses, still deep in their atavistic ignorance, prey to Conservative manipulations. And the mission of civilization included the creation of a secular political community that would substitute for more primeval bonds.

For the Méndez faction, by contrast, the Liberal community needed to be built from the bottom up, starting with the indigenous citizen-soldiers of the sierra villages. The incorporation of the masses to the Liberal project would necessarily involve negotiating and modifying Liberal policy, rather than simply imposing an already defined ideology. From such a perspective, Alatriste and his followers were illegitimate authorities who had from the beginning lacked commitment to the people and the villages. They were interested in personal aggrandizement rather than community and had committed countless abuses in their invasions of loyal Liberal towns.[41]

The particular popular, populist Liberalism that distinguished Méndez and his allies from the rest of the state, and that formed the postwar basis for the Montaña party in state politics, was thus constructed in conflict with the Alatriste faction between 1859 and 1861. Alatriste's broader alliances into the southern and southwestern plains of the state—an earlier version of "Llanura" Liberalism—forced the Mendistas into a more isolated, counterhegemonic position in which their only chance was to garner support from the indigenous villages and national guards in the expanded core area of Tetela, Jonotla, Xochiapulco, southwestern Zacapoaxtla, and western Tlatlauquitepec. The support of these Nahua and Totonac people, however, came at a price: the Mendistas had to take seriously the issues of ethnic and social justice, communal responsibility, political citizenship, and the just adjudication of lands being raised in popular struggles. Without their support, Méndez could not hope to offer an alternative to Alatriste. With it, he probably offered a more radical alternative—socially and politically speaking—than he and his inner circle had originally envisioned.

In the early months of 1860 the government in Veracruz began to take a more active role in the conflicts among Puebla Liberals and to lean increasingly toward Alatriste. Particularly as the tide began to turn against the Conservatives, the Liberals began to contemplate the reconstruction of a governing coalition at the national level. Thinking broadly, Veracruz politicians had to consider the relative power of Alatriste, backed by Liberal commanders in Tlaxcala, Teziutlán, Huauchinango, and southern Puebla, when compared to Méndez, backed by Zacatlán Liberals and the indigenous national guards of Tetela, Xochiapulco, and environs. It was the faction with the most political pull across the region—especially since it did not contain Indians and peasant radicals—that proved the most attractive.[42]

Factionalism within the Liberal camp continued to plague Puebla through 1861, however, and the previous conflicts in the sierra formed an important backdrop. When the Liberals finally defeated the Conservatives in the last days of 1860, rival Liberal forces prevented Alatriste from entering Puebla city. Yet following the pacification of the city under interim administrations in January of 1861, Alatriste once again held the post of governor through the end of July. Ironically, he resigned from office only a few days after publishing a congressional decree honoring Tetela's patriotism by changing the city's name from Tetela del Oro to Tetela de Ocampo.[43]

In early September 1861 the state congress named as interim governor Francisco Ibarra, national congressional representative for Zacapoaxtla. Juan N. Méndez became his secretary of the interior and militia affairs. A month later Ibarra called the state to popular elections for governor and congressional representatives. Electoral violence forced the use of militia and national guards, some of whom were brought from the highlands by Méndez. By the end of December most districts in the state were reporting their electoral results; but a few days later England, France, and Spain invaded Veracruz. In early January 1862, then, the combination of factionalism, electoral violence, and foreign invasion forced the declaration of a state of siege and the appointment of a military governor.[44]

The final chapter in Miguel Cástulo de Alatriste's military career was played out three months later in Izúcar de Matamoros, when he was captured and executed by Conservative forces after attempting to impede their movement from Guerrero toward the French in Puebla. Antonio Carvajal, his ally from previous sierra campaigns, had informed Alatriste of a nonexistent victory against the Conservatives. Alatriste had therefore moved confidently into battle with only a few men, expecting little resistance; instead, he was defeated and sentenced to death. He died a scarce month before the indigenous national guards from the Sierra de Puebla, the very same soldiers who rebelled against him and whom he personally disdained, distinguished themselves in the historic encounter with the French on the Fifth of May in Puebla city.[45]

Liberal Guerrillas and the French Intervention: From Victory to Retreat, 1862–1865

From the perspective of the relatively small and badly armed Mexican army, the battle on 5 May 1862 was indeed a great victory. Not only did it prove to be the sole large victory against the French, but it also helped delay the French takeover of Mexico City for an entire year. This historical centrality, both in military and symbolic terms, consolidated the Cinco de Mayo's place as a major national holiday. And everywhere in the Puebla highlands, oral tradition emphasizes the importance of the sierra population in making the victory possible.[46]

Written sources confirm the oral version. The Sixth Battalion of the National Guard, composed mainly of seasoned citizen-soldiers from Xochiapulco and Tetela de Ocampo, fought under the leaders they had grown to trust: Juan N. Méndez, Ramón Márquez Galindo, Juan Francisco Lucas, Juan Crisóstomo Bonilla. They fired the first shots against the French army and took part in three charges against the enemy line. They pursued the enemy in retreat, fought against the French's Conservative allies, and finally dispersed at the arrival of French reinforcements. Even Porfirio Díaz would later comment in his memoirs that the indigenous fighters in the Sixth Battalion had been crucial and courageous that day. What he did not emphasize, and none of the other observers seemed to note, was that the enthusiasm and effectiveness of the Indian soldiers was due to their shared sense of community and political commitment, built slowly and painfully over the space of several previous years of combat for a set of common ideals.[47]

Between 1862 and 1864 Liberals and Interventionists dug in across the Sierra de Puebla. While Conservative towns and villages began to declare themselves for the Intervention, leaders in the Liberal strongholds of the highlands negotiated the contradictory demands of local democracy and wartime security and exactions. The invaders and their local allies also got involved in the battle for the hearts and minds of the population. Indeed, throughout these years the French would combine populist propaganda concerning the abolition of taxes or the draft with major military campaigns against the Liberal army.[48]

When the Mexican army lost Puebla city in April 1863 and began its long retreat in front of the victorious Interventionist army, General Miguel Negrete moved into the sierra as military commander of the states of Puebla and Tlaxcala. Establishing his general headquarters in Huauchinango by early June, Negrete immediately began to reorganize the dispersed Liberal forces. He instructed the region's military commanders to requisition food, livestock, seeds, pasture, and ammunition; to seek out lead and gunpowder; to block trade to the enemy; to nationalize all relevant corporate property with the approval of his headquarters; and to require all males between the ages of fifteen and sixty either to serve in the Republican army or to present a rifle or horse to the relevant authorities.[49]

Scarcity of resources and problems with the draft soon began to divide Liberal commanders. Between June and August 1863 complaints came in from all parts of the Puebla highlands about abuses being committed with the draft and requisition of goods. In an area that had seen such heavy and continuous fighting during the 1858–1861 civil war, gathering resources and men in the villages was a delicate and complex affair. Already in the second half of 1862 officials had begun receiving protests from the villages about the heaviness of exactions. Simmering political conflicts, including district and land issues, also had a way of erupting at moments of stress. To top all this off, Negrete's policies were centered in the western sierra, oriented toward the interests of the Craviotos in Huauchinango and their white liberal allies. Thus, the Liberal presence on the eastern side, with the exception of the Xochiapulco national guard in Zacapoaxtla, tended to be composed of commanders from outside the area. Many of these officers treated the villagers like prey, collecting taxes and soldiers by force. And these gathering underground resentments would emerge strongly in the context of a new military offensive during the second half of 1863.[50]

In September, after an August decree by the Regencia of the empire had prohibited the draft, a major offensive by French and Conservative forces dislodged Negrete from Huauchinango and pushed him north to join the Liberal government in San Luis Potosí. As Huauchinango Liberal Rafael Cravioto explained in a letter to Benito Juárez in early October, the military and political situations deteriorated rapidly after Negrete's departure. The Liberals were unable to raise more national guard troops because they had no guns. Economically, the villages had been squeezed dry by a combination of emergency contributions, enemy occupation, and commercial paralysis. Politically, the Interventionists were still offering the abolition of all Indian taxes. Cravioto suggested that, in order to avoid "caste war," the Liberals should do the same.[51]

Cravioto's racial interpretation of the difficulties in the sierra was based on his recent experiences in the western highlands. On 24 September a commission from his forces had entered the indigenous village of Chiconcautla in order to gather the national guard tax for the month. Although the inhabitants had received the commission well, three days later the population surrounded the town garrison, and many Indians died in the ensuing battle. Cravioto concluded that, when faced with an immediate demand for money, the villagers had sought aid from the French troops in Zacatlán. And he became increasingly obsessed with the potential treachery of indigenous forces to the Liberal cause, writing to his brother on 10 October that the French were using much propaganda to attract them.[52]

The problem, however, went much deeper than French propaganda. In the case of Chiconcautla, we know from other sources that political authorities from the village had been conversing with the Conservatives since early

September, seeking protection from repeated Liberal taxation. This was hardly surprising, since Negrete's policies in the sierra had not been sensitive to the needs of the local population. Moreover, the behavior of outside Liberal commanders, when combined with the extreme economic stress caused by the repeated exactions of the previous seven years, had brought the region to the edge of rebellion. Added to this was the style of the Craviotos themselves, who were not of the villages and did not understand local problems. They tended to ride into the villages as outsiders and tax collectors; their positive role as patrons was limited to occasional legal representation or presenting small gifts.

The behavior of Rafael Cravioto around the Chiconcautla incident is particularly revealing in this regard, for he seemed mystified about how to prevent a similar occurrence in the future. Short of the total abolition of contributions, which would leave his forces without support, the only positive measure he could think of was to present a bugle to the Indians of another allied village. His main form of prevention, in fact, turned out to be negative. After the French occupation forces left Zacatlán on 14 October 1863, he and his brother Agustín led a campaign of revenge, executing and imprisoning leaders in several indigenous towns, killing the political authorities in Tepeixco, burning Chiconcautla, and imposing more forced contributions. Ultimately, it seemed that the Craviotos' way of combating disloyalty was to empty the villages of inhabitants. Instead, the result was the strengthening of popular support for the Intervention in many of the indigenous communities of Huauchinango and Zacatlán districts.[53]

Starting in April 1864, a renewed Interventionist offensive, partially inspired by the arrival of Maximilian and Carlota and their travel to Mexico City, further deepened the conflicts in the western sierra. Between June and December local Conservative forces from Chignahuapan carried the day with intermittent help from the French army. Despite a new alliance between Huauchinango Liberals and local plateados, Conservatives successfully drove a wedge between the Huauchinango-Zacatlán area and Liberals in Tetela de Ocampo. Faced with the choice between court-martial in Tulancingo or surrender with a promise of pardon, many Liberals in the western region began a process of negotiation. Finally, on 23 March 1865, escorted by a detachment of plateado cavalry, Rafael and Simón Cravioto and the plateado leader Antonio Pérez rode into Tulancingo, ready to work out the details of their surrender to the empire.[54]

The Interventionist cause was not so easily served along the eastern edge of the highlands, around Tetela, Xochiapulco, and Zacapoaxtla, during 1863 and 1864. A combined French and Conservative attack on Zacapoaxtla managed to dislodge the Liberals from the plaza in mid-September 1863, forcing military commander José María Maldonado's retreat to Xochiapulco. Liberal national guard forces countered, however, by repelling Interventionist attacks in Cuetzalan and Zacapoaxtla, retaking the latter town in mid-October. In the midst of a three-month battle for control of the region, Liberals successfully defended their control of Cuetzalan in late November. By the end of the year they could claim dominance in the area from Tetela de Ocampo, through Zacapoaxtla, into Tlatlauqui.[55]

An important explanation for this success was that Liberal policy in the eastern sierra was more respectful of village needs and indigenous culture, seeking to find common and creative solutions to problems as they arose. In contrast to the Craviotos, Zacapoaxtla's Liberal *jefe político* (district political administrator), José María Maldonado, understood that internal conflicts within districts and the aggressive actions of outside Liberal commanders had predisposed some populations, especially around the towns of Cuetzalan, Tlatlauqui, and Zacapoaxtla, toward an agreement with the Conservatives. Rather than carry out a campaign of fire and execution, at the end of October he decreed a pardon for all those who had collaborated with the Intervention. As he explained a month later, he was motivated by mercy rather than cowardice; those not taking advantage of his generosity would face violent punishment.

When the Liberals suffered a major defeat in Teziutlán in early January 1864, it was a good three months after the establishment of a strong Interventionist presence in the west. Even then Maldonado did not chalk it up to Indian treachery, instead pointing out that the Liberal rank and file had been gathered through a forced draft in Tlatlauqui and that the solution was to form a volunteer national guard force to defend Teziutlán. In the month that followed, Maldonado himself initiated talks between Tlatlauqui's representatives and the local Liberal commander, explaining that even if the Liberals occasionally treated the pueblos badly, they were better than the Conservatives, who always did so. The result of this initiative was an agreement between Liberal Colonel Ignacio Cuéllar and a commission from Tlatlauqui in which Cuéllar promised to protect the town from Conservative attacks in exchange for contributions to support his men.[56]

The differences between eastern and western sierras deepened further during 1864. On 18 March, shortly before the renewal of Liberal pressure in the highlands more generally, Maldonado issued a circular to the authorities in the villages of Xochitlán, Nauzontla, and Cuetzalan, north of Zacapoaxtla, emphasizing that the Liberal Reform Laws favored the poor. The abolition of the military and ecclesiastical *fueros*, he pointed out, extended legal protection to common citizens by removing from abusive soldiers and clerics the protection of a special court. In addition, the land laws "were designed to convert national property into private property, enriching a multitude of families; [they] were designed as well to distribute village communal property among the Indians in equal parts in order to meet their needs, without their having to pay anything." Those with larger properties, Maldonado continued, would pay taxes to the municipality to be used to finance education and other collective projects. He emphasized that only whites and Indians with more than one *fanega* (approximately 1.6 acres) of land would need to pay a tax on their *adjudicación* and that those who refused to do so should have their properties confiscated and redistributed to the poor. And he saved the best for last: "Since the traitors [to the Liberal cause] have proven themselves unworthy of consideration by the government," he concluded, "those who have communal property and do not seek a pardon immediately will lose their lands, which will be distributed as already described."[57]

Maldonado's policies proved particularly effective when combined with the indigenous populism of the Xochiapulco and Tetela national guards. The solidarity among these citizen-soldiers, facilitated by the officers they had elected to lead them, helped make Liberalism attractive to peasants in a number of indigenous villages. In September 1863, for example, when the Liberal forces had lost Zacapoaxtla and, pressured on both sides by a combination of Conservative and French soldiers, were reduced to the area between Tetela and Xochiapulco, Maldonado called a meeting of all the Liberal leaders. There he offered to leave the sierra under the control of Juan Francisco Lucas and migrate to join the Liberal government-in-exile in San Luis Potosí. Led by Lucas and other indigenous officers, the Liberals refused, promising to sacrifice all for the patriotic cause. This generous offer was publicized and sealed at a major Liberal parade on 27 September, where more than five hundred indigenous soldiers marched to the slogans of "Long live the Republic! Long live General Maldonado!" They topped off the occasion at a banquet, for which Lucas slaughtered several pigs from his properties.[58]

Three months later the village of Chilapa, part of the municipality of Zautla, petitioned Zacapoaxtla to become a part of the municipality of Xochiapulco. Among the reasons they gave for the transfer was that they maintained friendly relations with Xochiapulco, having formed a national guard detachment that fought side by side with the Xochiapulquenses. Not surprisingly, Maldonado rapidly acceded to the request. But the influence of Xochiapulco and Tetela went further than attracting friendly villages: it presented a Liberal alternative in times of trouble or dissension. In March 1863, for instance, indigenous villagers from Cuetzalan protesting abusive behavior by priests and political authorities addressed their petitions to Juan Francisco Lucas. When indigenous unrest accompanied the Conservative and French offensive in the district seven months later, it was Lucas who once again attempted to pacify the situation, warning Maldonado not to bring his forces any closer than Apulco. And in Tetela, when the lack of resources for national guard soldiers combined with the abuses of outside Liberal officers to bring tensions to the boiling point, a rebellion by indigenous soldiers on 8 October 1864 took place to the chant of slogans such as "Long live the Republic! Long live liberty! Long live the Liberal government and death to the tyrants!"[59]

All these incidents make clear the differences in the content, style, and practice of Liberal ideology between western and eastern sierras, which in turn resulted in dramatically different attitudes by the Liberal forces. In the west, the alliance the Craviotos formed with the plateados makes clear their limited understanding of village needs. Bandits whose social consciousness was limited at best, plateados had no commitment to the local population; their actions sometimes did more to help than to hinder the Interventionist cause. Certainly this was the case in Acaxochitlán in November 1864, when plateados shot one Indian woman in the head, killed her sister when she resisted being raped, kidnapped the three brothers in the family, and stole all of their livestock. In the east, by contrast, the tendency was for Liberal soldiers to use force to protect local interests. Thus, in late October 1864, only weeks after the incident in Tetela, six hundred Cuatecomacos moved into the village of Zautla to protect the land claims of the indigenous population in a border dispute with other landowners, granting the Indian villagers possession of the lands at gunpoint, then retreating immediately to their fortified positions.[60]

Despite repeated Conservative attempts, the combination of radical Liberal policies emanating from Zacapoaxtla and the military effectiveness of the Tetela and Xochiapulco national guards kept the area under Liberal control through December 1864. This resilience was not lost on the imperial government. Starting in January 1865, the Mexico City press began reporting official plans to do away with the rebels of Zacapoaxtla. And within the month, following the arrival in Veracruz of the volunteer Austro-Belgian Legion, the stage was set. As the only force responsible directly to the monarchs themselves, the Austro-Belgian Legion would prove to be the most effective counterinsurgency weapon and, at least initially, was quite successful. In a matter of weeks the Interventionist campaign in the eastern sierra began in earnest, and by mid-February the occupation of Zacapoaxtla had signaled the first Interventionist victory in an ongoing struggle for the hearts and minds of the local population.[61]

The Battle for the Eastern Highlands, 1865–1866

In March and April 1865 Zacapoaxtla proved a true challenge to the creativity of imperial policy. After a combination of French and Austro-Belgian troops took Zacapoaxtla on 17 February, the Liberal governor Fernando María Ortega, in conjunction with the Xochiapulquenses, remained on the offensive. Imperial authorities attempted to combine negotiation with military pressure, hoping to use the Austro-Belgian troops to create enough stability to make negotiations attractive. Key to this effort were the policies of José María Esteva, a moderate Puebla Liberal appointed to the position of *prefecto superior* for the state.[62]

Esteva had intimate knowledge of the region and of the origins of the Xochiapulco insurgency in the invasions of the haciendas Xochiapulco and La Manzanilla. Given the background of Liberal support for the villagers' cause, the high prestige and influence of the local Liberal Juan Francisco Lucas, and the prohibitive nature of the terrain, Esteva knew that mere repression would not solve the problem of rebellion in the sierra. He recommended instead that the imperial government indemnify the heirs of the haciendas, "leaving [the lands] to the possession of the village of Sochapulco [*sic*]." Esteva's request to attempt political negotiation, along with his appointment of the Zacapoaxtla conservative Pascual V. Bonilla to the position of local prefect, was approved by the emperor during the early days of April.[63]

Bonilla's assignment in Zacapoaxtla was part of a changing imperial policy throughout the sierra and more generally in much of central Mexico during 1865. Along with the appointments of Esteva—first as prefect of Puebla, soon thereafter as minister of the interior—it signified Maximilian's shift away from earlier, more regencia-dominated forms of political alliance. In a word, the emperor was attempting to legitimate his regime beyond the confines of the Conservative faction.

Aside from a clear interest in getting to know the country and in eliciting the broadest possible backing from the population, Maximilian also knew he could not continue to depend on the French army. The moment the Austrian monarch had arrived, the French commander in chief François Achilles Bazaine had informed him that the successful pacification of the main cities in central Mexico, accomplished already during 1863, warranted the immediate withdrawal of approximately half of the French troops. Although the emperor fought hard against any withdrawals, about a sixth of the French troops left Mexico in January 1865. This withdrawal must have reinforced the emperor's understanding that, in the long run, the empire had to move beyond reliance on the French army. If foreign troops could be used selectively to create enough stability so that political negotiation became viable, then moderate Liberals such as Esteva could be incorporated successfully into a broader coalition to buttress the monarchy. This policy initially seemed to work quite well in the western Sierra de Puebla, as the Craviotos and plateado leaders surrendered to the empire in March 1865. Bonilla represented this same vision in the east; yet because of the different balance of forces in that area, he was never able to apply it successfully.[64]

Bonilla's eagerness for negotiation in the Zacapoaxtla area lasted a mere two weeks. A couple of days after arriving in the town, he reported sending Juan Francisco Lucas a letter offering "all possible guarantees" if the Xochiapulquenses would surrender to the empire. What was "possible," however, was qualified to eliminate anything detrimental to "the national army, the honor of the Zacapoaxtecan people, and the landowners whose properties were usurped quite a while ago by the Indians in Xochiapulco who threw themselves into rebellion." If none of the goals of the Xochiapulquenses' struggle would even be recognized, the seriousness of the offer was in doubt from the beginning, and it is hardly surprising that an answer was not forthcoming.

Yet any kind of offer, sincere or not, ruffled the feathers of local Conservatives. Key among those opposed to any form of compromise was Agustín Roldán, the commander of the town's civil guard and an important force in local Conservative politics since the 1855 Revolution. According to Bonilla, Roldán and several others were stubbornly committed to "the triumph of one [political] party over another" rather than to the broader goals of imperial policy. Thus, the very day after Bonilla wrote the letter to Lucas, Roldán was saying "that once hostilities have begun one cannot suspend military operations for any reason, and that this would happen if I [Bonilla] continued my invitations to him [Lucas]."[65]

Bonilla's lack of commitment to serious negotiation, when combined with Conservative intransigence, quickly convinced him that the only alternative was military confrontation. By 19 April he was reporting that forces from Zacapoaxtla had chased the insurgents out of their encampments but that almost immediately the Liberals had retaken their old positions. Only by radically altering the balance of forces, he concluded, would it be possible truly to conquer the rebels. To accomplish this, he suggested that Xochiapulco be surrounded militarily by placing garrisons of three hundred men each in the villages of Tetela, Xochiapulco, and Huahuaxtla, arming Zacapoaxtla with special fortifications, and stationing an Austrian detachment there. Finally, Bonilla suggested, the Craviotos could be brought in to help as well, attacking the headquarters of the Liberal governor and commander in chief Fernando María Ortega.[66]

The best explanation for Bonilla's rapid about-face can be found in the unique difficulties with negotiation as a strategy along the eastern sierra. When Conservatives battled a popular Liberalism that called into question a great deal more than church property, the passionate entrenchment of both sides left no middle ground to claim. Under such circumstances military and diplomatic strategies were opposite sides of the same coin: negotiation would never work without the firepower to back it up. Yet if the very arrival of the Austro-Belgian Legion made negotiation in the eastern highlands possible, the legion's presence also swayed the balance in the Sierra de Puebla toward continued war.

Indeed, Conservative stalwarts proved the most successful allies for the Austro-Belgian Legion. Already on 3 April the Austrian commander Thun wrote to the emperor praising Bonilla's archnemesis Roldán. "An energetic opponent of the guerrillas," Thun wrote, Roldán

> has been constantly occupied, since the arrival of the Austrian troops, in furthering the cause of the Commanders and with it the cause of your Majesty, by his actions and good counsel. It was due to the skillful guidance of Roldan, who knows the local area very well, that the troops of your Majesty entered Zacapoaxtla on 17 February, practically without any losses. During repeated guerrilla attacks he conducted himself with utter fearlessness and thereby made the most favorable impression on his troops. Moreover, he is very knowledgeable about the local conditions and the battle methods of the Indians, so that we benefited repeatedly from his hints. It was his somewhat difficult task to secure the rapid deployment of the civil guard and their munitions, which he accomplished to our entire satisfaction.[67]

The combined policy of military pressure and diplomatic negotiation continued to fail through the rest of 1865. In May, after the failure of a first Austro-Belgian offensive into Xochiapulco, the Liberal forces agreed to an armistice. By early July, however, talks between the Liberal governor Ortega and the emperor had yielded nothing, and the Liberals returned to their combat positions. As Juan Francisco Lucas put it in a proclamation to the inhabitants of Zacapoaxtla ten days later, the Liberals had never recognized the legitimacy of the empire. Convinced after their observations that it was a government ever more dependent on foreign intervention, they had found continued war the only alternative.[68]

Throughout July and into August the battle raged. From Xochiapulco to Tetela, Austrian soldiers battled the unfamiliar terrain, frequent rains, and dense fog. Repeatedly they were ambushed, forced to retreat from the core region of Liberal control. Again and again they went back, with the Austrian commander Thun insisting they exert pressure on all fronts even if they had to retire every night to their garrison. In the first days of August, Thun himself led an incursion through Las Lomas toward Xochiapulco.[69]

At sunrise on 4 August, Thun came over the top of the hill separating Las Lomas from Xochiapulco with half of his troops and two cannon. They found Xochiapulco burned to the ground. In the reconnoitering and maneuvering that followed, a thick fog and light rain came down suddenly, encouraging the invisible Cuatecomacos to attack and forcing the Austrian retreat back to Las Lomas. That evening, Thun wrote, a messenger came from Juan Francisco Lucas offering a short armistice during which Lucas would speak to Ortega about ways to end the bloodshed. But Thun said Ortega was not a recognized commander, and Lucas would have to talk directly to Maximilian. "I retire today to Zacapoaxtla in order to retake the offensive tomorrow or the next day," Thun concluded. "Las Lomas is a place without resources or shelter, and the same is true of Xochiapulco, which at this moment no longer exists."[70]

From the perspective of the Cuatecomacos these events emerge in a somewhat different light. A messenger reached Xochiapulco in the early morning hours of 4 August to inform Juan Francisco Lucas and Juan Crisóstomo Bonilla that the Interventionists were about to attack. There was no longer any ammunition in the village, and people knew that the fight, if there was one, would have to be hand to hand, with machetes. The messenger told Lucas that the enemy was numerous, and they had cannon. "How many are there? Tell us once and for all!" exclaimed Lucas, shaking the frightened youth. "I don't know for sure, *tata*," the youth replied, "but I think each of us will get about eight or ten of them."

Lucas and Bonilla realized that a confrontation would be suicidal, yet neither could face abandoning their village to the enemy. Lucas, having evacuated his family, was the first to put a torch to his own house. The rest of the inhabitants followed his example, and within minutes the town was a burning red ball against the night sky. "It was dawn when the imperial troops could see the heroic town. A pile of smoking ruins, covered with ash and rubble, marked the spot where only minutes before had lived an industrious and flourishing population."[71]

Despite the burning of Xochiapulco, despite repeated incursions by the Austro-Belgian and imperial forces into the sierra, the Liberal national guards of Tetela and Xochiapulco refused to surrender. At various times during August, Thun showed himself optimistic that, when the weather improved, it would be possible to solve, once and for all, this "question of Xochiapulco." But through September this did not turn out to be the case.

Thun's services were soon needed elsewhere, in southern Puebla and Veracruz. In the second half of September, as the newly appointed commander of the Second Territorial Division of the empire, Thun began to make provisions for the "mexicanization" of the imperial troops. In a series of circulars addressed to different districts in the state of Puebla, he began to establish conditions for the creation of a model brigade for the National Imperial Army. In addition to volunteers, he wrote, the brigade would be composed of the abundant vagrants and deserters to be found in each district. Political authorities would be held responsible for covering the contingents assigned to them. The idea was to create a national army that could replace the French as they withdrew.[72]

Thun's policy of mexicanization formed part of a renewed effort by imperial policymakers, with the specter of French troop withdrawals continuously before them, to institutionalize Maximilian's rule. In addition to the proclamation of the death penalty for Liberals captured while in armed conflict, the formation of a national army constituted an assurance that the empire's allies would not be left vulnerable with the retreat of foreign troops. Another attempt at institutionalization was the reorganization of political districts to serve the needs of Interventionist and Conservative constituencies. All these strategies were tried in the Puebla highlands, and especially in the eastern region between Zacapoaxtla and western Veracruz, in the last months of 1865 and the beginning of 1866.[73]

Ultimately, the imperial battle for institutionalization was military, political, and ideological. It involved not only consolidating territory, both politically and militarily, but also convincing the population that negotiation or armistice with Liberal forces—particularly if followed by Austrian retreat—would not leave local Conservative supporters unprotected. It meant supporting all efforts in favor of the Interventionist cause, no matter how small. For example, when twenty-five women from Zacapoaxtla wrote a letter to Thun in late July, informing him that they had founded a charitable organization to help in the town's hospital, he immediately forwarded it to the imperial government, suggesting that the empress herself send them a letter of thanks. Institutionalization also meant dealing with the difficulties that revamped military policies—especially the increasing abuses of the draft—caused even among sympathetic populations.[74]

Institutionalization seemed to work quite well at the beginning. Additional pressure by Thun's forces on the Liberals in western Veracruz led, by the middle of January, to what everyone thought was the final capitulation and defeat of the eastern sierra national guards. Cornered in Papantla, unable to connect to allied forces under Méndez, Ortega, and Lucas in eastern Puebla and El Espinal, General Ignacio Alatorre surrendered to the Austrian troops on 15 January, setting conditions for himself and the rest of the area's Liberal forces. Within the month Méndez, Ortega, and Lucas had been added to the accords. At the pinnacle of imperial influence in the area, José María Galicia, the emperor's designated negotiator for Tuxpan, Jalapa, Jalacingo, and the Sierra de Puebla, moved into the area to anchor support for the empire.[75]

Galicia had an unbelievable capacity for compromise. He declared himself willing to commit his own personal fortune to cover large debts incurred by Liberal and Interventionist troops during the previous two years of conflict. He accepted as legitimate 2,500 pesos in personal credits run up by Juan N. Méndez during the campaign and was willing to reimburse him if Méndez then went into voluntary exile. He approved 20,000 pesos in additional damages caused by the conflict in the districts of Teziutlán, Papantla, Misantla, and Tlapacoyan.

Galicia was also willing to compromise politically. He accepted the fact that Alatorre, Lucas, and Méndez preferred formally not to recognize the empire, even though they were willing to lay down their arms. He traveled personally to the sierra to receive the surrender of the Xochiapulquenses. He experimented with the reorganization of political districts to better serve the needs or interests of previously dissident populations, naming new political authorities in all of them and hearing petitions from those who needed help. As a result, he was able to foster a climate of hope and moderation, fomenting the enthusiasm of Conservatives and neutrals alike as well as the cautious neutrality of dedicated Liberal fighters.[76]

The best proof of Galicia's negotiating talents lay in the effect his presence had in the Sierra de Puebla. Between January and February 1866 the mayor of Zacapoaxtla received twenty-four complaints from citizens whose interests had been damaged by the Conservative occupation and Liberal incursions of the previous two years. Again and again political officials recorded claims for such items as the roof on a house, a crop on a small field, a stove, or a saint's image. The average claim for damages was a little over

100 pesos, and many of the petitioners did not know how to sign their names. In fact, of the twenty-four claims, 70 percent were under 100 pesos, and only two were over 200. Clearly, these kinds of indemnifications represented the potential strengthening of the empire's social base at the local level.[77]

Ultimately, however, Galicia was not able to touch the core of the indigenous-popular Liberal project in the sierra. Ironically, the best evidence of this failure lies in the very document through which the Cuatecomacos declared their surrender to the empire. It is a terse text, stating simply that on 15 February 1866, and under the presidency of Juan Francisco Lucas, the military and civil officials of the "localities that under his orders had to this day defended the republican institutions" met to consider the terms of the surrender at Papantla. After a long and careful discussion that took into account the consensus among the enlisted men, "as well as the immense sacrifices that have been made to defend the republican cause [and that have made] impossible the continuation of the war against the Empire," the representatives of the soldiers and communities of the area agreed to the terms of the Papantla accords.

What is most important, however, is what the document did not say. It mentioned nothing about recognizing the legitimacy of the emperor or of imperial institutions, something that was quite common in similar documents. Instead, the text ended with a long list of names, indigenous for the most part, all followed by military titles or identification as mayor of one of the allied towns. The document was printed in the imperial newspaper as proof of the government's victory. But one could as easily read it to mean that all those who signed at the end stood ready to challenge the empire once again. As it turned out, they would not have long to wait.[78]

Galicia's carefully negotiated peace in Veracruz and the Sierra de Puebla lasted four months. After a new rebellion in Papantla in June 1866, General Thun and Maximilian accused Galicia of "abuses," and he was fired from his post. A more careful analysis of the situation, however, makes it clear that Galicia was not at fault. Indeed, the very drama of the eastern highlands case highlights some general contradictions between the broader policies of the emperor and the narrower interests of his staunchest supporters, contradictions that were also emerging elsewhere. As Pascual Bonilla had also learned during his brief flirtation with moderation in Zacapoaxtla, it was impossible for the empire, based as it was on the Conservatives and the church, truly to offer conditions of negotiation that would attract the more dedicated Liberals. Even the suggestion of talks evoked the suspicion of the Conservatives, on whom the emperor depended for political and military support.[79]

At best the imperialist alliance that Maximilian envisioned could have included the Conservatives, veterans of a long civil war with the Liberals; indigenous villages unhappy with their district capitals and with the abuses of Liberal troops; the foreign army and associated politicians; and the moderate Liberals. Such a broad base would have probably gone far toward reproducing the empire, even with the retreat of the French army. But the contradictions among these different bases of support were deep and numerous. Mexican Conservatives refused to collaborate with the Liberals or grant amnesty to the rebels. Foreign troops, most notably the special counterinsurgency forces like the Austro-Belgian Legion, racked up such a record of racist actions in the villages that they alienated potential indigenous support as well as moderate Liberals. Under such conditions the more constructive, creative, and conciliatory forms of negotiation—the kind that might truly attract the dedicated, more radical Liberals—simply could not work. In the end Maximilian's moderate Liberal policy led irrevocably to isolation and increased his dependence on diminishing, and ultimately counterproductive, foreign military support.[80]

Ironically, on the very same day that the Papantla accords went into effect, Napoleon was writing a letter to Maximilian announcing the irrevocable removal of all French troops from Mexico by the end of 1866. Over the next seven months, between January and July 1866, the imperial military situation began to fall apart. The combination of pressure from the United States and deepening tensions in Europe removed more and more of Maximilian's financial and military support. Spurred on by rumors of imperial crisis, Liberal troops began to score important victories against the best of the empire's forces, most notably in the north and south of the country. By August 1866 Liberal armies were encircling central Mexico from all sides, controlling most of the northern cities, moving east from Guerrero into Morelos, north across Oaxaca from Tehuantepec to Tlacotalpam. Many towns in the center of the country began to declare themselves against the empire.

An imperial cabinet crisis over the possible abdication of Maximilian nearly paralyzed the government in October and November. Then, on 28 November, Maximilian announced his intention to stay no matter what. Still, it was clear by the end of the year, as the French prepared for their final retreat, that the empire's days were numbered.[81] The question was not whether, but when and under what circumstances, the Liberals would regain control of the state. Under these transformed conditions the prologue to a different drama was being played out in the Sierra de Puebla.

Between June and August 1866, as all previous Liberal leaders and forces in the Puebla highlands reentered the fight, the imperial armies began to lose ground. By 9 September even the loyal imperialist division from Chignahuapan had gone over to the Liberal side. Faced with increasing military pressure and the deepening bankruptcy of the imperial treasury, which found it difficult to advance payments to the troops, the Austrians began more frequently to abuse the population and local officials or to defect to the enemy. Mexican commanders previously loyal to the empire also began to join the Liberals. At this time a sense of impotence began to permeate many official documents.[82]

In contrast to the gloomy years of 1864 and 1865, when the Juarista government was on the run and unable to communicate with its dispersed supporters, the Liberal mood was increasingly optimistic. During the second half of 1866 Porfirio Díaz, as commander in chief of the eastern Liberal army, hastened to name provisional civil and military authorities for the state of Puebla and to establish ground rules for the behavior of Liberal troops. Obeying the orders of higher commanders, local political and military officials began to systematize the requisitions of supplies and men, attempting to gear up for the final push against the empire. And especially in the first months of 1867, with the combined sieges of Puebla city and Querétaro taking shape, military requisitions increased.[83]

Overall, the general tone of Liberal requests and exhortations was one of unity. It was time to forget old rancors and divisions and join together for the good of the nation. True, some may have made greater sacrifices for the national cause in previous years, and judging from the numerous defections that had occurred, many of those who were beginning to swell the republican ranks had fought for or served on the imperial side. Now, however, it was time for all to contribute, side by side, without distinction. Such a broad call to unity worked relatively well during those last, heady months of the final offensive against the imperial forces. But once Maximilian was dead and buried, there were persistent questions and different perspectives—on how surrender to or collaboration with the enemy might affect one's right to citizenship; on what should be the reward for those who sacrificed all in the name of the republic; on what should be the interpretation of the Liberal reforms at the local level; on how, in the last analysis, the new Liberal nation-state should be constructed. These questions refused to die with Maximilian. The faint glimmers we get from the previctory documents illuminate the process by which distinct beliefs were nourished and nurtured and the expectations of various groups concerning the form that society would take after Mexico's "second independence."[84]

*Perched on the Edge of Victory: Alternative
Nationalisms and the Reconstruction
of Hegemony*

In the months before the final victory, sierra fighters began to smell the end of the conflict and to weigh the legitimacy of their military or civilian commanders. At times they could afford to be lenient. In their move through the sierra, loyal Liberals like Juan Crisóstomo Bonilla, Juan Francisco Lucas, and Juan N. Méndez did not balk at accepting the help of previously loyal Conservatives like Pascual V. Bonilla. They accepted the surrender of the forces from Chignahuapan and guaranteed peace and security to all Conservative inhabitants of the town. Even when Porfirio Díaz named Rafael J. García, a citified Puebla Liberal, to the provisional governorship of Puebla state with capital in Zacapoaxtla, the highland forces were generous enough to accept the leadership of a journalist who had never seen military action. Although García initially had doubts about the impact of his appointment, by early October 1866 he was writing to Juárez from Zacapoaxtla, suggesting a series of measures to facilitate the reestablishment of peace and civil guarantees in the area.[85]

The most tantalizing window we have on local expectations and visions for the future reveals the application of Liberal principles at the local level. Between January and June 1867, before the dust of battle had cleared, villages in the Sierra de Puebla—especially in the area around Tetela de Ocampo—became concerned with building and maintaining primary schools. School attendance was often spotty, especially under conditions of continued military mobilization, war scarcities, and the migration of families. Yet people could discern a different future in which, perhaps for the first time, educating their children would be possible. The inhabitants of the barrio of San Nicolás wrote to the municipal council in Tetela de Ocampo on 16 February, explaining that they had saved a hundred pesos from a communal system of agriculture and now wanted to invest it in a primary school. All in the barrio had agreed to help out in the project. "More than once," wrote the local justice of the peace,

> our desires have remained purely as projects, given that the critical circumstances through which we have passed have impeded [their realization]; but today, when we flatter ourselves with the hope of a stable and lasting peace, we have developed this project with the firm goal of finishing it with the cooperation and help of our [political] authorities, who, we repeat, provide abundant positive support for the prosperity and enlightened progress which for thousands of reasons we so badly need.[86]

The other major issue that emerged in the months before the Liberal victory was the adjudication of communal lands. A government circular issued on 4 March asked people in all the area's villages to meet and give their opinion on adjudication. The minutes of seven such meetings, from villages in the municipalities of Jonotla (Xonotla), Tuzamapan, and Tenampulco—key villages in the popular Liberal alliance—have survived. According to the minutes, the inhabitants in every village unanimously favored the adjudication process, but they stipulated several conditions: first, that the adjudications go always to the inhabitants of the village or district; second, that problems of borders or usurpation of lands be resolved justly and before adjudication; and third, that the lands in possession of members of the community be privatized without charge or tax, since all inhabitants had paid their taxes regularly and collaborated with the Liberal forces throughout the 1860s. The inhabitants of Jonotla and Tuzamapan emphasized that they had paid fifteen hundred pesos in 1863, while those from Tenampulco recalled having collaborated to build the hospital in Espinal.[87]

As the time for peace and Liberal reconstruction neared, people in the core Liberal region of the Sierra de Puebla began to imagine, for the first time in nearly fifteen years, what it might be like to build in peacetime. The available documents suggest that their vision emphasized education, private property, and the rights of all Liberalism's supporters to have their needs recognized and met. But their project was also popular and community oriented. They envisioned a Liberal nation-state in which political officials would support local education, prosperity, and enlightenment, and in which the contributions of the humble citizen would be justly rewarded and respected. The death of Maximilian made possible, at least in principle, the realization of this project; and the initial enthusiasm and generosity of sierra fighters was based on their confidence that such goals would be met. But as the Liberals moved from mobilization and resistance toward demobilization and the consolidation of power, it was not always clear which visions or projects would become practice. Scarcely a year after the emperor's death, the citizens of the Sierra de Puebla would once again discover, bitterly, the fragility of their "stable and lasting peace." They would also experience firsthand how quickly and easily Liberal politicians could forget their debts.

Victim to the Liberal statemakers' collective amnesia was one simple fact: along with the empire's changing fortunes at the international level, it was the tenacity and loyalty of forces such as the indigenous national guards in Puebla's eastern highlands that had ensured the triumph of Liberalism in Mexico. With the Juarista government in retreat, without access to weapons or money, these local grassroots forces kept up a war of attrition with weapons taken from the bodies of enemy soldiers. Often the first to mobilize, they were the last to surrender, and then only for as long as absolutely necessary. Many sacrificed all in the battle for a new order, envisioned as free from foreign occupation and local abuse.

The power and resilience of popular Liberalism, as we have seen, lay not with Liberalism itself but with popular culture. In the eastern Sierra de Puebla, complex combinations of communal legitimacy, national guard accountability, and the commitment of leaders to the bottom-up construction of a Liberal political community yielded a deep and enduring willingness to fight for and support the Liberal cause. In the western sierra, by contrast, Liberals fashioned a more hierarchical, elite-dominated coalition; the connection to popular political culture in many of the area's indigenous villages was left to the Conservatives. And the differential success and efficiency of the Liberal resistance on the two sides of the Puebla highlands was clearly reflected in the combat records of the two movements. If we envision them as concentric circles of support, we find that the core, in hardest times, was always the popular Liberalism of the indigenous national guards.

We have seen that this popular Liberalism was never a given but was constructed historically in a process of struggle, both between Liberals and Conservatives and within the Liberal camp. When Méndez and his supporters threw in their lot with the Nahua and Totonac national guards and villages of the central Puebla highlands, they did so in an effort to outflank their Liberal rivals. One could imagine that, with more hegemony over the Liberal movement throughout the state, Méndez would not have needed to take popular aspirations so seriously. But because he did, he and his supporters constructed a counterhegemonic Liberalism that locked in Liberal support in their core region. This alternative Liberalism would have lasting implications for the area, not only during the French Intervention but also for the rest of the nineteenth century.[88]

If Alatriste and his emerging "Llanura" Liberal coalition pressured Méndez from the Conservative side, it was the movement in Xochiapulco that provided him with a bridge toward the radical side. The role of this unusual population, and its even more unusual national guard, was central in all forms of Liberal coalition building. Ethnically Nahua, Xochiapulco was nevertheless a unique village, for it had no prehispanic or colonial tradition as such. It did not even possess a church. For all intents and purposes, it was a village in formation, a construction of its own guerrillas fashioned out of an hacienda. One might wonder whether a village more weighed down by ritual, lineage, and civil-religious hierarchies could have played such a pivotal role, mediating relations between mestizo Liberals and Indian villagers, helping to maintain relations with both Nahua and Totonac communities. In any case, Xochiapulco did. And the concentric circles of counterhegemony it helped to link, from small indigenous villages to the Liberal commanders of Tetela de Ocampo and even Zacatlán, buttressed Montaña Liberalism and helped defeat the French Intervention.[89]

Ironically, though, even as the struggles of populist and indigenous Liberals made possible the triumph of Liberalism as a whole, they also made more difficult the reconstruction of a hegemonic coalition that could carry forward the process of national consolidation. In the process of struggle between 1855 and 1867, these Liberals had fashioned strands of alternative nationalism and counterhegemonic Liberalism whose very presence in the liberal tapestry woven after 1867 would repeatedly challenge the centralization of power. Indeed, as politicians and military commanders had already discovered in the Sierra de Puebla, during the postwar years the central challenge was posed by popular political culture, which, distilled from the alternative nationalisms and Liberalisms constructed during the previous twenty years, did not have an immediate or necessary identification with any form of party politics. The only way to ensure popular support, in fact, was to incorporate at least a part of the popular agenda. To be effective, hegemony had to be built with counterhegemony. And the more the Juaristas struggled to centralize power between 1867 and 1872, the more a hegemonic political alliance proved illusory. But before we examine those struggles, we must first journey inside the indigenous peasant communities and examine the internal divisions and struggles through which popular political culture was itself constructed, transformed, and reproduced.

3   The Conflictual Construction of Community

Gender, Ethnicity, and Hegemony

In the first half of 1985 I made frequent trips to the central region of the Puebla highlands, driving a rented car over winding mountain roads to Tetela de Ocampo, Zacapoaxtla, and Xochiapulco. As I became better acquainted with the area, I began to understand why it had been possible to maintain an ongoing guerrilla resistance there. Zacapoaxtla seemed carved from a cliff, while Tetela stood protected between a river and a string of steep hills. Xochiapulco, perched on a narrow hilltop between two ravines that rapidly climb again on both sides to form two other mountain ranges, justly claimed its role as the quintessential stronghold of the movement.[1] Everywhere the red earth on the jagged hillsides was covered with luxuriant vegetation and clumps of evergreen and deciduous trees. In the afternoons the air would suddenly chill, while the clouds slowly dropped down, caressing the mountaintops with billowy white. The complaints I had read in military documents—about the frequent fogs and rain, about the harsh nature of the terrain—began to make a great deal of sense. This was a region where successful and continuous occupation was impossible for those who did not know the ground intimately and did not have social and family networks on which to rely.[2]

Between 1855 and 1872 Austrian, French, and Mexican armies experienced the difficulties of this region bitterly and directly. With only a thousand men on the field, most of them armed only with garrotes, the guerrilla movement that took shape in the central region of the Puebla highlands repeatedly fought its more powerful foes to stalemate. When faced with overwhelming odds, the guerrillas turned the harsh terrain to their advantage by relying on the consistent support and nurture they received from their communities. Through two decades of active combat, guerrillas were always careful to consult village leaders and to legitimize their decisions to enter combat by holding community assemblies. Aside from the ideological and political benefits, community support was also crucial at the material level, since only through local communal networks could soldiers keep up the flow of goods and intelligence information they required.

The importance of this communal connection was not lost on the guerrillas' adversaries. At one point during the 1868–1870 civil war, General Ignacio Alatorre, a veteran of the resistance against the French and leader of the repression campaign against his former comrades, found that he could not overcome them, even with an entire division of the regular army and twelve hundred national guard troops from Puebla city. He suggested that the resistance could be broken only by establishing a military colony in the area, which would then be in charge of maintaining the peace.[3]

To those of us living in the last decade of the twentieth century, the symbiotic relationship between communities and guerrillas is familiar. In the past generation scholars who struggled to make sense of an exploding postcolonial world called on multiple traditions in anthropology, political theory, and the "new" social history to fashion a vision of the peasant community and its "little traditions" as the motor of "Third World" revolutions. Facing the unacceptable disruptions of capitalism, peasants struggled to regain the solidarity, cohesion, and mutuality of their communal traditions, opposing this rich vision of a "moral economy" to the injustice and immorality represented by the new world order. In so doing, they became the allies and foot soldiers of nationalist revolutionaries, ironically moving "backward toward revolution" as their desire to regain a lost world pushed them irrevocably forward to the creation of a new one.[4]

This approach to the peasantry placed the masses at the center of historical processes, passionately arguing for the inclusion of communal and popular political cultures in our understanding of the "great transformations" the world had seen over previous centuries. In this sense we must not forget that it was an exciting and inspiring corrective to the top-down approaches it criticized. Yet at the same time scholars tended to idealize and homogenize the peasant community, constructing it as a seamless universe in which all agreed on how to define the moral economy and on what parts of the old world they sought to regain. Internal dissension, exploitation, or violence, no matter how important to the operation or definition of the community, tended to disappear from view. Perhaps inevitably, once scholars began examining peasant communities more closely, cracking open the smooth surface of solidarity, they rejected entirely the notion that these communities had ever manifested a unified counterhegemonic impulse.[5]

By placing internal conflict at the heart of the process through which community is constructed, my analysis of the Puebla highlands suggests a way out of this apparent dilemma. To begin with, I make no assumptions about the clarity or transparency of communal politics. Quite to the contrary. Communal consensus, when arrived at, was the product of complex articulations of interests, discourses, and perspectives within village society. Alliances among people of different ages, genders, ethnicities, and wealth were difficult to achieve, representing choices that excluded—as well as included—the visions and needs of different factions. The practice of alliance, moreover, often played with shifting boundaries between inside and outside, sometimes setting them around "the community" as a whole, sometimes around sectors of the village. Where the boundary was set—the very definition of "outside"—depended on the particular issue or conflict that had emerged.

In this sense the word *hegemony*, both as hegemonic process and hegemonic outcome, is also relevant to the analysis of communal politics. Achieving communal consensus meant constructing communal hegemony. Hegemonic processes, understood as the contestation, legitimation, and redefinition of power relations and cultural meanings, were constantly in motion at the village level. A multiplicity of perspectives or discourses were debated and articulated politically, through inclusion and exclusion. Distinct definitions and locations of community evolved in conflict and articulation with each other.

Community as a political concept, then, was already a hegemonic outcome of previous struggles. As such, it was a contingent creation, the product of conflict among a variety of potential communal projects. Community as networks of ethnic lineages and generational compromises; community as spatial or geographical entity; community as a cultural space in which identities were contested and negotiated; community as an "imagined" whole that engaged in confrontation and coalition with the outside world; community as a network of political institutions in flux and transformation, where the *república de indios* vied with the municipality, the cabecera with the sujeto—all these definitions and more engaged each other through specific sequences of struggle.[6]

It was this socially dynamic, heterogeneous community that served as the base for the guerrilla movement of the 1855–1872 period. Popular political cultures, themselves the outcome of these negotiations and renegotiations within villages and regions, then played a counterhegemonic role in broader confrontations over power. To modify a well-worn metaphor about guerrilla warfare, if the guerrillas were the fish and the communities the sea,[7] the fish needed to know a great deal about currents and navigation if they were to succeed.

The Community in the Nineteenth Century

In the Puebla highlands, village politics and communal institutions were in a constant process of change, negotiation, and adaptation from before the colonial period through the nineteenth century. Before the Spanish Conquest, patterns of exchange and conflict between ethnic groups and among several indigenous civilizations, as well as the differential constructions and negotiations of gender identities and relations within and among ethnic groups, helped define the form and exercise of power. Migration by Náhuatl and Nahuat groups from the central plateau and from Tlaxcala also modified the patterns of local politics. During the colonial period, institutions evolved through confrontations between the Spanish colonial project of domination and the internal divisions and hierarchies already present in sierra society. By the nineteenth century, ethnic, gender, and class conflicts pitted Indians against whites, one indigenous ethnicity against another, or sectors of the same ethnic group against each other.[8]

The negotiation and mediation of conflict created vital, changing institutions through which people constructed and modified communal political culture. What had emerged by the mid–nineteenth century, combining the disruptions and changes set into motion by colonialism with the new experiments in municipal government brought about by independence, was a new form of communal hegemony. Organized around a civil-religious hierarchy of officeholding that unified municipal and *cofradía* posts into a single cargo system, this new form of politics was a negotiated solution among communal factions—especially between younger and older men or spatially organized lineages and neighborhoods—over how to redefine and control power at the local level. Although not all men were equally successful within it, the cargo system did provide a sequential, age-defined path along which men could pass in their progressive attainment of communal authority and prestige.

By combining political and religious offices, and making all positions subject to surveillance by the *pasados* (the elders), the cargo system also provided for communal supervision over the new institution of the *municipalidad*—a different, and potentially divisive, source of local power and of mediation with the emerging postcolonial state. As we shall see, the Liberal Revolution of 1855 would usher in yet another series of local debates and conflicts over how best to respond to, and act on, the potentially revolutionary postcolonial prospects for citizenship and political participation. And as had happened earlier, the new changes would work themselves through layer upon layer of conflict and contentiousness in village society, all the way from families and lineages through the public debates of the communal assembly.[9]

The reproduction of the nineteenth-century indigenous community in the Sierra de Puebla involved negotiation and conflict at all socioeconomic, political, and cultural levels. Daily production and reproduction occurred in households and neighborhoods organized along kinship lines, and dispersed patterns of residence militated against easy political and cultural unification. At the same time, important political and ritual functions were concentrated in the cabeceras, those centers of local power that mediated with the broader economy and political system. Along the life cycle, moreover, kinship and ritual constructed ties and mediated conflicts within and between families, barrios, sujetos, and cabeceras.

Within the extended family, patrilocal residence was the norm after marriage. When a young couple moved in with the groom's parents, the bride labored under the supervision and authority of her mother-in-law. At the wedding the parents of the bride sometimes ritually expressed anger at the loss of their daughter and often were compensated with a small bride price. Only after the birth of several children was the wife granted the privacy of her own room and hearth. From that moment the young woman entered the generational scale of increasing influence that would bring her, as a mother of adult sons, the same privileges as her mother-in-law before her.[10]

Patrilocal residence, along with patriarchal control over land and other resources, reinforced control by older men over the labor of their sons. Ideally, new families broke away from the original family residence as they reached a point in their own life cycle where they had enough older sons to constitute a separate work group. Still, the tendency was for the new households to remain nearby. At the more intensive moments of the agricultural cycle, they formed larger cooperative work groups under reciprocal arrangements called *mano vuelta*. These groups, which operated on principles of kinship, fictive kin, and neighborhood, were organized and reproduced in ritual as well as work.[11]

The rituals that reinforced local forms of cooperation and labor control were organized around family altars and *oratorios*. When a son left his father's house, he would often take a couple of saints from the family altar to start his own. An oratorio, a small building housing a particularly important spirit or saint, was the responsibility of two separate lineages, often in different barrios. One lineage "owned" the saint and maintained the image and building, while the other served as godparents, providing the necessary goods and services for the celebrations. Fathers passed down responsibility for the oratorios to their sons, and it was bad luck to refuse. Relations between the two lineages responsible for an oratorio also extended into economic cooperation, including labor exchanges through mano vuelta, sharecropping, commercial or financial exchanges, and so on.[12]

Beyond these more local rituals, most males also participated in some way in the *mayordomías* responsible for the upkeep and veneration of the saints associated with the larger villages and the cabecera. Expenditures in goods, labor, and money involved whole families, with wives of *mayordomos* supervising the work of other women in food preparation, dressing the saint, and other tasks. Thus, men with the largest labor pool within their families had the easiest time fulfilling the more prestigious and onerous obligations. As Lourdes Arizpe observed for the twentieth century, "The strength and preservation of the Indian cargo system . . . was related directly to the maintenance of the norms of patrilocality and gerontocracy within the household group."[13]

It was on this cargo system, itself based on the patriarchal control of labor and other resources according to gender and age, that the system of communal politics rested. By the mid–nineteenth century the various ritual obligations associated with the mayordomías were interlaced with a series of civil posts tied to the municipal administrations of the sujetos and cabeceras. Although the religious cargos carried the greatest prestige, the men who proved able to hold all the posts in the civil-religious hierarchy evidenced the deepest commitment to service in their communities, as well as the capacity to marshal the necessary human and monetary resources to earn the respect of their fellow villagers. These then became the pasados, the most important and revered members of the community, who met in *juntas* to make all the important decisions. They nominated people to fill different posts; decided on a course of action in moments of crisis; mediated internal or external conflicts; and supervised all officials who represented the community in its dealings with the larger society.[14]

The relationship of elders to the community as a whole represented, in its clearest form, both the limitations and strengths of communal democracy. By definition, women and young men could not be pasados; yet the attainment of this status did not rest exclusively on economic or ethnic prestige. Quite to the contrary. The prestige associated with being an elder was constructed through a combination of service and sacrifice, through proving one's willingness to work for the benefit of the community. Holding local offices did not depend only on competence in the dominant language, either. Judges and local officials often did not speak Spanish well and sometimes did not read or write.[15]

Communal relationships were subject to negotiation and contestation at all levels. Within families, despite the rigid gender division of labor, strict patriarchal authority, and careful vigilance of young women's sexuality, there were some more flexible arenas where women and men, or younger and older generations, might confront each other. Generational confrontations occurred most frequently over the formation of households after marriage, when violent disputes between mothers- and daughters-in-law might force an early separation, especially if relations between father and son were also strained. Similarly, if the family of the bride was more prosperous or prestigious, the groom might be convinced to live matrilocally in exchange for the promise of land. But matrilocal residence was considered shameful, a sign of weakness or low status. Even in the twentieth century, when land scarcity had loosened the noose of patriarchal authority, "many prefer[red] to die of hunger before they [went] to live in their wife's house."[16]

The manipulation of matrilocality and patrilocality by women sometimes increased their authority or freedom within the family. Young wives could use the public shame associated with a return to their parents' house as a weapon against their husbands and in-laws, limiting or escaping from the worst kinds of physical abuse. Economically prosperous widows or older women could exert authority over the spouses of their children, forging arenas of autonomy and influence for themselves. And wives who did convince their husbands to live matrilocally increased their bargaining power with fathers and brothers, protecting the rights of their children to the family's inheritance.[17]

Although the strict gender division of labor tended to keep women within households, several female tasks provided space for negotiation and movement. One such task was buying and selling in the local *tianguis* or market, where women could interact with others and sometimes control the income from small transactions, such as selling the eggs from the chickens they raised and fed. Other "public" activities that fell on women's shoulders—sometimes literally—included gathering firewood, fetching water, and washing clothes. In all of these cases women created spaces for interaction and cooperation with other women and also—at least potentially—engaged in unsupervised interaction with unrelated men.

Fathers, husbands, and brothers attempted to limit, as far as possible, the independence associated with these activities. But beyond a certain point there was little they could do short of taking over the activity themselves. In such a context the following song from Tzicuilan is extremely suggestive:

You, young girl from Santiago, oh God, my love,
The day will come when we run away together,
The day will come when we run away together;
That's what I tell you, even if you really get angry,
I don't care who gets angry, your grandmother,
Your godfather, it doesn't matter.
Our love will be beautiful, oh God, my darling.

I shall wait for you, I shall wait by the water.
In your hand you will bring your jar, to carry the water.
I begin to tell you, I begin to say,
When will we run away together, when will we run away?

And you will answer, "You better move aside,
My aunt is watching, so is my godmother."[18]

The supervision of younger women by older women is central to the song as well. Godmothers, grandmothers, and aunts helped to control the behavior of younger girls and women, because older women with greater authority reproduced their position and privilege by making certain that younger women and men adhered to the established rules. Here we unlock the secret of women's stake in the systems of communal and patriarchal authority by analyzing the interactions of gender and generation. Women's entire sense of public and familial worth and prestige was embedded in the life cycle and in the passage from generation to generation. Their increasing autonomy—first establishing their own kitchen, with their own utensils and command over their own labor process; then commanding their young daughters' labor; and finally controlling their young daughters-in-law—depended on moving through the established cycles of family reproduction. And all of these transitions depended in turn on the bearing and nurturing of children. Small wonder that women calculated their age not in years but in terms of their place in the childbearing cycle.[19]

While men of different generations collaborated in their control of women's labor, sexuality, and reproductive potential, older women and men collaborated in the reproduction of generational authority and privilege. These crosscutting ties and conflicts, sometimes represented and worked out within families and households, were also at the root of communal politics. We have already seen how the council of elders, at the pinnacle of both gender and generational pyramids, was the key node of local power and legitimacy. But there was also a conflictual side, located in the cargo system itself and in the practice of communal assemblies.

The civil-religious hierarchy, though a clearly defined ladder of cargos through which all could theoretically pass, was in reality divided into an upper level (*cargos principales*) and a lower level (*cargos comunes*). Ideally, these levels were separated only by the age of the men holding them; but in reality not all individuals serving in the cargos comunes made it into the principales. The fact that the council of pasados oversaw the proceedings, nominating and approving candidates for the different positions, further buttressed the differentiation. Often the division also reproduced regional, ethnic, economic, and sujeto-cabecera distinctions, so that Totonac or poorer sujetos would have less representation in the upper reaches of the cargo system than would Nahua or more prosperous cabeceras. At the same time, however, these divisions were not set in stone. There was room for individual or group mobility into the status of elder or *principal*, depending on such factors as wealth, outstanding service or talent, service in war or rebellion (when younger men might evidence special qualities), and especially the separation of a sujeto population and the establishment of a new, autonomous cargo system.[20]

Some of these potential conflicts and divisions could be worked out in the communal assemblies. Distinct rules and systems of speech, as well as different codes of public behavior, competed for space within these assemblies. But they were also carefully constructed arenas of communal discourse in which interest groups, factions, or individuals sought collective approval for their projects or status. They had a well-established, almost ritualized practice with concentric circles of power represented within them. The use of language—whether Spanish, one or more indigenous languages, or some combination of them all—constantly helped rebuild relations of authority. Knowledge of Spanish, for example, represented a speaker's ability to mediate with the larger society and political system. But pasados who did not speak Spanish could call on their proven communal authority to bypass the symbolic power of the dominant language. In addition, women and younger men could, in the largest and most important communal assemblies, serve as a chorus of approval and disapproval, even if they could not speak up because they lacked generational or gender status or linguistic ability. Thus, local indigenous leaders, through the cargo system and council of elders, could counteract the accumulation of power by more acculturated mediators—whether in the position of municipal officials or municipal *secretarios*—by calling on the support of the community as a whole, reinforced within the discursive space of the assembly. Yet new leaders could emerge in the same space, bypassing some of the rigidities of pasado authority by calling on collective approval from the communal chorus.[21]

As practiced and reproduced in the Sierra de Puebla, then, the community was constantly reconstructed through a complex network of conflict and cooperation that tied women, men, and generations to each other in families, barrios, villages, and cabeceras. Crosscutting ties of generation, gender, and ethnicity defined the community as a combination of families, internally organized according to patriarchal age structure. Local leaders, always male, gained authority and prestige by holding office in a parallel structure of religious and political posts, in an ascending order of importance: the older a leader and the more offices he had held, the greater his authority. Ultimately, the council of elders oversaw all other forms of political activity. And it was this combination of families and elder patriarchs that gave the community its identity and legitimacy. "Our community, composed of its families and pasados," was a customary way of opening a political petition or other document.[22]

The relationship between family and community was reciprocal. The authority of elder males, as well as their responsibility to look after the common welfare, was clearly understood in both institutions. The maintenance of this authority in one institution reinforced its maintenance in the other. In the community pasados had the obligation continuously to earn their authority and prestige by advising, representing, and risking themselves for the common good. Patriarchs within families had parallel responsibilities. Just as pasados had to protect the community as a whole, male elders in families had to look after and protect their dependents. Given the interdependence of the two institutions, moreover, community authorities could legitimately intervene in families to preserve the mutuality of family reciprocal relations. An abusive patriarch threatened not only his own dependents but also the collective fabric of the community; thus, he had to be subject to community authority in the last instance.[23]

An excellent example of the interconnectedness of gender and community relations is provided by the case of Gabino Mora in the village of Los Reyes. In May and June 1868 the community of Los Reyes attempted to exile Mora. In the documentation provided by the *juez constitucional* of the town to the relevant authorities, it became clear that, among the various offenses committed by Mora (including public drunkenness, debt, lack of respect to local authorities, and so on) was that he constantly beat the Indian woman with whom he was living, slapping and punching her, sometimes chasing her with a knife. The juez went into detail on the treatment Mora gave his companion, concluding: "There are few occasions when this poor woman [*infeliz*] does not have her face bruised, because of the constant torment [*mala vida*] that he gives her." Interestingly—and in this context it is key to our understanding of the role played by a gendered ideology of reciprocity in structuring local relations more generally—Mora's mistreatment of his partner deserved the most detailed treatment of any of the charges. One can speculate that this was the case not only because of the actual harm done to the woman but also because Mora's unwillingness to accept his patriarchal responsibility dovetailed, culturally and symbolically, with his lack of respect for the patriarchal authority of local officials.[24]

It is in the mutually reinforcing relationship between family and community, and in the reciprocal obligations that tied different community and family members to each other, that we find the basis for communal hegemony. Justice for all was identified not with complete equality but with the reciprocal relations maintained by the "good" patriarch. Pasados were just if they protected their community and sacrificed themselves in the common interest. Municipal officials were just if they mediated equally between citizens and assured everyone's access to subsistence, as a good father would. State officials were just if they were responsive to the needs of all their "children."

In this context it is especially interesting that Juan Francisco Lucas, the most outstanding and prestigious leader of the guerrilla resistance, became known in his later years as *el patriarca de la sierra* (the patriarch of the highlands). He took seriously his obligation to watch over the common good, even as he grew older, wealthier, and more powerful. At one point, for example, he petitioned local municipal officials to carry out a *deslinde* (legal fixing of boundaries) between his estate and the neighboring village. As he explained in the document, it was not a question of solving existing conflicts but rather of preventing them. He wanted to make sure that everyone was happy with the boundary and that good relations were maintained. The role of the good patriarch was to guard the peace by acting justly.[25]

In a situation where the justice of the good patriarch functioned, then, everyone would benefit. Beyond the individual family or household, the pasados most embodied this principle. Their status reflected resources and commitment, authority and service; they earned it by personifying the ideal characteristics of the good father. The same characteristics also earned them the right to oversee and mediate political relations in general, keeping the peace between individuals as well as within the community as a whole. And as long as the elders did their job correctly and justly, everyone had the obligation to continue struggling for the common principles of communal hegemony. The best way to achieve justice was to assure the survival and viability of *las familias y los pasados*.

If communal hegemony was organized internally around a gendered and generational concept of justice, equally important to its overall reproduction was the form taken by relations with the broader society and economy. People who had the skills for such mediation—namely the education, language proficiency, and contacts to handle political or economic interactions outside the community—were still subject to the supervision and control of the collectivity, especially as embodied in the elders. They too had to earn the privilege of representing the community. Negotiations over who held the offices of mediation, including municipal *secretario* and *juez municipal*, usually balanced community prestige acquired through the cargo system with the skills learned in school, regional trade, or other sectors of the broader society. Compromises might entail a trade-off, with a locally prestigious but often non-Spanish-speaking or illiterate juez or alcalde serving alongside a ladino, mestizo, or acculturated Indian secretario.[26] But whatever the outcome in a particular case, the maintenance of communal consensus rested on the twin pillars of internal justice and successful mediation with the outside.

A Democratic Patriarchy: Popular Liberalism, Communal Hegemony, and the 1855 Revolution

Just as independence helped articulate emerging civil-religious hierarchies to postcolonial municipal institutions, the two decades of guerrilla resistance that followed the 1855 Liberal Revolution would introduce yet another wave of new dynamics into the reconstruction of communal consensus. From the 1840s economic and commercial growth had generated new opportunities in trade and agricultural production throughout the Puebla highlands. Most of these economic activities, like long-distance trade or commercial agriculture, were the province of men within existing divisions of labor. Additional opportunities for education and migration, moreover, opened alternative routes to economic and political influence for younger men, who might not need to wait around for their inheritances and might use new skills to build new alliances at the community level. Within municipalities and between villages, struggles over revenue or labor intensified, pitting one ethnicity against another, with the advantage on the side of dominant Nahua groups over less politically powerful Totonacos.[27]

The actual effect these changes had on the reproduction of communal hegemony varied a great deal from village to village, depending not only on internal economic and political relations but also on the ability of communal leaders to mediate with the outside. In this context it is especially interesting to note that in the Liberal villages of the central to eastern sierra, where popular Liberalism grew out of the contingent alliance between mestizo and indigenous Liberals described in chapter 2, the greatest amount of change and reconstruction seems to have taken place in internal concepts of communal hegemony. While not abolishing internal gender, ethnic, and generational hierarchies, the Liberal guerrilla forces along the central eastern Puebla highlands called into question the forms of hegemonic communal politics that had emerged between the late colonial and early postindependence periods. Organized in national guard forces where younger, indigenous, and less economically powerful men could gain access to prestige through physical bravery and loyalty, the Liberal movement constituted a challenge to the pasados' monopoly of power. The national guard's direct connection to the Liberal army, and thus to the local branches of the Liberal state, also provided an alternate route to mediation with the outside. Both internally and externally, therefore, the rise of a Liberal movement in the villages organized around the national guard battalions presented a new conjuncture in the ongoing construction of communal politics.

National guard soldiers and their leaders occupied this dual space in local political culture with a great deal of creativity and dynamism. They combined local indigenous concepts of community and collective responsibility with radical definitions of Liberal citizenship, nurturing a democratic vision of how society should be organized. According to this perspective, elected municipal officials should be responsible to all of the community's citizens, equitably distributing tax and labor obligations as well as revenues. National guards also used their position in local society, and the ideology of reciprocity that stood at the center of communal consensus, to conceptualize a more egalitarian relationship to the central state. At the state and national levels, the people should have the right to choose their own representatives and to demand responsiveness and access to political and economic participation for all. As defined by the national guards of highland Puebla, then, the nation was made up of all its citizens, and the state had an equal obligation to underwrite the prosperity of all.[28]

What emerged from this interaction of communal hegemony and Liberal struggle was, in the words of Judith Stacey, a "democratic patriarchy."[29] At its very center stood ongoing negotiations among male villagers over the sources and legitimation of local power and prestige. In these negotiations national guardsmen held new access to state power and control over the local means of violence and self-defense. Yet any reference to, or use of, communal solidarity by national guards of necessity went through the pasados. They were the custodians of "legitimate" communalism, the very embodiment of communal notions of justice, of the concepts of reciprocity and responsibility contained in the idea of the good patriarch. This mutual recognition of power and influence, then, underlay the construction of "democratic patriarchy."

But equally important to the concept was the oxymoronic tension between democracy and patriarchy. Democracy, in this case, meant the extension of influence and prestige to men who had previously been on the fringes of the system of communal power. Patriarchy signified the ongoing exclusion of women within the expanded definition of citizenship. And the oxymoronic tension was also present in the social and cultural struggles through which democratic patriarchy, as an emerging form of popular political culture, was built.

Democratic patriarchy was not only a negotiation among men but also an attempt by village peasants, both women and men, to confront the new political possibilities emerging with the Liberal Revolution. Literally in the heat of battle, the highland peasant guerrillas fought against Conservatives and on the side of Liberal elites to put their own stamp on the process of nation-state formation. They struggled to bridge the gap between their own dynamic and contested concepts of mutuality and justice and the ideas of individual freedom and equality contained within nineteenth-century Liberalism. Situating these ideas in a context of indigenous communalism and reciprocity, highland villagers tempered the individualism and strengthened the promises of equality they contained. In so doing, they fashioned a Liberal vision quite distinct, in class and ethnic terms, from that held by many citified intellectuals. At the same time, though, their vision was a gendered one in which the possibility of equality was necessarily mediated through existing patriarchal traditions and relationships.

The reconstruction of gender hierarchy within a guerrilla war meant that women were defined as "outside" combat, despite their presence in the villages and on the battlefields. Even if we restrict our attention to what was going on in battle, this was in many ways an arbitrary definition. As had been the case in most wars—especially before the industrialization and technological sophistication possible in the twentieth century—women served as camp followers and auxiliaries at the front, often differentiated from men only in that they did not carry weapons. In a guerrilla conflict, moreover, where the line between homefront and battlefront became increasingly blurred, women in the villages tended to become de facto combatants, confronting enemy incursions and the physical danger they entailed. This meant that women could easily become casualties, even if usually placed in the category of "civilians" or overlooked altogether in the gendered military reports that serve as my main sources. So why were women as a category excluded from combat? In her work on women and the military, Cynthia Enloe suggests that such an exclusion allows women's gendered labor for the war effort to remain invisible. This certainly seems to have been the case in the Puebla highlands.[30]

Contrary to the prevailing ideology, women's labor was crucial to the daily conduct of war. The local guerrilla forces, led from Xochiapulco and Tetela and based in a core area of five villages, needed about 150 to 200 rations of tortillas daily from each town. A ration of tortillas, according to the military requisition documents I have found, was composed of twelve tortillas. This meant that the women in these towns, in addition to the rest of their daily tasks, were engaged in making between 1,800 and 2,400 tortillas every day. When one takes into account all the related tasks— husking, degraining, and soaking the corn, hauling the wood and water, building the fire, grinding the corn, and making and cooking the tortillas themselves—the amount of additional work is staggering. As a point of comparison, Oscar Lewis records that in twentieth-century Tepoztlán before the introduction of a mechanized corn mill, the women in the Martínez family were forced to rise at two o'clock in the morning during the heaviest periods of the agricultural cycle to prepare rations for the three to four men headed for the fields. In the Puebla highlands, one must also consider that even if many of the combatants were from the same villages providing the rations, it is doubtful that any family provided a majority of its male members to active combat duty at any given moment. Thus, women's work was multiplied significantly by the war effort, giving the lie to the assumption that "women had to do this work anyway."[31]

The invisibility of women and their labor also delegitimized any right they might have had to independent reward on the other side of the conflict. In Tetela de Ocampo, for example, sixty-one separate municipal plots were adjudicated between 1867 and 1871 to individual townspeople, most of whom had participated in the resistance. Of those sixty-one adjudications, none went to women.[32] In neighboring Xochiapulco ten years later, land was given out to guerrilla fighters according to their rank in the guerrilla army. Women had access only as wives, mothers, or other family members.[33] And in an extreme case of the same sense of male entitlement, Domingo Ramos, an indigenous soldier from the village of Tzicuilan, decided, after the conflict was over, that he had a better right to the daughter of his fallen son than the mother did. The local judge refused his claim, arguing that Ramos had not contributed anything to the support of his grandchild in the two years since she had been born. Ramos then used his contacts in the local battalion of the guerrilla army to enter the house of the mother and try to take the child by force.[34]

As all the above cases demonstrate, the separation of women from the battlefield had important political and ideological implications. By increasing men's sense of entitlement to the rewards of conflict, women's marginalization from the status and rewards that came from war and political struggle helped paper over any ethnic or class cracks that might otherwise separate male combatants. Indeed, because only men's participation in combat was defined as a contribution to the war, the marginalization of women increased the size of the promised reward—in the shape of land and political participation—for male combatants, a result that is clear in the privatization of communal land by individual title as well as in the postwar exercise of universal male suffrage.[35] This sense of entitlement was most stark, perhaps, in the example of Domingo Ramos, where a former combatant saw his traditional ethnic and patriarchal right to control the next generation—further legitimated both by his own participation in the war and by the death of his son—as superior to that of the mother who had borne the child and cared for her since birth. Thus, in a very direct way general male entitlement helped to extend and reproduce support for the resistance among the male population of the villages, across potentially divisive class, ethnic, or generational lines.

War is not only battle, Nancy Huston has argued, but also discourse. Victory in war involves not only physical battle and the gaining of spoils but also the right to control how the story is told. In the long run it is the story, the narrative of war, that endures. And this narrative is defined not only by those who tell it but by those who listen: by those who witness and cry. In Huston's work women serve as mirrors and symbols; they define the ideological arena where war's victories are decided. Women are the outsiders against whom the war experience is defined. They are motive, pretext, booty, reward. Along with the nation, they are a valuable to be defended or claimed. They care for the troops, mother the soldiers, cry for the dead, suffer the rape of the enemy. "If women were not 'present in their absence' on the battlefield," Huston concludes, "*nothing would happen there worth writing home about.*"[36]

In the Puebla highlands the ideological separation of women from the battlefield also allowed them to become symbols of revenge between men. The victors could rape women as a part of their booty or as punishment of their enemies. Thus, during the 1858–1861 civil war, one Mexican troop detachment entered the town of Tlatlauqui repeatedly over a two-week period, purposefully singling out the indigenous neighborhoods and systematically raping the women as well as pillaging the houses. As the local official pointed out, there seemed to be no reason for the attack since the town gave them food, pasture for their animals, and all they demanded. The reason for the attack becomes clear only when we identify the different Liberal detachments involved. The invaders, under the orders of Antonio Carvajal, were allied with Miguel Cástulo de Alatriste, while the indigenous soldiers in the area had been collaborating with the Mendista forces under the command of Ramón Márquez Galindo, defending the region's Nahua and Totonac villages from the greed for land exhibited by Alatriste's Liberal allies in Teziutlán. Punishment for insubordination thus took the form of systematic rape. The message was clear to the Indian men, a group of whom followed the troops on their first visit, attempting to protect "their" women.[37]

Both in economic and ideological terms, then, the invisibility of women in the guerrilla war that raged in the Puebla highlands between 1855 and 1874 served to motivate male soldiers. Economically and politically, the definition of combat as "men's work" limited the conflict's rewards to men. Ideologically as well, war was defined in part as the defense of one's women. And the interaction of this defense with existing forms of communal hegemony helped to bind men across what were often extremely conflictual ethnic and generational lines.

The reconstruction of gender hierarchies, however, was only partially successful in overcoming divisions among men in local society. Civil war and national resistance, while unifying populations against a common enemy, also intensified demands for goods, labor, and soldiers. During the civil war (1858–1861), the French Intervention (1862–1867), and the internecine conflicts that followed (1868–1872), the villages provided daily rations, fighters, and even weapons for the local troops. Repeatedly, this support involved local authorities and others in unpopular requisitions. Small wonder that, by the 1868 conflict, Juan Francisco Lucas apologized to the juez in Huitzilan for having to ask, once again, for rations. It would only be 150 tortilla rations a day, Lucas promised; but even that entailed making, daily, 1,800 tortillas![38]

Often the requisitions, as well as the tensions and negotiations over them, took an ethnic form. Nahua or mestizo officials demanded goods, money, and men from subordinate indigenous villages. Resistance to requisitions was also often described in ethnic terms. In January 1863, for example, in the Nahua town of Cuetzalan, two local jueces municipales, both mestizos, blamed the area's indigenous population for their inability to meet their quotas. "The inhabitants of these locations," one of them explained on 5 January, "and especially the Indians, are leaving in droves, whether to distant *rancherías* or to other districts, because of which the census diminishes daily, and requisitions become impossible." The other followed up by suggesting, on 22 January, that his locality had trouble supporting the national cause because the Indians, dedicated to the production of *panela*, were frightened that their product would be seized and thus did not come down to Zacapoaxtla, making it difficult to collect taxes. In other villages as well, officials argued along ethnic lines for the reduction of rations, pleading the poverty or ignorance of Indian populations. In Jonotla in 1864, the villagers went as far as to call a junta de pasados to legitimize their plea.[39]

Internal conflicts could also deepen or take new turns with the stress and tension of war as the disruption of the always precarious balance of communal hegemony forced a political crisis. Such was the case in Xochiapulco between 1862 and 1863, when a seemingly normal consensus around the election of Juan José Español for *alcalde primero* quickly ran into problems with the rebellion of a sector of the local national guard. According to the minutes of a special municipal assembly held at the end of January 1863, a group of *vecinos* (respectable citizens) from the outlying barrio of Yautetelco refused to contribute their part to the taxes and other requisitions established to support the municipality and the resistance. Under the leadership of national guard captain José Gabriel Valencia, they were drinking to excess and committing all kinds of abuses, demanding to be attached to Zacapoaxtla instead of Xochiapulco. Within the month Juan José Español resigned from his post, explaining that he had personal interests to attend to but that, most important, the vecinos of Xochiapulco were accusing him of not being sufficiently assertive as a political official.[40]

In Xochitlán, a Nahua municipality with substantial mestizo and white populations, the political tensions intensified by war and requisitions stirred up animosities between Indians and ladinos. By July 1863 the citizens of Xochitlán had suffered repeated exactions at the hands of two mestizos: the alcalde Mariano Castañeda and the *comandante militar* Francisco Martín Peralta. They met in communal assembly to denounce both officials, whom they considered "incompatible with all sentiments that are human and just" and who they felt tended to bring about "the ruin of society and of individuals in our village." Having first cleared their actions with the relevant authority in Zacapoaxtla, they proceeded to elect a new comandante militar, who, in contrast to the previous officials, lacked a last name. Yet the troubles did not end that easily in Xochitlán. A year later the alcalde was asking for a leave from his post, explaining that he was poor and needed to spend time tending to his agricultural tasks. He did not know how to sign his name.[41]

Ethnic and political conflict overlapped and intermingled with tensions between sujetos and cabeceras. That was certainly part of the dynamic in Xochiapulco in 1862 and 1863, when the barrio of Yautetelco used the threat of joining a different cabecera as a weapon in its fight with the central population. In addition to war taxes, moreover, Yautetelco was protesting the local uses of revenue, concentrated predominantly in the center of the municipality. The alcalde Juan José Español, elected by ten votes in the cabecera, had a hard time convincing the outlying barrios of his legitimacy.[42]

Tetela de Ocampo, a much older cabecera racked with conflict among Nahua, mestizo, and Totonac groups, also faced the recalcitrance of its suje-tos. In July 1862, for example, the juez municipal of Nanacatlán wrote to the jefe político in Tetela to inform him that it was urgent that the cabecera cancel his village's quota of two beams for the bridge under construction. If not, the juez predicted,

> the result will be that the majority of the inhabitants of this town will leave and establish residence elsewhere. Because when I told them that we needed to provide two beams for the cabecera's bridge, they told me that if I want to I can go ahead, but the village will not move to find those beams, that they are ready to break off [from the cabecera] first. They also say that when it was our turn to build the bridge at Mapilco which is the one we use, you refused to help us, saying why should you cooperate for that bridge since you did not use it; well, today we have the same reason and say the same thing.[43]

Six years later, during the conflict following the manipulated state guber-natorial election, analogous difficulties faced the jefe político in Tetela in his relations with the rebellious anexo of Aquixtla, long a center of conservative mobilization. Throughout July and August 1868 the juez Francisco Domín-guez dragged his feet on providing soldiers and chasing deserters. Among the many excuses he gave for why he could never find the men he was looking for was that "many . . . had emigrated; others . . . have gone on long trips."[44]

The deepest underlying reason for sujeto recalcitrance was that, despite the democratic or popular Liberal promises of the guerrilla resistance, rela-tions with their cabeceras often remained hierarchical and tinged with ethnic domination. It was not at all unusual for the most resounding declarations of Liberal patriotism and equality to be made in the cabeceras, then sent out to the sujetos simply to be approved. Often the difference in power between mestizo or Nahua cabeceras and indigenous or Totonac sujetos was stark and clear.

In 1866, when Tetela declared against the empire once again on 12 August, the document produced was full of passionate and egalitarian language. The local citizenry, it said, wished "to gather under the tricolored republican flag all Mexicans regardless of party or condition." And, the document continued,

> Tetela engraved upon the forehead of its high cliffs the emblem of free men. . . . The mountains, sprinkled with the tears and blood of its sons, soften the heart and call out for justice before the Eternal; and that for this reason . . . [the townspeople] embraced, filled with joy, the republican flag offered to them, swearing to spill in its defense even their last drop of blood.[45]

After the document was signed, it was sent out to all the sujetos in Tetela district. A week later, in the Totonac village of Tuzamapan, the local juez reported that the local junta de vecinos had met to consider the document and, after a short discussion, had

> unanimously answered that since these villages are so insignificant in politics that they are not the ones who make or unmake the great thoughts, that they are always eager to take leadership from their old cabecera, and that in virtue of the fact that the cabecera has agreed to disavow the imperial government, we add ourselves to that agreement.[46]

A day later Jonotla concurred. Having consulted the "popular will," the authorities were told "that these villages have always followed the lead of their cabecera and have never raised objections to the decisions reached by their authorities, and that consequently they are in agreement with what was decided in the cabecera." To add irony to irony, however, Tetela did not accept these *actas* as valid, ordering its sujetos to declare their loyalty to the republic in more formally legitimate ways. This they did on 25 August, calling municipal meetings and duly recording the unanimous and democratic vote of all citizens present.[47]

It is important to remember, nonetheless, that the language of sujeto-cabecera relations, as part of ongoing local politics, always had two sides. The same village that one day declared its undying loyalty and submissiveness to its cabecera and agreed to what was asked could the next day use the same language to refuse compliance. In 1864, for example, the juez in Jonotla declared it impossible for the local citizens to meet the quota of war contributions being requested from Tetela. The pasados had met, he said, and requested that "I entreat you, as our father, to look on us as your sons and take our situation into consideration." Four years later the municipality of Tuzamapan also declared it impossible to contribute labor to the construction of the railroad, wishing instead to contribute money. All the villages in the municipality, wrote the local juez to Tetela's jefe político, "entreat you as the father of our district to look on them with consideration when assigning us our quota," for the scarcity and poverty affecting the villages was well known. At the same time, he concluded, as long as the jefe político was considerate, "we will obey your superior wishes."[48]

Thus, the sword of sujeto-cabecera conflict cut both ways. Sujetos that had difficulty with their cabeceras could use separation as a weapon of negotiation or simply attach themselves to a more acceptable cabecera. Thus, the village of Chilapa, part of the municipality of Zautla, petitioned to become part of Xochiapulco in 1863. Not only were they closer topographically, the villagers argued, but they had friendly relations with the Xochiapulquenses because they had all formed part of the same national guard battalion and fought together. The same year the village of Nauzontla, part of the municipality of Xochitlán, insisted that they pay war contributions directly to Zacapoaxtla because, despite the poverty and small size of Nauzontla, they had historically borne the greatest burden of municipal contributions. Paying with Xochitlán, they wrote,

> in reality is not in our interest: because that [town], although it has a large population and financially more fortunate citizens and is also a commercial town, still wants to even out the quotas with us, and on the other hand they get much assistance from the estate of doña Librada Castañeda, for we can say without a doubt that at the very most this village represents a third of the size of Xochitlán.[49]

In an equally smooth manipulation of the language of political hierarchy, the jefe político in Tlatlauqui wrote to Zacapoaxtla in January 1863, informing the military commander that Juan Francisco Lucas had come through his town demanding a loan of fifty pesos. The jefe had informed Lucas that, since Tlatlauqui was subordinate to Zacapoaxtla, it was there that the request needed to be approved.[50]

Once we move inside the community and examine its gender, ethnic, and other political hierarchies, it is difficult to romanticize popular Liberalism or guerrilla warfare. Women and subordinate ethnicities paid a high price, in labor and other contributions, for war; yet they received few rewards and even less credit. Sujetos were taxed unequally and sometimes signed inspirationally democratic documents because their cabeceras told them to. Mestizo authorities profited from the efforts of indigenous populations, and Nahuas minimized the contributions of Totonacs. Councils of elders made decisions that risked or took the lives of young soldiers.

At the same time, however, the intricate and contingent combinations of republican ideology, communal reciprocity, and political solidarity that emerged over two decades of battle made possible new forms of politics and offered, at least briefly, the glimmers of a more democratic alternative. At its very center stood the national guard battalions, which constituted a new discursive space tying communal politics to an emerging national project. Within this space young and indigenous males could experience relations where authority and prestige were not always conferred according to age, color, or social status. As a key locus of negotiation among men, the national guard contributed to the construction of a new form of communal hegemony based on a loosening of ethnic and age hierarchies. I have termed this new form of hegemony *democratic patriarchy* because, even though women and men contributed to its construction, men would benefit overwhelmingly from it.

Betwixt and Between: National Guards, Liberal Repression, and the Reconstruction of Communal Power

Liberal guerrilla warfare in the Puebla highlands increased the potential power of young and Indian men by making possible their participation in the national guard battalions that spearheaded the resistance. Officers were elected to head the battalions, often on criteria of dedication and bravery that had little to do with age or ethnicity. In the lists of combatants that have survived, it is common to find officers with no last name, followed by foot soldiers with last names. The national guard also played a new role in mediation with the larger society, since it was through its officers and the actions of its men in combat that villages were integrated into the Liberal movement, receiving recognition or rewards for their bravery and dedication.[51]

These changes generated tensions with older communal officials or practices that were partially and precariously tempered by a gendered ideology of family and community. In the national guard battalions, women's exclusion from combat and the exploitation of their gendered labor were embedded within an ideological and political construct that promised them—as well as other members of communal society—mutuality and reciprocity. In this context the promise of solidarity, of family responsibility and collective identity, was a powerful one that fired the imagination of both women and men.

A particularly good example of the power of this promise occurred in 1868, when the reconstituted Mexican state sent troops to the Puebla highlands to repress renewed political conflict. The commander of the federal army refused to negotiate, stating simply that the guerrillas had to lay down their arms unconditionally. In several of the guerrilla strongholds, soldiers met in community council to consider the situation. Even though they knew it meant the renewal of a bloody and unequal war, they declined the offer.[52] One of the documents they drafted in Tetela de Ocampo gave the following justification for their refusal:

> The citizens of our District conquered with their blood the fame of the land where they were born [against the French invasion], and . . . various fathers mourn the loss of their sons, many widows weep over the absence of their husbands, and many more orphans suffer from lack of the nurture their parents' physical labor used to provide them. With this in mind, how can the fathers, brothers, and friends of these victims abandon the weapons that the dead hallowed with their blood, having carried them until the end of their days?[53]

This is a compelling image. A powerful ideology bound all in a common fight for the good of the collectivity. Women and men, young and old, found solace and meaning in it. Yet not all benefited to the same extent.

Basing a popular guerrilla movement on existing communal and familial networks reproduced the subordination of women, limiting the development of alternative democratic institutions. At the same time, the intense communal controls and village participatory politics that emerged during guerrilla warfare limited private patriarchal power and individual accumulation, conditioning the form of gender hierarchy and relegitimizing the communal base of women's status and prestige. In the Puebla highlands, then, the interaction between communal democracy and patriarchal or generational power fashioned this powerful yet contradictory discourse of democratic patriarchy: a communally based, inclusive form of mobilization that rested ultimately on the continued subordination of half of that community. This discourse provided a language of reciprocity and of mutual obligation that inspired people to action, providing as well a yardstick with which to measure the accountability and responsibility of leaders to followers and of all individuals to each other. Yet it also continued to reproduce lines of authority and submission that impeded the emergence of a more purely egalitarian political culture.

In effect, the unwritten condition for access to community benefits and protection was an acceptance of the existing division of patriarchal power. From a gender-centered perspective, this fact helps us explain how women, as conscious actors who chose among really existing, imperfect alternatives, could ultimately help reproduce their own subordination. A democratic patriarchy—resting as it did on a reciprocal definition of patriarchal responsibility and privilege and giving the community ultimate sanction over the behavior of abusive private patriarchs—was better than unbridled private power. Community tradition legitimized the vigilance of both public and private relations that helped to uphold the rights of the weak against the abuses of the strong. In addition, upholding community practice and ideology in the face of commercialization and differentiation might allow women to recover the eroding importance of their subsistence tasks and domestic work.

Access to community support was predicated, however, on the acceptance of the basic patriarchal order. Scoring partial victories, either as women or as members of a class or ethnic group, meant reinforcing the overall structures of gender hierarchy. Under existing conditions, accepting the hierarchies embedded in communal hegemony was a precondition to preserving communal cohesion. Indeed, from the standpoint of men, gender hierarchy transcended divisions of ethnicity and class by giving all a stake in the reproduction of a collectivity defined in male terms, where combatants were united in the common defense of "their" women and in their exclusive entitlement to the political and material rewards of the struggle. And the strength of popular Liberalism as counterhegemonic politics rested, paradoxically, on this hierarchical solidarity.

Given the interlocking systems of gender and generational power at the local level, the same gendered ideology that bound together younger and older men also reproduced the legitimacy of familial gerontocracy. As long as younger national guards monopolized mediation with the outside through their relations with the Liberal state, the rearticulation of communal and familial discourse would serve them well. Things would change, however, after 1867.

With the defeat of the empire and the reestablishment of the republic, the power and autonomy of popular Liberalism began to decline. The disentailment of community lands began in earnest by 1868, and the importance of a unified communal response loomed large. Under such conditions the independent power of the national guards began to decrease and the pasados easily stepped back into the limelight, reorganizing the very same discourses of familial and communal responsibility articulated by their younger rivals.[54]

Communal hegemony once again was reorganized around a revitalized generational axis. This reorganization provides the best explanation for the fact that in 1869, when the Nahua villages near Cuetzalan, unhappy with the abusive privatization of communal lands going on in their region, participated in a regional rebellion in alliance with the national guards from Xochiapulco and Tetela de Ocampo, officials at the Mexican Defense Ministry were confused about what to do with the captured guerrilla leaders. All the military sources insisted that these leaders were dangerous and should be sent into internal exile. Yet officials in Mexico City had a hard time believing this judgment: the average age of the prisoners was ninety-two![55]

But perhaps the best evidence for this new revitalization of generational politics is to be found in the transformation of Juan Francisco Lucas. Born in 1834, his baptism certificate records no last names for either of his parents or for himself. At age twenty-one he joined and soon led the national guard battalion from Xochiapulco, rising in a single decade to the rank of general, carrying on a personal correspondence with the president of the republic, and becoming a compadre of Porfirio Díaz himself.

Lucas's youth and lack of connection to a regular cargo system might have given ethnic leaders pause. This ambivalence is certainly reflected in two petitions from the pasados and authorities of Cuetzalan in 1863, which refer to him alternatively as "Señor Capitan Don Juan Francisco Lucas" and "Señor Don Juan de Politico," almost as if they thought he was masquerading as a political authority. At the same time, though, throughout the years of the Liberal Revolution he held ultimate say in the region under his command, even as he respected communal leaders and authorities. Perhaps things changed after 1867, when some of his former allies turned against him and he found among his new allies many of the older pasados whom he had earlier challenged or circumvented.

In 1868 Lucas married Asención Pérez, daughter of one of Tetela's wealthiest and most prominent mestizo citizens, ultimately inheriting one of the few larger *fundos* in the region and using it as base for the ongoing rebellions in the sierra. In the end, as we have seen, he would be known as *el patriarca de la sierra*. But at his wedding in 1868, still three months short of his thirty-fourth birthday, General Juan Francisco Lucas lied about his age. In declaring himself thirty-five, he symbolically recognized the changes already in the wind. For the rest of the nineteenth century, the popular Liberalism of the national guards would have to sacrifice potential democracy for communal survival. Twenty-year-old national guard captains would once again surrender communal space to pasados and their allies.[56]

Yet the most important lesson we have learned, by traveling inside the community during periods of political change and strife, is that all transformations in the Sierra de Puebla have occurred at the intersection of complex internal hegemonic processes and the successive waves of confrontation with colonizers, conquerors, and other outsiders experienced since the prehispanic period. The tendency of younger men to rise and challenge generational authority, in contexts of war or political flux, is a recurring one in this context. Compromises among generations, ethnic groups, and villages had helped fashion, by the late nineteenth century, at least three institutional and discursive transitions in local society: the ladder of civil posts associated with colonial *gobiernos de república*; the civil-religious hierarchies articulated, after independence, with the new municipalities; and the seemingly ephemeral democratic patriarchy of pasados and national guards in the 1855–1867 period. With the 1910 Revolution, village-based militias would once again attempt generational and ethnic negotiations with communal leaders; once again they would involve gendered relations of power.

4   Alternative Nationalisms and Hegemonic Discourses

Peasant Visions of the Nation

In the Xochiapulco municipal building in 1985, in a room beside the main office, there was a display of memorabilia from the resistance to the French Intervention. Alongside two small cannon captured from the Austro-Belgian Legion and two large, corroded cannonballs stood a wooden cabinet with glass doors, full of human bones. I asked the young municipal assistant hovering over me whose bones they were. He confirmed the explanation on the sign hung on the display: they were Austrian bones, dug up in the central plaza of the town about ten years before when the municipality was building a basketball court.

According to local memory, the bones were the remains of a major encounter in the village, when the Austro-Belgian Legion had invaded Xochiapulco. The whole population had evacuated the village before the Austrian advance, fleeing into the surrounding hills. The foreign soldiers had occupied the town, camping out in the central plaza. Then at two in the morning, dragging themselves laboriously on their stomachs through the thick fog, their machetes between their teeth, Xochiapulco national guard soldiers descended from their hiding places. Stealthily evading the sentries in the heavy fog, they pounced on the sleeping invaders. After the massacre the dead had been buried in the plaza, to be uncovered more than a century later and placed on display.[1]

My purpose in this chapter is to engage in a process of excavation analogous to that of the municipal workers who built a basketball court in Xochiapulco's central plaza. In my case, however, the product of the archaeology will be not bones, but discourses. By focusing on the ideological, cultural, and political strands that are obscured during the process of construction of nationalism, I will provide a different perspective on the process as a whole. On the one hand, I will exploit the oxymoronic tension in the term *peasant nationalism* in order to explode our customary political understandings of both words included in it. On the other, I will provide a context for understanding how apparently ancient rural issues—

land, political demarcations, private versus communal rights—can become part of an emerging popular nationalism, changing its contours and being changed by it.

My conceptual starting point will be the idea of discourse as the product of an open-ended process of cultural, political, and ideological interaction. Particular ideas, concepts, or perceptions can become articulated with each other, as elements, either by emphasizing lines of similarity or by using difference to construct boundaries of antagonism. Whether two elements are joined in a discursive field by an emphasis on their similarities or divided by a discursive frontier that focuses on their differences, the identity of the elements is changed through the practice of articulation. In the case of nationalism, then, it makes sense to concentrate not only on the major discursive elements in the final product but also on the process of construction itself. Through open-ended processes of articulation, nationalist discourses are formed from already existing elements and newly emerging ones. By connecting these elements along new lines of equivalence and antagonism, social and historical actors transform the meaning of both old and new.

In the Sierra de Puebla between 1850 and 1876, practices of equivalence and antagonism created hegemonic discourses through the incorporation or submergence of particular practices and ideas at the communal, regional, and national levels. At each of these levels, already constructed discourses interacted with and modified each other. The ultimate products were already "official stories" that buried counterhegemonic elements in smoothed-out discourse that purported to speak for the whole community. Only by uncovering the elements of alternative nationalism and popular political practice buried within the remaining "official stories"—at the community, regional, and national levels—can we begin to understand the complex and conflictual processes through which rural folk, and their urban allies and antagonists, perceived and dealt with the painful political, cultural, and social questions surrounding the construction of a nation.

A methodological problem I have faced in this chapter involves the order of presentation. While doing the research, I began by reconstructing the historical narrative of events, conflicts, and political alliances in the Sierra de Puebla between 1850 and 1872; I then gleaned the discursive elements from the documentary evidence through a process of textual analysis. Only at that time did it become clear to me how most of the elements of the nationalist discourses I was studying had both a previous existence and a reorganized and transformed presence in the changing political alliances and opportunities of that period. My struggle with the presentation of these materials, however, is an entirely different question. I have compromised by combining historical narrative with an analysis of discourse in discrete temporal fragments. The definition and order of these fragments presupposes a relatively traditional chronological periodization; but by putting it to a new purpose in this chapter, I hope to transform it, at least in part.

Building the Boundaries: Populist Conservatism and Communitarian Liberalism

In 1850, when the indigenous peasants of Xochiapulco and La Manzanilla haciendas first rebelled against the landowners and their allies in Zacapoaxtla, they also involved themselves in the building of a new nationalist discourse. As we have seen, they entered this new discursive space through their meeting with Juan Alvarez, leader of the Liberal Revolution and a well-known populist *cacique* from "El Sur." In exchange for supporting Liberalism, the Xochiapulquenses were promised land and municipal autonomy. From this first point of articulation—in which Liberalism as a political movement was tied, through the practice of equivalence, to peasant access to land and to local political independence—the peasants of Xochiapulco and their allies would build discourses on nationalism that dynamically tied local and regional struggles for social and ethnic justice to a broader vision of how to "make" a national polity.

Throughout the Sierra de Puebla the issues of landownership and political independence could serve as poles around which to arrange discursive fields concerning the contestation of power. Land issues concerned access to resources, both private and communal. They involved the definition of overlapping rights to common lands and forests, both between communities and between individuals resident in a single village; likewise, they involved individual rights in collective property and disputes over their potential privatization. A discourse on land could also embrace community membership and the responsibilities attached to it. Finally, land issues also connected to questions of religious ritual and political demarcation. Plots could often be set aside to meet the obligations of particular cofradías. And when villages were broken into newly autonomous municipalities or divided between distinct political districts, the process often left unresolved questions of boundaries and rights in the contested terrain along the edges of each population center.[2]

Political independence was also the tip of an entire iceberg of articulated issues. Conflicts between villages over the demarcation of political districts involved confrontations over the control of land, revenues, and labor power. Often these were contests between existing and emerging coalitions of the locally powerful. Given the interrelationships between political and religious districts, moreover, local battles over political power might draw in the clergy, with both sides seeking the support of local priests. In the cargo systems, too, the intersections between religion, ritual, and political power could be intricate and intense.

In addition to questions of autonomy, discourses about political independence debated the definition of political participation. The old debates surrounding political participation in highland indigenous communities ultimately involved a contested process of constructing legitimate political arenas, in terms both of who could have a voice and of who could stand for elective office. At the communal level, especially with the establishment of cargo systems, these arenas of participation were delineated along gender and age lines, with further spatial distinctions between barrios that were often ethnically distinct. In the region's indigenous villages legitimate political power and participation tended to concentrate in the hands of older Nahua or mestizo men, while district or regional political arenas were mainly constructed around centers of mestizo or Spanish power and settlement. In this context local elections, by providing a space where alliances and bargaining between political factions could go on, were usually about the reproduction of existing power relations.[3]

The discursive threads of land and political independence could be woven into a tapestry that contained most arenas of conflict or debate in highland political culture. Land connected through community to religion and ritual; then through village cargo systems or parish priests to political demarcations and political participation; then back through political demarcations to conflicts over property; and then back to land again. Depending on when and where one started and the particular lines of equivalence or antagonism first constructed, the rest of the elements would fall into place in very different combinations. Clearly, Xochiapulco's particular way of articulating local discourses to an emerging national Liberalism was only one of many. Different people, factions, and communities in the Sierra de Puebla made their choices among the many possible discursive alternatives available to them through the medium of specific conflicts and coalitions.

One such moment in highland Puebla was the rebellion against the Liberal Revolution that began in Zacapoaxtla in December 1855. The Plan de Zacapoaxtla—an attempt by Conservative regional notables to put together a counterdiscourse tying local issues to an anti-Liberal agenda—and the ensuing uprising pitted military officers and parish priests against a young and struggling Liberal government. In articulating a local anti-Liberal discourse, Conservatives chose as their point of departure the Catholic religion and its unifying effect among Mexicans otherwise divided in myriad ways. "It is unquestionable," read a paragraph often reproduced in the various manifestos of the movement,

> that the only tie that still binds our people, so embattled by scandal, defection, and anarchy, is the religious sentiment so deeply embedded in the heart of all Mexicans, not only because they see this sentiment tied to the traditions of our primitive society and to the memory of our fathers, but because they instinctively know that once this sacred tie is broken, the only future for our homeland will surely be dissolution and ruin.[4]

Through this entry point, parish priests often became the leaders of the movement in the villages, using their influence in local political affairs to call for a return to the Conservative laws of 1836 or the Conservative constitution of 1843. From the time of the first Zacapoaxtla plan through the various Conservative uprisings in Puebla state during 1856, priests were the instigators or contact people. They led communal assemblies, were executed, were stripped of their goods, or were forced to present financial guarantees that they would no longer involve themselves in politics before being allowed to return to their parishes. Liberal government officials not only ordered the punishment of rebellious clergymen but commented openly in their letters and reports about the role of the church in Conservative rebellion.[5]

The clergy's clear conspiratorial role made it difficult for Liberals in positions of power to be sympathetic regarding any aspect of religion. They connected Catholicism to the abusive power of priests and publicized as many incidents of this abuse as they could find. In one such incident the priest in Ixtacamaztitlán refused to bury the dead infant of the illiterate Indians José Lorenzo and María Josefa because they did not have the money; when María Josefa protested, the priest slapped her. The prefect of San Juan de los Llanos district had a field day: not only did he order an immediate burial for the baby, but he sent the case to the national newspapers, where it was published under the title "A Priest Similar to Many." Certainly there was enough evidence of abusive behavior to keep Liberals happy: for instance, Father Venancio Gavino López, parish priest in Zapotitlán, recognized in his last will and testament eleven illegitimate children.[6]

Such intense hostility toward religion, however, made impossible any attention to the importance of ritual in local political culture. In 1857 in Tulancingo, for example, General Manuel F. Soto reported a Conservative conspiracy in the darkest of tones, accusing the clergy in the locality of refusing to swear loyalty to the Liberal constitution and of stirring up the rural population against the government. He needed reinforcements, he wrote, to avoid problems "in a town where priests and reactionaries have always dominated." Yet the issue at hand turned out to be somewhat less than apocalyptic. People were interested in having the Holy Week processions that year as usual.[7]

In other instances as well, a by-the-book Liberal reaction to requests for approval of communal rituals confused clerical hierarchy with religion and closed off potential articulations between Liberalism and popular culture.[8] In the worst cases Liberal articulations of racism with anticlericalism resulted in ugly representations of indigenous peasants and of popular religion that pushed rural folk into the arms of the very enemies the Liberals were condemning. Such was the case in a letter received in 1865 by Rafael J. García, later governor of Puebla, from a Liberal friend, a Señor Arellano. The people remained the same through all political convulsions, wrote Arellano.

> Their erroneous customs in the area of religion, instead of becoming more enlightened, are further darkened in the chaos of their ignorance, and slowly they walk to the edge of the precipice. The Indian works the whole year, suffering the worst privations; he lives almost naked and badly fed; yet he is obsessed by money, only money, and for what? It pains me to say it: to invest in functions called religious, and in every church they have a multitude of statues, and none is kept from taking the throne, or going out to the street in its yearly procession.

And no matter how paradoxical this behavior might seem, Arellano concluded, it was an infallible truth, along with the fact that these abuses always benefited the clergy.[9]

The discursive antagonism between Liberalism and religion thus limited the possible articulations between Liberalism and communal hegemony, opening potential spaces for Conservative populisms through the connection of religion to ritual. Such was clearly the purpose of the communal assemblies held in Zacapoaxtla and Zapotitlán in late 1855, both called and led by the local parish priests. Bringing together political officials and notables from the various surrounding villages, the priests used the assemblies as forums to bemoan the failure of the Alvarez government and the danger to Catholicism its policies represented. The documents elaborated at the meetings declared the districts in rebellion against the Liberal government, accepted the 1836 laws, and garnered the signatures of as many people as possible. Particularly in the case of Zapotitlán, the authorities from the various anexos signed only with a cross, unable to write their names. At the very bottom of the document, the local notable Pascual Mansilla declared that he signed "in the name of the multitude of Indians who cannot write, from all the surrounding villages."[10]

This attempt to articulate populism with Conservatism through religion was successful in a variety of towns and villages, particularly in areas with conflicts between cabeceras and anexos or in places where the Catholic church had a populist presence. In Chignahuapan, for example, the local parish priest had been extremely generous in his loans and aid to the community. But as these examples bear out, religion was simply an entry point to an entire articulation that connected political independence and participation to control of land, labor, and revenue and finally to general questions of conflict over power.[11]

In this context there were always boundaries to what could be constructed. From the perspective of Conservative leaders, the potential populism of the anti-Liberal articulations might easily get out of hand. So it happened in the town of Huamantla, in the territory of Tlaxcala and along the sierra's western flank. In January 1856 a group of eighty people gathered and, to the rhythm of wind instruments, marched to the house of the local priest, then to that of the local colonel. Taking both authorities with them, the crowd proceeded to the house of the prefect and announced their intention to support the Conservative general Güitián, who had joined the Zacapoaxtla rebellion after having been sent out to repress it. Neither the priest nor the colonel would take responsibility for the movement, and when the prefect asked who was the leader, the crowd responded, "The people." "Since there wasn't a single notable person among them," the prefect reported, "on whom I could place the responsibility, I thought it convenient to send them away, telling them to return quietly to their houses without disturbing the peace, and they obeyed me in a docile fashion, dispersing in a moment." The whole movement, it seemed, had been prompted by the rumor that Güitián, along with 250 men, was about to arrive in Huamantla. But when the crowd tested the waters, rounding up the usual Conservative suspects in the persons of the local clergy and military, they found conditions were not right, probably at least in part because the initiative did not come from above.[12]

If religion served as the point of articulation downward, toward communal processes of hegemonic politics, the Catholic church as an institution under siege by Liberalism served as a point of articulation that led sideways to the military institution, which was in a similar position. It is interesting to note, in this context, that the Zacapoaxtla plan also criticized Liberalism's lack of respect for established military officers. This helps to explain why, during the two months between the original Zacapoaxtla declaration and the formation of a special national army, four different military expeditions sent to the sierra to repress the rebels all joined them instead, ultimately taking Puebla city. When the Liberal government was finally able to repress the Conservative Puebla revolution in March 1856, it was only with an army formed expressly for that purpose and composed mainly of national guard rather than regular army soldiers.[13]

The Liberal victory in Puebla helps us map the lines of discursive conflict between Liberals and Conservatives over how to articulate popular political culture. We have already seen that Liberal discourses were generally antagonistic to religion, abandoning the territory of ritual to Conservatives. At the same time, the Conservatives could not entirely dominate the terrain of populist construction because of the hierarchical representations of power within their movement. As the case of Huamantla suggests, Conservative populisms worked best when controlled from above. Conservatives wanted to incorporate communal hegemonic discourses not to change relations in the communities but to reproduce and further centralize them. To this the Liberals opposed an alternative discourse whose point of departure was political decentralization and the democratization of property rights.

Here was a different view of community and communal hegemony whose center was not ritual and political power but instead political participation and individualized access to land. This vision of community worked especially well in Xochiapulco, an hacienda with no previous communal tradition or local civil-religious hierarchy, where political participation among equals and individual access to land was opposed to political, social, and economic control from the outside. We have already seen, in part, how the story might have been different in other villages, where both discursive poles in the Liberal agenda might cause internal struggles over legitimacy in property rights or political access.[14] Yet in the end, by raising the issue of power and its potential decentralization, liberal attempts at populist discourse created the potential for new dynamics not only at the communal level but at regional and national levels as well.

In this context the role of the national guard battalions in the struggle for Puebla becomes even more crucial. The national guard, by providing an alternative political arena for younger and indigenous men within the villages, challenged the factions of powerholders who were in control of communal politics. These national guard battalions also provided a vehicle for the articulation of a Liberal populist discourse. In contrast to Conservative populisms, this discourse did not proceed from religion to ritual to traditional lines of power. It began instead from democratization and political decentralization and moved through the individualization of land rights to the creation of a new political leadership. The potential promise contained in this alternative communal discourse is highlighted in the effectiveness of Liberal national guards against the regular army and its Conservative village guards. But in Puebla in 1856, the lines were just beginning to be drawn. They would continue to be contested and articulated, in a dizzying number of combinations, village by village, throughout the next twenty-five years.

After the Conservative defeat in Puebla, the next conflict that provided a medium for renewed discursive constructions was the three-year civil war (1858–1861), and in particular the internal divisions within Liberalism that were fought out in the sierra between 1859 and 1860. I have already dealt with the details of the split between Méndez and Alatriste (see chapter 2). Suffice it to recall here that, in the context of competition with his rivals, Méndez sought indigenous allies in previously Conservative communities. Perhaps for the first time he took seriously the democratic potential of Liberalism in a communal context. The result was a rethinking of democratic participation and community property rights within an expanded Liberal definition of autonomy and political decentralization.

This rethinking of democratic participation entailed not only the incorporation of new groups and communal constituencies into an already defined Liberal agenda but also the very transformation of Liberal discourses and agendas in interaction with popular political culture. It produced an especially radical and decentered form of Liberalism. In an attempt to reflect its popular, everyday, and inclusive nature, I will refer to it as "communitarian" Liberalism. This term reflects both the contradictions inherent in collectivizing Liberal principles and the internal communal tensions intensified by a coalition with Liberalism. It suggests as well that, under the extraordinary conditions created by civil and foreign wars, a whole host of notions and elements not found routinely within Liberalism might become a part of it.

Elaborated during ten years of civil war and foreign intervention, communitarian Liberalism united the broadest possible coalition for the confrontation with Conservative and foreign enemies. The frontiers of discursive antagonism became especially flexible in this context, allowing for the articulation, through equivalence, of elements that otherwise might not have formed part of Liberal discourse. The flexibility of boundaries sometimes produced ambiguous connections among elements, or unclear, almost floating promises and expectations. In many of these cases contradictions would resurface when the emergencies of war were over. Meanwhile, the stage was set for the evolution of particularly powerful and innovative forms of alternative popular nationalism.

To illustrate the forms of articulation that could occur within communitarian Liberalism, I will analyze some examples of discursive construction occurring in the Sierra de Puebla between 1859 and 1867. Three of them are related to the issue of land and municipal politics and demonstrate the flexibility of articulations through equivalence in this period. The fourth, more difficult to pin down, is the growth of a "floating" sense of entitlement, of a variety of expectations regarding how "good" citizens would be rewarded after the conflict. In all four cases, however, the very ambiguity of discursive frontiers elicited dramatic political and cultural creativity on the part of rural populations.

Stretching the Boundaries: Conflict and Coalition, 1858–1867

In 1859–1860, when a dispute among Liberal factions in the Puebla highlands erupted in the interstices of the Liberal-Conservative civil war, the faction led by Juan N. Méndez and Ramón Márquez Galindo connected through the Xochiapulco national guard to the Totonac communities of Tenampulco and Tuzamapan. A distinct interpretation of Liberal land laws on disamortization of communal or municipal properties underlay this alliance. As is well known, the original Liberal laws on the privatization of corporate properties applied equally to church and communal lands, calling for the privatization of both in the interest of developing a market society of individuals who could all be equal before the law. In practice, however, such principles proved to be illusory.[15] After the original passage of the disamortization law in June 1856, therefore, Miguel Lerdo de Tejada issued a series of clarificatory decrees concerning the disamortization of small municipal or communal properties. These decrees can be seen as an alternative interpretation of how Liberal law could be applied to the communal and smallholding peasantry. It was to this alternative tradition that the Méndez-Xochiapulco-Tenampulco alliance attached itself, stretching its boundaries in the process.

Lerdo explained in his original and most important circular of 9 October 1856 that attempts to apply the June land laws had generated confusion. Certain individuals, he said, "are abusing the ignorance of poor peasants, and especially the Indians, to make them see the disamortization law as opposed to their interests, [but] whose principal purpose was, quite to the contrary, to favor the most humble classes." There were also abuses, according to Lerdo, in the application of the June law. Most important, the poorer peasants were being left out of the adjudication process because they did not have the money to pay the necessary fees or because speculators beat them out in presenting petitions to adjudicate specific plots. It was necessary to remedy these abuses and to convince the poor smallholding peasantry that the law was meant to benefit them; otherwise, "the law would be nullified in one of its principal goals, which was the subdivision of agricultural property." Thus, Lerdo ordered that all plots whose value was under two hundred pesos be adjudicated for free and of necessity to their de facto possessors unless they clearly and specifically renounced their right to such plots.[16]

A month later, in a case brought before the president by the village of Tepeji del Río, the democratic interpretation of the Liberal land laws was pushed even further. The villagers of Tepeji had requested, only a week after Lerdo's original circular, that their common plots in individual usufruct ("de repartimiento") not be included in those affected by the adjudication procedures. The president chose instead to declare the tradition of communal property, which he interpreted as the Spanish crown extending ownership of land to indigenous communities while prohibiting its sale or transfer, to be entirely relevant and legitimate in a Liberal context. Thus, he declared,

> the relevant lands should be held and enjoyed by the referred Indians in absolute property, receiving thus the right to pawn, rent, and sell them, and to dispose of them as any owner does of his things, and without the mentioned Indians needing to pay any cost, since they are not receiving the lands in adjudication, since they already owned them, but simply are being freed of inappropriate and anomalous impediments attached to that ownership.

In this interpretation Liberal legislation modified communal property rights only by allowing the free circulation of the plots. The identity of the proprietors and the tradition of proprietorship should remain otherwise unchanged.[17]

The Méndez-Márquez alliance took this kind of interpretation as its starting point when it protected the rights of Totonac Indians over those of white vecinos in the adjudication of municipal land in the Teziutlán-Tenampulco area. The contested terrain between districts, in this case where Teziutlán, Tlatlauqui, and Jonotla all bordered on one another, became especially difficult to define during processes of adjudication. Commercial agriculturalists from Teziutlán had rented or possessed lands in these regions, prime tropical lands for livestock or other commercial uses, and wished to privatize them. Municipalities were also not clear on where the dividing lines stood between them. Under such circumstances the allies of Alatriste in Teziutlán began a process of Liberal disentailment that they hoped would benefit them. They used the most literal interpretation of the June 1856 law as their guide: land to whoever possesses it at the time. Márquez and Méndez, by contrast, articulated the claims of villagers to the spirit of the 1856 law, as represented in the clarificatory circulars and decrees of October and November, and supported indigenous self-defense actions against white landowners adjudicating themselves municipal properties.[18]

When Rafael Avila, vecino of Teziutlán and a local political official named by Alatriste, protested Márquez's actions in his town, he couched the protest in terms of the first interpretation of Liberal land law. "Márquez's provisions regarding land continue to give bad results," he wrote, "because today all the Indians from Tenampulco not only want to grab part of my lands but now they want them all, and about half of those that belong to this municipality, and they have already tried to take possession of them with weapons in their hands." Avila further accused Márquez of offering weapons to the peasants from Tenampulco and El Chacal in order to expel Teziutlán vecinos from municipal lands, predicting there would be a "caste war" if Alatriste did not take stern countermeasures. From Avila's point of view, his predictions began to come true three days later when indigenous soldiers sent by Márquez invaded the town and sought to arrest the local officials in charge of the disentailment process.[19]

Yet it is instructive to view the conflicts from the perspective of the other interpretation of Liberal law. If the original and legitimate right of proprietorship was the grant given indigenous communities by the Spanish crown, and if indeed one of the main purposes of Liberal land legislation was the redistribution of land, then the indigenous peasants of Tenampulco, Tuzamapan, El Chacal, Jonotla, and associated villages had a better right to disputed municipal lands than did the wealthier white inhabitants of Teziutlán. Moreover, since these peasants had not renounced their right to the land in any legal or explicit way, any process of adjudication being carried out in Teziutlán was not only illegitimate but illegal. Indeed, in light of the circular of 9 October 1856, Avila and his ilk might well be considered "speculators." In this context the actions of indigenous peasants, when they attempted to recover the lands and to arrest the political authorities in charge of adjudications, were legally justified.

In the Sierra de Puebla, then, through specific alliances, conflicts, and discursive practices, an alternative interpretation of Liberal land law already present in debates within the Liberal state was articulated to an emerging regional discourse on the meaning of property. In this context the ownership of land was neither foremost nor most legitimately a question of individual or private rights but was instead interconnected with histories of common right and usage dating back to the Spanish conquest. In conflicts over land, moreover, the humble and indigenous had greater legitimacy simply by their status. They were owners unless they expressly and publicly said otherwise. Small wonder that the indigenous peasants of the Tenampulco-Tuzamapan area gave Márquez and Méndez their enthusiastic support. Small wonder, too, that the remaining factions of white Liberals in Teziutlán, Huauchinango, and Zacatlán, as well as the southern *llanuras* of Puebla state, did not. That both continued to fight against Conservatives, and later French Interventionists, exemplified the problematic unity of communitarian Liberalism.

During the French Intervention two other moments of discursive construction further developed the alternative Liberal discourse around communal land. Both occurred in 1864, at a moment when the region was under attack from Interventionist forces. Both had as their prime inspiration the need to maintain or expand the coalitions fighting against the invaders.

In March 1864 José María Maldonado, then military commander of Zacapoaxtla, issued a circular to the commanders of the indigenous villages of Xochitlán, Nauzontla, and Cuetzalan explaining the Reform Laws. As we have already seen, Maldonado's main message was that the laws of reform had as their first beneficiaries the humble classes, saving them from the abuses of a priestly elite and giving them access to land; he was interested in expanding the popular base for his resistance.[20] But what is most interesting for our purposes here is that his circular's discourse on land built on the tradition already detailed. It connected to the national circulars and resolutions of October and November 1856 as well as to the articulations occurring in the 1859–1860 conflict between Méndez and Alatriste.

According to Maldonado, the purpose of the disamortization laws was "to turn national property into private property, enriching multitudes of families," and he argued that "communal lands in the villages should be distributed among the Indians in equal parts in order to meet their needs and without their having to pay anything." Yet despite his attempts at carrying out these dispositions in the fairest possible way, he continued, some people had felt their interests had been hurt, in particular those who, "abusing the authority they had held, had grabbed for themselves the communal lands existing in the highlands, to the detriment of the villagers." Thus, he ordered the village commanders, it was their duty to enforce the law and to make sure that all white landowners ("de razón") and those owning more than one fanega of land paid the necessary taxes in order to make their adjudications legal. Those who were unwilling to do so would lose access to the land, which would then be distributed among the poor.[21]

To this point Maldonado built on existing alternative discourses, selecting community members and poor Indians as especially entitled to justice under the reforms. In his discussion, as in the previous examples, property rights were tempered with justice and put in the context of redistribution and a commitment to equality. But Maldonado went even further: he connected the right to property to defense of the nation. "Since traitors have proven themselves undeserving of consideration by the government," he concluded, "all those who possess communal land in the villages and do not immediately seek a pardon will have the lands taken away and distributed [to the poor]."[22]

In connecting the defense of the nation to entitlement to property, Maldonado opened up a new line of equivalence along which to articulate a popular Liberal discourse. Along this line the ownership of property was not simply an individual issue; rather, it became reembedded in questions of collective behavior, collective good, and community responsibility. The community and its representatives had the right to judge who was deserving and who was not, according to political and moral principles. And those who did defend the nation—soldiers of whatever rank—were entitled, by implication, to own land.

An analogous articulation occurred in December of the same year, when the Liberal governor of Puebla state, Fernando María Ortega, signed a decree giving Xochiapulco formal ownership rights over the lands of haciendas Xochiapulco and La Manzanilla as well as the lands of the extinct village Xilotepec. In a direct follow-up to the original pact with Juan Alvarez, Ortega also granted Xochiapulco independent municipal status, making it a *villa* instead of a simple pueblo, and calling it "Villa del Cinco de Mayo." As the new name for the community attests, the decree was justified in a discourse of entitlement concerning the rewards that "good" citizens received.

The state had the right to grant land in such a context. The three justifications appearing at the beginning of the decree were that the state has the right to reward the services of citizens and populations; that the inhabitants of Xochiapulco "have given eminent service in the noble cause of Mexico's independence, and their soldiers among other brilliant actions of war distinguished themselves in the glorious battle of the Fifth of May"; and that, for the public good, it is sometimes necessary to take over property, after having estimated and paid its just price. The state was designated, in the decree, as the mediator between Xochiapulco and the hacendados. Legitimate access to land was granted, through a series of nested justifications, to all members of the community because of the village's role in the resistance to the French but also, according to rank, to the soldiers who had fought on the Fifth of May.[23] In the end, therefore, the issue of private property, and of access to it, was set in the context of service to the nation and to the community.

Although access or right to land was the entry point in this discourse of entitlement, other rights were also articulated through the concept of entitlement, most clearly in Ortega's decree of December 1864. People who defended the nation were good citizens and thus entitled to land, political independence, political participation, education, economic prosperity, and so on. By using defense of the nation as the common point of access, this discourse decentralized power and privilege as nodes of entitlement and replaced them with bravery and service, much in the same way that the national guard presence shook up existing hegemonic coalitions within the communities. A discourse of entitlement thus established, in a floating and hazy way, the possibility of a more democratically organized political community, one where membership and rights depended on behavior rather than on birth, age, class, ethnicity, or regional origin. At least until the defeat of the Intervention, these free-floating discourses of entitlement and citizenship worked extremely well in keeping together the broad coalitions defending the republic. But there were dangers to communitarian Liberalism as well. Once the end of the conflict caused fighters to claim their rights as citizens, no one was really sure what these rights entailed. Debates over their definition would be felt in Mexican politics throughout the nineteenth century and into the twentieth.

Indeed, with the defeat of the French Intervention and the execution of Maximilian in 1867, the political alliances that underwrote the construction of Liberal discourse began to change. No longer was the main goal the defeat of a powerful military enemy. Increasingly, the newly emerging Liberal agenda centered around the reorganization and institutionalization of power. As this process occurred, the flexible discursive frontiers, fashioned during war to facilitate broad and floating practices of equivalence among elements, began to harden. As Liberal soldiers began to envision the rewards to which they were broadly entitled for having defended the nation, attempts to reconstruct tighter frontiers of antagonism met with strong and concerted resistance.

Former Liberal allies worked out the meanings of popular discourses on land and municipal autonomy—and of the more "floating" definitions of citizenship, political participation, and access to resources and prosperity—in the context of the political and military confrontations generated by reconstruction. In the Sierra de Puebla three specific struggles were crucial: the rebellion over the election of a state governor in 1868; the Arriaga rebellion of 1869 and associated uprisings through 1870; and the local movement associated with Porfirio Díaz's revolt of La Noria in 1871–1872. While each conflict was organized around a slightly different political and discursive center, all three involved the definition of interconnected elements in communal, regional, and national Liberal discourses. I will therefore combine a general consideration of the discursive themes that applied to all three rebellions with a more specific discussion of their interactions in each political moment. Finally, I will ponder the more general problem of building a national hegemonic discourse, the monumental task faced by Liberal politicians in late-nineteenth-century Mexico.

Shrinking the Boundaries: Reconstruction Through Repression During the Governor's Rebellion of 1868

Beginning in the first months of 1867, before victory against the Intervention was complete, people in the Puebla highlands began to debate what the future would look like. If we can judge from surviving documents, their highest priorities were land, education, and compensation for sacrifices made during the war. In many ways these questions were connected. The poverty and scarcity brought on by the war made support for schools or returning soldiers difficult to come by. Families desperate to eke out a living found it impossible to send their children to school.

The question of land was also connected to subsistence. The overlapping titles of adjudication issued during the war often made the definition of property rights even more confusing in the postwar period. These questions were also interlaced with notions and expectations of entitlement whose hazy, floating quality had been crucial, as inspiration, during the fighting. During peacetime, however, these expectations returned to haunt villagers as they tried to define their rights and determine to whom they must turn to have those rights recognized.

The definition of rights was made even more complicated by the general economic depression that rocked the country at the end of the war. Between February and July 1867 the mayor of Tetela de Ocampo learned that funds were so scarce in Puebla city that municipalities and national guard soldiers could expect no compensation for losses suffered during the conflict. By August of that year individual fighters could do nothing but apply for one of the honorific medals decreed by the national state in recognition of bravery. According to letters sent out by the state government in July, political officials had no recourse but to tax local merchants to provide national guard soldiers with a week of severance pay. Officials were also encouraged to make a list of the dead or disabled so that their families could apply for pensions.[24]

Such problems were perhaps inevitable after ten years of violence. Yet, as municipal officials in Tetela discovered, villagers had high expectations for peace. One such expectation was, as we have seen, the development of education. Already in February the people of San Nicolás barrio were looking forward to its advancement during an era of "lasting peace." In the following months, however, communities throughout the district faced local problems with school attendance and financing, problems deep and difficult enough to cause the resignation of teachers and confrontations between some local officials and vecinos.

In a letter to Tetela's jefe político in late July, municipal officials from Aquixtla explained that their five schools were financed with the Chicontepec tax—when it was possible to collect it. Given the scarcity of maize, families were migrating in search of seed. The teacher from one of the schools had finally left because they owed him twelve pesos. Whether because they were not paid or because the children simply did not come to school, other teachers also left their posts in the first six months of 1867. Yet the villagers kept on, demanding resources from the state government to cover the sustenance or construction of schools. In some cases they even held communal assemblies to legitimate renting municipal lands to pay for education.[25]

Another postwar debate was over the disentailment of communal lands. In communal assemblies held during March 1867, several villages, building on the regional discourses constructed during the civil war and the Intervention, connected popular access to communal land with bravery and with contributions made to the cause of the republic. Among the documents that supported village efforts was an 1864 letter from Zacapoaxtla's jefe político to the community of Cuetzalan, in which he emphasized that traitors who had not taken advantage of the 1863 pardon would not have legal access to communal land and that these properties should be repossessed and distributed among "peaceful citizens."

In March 1867, then, while the fighting was still going on, the communities of Jonotla, Tuzamapan, and Tenampulco—the same who had joined with Méndez in 1860 to articulate a Liberal counterdiscourse on land—held assemblies to consider the Liberal government's circular on disentailment. All three agreed with the privatization as long as all adjudications went to inhabitants (vecinos) of the village or the district; the disentailment of the plots held by vecinos was done without charge; and all preexisting problems of boundaries and land usurpations were resolved ahead of time and with justice. Perhaps most interesting, however, was the justification given for exemption from fees in the adjudication. Since the villages had collaborated assiduously and paid all their taxes during the 1860s—that is, during the wars—now they were entitled to their properties without charge. Jonotla and Tuzamapan mentioned especially the thirteen hundred pesos they had contributed to the resistance in 1863, while Tenampulco recalled always being on time with its contributions, plus having provided labor to build a field hospital in Espinal.[26]

Also related to these issues of entitlement was the treatment of those citizens who had collaborated with the invaders. As we have already seen, from the very early part of the war against the French the citizens of the Sierra de Puebla had been led to believe that resistance to the invasion would result in preferential access to resources. In June 1867 the state government transcribed further orders from the high command of the Eastern Army, exempting from fines and confiscation of property only those citizens who had occupied municipal office without salary during the French Intervention. Small wonder, then, that when Benito Juárez issued the Convocatoria for national elections in August 1867, people protested the idea that those who recognized or served the empire should be forgiven.[27]

Within these broader debates about collaboration with the empire, deputies in the Puebla State Congress argued over exemptions to the congressional decree of 25 January 1868, which gave state employment preferentially to those who had fought against the empire and prohibited anyone who had received a salary from the imperial government from holding a public post. The debates around exemption were passionate and deeply gendered. Those who sought pardon justified their behavior in terms of their families. In response, the *serrano* deputy Juan Crisóstomo Bonilla told the story of Mexicans whose heroism forced them to burn their own houses before submitting to the enemy, a clear reference to Xochiapulco. While the same level of heroics could not be expected of everyone, Bonilla continued, at least Liberals could have refused to take a public post. When a deputy suggested that a contradiction existed between duty to family and duty to country when sons needed bread and daughters were about to become prostitutes, another serrano congressman answered that many dedicated Liberals who had undergone misery without serving the empire were now entirely forgotten by their country. Finally, a last passionate speaker asked, Who now thinks about the widows of the heroes of the resistance? Yet in the end a majority of the petitions for exemption were approved.[28]

It is especially clear, from these debates on the rehabilitation of state bureaucrats, that floating promises of entitlement and rewards meant very little when the task at hand was reconstitution and centralization of state power. No matter how heroic an individual's service to the nation, political loyalty, social class, and administrative skills were much more important than war record or previous political stripes. This would become clear once again in the election for state governor, which pitted Juan Nepomuceno Méndez against Rafael J. García. Wounded after leading the Sierra de Puebla's Sixth National Guard Battalion in the first charge against the French on 5 May 1862, Méndez had a stellar military record dating all the way back to the Liberal Revolution and the three-year civil war. He had confronted French and Austrian troops on the battlefield throughout the 1860s, becoming an important figure in the heroic Eastern Army. By contrast, García had a one-page military file that recorded his honorific title of brigadier general, granted by Minister of War Ignacio Mejía in November 1867. This title was given a scarce couple of months before the election for governor and was most likely a reward for García's loyal service to Juárez during the political struggles of that year. Indeed, García's only claim to fame during the Intervention was that he was persecuted and placed in jail by the Imperial government for publishing, in his Puebla newspaper *La Idea Liberal*, an editorial suggesting a plebiscite on the empire.[29]

These were some of the underlying issues confronting the Puebla State Congress when it met on 15 February 1868 to consider the results of the state election for constitutional governor. During the previous six months the primary presidential elections and the contest for state congress had served as dress rehearsals in the conflict over which Liberal faction would control state politics. As provisional governor during these battles, García had done Juárez's bidding, struggling town by town to construct political majorities against Méndez, whose wartime record defined him as an ally of Juárez's rival, Porfirio Díaz. While Juárez's presidential victory was never in doubt, state congressional elections yielded a complex set of crosscutting alliances in the legislature. And in terms of numbers the elections for governor constituted a clear popular victory for the Mendista forces.[30]

In local elections held in every district, under the principle of universal manhood suffrage, no gubernatorial candidate had received the majority mandated by law. When the congressional electoral commission met to consider the results, it found that Méndez had received 48.5 percent of the vote, while García, Ignacio Romero Vargas, and Fernando María Ortega had received 18.1, 16.4, and 5.2 percent respectively. The commission's majority felt that Méndez should be declared the winner: there had been irregularities in two of the state's electoral districts, and if the tallies from these two districts were annulled, Méndez had a majority of the popular vote. The commission's minority disagreed, however. They pointed out that Méndez had a majority only if all the votes from the two questionable districts were annulled but not if the clearly illegal votes were annulled and the rest left to stand. The minority therefore argued in favor of a congressional vote among the four top contenders.[31]

These, then, were the undercurrents at work on 15 February, with control of a key state in the balance for the Juaristas. Méndez's allies in Congress, led by his fellow resistance fighters and war heroes Juan Crisóstomo Bonilla and Ramón Márquez Galindo, were understandably suspicious of the minority position. In a first impassioned speech on 15 February, Bonilla told a packed and emotionally charged auditorium that certain members of congress sought to delegitimize Méndez by rejecting the majority position of the electoral commission. This rejection, Bonilla concluded, would be an annulment of the popular will.[32]

Before it was possible to vote on the majority and minority positions, however, the congressmen needed to decide whether Romero, both a member of congress and one of the contenders for governor, could vote without conflict of interest. Romero offered to retire his name from the candidates' list in order to stay and, after some debate, was allowed to do so. With Romero present and voting, the majority position was defeated by one vote, eliciting passionate protests from Márquez and Bonilla. Both serrano congressmen insisted, in separate speeches, that some of their colleagues were colluding against Méndez. After the minority position, without Romero's name, was approved for a vote, Bonilla stood up. "As an honest man, my conscience rebels against this procedure," he concluded, "and I am leaving, because I cannot continue to form a part of a legislature that violates the law and scorns the popular will."[33]

When the vote for governor actually took place, Rafael J. García won by a vote of nine to two. Six members of congress previously voting had either left the assembly, as Bonilla did, or expressed their alienation by not casting a vote.[34] Through internal manipulation and conflict and a questionable call on Romero's presence in the assembly, a candidate supported by less than one-fifth of the electorate defeated another with nearly one-half of the popular vote. Technically, of course, procedure had been followed—at least most of the time. But when a population had just emerged from foreign occupation with claims and expectations about the rewards to which their resistance had entitled them, such a clear rejection of a war hero and of "the popular will" could have explosive results. To the chagrin of Juárez, García, and all their allies, that was exactly what happened. First, however, the discourses of rebellion would be articulated slowly and painfully, over a period of three months. At their center lay broken pacts of entitlement and political participation.

García's supporters tried to depict the sierra rebels as irresponsible, violent people who thoughtlessly joined an uprising to further the personal ambitions of a militaristic leader. Yet the people in the highland villages most closely tied to Méndez during the previous ten years of struggle— Tetela, Zacatlán, Xochiapulco, Jonotla, Tuzamapan, Tenampulco—were not really interested in rebellion. People were "very tired and ... desire[d] peace," Juan Francisco Lucas had written to Juárez in October 1867. Referring to Xochiapulco, he continued: "This municipality has suffered much there was no other town that suffered as we did on our entire front everything was burned by the invaders, and if we do not work every day there is nothing for the subsistence of our families."[35] Although the intensity of Xochiapulco's experience had indeed been unique, other villages shared the same sense of fatigue, of yearning for peace and better times. Under such circumstances only the most direct and violent insult to their hard-won rights and independence could possibly make them change their minds. Between February and June 1868 the election for state governor was successfully constructed as such.

The effort began with a letter from five of the six Puebla congressmen who had refused to vote in the last part of the 15 February session. Published in the national opposition newspaper *El Monitor Republicano* less than a week after the event, it blamed Romero directly for the illegal outcome in favor of García. In the next few days some of the strongholds of Mendista sentiment in the sierra held village assemblies to discuss the election results. We have an account of such an event in Zacatlán on 25 February, prompted by the arrival of four hundred rifles from Tetela de Ocampo. According to Rafael Cravioto, a Juarista Liberal in neighboring Huauchinango:

> A great multitude of people came out to receive them [the rifles] with the military and governmental authorities, and music [was played], fireworks were set off, and the church bells were rung. A cry went up: Long live citizens Juan Méndez and Vicente Márquez, and death to the governor Rafael J. García and to the [local] jefe político Dimas López [a García appointee]. They finished off this scandal by tearing down all the government decrees posted in public places.

Immediately afterward, according to Cravioto, a municipal assembly was held. Political authorities, municipal employees, and notable citizens all signed an *acta* protesting the election of García as governor. In the following weeks this acta, along with several signed in other sierra municipalities, was forwarded to the congress in a formal and legal protest against García's election.[36]

The Liberal discourse formulated in these petitions was organized around two central elements. One was the people's right to decide political outcomes through the medium of elections and to have that right protected through respect for law and for the right to petition. The other was that popular participation in the wars of the previous decade had entitled people to sovereignty and to social and legal guarantees, all of which were being trampled by manipulative politicians. In Zacatlán the municipal secretary Pablo Urrutia emphasized that the events were especially "undeserved by a noble, courageous, and generous people, who had conquered, through the sacrifice of their own blood, their freedom and their most precious [legal and social] guarantees." In Tetela the node of moral outrage was the abuse of confidence perpetrated by the congressional deputies on a naturally patient and simple people.

> It is a sad thing, sir, for the villages, people who by their very nature
> are tolerant, . . . [but] cannot be so when they are humiliated, their
> rights and sovereignty wounded and trampled upon, and with the
> further aggravating circumstance of abuse of confidence, abuse of
> the simplicity and innocence of the people.

The only way to redress these grievances, all the actas agreed, was to declare García an illegal governor and to give the post to Méndez, the legitimate contender who deserved popular support.[37]

Although the petitions were presented to the congress by Ramón Márquez Galindo, the deputies refused to hear them because they had not been presented through appropriate channels. No one saw fit to point out that the congressional refusal placed the petitioners in a political cul-de-sac: the appropriate channel was the governor; yet by presenting the petitions to him, the villages would have been forced to recognize the authority against whom they were protesting in the first place. No single deputy, moreover, was willing to take the petitions on personally, which would have been an alternative route to formal consideration. Thus, the petitions were not admitted, and Márquez Galindo took them back.[38]

The petitions became a political hot potato, tossed back and forth between the congress and the governor, between the state and federal governments, between the sierra villages and the state government. For the people in the sierra, this refusal to hear the actas further legitimated their right to rebel.

No one in the government wished to disavow the petitions entirely, since this would have questioned a sacred Liberal right. The federal government needed to get to the bottom of the controversy in order to close off all legitimate ground for rebellion. García's legitimacy also rested on being reasonable about the petitions. And the congressional deputies were eager to show they had acted legally and according to principle.

The fate of the petitions in the state legislature was officially reconstructed, in a three-stage process, between April and May 1868. Even though García agreed with Juárez that considering the actas would remove all legal pretext for an uprising, he was initially convinced that the documents had never been presented because they had not passed through his office. By early May he was writing to Juárez that he planned to use his influence in congress to get an official declaration that the petitions had never been received. In a secret session on 7 May, however, during which the legislature debated the rebellion in Zacatlán and authorized a military expedition to the area, the actas came up once again, and the deputies were forced to admit they had seen the documents. Despite a long and defensive discussion about legitimate channels and lack of time to consider the documents, the approval of a military expedition badly muddied the moral waters. On the next day the three representatives from the sierra districts stopped attending the sessions.[39]

This was still not the end of the issue. In a third stage of official reconstruction García sent an official note to the congress more than two weeks later, asking that they reach a formal decision on the actas. In the meantime he suspended preparations for the military expedition already authorized. García explained that he wished to avoid spilling blood and that this last legal alternative might change the minds of inhabitants in the sierra districts, who, believing that the congress had simply refused to hear their protests, "judg[ed] therefore that they have exercised their right to petition in vain." In an immediate special session congress declared formally that it recognized the right to petition, as long as it was done through appropriate channels. But given the election law of 1868, which stipulated that no protest against the legality of the election could be heard beyond the day of the election, it was impossible to hear protests regarding the change or nullification of the election procedures. Thus, in perfectly circuitous official language, the illegitimacy of the sierra rebellion was constructed.[40]

Meanwhile, in the sierra itself municipal and communal assemblies in many villages took the final step in articulating a legitimate discourse of rebellion during the first few days of June. A municipal assembly in Tetela declared that town in rebellion against the state government on 1 June, naming Juan Francisco Lucas commander in chief of the northern front. Over the next week communal assemblies discussed and approved that document in Zapotitlán, Jonotla, Escatlan, Zoquiapan, Huitzilan, and Tuzamapan. On 10 June, Juan Francisco Lucas established the formal bases for governance during the rebellion. He made clear in a letter to the jefe político in Tetela that all relations with the federal government should remain normal, for the revolt had nothing to do with the national state. As of mid-June, therefore, most of the highlands was in revolt. The process of open confrontation and repression had begun.[41]

I treat the military and political implications of the rebellion in chapter 8. For now, suffice it to say that the federal government did not accept Lucas's separation of state and federal issues, sending a division of the federal army to the area to help in the repression. Ignacio R. Alatorre, previously a comrade in arms of the serranos during the French Intervention and more recently known for his successful repression of a movement in Yucatán, led the governmental attack. The presence of the federal army raised two new questions for the rebels, each of which was resolved through debate in municipal assemblies.[42]

The first was whether or not to confront the federal army. As Juan Francisco Lucas put it in his call for a general assembly of representatives from all the rebellious districts, the presence of the federal army "has put these villages in the painful position of choosing either to accept the shameless trampling of their rights or to compare the strength of their weapons against those of the federal army." The choice was left to each district. In the end all attempted to avoid confrontation with federal forces while maintaining in principle the right to question García's legitimacy.

Alatorre put the question to Lucas on 9 July, when he wrote an official letter from Tlatlauqui demanding to know Lucas's plans. Lucas's answer showed how deeply he felt the dilemma, yet in the end he stood by the principles of the revolt. "In the districts that form a part of this front," he wrote, "and that consider me their leader," there had always been respect for the federal government. That had been demonstrated repeatedly in the past days, as the national guard battalions evacuated Teziutlán, Tlatlauqui, and Zacapoaxtla before the federal advance. But in the name of the districts he represented, Lucas continued, it was important to point out that this respect

> could not make the villages sacrifice their conscience by recognizing
> don Rafael García as legitimate constitutional governor of the state

of Puebla, since the fact that his election was null and illegitimate can be perceived by all the citizens.

We still trust that the supreme magistrate of the nation will not want to impose upon us this painful sacrifice, which would be tantamount to admitting that the right of the people to elect a governor is nothing but a vain whim.[43]

Negotiations continued for another week, leading to a personal meeting between Alatorre and Lucas on 17 June. But a basic antagonism emerged between the rebels' core argument that the people had the right to decide and the government's bottom-line need to defend the principle of authority. This antagonism was clear in the two generals' distinct understandings of the 17 July agreement. Alatorre reported to the minister of defense that Lucas "offered to inform his subordinates that he wished to separate himself from the political question of the sierra, putting down his weapons before the federal government." Lucas thought he had offered to take the issue of surrender back to the districts he represented and discuss it in municipal assemblies. By 26 July all the communities and national guards in rebellion had discussed the issue, and all had agreed that surrender was impossible under the conditions presented. In his answer to Alatorre, therefore, Lucas explained that after consulting the national guard forces and officers under his command, the answer was

> that with the deepest sentiment, they see the humiliating conditions that [the federal government] wants to impose on them, and that before accepting these they are willing to sacrifice all, even their very lives, for they are conscious that they have not committed any crime, but that quite the contrary they have made heroic sacrifices in the name of national independence, and in the name of those very same national principles and of liberal principles, if they would allow themselves to be disarmed of their weapons, the majority of which they took off [the bodies of] the foreign enemy and Mexican traitors, they would no longer be deserving of the name "citizen."[44]

The second question the rebels needed to answer was intimately related to the first. In the context of a possible confrontation with the federal army, were they willing to lay down their weapons unconditionally? Lucas made clear in his letter to Alatorre that the answer was no. The weapons in the hands of the sierra national guards took on great symbolic value. They were more than their mode of defense. They represented the people's earlier struggles, and what the soldiers felt entitled to; indeed, the weapons almost became their medals. Whether in Tetela de Ocampo on 22 July, when the national guard agreed in municipal assembly to keep their weapons, or at the Apulco Pass outside Zacapoaxtla on the twenty-sixth, when the national guard soldiers from that town disagreed with their officers on the very same issue, the weapons came to symbolize entitlement through bravery.[45]

The Tetela document, signed by all the members of the national guard, is particularly coherent on the issues involved and merits close analysis. The document states at the beginning that to give up their weapons would deprive the national guard of the laurels they won on 5 May 1862 and at the sieges of Querétaro, Mexico City, and Puebla city. The national guard soldiers had always used their weapons in defense of republican institutions. Even the foreign invaders never tried to impose unconditional disarmament. The local soldiers had sacrificed everything, suffering hunger and many other calamities, in defense of the republic. The specific formulation deserves to be quoted at length:

> Decimated, the Citizens of the District conquered with their blood the fame of the land where they were born and where various fathers mourned the death of their beloved sons, many widows weep over the absence of their husbands, and a multitude of orphans feel the lack of food that the physical labor of their parents previously provided them: With this in mind how could the fathers, brothers, and friends of these victims abandon the weapons that they have sealed with their blood, carrying them until the end of their days?
>
> And finally; understanding it to be their duty to conserve their honor, their glory, their dignity as Citizen-soldiers [*Ciudadanos milicianos*], the general interests of the District and the private ones of each individual and finally their rights as free men, in honor of their compatriots [*paisanos*] who were sacrificed while defending republican institutions, they declare: that it is their entirely free [*plena*] will to keep in their possession the weapons they carry.[46]

In the process of struggle, then, hemmed in by a lack of alternatives, the citizen-soldiers of the Sierra de Puebla constructed complex discourses about rebellion and refusal to surrender. These discourses began from moral outrage. Although articulated differently in each village or communal assembly, they all centered on broken pacts, on covenants that had been built on the battlefield, through death and privation, over an entire decade. These covenants had been shattered by a series of simple acts: disregarding the popular will in an election; ridiculing the right to petition through circuitous official doublespeak; and sending in federal troops, commanded by a former comrade in arms to demand unconditional surrender and disarmament.

In the face of these conditions, even as they were being treated like common criminals or intractable enemies, the serranos gathered up the threads of a tattered popular Liberalism. They wove the strands stubbornly and patiently, through unequal battles, village disagreements, and renewed loss of life and blood, into a new and more specific pattern of alternative nationalist discourse. In their documents and assemblies they remembered who they were, where they had been, what they had done, and ultimately what they felt entitled to expect from a national government. In 1868 they were defeated. But those who lived to fight again took with them the lessons of that year. In the starker, more militant regional political culture they helped build, it was bravery, constancy, and service—rather than privilege, wealth, and connections—that earned the title of Citizen, with a capital C.[47]

The Struggle Within:
Alternative Nationalisms, National Guard Soldiers,
and Communal Hegemony in 1868

The political culture emerging in the Puebla highlands was itself a product of internal hegemonic processes, within and between communities. As had been the case during the Intervention, the cabeceras of Zacatlán and Tetela led the movement, sending their declarations out to their anexos to be heard and acted on. In Jonotla and Tuzamapan the language of response to Tetela was hierarchical, using such phrases as "obeying" or "following orders." Within the municipalities and villages as well, communal assemblies were hegemonic processes. The literacy of the secretarios and the presence of the pasados constructed particular types of political spaces in which not all possible positions could be heard effectively. We do not have access to the counterdiscourses murmured along the edges of the crowd. What did the widows so reified in the Tetela national guard document have to say about the struggle? Perhaps they would have preferred peace to another war, caring less whether their husbands' blood-covered weapons were hallowed by further loss of life. Perhaps they wanted to labor for their children and families rather than for yet another round of tortilla rations delivered to the troops.[48]

We also lack specific information on the renegotiations between pasados and national guard soldiers once the latter lost bargaining power with the federal government and consequently lost influence in the communities. One source of clues is the Tetela national guard document, where the national guard's weapons symbolize citizenship in two distinct ways. One argument for keeping the weapons is that they represent the losses suffered

by families and communities: the dead lived up to their communal responsibility, and their sacrifice in turn obligates the living to pay back their debt
to the dead. The other argument for refusing disarmament is that the weapons symbolize the glory and dignity of the citizen-soldiers and thus also the
interests of the political district, the individual rights of all citizens, and
ultimately their abstract general rights as "free men." If the first argument
represents the communal hegemonic process and leads finally to the pasados, the second argument is the counterhegemonic Liberal process of the
national guards. The two meet as equals in the unanimous, public refusal to
surrender and in their common fight against the federal government. They
thus share the effort to revindicate and reclaim the struggles and sacrifices
of the previous ten years, struggles and sacrifices once again represented in
the central articulation of weapons and citizenship.[49]

A second source of clues about communal negotiations is the presence of
indigenous elders among the prisoners taken in battle from Cuetzalan. In
most rebellious villages in the sierra in 1868, concepts of entitlement were
articulated predominantly through questions of political legitimacy and
participation. In Cuetzalan, by contrast, communal and popular Liberal notions of property in land served as the centerpiece of negotiations between
national guards and pasados. Victims of a concerted push by entrepreneurs
from Zacapoaxtla, who were using Liberal disentailment as a wedge to separate indigenous villagers from their lands, national guards and pasados together negotiated a common strategy of defense of communal property. The
discourse of rebellion in Cuetzalan was therefore organized mainly around
the question of communal disentailment, deepening an already existing
Liberal counterdiscourse while confronting the federal army. National
guard soldiers protected other community members and, in conjunction
with the elders, led them in direct actions against the fences and improvements erected by the interlopers.[50]

Already during the French Intervention, earlier struggles over common
land in Cuetzalan, especially in the indigenous barrio of Tzicuilan, had
helped formulate a popular Liberal discourse on land. In 1862, while José
María Maldonado was military commander in Zacapoaxtla, two alcaldes and
fourteen pasados from Tzicuilan had complained that several recent vecinos
in Cuetzalan had been allowing their cattle to damage the crops of the barrio.
Given Maldonado's reputation for "ideas . . . highly liberal," he would un-
doubtedly "incline [him]self to be a decided supporter of the weak and
especially the Indian race that always suffers [at the hands of] its domina-
tors." Maldonado indeed lived up to his Liberal reputation, working out an
agreement between the villagers of Tzicuilan and the three white vecinos in

which all cattle needed to be removed from the area. Ultimately, Maldonado also supervised the rental of communal land to two of the three vecinos for a period of five years.[51]

As a part of communitarian Liberalism, expectations about disentailment in Cuetzalan were thus well developed. Full-fledged, these expectations would come home to roost in the postwar period. In January 1868 the villagers of Tzicuilan rebelled against what they saw as the continued abuse of their communal land rights. The villagers echoed many of the notions of entitlement earlier presented by the communities of Tuzamapan and Jonotla. This echoing is particularly clear in a letter from Francisco Agustín, Cuetzalan's national guard captain, to Ignacio Arrieta, the district's jefe político. According to Agustín, the people of Tzicuilan barrio considered their rights in communal land to be buttressed by what Guy Thomson has called "a contractual association" with Mendista Liberalism.[52] As we have seen, that association was itself based on the complex construction of a popular Liberal counterdiscourse on land since the 1850s.

Between February and June 1868 rebellions in Zacatlán, Tetela, and Xochiapulco centered around the election of García but intertwined politically and militarily with ongoing unrest and rebellion in Cuetzalan. In late February the indigenous villagers of Tzicuilan and the white citizens in Cuetzalan reached an agreement with the mediation of Juan Francisco Lucas. It allowed the *adjudicaciones* to continue in the hands of a commission that would define which lands were to be left as *ejido* (collective communal property that was legally untouchable under the terms of the Land Law enacted 25 June 1856) and common mountain land and which could go up for adjudication. Yet in late April, Tzicuilan's municipal officials, pasados, and national guard soldiers were still disputing the boundaries defined by the commission. They demanded clearer explanations from the jefe político and other authorities and insisted on redress. "That alcalde and those who call themselves pasados," the commission's report to Zacapoaxtla's jefe político predicted, would not cooperate with the orders presented to them.[53]

Through the beginning of the general armed conflict in the sierra in June and July, Tzicuilan's national guard soldiers, elders, and other villagers resumed direct action. They pulled down walls, destroyed coffee crops, and attacked the residences of white vecinos in the area. For political, ideological, and military reasons, an alliance with the serrano rebels to the south therefore made a great deal of sense. Indeed, Pilar Rivera, Tetela's national guard commander, reported from Apulco Pass on 25 July that federal troops had managed to arrest Francisco Agustín "from Quetzalan [*sic*], who was coming with one hundred Indians to get arms in Xochiapulco." In his orders to Rivera on the same day, Lucas warned him to stay alert for the arrival of the Indians from Cuetzalan and informed him that rations for the soldiers would also be coming from Cuetzalan and Xochitlán.[54]

These intersections and articulations among local struggles also allowed Ignacio Arrieta, juez municipal of Cuetzalan, to use the presence of federal troops as a cover broadly to repress the movement in Tzicuilan and associated barrios. By mid-October approximately twenty indigenous prisoners from Cuetzalan had ended up at Alatorre's general headquarters in Zacapoaxtla. Identified as leaders of the movement, they had been arrested in Apulco at the end of July and in several encounters with and raids on Tzicuilan's and Tzinacantepec's national guard soldiers. Those considered capable of military service—one assumes the younger national guard soldiers—were drafted into the army. The rest, elders among whom the youngest was 64 and the oldest 104, were sent to internal exile in Yucatán.

The pasados and their relatives in Cuetzalan repeatedly petitioned for the release of the old men. Although the surviving elders were returned from Yucatán within several months, state and local officials resisted their release from house arrest in Puebla city well into 1869. The officials argued that "they had positively been among the conspirators in [Cuetzalan] . . . and were only turned over to the second division [of the federal army] once all attempts at leniency had proven useless."[55]

In the initial petition to Juárez, the kinsmen of the pasados insisted that their village had been forced to participate in the movement led by Juan Francisco Lucas. Being powerless, they said, they had no choice in the matter. While Lucas, the movement's leader, was free, a few poor old men were in prison, and "the Indian families of our unfortunate kinsmen are dissolved in tears [seeing that their relatives] are condemned to die in the burning regions of deadly Yucatán." Yet later in the document the petitioners softened their earlier claim, suggesting that "this is not the place where we should say whether or not we wished to defend General Lucas's plan." Instead, they wished only to point out that in 1862 "we resolved to support the flag that with such honor had been carried by the illustrious citizen Benito Juárez; and the Austrian legions and the French army and its allies were unable to force us to change our minds."[56] The specific language of the document did not belong to the petitioners, since none of them knew how to read or write. Waiting in Jalapa, Veracruz, for news of their relatives, the kinsmen from Cuetzalan most likely engaged the services of a local *tinterillo*, a small-time lawyer who specialized in this sort of thing, to embellish the words into something worthy of a president's eyes. Yet the connection to the resistance against the French was always there, in subsequent petitions from the elders as well, very much a part of local discourse.

Again and again the pasados returned to three basic themes. The first was that they were not directly a part of Lucas's rebellion but that Ignacio Arrieta had used it as a cover to arrest and repress them. The second was that they had been political officials in their villages, authorities who upheld the law and did not rebel against the government. And the third was that they had defended constitutional principles and the Liberal cause throughout the last ten years of war.[57]

Evidence from Apulco Pass suggests that claims of innocence in the broader sierra rebellion were untrue, although probably de rigueur in any request for freedom. Given what we know also about internal community tensions—between older and younger men, between pasados and national guards—the various fissures in the documentation may well reflect interior discord over the costs and process of the rebellion. But what emerges most clearly from the combination of different documents is that legitimacy, as defined by defense of Liberal and constitutional principles, was at the center of the petitioners' own self-identification. As Indians from Cuetzalan, communal officials, national guardsmen, or simply members of the community, they were entitled to their rights because no one—not the Austro-Belgian Legion, not the French army, not even Mexican Interventionists—had been able to interfere with their support for republican institutions.

And so we come full circle in this discourse of entitlement: from the original construction of an alternative interpretation of Liberal land law, through the justification of rights, to participation and resources as rewards for bravery and defense of the nation, to the articulation of discourses of rebellion around broken pacts of political participation and responsible adjudication. This was the form taken by an alternative Liberal populism in the Sierra de Puebla during 1868. This was the Liberalism that supported the Montaña party and Méndez against the centralizing Liberalism of Juárez and his ally García.

In 1868 the central axis of struggle was the governor's election and the issues of political accountability, respect for the popular will, and the right to petition. In this sense the rebellion in Cuetzalan, centered on issues of land privatization, remained on the fringes of the broader serrano movement. That would change quickly in the next few months, however. Villages throughout the highlands began to confront the same questions, comparing the floating promises of communitarian Liberalism to the much starker realities of who was getting common lands and how and why they were getting them. The new uprising in late 1869 would reverse the order of the issues. From a much narrower political rebellion quickly evolved a broad movement that challenged, from within, Liberal practice on land adjudication.

The Struggle for Land and Citizenship: Popular Liberalism and Communal Property, 1869–1872

Although matters had come to a head more quickly in Cuetzalan, by the later months of 1868 the mess that was de facto Liberal land policy had gotten out of hand in many villages. The practice of communitarian Liberalism was contradictory on the issue of land. While Liberals made inclusive, populist promises about the people's right to property, they celebrated rental agreements and adjudications that more often than not violated that very same right. Between 1858 and 1867 Liberal officials had carried out adjudications and rental agreements on municipal properties in a fairly ad hoc way, usually to raise funds for the war effort. In so doing, they filled a vast graveyard with broken and overlapping promises that would come back to haunt them.[58] Starting in the second half of 1868, the ghosts of broken promises invaded the Sierra de Puebla along three broad fronts.

The first front involved disputes over boundaries between districts or municipalities. Many disputes were extremely old, dating back to previous separations of one municipality or district from another. The need to privatize or disentail all municipal property increased the importance of a clear boundary, since each individual municipality would receive the right to privatize what was considered theirs. Particularly on the frontiers, where overlapping usufruct was often the rule, conflicts could deepen and continue for years. Often they were exacerbated by renters of municipal lands, who extended the edges of their plot and then presented a petition for adjudication in one of the two municipalities.[59]

Disputes between Jonotla and Tuzamapan, for example, were generated at least in part by rental agreements and attempted adjudications. According to Antonio Sánchez, juez from Tuzamapan, the representatives from Jonotla had arrived at a conflictual meeting of both communities on 14 May 1868 claiming that only Jonotla would have access to certain lands because they had disentailed them. Sánchez argued that this claim was in direct contrast to what had occurred before, when both municipalities had lived "enjoying the lands in unity and harmony." It was necessary for the federal government to decide on the disagreements of the adjudication, since people from Tuzamapan had also disentailed land in the disputed areas. In the end,

Sánchez insisted, "all we want is peace and unity, since the lands where all these villages are located belong to all of us, without distinction." The juez from Jonotla, Francisco Rodríguez, countered that his village wanted only to define the boundaries of the plots adjudicated in March 1867, but the people from Tuzamapan had refused. He added that people from Cuetzalan and Zacapoaxtla had also usurped Jonotla's lands and that a commission should therefore be appointed to look into the matter.[60]

By the first half of 1869 deep and widespread conflicts between municipalities prompted action by the state congress. On 22 May congress issued a decree by which villages were obligated to resolve their differences over lands by naming "árbitros amigables componedores," or individuals with a reputation for honesty and rationality who would oversee a process of arbitration between the two parties. According to the decree, representatives from each municipality would select an arbiter and draw up a notarial contract with him. Once the sides had named their arbiters, the two would examine the land together and reach a decision within two months. The day following the decision, formal markers would be fixed clearly to designate the boundary. Several communities in the sierra attempted to fulfill the terms of the decree in the months that followed, but conflicts continued well into the 1870s.[61]

The second front of conflict over disentailment concerned the identity of those who adjudicated communal lands as well as the different kinds of property affected. In dispute were the rights of individuals and communities, outsiders and vecinos born in the village. In February 1868, for example, the vecinos of Nauzontla protested the disentailment of the pasturelands named Xiliapa to Rafael Bonilla, a resident of Zacapoaxtla. "From time immemorial," they explained, Xiliapa had been a common grazing area. Several inhabitants of Nauzontla had suggested that it be divided among "the poor who have nowhere to sow their crops." The authorities of Jonotla and Escatlan protested the privatization of property to José María Ortuña and Benito Vásquez in December of the same year, insisting the lands had already been adjudicated in favor of the communities in March 1867. "First must come the proletarian class, before the interests of an individual," they wrote. And in August 1870 the alcalde of Tuzamapan legitimated his protest against Lauriano and Gavino Mora, who possessed plots in individual usufruct in Los Reyes and were planning to sell them to outsiders from Cuetzalan, by saying that "those little pieces of land belong . . . [to the] *pueblo* ["village" or "people"]."[62]

The issue of overlapping rights was immeasurably complicated by rental agreements. It was established local practice to rent communal lands called *propios* to outsiders as a way to increase communal revenues or pay for a yearly fiesta. Yet these rental agreements could then become permanent simply through the practice of adjudication. This was unacceptable to the villages.

Luis Cabañez, an entrepreneur from Papantla, used precisely this kind of strategy when he rented the lands of Poza Larga in 1864, during the war of the French Intervention. He paid six years in advance. Then, in his request for adjudication to the jefe político in Tetela, he explained that he needed the lands as a cattle path for his *finca* San Pedro. He charged that all other attempts at adjudication by neighboring villages were illegal because they did not possess the land. Besides, their real purpose was to retain communal possession.

Octaviano Pérez had a similar purpose in mind in Tzicuilan in 1864, when José María Maldonado rented him a piece of communal property. Pérez managed to adjudicate it five years later, in May 1869. In fact, he had migrated to the municipality in question and established residence first, becoming a vecino as a strategy for land privatization. In this context, it is perhaps not surprising that Juan Rosas, originally from Nauzontla, was kicked out of Jonotla after a six-month residence in 1868 in the midst of the furor over adjudications. Yet in his protest to Tetela's jefe político, he expressed his consternation because he had participated in all the pueblo's *faenas* or work parties and therefore saw no reason for his removal.[63]

In some cases these disputes dragged on painfully, multiplying ill will on all sides. In the hotlands between Tenampulco and Tuzamapan, an area with much commercial potential, the communal properties of La Junta de Apulco and Paso de la Canoa underwent a series of overlapping adjudications and disputes between 1867 and 1870. It seemed impossible to reach an agreement despite repeated meetings among representatives of the different villages and despite renewed petitions by all the entrepreneurs involved. At one point the village of Tenampulco declared part of the area its ejido only to find that several villagers had already carved out plots in the area. Officials in Tetela, without consulting local authorities, adjudicated some of the same territory to the entrepreneur Pascual Sánchez. The lands claimed by Vicente García had been collectively owned by the villages of Jonotla, Tuzamapan, and Tenampulco, making even more difficult any kind of demarcation. And finally, when the vecinos disputing Sánchez's adjudication in El Chacal, "leaving aside their rights, offered citizen Sánchez, that they would give him a part of what he had claimed, all his pasturelands . . . and all he wished to take in land from the uplands," Sánchez refused. Clearly, the lowlands were the prime territory.[64]

Disentailment continued, seemingly unabated despite the controversies, between 1869 and 1871.[65] Yet because of ongoing litigation or protest in individual cases, local governments were also forced further to develop alternative interpretations of Liberal land law. Contestation over these new interpretations constituted the third front of conflict over disentailment.

People used their interpretation of existing Liberal land legislation to defend village rights and access to resources. Article 8 of the 1856 Land Law was especially useful to the communities because it exempted from expropriation, in the case of municipalities, "ejidos and lands destined exclusively for public use by the populations to which they belong." Also valuable were the later decrees in the same year that reinforced the right of smallholders preferentially to privatize their plots.[66] Responding to state requests to define ejido lands, communities elaborated detailed and well-informed petitions, further extending and transforming the meaning of existing Liberal land policy.

Between 1868 and 1870 the villages of Xochitlán, Yancuitlalpan, Tzicuilan, Xocoyolo, Nauzontla, Jonotla, Tenampulco, and Tuzamapan declared ejidos. The discourses and political conflicts underlying these petitions were extremely complex. Often the lands declared to be ejidos were precisely those under dispute with individual entrepreneurs. The petitions also initiated tugs of war with the local jefes políticos. Villages would attempt to declare large tracts of territory as common lands, then prepare to negotiate smaller pieces once their initial requests had been denied.[67]

Most striking throughout is the conscious and concerted engagement with Liberal discourses on land. Village documents strain at the edges of what is acceptable within Liberal discourse yet at the same time claim legitimacy within it. In November 1868, for example, the juez of Xocoyolo wrote to the jefe político in Zacapoaxtla wanting to know how his village could claim the only communal virgin forest left to them. The wood had great public utility, and the village wished to claim it before "someone else from outside adjudicated a piece." Was it possible, he wondered, "to denounce only once for the village [as a whole], or does each vecino need to denounce separately the number of *almudes* [land measure equal to approximately 3,300 square meters] needed?"

Between December 1868 and January 1869 the authorities and vecinos of Santiago Yancuitlalpan also negotiated with Zacapoaxtla's jefe político, suggesting several common lands as their ejidos. Throughout the legitimation of their request referred to the June 1856 law: "since the law of 29 [*sic*] June 1856 and later superior decrees give the villages ejidos for public use"; "since it is so necessary and indispensable for this village to declare a plot as ejido for public use, and since article 8 of the Law of 29 June 1856 grants it to us. . . . " Similar discourses were used by Tzicuilan, Jonotla, and Tuzamapan in 1869 and 1870. In August 1870 Jonotla also mentioned Lerdo's circular of October 1856, making a further oblique reference to Juárez's decision on the case of Tepeji del Río by saying that, since the original formation of the pueblos, each individual vecino had recognized the land occupied as their property. And in November of the same year Tuzamapan went as far as to declare that the purpose of the ejido was to provide funds not only for the needs of the municipalities but also "for the religious communities" in their yearly fiestas.[68]

The ongoing tug of war between official policy and communal practice forced new strategies on Liberal policymakers and provided opportunities for articulating discourses of legitimacy and citizenship. In Yancuitlalpan in January 1869, for example, the acta establishing ejido land was legitimized by claiming the combined terrain of democratic citizenship and respect for tradition and communal authority:

> We the undersigned in the name of the pueblo in general, [and] called to this session by established custom, in all that has to do with the public [interest], to hear the opinion of those people with greatest influence who have held office in the administration and today are named *pasados* . . .

In Jonotla as well, in August 1870, those signing the petition did so "in the name of all the communities in this municipality and each one of the individuals that form a part of it." And in Tuzamapan two months later, the municipal assembly came together "after having celebrated a popular [town] meeting in which all the vecinos of the village preceded by their authorities discussed sufficiently the need for an ejido to serve the public for livestock grazing."[69] Thus did the villages of Zacapoaxtla and Tetela districts redefine and reorganize Liberal discourses on land and citizenship, not only through rebellion but also through legal action. Between 1869 and 1872 unredressed grievances on both counts simmered only slightly below the surface, facilitating the inclusion of these villages in political movements that called for a reorganization of power. Yet such inclusion was never automatic or simple, as evidenced by the Arriaga rebellion of 1870.

Francisco Javier Arriaga had no clear political agenda when he took Apulco Pass in November 1870, declaring himself in rebellion against the Lerdo-Juárez government and in favor of the 1857 constitution and the "Michoacán plan." A commander of the Zacapoaxtla national guard, Arriaga possibly still harbored resentments toward the jefe político Juan Francisco

Molina, who during the 1868 rebellion had surrendered to the federal army and imprisoned several of the national guard officers who refused to turn in their weapons. Molina's manipulative and self-serving attitude during those months had gained him much favor with the state and federal governments, to the detriment of other ambitious locals in Zacapoaxtla district, Arriaga among them. Whatever his motives, however, Arriaga was not inspired by a wish to support the pueblos in their struggle to keep control of the disentailment process. Only a few years later he would be one of the entrepreneurs wishing to complete the adjudication process in his favor. But in the context of 1869–1870, with political and discursive lines as they were, Arriaga's strongest allies turned out to be precisely those communities and national guard forces most interested in redefining Liberal privatization of property.[70]

Arriaga knew well that the key to successful mobilization lay in convincing Xochiapulco to join. Although rumors abounded about Xochiapulco's participation, it does not seem that Arriaga's initial declaration was enough to convince Lucas or any other leader of that village's national guard. Ironically enough, it would be the federal army itself, with the ubiquitous Alatorre at its head, that provided the reason to involve Xochiapulco and generated yet another major military uprising in the area through the middle of 1870.[71]

Alatorre explained in his telegraphed report of 3 December 1869 that the Sixth Battalion of the federal army—with twenty-two officers and four hundred soldiers—had marched from Zacapoaxtla to Xochiapulco on 2 December. It had done so "peacefully," according to Alatorre, simply to find out what that pueblo's intentions were in the Arriaga conspiracy. José María Vásquez, lieutenant colonel in command of the Sixth Battalion, reported reaching Xochiapulco about midday and finding the village entirely deserted. When he consulted Alatorre, the commander in chief ordered him to do all that was possible to inform the local inhabitants that the army offered them "all kinds of guarantees." If there was no answer, the battalion should return to headquarters the next day. In his official report Vásquez wrote that

> I did all that was humanly possible to publicize this; but when I saw my efforts were having no result, since even the last women of the village were gone, and given the dark and fog of the night, I ordered the battalion to form and camp out in the central plaza.

Although the soldiers set up sentries, these were powerless in the attack that followed, which according to Vásquez occurred around two in the morning.

> The enemy, numbering between six and eight hundred infantry and favored by the dense darkness, came into the village cautiously and in all directions among the various vegetable gardens that exist there, using all the precautions they knew, since the tracks we found afterward suggest they carried out their operation dragging themselves on their stomachs.

Pouncing on the sleeping soldiers, the Xochiapulquenses began the attack by giving, in Vásquez's words, "a savage howl."[72]

"The truth be told," wrote another officer in the Sixth Battalion, "they pressured us severely." A little before dawn, after managing to secure the wounded and the remaining ammunition in Juan Francisco Lucas's house, the survivors from the first attack built trenches in the central plaza. Surrounded by guerrillas, they fought a long and intermittent battle until reinforcements arrived, approximately twenty-four hours after the first ambush. "After having chased the enemy as far as possible," wrote the commanding officer of the reinforcements in his report, "I began to prepare a transport for the wounded, burying one officer and forty soldiers, ours, who had died in the battle, and fourteen enemy dead."[73]

Alatorre used the encounter in Xochiapulco to legitimize an intensification of repression throughout the area. He declared a state of siege in Zacapoaxtla district on 3 December because

> without this measure my military operations in the area would be useless, since here the majority of the inhabitants are unfamiliar with the principle of authority, because of the lowliness of their customs and their marked tendencies toward scandal and licentiousness, as well as their ferocious instincts to destroy all those who are not of their race; . . . the inspiration for this measure is the treacherous attempt perpetrated against the Sixth Battalion last night in Xochiapulco.

Actually, given the details of the events on 3 and 4 December, it seems fairly clear that Alatorre ordered the invasion of Xochiapulco precisely to force a reaction, which would then allow him to step up repression. Otherwise, why send an entire battalion, composed of four hundred fighting men, on a "peaceful" mission to inform a village—whose entire population, including children, women, and elderly—was probably not much more than twelve hundred—that they had all the guarantees before the law? Could such a message not have been equally well delivered by a single messenger?[74]

The Second Division of the federal army had attacked Arriaga's rebels at Apulco Pass on 30 November and found no rebels from Xochiapulco or

Tetela. Nonetheless, Alatorre sent an order to Juan Francisco Lucas on the hacienda Taxcantla. If Lucas did not appear in Zacapoaxtla, Alatorre would consider him in rebellion against the government. Lucas answered that he was sick and that Alatorre could send the necessary information in writing. Allegedly pushed on by some of the political officials in Zacapoaxtla, who assured Alatorre that Lucas had a huge stash of arms and ammunition, as well as by his own ambitions and growing enmity with the Nahua general, Alatorre formed his plan. In the weeks following the invasion of Xochiapulco, the federal army once again burned that village to the ground, the second time in five years its inhabitants had suffered such a fate.[75]

Even as these specific events provided the spark that rekindled rebellion in Xochiapulco and drew to it dispersed troops from throughout the sierra, the tinder was, as elsewhere in the highlands, the neglect of promises around land and citizenship made during the period of communitarian Liberalism. For Xochiapulco these promises were organized discursively and politically around the Liberal governor Fernando María Ortega's original 1864 decree that had granted the village autonomous municipal status and legitimate right to the lands of the former haciendas Xochiapulco and La Manzanilla. In the months between December 1869 and June 1870, Xochiapulco led soldiers from the villages in the districts of Teziutlán, Tlatlauqui, Zacapoaxtla, San Juan de los Llanos, and Tetela in a military confrontation over these basic demands. They fought for land and political participation, as rewards for and recognition of popular sacrifices in the cause of the nation.[76]

By June 1870 the local and regional options for rebellion and redress had played out to stalemate. On the one hand, the state governor, Ignacio Romero Vargas, explained to the ministry of defense that a complete military victory was impossible. Facing a thousand guerrillas, most armed only with garrotes, Romero calculated that the government would have needed four times as many men, during an eight-month campaign, across the whole sierra from Teziutlán to Chignahuapan, from San Juan de los Llanos to Tetela de Ocampo, in order to win militarily. Already this could not be accomplished because of the government's lack of resources. But even if it could have been done, he emphasized, the origin of the rebellion—in issues of land and of political conflict between Zacapoaxtla and Xochiapulco—would not have been resolved. So the only route was pacification and negotiation.[77]

On the other hand, by April and May 1870 increasing resistance from allied villages made financing and feeding the rebel troops a problematic venture at best—small wonder, when a generation of war and violence had left the sierra "a desolate field, a mountain of ashes, a desert where one hardly distinguishes the places where the houses and cabins of the peasants used to stand." In their surrender, signed on 3 June by eighty-one officers and soldiers from a number of different communities, the rebels still recalled their participation in the wars against the French Intervention, remembering the Fifth of May and other battles. But when they agreed that "civil war had been the principal obstacle to the progress of the republic," a new note crept into the document, one of resignation to the present balance of forces. Democracy, in this context, stopped being the fulfillment of Liberal promises and became respect for constituted authority.[78]

Yet it took a full year, and much struggling against the current of establishment opinion, for Romero Vargas to gain congressional approval for the final pacification agreement. In a report to the state congress at the end of October 1871, Romero compared the price of pacification to what a complete military victory would have cost. Instead of an estimated expenditure of 300,000 pesos across eight months, Romero had promised to pay 10,000–15,000 pesos, spread out over public works, schools, and musical instruments for municipal bands. He approved the separation of Xochiapulco from the district of Zacapoaxtla and its addition to Tetela district. He created the new district of Alatriste, to include the municipalities of Chignahuapan, Aquixtla, and San Francisco Ixtacamaztitlán, all of which had long-standing and violent disagreements with their respective cabeceras. Finally Romero recognized the legitimacy of Ortega's 1864 decree. Thus, the state at last took responsibility for the expropriation of lands from the former haciendas Xochiapulco and La Manzanilla and their distribution to the national guard soldiers from Xochiapulco who had defended their country against the French.[79]

Romero was able to rest on his laurels as peacemaker for a mere two weeks. By mid-November 1871 Xochiapulco had declared in favor of Porfirio Díaz in the revolt of La Noria. The whole Sierra de Puebla, most notably Tetela and Xochiapulco, became an important center of mobilization, occasionally serving as headquarters and hideout for Díaz himself. Juan N. Méndez was named commander in chief of the region's Constitutionalist—otherwise known as Porfirista—army. Juan Francisco Lucas and Juan Crisóstomo Bonilla held important military posts.[80]

What was new about La Noria, both nationally and from the perspective of Puebla's serranos, was that it was not simply a regional rebellion. Over the next six months it represented a deep military and political challenge to the regime of Benito Juárez. By fixing his own reelection through the manipulation of the national congress, Juárez had broken some key connections in his alliance. If we are to judge from the Sierra de Puebla, moreover, the repression and authoritarian centralism of the previous five years had finally angered the entire country. The only thing that seems to have stopped the success of the La Noria revolt was Juárez's death. The subsequent confusion among regional leaders made effective Lerdo's policy of selective co-optation and amnesty. From the perspective of the Porfirian forces, however, this was only a temporary setback. In 1876 the Sierra de Puebla joined with other regions in the uprising of Tuxtepec, finally carrying to power their old ally and comrade, Porfirio Díaz.[81]

The Archaeology of Discourse:
The Plan of La Noria in Regional Perspective

Let us return to the bones buried in Xochiapulco's central plaza, uncovered in the 1970s during municipal improvements and placed in a cabinet in the municipal building. We can now say with fair certainty that they are not Austrian but Mexican. Given the number of battles fought in Xochiapulco between 1864 and 1872, there could well be some Austrian bones buried somewhere in the central plaza, in a deeper archaeological layer, waiting to be discovered in a subsequent public works campaign. But the timing of the attack on the Sixth Battalion of the federal army in 1869, plus the profound similarity between surviving oral memory and the reports we have of the later ambush, make clear that the first bones to be uncovered belonged to Mexican soldiers.[82]

Following the report of the officer who organized the original burial, there was a curious intimacy to this common grave. Xochiapulquenses lay next to the federal soldiers they had killed, officers next to enlisted men. Mexican soldiers who had probably fought the French together, only to confront each other on a dank and foggy sierra morning in an ambush portrayed as the triumph of barbarism over civilization, were finally reunited underground. A century later their descendants retrieved them, labeled them Austrian, and displayed them all together. The ironic appropriateness of this intimacy, as well as its inaccurate display behind glass doors in Xochiapulco's municipal building, becomes all the greater when we realize that the checkered history of these bones is strangely paralleled by that of regional-popular Liberal discourses on the nation. Repressed in battle, these discourses too were buried by official stories of nation-state formation, to be dug up during the Revolution of 1910, mislabeled, and displayed in curious intimacy next to their enemies.[83]

But in addition to the inaccuracy and irony of these discursive manipulations, their effectiveness has also prevented us from digging out the complex and multilayered meanings of Mexico's political history from 1855 to 1876, better to understand not only the Porfiriato but also the Revolution of 1910. Later I will have occasion to return to the broader implications of this fact. For now an analysis of the Plan de la Noria from the perspective of the Sierra de Puebla can provide an initial example of the discursive richness that has been buried alongside popular Liberalism.

According to Daniel Cosío Villegas's influential commentaries, the Plan de la Noria is not an important political document. Aside from its brevity, "passable prose," and "effective demagogic language," Cosío Villegas writes, the plan is poor because

> the analysis of the ills affecting the country is superficial and barely goes beyond laying personal blame on the bad head of state; its positive part, that concerning the cures available for the national ills, has few ideas; and even more, Díaz does not even make his the few solutions he suggests, instead confessing to have gotten them from others, which then explains why he leaves to a constituent assembly the task of looking over the country's situation in order to find the way of improving it.[84]

Cosío's explanation for these lacks is that the plan was simply a personalistic document, inspired by little beyond Díaz's desire to attain power. Yet if we examine the plan from below, some of its apparent weaknesses are transformed into strengths. Familiar language connects it to the experiences of localities over the previous generation.

The bulk of the plan is dedicated to explaining the situation of the country, one of crisis and political illegitimacy. The centralization and reproduction of power has caused a series of abuses, including the indefinite reelection of the executive and the increasing domestication of the legislative and judicial branches. "Various states have been prevented from installing their legitimate authorities and are under the sway of unpopular and tyrannical governments, imposed by the direct action of the executive."[85] Certainly this description fit the case of Puebla, still in 1871 governed by Ignacio Romero Vargas, whose illegal 1868 maneuver in the state congress facilitated the questionable election of Rafael J. García over Juan N. Méndez.

> The army, glorious personification of the principles conquered from the Ayutla Revolution to the surrender of Mexico [City] in 1867, which should be listened to and respected by the government in order to preserve the gratitude of the people, has been vilified and debased, forced to serve as the instrument of odious violence against the freedom of popular suffrage, forcing it to forget the laws and customs of Christian civilization in . . . [numerous] massacres that make us return to barbarism.

The national guard soldiers themselves could not have put it better. Restated here were their expectations of entitlement: as the "glorious personification" of Liberal principles, they deserved to be respected and thanked; instead, they had been repressed by their comrades from the war against the French, regular army soldiers who were now forced to kill their own kind. And what worse vilification of the heroic reputation of the army than to have it step in to enforce questionable electoral results, as happened in the Sierra de Puebla in 1868?

What follows in the plan is the criticism of Juarista economic and fiscal policy, a critique rightly denigrated by Cosío as showing little economic sense or sophistication. But from a regional perspective—in a situation of widespread economic depression when the widows of fallen soldiers and the veterans themselves were unable to collect on pensions, when municipalities lacked the funds to open schools or rebuild public buildings—the assertion that federal funds were "more than sufficient to [cover] all public services" must have sounded awfully attractive. So did a phrase much later in the document, where, in a new reference to internal repression by the army, Díaz wrote, "They have soaked the hands of [the nation's] brave defenders in the blood of the vanquished, forcing them to change the weapons of the soldier for the ax of the executioner." This rhetoric was buttressed only a few lines later by Díaz's assertion of his obligation to "my comrades in arms with whose cooperation I have been successful in many difficult enterprises."[86]

The recurrent theme throughout the first pages, then, was the recognition of the people's contribution to the Liberal Revolution and to its defense against Conservatives and Interventionists. A small group of powerful men was perpetuating itself at the summit of power, refusing to recognize national guard soldiers or listen to local needs and criticisms, trampling the electoral will of the people. "We will fight, then, for the cause of the people, and only the people will own the victory." Give back to the people their justly won victories—this is what regional constituencies heard. "The constitution of 1857 and electoral freedom will be our banner; less government and more liberty our program." Decentralization of power, more local and regional autonomy—this was also an important element in the communitarian Liberal discourse of the war years.[87]

The other key theme in Cosío's criticism of the Plan de la Noria is that Díaz refused to stand behind a specific and substantive plan of reform, proposing instead that a convention of three popularly elected representatives from each state decide the course of policy. Yet again, in the context of combining regional needs and discourses within a responsive national movement, this approach seems to have made the most sense. This would have been the case especially if Díaz's prediction about the convention came true: "The delegates, who will be pure and honest patriots, will take to the convention the aspirations and ideas of their respective states and will know how to formulate with loyalty and sustain with interest the needs that are truly national." There was no stacked deck, in other words. People chosen by popular election would decide the course of the country. Díaz promised to abide by the decisions of the convention, which, in contrast to Cosío's interpretation, was not a constitutional but rather a Constitutionalist—the name given to the Porfirista movement—convention. To ensure no misunderstanding about where the power should lie, among his suggestions for possible reforms Díaz listed the following: a direct election for president; the installation of popular tribunals to judge the accused; and a guarantee of resources and autonomy to municipalities. And the final, oft-quoted flourish: "That no citizen shall impose and perpetuate himself in power, and this shall be the last revolution."[88]

The frequency with which the last phrase is quoted is directly related, of course, to its irony: the man who wrote the document perpetuated himself in power so long that he brought on the greatest revolution of Mexican history. Yet to leave it there, especially with some knowledge of existing regional discourses in the Mexico of 1872, is too facile.

A different, more populist, more responsive interpretation of the Plan de la Noria does not transform Porfirio Díaz—or Juan N. Méndez or any other general—into a popular hero. It simply demonstrates that, in the ongoing formation and transformation of nineteenth-century Mexican Liberal discourses, the plan was an important, experimental articulation. Through the practice of equivalence it brought together ready, although increasingly frayed, discursive elements from popular Liberalism. This was its great attraction, and it goes much further than a simple patron-client or *caciquismo* model in explaining the popularity of La Noria in the Sierra de Puebla and other areas of Liberal resistance to the French.

Once the conquest of national power became a real possibility, however, this same experimental articulation was transformed into a weakness. Cosío's perspective is more relevant here and helps us explain the modification of the Plan de la Noria in Ameca in April 1872. In the modified version, the discursive codes and references pertaining to the previous ten years of war and sacrifice were gone; so were the statements of trust in the wisdom of the people. In their place was the suggestion that the president of the Supreme Court become provisional president when the movement succeeded, a clear effort to mend fences with Lerdo and his followers. Appended was a specific and much more orthodox program to be installed once the movement took power.

This tension between the decentralization and regional articulation of interests, and the need to revindicate the principle of authority and the centralization of power, lay at the center of all Liberal debates and practice from the time of the Ayutla Revolution and the Constitutional Convention of 1856–1857. It reemerged during the Restored Republic in the conflict between Juarismo and the defenders of communitarian Liberalism. It emerged again between the two versions of the Plan de la Noria. It would reemerge once more in the contrast between the early and the late Porfiriato.[89]

2

COMMUNAL HEGEMONY
AND NATIONALIST DISCOURSES
IN MEXICO AND PERU

5   Contested Citizenship (2)

Regional Political Cultures,
Peasant Visions of the Nation,
and the Liberal Revolution in Morelos

In August 1864, shortly after taking the throne of the so-called Second Empire of Mexico, Maximilian of Austria received a petition from the village of Tepoztlán. The five men who signed it, notables and political officials from the community, began by thanking the monarchs for the gracious reception they had given the commission from Tepoztlán that had traveled to Mexico City in June to congratulate them on their coronation. The notables then explained, at great length, the genealogy of Tepoztlán's legitimacy as a village, dating back to precolonial times ("la gentilidad") when it was already part of the Aztec empire ("basto y antiguo Imperio megicano"). After the conquest the village's most important founding moment was in the *reales cédulas* granted by Philip II of Spain and his successors, confirmed by new petition in April 1648. Unfortunately, the notables continued, by the end of the wars of independence the village's land titles had been lost. According to oral tradition, this loss was due to treachery. Already by 1824 the lack of land titles had led to some attempted land grabs along the village's eastern boundary. But in 1842 the town was still receiving rent for use of pastures from one of the neighboring haciendas.

The representatives of the village then warmed to their subject. Starting in 1826, and despite its lack of antiquity when compared to the community, the hacienda Oacalco began to usurp lands from Tepoztlán along three different borders. Village officials had tried desperately to find the lost documents, knowing that this was the only possible way to stop the hacienda's expansion. But even though they traveled on several occasions to the national archive, they were unable to find the documents. Then, between 1845 and 1849, the pace of usurpation had picked up. By the latter year the hacienda had reached the suburbs of a couple of Tepoztlán's smaller outlying anexos. In the same year a local political authority considered treacherous celebrated an agreement with the hacendado, formalizing the boundary that existed at that point.

Another village representative traveled to Mexico City in 1853 and found the titles in the national archive. They were properly stamped and authorized on 6 May, and the villagers were ecstatic. They asked for a new measurement and paid for it at great sacrifice. But given the 1849 agreement, the judicial authorities found in favor of the landowner and threatened to fine the village nine hundred pesos if it ever brought the case to court again. At that point the question was legally buried. The pueblo had spent all its funds on lawyers and judicial fees.

The owner of Oacalco did not move again until May 1864, when he managed to convince a local judge to give him possession of yet another hunk of village land. With this, the villagers explained, the situation simply went too far. "And it is not fair, Sire," they wrote,

> that our pueblo should suffer any longer. Since you took the throne, the hour of justice has sounded in Mexico and we no longer fear the long delays and high costs of a court case. Neither do we fear injustice and instead we rest in the protection Your Majesty offers to the Indian pueblos who have been the most unfortunate.

In the conclusion to their petition, Tepoztlán's representatives asked the emperor for four things: first, that the agreement of 1849 be declared null and void; second, that the new boundaries be congruent with those measured in 1853 after the legitimate and original titles were found; third, that existing conflicts with other neighbors be resolved amicably through the comparison of the respective land titles; and fourth, that the emperor himself, as an impartial judge, decide the case. "For," the petitioners concluded,

> if the pueblo's bad luck be that the case goes to the ordinary courts, of course—and we know, Sire, that you will see fit to forgive us— we will give up the case entirely; we would return to our village and tell them, "Resign yourselves, your luck has not been decided, God still wants to try your patience, live in peace and wait."

Throughout the petition, which the signers insisted they had composed themselves without outside help, the discourse articulated is conservative, even colonial. The justice of the villagers' claims is traced to their precolonial identity as a part of the Aztec empire, an identity then recognized and granted full legitimacy by the Spanish crown. This combination of ethnic identity and colonial corporate privilege was engraved, almost magically it seems at times, in the colonial land titles the pueblo possessed. When these titles were lost—not coincidentally around the time of independence—the immediate result was usurpation by the haciendas. Only with the arrival of a new monarch did it seem possible for the villagers finally to regain the justice lost during the intervening years. They attempted to do so by throwing themselves on Maximilian's mercy, paternal benevolence, and royal impartiality, emphasizing that they would retire all claims if the matter returned to the ordinary courts.[1]

The interpretation of this document is complicated by the fact that it comes from Tepoztlán, a village with a long Liberal tradition dating back to the 1855 Revolution. The Tepoztecos constituted one of the most important national guard battalions to defend the Liberal Revolution in Puebla in early 1856. Between 1858 and 1860 they formed the core of the Liberal Brigada Leyva, battling Conservatives throughout Cuernavaca district during the 1858–1861 civil war. Then in 1910 Tepoztlán would emerge again as an important center of Zapatista organizing. Yet in the middle of these two historical periods, during which Tepoztlán proved to be a radical and socially progressive town, sits a conservative, colonial document.[2] Such a fact defies linear interpretation; how do we explain this apparent contradiction?

One place to begin an explanation is by noting that Tepoztlán was not alone in generating such a contradiction. In the same year of 1864 the village of Anenecuilco—made famous by the work of Jesús Sotelo Inclán and John Womack, Jr., as the birthplace of Emiliano Zapata and the Zapatista revolution—also presented a petition to Maximilian. Although we do not have a copy of the original petition, we do know that on 5 January 1865 Maximilian resolved it negatively, basing his decision on the disamortization law of 1856, which, in his interpretation of the moment, denied villages the right to collective or corporate property.

We know that Anenecuilco, too, had a long radical and Liberal pedigree. Supporters of Morelos during the siege of Cuautla in 1810, they formed a part of the district that rebelled in favor of Juan Alvarez in 1850 and 1854. Along with Tepoztlán, they had been searching for their land titles in 1853 and 1854. In the early 1860s former Liberal fighters from the area also led a strong campaign against the plateados. In the 1870s the village would support the rebellions of Porfirio Díaz, once again in order to regain the lands taken by neighboring haciendas, finally to rebel against their earlier allies in 1910 and form one of the central cores of Zapatismo. So here as well we find this momentary apparent contradiction in 1864. What had happened?[3]

If we examine particular discourses in formation at the local level and place them in the context of changing political circumstances and alliances, it becomes clear that both Conservative and Liberal projects for the organization of national power had something to offer rural peoples. As peasant leaders struggled to justify and legitimize their villages' political identities and access to land, they found that a variety of discourses, political practices, and alliances helped condition the struggle for local social justice. While attempting to articulate discourses of legitimation that could convince village factions to support the new strategies, local leaders discovered they must also provide convincing explanations to potential regional or supraregional allies. Through this multifaceted and creative process, rural people participated in the formulation of nationalist discourses, both Liberal and Conservative, and, by pressing at their boundaries, expanded the participatory potential of both.

This type of approach suggests that Liberal and Conservative discourses evolved in relation and contradiction with each other, through a mutual process of interrogation, not only among urban intellectuals but also in the villages, small towns, and regions of nineteenth-century Latin America. An interlocking series of dialogues—among villagers as well as citified politicians, within and between regional factions, and between rural people and state officials—helped form these discourses. In this context it is particularly useful to return to the Tepoztlán petition and consider a second discourse buried within its pages, a discourse organized around the broken promises of the Liberal Revolution and around the delegitimation of the local leaders who gave that revolution their support.

In 1854, according to the signers of the document, a section of the village joined the Ayutla Revolution with the hope that doing so would bring them justice on the land question. All it brought was death, however, and only two of the original Liberal fighters survived: "in the government of Albares [*sic*] and Comonfort, despite the services rendered for the cause, no one looked with interest upon the just needs of the pueblo." And things got worse with Zuloaga and Miramón. It was at this moment that the two surviving Liberals called for revolt in the civil war, again referring to the land claims. By this point, the petitioners continued, many local people had had enough; but their protests were in vain.

> In vain the notable and sensible men of the village intervened; in vain they argued that violence would give the people nothing but death and mourning and that the pueblo would not get justice for its claims through violence. They were not heard, and as had been predicted our village became a stage for anarchy so horrible that our society was threatened to its very foundation. Fathers were taken violently from their children; sons from their parents; husbands from the conjugal union; and brothers and friends one from the other, [all] to a revolution no longer prompted by the national interest but by the most ignoble passions. Thus triumphs the seduction done from afar by strangers styling themselves as leaders who then forgot the poor unlucky ones who had fought at their side. Around

one hundred men died in the revolts between 1854 and 1860, leaving many families in misery and a multitude of innocent, suffering orphans. Those first courageous leaders who had thrown themselves into revolution, under the pretext of doing good for the village, were dragged to their tombs without leaving their people anything but a sad memory.

And this was why, according to the petitioning villagers from Tepoztlán, the Intervention and empire were to be celebrated: not because they challenged Mexico's independence—which they did not—but because they would bring the peace and justice promised yet denied by the Liberals.[4]

Peasants and other rural people in Morelos struggled, over generations, to fashion political discourses that would tie them effectively, and with social justice, to an emerging "imagined community" at the national level. As we can see for the case of Tepoztlán, factions within the villages struggled with each other, rising and falling in prestige depending on changes at the regional and evolving national levels. Village leaders and their supporters confronted and tried to make sense of these changes; in so doing, they created and contested different visions of the national polity and of their own participation in it.

In the long run, as we have already seen for the case of Puebla, none of the alternative nationalist discourses—nor the political practices prompted by them—were successfully incorporated into the process of national reconstruction and consolidation in Mexico during the latter nineteenth century. Yet through the very processes of participation, political creation, and repression, rural people transformed both themselves and the polities they struggled to expand. Not only did popular creativity and political action put identifiable marks on the state being constructed over these years, but the popular political cultures formed and transformed over the second half of the nineteenth century have reemerged repeatedly in the twentieth. In this chapter I unearth these alternative nationalist discourses for the case of Morelos, not only to understand what has gone before but also to establish an open dialogue with what has come after. In so doing, I hope to provide new perspectives on both.

El Sur, 1810–1855:
The Problematic Construction
of an Alternative Political Culture

Three times between 1810 and 1854 the people of Cuautla Morelos participated in movements that rose to challenge the existing balance of power.

During the first half of 1812 Cuautla became the centerpoint of José María Morelos's attempted insurgent encirclement of Mexico City. Although unsuccessful in holding Cuautla against royalist siege, Morelos was nonetheless able, with the help of local allies ranging from estate managers and priests to villagers and laborers, to fortify and control the town for a period of approximately four months. Then in 1850, in the aftermath of the U.S. occupation of Mexico, the Indian neighborhoods of Cuautla invaded the hacienda Santa Inés. The local national guards, still organized from the resistance to the occupation forces, refused to repress the invaders, arguing that justice was on their side and with all members of "the popular class." Finally, in December 1854, a local shoemaker led an urban uprising in Cuautla with the apparent complicity of the entire population, including the local political authorities. The military commander sent to repress the rebels found it hard to bring anyone to justice, since he accurately observed that he would have to bring to trial the entire population of the town.[5]

Precisely because it was not unusual, Cuautla provides a good entry point into the complex and overlapping layers of regional political culture that were being constructed, contested, and reconstructed in the Morelos region between 1810 and 1855. Urban artisans, priests, workers, and merchants, in varying forms of alliance with the peasants and day laborers of surrounding villages and haciendas, stood up against the abuses of landowners, large merchants, and politicians. Often the abusers were peninsular Spaniards; throughout the nineteenth century many of the sugar haciendas and larger commercial establishments in the districts of Cuernavaca and Morelos remained in Spanish hands. Small wonder, then, that a recurrent battle cry throughout these years was "*Mueran los gachupines*" (Death to the Spaniards)—a cry directed in particular at the exploitative, gouging Spaniards who deserved the insult *gachupín*.[6]

Because so many of the prosperous hacendados, merchants, and technicians in the area were Spaniards, even after independence, the term *gachupín* was also bound up with other recurrent themes of rebellion. Villages and haciendas confronted each other over the use, misuse, and appropriation of land, water, and forest. Village and hacienda economies competed over labor and markets and over the allegiances of local political officials. All these issues helped define and shift battle lines and intersected at various points with the problem of an enduring Spanish presence. Thus, the expulsion, and later the murder, of Spanish citizens was always connected with other vindications or grievances. The targets were hacendados who expropriated village resources and even raised private armies to repress peasant soldiers; technicians, hacienda administrators, and accountants at the hacienda stores who exploited peasants directly; and urban merchants who traded with the haciendas, lent money at exorbitant rates, and aided landowners in buying off political officials.[7]

Cuautla also serves as an interesting example of another element in regional political culture. Throughout the first half of the nineteenth century, particular towns and villages wove patchworks of localized alliances into broader regional movements. During the independence struggles around Cuautla, for example, the popularity of the insurgent cause was particularly great to the west of the city, in the sierra region including the towns of Tlaltizapán and Yautepec. The former village, according to royalist sources, had rebelled en masse at the prompting of a single insurgent leader. The latter town, along with the nearby hacienda of Temilpa, was the center of operations for the insurgent leader Francisco Ayala. When Ayala and his two sons were captured and killed in the royalist mopping-up operations that followed the fall of Cuautla, it is indicative that their bodies were strung up in Yautepec and Tlaltizapán. At the same time, though, Ayala was the subject of an oral tradition that extended across Cuautla to Jonacatepec and Jantetelco.[8]

In both 1850 and 1854 the town of Cuautla served as the central organizing arena for popular movements. Again, however, the town was not isolated from the surrounding countryside. In 1850 it was rumored that a great many villages to the west, from around Puente de Ixtla, had also been involved. In 1854 mobilizations continued as far south and west as Tepalcingo even after they had been repressed in Cuautla. And to further extend the connections in 1854, the authorities in charge of keeping order reported several leaflets and slogans throughout the area—from Cuautla to Jantetelco, from Tepalcingo to Jojutla—that linked the conflicts to the movement being organized by Juan Alvarez in the neighboring state of Guerrero.[9]

Since the late eighteenth century a series of struggles and reorganizations of sociopolitical space had connected the political culture emerging in Cuautla, Cuernavaca, and environs to protests and social movements extending from Michoacán in the west, through Guerrero, and into southwestern Puebla and Oaxaca. An important characteristic of the independence movement in this region, which would be reproduced in later mobilizations and political struggles, was the weaving together of village or local movements through alliances between leaders. Usually men of influence and prestige within smaller areas, these *caudillos* then formed broader coalitions that operated on the basis of negotiated convergences among constituencies. Morelos himself, for example, negotiated a series of alliances with the likes of Nicolás Bravo, Hermenegildo Galeana, Vicente Guerrero,

Juan Alvarez, and Francisco Ayala. Each of these men "brought" into the coalition their local constituencies, built through a series of reciprocal though unequal interactions.[10]

Between 1810 and 1840 Juan Alvarez and Vicente Guerrero, surviving populist leaders from the wars of independence, built on these existing regional connections. They constructed a radical federalist coalition of peasant villages, local caciques, provincial elites, urban artisans, and petty merchants. They drew on the traditions of popular rebellion and anticolonialism built up in the region since the 1780s, which had combined resistance to the Bourbon reforms with a strong hostility to Spanish merchants, landowners, and state officials. In the postindependence years continued Spanish control of larger properties and important commercial networks gave additional meaning to the independence slogan "Mueran los gachupines," not only in Cuautla Morelos but throughout the area. And by the 1830s struggles among local notables and provincial leaders over taxation, municipal autonomy, and rentals of municipal land combined with village conflicts over land and political power in the context of a transition from *república* to municipal government. For politicians with their eyes on Mexico City, these regional patterns fed an intensifying debate between centralist and federalist models of political organization, as diverse factions attempted to broaden their coalitions in order to become contenders in the struggle to "make" national politics.[11]

Peter Guardino has convincingly shown that rural conflicts in Guerrero between 1820 and 1850 were not mainly about land—at least not in the sense familiar to historians of the later nineteenth century. In many areas the unifying factors seem to have been resistance to taxation and to political centralization, as rural populations struggled to limit the head taxes levied on them and to maintain or achieve some degree of municipal autonomy. In both the 1830 civil war and the conflicts of the 1840s, these issues interlocked with anti-Spanish and antiforeign mobilizations, for villagers often interpreted the 1820s legislation expelling Spaniards as also legitimating the expulsion of non-Indians from municipal government and village lands. In the cases where land was a factor, the conflicts were generally not between communities and haciendas but instead between municipal governments and *oficiales de república* over the ownership of communal lands.[12]

In the districts of Cuernavaca and Cuautla Morelos (what is today the state of Morelos), by contrast, issues of municipal autonomy, taxation, and anti-Spanish feeling intermingled by the 1840s with more recognizable forms of hacienda-community conflict. Part of the difference had to do with the history of commercial production in this region. Already in the late colonial period haciendas and communities in the districts of Cuernavaca and Morelos had confronted each other over the competition between two market-oriented and relatively dynamic systems of production. In the villages peasants produced subsistence crops and fruits and vegetables for the Mexico City market. People moved back and forth among a variety of urban occupations, commerce, agriculture, and occasional wage labor. The hacendados, for their part, were not interested in using coercion to retain a resident labor force but in enlisting the aid of state officials in their struggles to discipline labor and neutralize competition from the village economies. This meant cooperation from local political and judicial authorities in cutting communities off from their access to water and other resources and sometimes evicting tenants who would not cooperate with hacienda administrators.[13]

Despite regional differences, various local alliances were unified into a broader radical coalition by the common need, felt throughout the villages of El Sur (see map 5), to confront the reorganization of power set into motion by the transition from *república* to municipal government. As would become clear by the 1840s, federalism allowed for greater municipal autonomy in the working out of these local issues, where control over land, revenue, and political office were being contested along lines of ethnicity, age, class, and geographical space. Centralists, by contrast, tended to support the consolidation of larger municipalities and their control by mestizo or white vecinos, with predictable consequences at the community level. Thus, peasants in Guerrero and Morelos—whether confronting the encroachment of the hacienda, manipulation by corrupt municipal officials, higher rates of taxation, or some combination of all—could agree on the need to fight for a decentralized polity in which municipalities could work through these new issues in a relatively autonomous fashion.[14]

By the 1840s, then, the combined practices and experiences of the previous generation came together to generate a broad agrarian movement in Guerrero and neighboring areas. What catalyzed the movement in Guerrero was a worsening of land conflicts in the Chilapa area, in combination with generalized protest against an increase in the head tax. Around the same time, conflicts over land, markets, water, and other resources had been intensifying in Cuernavaca and Morelos, along with municipal and taxation issues. In Mexico City as well, the political stakes began rising rapidly in the 1840s. Regional, economic, and sociopolitical conflicts among elite factions formed the backdrop for various attempts to consolidate broader political alliances and thus, at least potentially, to build and retain state power. Some caudillos initially active during independence, like Bravo and Alvarez, saw

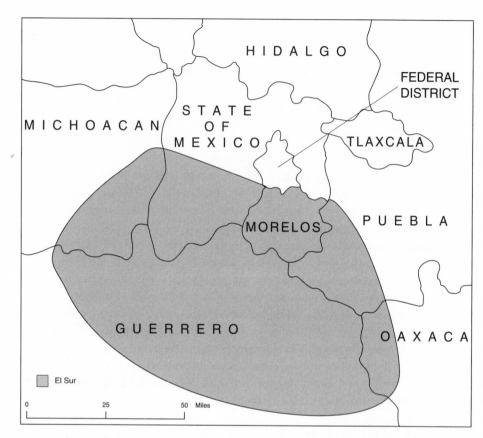

Map 5. El Sur (shaded area). *Note:* Until 1869, Morelos was the third district of the State of Mexico.

the agrarian movement in El Sur as a potential stepping-stone in the making of a national politics during these years. And this possibility would emerge with particular force for Juan Alvarez, not only during the U.S.-Mexican War but again during the Liberal Revolution.[15]

From the 1840s the formation of the national guard battalions allowed Alvarez to cultivate a new relationship with the rural population in El Sur. According to the relevant legislation these battalions were organized by village, made up of volunteers, and elected their own officers. Especially during the U.S. occupation, with the regular army in complete disarray, the national guard battalions in the Morelos-Guerrero area served as the first line of defense against the invaders. Under their local leaders—usually village merchants or local notables such as Amado Popoca of Tepalcingo, José Manuel Arellano of Tetecala, and Manuel Casales from the

Rancho de los Hornos in Tlaquiltenango—village dwellers from Cuernavaca and Morelos districts stood up against the foreign army. As commander of the southern division of the army, Juan Alvarez was their immediate superior, and he also distinguished himself against the foreign occupation forces. By the end of the occupation the battle against a common enemy had deepened the solidarity between the national guard battalions and the villages of El Sur. And these deep connections were further manifested in the support national guards provided to village social and agrarian movements during the early 1850s.[16]

In fact, in 1850 the prefect of Cuernavaca had already informed the government of Mexico state that "all the pueblos were discontented and alarmed because of the last revolution [led] by Arellano, which had tried to destroy the haciendas."[17] He was referring to a series of conflicts to the south and east of Cuernavaca city in which the villagers of San Francisco Chicolula, Xochitepec, and Tlayacapan had, between 1848 and 1849, confronted the haciendas Miacatlán, Chiconcuac, San Vicente, and Oacalco. With the support of the national guard, most notably that of Lieutenant Colonel José Manuel Arellano, head of the Tetecala battalion, the villagers had moved or destroyed boundary markers between communal and hacienda properties. In the case of Chicolula and the hacienda Miacatlán, the peasants had also threatened to destroy the dam that managed the irrigation water. In addition to these dramatic confrontations, Tepoztlán had battled the hacienda Oacalco over land; Jojutla had confronted the local notable Joaquín Fandiño over the new hacienda he had carved from communal lands; and Puente de Ixtla had tussled with the hacienda San Gabriel regarding the location and control of the local market *(tianguis)*.[18]

Alvarez was not amused by the actions of the national guard commander Arellano in Tetecala, particularly since the events had occurred in 1848, while U.S. troops were still stationed in nearby Cuernavaca city. He chastised Arellano severely, writing to him that his commission did not entitle him to get involved in other people's affairs. While temporary, the rift between Alvarez and Arellano reflected in part the different organization of the agrarian movement in the Guerrero and Cuernavaca subregions of El Sur. Not only was land a more immediate issue around Cuernavaca, but Alvarez had less direct influence in that subregion.[19]

But a deeper question emerged as well. Landowners, provincial notables, villagers, and townspeople could all agree on the need for federalism and represent this unity through the creation of national guard battalions. But in the end they might develop quite different visions concerning the final goals of federalist policy. For federalist politicians and notables like Alvarez, on the one hand, the ultimate goal was national power, or at least the ability to negotiate participation in a national coalition. For villagers and townspeople, on the other hand, the more direct issues were social justice, access to resources such as land, and the responsiveness of local political institutions. It was the negotiated convergences between these two visions, and the working out of the contradictions between them, that ultimately generated—by the mid-1850s—the Alvarista form of radical federalism qua liberalism that would propel the Ayutla Revolution.[20]

For the federalist and Liberal politicians gathering around Alvarez, the need to find allies outside their social class forced them to take seriously the issues being discussed in the pueblos and communities of El Sur. Taking these issues seriously turned out to be a key component in winning Mexico City in 1855. In the years immediately preceding the Liberal victory, new and broader mobilizations—again involving national guard support and claiming a connection to Juan Alvarez—took place in Cuautla, Tepalcingo, and Jonacatepec. Beginning in Cuautla in 1850, these mobilizations spread and melded into each other. Over the next three to four years they created a general climate of unrest that uneasy hacendados called *la guerra de castas* (caste war). These movements served as the initial and the final impulse that propelled Juan Alvarez into the presidency with the Liberal Revolution of mid-1855.[21]

The Liberal Revolution in Morelos: The Genesis of an Alternative Nationalism, 1850–1855

Beginning at six o'clock on the morning of 17 October 1850, an alliance of national guard soldiers and approximately five hundred inhabitants from the popular indigenous neighborhoods of Cuautla Morelos began to tear down the boundary markers separating the hacienda Santa Inés from the northern barrios of the town. Continuing into the next day, the participants measured out new streets in the cane field known as San Martín, symbolically claiming the territory for use by the barrios. When the subprefect of Morelos district ordered the national guard commander to take his battalion to the site and restore order, arresting those responsible, the soldiers refused to do so. As the commander explained in his note, the soldiers based their refusal on the fact that for more than a year the people of Cuautla had been petitioning the government for redress in the face of hacienda expansion, "exasperated because they did not have land to live on." Only after seeing these legal petitions come to nothing did they decide to take direct action.

For this reason, being convinced that the people have the right to rebel "when the law is ineffective," the soldiers felt no crime had been committed: "they could not take up arms against their brothers and against their own rights since all belonged to the popular class, but . . . they insisted they would obey authority whenever it was necessary to contain real disorder."[22]

This movement could be repressed only from outside, with a combination of hacienda guards and troops brought from elsewhere in the state of Mexico; and this fact is central to our understanding of the political alliances involved. The commander in charge of the repression understood quickly and well that everyone in the town, all the way from the municipal officials to the national guard battalion to the parish priest, had some kind of role in the uprising. In this multileveled and multifaceted coalition, the unifying discourse was a Liberal one of rights and contract. People had the right to petition the government about their grievances and the right to be heard. If the government or the law did not work on their behalf, an implicit contract between state officials and the citizenry would be broken; direct action was then legitimate. Thus, the national guards insisted that no disorder had occurred and no laws had been broken. But equally important, the national guards refused to take up arms because of political solidarity: "All belonged to the popular class."[23]

The language of the rebellion prompted its opponents to insist it had been backed by "anarchist machinations." Yet one does not have to resort to such well-worn accusations to understand the coherence of the discourse presented by the rebels. In 1850 the peasants, Indians, and national guard soldiers in Cuautla experimented with a Liberal articulation of the popular political discourses that had been emerging in El Sur since the wars of independence. Composed in about equal parts of anticolonial, anti-Spanish, and antilandowner traditions and political practices, these discourses, which had accumulated during the independence period, had carried over into the mid–nineteenth century. Village peasants, artisans, rural soldiers, provincial intellectuals, and populist caciques then elaborated them into radical federalism and alternative visions of citizenship.[24]

In the particular construction of popular discourses elaborated by the Cuautla rebels in 1850, antilandowner and anticolonial elements were articulated through the concepts of citizens' rights, social contract, and the common political identity and interests of the people or "popular class." The actions of the people against the hacienda were justified because citizenship rights—specifically the right to be heard and to a just livelihood—had not been respected or upheld. The unity of all sectors of "the people" was important because of their common interest in these citizenship rights. Politically, culturally, and spatially constructed, this unity would be activated and reactivated, again and again, over the next decade.

A week after the start of the rebellion, Colonel José de la Piedra reached the city. He was convinced by local authorities and the parish priest not to disarm the national guards immediately but rather to allow them to present their weapons to the municipality within four days. This, de la Piedra noted, was the prudent strategy. It allowed for an investigation of the issues existing between the villages and surrounding haciendas.

Officials in Mexico City, however, did not see it quite the same way. They demanded by return mail that de la Piedra disarm the guard immediately and turn the leaders over to the relevant judicial authorities, lest the show of leniency encourage further lawlessness. The colonel reacted strongly to the criticism, accusing local landowners of seeing his prudence as weakness. From his perspective he had no other choice. The entire population of the city had been involved in the uprising, and a more repressive strategy would have only increased tensions, causing further violence, possibly even the burning of cane fields. Besides, how did one choose the leaders to prosecute in a population that had stood as one?[25]

Some of the weapons from Cuautla were ultimately recovered and redistributed to apparently loyal national guards in other villages. Yet the threat of continued mobilization remained, for the leaders of the movement were in hiding and none of the issues had been resolved. And the climate throughout the districts of Cuernavaca and Morelos continued to be tense in the next several years. In Cuernavaca, according to the military commander Ramón Parres, caste war had threatened since the late 1840s, organized first around the demand for "restitution of the land and water haciendas had usurped from the pueblos," then around the presence and behavior of Spaniards in the area. By 1852, when Parres sent his report, unrest was leading to a war similar to the "socialism" existing in Yucatán.

In Morelos district the next year, a popular uprising in Tepalcingo (see map 6) resulted in the murder of the local alcalde, his wife, and several other local notables. The ensuing repression involved the arrest of many local citizens, including the Liberal commander and Alvarez ally don Amado Popoca, and the abolition and disarming of the Jonacatepec and Tepalcingo national guards. Even these actions did not stem the tide of rebellion, however. In March 1854 Miguel Franco, a political official in Jonacatepec, wrote to the commander in chief of the southern front complaining about possible renewed outbreaks of political violence in his area. He had found a leaflet favoring Juan Alvarez exhibited in a public place, and he feared revolution.[26]

Map 6. The State of Morelos (Cuernavaca and Cuautla Morelos districts)

The threat from Alvarez, and his national guard allies at the local level, was real enough. Composed in about equal parts of populist rhetoric and the memory of past political alliances, Alvarez's call to arms against Santa Anna was perhaps best summarized in a document he issued from Ciudad Guerrero on 1 October 1854. Among the strongest themes in the proclamation was the long history of struggle for justice that existed in El Sur, on "this soil abundantly irrigated with the blood of our illustrious victims in [the cause of] Independence and liberty, . . . the homeland of the clairvoyant, unfortunate Guerrero." The goal of this struggle, according to Alvarez, had been equality, peace, and liberty:

> The inhabitants of El Sur want the nation to be represented by Mexicans of any origin, with the only expectation that they be patriotic, honest, and that they refuse the pernicious influence of those classes that call themselves privileged in order to exploit the people, who feed upon the people's blood and insult them [by wearing] luxurious clothes.

The inhabitants of El Sur, he assured his audience, would always fight for "holy liberty," looking forward to a time when there would be "peace, liberty, love of work and family, and honesty in government." They would fight until "there is one law for all, and guarantees for the citizen, until [social] classes stop sucking the substance from our homeland, until divisions between brothers have disappeared: let us swear homeland and liberty: let us unite to make the tyrant eat dust, and the nation will be saved."[27]

And unite they did in the Morelos and Cuernavaca districts as well as in other parts of El Sur. The pace of mobilization picked up throughout the area, despite government attempts to repress the Ayutla movement by arresting all those individuals who had voted for Alvarez in the popular juntas held in early December 1854. In Cuernavaca, for example, the military commander wrote to the defense minister about a meeting of rebels that had occurred on lands belonging to the haciendas Temisco and San Vicente. Led by Isidoro from Xochitepec (later identified as a national guard commander and held responsible for further anti-Spanish violence), this meeting by itself would have been of little consequence, the commander admitted. Yet it was important because it

> indicated that the reorganization of the villages in this district is well underway, in order to destroy the properties and the Hispanic-Mexican race, [something that has been] premeditated for many years, and it would be most convenient that, whatever this turns out to be, it be nipped in the bud and that those involved receive exemplary punishment.[28]

We will probably never know how much of this incident was constructed by the rebels and how much by the repressive attention it received. But the volatile context in which the incident occurred, as well as the political role of Alvarez in stimulating the various local mobilizations, cannot be denied.

By mid-December a conspiracy in Alvarez's favor had broken out in Cuautla. At nine o'clock on the night of the sixteenth, to the call of "Long live Morelos and don Juan Alvarez," the conspirators managed to chase the local military commander, Manuel Céspedes, out of town and force him to take refuge on the nearby hacienda Coahuixtla. The next day the commander of reinforcements sent from Mexico City found that a hundred rebels had laid siege to Coahuixtla. They ultimately forced the administrator to open the hacienda's doors to avoid the burning of the cane fields that remained after the previous night's arson. The rebels then entered the property, carrying off horses and weapons. The commander reported from the hacienda Tenextepango that he had decided not to attack Cuautla Morelos itself because the rebel force had swelled to four hundred or more and had provisioned themselves well "from some haciendas, villages, and private homes in the general area."[29]

The rebellion spread dramatically in the next twenty-four hours. On 18 December the military commander from Cuernavaca reported that the road to Puente de Ixtla had been cut by the rebels, and it was no longer possible to charge the toll there. On the same day Céspedes reported from the hacienda San Carlos that the rebels had established trenches in the streets of Cuautla, occupying all principal points and all entrances to the town. To remove them he would need a force of three hundred infantry and a mountain cannon (*arquebus de montaña*). Predictably enough, the minister of defense was not amused. In a letter to Céspedes the next day, he wondered

> how a few men who have just carried out an uprising in an insignificant village, without leader, weapons or ammunition, have been able in so few hours to put together a force so imposing that it cannot be repressed by 113 cavalry, 45 [reinforcements] under Lieutenant Colonel Saldivar, 60 that you have, and the auxiliary force under General Cirilo Tolsa, for all these [men] compose a larger organized force than that led by the miserable cobbler who heads the uprising in Morelos.

Despite the sarcasm, the ministry did send what Céspedes had requested, although emphasizing once again that it was to help with "the totally insignificant rebellion" in Cuautla Morelos.[30]

Although reinforcements turned the tide against the rebels in Cuautla, Alvarista mobilization continued to swell in the region as a whole. "The seduction of Alvarez, through persuasion or force, continues to extend itself in these districts," reported Cuernavaca's military commander on December 23.

> From all points and villages I get requests for men and arms; . . . [the rebels] enter defenseless communities like they did in Tlaquiltenango, picking up weapons, money, and horses. They equip themselves very abundantly and drag along many who had not thought to go with them.

Events like these multiplied with such alarming rapidity in the first days of the new year that, before the first week of 1855 was up, the government in Mexico City found it necessary to organize a systematic occupation of Cuernavaca and Cuautla Morelos. Throughout January detachments of federal troops collaborated with hacienda police in an attempt to bring the region under control. That they failed was made clear by events later in the year. At the same time, military commanders set a pattern of racist confrontation with the local population that would be repeated, time and again, over the next decade.[31]

An important center of repression in early 1855 was the southwestern fringe of Cuernavaca district, including Puente de Ixtla, Tetecala, and Jojutla. This was an area easily connected, in spatial terms, to Guerrero and the Alvarista movement. Between 6 and 13 January officials reported rebel actions on the haciendas Cocoyotla, San Nicolás, and Treinta Pesos, as well as in the villages of Tetecala, Tlaltizapán, Jojutla, Puente de Ixtla, Tlaquiltenango and Tetelpa. The pressure was intense enough to supply a growing rumor mill that placed insurgents even where they could not possibly be. The panic that spread through the haciendas made defense difficult and almost halted the cane harvest for lack of workers.[32]

But perhaps the most frustrating part, from the perspective of those involved in the repression, was the close connection the insurgents had with the land and the local population. The military commanders could not get the collaboration of the villagers in the areas they occupied. In one case an officer was reduced to paying for information because no one would collaborate for free. Even when government forces managed to locate and pursue the rebels, it was impossible to catch them. They dispersed without engaging the large detachments, separating into several smaller groups and heading for the protection of the ranchos located in the uplands, or so-called temperate lands (*tierra templada*), that ringed the valley. General Francisco Güitián reported from Jojutla that the largest gathering point was Rancho de los Hornos, home to the leader Manuel Casales. It was an effective hideout because the paths leading to it were so narrow that the cavalry could not operate. Thus, Güitián requested additional infantry to remove the rebels from the nearby hills.[33]

The other center of rebel activity, and hence of government repression, extended from Cuautla to Tepalcingo in Morelos district. Nestled against the Huautla Mountains, whose passes also led toward Guerrero, Tepalcingo often served as a rebel stronghold. On his way to Cuautla to bring matters under control, General Nicolás de la Portilla was informed, while on the hacienda Tenextepango, that a raid was in progress in Tepalcingo. Portilla and his men arrived by night to find a most confusing situation. Although the invaders had escaped, they had left loot, papers, and victims dispersed throughout the town. According to Portilla, "the disorder was horrible: clothes and other effects strewn in the streets; the lamentations of raped women; the priest robbed and beaten [*estropeado*]; the mayor and municipal subsecretary tied up." Two times in his report he compared what he had seen to the acts of the "barbarous Indians" of the north—seemingly a reference to unconquered tribes like the Apache—even though, he said, these events occurred so close to the capital city. He also claimed that all the women had been raped, except for a few who had managed to escape. "The leader is Juan Pablo Sanchez *pinto suriano* ["southern darkie" or "painted one"]," Portilla continued; "the cry on all their lips as they robbed was Long live the Virgin of Guadalupe, long live Villalva, and long live Alvarez."[34]

Portilla's perspective was less than objective. His initial report is full of clues in this regard: the comparison of the Liberal guerrillas to what he calls "barbarous Indians"; the incendiary and unsubstantiated claim that almost all the women in the town were raped; his use of the word *bandit*, rather than one of the commonly used words for *rebel*, such as *pronunciado* or even *faccioso*; and his invocation of the term *pinto suriano* when referring to the leader of the band. His later correspondence, as he attempted to reestablish order in the district, adds proof to the charge that racism prevented him from seeing or reporting incidents clearly. He continued to refer to the rebels as bandits even as they spread political leaflets in the villages. He also created an image of Indians as barbarous and wild, arguing that

> Jonacatepec and Tepalcingo are very eccentric, [being located] up against the mountains which through Huautla go to the department of Guerrero: I am not worried about Jonacatepec, because it seems that this village is unified and somewhat intrepid; not so Tepalcingo, where the destruction occurred a few nights ago, whose inhabitants generally are Indians, and those who are not, are known for their proverbial cowardice.[35]

Whatever attempts were made to minimize the political importance of the Alvarista movement, its depth and support in the villages is most clearly mirrored in the repressive methods used. All rebels caught with weapons in hand were summarily executed and their bodies hung on public display in the plazas of villages considered rebellious. José María Costa, executed in Jojutla, was hung on the road from that town to Tlaquiltenango. The bodies of two others recovered on the road were hung in Jojutla as well, for Güitián was convinced that several of the leaders were from there. And after the nocturnal raid on Tepalcingo, the four prisoners Portilla had executed by firing squad were all hung in the plaza of that village.[36]

Simmering in this cauldron of racism and repression was the Conservative belief—held, as it turned out, by a surprising number of moderate Liberals as well—that the words *barbarism, Indian,* and *democracy* could be used as synonyms. For some, such as Lucas Alamán, the equation went back to the wars of independence and to Hidalgo's assault on the Alhóndiga; for others, it was formulated during the Ayutla Revolution. Nowhere was it more succinctly expressed than in a piece reproduced in

Mexico City's *Diario Oficial* on 19 May 1855, when in a comment on an editorial appearing in Toluca, the editors of *El Universal* allowed themselves to speculate on what could be expected from a government headed by Juan Alvarez. Describing Alvarez as a "semibarbarous Indian, his chest bare, a kerchief tied around his head, and displaying his black skin before the eyes of an astonished civilization," they imagined him taking over the presidential palace accompanied by his pintos. He would appoint as the givers of his laws "those lost men, stained with the blood of their brothers," men "who have learned to make [laws] through pillage and murder." Then, the editors continued, "we would see those terrible acts of vengeance that so please the demagogues, those *glorious* acts of popular justice, in which the hordes learn the tremendous task of making sacrificial victims, until now the only known method for exercising democratic rule." And the editors concluded on a somber note, reminiscent of Portilla's reactions in Tepalcingo: "When we reflect on what a government by D. Juan Alvarez would look like, we are sometimes reminded of the invasion of the barbarians from the North into the Midday [*sic*] of Europe, and it horrifies us to think of it."[37]

Yet if we turn the lens around and examine the picture from the perspective of the rural dwellers and small merchants that made up the bulk of Alvarez's support in Guerrero, Morelos, and Cuernavaca, the horror quickly dissipates. Alvarez, Villalva, Casales, Arellano, Popoca—all these men were upstanding citizens in their localities. Mestizos, ladinos, creoles, or Indian notables, often property owners, they garnered the support of village populations through a combination of reciprocity and astute politics. While the cry of "Long live Villalva, long live Alvarez" served as a discursive marker for Conservatives and moderate Liberals alike, signifying pillage, barbarism, and blood, for the national guard soldiers and villagers of Cuernavaca and Morelos the cry invoked two generations of shared experience in the construction of an oppositional political culture. Sometimes it was connected to José María Morelos and Vicente Guerrero as well; always it unearthed memories of common aspirations to peace, liberty, and equality, to the sentiments expressed in Alvarez's proclamation of October 1854.[38]

This was, in the end, what "El Sur" meant, as a cry for unity or the subject of debate, to villagers from Tepoztlán to Tepalcingo. Of course, not all individuals in a community would have agreed that the call was to be supported or endorsed. Intense debates must have ensued about the strategy and meanings attached to the Ayutla Revolution. Beyond the active members of the national guard battalions, in each village there were always substantial neutral populations of *pacíficos*, as well as those who strongly believed in the opposite side. And as we shall see, there was plenty of room for debate. Would the Alvarista Liberals truly live up to their promises to the pueblos? Would communal lands be returned? Would just and autonomous municipal governments be established?

The answers to these questions would be learned painfully and bloodily in the next few years, in repeated confrontations with Conservatives and among Liberals, over the meaning of revolutionary Liberalism and democratic citizenship. But in August 1855, as Juan Alvarez and his allies rode a crest of popular support into Mexico City, history seemed to be on the side of those in the villages who had argued long and hard, in the assemblies where communal hegemony was constructed, for an alliance with the Ayutla movement. Agustín Trejo of Tepoztlán, Guadalupe Rubio of Coatlán del Río, Isidoro Carrillo of Xochitepec, José Manuel Arellano of Tetecala, Manuel Casales of Tlaquiltenango, Amado Popoca of Tepalcingo—all of these national guard commanders lived to expect their day in the sun. Perhaps they preened themselves in communal meetings or strutted just a bit as they walked through the plaza after Alvarez sat in the presidential chair. Yet the Conservatives regrouped in Puebla only a few months later. Once again the national guard commanders and their village comrades would be called on to defend the Liberal cause. And when the dust of Puebla cleared, they found themselves blocked from partaking of the fruits of the victory they had made possible.[39]

Radicalization and Repression, 1856–1860

Between December 1855 and March 1856, even their detractors had to admit that the national guard battalions from Guerrero and the districts of Cuernavaca and Morelos played key roles in defeating the Conservative revolution in Puebla. The Puebla campaign—the first big challenge faced by Ignacio Comonfort after he took over the presidency from Alvarez—demonstrated once again the importance of the national guard organization within the Liberal Revolution. After the promulgation of the Conservative Plan de Zacapoaxtla in December, every one of the regular army battalions sent to repress the movement ended up going over to the rebel cause. In this sense the presence of the national guards in the campaign on Puebla city was crucial to the Liberal victory and was recognized as such. But once the soldiers began to return home, the balance of forces changed quickly and dramatically.[40]

While the cannons that took Puebla were still hot, a commission of hacendados from Morelos and Cuernavaca districts wrote Comonfort a letter about the situation in their region. Congratulating the president on his victory, the landowners went on to request vigorous action against the grave problems they and their properties were suffering. Already the first returning national guards had been threatening political authorities, and the people from Xochitepec—one of the centers of earlier national guard mobilization—had called for the surrounding villages "to throw themselves on the haciendas." In addition, the soldiers from Xochitepec had fired on a detachment of the *resguardo* (hacienda police). The hacendados therefore requested that the remaining forces from Guerrero not cross through their districts when returning from Puebla and that detachments from the regular army be stationed in Cuernavaca and Morelos. In combination with the resguardo, these detachments could nip the rebellion in the bud. Doing so, they continued, would return

> to our authorities the prestige they have almost lost on seeing themselves at the mercy of so many armed bands and military commanders as have existed around here, who have gotten pleasure from mocking the orders of the prefects and have even dared to threaten them.

This was the moment that would decide the future of their districts, the landowners concluded. Their salvation was in the president's hands, and it was impossible for the members of the commission to believe that Comonfort would ignore their plea. Just to make sure, they included a veiled threat. If the government did not take immediate action, there was the distinct possibility that

> the immense capital invested here would disappear; and that the large sums we spend annually for the benefit of all the inhabitants would end up outside the country, used there to buy the best fruits of the richest soils of our country. The terrible plague of caste war that is about to descend in that region would soon flood the entire country, and there would be born the new scourge of socialism.[41]

Only a few days later, in April of the same year, the predictions of the landowners were buttressed by events in Cuautla and environs, where an alliance of returned soldiers and hacienda laborers once again began to confront the owner of the hacienda Santa Inés. According to the estate's owner, Luis Róbalo, a good number of the workers forced the rest of the labor force to lay down their tools, threatening them with machetes. More than two hundred rebels then headed off to Tepalcingo, an important national guard stronghold, apparently to plan a more generalized assault on the area's haciendas. As proof of this broader plan, the prefect of Morelos cited further incidents on the hacienda Cocoyoc, where a large number of individuals had prevented work and stopped the irrigation water. The general goal of the movement was, according to the prefect, to increase wages on numerous estates in the district. And General Nicolás de la Portilla, again sent to the area to investigate the situation, corroborated the general sense of disorder and loss of control. He emphasized numerous murders of political officials, violent threats to landowners who did not accede to wage increases, and attempted arson on the cane fields of the hacienda Santa Inés.[42]

The agrarian movement of 1856 articulated a Liberal discourse similar to that formulated in Cuautla in 1850. An alliance of rural laborers, village peasants, and national guard soldiers demanded an increase in wages for hacienda workers, undertaking a form of wildcat strike to make their point. According to Portilla, lands previously in the hands of hacendados had also been reclaimed by armed peasants, as in the de facto actions of 1850. Armed peasants then cultivated the reclaimed lands.

In 1850 the rebels had been accused of anarchist manipulation; in 1856 they were accused of socialism. "Socialist principles have spread through our fields," wrote the administrator of the hacienda Atlihuayan, "and our workers are rebelling to demand the most absurd wage increases." The movement, however, could just as easily be understood as an extension and systematization of the same Liberal principles of citizenship rights—the right to be heard and the right to a just livelihood—that had inspired rural people in 1850. As had been the case in 1850, and despite the dominance of Liberals in the state apparatus, the government responded to the rural movement with repression, beginning a systematic offensive against the villages and the national guards.[43]

After the landowners' March request, Comonfort quickly authorized Nicolás de la Portilla, of earlier repressive fame in the area, to move against the region's pueblos. Comonfort here foreshadowed his later support for the Conservatives and the Plan de Tacubaya.[44] With Comonfort's authorization, moreover, Portilla employed the same tactics he had used earlier under a Conservative government.

Portilla violently occupied and disarmed the Liberal villages in the Cuernavaca and Morelos area. In Tepoztlán a soldier in the local national guard was killed by the invading force under Portilla's command. Establishing an alliance directly with the landowners and their private police, Portilla organized a counterinsurgency campaign against forces that, only two months before, had served in Puebla on the same side he was now representing. He justified his actions by building directly on his earlier racist formulations in the area. Thus, an analysis of his personal discourse sheds additional light on the ongoing development of a broader Conservative, as well as moderate Liberal, perspective on the connections among the concepts of democracy, race, and barbarism.[45]

Portilla's view of the situation in Cuernavaca and Morelos was based on three fundamental tenets. First, Portilla invoked a racial dehumanization of the villagers, just as he had dehumanized the indigenous population of Tepalcingo in 1854. In his letter to General Angel Frías in preparation for the attack on Tepoztlán, he justified the need to start out early, at 5:00 A.M., "because the Indians are warlike [*por ser la indiada belicosa*]." Second, Portilla associated indigenous peasant soldiers with disorder and banditry— again reminiscent of his attitude in Tepalcingo two years before. In his original report to the defense minister about the situation in Morelos, he referred repeatedly to the soldiers returning from the Puebla revolution as bandits and thieves, implicating Alvarez in the original problem because he had distributed weapons in the region in August 1855. Access to weapons and horses, argued Portilla, was one of the roots of the problem. It had made the peasants unruly, willing to confront the landowners and political authorities; the result was social chaos, with peasants attacking property and peaceful citizens, even though they portrayed their depredations as a defense of liberty.

The third element in Portilla's discourse was his attempt to distance the present village soldiers from the "glorious" national guards that had fought in Puebla. The people in Morelos and Cuernavaca, Portilla argued, were led by individuals who "don't know how to read or write and therefore become puppets in the hands of malicious manipulators, who can do what they wish with them." Thus, they needed to be disarmed and a real, lawful, national guard put in their place. One presumes that this new national guard would have real commissions and military titles, in contrast to the relatively egalitarian forces left in the area by Juan Alvarez during his retreat south. Yet even in this letter Portilla showed his ambivalence, concluding with a contradictory paragraph in which he admitted that

> it is interesting to note that all these armed folk I am referring to were ordered to go to Puebla to destroy the reactionaries, and they were a formidable force, as is well known; and with the exception of a few individuals from Tetecala led by don Manuel Arellano, the rest deserted, entire companies, committing terrible crimes, like those committed by a company from Tepoztlan. . . . Arellano has a very unfavorable background, for he was sentenced, in 1848, to prison in San Juan de Ulúa, for robbery.[46]

Portilla attempted to resolve the contradictions in this paragraph by implicating Arellano in crimes against property. Yet herein lay the crux of his dilemma and of that faced by most Liberals who had either property or social standing. In the heat of the battles that defined their seizure of power, it was the village soldiers, the peasant national guards, who snatched the victory. The national guards were the dedicated fighters, the battalions that did not change sides, the ones that led the charges against the enemy. Once the dust had cleared, however, the same fighters, by their very presence, stretched the definitions of citizenship. They demanded equality as well as liberty, justice as well as private property. Thus, they could not be the national guards, the citizen-soldiers the Liberal leadership required. The "real" national guards should follow orders, hold legitimate commissions, know how to read and write. They should discharge their duty as laborers rather than demanding higher wages or challenging the boundaries of the large estates. Yet there they were, these illiterate, stubborn soldiers, claiming their due as national guards and sealing the military victory of the movement as a whole. What could be done with them?

The case of Portilla is a particularly good example of how these questions divided Liberals, establishing a murky frontier between their moderate camp and the Conservatives. Although Portilla's first repressive campaign in Morelos occurred under a Conservative administration and his second under a Liberal one, the discourse and practice of both was virtually identical. When it came to social unrest, popular democracy, and the protection of private property, the dividing line was not between Liberal and Conservative parties but between moderate and radical Liberals. This would remain so through the French Intervention and the Restored Republic and into the Porfiriato. The Conservatives in Cuernavaca and Morelos—landowners and large merchants, Mexicans and Spaniards—were repeatedly able to use the image of a chaotic, barbarous democracy to drive a wedge through that crack in the Liberal alliance.

Nowhere is this strategy clearer than in the many Spanish and Conservative campaigns, between 1856 and 1860, against Liberal soldiers for alleged conspiracy to murder Spanish citizens. Elsewhere I have dealt in detail with the dramatic case of the raids and multiple murders carried out in December 1856 on the haciendas Chiconcuac, Dolores, and San Vicente that belonged to the Spanish citizen Pío Bermejillo. An extensive campaign by the Spanish government, which included breaking off diplomatic relations, caused a major crisis for Comonfort's Liberal government. The main thrust of the campaign was that the crimes had been committed by members of the national guard of Xochitepec, including its leader Isidoro Carrillo, and that

Alvarez and several of his officers had been implicated. Thus, according to the Spanish and Conservative versions, the Ayutla Revolution was, from the very start, tainted by the participation of bandits. It would lead irrevocably toward the kind of disorder that resulted in the assassination of Spanish citizens in the Cuernavaca area.[47]

The Spanish and Conservative version of events claimed further that the 1856 murders were not an isolated incident. Even a cursory examination of data from the period 1855–1858 yields eight additional cases in which violence was committed against Spaniards in the Cuernavaca area. Five of the eight involved merchants, often in the context of sacking stores in some of the towns; the other three involved Spaniards resident on haciendas in the region.

In most of these cases national origin was apparently not the main issue. Rather, it was the behavior of particular people—as merchants, hacienda administrators, or allies of the opposing political faction—that forced the issue. At the same time, however, it is undeniable that in three of these cases Spaniards were targeted specifically for their nationality. In August 1858, for example, troops invaded the town of Zacualpan Amilpas and raided the commercial establishments of a number of Spanish citizens, crying "Mueran los gachupines!" In Xochitepec a similar attack had been carried out a year earlier with the same slogan.[48]

The racial motives emerge with particular clarity in the case of Yautepec. On 22 August 1858 a band of sixty to seventy Liberal guerrillas invaded the town, going immediately to the house that lodged the soldiers from the Iturbide battalion who were protecting the town. They killed the sentry and disbanded the forty soldiers, some of whom then joined the invaders. According to the Spanish merchants who declared themselves victims of the action, this combination of guerrillas, soldiers, and other locals then sacked the houses and stores of three Spaniards—Manuel María Rubin, Manuel Abascal, and José Ros y Prats. As the troops carried out their attack, they yelled, "Long live Don Juan Alvarez, long live Federalism! Constitution of 1857, death to the Spaniards!" Later, Rubin, Abascal, and Ros y Prats described the events: "Those ferocious men searched for us, house by house, in order to kill us, and despite the existence of other Mexican stores and of other inhabitants with wealth, only our three houses were sacked, only Spaniards did they wish to assassinate, and only the interests of Spaniards resident in this town have been harmed."[49]

The testimonies of other witnesses or participants in the events tend to contradict some of the assertions made by Rubin, Abascal, and Ros y Prats, particularly their claims that the whole town's population was complicit in the events, that there was a larger conspiracy against the Conservative government, and that only the property of Spaniards was affected. Several Mexicans were also victims of the raid, especially those with political posts or larger commercial establishments. The only proof of a larger conspiracy was a small supply of wet gunpowder and the testimony of a frightened teenager. Yet despite these discrepancies, all of which point to the exaggeration of events by the Spanish merchants, other testimony does confirm that the invaders had close connections in the town and that a good proportion of the prominent merchants and political authorities targeted by the Liberal guerrillas were Spaniards.[50]

The Mexican government was interested in portraying the incident as the work of a bandit gang, unpredictable and uncontrollable. This would classify the event as an "act of God" rather than a political act subject to reparations claims. The ability of a political group to operate with impunity so close to Mexico City, moreover, would also reflect poorly on the government in power. By contrast, the Spanish merchants and their representatives were interested in presenting an airtight case for a political conspiracy, which would then give them the best possible motive to claim reparations. Whatever interpretation we place on the interests involved, however, the apparent Liberal identity of the invaders merits further exploration.[51]

The raid on Yautepec was only one of several indications of widespread Liberal activity in the Cuernavaca area. Several Liberal commanders, including Agustín Trejo of Tepoztlán, remained active and at large after the Conservative victory in Mexico City. In October 1858 Pío Bermejillo, the victim of attacks and murders on his properties in December 1856, reported that his administrator had seen "[Isidoro] Carrillo, Casales, and all the [guerrilla] leaders from this area go out together toward Yautepec, and together they make up quite a large number." Bermejillo insisted that "Carrillo is delirious for revenge, and the plan is set [once again] to invade these estates." Bermejillo feared a repeat of the actions that had taken place on his three haciendas in 1856, for which Carrillo's brother and brother-in-law had recently been executed in Mexico City. Many of those implicated in the earlier raids had not been brought to justice, Bermejillo insisted, and they had joined forces with Carrillo and Casales. If something was not done, Bermejillo concluded, his properties as well as the lives of the Spaniards living on his estates would once again be in grave danger.[52]

Yet it is often difficult to separate fact from incendiary allegation. When the newspaper *Mexican Extraordinary* reported, in March 1858, that a Spaniard had staggered into Cuernavaca with multiple machete wounds to the head, the hacienda owner Leonardo Fortuño explained in a letter that the individual in question was a Mexican employee of his. The man had gone to Cuernavaca after receiving first aid on the estate for wounds he had suffered while defending the property from Liberal rebels.

In other cases Spanish citizens used the atmosphere of contention around them to create a confrontation and then magnified the incident. Manuel Ruiz de Vallejo, for example, complained to the French minister responsible for Spanish affairs that he had been badly treated by Liberal soldiers in Puente de Ixtla in 1857. Yet Miguel Negrete, the commander of the force, reported that he had actually imprisoned Lieutenant Oñate, who had fought with Ruiz, keeping the officer in jail for eight days. Only later did Negrete find out that Ruiz had gotten Oñate drunk and had insulted Mexico before Oñate reacted.[53]

The killing of several Spanish prisoners taken from the hacienda San Vicente in 1860, attributed to a Liberal brigade under the command of General Francisco Leyva, provides an especially clear window on the complexities and contradictions of "the Spanish question." The general contours of the incident are clear: Leyva's troops had taken prisoners from several hostile haciendas; after the arrival of Conservative troops, four prisoners were shot in the middle of a disorderly Liberal retreat. The prisoners may or may not have been escaping; even those doing the shooting may not have known. Such events happen in most wars, and most officers do what Leyva did. They attempt to establish a record of responsible behavior, and they investigate events that do not seem to fall into place. Leyva did in fact undertake a brief judicial investigation, ultimately emerging with as sympathetic and believable a version of what happened as he could muster, and in this and other ways his behavior was fairly average.[54]

The situation was portrayed otherwise by the Mexico City press and Spanish diplomatic representatives. In a letter to the representative of the French emperor in charge of Spanish citizens, the Spanish consul Telésforo G. de Escalante likened the 1860 murders to those occurring in 1856. Only now, he argued, they were being committed directly under the Liberal banner. Francisco Leyva had taken over as Villalva's successor, leading the same "gang" (*gavilla*) in similarly barbaric actions in the name of "progress."

Although much of Escalante's version was not supported by the testimony given on both sides during the government inquiry, the Liberal government in Veracruz danced to the Spanish piper's tune. The reason was made clear in a memo that the minister of international relations sent to the Defense Department on June 29. The Conservatives were carrying out a campaign against the Liberals in Europe, he explained, and were highlighting all the excesses committed during wartime. This publicity would result in a lack of confidence with the Liberals among Europeans, which would cut Liberal lines of credit and bring to an end all programs of European colonization. Ultimately, then, the exigencies of finance and image won out over the need for solidarity in the Liberal camp.[55]

This incident, and the consequent removal of Leyva as commander of his brigade, destroyed the force entirely. Although Leyva was kept under house arrest in Veracruz for two months, the charges against him were neither made to stick nor formally dropped. By mid-1861 he had been reassigned to the federal army in Mexico City. In the meantime, the soldiers of his brigade were caught in the political and diplomatic crossfire. By mid-September 1860 the bulk of the Leyva Brigade—made up of the Tepoztlán battalion—had simply dispersed. They would stay in their village, cultivating their lands, nursing their wounds, and cleaning their rifles until the French intervened in Mexico.[56]

How did the Tepoztecos, going about their daily business in their village, perceive these events? Certainly the national guard commanders and Liberal soldiers no longer strutted or preened. Perhaps occasionally an older woman, made freer by her station in life, might say to their faces what others in the village would only comment behind their backs: that it was enough.

At first, they must have said, the Liberal faction in Tepoztlán had prestige. They had gone with Alvarez all the way to Mexico City, then helped beat the Conservatives in Puebla. For their pains, they were rewarded with Portilla's invasion in 1856. Even then many held firm. Between 1858 and 1859 they joined conspiracies against the Conservative government, and some even helped smuggle arms into the village. Many joined the Brigada Leyva, and Tepoztlán became Leyva's central headquarters. But to top it all off, the Liberal government repressed them again, trusting some gachupín over their loyal commanders. Just look what happened to Ramón Oñate! When he was a lieutenant, Negrete put him in jail because he beat up a gachupín who spit on Mexico. When he became a captain, in charge of the Tepoztlán infantry in the Leyva brigade, some more gachupines said he talked ugly and waved a pistol at those prisoners they took on San Vicente. So they took him down to Cuernavaca, as if he were a common criminal, and made him testify. Well, that was enough, they must have said. Have we gotten back even a finger of the land taken from us? Where is the peace and justice that *el tata* Juan promised? The Liberals are just like all the others.[57]

And so it seemed. When Leyva wrote to the minister of defense in June 1861, suggesting that he might go back to Cuernavaca to raise a new force and promising he could have between five hundred and seven hundred men ready in a week, the government turned him down. Thank you, said the note dated 2 July, but we already have all the men we need. Leyva tried again after the French invasion, promising to raise a thousand men in the area of his influence. The president decided to send him to Guerrero instead.[58] If the Tepoztecos had had enough of the Liberals, it seemed that the Liberals, too, had had enough of the Tepoztecos.

The Interventionist Interlude and Experiments with Imperial Politics, 1862–1867

By the time of the French Intervention and Regencia (1862–1864), the villagers in Morelos and Cuernavaca districts had reached an impasse. During the social and political movements of the previous decade, they had constructed radical and sophisticated popular discourses around notions of Liberal rights. They had articulated the rights of individual citizens, particularly as members of the "popular class," to the just distribution of lands, a living wage, and the participation of "the people" in the construction of a national polity. Socially and spatially, they had built alliances among hacienda laborers, village peasants, and national guard soldiers. In both 1850 and 1856 it was possible to see connections to the broadly popular political discourses that had been emerging in El Sur since the wars of independence.

After Comonfort became president in December 1855, however, Liberal statemakers faced a difficult dilemma in relation to their peasant allies. While the national guards had been their most reliable allies, both politically and militarily, the guards had also demanded that issues of land rights, social justice, and municipal autonomy be taken seriously. These demands, in turn, dramatically radicalized the agrarian social movements that buttressed and protected the guards, raising the specter of caste war.

In part as a reaction to these demands, Liberals in positions of power elaborated racist, exclusionary discourses and practices of social control that shared much with the Conservative position. One manifestation was the repression and disarmament of the national guards in 1856, after which Agustín Trejo of Tepoztlán and other Liberal commanders were reduced to a marginal and illegal existence on the boundaries of villages and haciendas. In addition, various trials were carried out by Liberals against soldiers accused of murdering Spaniards, starting in Chiconcuac in 1856 and ending in the same place in 1861. The consequence of these policies was the repression or destruction of several Liberal forces, from the Xochitepec national guard to the Brigada Leyva. And all of these actions were justified through racist discourses that excluded peasants and Indians from the construction of a national polity.

Under such circumstances it is not difficult to understand why the villages were in a crisis by 1861. What had Liberalism done for them? Had it brought anything but death? Village consensus, always a fragile and contested political construction, must have broken down by this point. People did not know whom to support. So they lifted their fingers to the wind and waited, scrutinizing the currents and crosscurrents with care.

What they found differed significantly from west to east, depending on the activity of Liberal forces and the proximity to Guerrero and Alvarez's headquarters. In Guerrero, in the mountains around the town of Teloloapam and in the whole region south of the Río Mescala, the Liberal movement was unconquered by Conservative and imperial troops. There, and in Alvarez's general headquarters at his hacienda La Providencia, Liberal strategy was formulated and debated and new guerrillas trained. In Cuernavaca district between 1861 and 1864, guerrillas in touch with Alvarez continued to identify themselves clearly with the Liberal cause, maintaining a base in the area's villages and generally taxing populations or individual travelers on the road in a relatively polite and "legal" way. In some parts of the district loyalty to the Liberals deepened over these years. In the Sierra de Huitzilac, directly south of Mexico City, villages became known for such a complete dedication to the cause that one desperate imperial official was prompted to suggest that several of the pueblos be destroyed and their inhabitants relocated in the cities in order to make the region a free-fire zone. In the municipality of Tetecala, by contrast, support for the Liberals was more conditional.[59]

In the villages of Jojutla, Puente de Ixtla, and Tlaquiltenango in October 1863, a band of approximately one hundred Liberal guerrillas made the rounds asking for money, horses, and provisions. While only a few people showed up when local authorities demanded that the villages confront the Liberals, villagers did expect reciprocity for any support they offered, whether tacit or active. In Puente de Ixtla, for example, when a guerrilla leader demanded one thousand pesos from the municipal president, the political official responded that the pueblo would give nothing until the guerrillas gave back the agricultural land at the borders of the village that they had been occupying illegally. When the official later saw that the men were not living up to the agreement made by their leader and were instead continuing to rob horses, he gathered a force of locals and drove the guerrillas out of town. Yet the complexity of these relations did not mean that local men were willing to collaborate with the repressive forces under the command of the Regencia. Quite to the contrary. The repression in Cuernavaca district was ultimately organized from the haciendas by an alliance of administrators who then demanded support from the government, or by imperial officials who then demanded aid from the haciendas.[60]

The situation was somewhat different in the district of Cuautla Morelos, where local villagers were even more ambivalent about the political factions contesting power. The comparative weakness of the Liberal presence, when combined with the widespread brigandry of the plateados, muddied the sociopolitical waters for all parties involved. Although sometimes supportive of the peasantry's social demands, the plateados were more often allied with landowners, abusive priests, and even abusive political authorities. Often they robbed indiscriminately from peasants and small merchants attempting to take their goods to market.

In 1862 Liberal forces in the area got into difficulties with each other because one had accepted into its ranks a number of notorious plateados, known for terrorizing local villagers across a band of territory from Ameca in the north through Jantetelco and Jonacatepec in the south. According to the Liberal government's report on the incident, two Liberal forces fired on each other after the bandits in one force, fearful that they would be recognized, began to shoot in an effort to create a diversion. As the local official explained, people in the villages did not fear the bandits when they appeared as such, but only when they managed to masquerade as soldiers of the government.[61]

In the villages of Jantetelco and Jonacatepec, plateado gangs were constantly in operation by 1863, aided and abetted by village and hacienda notables. Even if the gangs often took the name of "defenders of liberty," their behavior against the local population was quite indiscriminate. When it came to attacking bandits, therefore, the local vecinos were willing to collaborate with the Regencia. And that was exactly what happened on 26 December, in Rancho Las Piedras, hacienda Tenextepango. A force of 120 men organized an ambush of the gang of plateados whose custom it was to congregate there. As they stood on the green hillsides to the south of Cuautla, though, sixty imperial cavalry and sixty volunteers from the village of Mapazlán saw pass behind them a guerrilla force. Composed of around two hundred infantry, this force was led by the liberal commander Francisco Leyva. "When the men from Mapazlán saw the force," reported the local military commander from Yautepec,

> they said they were going back to their village and they refused to attack Leyva even though such an attack would surely have been successful because he did not see them. This is because don Rafael Sanchez, head of the men from Mapazlán, had once served under the orders of Leyva.[62]

Thus ended what might otherwise have been an important moral and military victory for the imperial forces of the Regencia, much more so than a routine sweep of the local bandit gang. The villagers' refusal to fight against a prestigious Liberal military commander such as Leyva evidenced a lack of commitment to the Conservative cause. And in oral memory Sánchez was later remembered in the area as an intrepid Liberal fighter who proved his worth against the plateados.[63]

What east and west had in common, then, was a suspicion of the Liberals and a lack of enthusiasm for the Conservatives. In a sense the arrival of Maximilian—a monarch, but not a Spanish one—provided a way out of the conundrum, giving fresh life to the anti-Liberal factions in community politics. In this context it is easier to return to the 1864 petitions from Tepoztlán and Anenecuilco and see them in a new light.

There is some evidence to suggest that different political persuasions attracted distinct social strata within the communities. The Liberals generally attracted support from a broader spectrum, all the way from small merchants or agriculturalists to the itinerant day laborer. Thus, while the national guard soldiers from Xochitepec who participated in anti-Spanish actions—Trinidad and Isidoro Carrillo, among others—tended to be nearly landless men who worked for the estates or rented small pieces of land within their borders, the national guard captain Agustín Trejo and the Liberal alcalde Pascual Rojas were more educated men. Rojas, for example, wrote to his mentor Juan Alvarez protesting Portilla's invasion of Tepoztlán with a detailed explanation of the local meaning of Liberal institutions, providing an impassioned defense of the local justice and autonomy his village deserved after the sacrifices they had made in the Liberal cause. Trejo, meanwhile, sent Juan Alvarez a well-written and politically informed note about Portilla's persecution of the national guard. And both leaders were joined in this intermediate status by the likes of Amado Popoca, a relatively prominent merchant from Tepalcingo who could also use impassioned language in the cause of Liberalism.[64]

At least in Tepoztlán, though, local Conservative leaders were more exclusively from the village elite. The five men who signed the 1864 petition were from an entirely different stratum than Trejo. Proud of their education, they used big words in their petition and made clear that no one had helped them. They connected to their own Aztec past despite their personal distance from the more humble elements of Nahua ethnicity and tradition. They were not interested in the rights provided by Liberal citizenship but instead in the lands allocated to them through ancient ethnic identity and corporate privilege.[65] Theirs was not the anticolonial, anti-Spanish, antilandowner discourse elaborated in El Sur since independence.

We do not know the exact extraction of the different political figures in Anenecuilco. On the one hand, Don Narciso Medina headed the petition to Maximilian that asked for the return of communal lands in 1865. José Zapata, on the other hand, supported the renewed Liberal offensive in 1867, allying with Leyva and chastising Medina for hiding political fugitives. They would reconcile in the early 1870s, when their common concern for village land rights prompted them to support Porfirio Díaz.[66]

But who was right in 1865? In Tepoztlán, was it Agustín Trejo, Pascual Rojas, and the other dead or marginalized Liberal leaders, or was it the five learned men who promised the return of village lands? In Anenecuilco, was it Narciso Medina and José de los Santos, who attempted to vindicate communal rights through collaboration with a foreign emperor, or was it Rafael Sánchez and José Zapata, who were at different points abandoned by Francisco Leyva? In the final analysis, what was more important—loyalty to faithless allies, or the possibility of finally getting justice on the land question?

Between 1864 and 1867 villagers in Anenecuilco, Tepoztlán, and many other Morelos pueblos would hotly debate this question. The answers were not easy or clear, and Maximilian further muddied the waters by elaborating his own promises of social justice, prompting villagers from throughout the region to write their own petitions to him. Indeed, Maximilian's struggle to make sense of Mexican agrarian relations, coming as he did from the European tradition of the "enlightened monarch," yielded a populist opening through which the Morelos villages would continue to pursue their claims.

Initially, however, Maximilian's responses to the Tepoztlán and Anenecuilco petitions were largely straightforward Liberalism. In the case of Anenecuilco, the minister of justice informed Cuautla's prefect on 5 January 1865 that

> his Majesty the Emperor has seen fit to resolve: that according to the law of 25 June 1856, civil corporations cannot hold property in common; and that the vecinos of that pueblo should seek individual restitution for the damage done to their personal interests by the events they mention.[67]

For Tepoztlán, whose petition was not answered until 2 May, Maximilian decreed precisely what the petitioners had emphasized they did *not* want: that the titles be turned over to "a lawyer known for his honesty and learning" in order to assess the village's chances of success in litigation. In both cases, therefore, Maximilian emphasized the sanctity of private property, interpreting existing Liberal law in the narrowest and most literal sense. This was the case even though other possible interpretations already existed based on the clarificatory circulars of October 1856. (See the discussion in chapter 4.) Not only was this reaction unsatisfactory for the Conservatives who had invited Maximilian to Mexico, but it was also frustrating to the villages that had pinned their hopes on him.[68]

By January 1866 the lawyer appointed to Tepoztlán's case had reached his verdict. Despite the existence of a good prima facie case in Tepoztlán's favor, he noted that the inevitable lack of clarity in the reference points listed as boundary markers meant that the government should support a new deslinde that did not go through the courts. Despite this relatively positive finding, however, the Tepoztecos made their dissatisfaction known. In a letter sent to the emperor with the lawyer's judgment, the alcalde of the village repeated emphatically that the village did not want to go to court and that the matter should be turned over to Maximilian. This new wrinkle seemed to stall the case once again, and papers were shuffled back and forth between different government offices, without a verdict being reached, until August.[69]

Meanwhile, however, the owner of the hacienda Oacalco, taking advantage of the apparent confusion in the case, went ahead and carried out his own new deslinde, putting up *mojoneras* or boundary markers without the consent of village officials. In response to a new protest by Tepoztlán, the landowner wrote to the prefect that the 1856 land law protected him and that he simply could not continue waiting around while disgruntled villages presented more and more petitions. Sooner or later the right of property had to be respected and decided, once and for all.[70]

Yet in September 1866 Maximilian—essentially overturning his earlier judgment, which would have supported the hacendado's use of the 1856 land law—emphasized the village's right to litigate for its lands as a corporate unit. The prefect was ordered to

> concede or deny the pueblo of Tepoztlán's right to litigate against the hacienda of Oacalco, in keeping with the precise provisions of the Law of 1 November 1865 about land and water rights, as long as it involves issues of property or possession. For this it is necessary [to present] only the copies of the respective titles and expressions of rights made by the interested parties . . .

In addition, Maximilian ordered that Tepoztlán should present its complaint about the hacienda's recent illegal deslinde to the relevant court. But what is most striking here is the change in policy from the earlier answer to Anenecuilco and the final answer to Tepoztlán. What had happened in the meantime?[71]

The evolution of Maximilian's agrarian policy, as Sotelo Inclán has made clear, must be seen in the context of two major tendencies: the progressive loss of French financial and military support, which forced the emperor to rethink the contours of his alliance within Mexico; and the continuous social and political pressure put on him by rural conflict and peasant demands. Under these circumstances peasant pressure forced open the possibilities of official discourse, allowing the more emancipatory elements to flow forth, much as had happened under the Liberals. Not coincidentally, it was precisely the period between April 1865 and September 1866—the very same months in which the Tepoztlán case was under contention—that Maximilian's agrarian policy turned completely around.[72]

Between 1865 and 1866 Maximilian attempted to win over the poor and indigenous classes of Mexican society, those grouped under the euphemism *clases menesterosas*. In addition to the Junta Protectora de las Clases Menesterosas, founded in April 1865 under the presidency of the Nahua intellectual Faustino Chimalpopoca, Maximilian put into effect a number of decrees concerning village lands and rural labor laws, all translated into Nahuatl and designed to increase his popularity across class and ethnic lines. It is interesting to note, in this context, a direct parallelism between the decrees being promulgated on agrarian issues more generally and the new challenges facing the imperial government in the case of Tepoztlán.[73]

In April 1865, precisely between the refusal to consider Anenecuilco's petition on communal lands and the delegation of the Tepoztlán petition to the arbitration of a lawyer, Maximilian decreed the organization of the Junta Protectora. The junta's purpose was to hear complaints of villagers and other "humble folk" on issues of land and labor disputes. In November 1865, after the junta had already been flooded by complaints from hacienda and village peasants about their treatment and expropriation by hacendados, Maximilian promulgated his decrees on rural laborers and arbitration of differences over land and water rights. And in June 1866, shortly before the final resolution on Tepoztlán, the emperor promulgated his laws on the rights of pueblos to common lands.[74]

The problem with these emancipatory promises, however, was soon clear to villagers everywhere. If people attempted to use the laws to their advantage, they collided with local officials who inevitably supported the cause of the landowners. And ultimately, it was precisely on these officials that the imperial edifice stood. Without exception, the populism of the imperial government quickly melted before the glare of the local political authorities.[75]

An excellent example of this contrast between promise and practice occurred in Cuernavaca district between June and August of 1866. Don Juan

Núñez, designated protector of the indigenous villages in the district, presented a series of petitions to the imperial government on behalf of the village of Xiutepec and others. In an attempt to get enforcement of an earlier decree removing the abusive alcalde Sixto Valero, villagers had presented two additional requests to the government over a period of six months. Valero had been in complicity with local hacendados over several years, aiding the haciendas Temixco and Treinta in their attempts at land accumulation. In the process several of the area's villages had found that the territorial markers separating them from the great estates had actually reached the outlying houses. But every time an order came down from the government to remove Valero, the departmental council—where he apparently had friends—ignored the order.

Núñez thus requested the removal of Valero and the resolution of the land issues affecting his clients. Within two weeks of the first petition, however, Núñez's clients were protesting his false arrest. And when the final decree "resolving" the case came from the Junta Protectora, it simply urged the emperor to sign a separate decree protecting a village's *fundo legal*, so that haciendas could not usurp land right up against the houses. Although Maximilian recognized the villages' rights to an ejido or fundo legal in September 1866, the contradiction between promise and practice remained.[76]

A similar incident in eastern Morelos, around Cuautla and Yautepec, stands as the best proof of the ongoing problems encountered by the imperial government in winning the hearts and minds of the agrarian population. In September 1866 Juan Cataño y Calvo, a merchant and small-time miner from Cuautla Morelos, was named president of the Junta Auxiliar de las Clases Menesterosas formed for Morelos. Within days word of his appointment had spread across the villages of the district, and when Cataño was in Jonacatepec on business, several of the communities in Zacualpan municipality requested his intervention on land and other issues.

Apparently quite enthusiastic about what the imperial government might do for the peasants of the area, Cataño traveled to each of the communities and held assemblies in the plazas. He rang the church bells and gave speeches about the mercy and justice awaiting rural people under the empire. People got quite excited and began crying "Viva!" to Faustino Chimalpopoca and Maximilian, setting off firecrackers as part of their celebration. The subprefect of Cuautla then arrested Cataño, along with his son and an aide on the junta auxiliar, for stirring up the population and disturbing public tranquility. When the case reached the imperial authorities in Mexico City, it became clear that Cataño had been appointed to head a junta auxiliar for the municipality of Morelos only, while he had assumed he had jurisdiction over the entire district. In the end the junta protectora in the capital city fired him from the position for overstepping the boundaries of his authority. Nothing was done for the villages that had presented their petitions to Cataño.[77]

From the perspective of an emperor anxious to buttress his power, imperial policy to protect the rural population actually backfired. Although the policy raised hopes about redress of grievances, it lacked a mechanism to enforce its socially progressive provisions. Thus, it simply opened up peasants and other rural folk to the repression of local authorities, whose first loyalty was often to the landowners in their district. In this context it is hardly surprising that, even after the most progressive forms of agrarian legislation had already been enacted, the imperial government was unable to gain the loyalty and wholesale support of the villages. While the emperor and other national political figures were anxious to paint themselves as the protectors of the Indian communities, no one was capable of meeting the deeper sociopolitical challenge presented by the balance of power in the countryside.

Hanging the Peasants Out to Dry: Alternative Nationalist Discourses During the Liberal Revolution, 1855–1867

From the standpoint of Morelos villagers, Liberal presidents and European monarchs proved themselves equally incapable of participating in the kind of emancipatory social project presented by the national guards and agrarian social movements of El Sur. At the same time, however, the military strength of those movements sealed all the Liberal victories—in 1855, in 1856, and finally in 1867. It was also the political and cultural creativity of agrarian social movements—particularly concerning issues of communal lands and political citizenship—that forced the articulation of new and radical elements into both Liberal and imperial discourses. In this sense, we would do well to reverse our perspective on this period: instead of seeing peasants as reacting to what was offered to them by Liberals, Conservatives, or imperialists, we need finally to admit that most of what was creative or new in the 1855–1867 period—under Liberal regimes as well as the empire—was put there in response to peasant pressure and contestation.[78]

At the same time, a close analysis of this period also shows that creativity and military strength did not translate easily into ongoing participation and influence. Quite to the contrary. In part because of the danger represented by agrarian social movements, both Conservatives and Liberals promised change, but they repressed instead of delivering on their promises. Under the Liberals the agrarian social movements and radical Liberal discourses in El Sur were first articulated to the original federalist and radical Liberal project of Juan Alvarez and the Ayutla Revolution. Under Comonfort, and only a few weeks after the Puebla victory, these same movements and discourses were disarticulated from the reorganized Liberal coalition through justifications already well known in Conservative thought: Indian peasants were semibarbarous and therefore responsible for transforming democracy into bloodshed and mindless carnage. Once peasant movements and alternative nationalisms were disarticulated from the coalition, however, the Liberals cut off their own transformational potential and began to lose ground. Comonfort, responsible as president for the repression of the Morelos national guards, also served as interim president after the Conservative coup of 1858.

Between 1865 and 1866 Maximilian attempted to articulate some of the same emancipatory elements from radical agrarian discourses into an enlightened monarchical project. He was unsuccessful because—unlike Juan Alvarez—he did absolutely nothing to confront the balance of power in the countryside. Even as progressive agrarian laws multiplied on the books, raising the hopes of villagers in many parts of the country, in the pueblos nothing changed.

Yet from the perspective of rural politics something did change in the long run. The alternative national visions created over the decade of the Liberal Revolution, while repressed politically and militarily, were not exterminated. They remained part of local political culture, emerging time and again during periods of unrest or political fluctuation. Despite brief flirtations with early Porfirismo, no movement or coalition incorporated these various forms of local emancipatory discourse. They were left hanging, without a solid foundation, through the Restored Republic and into the Porfiriato. Only with Zapatismo was the foundation finally provided.

6   From Citizen to Other

National Resistance, State Formation,
and Peasant Visions of the Nation
in Junín

In the central highlands of Peru, the district of Comas perches on an escarpment that divides the Tulumayo River into two branches, one heading southwest into the Mantaro Valley proper and the other heading down toward the eastern jungle (see map 7). Along the eastern margin of the Mantaro Valley region, the villages of Comas district have been prominent in the various military uprisings and conflicts dotting Peruvian history. In 1752 Juan Santos Atahualpa took Andamarca in an ill-fated effort to begin his conquest of the highlands. In 1968 the Cuban-inspired Movimiento de Izquierda Revolucionaria (MIR) attempted to establish a guerrilla *foco* in the same area, suffering as quick a repression as Juan Santos. In the mid-1980s the Maoist guerrilla group Sendero Luminoso (Shining Path) also made Comas one of its attempted entry points into the central highlands. And in between, in March 1882, the Comasinos themselves organized an attack against a detachment of the Chilean occupation forces, initiating a regionally inspired guerrilla war that fought the foreign army to stalemate. Indeed, the local guerrilla force survived much longer than those from the outside that preceded and followed it, managing to hold on, despite repeated military expeditions, into the first years of the twentieth century.[1]

Given this history, it makes sense to begin our story of alternative nationalisms in Junín with the contrast between two events occurring in the community of Comas, one in 1882 and the other in 1888, which are almost mirror images of each other. In May 1882, two months after the successful ambush of a Chilean detachment at Sierra Lumi, the military commander Ambrosio Salazar y Márquez was arrested and imprisoned in Comas. A group of villagers was angry with him for not distributing to the community the weapons picked up during the ambush, plus some given to him by a local hacendado. Salazar had instead given the weapons to young men from the valley towns, "believing," in the words of the local historian Eduardo Mendoza Meléndez, "that they would be better used that way."

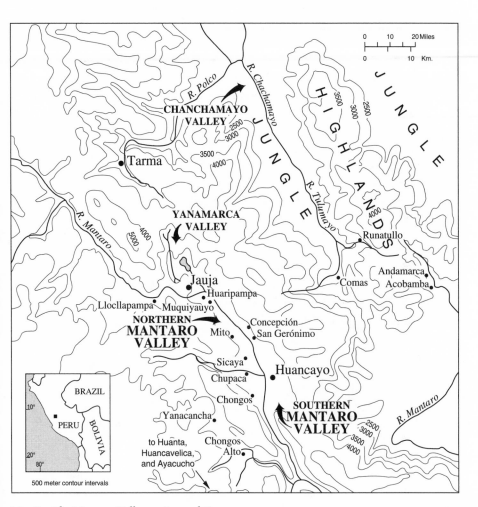

Map 7. The Mantaro Valley region and Comas

Nearly six years later, in February 1888, the radical lawyer D. D. Osambela was also jailed in Comas. In this case the reason seemed to be exactly the opposite. By arming the villagers and encouraging them to resist the national government, advising them to form their own federation of districts independent of the central state, Osambela had made the area vulnerable to outside repression and called down on himself the active opposition of a significant sector of the local population. Interestingly, both men were also freed by local villagers, providing evidence that the community was not united in either of the cases.[2]

Why did such different actions prompt such similar reactions from the Comas population? An easy answer would be that the two acts of imprisonment were carried out by opposing factions within the village. But such an explanation does not stand up to closer scrutiny. In 1882 the people who led the move to imprison Salazar were not political authorities and had not been leaders in the earlier Sierra Lumi ambush; nor did they appear as major protagonists in the later political conflicts either. The strong communal participation in the ambush and Salazar's failure to trust local guerrillas probably angered some of the community's average citizens enough that they contemplated, and carried out, his imprisonment. In 1888, by contrast, people on both sides of the confrontation had been important participants in the earlier guerrilla struggle. Here the division seemed to be a new one, over how to confront the political realities of postwar Peru. Thus, the two events in Comas, although revealing internal disagreements, were not simple factional battles. In different ways both represented complex political conflicts over the proper role for allies from the outside and over what stand to take vis-à-vis emerging national coalitions.[3]

Separated by less than a decade, these two events help us map the debates held in Peru's central sierra communities around their possible inclusion in an emerging national polity. In contrast to Morelos and other parts of El Sur in Mexico, where peasants had participated actively if problematically in the political and ideological construction of such a polity between 1810 and 1855, in Peru the Chilean occupation helped raise, for the first time in the nineteenth century, a "national question" to which rural peoples could actually contribute an answer. In this chapter I examine the struggles of peasants in Junín to construct unifying discourses about what they were willing to risk for the construction of a national polity. Whether they were mustering the initial willingness to fight, struggling over the narrative of completed battles, demanding legitimacy as soldiers and citizens, or debating the form of their reintegration into the postwar sociopolitical order, the villagers and townspeople of the central highlands helped forge new perspectives on the meaning of the nation.

The Historical Construction of Alternatives: Junín to 1879

At the time of the Spanish Conquest, the central highlands region was still known as the locus of the ethnic kingdom of the Huancas. Rankling under their recent conquest by the Incas, the local *kurakas* (ethnic leaders) made an alliance with the Spanish conquerors in exchange for special privileges. From this arrangement came, according to one interpretation of the region's history, the traditional lack of Spanish haciendas in the area and the enduring strength of the region's village-based economy. A strong and dynamic village sector, under the leadership of Huanca kurakas and their descendants, dominated local commercial production and exchange, connecting broadly to Lima, the mines of Huancavelica, and the mining economy of Cerro de Pasco. Before independence, land usually accumulated in the hands of the families that could trace their line back to the kurakas. Until the nineteenth century the political culture of the area centered in the villages and towns. Within the villages themselves, there was ethnic conflict and contentiousness over the control of labor and land. In the region as a whole, substantial intermarrying occurred between the Huanca elites and Spanish families settled in the provincial towns.[4]

There were important variations within the general pattern. In the south-central part of the Mantaro Valley, especially along the river's western bank, Huanca kurakas had carved private livestock *estancias* out of communal uplands with the express purpose of expanding commercial herds in the trade with the Huancavelica mines. They used their position as ethnic lords to cement exploitative relationships with local shepherds. By contrast, in the northern part of the Mantaro Valley, and especially around Jauja, the Huancas established a more indirect presence by intermarrying with indigenous and Spanish elite families. Commercial production around Jauja was oriented toward the mines of Cerro de Pasco and the Lima market.[5]

Added to these economic and sociopolitical differences were variations in ethnic relations. A key locus of power in the Huanca kingdom, the western bank of the Mantaro River had also been a center of Inca political reorganization. As a form of social control, the Incas had brought in ethnically distinct colonizers, or *mitmaqs*, to live side by side with the Huancas. When placed atop this complex ethnic map, the Spanish policy of *reducción* created multiethnic villages in which the various barrios in effect represented ethnically diverse *ayllus*, many of them not originally Huanca, coexisting within a single political demarcation. Much of this internal diversity, moreover, was organized spatially. Huanca centers of power were in the lowland areas near the river, whose inhabitants might be identified as *wari*; the other ethnic groups were located farther upland and defined as *llacuaz*. By contrast, in the northern area less ethnic conflict seems to have occurred within villages, with the ethnic ayllu lines conforming more clearly to colonial community demarcations.[6]

The potential conflicts on the Mantaro's western bank emerged with particular clarity in the 1780s and 1790s, when the decline of production in the Huancavelica mines combined with internal dissension in the Dávila-Astocuri-Apoalaya lineage. Tenants on the increasingly privatized estancias joined with communal officials and peasant households to contest the boundaries of kuraka holdings. The confrontation went on for nearly two decades, leading ultimately to the weakening of the lineage and, after independence, the transference of much of the high pastureland to a new generation of white creole landowners. But the issue of boundaries, murky from the start because of the way kuraka landowners had privatized customarily communal and ethnically based access to resources, would continue to haunt the new hacendados for more than a century.[7]

Alongside the ethnic and socioeconomic conflicts in village life, and sometimes embedded within them, were the attempts to construct and reproduce communal consensus. The village councils and community assemblies articulated communal discourses through the inclusion and exclusion of factions and opinions, constructing the hegemonic political culture of the *comunidades de indios*. It was precisely in this dynamism that the strength of the communities lay. By confronting disagreements and debating options, villagers participated in the ongoing renewal of communal hegemony, painfully carving out the unity needed at crucial political junctures.[8]

I have argued elsewhere that the central highlands, in contrast to most other regions of the Peruvian viceroyalty, mobilized fairly strongly in favor of independence from Spain. This mobilization reflected the particularities of the regional political culture constructed during the colonial period. An alliance of creole entrepreneurs and village notables supported the army of San Martín, ultimately inheriting the regional economy from ruined Spanish and kuraka families. But in addition to the success stories of these individuals, some villages in the region preserved a more collective memory of their participation against the Spanish armies. Their remembered narrative stressed the alliance of different communities, ethnicities, and social strata in a common quest: the establishment of an independent nation. It would emerge again, two generations later, during a new military invasion.[9]

In the meantime, however, the destruction of the wars of independence resulted in political regionalization, economic stagnation, and a strengthened peasant subsistence economy until the middle of the nineteenth century. Only after 1850 did new mining, commercial, agricultural, and livestock activities begin to revive complex and diverse village economies. By 1870 the regional economy showed strong dynamism and internal differentiation. Everywhere the result was conflict between communities, especially between cabeceras and the anexos dependent on them, over access to resources—pasturelands, commercial routes, taxes and labor rents, connections or influence in the closest centers of political power.[10]

In addition to reflecting the increasing sociopolitical tensions of economic revival, the conflicts between cabeceras and anexos also showed the contradictions in postcolonial attempts at political reform. The Law of Municipalities included in the 1860 constitution gave ultimate control over taxes and labor drafts to the municipal and provincial councils, decentralizing access to revenue. At the same time, this policy increased the attractiveness of independent district status, since anexos could, by declaring independence from a cabecera, directly control local rents, political posts, and communal work parties. Villages that remained anexos—especially while growing economically or demographically—found that they contributed more than their share, in resources and labor power, to the cabecera of their district.

A further source of contention was the electoral process itself. Between 1856 and 1867 three different constitutional conventions debated the conditions for citizenship and suffrage. In 1856 the right to vote was granted to males over age twenty-one who owned landed property or had served in the army; this made it possible for many communal peasants to exercise the right of suffrage. In 1860 the right to vote was linked to the payment of taxes and *contribuciones*; in 1867 all citizens above the age of twenty-one were allowed to vote. The promulgation of these constitutions through electoral law gave control over elections to local notables at the municipal level. The meaning of citizenship and suffrage were thus worked out from one municipal elections board to the next, as political officials translated local vote counts into influence on provincial representation in the national legislature. Not only did electoral law further increase the importance of municipal autonomy for the villages, but it also gave communities additional room to negotiate in regional political coalitions.[11]

Near Jauja, in the northern Mantaro and Yanamarca valleys, the socioeconomic and political contentiousness of the 1860s and 1870s had relatively benign results. The economy in the region rested on an alliance of Jaujino merchants and elites in the communities, an alliance that gave impulse to commerce, seasonal migrations to the mines, and *arrieraje* (mule driving). Communities produced livestock and agricultural goods for a regional market organized around the mines of Cerro de Pasco and Huarochirí. Commercial agriculture took place on small or medium-sized plots, located in the villages and belonging to merchants from Jauja or from the communities themselves. The combination of community livestock and agricultural production, arrieraje and local commerce, and occasional migrations to the mines allowed indigenous peasants to reproduce their own local economies while participating in a relatively autonomous way in the economic life of the region as a whole. Finally, from around 1840 mestizo merchants were already living in the villages, owning property and often marrying women from local prestigious families.[12]

Politically as well, local conflicts were channeled through already established relationships, as village merchants and farmers manipulated their patron-client ties to other, more powerful people in the cabeceras or towns. At least until the end of the 1870s, these relations proved flexible enough to remain firm. Although we know of two villages—Acolla and Muqui-yauyo—that petitioned the national government for independent district status, these petitions were handled through existing networks and remained in process for a long time, without the situation escalating into violence. Asymmetrical yet reciprocal patron-client ties supported multi-ethnic and multiclass cooperation, and conflicts were generally resolved successfully within existing networks.[13]

South of Jauja, along the Mantaro's eastern bank, a slightly different pattern of political tensions obtained. The creation of the new province of Huancayo in 1864, which brought the southern half of the Mantaro out of Jauja's orbit, also reshuffled district and electoral lines. Some anexos were reassigned to new cabeceras; relations among peasant communities, and with the hacendados and merchants concentrated in the larger towns of Concepción and Huancayo, also changed. But perhaps most important, the readjusted lines of power seem to have strengthened the importance of the valley towns—Concepción, San Gerónimo de Tunan, Huancayo—in the demarcation of political and economic space in the new province. These issues would emerge with greater strength during the War of the Pacific.[14]

In contrast to the area around Jauja and the eastern Mantaro, the Mantaro's western bank experienced much more open and violent confrontations between pastoral anexo villages and their lowland capitals. In 1874 the National Congress authorized the creation of the new district of San Juan, separating the *puna* (upland) communities from the control of Chupaca. Violence exploded between lowland authorities and highland shepherds. The prominent mestizo descendants of the kuraka families, settled in Chupaca, wished to retain control of upland resources in an increasingly dynamic commercial economy. Through the municipal council these merchants and political authorities had continued using highland "communal" pastures, marketing puna livestock, and monopolizing money and labor taxes to make improvements in the district capital. Highland shepherds, however, wanted to make more effective and independent use of pastures, livestock markets, and local revenue by controlling their own municipal institutions.

A long history of spatial and ethnic differences underlay the conflict. The lowland communities, whose fertile lands began at the edge of the river, had historically been the centers where power and population were concentrated. From prehispanic times, however, highland and lowland populations in the Chupaca region had come from distinct groups. After the Spanish Conquest Indian notables had used their political and economic power—concentrated in the more developed lowland communities—to colonize upland resources. With demographic and economic growth in the nineteenth century, other population centers had begun to emerge in the middle and upper reaches of the district. Slowly these dependent concentrations of shepherd families stopped tending the flocks of lowland notables in exchange for agricultural products and access to pasture; instead, they began to seek out independent outlets for their increasingly valuable livestock products and attempted to gain access to their own agricultural plots.[15]

The conflict in the 1870s thus helped to re-create, in a new form, tensions already constructed between *waris* (lowlanders) and *llacuaces* (uplanders). Indeed, waris from Chupaca went as far as to invade the high zone, beating and wounding several people and stealing sheep and mules. The leader of the invasion was Bartolomé Guerra, the *gobernador* of Chupaca and a direct descendant of the Ibarra-Apoalaya clan. Ethnic conflict also reappeared in the documents protesting the creation of the new district, in which the Chupaquinos insisted that the puna had no real communal tradition, housing only the shepherds who worked for members of the lowland communities.[16]

In addition to the economic, political, and ethnic problems between villages, another situation on the Mantaro's western bank contributed to creating and maintaining such high levels of tension. In protests about the creation of San Juan district, the inhabitants of Chupaca insisted that the new demarcation was the brainchild of the large landowners of the puna, who wanted to divide communities among themselves in order to expand the large estates into communal pastures. Part of this accusation was true, connecting to the political reforms of the 1860s and to the creation of the province of Huancayo in 1864. The inhabitants of the upland ayllus, especially those from Yanacancha, had sought the aid of the nationally prominent Valladares family (owners of the hacienda Laive and residents of the recently created province of Huancayo) in drafting and promoting the law that created the district of San Juan. Bartolomé Guerra, for his part, was related to José Jacinto Ibarra, the national congressional deputy from Jauja throughout the 1860s and president of the congress in 1867, when the two new deputies from Huancayo province cut Jauja's representation by a third.[17]

Whatever the personal intricacies of these alliances, however, it is clear that the presence of a new and more powerful hacendado class in the area substantially modified the local balance of forces. Under conditions of economic expansion, where the control and marketing of livestock was a key point in the regional economy, hacendados competed with merchants from the lowland communities for access to the labor power of the puna shepherds. Such competition sometimes occurred on the haciendas themselves, since some prominent Chupaquinos were prosperous enough to rent large holdings. Large landowners and village merchants were also involved in head-to-head competition over pasturelands. One reason for this competition was that the customary pastoral rights privatized by the Apoalaya-Astocuris—rights that themselves supported extremely murky and flexible boundaries—justified both hacendado and Chupacan claims to the same pastures. In addition, the dislocation and destruction of the wars of independence had left much land vacant on the puna, and shepherd families had moved onto it during the nineteenth century. Thus, once the expansion and improvement of hacienda herds began in earnest in the 1860s, the new class of landlords had renewed and intense motives to claim ownership of these territories.[18]

In the southwestern Mantaro Valley, therefore, and in direct distinction to the northern and southeastern zones, villages were in the middle of an extremely complex conflict in the years immediately preceding the War of the Pacific (1879–1884). In a general context of economic dynamism, several social and ethnic groups were vying for control of the most important resources, including pasture, livestock, and labor power. On one side, a new class of landowners needed resident laborers and new *canchas* (pastures) for grazing their larger flocks; but the neighboring highland pastoral communities, involved in their own attempt to expand livestock production and in conflict with the wari communities, wanted to retain independent control over land and did not need to work for the hacendados. On the other side, the lowland communities, wanting to maintain dominance over the llacuaz economy in their districts, could one day ferociously beat up the shepherds and the next day evoke communal unity in the face of a common landowner threat. These complex and contradictory lines of alliance and conflict would complicate themselves even further during the war with Chile.

Guerrilla Warfare and Peasant Visions of the Nation in Central Peru, 1881–1886

The crisis of the War of the Pacific intensified already existing tensions and conflicts throughout the central region. Although the war did not reach the area directly until 1881, battalions for the defense of Lima were organized in the region through conscription, bringing the draft violently into much of the zone. Yet even the draft seems to have been experienced differently in the northern and southern Mantaro. In the latter the most powerful landowners took direct responsibility for filling the units, traveling personally to the villages and haciendas to enroll the peasants. In Jauja, by contrast, local merchants used patron-client relations to fill quotas with their associates and followers from surrounding communities. Either way, however, the war was initially but a shadowy presence in the daily experiences and routines of central highland peasant communities.[19]

After the Peruvian defeat at Miraflores, the situation in the central highlands changed drastically. General Andrés Cáceres, perhaps inspired by the recent Mexican victory against the French Intervention, traveled to the central region to organize resistance to the Chilean occupation. Cáceres envisioned a multiethnic and multiclass national front, with bands of guerrillas or *montoneros*, organized village by village, supporting a small regular army. Village priests, municipal authorities, wealthier peasants and local merchants—people who were, in Cáceres's word, *idóneos*, or properly adapted to local custom and language—would head the montoneras, serving as the strong links in the alliance at the local level. Provincial political authorities and notables from the valley towns organized and led the regular battalions, while landowners and wealthier merchants showed a general initial willingness to finance the regular army.[20]

Given the political situation in the prewar years, Cáceres's concept of a national front operated quite differently in the various subregions of the Mantaro Valley. The "strong links" in the alliance—the notables familiar with community politics and local issues—were precisely the people who, in the southwest of the valley, had been central figures in violent conflict. These previous ethnic, social, and political tensions, when combined with the more constant presence of the Chilean army, led ultimately to the breakdown of class, ethnic, and national collaboration along the Mantaro's western bank. In the Jauja area, by contrast, several merchants and small landowners participated in the organization of village montoneras, and most maintained their solidarity with the Cacerista resistance throughout the Chilean occupations. To the west of the river, on the northern bank, the villages of Sincos, Llocllapampa, Muquiyauyo, and Huaripampa also resisted the Chilean army in 1882 under the leadership of local elites, village priests, and Cacerista officials from Jauja. Thus, in the northern area the more robust prewar relations of patronage and clientele buttressed the broader alliances necessitated by the war.[21]

A third pattern obtained along the southeastern bank of the Mantaro. The potential tensions created in the earlier political reorganization—between cabeceras and anexos, between valley towns and upland villages—emerged in the context of battle and pitted different ethnic and communal interests against each other. Within the folds of a common defense, which continued to work well enough to provide some of the most dramatic victories against the Chilean army, class, ethnic, and subregional tensions successively boiled and simmered, providing a complex backdrop to the confrontation with a foreign invader.

In the early months of 1882, then, as the villagers of the Mantaro Valley debated what to do about the presence of the Chilean army, a variety of distinct "founding moments" emerged that would color the meaning and process of the resistance for years to come. The initial challenge facing all communities was fairly straightforward. After the Chilean expedition had forced Cáceres's retreat to Ayacucho, any village that challenged the invaders would necessarily face a superior and repressive force, usually without the benefit of many weapons. With the odds so stacked against them, it is hardly surprising that some villagers were reluctant to take up the cause of the national resistance, at least not until the alternative looked equally bad. But the way in which villages met this challenge reflected deep differences in local power relations, as well as distinct forms of alliance or conflict with the Cacerista high command and its representatives.

As an entry point into considering these differences, I will analyze the oral memories of the war that have survived and been recorded in these various subregions of the central highlands. While clearly not the only important or authoritative versions of events, these memories have embedded within them some of the conflicts and disagreements that occurred in the region during the Chilean invasion. Through a comparison of the versions for each case, it is possible to begin unraveling the intricacies of local conflict, politics, and consciousness.

Let us begin with the case of Comas, for many reasons a crucial one if we are to understand the guerrilla offensive in the first half of 1882. The second Chilean expedition to the central highlands, led by Colonel Estanislao del Canto, reached the Mantaro Valley in early February of that year. According to the version presented in his own memoirs, Ambrosio Salazar y Márquez passed through Comas on 8 February, only a few days after the Canto expedition had arrived in the central sierra. Originally from the village of Quichuay, part of the lowland district of San Gerónimo de Tunan, Salazar had been forced to interrupt his legal education in Lima with the advent of the war. He was carrying a commission from Cáceres and suggested the formation of a guerrilla force. But Salazar, educated in the prestigious Colegio de Santa Isabel in Huancayo, a professional man and village entrepreneur, dressed in European clothes and working as an accountant on the hacienda Marancocha, was initially rejected. Only two weeks later, on 24 February, did the district mayor write to Salazar and request his help. What had happened in the interim was that a Chilean detachment had been reported on its way through Comas district, en route to sacking the hacienda Runatullo.[22]

Here the different versions of events begin to diverge. According to Salazar, the decisive moment came when the Comasinos received, within a very short period of time, two different warnings about the possible effects of the Chilean presence. The first was a letter from Pedro Teodoro Reyes, the priest in charge of Jauja's provincial council, requesting livestock to feed the Chileans stationed in that city. The second was the visit from the Chilean detachment. Salazar recalled that the political authorities of the district then wrote him that he had been unanimously elected commander of a local guerrilla band, and they requested his presence to help plan the ambush of the returning troops. Salazar reported to Cáceres that he had organized the villagers in two lines, one with thirty rifles and the other with fifty *galgueros* (soldiers ready to push *galgas*, or huge boulders, down a hillside). When the Chileans marched through Sierra Lumi pass, they were resoundingly defeated and all their booty, horses, and ammunition confiscated.[23]

Luis Milón Duarte, an important landowner in the central highlands who collaborated openly with the Chileans, presented a very different version of the same events in his memoirs. Initially, he wrote,

> the Indians received them with much humility and gave them guides, and [the Chileans] left, emphasizing that on their return they would expect good food: the gobernador and mayor responded fine, *taitay* [father]; when the [detachment's] representatives had traveled several blocks, the mayor caught up with them to ask them for a little list [*listita*] of what they expected upon their return.

As we know, however, and as Duarte himself points out, when the detachment came back through the area on 2 March, the newly formed montonera from Comas was waiting in ambush at Sierra Lumi canyon. The entire community—according to Duarte, the women participated as well—rolled huge boulders onto the trapped soldiers from the surrounding cliffs. What happened between 24 February and 2 March?

Duarte recounts a picturesque version. The Chileans, he says, were accompanied by two guides: Luis Loero, an Italian citizen; and a certain Olivera, previously an employee at the Convent of Santa Rosa de Ocopa who had been fired for his ill conduct. The Chileans made the mistake of asking Olivera to make up the list of provisions the Comasinos should have ready. Duarte insists that, of his own initiative, Olivera put as the first item "fifteen young virgins [*doncellas*]." This request prompted a furious discussion in the village, and a communal assembly was called for the next day. According to Duarte, "the poison had already reached the bloodstream." His version deserves to be quoted at length:

> A peaceful people, who twenty-four hours before had humbly attended to the needs of the Chileans and said good-bye to them with the utmost humility and resignation, became furious. The Chileans, they said, have to return along the same road they have taken, and it goes along a series of passes easily dominated from Comas. They remembered the traditions from the wars of independence, which narrated how the "San Fernando" Battalion from Carratalá had been destroyed by boulders along the same road. They insisted that many of those who had witnessed the attacks on the Spanish still lived. . . . The complete lack of rifles in the village, where the only weapons were shotguns for hunting deer, sealed the plan. "Those who have insulted our community don't even reach thirty [men]," they said. Recently arrived travelers confirmed they had seen no reinforcements on the road. And so the resistance was prepared.

This is certainly a mythical version of the events. Duarte wrote his memoirs with the general purpose of justifying his collaboration with the occupation forces and demonstrating that once the Peruvians had been defeated in Lima, there was no longer any valid reason to fight. Interested in delegitimizing the motivations of those who chose to continue the resistance, he argued against leaders such as Cáceres, who felt it was possible to rely on irregular peasant forces to harass the Chileans and improve the terms of the surrender. Thus, he interlaced his text with comments denigrating the peasantry's capacity for political consciousness and minimizing their potential as soldiers. In this context his use of the incident with Olivera and the fifteen virgins is very specific. Without a direct threat to their women—a threat to which even animals will respond—a humble, resigned, and passive group of Indians would have remained just that. Once the "poison reached the bloodstream," however, the transformation was immediate. In such a context, since the purpose of the incident is to deny political sophistication and complexity to the peasants' motives, it is important to question its credibility.[24]

If we compare Duarte's version with the oral memories of these events in Comas, some striking parallels emerge. The communal versions, written down first by the local schoolteacher Rafael Concha Posadas in the 1930s, then in the 1980s by the Historical Commission of the Peruvian Army as part of the centennial celebrations, agree with Duarte that Salazar had no important role in planning the ambush. The Chileans spent the night of the twenty-fourth in Pumamanta, a small community nearby, before arriving in Comas. While there they mistreated two old men and gang-raped a young girl until she died. The next day, when they arrived in Comas, they were treated well precisely because the people knew about what had happened in Pumamanta.[25]

In contrast to Duarte, who saw the pliancy and humility of the Comasinos as typical and thus unproblematic, the oral memories in Comas itself explain the villagers' initial peacefulness by recalling Chilean savagery. Yet even here the two narratives have something in common. Among the items the Chileans ordered readied by their return, in addition to one or two *pachamancas* (the equivalent of two to four steers, ready to eat), other food items, and two thousand soles in cash, were (depending on whose figures one uses) somewhere between fifteen and twenty-five virgins. As in Duarte's account, the virgins serve as a symbolic marker to catalyze the resistance.

What the two versions do not share is the political implications of this discursive marker. For Duarte, the request for virgins provides the only explanation for the resistance, since he believes that the indigenous peasantry of the central highlands "felt the warmth of patriotism only when the invasion touched their reduced patrimony; the cow, the sheep, the chicken, the agricultural plot, and especially the brutal affronts against their women." For the Comasinos, though, the demand for virgins set into motion a complex political discussion. A communal assembly followed, with the convocation of all surrounding villages. Consensus was achieved through debate and disagreement, finally yielding a plan for the ambush.[26]

The Comasinos further remembered that an appeal to Cáceres for help was turned down and that the village had only five armed men as sharpshooters; these were backed up by a communal barricade of galgueros. Armed with slings, the women of the community occupied a separate hilltop under the leadership of Candelaria Estrada. After the ambush was over, the women mutilated the corpses of the Chileans, screaming in Quechua, "Here, take them, Chileans, the virgins you wanted, all nice and combed!"[27]

We may never know with certainty which of the surviving versions is closest to the events at Sierra Lumi. More important, in any case, is to use the contradictions as entry points into an understanding of the internal conflicts of the Comas resistance. One of the key elements here is the role of Ambrosio Salazar y Márquez. Did he participate in the ambush? How important was he in the organization of the montonera?

From Salazar's own perspective, of course, he was central. If one follows his correspondence with the Cáceres high command, it becomes clear that his organization of the Sierra Lumi ambush, and his leadership of the Comas montonera, became his ticket to prominence in the Cacerista faction. It earned him the rank of lieutenant colonel and the place of second in command of the Concepción battalion that followed Cáceres north to Huamachuco. It ultimately sealed Salazar's political appointment during Cáceres's presidential administration. Indeed, the purpose of his memoirs, which were written twenty years after the fact, was to show the government—much as Bernal Díaz del Castillo had tried to show the Spanish crown three hundred years before—how crucial he had been. If we think of Salazar's memoirs as a contemporary *documento de probanza*, therefore, his claims about the centrality of his own role should be taken with many grains of salt.[28]

On the other side, the Comasinos, and in particular those notables in the community whose leadership during and after the War of the Pacific was challenged by Salazar's claims to exclusivity, wished to deny Salazar's role entirely. These notables and local intellectuals—schoolteachers, mayors, descendants of the political authorities of the time—wished to demonstrate that the community organized the ambush at Sierra Lumi of its own volition. The district authorities called for the participation of all surrounding communities. Some individuals and barrios did not live up to their responsibility, according to the memories that survive; but in general the community acted in concert, heroically and autonomously. And the names of the leaders seem to roll religiously, ritually, from the tongues or pens of the narrators.[29]

There are clues, however, that neither the process nor the memories were quite so unified. The women had their own autonomous barricade; it was they who mutilated the Chilean corpses. What would they remember if asked? Perhaps that they were avenging the rape and death of the young girl in Pumamanta; perhaps that they gave the Chileans the death blow with their slings; perhaps that it was they, rather than their men, who demanded action in the communal assembly. Were all men in agreement? In the apparently official report of the action at Sierra Lumi, written by the political officials of Comas district, there are accusations against one of the local authorities, who did not himself participate although he organized men from surrounding villages for combat. According to this document, his refusal to join explains the lack of a total victory.[30]

In all of this contentiousness, the success of the action at Sierra Lumi greatly increased its value as symbol and political currency. If Salazar was not there for the action itself, he certainly presented himself in the community almost immediately afterward to organize the narration of it. If the women of the community were crucial to the original decision to resist, the men—and especially the political authorities—appropriated it as soon as its importance became clear. And even though Salazar himself does not mention it at all, perhaps for obvious reasons, it is important to emphasize once again the symbolic role played by the image of the virgins.

In several places in the central highlands, it is said that the Chilean army demanded virgins along with provisions. Of course, we cannot be sure if the Chilean commanding officers did or did not make it their custom to demand virgins from the conquered villages. What we do know, and in any case what interests us here, is that the demand for virgins always marks the break with neutrality, the moment when it became impossible to abstain from action: the final, inevitable decision to seek revenge and reparation. The demand for virgins is thus a discursive marker designating communal unity in the face of a common threat. Communal unity, achieved through a conflictual process of argument and debate, is represented in a gendered way, with reference to one of the most basic and inalienable symbols of patriarchal power: control over women, and in particular over the sexuality and reproductive potential of daughters.[31]

As a point of comparison, it is also important to examine the debates that occurred, around the same time, on the Mantaro's western bank. Cáceres's representatives were active there as well, trying to convince the villages to form montoneras. Bartolomé Guerra, a political official and landowner from Chupaca and one of the participants in the confrontations with San Juan in 1874, was one such representative. So was José Gabino Esponda, a mestizo notable from the district of Sicaya who traveled through the villages on 20 February, counting weapons and trying to organize guerrilla forces. Finally, Corporal Tomás Laimes, a veteran of the battles of San Juan and Miraflores and originally from Huanta, Ayacucho, would join with the local notable Ceferino Aliaga to organize the resistance in the upland communities of Colca, Chongos Alto, and Huasicancha (see map 8).[32]

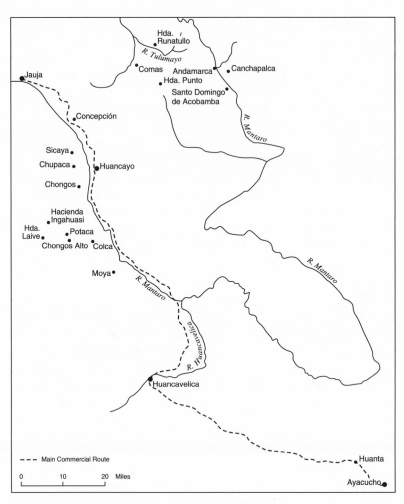

Map 8. The southern Mantaro Valley and Ayacucho

Until the beginning of April 1882, the western bank villages were on the margins of enemy activity, which was centered east of the river. After two months of exactions, however—and prompted by the recent naming of a Cacerista subprefect in Jauja—the villages along the northwest bank began to rebel. People in the village of Muqui cut the bridge that crossed the river. In response, Colonel del Canto began to organize a general offensive against the western bank communities. As a part of the offensive, he wrote to the district of Chupaca on 10 April, demanding provisions and, according to oral tradition, two hundred virgins. Chupaca called an open town meeting (*cabildo abierto*) to discuss the situation. The same general action, with some variations, was occurring in the majority of the villages in the area.[33]

The two versions of events we have for Chupaca are especially interesting because they show the ethnic and class tensions, as well as the problems between cabeceras and anexos, contained in the debate. Teogonio Ordaya and Aquilino Castro Vásquez, both schoolteachers from the town, agree in their histories informed by oral tradition that a communal assembly was held on 12 April to discuss what to do about the virgins requested by the Chileans. They also agree that this original meeting was marked by conflict and that it resulted in the ouster of the original political authorities. But here their versions diverge somewhat, providing a key entry point into local conflicts.[34]

According to Castro Vásquez, the majority of those present at the original assembly felt that it was important to give the Chileans as many virgins as possible, although the political authorities—notable and educated, usually mestizo—did not agree. Still, the assembly respected the opinion of the majority, and

> letters were sent to the political officials in the twelve anexos of Chupaca, ordering them to send, as quickly as possible, ten women from each anexo. The officials in the anexos perceive the order as a slap in the face and react angrily, especially Casimiro Gutarra and Esteban Macucachi, representatives of Huamancaca Chico, who threaten the district authorities.

Faced with a possible rebellion by the anexos, district officials decided to round up prostitutes to send to the Chilean army. They found only six, however, and all of them in the district capital! Only at this point, and after a new gobernador was named, did the possibility of resistance come up.

Another popular meeting was called by the new gobernador of the district, the recently installed Cacerista subprefect from Jauja, and Ceferino Aliaga, who already commanded a functioning highland montonera in Chongos. Those present reached a consensus to fight the Chileans, even without weapons. According to Castro, the discourse at the meeting helped to unify the villagers, recalling the previous moments in history when internal differences had been overcome to confront a common enemy. Key in the unifying message was, once again, the Chilean request for virgins and the consequent need to defend the district's daughters.

> Chupaquinos: You who have fought against the Spanish next to Manco Inca and Titu Cusi Yupanqui; you who have fought against Carratalá next to the embattled Bruno Terreros; you who have never trembled before your enemies; now at this supreme moment,

when you confront your destiny, you will have the courage to confront these intruders from the south, who would sully your daughters.[35]

Ordaya's account, as recorded by the Permanent Historical Commission of the Peruvian Army in 1982, is more contradictory. Initially he is vague about why the original governor of the district was replaced: "He must have committed some errors." Yet later in his account he recalls two additional communal assemblies: the first to name new authorities on 13 April; the second on 14 April, during which "*los emponchados de Cunas*" (those from the area near the Cunas River, the upland tributary of the Mantaro River, who wore ponchos rather than coats or jackets) organized the defense of the district. By the end of his account, moreover, he explains that, when the first account of events was published in Chupaca in 1923, people criticized its author for saying that the Chileans had demanded virgins; this simply could not be true.

> But through this commentary started a long discussion and the conclusion was reached that the [Chilean] headquarters had made the demand orally rather than in writing, . . . [and the mayor] had already asked Iscos, Ahuac, everywhere, to put together a group of ten or fifteen young girls. And this is the way that in Chupaca there had been named around ten girls, but in the next assembly they refused to obey the order . . . , and then all the leaders from these villages got together and agreed not to accept and to confront the enemy by organizing guerrillas.[36]

The discourses in Comas and Chupaca are strikingly similar. In both places the villagers themselves took the lead in organizing the resistance, holding communal assemblies where relatively autonomous if contentious decisions to resist were hammered out. In both communities the defense of women, and especially of virgins, emerges as the culminating motive for confrontation. The virgins are the gendered symbol of unity among ethnically and spatially defined factions, the discursive marker that designates a moral frontier beyond which resistance was inevitable. In both cases as well, at least one version of events emphasizes the memory of the wars of independence, especially the struggle against the Spanish battalion of Carratalá.

In Chupaca the memory of the Huancas allying with the Incas to resist the Spanish conquest provided an additional unifying image. Today we know that the Huancas allied with the Spanish against the Incas.[37] But at the particular moment of the Chilean invasion, oral memory seems to have worked in reverse.

In both Comas and Chupaca, then, unifying images brought people together across ethnic, gender, and political lines; but the internal dynamic of unity was distinct in each case. Perhaps not surprisingly, given the prewar pattern of struggle between upland and riverside villages around Chupaca, the element of ethnic conflict emerges with particular clarity in these versions of wartime events. The upland villages of Chupaca district—the anexos, the ones who wear ponchos, the llacuaces—were the most combative, yet also the politically marginalized junior partners, of the resistance coalition. The indecision of the district's mestizo authorities, and their attempt to force the indigenous anexos to bear the burden of the Chilean demand for virgins, created the impasse that allowed the less powerful puna villages to assert themselves. In the context of earlier conflict and confrontation over district lines, the indigenous llacuaces then rebelled, electing new and decisive local authorities. With the help of the Cacerista subprefect and the commander of an already formed upland montonera, they finally imposed heroism on a vacillating mestizo and wari elite.

In Comas, by contrast, the authorities in the district cabecera emerged as the heroic force. They exerted leadership against the personal ambition of Salazar and convinced the people to take on the Chileans in true communal unity. In this case, therefore, the main line of ethnic contention was between Comas and the valley communities, as represented by Salazar, rather than between cabeceras and anexos in Comas proper. Ultimately, this greater ethnic unity between cabeceras and anexos, between upland and lowland subregions, would be reflected in the form and style of struggle engaged in by the Comas montonera throughout the war and immediate postwar years.

The situation was different in the northern Mantaro, as represented by the village of Sincos. There the model that Salazar would have preferred for Comas actually did materialize. Outsiders in touch with the Cáceres high command summoned the communal assembly and wrote up the results. On 11 April 1882 fourteen men from the village, led by the Jauja notable José María Béjar, signed a document declaring that "all the sons of the village unanimously and voluntarily offered to take up arms in defense of the national honor." Just to make sure that such unanimity was preserved, however, a soldier who failed to show up in defense of the nation would be fined four soles for the first offense, eight for the second, and so on. "And in addition," the document went on,

> none of us will be able to leave the force under any pretext, without first proving the legality and justice of this separation, and until their innocence is proven, those who infringe on this sacred duty will have their lands confiscated, and they will be considered traitors.[38]

In Sincos, therefore—and by analogy in much of the northern Mantaro—village participation was organized more formally, through a clear chain of command. The punishments for those unwilling to participate, or to second the "unanimous" decision taken by fourteen village men, included monetary fines, confiscation of property, and formal definition of the dissenter as a traitor.

The difference in these "founding moments" of participation in a national resistance reverberated through the subsequent elaboration of nationalist discourses. In much of the northern Mantaro the legitimation of villagers as soldiers and citizens took a relatively unproblematic turn, as reflected in the oral memories surviving around Jauja, Muquiyauyo, and Huaripampa. For Huaripampa, the story of the creation of a montonera by Father Buenaventura Mendoza uses the same symbolic marker as do the narratives from Chupaca and Comas: the violation of the chastity of women. Yet beyond that, the narrative is unproblematic and straightforward. Around Acolla no memory of a local battle has been recorded. On the contrary, oral tradition has it that seven Chileans who were passing through were murdered and their heads placed on display in the public plaza. When Cáceres passed through a short time later, he promised to elevate Acolla to district status as a reward.

In the northern part of the Mantaro Valley, therefore, oral tradition seems to confirm that a united front among the peasants, their political and religious authorities, and the local Jaujino elite remained generally successful. All joined together against the invader; the heroes of the battles included both Indians and priests. Because the alliance led to political rewards in the form of new district cabeceras, it would be maintained during the years of national reconstruction.[39] Thus, the pueblos of the Jauja subregion did not develop alternative nationalisms that claimed expanded political space for peasant communities in a reconstructed national polity. Instead, they were granted specific rewards within more hierarchical political relationships, and they accepted them.

The story was something else again in the areas with more autonomous forms of participation and discourse, where villages repeatedly struggled to maintain control over the content of their stories and over the terms under which they would be recognized as citizens and national combatants. In the postwar years, as confrontations with the state dragged on, some of the villages or villagers showed they were willing to accept relatively minor concessions in order to end the conflicts. But their previous record of autonomy, militancy, and rebelliousness weighed against them with state officials, and rarely were they offered even a fraction of what the northern Mantaro districts received as a matter of course. Even in the cases where the offer was made, it was not delivered. In the end, therefore, the reintegration of the more autonomous districts proved bloody, painful, and at best partial. Junín's alternative nationalisms were constructed precisely under such problematic and fragmented conditions.

An early moment in this autonomous and painful construction came in April 1882, in the thick of the guerrilla campaign against the Chilean army. The montonera from Acobamba entered the hacienda Punto, belonging to the local landowner Jacinto Cevallos, asking for provisions. In an exchange of notes with his administrator, which was intercepted by the Acobambinos, Cevallos called the guerrillas "barbarians," in effect denying them their identity as citizen-soldiers. The guerrillas' answer was swift and angry and has been analyzed at length elsewhere. What is important to emphasize here is the articulation, within their discourse, of three basic elements: the connection of patriotism and citizenship to the defense of the "patria" against the Chilean invasion; the contrast between Cevallos's treachery in communicating with the Chileans and the guerrillas' reasonable and just behavior as citizen-soldiers under the command of Andrés Cáceres; and the guerrillas' repugnance at Cevallos's duplicity in calling them barbarians while collaborating with the enemy. Woven together into a discourse about the defense of the nation, these elements yielded a notion of citizenship rights that transcended ethnicity and social class: "Any hacendado should tolerate us as patriotic soldiers."[40]

As citizens first and Indian peasants second, the Acobamba guerrillas had as much right as any other group of soldiers to request provisions and weapons and to retain the booty taken in battle. But as their letter to Cevallos makes clear, these rights were not granted to Indian peasants by the landowners in the southeastern Mantaro. The guerrillas from Comas would also discover that even the Cacerista officials, generally mestizo authorities or merchants from the communities along the Mantaro Valley floor, thought that some citizens were more equal than others. When given a choice between their indigenous peasant allies and a more expedient coalition with landowners and valley notables, Cacerista officers tended to choose the latter. It is in this context that we can best understand Salazar's imprisonment in Comas.

In Comas and surrounding communities, the conflict with Salazar, and through him with the valley centers of political and military power, intensified quickly in the months after Sierra Lumi. The main issues were access to arms and ammunition and the organization and "regularization" of the Comas montonera. On both issues Salazar was interested in establishing the control of the force by mestizos from the valley towns, especially from Concepción; and he ran into difficulties with some of the Comasinos. The conflicts came to a head at first when Salazar chose to give the weapons obtained at Sierra Lumi, along with some extra guns donated by a local hacendado, to young men from the valley rather than to the Comasinos themselves. This decision resulted in a group of villagers holding Salazar— along with a Cacerista adviser who had just arrived—prisoners in the community. Although the two prisoners were apparently freed by communal agreement, a Cacerista column nevertheless entered the area, helping to reorganize the Comas guerrillas into a single column of a broader force ordered to attack Concepción. By early July 1882 the new forces, suitably reorganized and under the command of valley officers, began their campaign. Seen in the light of these underlying issues, the victory of Salazar and the Comas column in Concepción on 9 July, represented by the former in such heroic terms in his memoirs, takes on new, more complex hues.[41]

An additional complication faced by the village montoneras in the southern Mantaro was the need to confront landowners who collaborated with the Chileans. This was one of the subtexts in April 1882, when the guerrillas from Acobamba confronted Jacinto Cevallos. Thus, the initial invasion of Punto, which seems to have occurred in the same general period between May and July 1882, must be seen as a direct reprisal by the montoneros against a treacherous landowner. Something similar occurred west of the river, when in June 1882 Luis Milón Duarte, already a known collaborator, arrived at his hacienda Ingahuasi. There, according to his own version, he was confronted by an upland montonera:

> When the commander arrived he said he had an order to arrest me, given by a pseudo prefect in Huancavelica, even though I was in territory belonging to Junín, "and that the order to capture me was because I was spreading propaganda for peace." . . .
> They took me prisoner and took control of my farm, which they sacked for many days, taking out herds of livestock.

Here too the occupation of the hacienda was a reprisal for treason; Duarte's captors obeyed an order from above. Duarte describes in his memoirs how the guerrillas took him to Huancavelica and, without causing him the least harm, deposited him in Cáceres's camp.[42]

On the southwestern bank of the Mantaro, the confrontation between peasant guerrillas and treacherous landowners intermingled with the legacy of conflict between waris and llacuaces from before the war. Duarte was captured, after all, by an upland montonera, which was independent, llacuaz, formed earlier, and more dynamic than the riverbank guerrilla bands. By taking him to Huancavelica, they demonstrated an independent and direct connection to the Cacerista high command. From the very beginning, therefore, the two types of guerrilla forces on the Mantaro's western bank operated separately. One operated near the riverbank and was led by Cacerista officers who had earlier served as political authorities in the conflicts with the puna communities. The other was composed of upland shepherds who preferred an alliance toward the south with Huancavelica and Ayacucho, an alliance facilitated by the connections of its leader Tomás Laimes.

There was competition between the two montoneras. The puna guerrillas, considering themselves autonomous, refused to obey orders from the riverbank commanders, who only a few years before had headed the effort to keep them dependent on the lowland district capitals. Given the depth of prewar conflicts between communities and with landowners, these internal ethnic differences predominated. Each faction sought an independent line to the Caceristas, rather than taking opposite sides in the broader political battles.

Throughout 1883 the llacuaz guerrillas carried out successful rearguard actions against the third Chilean occupation force. After the Iglesista collaborator Luis Milón Duarte attempted a political reorganization of the area in early 1884, they adopted more militant and violent tactics. In addition to executing prisoners whom they considered traitors—such as Narciso Giráldez, Guatemalan Consul Wheelock, and a recalcitrant gobernador from the community of Moya—Tomás Laimes and his comrades Briceño, Santisteban, and Vílchez led a campaign of increasing terror against villagers who would not collaborate and guerrillas who did not submit to discipline.

From the perspective of landowners and merchants in Huancayo and Concepción, and in particular of those who owned property on the Mantaro River's western bank, these actions were simply those of bloodthirsty bandits who pretended to be fighting in the name of the nation. Nor did the villagers from rival communities such as Moya or Potaca, where the guerrillas carried out the bulk of their disciplinary actions, look kindly on the montoneros. Yet in the last analysis the llacuaz guerrillas' increasing violence must also be put in the context of the increasing military, political, and economic pressure they faced in 1884, when the Chilean alliance with the Peruvian landowner Miguel Iglesias upped the political stakes and began to change the lines of alliance in the area.[43]

In Comas the lines of alliance had begun to change even earlier. As we have seen, the conflicts between the Comasinos and the valley commanders had already erupted before the battle of Concepción in July 1882. From the time of the Sierra Lumi ambush, Salazar had been attempting to use the energy and combativeness of the Comasinos to his advantage. In the official battle reports to Cáceres, he took full credit for the attack, even though it is unclear whether he was actually present at the battle or arrived shortly thereafter. He took control of the weapons captured at Sierra Lumi and distributed them to his more prominent allies from the lowland communities, leaving the Comas guerrillas unarmed even though they had won the weapons in the first place. Thus, from the very beginning both the narrative and the spoils of battle were being taken away from Comas's citizen-soldiers. The imprisonment of Salazar, his subsequent release, and the arrival of a Cacerista regular army battalion to "reorganize" the guerrilla force were only the first skirmishes in a twenty-year political war the Comasinos would be forced to fight. Whether among themselves or with others, the people of Comas battled stubbornly, over an entire generation, to regain control of their narratives, their battles, and their booty.

After Concepción, and despite repeated actions in the area through 1883, the Comas montonera returned home. Already jaded in their alliance with the Caceristas, they continued to insist on the legitimacy and autonomy of their actions. The events of 1884 and 1885 would find them occupying the haciendas in their area, the property of collaborationist landowners, and selling the livestock for money with which to purchase the arms Salazar had refused to give them.[44]

The divisions within the peasant resistance, as well as the implications these would have for Cacerista policy, were not discerned clearly until the Chilean army ended their occupation of Peru. Until then the principal priority for political alliance was still, from the Cacerista point of view, the national resistance. As we have seen, however, the situation had begun to change by the end of 1883. With the Chilean departure, the new conflict emerging was internal, between the Caceristas and the supporters of Iglesias, over who could control the state and begin the reconstruction and reunification of the country. In this new situation the priority of alliance changed; the goal became the presidential palace. With this in mind Cáceres must have asked himself: where is the most potentially fertile ground in the central sierra? His answer was not, nor could it be, in the communities with the most independent guerrilla forces.[45]

In the two years between the Chilean departure and his ascent to the presidency, Cáceres showed himself to be an extremely clever politician in his dealings with the central highland montoneras. In June 1884 he accepted the Ancón Treaty, marking the end of the national resistance and the beginning of the civil war. The following month, as he began his confrontation with Miguel Iglesias, he also began repressing the independent montoneras in Comas and the puna communities of the western bank. At the same time, he gave greater importance to the alliance of merchants, small landowners, and peasants represented by the montoneras near Jauja and in the lowland communities along the Mantaro. This well-planned change in the balance of forces among the region's guerrilla forces would serve him well in 1885, when the montoneros along the river's western side, suitably reorganized under the Chupaca notable Bartolomé Guerra, formed the first line of resistance against Iglesias's "Pacifying Army."[46]

A clever policy, from the point of view of national unification; but it was something else from the point of view of the independent montoneras, those indigenous peasants who risked all to defend "our most amiable homeland."[47] Around Comas the villagers who had fought the Chileans at Sierra Lumi and Concepción; who had initiated and ended the central highlands resistance with dramatic victories against the invaders; who had confronted collaborationist landowners—these same villagers now found themselves caught between attempted hacendado reprisals and Cacerista "reorganization." In the highlands to the southwest of Chupaca, the llacuaces who had inspired the resistance in the first place; who had stayed with Cáceres throughout and fought in his name; who had been insulted by Chileans, Peruvian hacendados, and even wari officers—these same llacuaces were now repaid with contempt and repression by their riverbank enemies. Ultimately, therefore, the punishment fell on those who had suffered most directly from the invading army.

Let us begin with the dramatic case of the commander Tomás Laimes, executed in Huancayo's central plaza in July 1884. Many authors writing about Laimes have emphasized that, when Cáceres called him into Huancayo in mid-1884, he came willingly and peacefully. First he underlined his legitimacy and importance as a soldier and defender of the nation, replying to Cáceres's initial messenger, the mestizo commander José Gabino Esponda: "Tell Cáceres that I am as much a general as he is, and if he wants me to go to Huancayo he must treat me as equal to equal." He and his followers came proudly, expecting, in Gavin Smith's words, "to be respected and treated on equal terms by the professional army." Instead, Laimes and his fellow commanders were brought before a military tribunal and summarily executed, even though until the last they continued to insist that their actions were legitimate within the terms of war.[48]

What were the accusations against them? Not following Cacerista orders, as given by José Gabino Esponda, an officer from the rival riverbank district of Sicaya; yet Esponda, part of the wari elite never obeyed by the puna guerrillas, certainly had an ax to grind in the affair. Laimes was further accused of sacking the haciendas Tucle, Laive, and Ingahuasi, all of which belonged to landowners who had collaborated with the Chileans. Laimes was also charged with executing several individuals, including the indigenous governor of Moya, and with mutilating numerous villagers by cutting off their ears. He never denied any of the charges of murder or mutilation, simply stating that his victims had all been traitors. The final charge was that Laimes had crowned himself Inca emperor. On this he hesitated, finally admitting that he had probably done so, but only when drunk.[49]

Over the next fifty years or so, the contested image of Laimes became one of the points around which distinct narratives of the guerrilla war were constructed. From Huancayo and among local scholars, one gets a picture of Laimes as a bandit who pretended to support the nation in order to sack and pillage, keeping control of his territory through pure terror. Often thrown in here is a racist image of Laimes, drunk and disorderly, crowning himself Inca emperor. To these portraits, based in large part on the version of his trial printed in the Lima newspaper *El Comercio*, is added a new narrative of his death, written by the Aprista politician Carlos Prialé Morales in 1937. According to Prialé, who witnessed the event, Laimes went to his death "with all the signs of a bad man, more dead than alive, weeping and in a cold sweat."[50]

Yet the image of Laimes, and of the guerrilla struggle he led, is different in the highland villages themselves, especially among the descendants of the peasant soldiers who fought with him, accompanied him to Huancayo, and returned to the highlands after his death to continue their occupation of hacienda lands. According to the versions recorded by Gavin Smith in Huasicancha, the montoneros were unified behind Laimes and "showed great tactical skills and cunning but were constantly betrayed by outsiders." Indeed, Smith reports that as late as 1981 Huasicanchinos showed him "where we [sic] ambushed the Chileans . . . [and] hid during the guerrilla war." The recorded oral memory of Laimes's death is also different: he is supposed to have died in ambush, "on his way to a conference with his cofighter Cáceres, . . . unarmed because he trusted his companion-in-arms." As we have seen, this image of trust and equality is much more in keeping with the events surrounding the execution than the story presented by local historians in Huancayo.[51]

A last element that needs further exploration is the charge that Laimes had himself crowned Inca emperor. This charge recalls Eric Hobsbawm's oft-quoted assertion, based on Henri Favre's work, that Laimes is remembered as Túpac Amaru. When discussing the issue, Nelson Manrique skirts both its possible millenarian implications and Laimes's potential alcoholic motivation. Yet Smith has found no memory connecting Laimes to Túpac Amaru in twentieth-century Huasicancha, pointing out instead that local fiestas often have figures of Incas and a plentiful supply of alcohol. This description would also apply to many parts of the Peruvian highlands in the eighteenth and nineteenth centuries, especially for the widespread Andean dance of the *Capitán*, which we know was danced in the western Mantaro region in the 1880s. I therefore wish to suggest that, when Laimes crowned himself Inca, he was dancing the role, or cargo, of the Inca in a local version— probably underground and illegal, possibly revisionist—of the Capitán.[52]

As interpreted by Burga and others, the Capitán was a dance consolidated in the eighteenth century as a reenactment of the Spanish capture of Ata- hualpa. Within it, the figures of the Capitán and the Inca danced in ritual conflict. The Inca was the symbol of conquest and defeat, while the Capitán represented the dynamic conquering force, dancing with his head raised to the beat of loud music and accompanied by "weapons and horses." Accord- ing to Burga, at least for twentieth-century Cajatambo, the outcome of the ritual conflict varied a great deal from village to village. At times the con- frontation was resolved with a single dance of unity. At other times the capture of Atahualpa was followed by the payment of ransom, and then each *cuadrilla* of dancers retired to its own barrio to continue dancing. Thus, the dance seemed always to have had room in it for symbolic manipulation, depending on local political and social conditions. Even though the Inca often stood for defeat and tragedy, he could also become a figure of defiance and resistance, representing the majority of the indigenous population. "The cargo of the Inca is so identified with the Indian majority," writes Burga, "that Luis Pardo, the legendary bandit from Chiquián, when he wished to demonstrate his rebellion against the established order, took the cargo of the Inca in the fiesta of Santa Rosa in Chiquián in 1900."[53] Did Laimes do the same in the early 1880s?

Much contextual evidence suggests that he did. To begin with, we know that dancing the Capitán in the villages of the southwestern Mantaro was a controversial act in the first half of the 1880s, having been prohibited re- peatedly by the Huancayo municipal council. The only time when the dance was allowed by the council was in late 1882, after the end of the second Chilean occupation. A partial explanation for these prohibitions, even perhaps for the one leniency, can be found in Carlos Samaniego's analysis of the dance, which he says was also extremely popular in the area during Independence. The Capitán, Samaniego writes, is "military in style and express[es] the form in which the population has participated in the wider society from the beginning of the colony: through the army." Thus, the Capitán could have served as a symbolic theater in which communities reenacted and strengthened their unity vis-à-vis the invaders; it could also have served the purpose of acting out military defiance and rebellion.[54] In this context, what did Laimes's possible enactment of the Inca mean?

It is interesting to note that Samaniego's description of the Capitán does not mention the Inca figure. Could it be that the version of the dance in the central highlands had entirely eliminated the figure of the Inca? Given the Huancas' alliance with the Spaniards during the conquest, it is tempting to say that it had. Yet we know that in the eighteenth century the movement of Juan Santos Atahualpa, as well as Túpac Amaru, struck a sympathetic chord in the region. Perhaps the oral versions of the dance collected by Samaniego in the twentieth century, after the dance had undergone several major transformations, referred to later variants from which the Inca had been eliminated. In the nineteenth century there may well have been an Inca cargo taken by Laimes, in symbolic representation of the ethnic unity of his resistance movement and of its defiance of the established order.

The other possibility is that, in fact, the Capitán customarily danced in the central highlands did not have an Inca and that Laimes intentionally created one. Here one could speculate that, being from Huanta, Ayacucho, Laimes could have imported the Inca from one of the fiesta traditions in his birthplace and used it in an attempt to unify the broader guerrilla movement. In this way an existing political and military connection—as demonstrated in Duarte's description of his being taken to Huancavelica by the llacuaz guerrillas operating on his hacienda Ingahuasi—was reproduced and strengthened on a ritual plane.[55]

We may never know whether Laimes danced an existing cargo or created one. In either case, however, he was not crowning himself Inca as a political act central to his movement. As his answer to Cáceres's messenger and his subsequent testimony at his trial make clear, Laimes based his legitimacy not on connections with the Inca tradition but on his behavior and prestige as a defender of the nation. His followers, moreover, obeyed him not because he was a reincarnation of Túpac Amaru but because they believed in him and the movement he led or because they were subject to the draconian discipline of the movement's last year.

Thus, we must discard an interpretation of this guerrilla movement as yet another example of a one-dimensional "Andean utopia." Instead, we have a creative manipulation of ritual and fiesta traditions and symbols, the use of a cultural arsenal in new and politically significant ways. And this is the central point. In Laimes and his followers we find a complex and innovative local movement, tied into emerging debates over the construction of the national polity. This is how Inca symbolism was used: not as a backward-looking ethnic isolationism but as a ritual expression of the need to break open definitions of citizenship and nationhood in order to include the indigenous majority.[56]

The struggle for inclusion took another form in Comas after 1882. On the surface this new struggle resembled that of the southwestern Mantaro, as the Comasinos occupied several haciendas belonging to local collaborators and expropriated livestock herds to provide sustenance and cash for weapons. But the struggle of the Comasinos between 1884 and 1887 focused more intensely on the issue of the livestock extracted from the area's haciendas—which came to symbolize the legitimacy of their montonera in the resistance—and thereby the villagers' rightful claims as citizen-soldiers.

From 1884 the landowners of the area—including the Valladares brothers, Jacinto Cevallos, and others—struggled to define the Comasinos' possession of cattle from their haciendas as theft. In an *expediente* presented to the Cacerista forces in mid-1884, the hacendados were able to convince Cáceres of the legality of their claims. We can at least speculate that the timing of the request—made right around the time of Laimes's execution—was particularly felicitous. Cáceres was at that moment emphasizing social control in his attempt to reorganize his army for the impending civil war with Iglesias. The content of Cáceres's resolution, and the language of Prefect Guillermo Ferreyros's letter communicating it to the Comasinos, are especially revealing, since they describe the situation as a simple matter of defense of private property and do not comment on the circumstances under which the livestock was removed. Ferreyros's letter deserves to be analyzed in detail.

Ferreyros prefaced his letter to the gobernador of Comas district with a transcription of Cáceres's resolution. This document gave him the power to decide which was the best way to ensure the return of Valladares's livestock from the haciendas Runatullo, Pampa Hermosa, Curibamba, and Ususqui, as well as to bring the "criminals" to justice. If the villagers obeyed the order to return the animals, Ferreyros wrote,

> this Prefect's office . . . will give all sorts of guarantees to the individuals from those communities, for they will not be persecuted or molested for the mistakes they have made, which will be forgotten; but in the opposite case [i.e., if the villagers do not obey the order to return the animals], this office will give the most efficient and immediate orders to capture the delinquents, as has been ordered by his Excellency the General, and impose the most severe and exemplary punishment, that their grave crimes deserve.[57]

Ferreyros portrayed himself as generous by making clear that he would forgive the Comasinos if they obeyed his orders. He was generous, however, not because he recognized any legitimacy in the actions of the villagers but rather because he was placing himself in a paternal position vis-à-vis people who had shown themselves unworthy of equal treatment. In the end both Cáceres's resolution and Ferreyros's letter stripped the Comasinos of their identity as soldiers of the nation, transforming them into common delinquents. The prefect, by extending a fatherly offer of forgiveness, also took away any illusion of equality as citizen-soldiers the Comasinos might have harbored.

With one exception—apparently, some people from the district met with government representatives at the convent of Santa Rosa de Ocopa to try to hammer out an agreement—the villagers of Comas district refused to obey repeated government orders to return the livestock. In general, their position seems best represented by an 1887 letter from representatives of the village of Parco that detailed the contributions made by Comas district to the resistance against the Chileans. In recognition of their service to the nation, the representatives requested a decrease in the livestock owed to Valladares and identified more than eight hundred cows, steers, and horses taken from Valladares's haciendas as those the Chileans were bringing back from their own raid when attacked at Sierra Lumi. In conclusion they requested "that the cattle taken at Sierra Lumi from the common enemy can be considered as a sort of booty of War."[58]

The Caceristas proved unable to accept the arguments of the Comasinos. From their perspective, the Caceristas had three alternatives for political reorganization in the central highlands. They could ally themselves with the most autonomous and active montoneras, those who had collaborated most directly with Cáceres. They could ally themselves with the mestizo village elites, who had the closest connections with the urban and commercial powerholders in the region. Or they could try to reconnect with the local landowners. The last option proved complicated, at least during the civil war, because landowner collaborationism during the occupation tended to connect the hacendados with Iglesias. The first possibility was also difficult unless Cáceres was prepared to accept some form of social revolution. How could he depend on peasant leaders autonomous enough to consider themselves his equals or to demand hacienda livestock as booty of war?

Worse yet, having thrown in his lot with the Salazars, Espondas, and Guerras of the resistance, Cáceres could not change strategies in midstream. The best alternative—the most politically and militarily effective one during the civil war and perhaps the only practical one—was an alliance with the mestizo elites in the villages. Since they had already fought in the resistance, these groups had prestige at the local level and influence in their communities. They also had social position and practice mediating with urban power groups.

In this way we can explain clearly why Cáceres chose his allies from among the notables of the western riverbank communities, naming Bartolomé Guerra general commander of the central sierra guerrillas during the civil war of 1884 and 1885. We can also explain why the guerrillas from the Jauja region were Cáceres's most enthusiastic supporters in that conflict: it was there that the Cacerista strategy worked most smoothly. Toward the south and east, however, the situation was a great deal more difficult, and it would continue to be so for years to come.[59]

The Failure of Hegemony in Junín: State Repression and Peasant Resistance, 1885–1895

In contrast to Mexico, where the defeat of a foreign army was both a cause and an effect of the internal victory of the Liberal army and Liberal party, in Peru the departure of the Chilean army underlined the defeat of a divided Peruvian polity. By announcing his willingness to accept a treaty with territorial concessions, the northern landowner Miguel Iglesias became the designated leader of the peace negotiations that led to signing the Treaty of Ancón on 20 October 1883. Three days later, in the wake of the Chilean retreat from Lima and using Chilean weapons, Iglesias took control of the capital city. Until the Chileans completed their withdrawal from Peruvian territory in August 1884, Iglesias attempted to build a viable governing coalition. But beyond the approval of the Ancón treaty by the 1884 Constituent Assembly, and even by General Andrés Cáceres in June of the same year, political consolidation eluded Iglesias.[60]

The problem was that ending a foreign occupation was not the same as bringing about national unification. As became painfully clear in the following months, the Chilean departure in August 1884 was only the beginning of a civil war over who would supervise the reconstruction of the Peruvian state. Although Cáceres had the political advantage, untainted by collaboration with the Chileans, his initial attempt to take Lima at the end of August 1884 proved a bitter failure. Lacking supplies and men, the defeated hero of La Breña wandered through the highlands for months, attempting to rebuild his army. As had been the case during the La Breña campaign, Cáceres's most effective support came from the central part of the country, between Jauja and Ayacucho. Once again the village montoneras and Indian guerrillas of the region decisively turned the conflict in favor of the Caceristas. Yet many battles and much loss of blood would still ensue before the Cacerista army took over Lima in December 1885, installing Cáceres as provisional president and beginning the consolidation of state power.[61]

In the months that followed the original Cacerista defeat in Lima, a division of the Iglesista army, known as the Pacificadora del Centro (Central Pacification Army), traveled into the central highlands. Led by Colonel Pedro Más, its main task was to place villages in the La Breña stronghold under Iglesista domination. Representatives traveled through the district capitals of the area, calling municipal assemblies to establish political officials and inquire about the needs of different villages. But the division's presence was essentially military, as evidenced by the constant battles and skirmishes between sectors of the Pacificadora and the village montoneras in Junín and Huancavelica.[62]

Between November 1884 and February 1885, the indigenous peasant guerrillas constituted the only effective and organized resistance to Más and his expedition. From Huancayo to Huancavelica to Huanta, from Ayacucho to Acobamba to Chongos Alto, the montoneros constantly harassed the Iglesistas. Between November and December of 1884, Más was forced to send special expeditions to Acobamba and Huanta to deal with rebellion. In Huancavelica fifteen hundred Indian guerrillas yelled "Viva Cáceres!" as they plunged into battle, burning and sacking the houses of Iglesistas. Commanders commented, moreover, on the centrality of Huanta in the reorganization of dispersed guerrilla forces.[63]

But the most dramatic guerrilla actions occurred in the Mantaro Valley, especially in the upland villages belonging to the districts of Colca and San Juan, on the border between Junín and Huancavelica. In early December 1884 the Iglesista prefect Andrés Recharte wrote to the War Ministry from Chongos Alto:

> Yesterday I reached Colca, on the border of this department, and the people, on the approach of the pacification forces, all fled to join the Indians of Vilca and Moya in the neighboring department of Huancavelica, where they are still in rebellion and agitating other neighboring villages. In the village of Colca I have been unable to constitute authorities of any kind, for I found not a single man. The same thing happened to me in this place, where I have found only women and very elderly men.[64]

Recharte promised to pacify all the communities in the region over the next several days, but this proved impossible because the villagers simply fled into the puna, attacking Recharte's soldiers from the surrounding hills. The next day, while still in Chongos Alto, Recharte was informed that the Cacerista priest Father Peñaloza, leading the combined indigenous forces from the villages of Vilca, Moya, Huasicancha, Potaca, Quishuar, and Chongos Alto, was preparing an attack. While they were still assessing the situation, Recharte's forces were surrounded and ambushed, then compelled to flee downward to the village of Chupaca. As the Iglesista officer José Godinez would comment a few days later, this lack of success or "imprudence" on the part of the prefect only gave the montoneros additional confidence. Until the end of 1885 they maintained a liberated zone of sorts in their area, collaborating with the Cacerista forces under the command of Peñaloza or Bartolomé Guerra yet maintaining partial autonomy of leadership and organization.[65]

This autonomy made Iglesista control of the punas illusory. Even if officers from the Pacificadora placed more pliant political authorities in the riverbank districts, the upland regions remained in rebellion, foiling all attempts to bring them under control. And in the end these upland montoneras sealed the Cacerista victory. When Cáceres and his army outflanked the Pacificadora in Huaripampa, managing to move on to Lima and surprise Iglesias, the upland guerrillas collaborated by cutting bridges across the Mantaro, isolating a sector of the Iglesista forces near Chupaca and facilitating the movement of the rest of the Cacerista army under the command of Remigio Morales Bermúdez. Yet despite this advantageous position, Morales Bermúdez reported, and even though numerous guerrilla commanders sent him letters begging to confront the Iglesista army under his orders, Morales decided to avoid further bloodshed and march to Lima, where he was sure the conflict had already been decided in favor of the Caceristas.[66]

Although Morales Bermúdez explained his lack of action against the Pacificadora in benevolent terms, writing that he wished to avoid further "bloodshed between brothers," an additional motive was his desire to disband the guerrillas. Although their autonomy had given victory to his side, he also feared it might prevent reunification. In his final report to the recently established Cacerista Defense Ministry, Morales wrote that the original village authorities who had been replaced by Relayze and the Pacificadora had begun returning to their posts,

> called by the villagers as an indispensable way to pacify the guerrillas who have confidence only in these authorities.
>
> Understanding the dangers of leaving these guerrillas mobilized, I managed to convince them to return to their homes, reminding them of the victory of our side with the establishment of a government that will return to the country its lost confidence.

With victory assured, the Caceristas no longer needed the guerrillas. Their active presence, in fact, could easily be transformed into a threat. Time to go home; and, by the way, thank you for your help.[67]

Six weeks later the arrival of Bartolomé Guerra further buttressed the changing balance of power in the Mantaro Valley. Cáceres gave this notable from Chupaca extraordinary powers, as a special envoy of the central government, to collect all weapons and "other items belonging to the state" from the guerrillas. The anger felt by the upland montoneros at Guerra's presence must have been great, considering the man's past history as a leader of invasions against puna autonomy. Indeed, Cacerista officials would have done well to heed more closely the warnings of Prefect Antenor Rizo Patrón about the agitation still existing in many villages:

> Because of the state of war in which they have found themselves during the last years, which, given the natural lack of culture in these populations, makes them believe that it is still not the time for urgent demands, such as for example the return of the weapons, which belong to the state, but which they nonetheless have become used to seeing as their own.[68]

Whose weapons, whose lands, whose cattle? These would be the important questions debated by peasant guerrillas and Cacerista officials over the next few years. As had been the case in the Sierra de Puebla, moreover, control of these specific items also signified control of the narratives and victories. Given his local political record, Bartolomé Guerra was not the one to negotiate a compromise in such a situation, a fact that would become increasingly clear over the next several months. So would the fact that, if the Cacerista state wished to reestablish control over the region, disarming the peasant guerrillas was simply not enough. The Caceristas also needed to build a hegemonic consensus—in the sense of recognizing and incorporating the demands and expectations of Cáceres's most assiduous and effective allies.[69]

Consensus did not mean the same thing in all subregions of the central highlands. The simplest case, where control was not even an issue, was in the villages near Jauja. Having remained mobilized in easy alliance with the Caceristas throughout the war, these communities were rewarded in 1886 with the creation of two new districts: Acolla, in the Yanamarca Valley; and Muquiyauyo, on the northwest bank of the Mantaro River. Here the wartime coalition among local merchants, small landowners, and village notables was buttressed by the policy of district creation, for it was precisely people in these networks who held office in the new municipal governments.[70]

In the uplands along the Mantaro's southwestern bank, by contrast, the failure of disarmament left few clear options in the hands of the Cacerista state. The established practice of mediation through local notables was not effective in this case, since the Cacerista allies willing to attempt it—such as Guerra himself—were from the riverbank communities implicated in the region's land and ethnic battles since before the war. At the same time, however, the execution of the region's independent commanders in 1884, when combined with the reorganization of the montoneras against the Pacificadora, did give the Caceristas an opening, however minor. Through this crack the Comisión Especial del Supremo Gobierno (Special Government Commission) moved into the area with the express purpose of resolving existing land conflicts and giving upland communities a direct line to the central government.[71]

Since September 1886, two and a half years before Special Commissioner Emiliano Carvallo traveled to the central sierra, congressional representatives from Huancayo province had been putting pressure on the Cacerista state to return the haciendas invaded by the montoneros to their "legitimate owners." After the failure of disarmament in early 1886, however, the only way to do so would have been to send a military expedition against the upland villages. Such an expedition would have constituted a direct attack against Cáceres's most faithful allies during the recent civil war, in the name of a group of landowners who had eagerly collaborated with the Chileans and then with Iglesias. This the Caceristas were not prepared to do, even after peace had been declared. The special commission seemed a workable compromise.[72]

Arriving in the area near Potaca and Chongos Alto in April 1889, after repeated pressure from provincial authorities and national representatives, Carvallo heard petitions from communities and private landowners about land usurpation and about the need to establish clear boundaries between holdings. In each case the general procedure was quite similar. On request by one of the parties, Carvallo asked both sides to appear at his office with their land titles. These were then compared, and often each side would designate a representative to walk the boundaries with state officials. Most individual owners admitted that, even if the existing boundary was not acceptable, the communities had been in possession of the disputed lands for more than one year. Carvallo would then support—in an administrative capacity (*apoyar administrativamente*) and under the terms of the Peruvian civil code—continued possession and tenure by the communities. Carvallo expressly stated that the hacendados still had the right to take the matter to court and that permanent land title was not being given to the communities;

but, as he put it in his decree supporting the community of Uñas over Josefa and María Jesús Cárdenas, "[It] is in the interest of social order to support the party in possession."[73]

Between 1884 and 1889 the general Cacerista policy along the southwestern Mantaro mixed repression with concession, political marginalization with administrative recognition. The willingness of the central government to appoint a commission to hear officially the claims of peasant villagers, despite extreme hacendado pressure to repress and dispossess the Indians, rested in part on the earlier repression and reorganization of the montoneras. Also key to this balancing act was the distinction between administrative possession of the disputed lands—which the state supported—and legal title, which only the judicial system could grant. In the end, therefore, the renewed presence of the Cacerista state in this subregion was effective precisely because its officials claimed a cautious middle ground between the aspirations and expectations of peasant guerrillas and the demands of local landowners.

The story was different in the Comas region. In contrast to the southwestern Mantaro, villages in the Comas area did not participate actively in the campaigns against the Pacificadora. True, they were perceived by Iglesista officials as in rebellion against the government, and they lived up to their reputation during the pacification campaign by assassinating a local political authority from Apata who was collecting the personal head tax (*contribución personal*) in May 1885. But with the exception of Acobamba village, they participated less in the Cacerista campaign during the civil war than did the villages of Huancavelica, Ayacucho, and the Mantaro's southwestern bank. Their rebellious position, therefore, was perceived as autonomous by both sides—a perception that would affect the policy decisions of the Cacerista state in their case.[74]

In the Comas area, as we have seen, the bones of contention for the guerrillas were both land and cattle. Since the Chilean occupation, the montoneros from Comas and environs had been in control of the haciendas Punto and Callanca. In addition, they had taken livestock from several of the surrounding properties, especially the hacienda Runatullo belonging to Manuel Fernando Valladares, through much of the conflict. We have seen as well that, since 1884, Cacerista officials and village representatives had been debating the legal definition of this livestock. Caceristas considered it stolen property; Comasinos, legitimate booty of war. From the standpoint of the villagers, moreover, their definition was additionally legitimate because Valladares, despite the many sacrifices made by the peasant guerrillas against the "common enemy" and in defense of his property, did not deign to protect us not even with one rifle, much less with ammunition in order to defend this hacienda from the common enemy. This was the origin of taking some cattle from that hacienda to use in order to buy rifles and some ammunition and gunpowder, elements necessary for "War."[75]

The situation got worse, not better, with the consolidation of the Cacerista state. On 25 January 1888, two years after Cáceres had taken control of the central government, three political authorities from Comas who had previously participated in the montonera—Rufino Llauco, Nazario Valero, and Mariano Sánchez—wrote a letter to the authorities and notables of Uchubamba, to the north of the Comas area. They invited the villagers from that area to take part in a new and autonomous federation of districts, which would take care of commerce, justice, education, and the common defense. They mentioned an outsider, a judge from Ica, who was serving as intellectual adviser and urged the Uchubambinos to participate. The local justice of the peace thought better of it, however, and instead forwarded a copy of the invitation to the subprefect's office.[76]

This letter to Uchubamba has been analyzed in great detail several times. For my purposes here, the letter's basic message concerned the need for autonomous political organization, backed by arms if necessary. But perhaps most important, it spoke of citizenship rights in the context of a national polity, even though such a polity was conceptualized as a "federal state" or a state within a federalist system. There was a social contract within the proposal to Uchubamba. In exchange for providing arms and men in situations where defense was needed, citizens received promises of freedom, local autonomy, and free elections of political authorities, as well as the right to participate in the general improvement of commerce, industry, education, and justice.[77]

Manrique has speculated on the socialist implications of such a project, suggesting that Osambela might have been a political militant and that the peasantry was not ready to listen to such an advanced message. One might even discern in the proposal an anarchist flavor or a radical liberal pedigree by comparing some of the discourse on rights and social contract to what had emerged a generation earlier in central Mexico. The concept of free elections might speak as well to the changes in electoral law ongoing in Peru since the 1850s.

What is clear from this letter is that one faction of the village leadership was fed up with the lack of response from the Caceristas and wished to take matters into their own hands. Osambela, whether socialist, anarchist, or simply radical in some less defined way, was a useful ally for this group. The consequences such action could bring down on the community as a whole, however, were problematic. This painful reality, rather than the lack of "advanced" consciousness on the part of the peasantry, helps explain the divisions in Comas. This was the question in contention when, on 1 February, a faction of the village wrote a letter to the subprefect denouncing Osambela and his followers.[78]

When rumors reached Comas that the authorities knew of the letter to Uchubamba, a group of vecinos led by Esteban Paytanpoma—also active in the montonera—signed a letter to the subprefect disavowing the actions and plans of "four individuals, . . . who seduced by the mentioned *Docto* [learned man, or doctor] allowed themselves to be guided." They insisted that the majority of the villagers did not agree. On the same day the authorities who had signed the original invitation to Uchubamba joined other local notables, including at least one additional prominent guerrilla leader, in signing another letter to the subprefect, insisting that they had never contemplated taking up arms against the government. Yet the very next day, according to the gobernador from Concepción, the judge from Ica led his allies in a march to Andamarca with plenty of rifles and ammunition and was said to have mobilized Punto as well.

Internal disagreements continued. Sometime in the first half of February, Osambela was jailed in Comas. But Jauja's subprefect reported that Mariano Sánchez, Nazario Valero, and others organized an assault on the jail early on 13 February, freeing Osambela and nearly killing the local gobernador. And whatever the truth of specific claims or counterclaims, by August events in Comas had called down upon the district the first national military expedition, led by the Cacerista subprefect Andrés Freyre.[79]

The events of the first half of 1888 made the Cacerista state a great deal more open to a military solution in the Comas area. In August 1888, when congressional representatives from Jauja and Huancayo demanded to know what was holding up state action on the usurped haciendas, the government was ready to act. Scarcely a month later, in September, the Ministry of the Interior ordered that the prefect use the necessary forces from the Callao Battalion for an expedition to Punto and Callanca. It was only because the prefect lacked time and funds that the expedition did not depart until December.[80]

The experience of this expedition underlined both the difficulties faced by regular troops in the Comas area and the ongoing disagreements among factions of the local population. After a short engagement at the entrance to the hacienda Punto, the guerrillas retired to the surrounding hills, where "protected by the topography . . . , the dense underbrush . . . and the thick fog that envelops those regions at this time of year," they harassed the troops with constant gunfire and threat of ambush. The situation changed, however, when representatives from the community of Canchapalca traveled to the hacienda and indicated their willingness to negotiate. Lieutenant Colonel José Alarcón was attacked by the Comasinos when he arrived in Canchapalca to work out an agreement, but local villagers protected his retreat to Punto. Once again fragmented, the rebels decided to accept the prefect's new offer to negotiate, sent from the hacienda Llacsapirca in early January to the communities of Acobamba, Yanabamba, Canchapalca, and Comas. In an agreement signed by all interested parties, including the owner of Punto and Callanca, Jacinto Cevallos, the haciendas were to be bought by and divided among the different communities.[81]

The agreement involved exchanging land for cattle. Cevallos was willing to part with the land, probably in great part because the communities and hacienda peons had been in de facto possession for seven years. In exchange, he received twenty-five hundred head of cattle and a promise to respect existing territorial boundaries. From the standpoint of the state, this agreement would help resolve the perennial conflict over livestock, unresolved since 1884. And the villages could ensure the retreat of the military expedition in exchange for a promise of future livestock deliveries. But there was another angle as well: an attempt to exploit existing political divisions between and within the villages of the Comas area.

The majority of the hacienda Punto was given over to the village of Acobamba and its anexos, and a smaller section was given to Comas and its anexos. The hacienda Callanca was turned over to three prestigious vecinos of Comas to administer as they saw fit. Their only obligations were to take an inventory of the belongings on the hacienda and to turn over the property to Cevallos when asked. The unspoken obligations were quiescence and surveillance in the area. In this sense, it is not surprising to note that the name of Esteban Paytanpoma, lead signer of the original letter denouncing Osambela and his allies, also headed the list of vecinos granted the right to administer Callanca.[82]

When Emiliano Carvallo reached the area in May 1889, the agreement from January was already unraveling. Acobamba had met its initial livestock obligation only in part, and Comas had not remitted any cattle at all. The three Comasinos sent to inventory the hacienda Callanca found nothing worth reporting, whether in cattle or any other property; thus, no inventory was taken. Carvallo decided that the communities had received the best offer possible and that he could not extend the deadlines of payment; thus, he ordered the return of the haciendas to Cevallos. Yet as late as March 1890 the subprefect in Huancayo was unable to make the villagers comply, even after ordering the arrest of the local gobernador.[83]

In fact, matters worsened in March 1892, when Manuel Fernando Valladares filed a new protest that accused "the same Communists [*sic*]" of invading part of his hacienda Runatullo and preparing its land for planting. After serious investigation, which included a visit to the area by several representatives of the government, Valladares's complaint was declared baseless: the villagers had been in possession of the disputed lands for a long time. In the end, state authority was still elusive in the region. In an administrative report of June 1893, Andrés Freyre, the same subprefect who had led the expedition in January 1889, was forced to write that "the rebels" of Comas were the only ones who still would not pay the contribución personal that they owed.[84]

The contrast in effectiveness of Cacerista policy between Comas and the southwestern Mantaro is perhaps best explained by examining the different patterns taken by relations among hacendados, the state, and the peasant communities in each case. In the southwestern Mantaro the earlier Cacerista execution of peasant leaders, when combined with the availability of reliable community allies in the riverbank villages, lessened the state's need to rely on the landowners for pacification in the area. This combination underwrote the success of Carvallo's attempt at hegemony, which merged the partial incorporation of peasant demands with overall political control by the riverbank commanders and the concession of the judicial branch to the hacendados. In Comas, by contrast, Cacerista officials first tried military repression and in the absence of reliable community allies were forced to collaborate with landowner Cevallos from the start. After the military expedition made clear the divisions within rebel ranks, local authorities attempted a compromise that took advantage of these splits, using the judicial branch to exchange land for cattle. But when the peasants did not fulfill their part of the bargain, Carvallo was forced to order the haciendas returned to Cevallos. In the Comas case, therefore, the Cacerista state's post facto attempts at hegemony more clearly and exclusively served the interests of the hacendados and were not effective.

A Balance Sheet of Cacerismo: The Othering of the Peasant Guerrillas

When Emiliano Carvallo completed his tour of the central highlands, the balance sheet of Cacerista pacification was mixed. It combined complete success in the Jauja area with partial victories along the Mantaro's western bank; in the Comas region the guerrillas lived to fight another day. We cannot know what was on Carvallo's mind as he sat in Tarma in July 1889, fresh from his encounter with recalcitrant Comasinos. Perhaps he focused on the frustrations of trying to make peace between seemingly intractable enemies. What we do know is that on 11 July he sent to Cáceres a fifteen-page proposal for the abolition of all communal property.

Carvallo began his proposal by giving a historical analysis of communal property during the colonial period, explaining how, despite early republican attempts to privatize village holdings, communal tenure continued to exist in most areas, "a throwback to an era of economic backwardness, . . . and with the same problems [it] had in the times of the viceroyalty." In Carvallo's opinion, communal property by definition led to economic backwardness because "private property stimulates work, while communism discourages men and favors laziness." Given the confusion of early republican policy, he continued, things had gotten to the point of "returning unconsciously to the colonial agrarian regime." A new law was therefore needed in order to "lift the Indian from his submission and dejection."[85]

Carvallo's proposed law would privatize all communal holdings in the intermediate agricultural zones while keeping puna pasturelands in collective tenure. Each head of household would receive a set amount, according to marital status and the land's access to irrigation. The distribution would be done by a three-person commission, composed of a delegate from the provincial council, a lawyer, and an engineer. All lands left at the end of the distribution would be sold at two-thirds their legitimate assessment and the proceeds turned over to the municipal council of the provincial capital in order to finance primary education in the towns and villages of each province.[86]

As far as we know, this proposal was not put into effect. Although not important as state policy, it does reflect an emerging consensus among Cacerista officials that, as of 1890, began to reverse remaining populist impulses toward a broad national coalition. In his document Carvallo emphasized the backwardness, ignorance, laziness, and lack of education of the Indians, blaming it all on the survival of communal land tenure. He said that the Indians were in the same state in which they had been during the colonial period. Such inferior beings obviously could not be citizens; only through a combination of land privatization and public instruction would they become so. In other words, they needed state tutelage before they could be full members of the national community.

These sentiments were echoed in the congress between 1890 and 1892. The legislature amended the constitution to limit the right to vote to those citizens who knew how to read and write and then amended the municipal and electoral laws to fit the new status quo. As the report of a special senate commission put it in 1892, with regard to the electoral law,

> the making of a good electoral law, in conformity with the demo-cratic principles that serve as a base for our constitutional system, comes up against the frustration presented by the lack of culture among our popular masses, the majority of whom do not know how to read or write and do not understand the most trivial of the citi-zen's rights and responsibilities.[87]

A similar argument was made in 1891, when congressional representatives called for the abolition of the puna district of San Juan and its return to Chupaca. There had been no reason to create such a district, they wrote. Even if San Juan had existed legally since 1874, only in 1888 had the prefect of Junín actually ordered the designation of political authorities. Even then the only post filled was that of gobernador, "because in the district there is no other person capable of carrying out the duties of the other offices, and this lack reaches such a deplorable extreme that the district does not possess a single school." The central government accepted the arguments and abol-ished the district of San Juan in October 1891.[88]

This emphasis on the backwardness and barbarity of Indian peasants had been present in the discourse of central sierra landowners since the War of the Pacific. It had informed Jacinto Cevallos's original letter to the adminis-trator of his hacienda Punto, when Cevallos had balked at provisioning the Acobamba guerrillas. It permeated Luis Milón Duarte's memoirs, serving as the prime justification for his collaboration with the Chilean army. What was different about the Cacerista version was its emphasis on education, literacy, and private property as the central tenets of civilization and citizen-ship. Gone were the wartime qualifications of bravery and resisting the invaders. With a few strokes of the pen, Cacerista policymakers managed, as of 1890, to transform Junín's citizen-soldiers into barbarian "others." Offi-cial amnesia proved a wondrously effective political weapon.

Why did this happen? Throughout the 1880s and into the 1890s the common aim for most of Junín's montoneros had been to vindicate them-selves as citizens and soldiers, to rebut the accusations of criminality flung their way since 1884. Their fundamental desire was to have their contri-butions to the national resistance recognized. This was also what stuck in the craw of the Caceristas. Although open to the use of guerrilla forces, Cáceres had always thought they should serve in an auxiliary capacity. The problem in Junín was that the montoneras refused to remain subor-dinate. In declaring their autonomy, they forced the Caceristas to strip them of their legitimacy.

This is the core explanation for the "othering" of Tomás Laimes, the puna guerrillas, the Comasinos, and, by implication, the highland peasantry in general. Because Laimes and his movement were autonomous, and because Laimes committed the crime of declaring himself "as much a general" as Cáceres, he was transformed into a drunk and bloodthirsty Indian, crowning himself Inca emperor in a fit of millenarian hallucination. Because the Comasinos had defeated a Chilean detachment on their own and refused to follow Cacerista direction, the cattle taken in war became proof of common delinquency and criminality. And thus the agency of the most active and committed national soldiers was taken away in order that their autonomy might not become a threat during national consolidation. Citizens who had earned their status by risking their lives and villages in the defense of national territory were "othered" as illiterate, lazy, backward Indians.

As we begin to understand the process of state formation in postwar Peru, we must continue to uncover the stories and listen to the voices that portray the Comasinos and Tomás Laimeses as dynamic, creative, politically central actors. Without these guerrillas, Cáceres would not have brought the Chilean occupation to a standstill. Without these citizen-soldiers, Cáceres would not have become president. Some oral histories and written documents make their contributions very clear. We must continue to listen to these recently revealed stories and to consider their implications carefully.

7 Communal Hegemony and Alternative Nationalisms

Historical Contingencies and Limiting Cases

In the four decades between the U.S.-Mexican War (1846–1848) and the end of the War of the Pacific (1879–1884), the people who inhabited the rural villages of Puebla, Morelos, and Junín confronted the challenge of how to participate in the making of a national politics. Although events and conflicts in the three regions differed greatly, nationalist guerrillas in all three operated in analogous and complex political contexts. Born of and nurtured by local processes of communal hegemonic politics, their movements were also part of broader struggles to centralize power that involved conflict among diverse regional political cultures.

Defined as combinations of beliefs, practices, and debates around the accumulation and contestation of power, these regional political cultures set the contours for the class and ethnic negotiations and alliances that helped form the state. They were formed and reformed in regionally and historically specific struggles over control of resources and people and over the meaning of actions, events, and relationships. Internally conflictual and variable, these regional political cultures were intermediate arenas of alliance and political practice, where the hegemonic politics of community intermingled with the discourse and practice of other groups. Each affected the form taken by the rest. Once regions became involved in the making of a national politics, that process would also have a reciprocal effect on the regional cultures themselves.

By the second half of the nineteenth century, the accumulated debates, loyalties, and grievances in each region formed the political backdrop against which national politics would be constructed. Nationalist guerrillas in Puebla, Junín, and Morelos emerged from and were responsive to their respective communities, yet they also operated in these broader arenas of alliance where notions of justice and definitions of citizenship were being contested. Depending on the context, therefore, the actions and discourses of the guerrillas could be either hegemonic or counterhegemonic. In the villages, where decisions to participate in a particular conflict and on a particular side were debated and legitimated according to local notions of justice, communal obligation, and reciprocity, political practices and discourses were embedded in communal consensus and were thus hegemonic. At the regional and emerging national levels, when guerrillas used the relatively more inclusive and egalitarian discourses and practices of communalism to challenge accumulations of power and elitist definitions of citizenship, their practices and discourses were counterhegemonic.

In this chapter I will explore the boundaries of the process by which rural peoples constructed alternative nationalisms. I will show, on one side, how the construction process was flexible and contingent, composed of multiple and ongoing conflicts over power at the communal, the regional, and the emerging national levels. Each example of alternative nationalism was regionally and culturally distinct, even as they all emerged through analogous processes. But I will also show that not all rural people were able, through their dynamic and complex political interactions, to construct alternative nationalisms.

Here the limiting case of Cajamarca will be crucial. Despite the active participation of peasants and other rural folk in the movements of the late nineteenth century, no alternative nationalisms emerged in this region. In contrast to Cajamarca, the three regions of Morelos, Puebla, and Junín all possessed a strong communal tradition. Even as this tradition was reconstructed and modified in diverse ways, it provided a relatively autonomous political arena for processes of local hegemony. This local arena, and the relationships and discourses that I have been calling *communal hegemony*, provided rural peoples with the political and cultural resources to confront, modify, and participate in the regional and "national" processes of state formation in a more autonomous fashion. In all three cases where this communal tradition existed, then, some form of alternative nationalism emerged over the second half of the nineteenth century. In Cajamarca, with a weak communal tradition, it did not.

Communal Hegemony, Regional Political Cultures, and National Coalitions: Morelos, Junín, and Puebla in Comparative Perspective

It is nearly impossible, in comparative history, to find perfectly commensurable apples. One usually ends up with a basketful of shapes and colors that includes not only apples and oranges but pears and grapes as well. But the greatest potential creativity and discovery lies precisely in this lopsided, crowded, and dynamic basket, through the comparison of open-ended and rich case studies. This is so because the lack of fit, of commensurability, is the first and most important clue that a larger boundary or antagonism exists between cases. Thus, lopsidedness, rather than being a fault, offers an entry into analytical richness and productivity.

There is an important qualification here, however. Comparison of this kind is successful in direct relation to the honesty of the one doing the comparing. The three cases of Junín, Morelos, and Puebla are different not only because of intrinsic variations but also because of the research processes I underwent in each case and the different historiographies existing for each one. Although I cannot control entirely for the effect these factors must have on the comparison, by stating them I can put all my research cards on the table and allow the reader to play with the same deck I have at my disposal.

For Morelos, research conditions and options forced me to rely mainly on documentation in national archives, especially military and government reports. I have been able to supplement this documentation with some anthropological studies and the oral histories reproduced by Sotelo Inclán, but there is still a more "outside" flavor to the analysis that tends to favor the description of events rather than a deep analysis of perceptions. The existence of the 1910 Revolution, moreover, and the myriad current debates about the role of the masses in that upheaval together tend to connect my narrative to an already existing "heroic" vein. This is especially true for Morelos, because the role of the Zapatistas in the 1910 conflict is engraved on the very foreheads of Mexican schoolchildren and Mexicanist historians. As I narrate earlier conflicts and popular political movements, therefore, I tend to fall effortlessly into a packaged epic form, championing the constant struggle of the Morelos peasantry against oppression, a struggle that would necessarily culminate in Zapatismo. I have been able (and willing) only partially to correct for this tendency.[1]

In the Sierra de Puebla, by contrast, I was able to do a great deal more work in municipal archives and even some oral history in Xochiapulco. The lack of a historiography as comparatively rich as the one for Morelos has also given me more freedom in the narrative, for I have found fewer pitfalls along the way. Moreover, my ability to spend more time in the region, when combined with a particularly rich anthropological literature, has yielded a more detailed data base from which I felt more comfortable in generalizing about perceptions, ideology, and internal community relations. This freedom is reflected in the space I have given this case study in the overall work.

For Peru, fifteen years of research on the central highlands resistance conducted by Nelson Manrique, me, numerous regional historians, and the Permanent Historical Commission of the Peruvian Army have yielded a much richer, more detailed "inside view" in which a variety of versions compete with each other for hegemony. While many of these versions are also written in a heroic vein, the ability to confront them with each other, to mine the contradictions and conflicts, allows us to move more successfully beyond the epic narrative. This transcendence is also facilitated, ironically and painfully enough, by the lack of a popularly based transformation of Peruvian politics that successfully incorporated highland social movements. In Mexico the history of nineteenth-century nation-state formation goes on between two "bookends" where the rural masses played meaningful roles in movements for social transformation—the wars of independence and the 1910 Revolution. In Peru the analogous bookends are moments of suffering and repression: Túpac Amaru and Sendero Luminoso.[2]

With these differences laid out, it is now possible to compare more honestly the emergence of alternative nationalisms in the three regions. The nature of these alternative discourses, as well as the timing and process of their emergence, varied along three conceptual axes: the form and dynamics of communal politics; the nature of existing regional political cultures; and the process by which each region was inserted into an emerging "national question." In constructing my comparison, I will rely on a chronological narrative, beginning with a review of the earlier history, moving on to the moment and process of confrontation, and ending with an analysis of the results in each case. It is important, however, to remember that this periodization is a narrative device rather than a natural or inevitable feature of the data.

By the time the villagers of Morelos, Puebla, and Junín confronted the making of a national politics, the communities they lived in had undergone numerous and diverse processes of construction and reconstruction. In the Puebla highlands, precolonial, colonial, and postcolonial histories had all involved complex and multifaceted ethnic and spatial conflicts. Widespread, recalcitrant confrontations between cabecera and sujeto villages were a particularly long-lasting form through which these conflicts had been expressed, highlighting the flexibility and contingency of all community boundaries. In such a context, where differences of gender, generation, wealth, and ethnic identity were constantly and dynamically contested, communal assemblies served as crucial arenas where consensus could be built through the establishment of hegemonic alliances and coalitions around elders or pasados, the "good patriarchs" who represented the village (see chapter 3).

In Morelos as well, we know from existing anthropological and oral historical materials that gender, generation, ethnicity, and wealth were central elements in the construction and contestation of communal hegemony. As recorded by Sotelo Inclán, for example, one of the important influences on Emiliano Zapata's early life was his uncle José María Zapata, a guerrilla fighter during the Liberal Revolution and French Intervention. One of the elder Zapata's favorite sayings, from a list he used to give advice to the young, was "Skirts are for women, bullets for men."[3] This clear distinction between private and public matched nicely with the more general traditions of village government, which, again according to Sotelo, involved

> almost always maintaining, according to patriarchal tradition, the older men in the higher cargos and the younger beginners in the lower ones; but it was possible for a young man with special gifts to become the head. This did not mean that the elders lost their authority or preeminence, because their advice was always heard, and they received [respectful] treatment by being called "uncle" or "tata."[4]

The oral histories and community studies of Tepoztlán emphasize the division between public and private and the marginalization of women from politics and armed conflicts. In Oscar Lewis's oral history of Pedro Martínez, for example, Martínez comes back repeatedly, over his entire lifetime, to the separation and contradiction between family and politics, between women and children and the public life of men. In the case of the 1910 Revolution, he justifies leaving the Zapatista army less because of the feud he was admittedly having with his commanding officer than because his wife and children would starve without him.

> That's why I left the army, for my wife. How I loved my wife! I didn't leave because I was afraid to fight but because of my wife, who had to find food for herself and the children. I said to myself, "No, my family comes first and they are starving. Now I'm leaving!" I saw that the situation was hopeless and that I would be killed and they would perish. Especially because my colonel hated me and wanted to kill me.[5]

Yet later on, when discussing his participation in a community road-building project to help his village, he reaches exactly the opposite conclusion:

> All through the Lenten season I didn't earn a *centavo* for my family because I helped build the road. It made no difference to me that my

wife and children might starve. It couldn't be helped because I was working for my village, which counted for more.[6]

Ethnic and spatial distinctions, often overlapping and reinforcing each other, are also clear in the anthropological studies of Tepoztlán. According to Lewis, people referred to "the inhabitants of the smaller and poorer barrios of San Pedro, Los Reyes, and San Sebastián as *indios*."[7] And in Martínez's memories of the 1910 Revolution, spatial and ethnic distinctions also overlap in his memory of the troops of Genovevo de la O, from the Sierra of Huitzilac, where he implicitly equates Indian identity with special ferocity.

> Zapata and Genovevo de la O got everybody around there to rise up. Genovevo de la O took all of Ocuila and Chalma, all that sector. He aroused the people, all Indians, the ugly-looking kind from up in the mountains. And he attacked the trains. It didn't take long before he was well armed. He was the very first to have Mausers. Zapata's men had only rifles.[8]

In both Morelos and Puebla, ethnic, gender, and spatial hierarchies helped organize local life, and communal hegemony was constructed along gender and generational lines. Yet the two regions differed in the particular ways that these common elements were combined. In Morelos, by the time of the Liberal Revolution, ethnic distinctions within and between villages, and struggles between cabeceras and sujetos, were more submerged within a map of conflicts that gave primacy to the division between pueblos and haciendas. Internal divisions emerged over matters of collaboration with hacendados or complicit local authorities rather than over matters of revenues, religious cargoes, public works, or other internal issues. Communal hegemony, while also constructed around the image of the "good patriarch," thus revolved around a patriarch whose main claim to prestige and trust came from his willingness to confront exploitative outsiders. While internal conflicts, squabbles, and factionalism continued to exist, the patriarch's principal obligation was to save the village as a whole from outside expropriation. In the Sierra de Puebla, by contrast, although both inside and outside sources of prestige were also crucial, the balance was still, by 1855, toward the inside.

We have already confirmed the existence of gender, ethnic, spatial, economic, and generational dynamics in the case of Junín (see chapter 6). In the Peruvian central highlands, communal constructions favored both "inside" and "outside." Communities in Jauja and Comas tended to draw the ethnic or spatial line more directly around whole villages or groups of villages, whereas along the western Mantaro ethnic and spatial conflict was an important element of the internal hegemonic process. Larger communities were divided between wari and llacuaz, those who no longer wore ponchos and those who did. As was the case in Mexico, people worked out conflicts and rebuilt hegemony in the communal assemblies. Overall, then, internal and external tensions were resolved everywhere through building community consensus.

In all three regions processes of communal hegemony conditioned and were conditioned by the formation and transformation of regional political culture. After independence from Spain all three areas entered a period of economic stagnation and retrenchment that favored peasant and subsistence production. But already by the middle of the nineteenth century, all three showed signs of recovery and expansion. Although in different ways, this recovery meant a reencounter with commercial production and with hacendados interested in profiting from new markets.

In Morelos (see chapter 5) the construction of a radical federalist political culture in El Sur came into conflict with the extensive economic and political power of a centralist conservative landowner class. Especially after 1840, renewed confrontations over land, water, and other resources sharpened the tensions between villages and haciendas. These conflicts intensified the allegiance of pueblos and radical caciques to an emancipatory agrarian program and gave new meaning to the familiar slogan "Mueran los gachupines." In an increasingly polarized political situation, landowners and their allies raised the specter of caste war to split the opposing federalist alliance. By 1850 existing ethnic or spatial divisions among pueblos in Morelos were clearly subordinated, within regional political culture, to the common confrontation with a powerful landowner class.

In the Puebla highlands, by contrast, ethnic and spatial divisions within and between communities combined with distinct patterns of commercial production, marketing, and accumulation to generate three different subregions. Along the western highlands an entrepreneurial merchant-landowner elite centered in Huauchinango exploited the labor of peasants who inhabited ethnically fragmented indigenous communities. Neighboring villages confronted each other in recurring conflicts over land, and Huauchinango's powerholders established vertical patron-client ties with the communities by representing them in these cases (see chapter 2). Pueblos wishing to resist these networks of domination tended to ally with Huauchinango's rivals in Tulancingo, a traditionally Spanish and Conservative city whose elite competed for markets in the nearby Pachuca mines. Along the eastern sierra, by contrast, lines of conflict tended to be drawn over markets. Since the colonial period the white creole elite in the cabecera of Zacapoaxtla had controlled the intricate system of indigenous markets connecting the region's numerous Nahua villages. By the 1840s, however, increased commercial opportunities in trade with Veracruz had encouraged Indian merchants to seek out independent connections. Attempts to expand sugar production on the few larger properties of the area also led to a confrontation between the owners and resident laborers of the haciendas Xochiapulco and La Manzanilla, and these two properties would be transformed into the center of rural rebellion for the region as a whole. In the central region of the sierra, commercial and mining activity encouraged a more egalitarian political style, with less direct forms of exploitation along ethnic lines. Yet within the district of Tetela several sujeto villages were ethnically Totonaco and constantly resisted the more direct extraction of revenue and labor by their mestizo and Nahua cabecera.

As in the Puebla highlands and in contrast to Morelos, villages in Peru's central sierra were united neither by a concerted and powerful landowner threat to unite them nor by an alternative radical coalition of the kind Juan Alvarez offered to the pueblos of El Sur. Regional political culture was therefore more fragmented in its construction, with diverse subregions existing side by side (see chapter 6). The legacy of Huanca power had helped reconstruct ethnic and spatial conflicts within communities along the Mantaro's western bank, encouraging as well the accumulation of extensive lands by the descendants of the Huanca elite. By the 1840s these larger properties had passed into the hands of a new group of creole entrepreneurs, changing the balance of power in the region but not uniting all villagers against them. Quite to the contrary: during the 1870s some of the upland communities, interested in gaining independence from their riverbank cabeceras, occasionally allied with the new hacendados. In the Jauja region of the northern Mantaro, by contrast, patron-client ties helped anchor a coalition of village elites and merchants from the towns that diffused tensions and contradictions relatively well. And in the Comas region conflicts with local landowners and riverbank communities were kept at bay in the period before the war since the physical separation of Comas district from the Mantaro proper seemed to encourage the dispersion of tensions with valley powerholders. It is important to emphasize, however, that in Comas and the western Mantaro, a new group of innovative landowners did present a potential problem for the villages, in many ways parallel to the conflicts in Morelos and on Puebla's haciendas Xochiapulco and La Manzanilla.

Each of these diverse regional political cultures faced a major challenge when confronted, sometime between 1855 and 1881, with a "national question," a new situation in which broader coalitions for making national politics were both necessary and possible. In Mexico this challenge occurred in the years between the U.S.-Mexican War and the French Intervention (1846–1867); in Peru the challenge was represented by the War of the Pacific (1879–1884). In Puebla and Morelos the first conditions for participation in a national coalition were strikingly similar. Xochiapulco and La Manzanilla, as well as a good proportion of the villages of Cuernavaca and Morelos districts, allied with Juan Alvarez in exchange for promises of land and municipal autonomy. In Peru's central highlands, by contrast, Andrés Cáceres organized a guerrilla resistance on a multiclass, multiethnic model, but his allies were village montoneras subordinate to local notables and merchants, who were themselves subordinate to the Cacerista high command. In the long run, however, the military effectiveness and dynamism of all the rural irregular forces would give them an autonomy and radicalism not originally envisioned by the national-level leaders who had allied with them.

In Morelos the response of communities to the raising of a "national question" was swift and sophisticated, in part because of the long history of alternative political cultures and radical agrarian projects in the region. By the early 1850s the pueblos had elaborated a sophisticated and radical liberal discourse, which continued to expand and evolve through 1856. This high degree of sophistication, when combined with the military importance of the area's national guard forces, gave the Morelos villagers significant influence within the Alvarista coalition. Early on that centrality forced Liberal statemakers to face the contradiction between their need to expand their national-level alliances and their obligation to be responsive to local and regional issues of social justice. By 1856 they had resolved this dilemma by repressing the national guards.

Events moved a little more slowly in Puebla. It was only during the Liberal-Conservative civil war (1858–1861) that the contradictions between moderate and radical Liberalisms—constructed ethnically and spatially as *llanura* (whiter "lowlands") and *montaña* (mestizo and Indian "highlands")—began to emerge. Yet even here the dilemma was worked out through conflict among local Liberal factions. Negotiation among the towns and villages of Tetela, Xochiapulco, and Tetela's Totonaco sujetos resulted in the emergence of a new radical Liberalism. This radical Liberal coalition, still untainted by national repression, served as the most dependable and militarily dynamic ally throughout the French Intervention and Second Empire. In their discourses, the villages within the Xochiapulco-Tetela alliance creatively stretched the boundaries of more moderate forms of Liberalism with their communitarian varieties. The contradictions sealed in Morelos by 1856 would emerge in Puebla only during the Restored Republic (1867–1872).

Junín shared more with Puebla than with Morelos on these issues. Although the processes of political growth were distinct in Comas and the west bank of the Mantaro, in general the alliance with the Cacerista army stayed firm through the Chilean occupation. The alliance lasted in part because of the occasional presence of the Cacerista regular army in the Mantaro Valley, which tended to give the montoneras quite a bit of de facto autonomy. Only with the Chilean departure and the beginning of the internal civil war would the question of guerrilla autonomy and radicalism, along with their legitimacy as citizens and soldiers, be placed on the political agenda. As in the Puebla highlands, a contradiction between national power and regional social justice would emerge in Junín only with the end of the international war. Once this occurred, the variants of alternative national discourses would run the gamut from the noncombative, patron-client variety found in Jauja, through Laimes's creative manipulation of ethnic ritual and Inca symbolism, to the conceptualization of a radical "federal state" by a faction of the Comasinos and their radical outside adviser Osambela.

In all three regions the prominence of the villagers' military, political, and cultural contributions forced national leaders to consider at least a part of their demands. It is this general fact that helps explain the attempts made by politicians as diverse as Juárez, Maximilian, Díaz, and Cáceres to construct coalitions and articulate discourses that would include a portion of the rural social movements that had supported them. These various attempts at hegemonizing were, however, only partially successful: Maximilian maintained his position in Morelos for perhaps a year; Cáceres was clearly successful only in Jauja and perhaps on the Mantaro's western bank; and Díaz succeeded in Morelos and Puebla for perhaps a decade or so. Ultimately, all governments of national reconstruction faced the need to repress some of their former allies. And in all three cases the repression was conceptualized and legitimated through racist discourses that "othered" the Indian peasantry.

An important general conclusion, therefore, is that the images of backward, isolated Indian peasants that became so common in Morelos, Puebla, and Junín during the late nineteenth and early twentieth centuries were partially (re)created in these earlier periods of repression. The view of Emiliano Zapata as a bloodthirsty Indian bandit, against which Jesús Sotelo Inclán so effectively wrote, had been tried out on Zapata's ancestors first. The image of passive and ignorant Nahua or Totonaco villagers willing to serve any cacique master, confronted in the 1970s by radical ethnographers of the Sierra de Puebla and to this day in some histories of the area, were partially formulated as justification for the repression of radical Liberal movements. And the image of the Mantaro's Indian uplands as wild and atavistic, reinforced in recent years by the emergence of Sendero Luminoso, underwent one of its many reconstructions during the repression of Laimes and the Comasinos.

This kind of "othering" is, of course, not unique to the areas studied: it has a long history that begins at least with the beginning of colonialism.[9] Given the amazing longevity and fortitude of this perspective, it is perhaps not too repetitive to emphasize once again the creativity, dynamism, complexity, and variety of the alternative nationalist discourses formulated in these regions during the second half of the nineteenth century. Although they all centered around claims to citizenship, political participation and autonomy, and social and economic justice, each had a distinct timing and dynamic. Although they were all formulated in dialogue with emerging "national questions," each built on the traditions of alliance and communal hegemony existing in regional political cultures. Finally, although they all reached a contradiction between social justice claims and the ongoing unification of a national coalition, each did so distinctly and at its own pace.

Only by emphasizing this deep diversity within broad commonalities can we understand how, in Morelos and Puebla, the same general discourse on family and mortality emerged in two different villages within three years' time but with exactly opposite meanings. In Tepoztlán, when local representatives petitioned the imperial government to return their lands in 1865, they explained that during the Liberal Revolution "fathers were taken violently from their children; sons from their parents; husbands from the conjugal union; and brothers and friends one from the other." Three years later in 1868, when justifying their behavior to the federal government, the local soldiers of Tetela explained that during the Liberal Revolution and the French Intervention, "various fathers mourned the death of their beloved sons, many widows wept over the absence of their husbands, and a multitude of orphans felt the lack of food that the physical labor of their parents previously provided them." In Tepoztlán the discourse of loss and death helped legitimate the decision to abandon Liberalism because of its broken promises; in Tetela it explained why local soldiers could not lay down their arms but must continue to defend their view of what Liberalism meant and continued to mean for the rural villagers of the sierra.[10]

The "National Question" and the Great Estate: Cajamarca as a Limiting Case

In contrast to my other case studies, peasant communities had not placed significant limits on landowner control of labor and regional politics in the

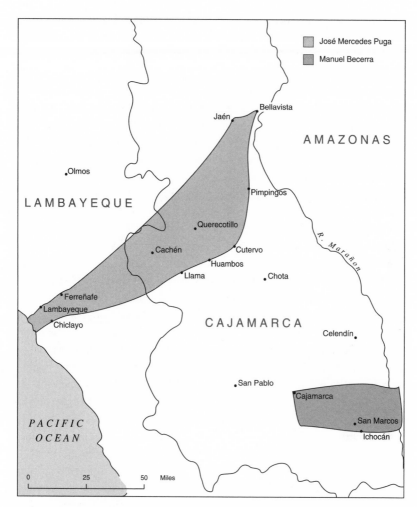

Map 9. Areas of guerrilla influence, Cajamarca

Peruvian department of Cajamarca, located in the northern highlands (see map 9). One important explanation lies in the much weaker peasant communal tradition found in Cajamarca. Even before the Spanish Conquest, communal structures did not have strong native roots but had been imported from the south during the Inca conquest. By the time of independence from Spain, existing villages of smallholders had little if any sense of institutional cohesion, communal land, or communal tradition of struggle. Although the great estate faced opposition to its process of territorial expansion, it had not confronted the concerted, powerful, and viable communal resistance its counterpart had faced in Morelos. And the hacendados had not been forced to grant political space to the villages as they had in Junín and the Puebla highlands.[11]

A second factor contributing to hacienda dominance was the lack of economic alternatives available in the regional economy during the nineteenth century. Beginning in the late eighteenth century, the decline of the area's *obrajes* (textile workshops) encouraged the local economy to turn in on itself. In quite the opposite way from Morelos and Junín, where the proximity of urban or mining markets generated strong opportunities for commercial production in both hacienda and village economies, highland Cajamarca seems to have remained an economic backwater in the years before the War of the Pacific. Local peasants had few alternatives, whether in the form of markets for their surplus production or opportunities for occasional wage labor in mining or other sectors. The hacienda, and therefore the hacendado, was the most powerful social, economic, and political force in local life. The basis for this power was not always direct control over people but rather a monopoly on the land itself. Thus, while only 30 percent of the department's inhabitants lived on the great estates—which is not all that different from the municipalities in Morelos or Junín with the highest concentration of hacienda population—in Cajamarca the great estate controlled over two-thirds of the entire land area. The majority of the region's inhabitants therefore depended on the hacienda for access to resources, even in the cases where they did not live directly on the properties.[12]

This combination of economic, cultural, and political conditions generated quite a distinct regional political culture. Those hacendados who succeeded in reproducing their position in local society did so by keeping private armies on their estates and developing patron-client relations with the smallholder villages near their properties. Conflict tended to occur among factions loyal to different landlord powerholders, taking the form of contestation between families or clienteles. Ultimately, while there were cases of peasant resistance against the hacendados, the crucial source of conflict in prewar Cajamarca was competition among landlords as they attempted to establish the most complete hold over their areas in order to maintain and reproduce their status. In stark contrast to Morelos, neither the landlords nor the villagers were able to build a unified political position. The former fought among themselves for influence and prestige; the latter did not generate an autonomous radical project that could conquer space in regional political culture.[13]

Systems of land tenure, population patterns, and the construction of regional political culture varied substantially in Cajamarca department's northern province of Jaén. A frontier region with a relatively sparse population, but whose economy had long been based on the commercial exploitation of tropical crops, Jaén had undergone a significant commercial expansion in the decades before the War of the Pacific. Traders from Chota province and the departments of Piura and Lambayeque entered the area seeking to buy supplies of cattle, cacao, coffee, cascarilla, and other products. The opportunity to rent a sizable proportion of the existing great estates, which belonged to a state-controlled charitable agency called the Beneficencia of Jaén and were dedicated mainly to the breeding of cattle and sheep, also attracted entrepreneurs from surrounding provinces. Commercial expansion and hacienda rentals thus concentrated a higher percentage of Jaén's population on haciendas than was usual in the rest of the department. Despite the overall thinness of population in the province, more than 40 percent lived on great estates, according to the 1876 census.[14]

For local smallholders and peasants, accustomed to the greater autonomy of a frontier trading economy, the influx of "outsiders" from Chota associated with large landholding or interprovincial commerce generated hostility and local conflict. Since these outside entrepreneurs expanded commercial agriculture mainly by renting lands through the Beneficencia, which obtained funds by administering state properties, smallholders tended to equate their presence with the extension of state authority. Scattered evidence further suggests that they saw state incursions—especially in the form of the contribución personal—as yet another invasion of outsiders that went along with commerce and commercial agriculture. A militantly antistate political culture emerged at the local level, oriented toward the removal of exploitative strangers and of an abusive, intrusive state. As we shall see, this political culture would have important implications for the type of movement developing in this province during the War of the Pacific.[15]

In contrast to Jaén, where the landowners renting state properties had a more direct connection to, and dependence on, state officials, in Cajamarca province many landowners defended the sanctity of their properties' boundaries by not allowing state officials to cross into their estates when chasing criminals or collecting taxes. Hacendados also hid bandits on their land in exchange for personal loyalty and in some cases even protected neighboring peasants who were resisting taxation or conscription. The peasants, for their part, preferred a local patron's protection against state exaction to the only available alternative: taxation by the landlord *and* the state. Only when hacendados competed with each other for influence did the role of the state become relevant. Before the War of the Pacific the participation of local landowners in factional battles at the national level can best be explained in the context of local intra-elite competition.[16]

Jaén and Cajamarca provinces thus presented distinct prewar patterns of internal conflict and different relationships to the emerging state structure in Lima. In Jaén interclass hostility over commercial expansion predisposed outside landowners to accept state aid in extending commercial agriculture while increasing peasant resistance to state exactions. In Cajamarca peasants and landowners both viewed the state with suspicion, preferring the existing status quo to an unclear and disruptive form of change. The only exception seemed to be the weaker landowners, who, by seeking state aid in their unequal battle with their stronger colleagues, forced the political involvement of the more influential Cajamarca hacendados as well.

Indeed, the construction of regional political cultures in Cajamarca made it difficult for any group to see the state as a potential ally, for peasants and landowners tended to be hostile and suspicious toward the expansion of a state authority they did not think would bring them any benefits. This hostility was in direct contrast to the situation in Morelos, where since independence landowners and peasants had each participated enthusiastically, although on different sides, in the struggles between Federalists and Centralists, Liberals and Conservatives, to centralize and reproduce state power. It was also different from the situations in Puebla and Junín, where—despite less dramatic polarization between communities and haciendas—political stalemates emerging from conflicts over municipal autonomy, access to land and revenues, and the changing nature of markets encouraged all to seek new alliances in the emerging national arena. In the northern Peruvian sierra, by contrast—with the exception of entrepreneurial groups in Jaén—the existence of an effective system of private landowner power diminished the relevance of state interventions for all parties involved.

The final element that helped define this political culture was the specific insertion of the northern Peruvian sierra into the War of the Pacific. When Nicolas de Piérola abandoned Lima to Chilean occupation in January 1881, he established camp in Jauja and divided the country into three large zones of resistance. The northern zone, under the control of Admiral Lizardo Montero, had its headquarters in Cajamarca. In contrast to the northern coastal departments, which had been subject to Chilean invasion and occupation since 1880, Cajamarca was spared the presence of Chilean soldiers until mid-1882. Even then the actual occupation, while quite destructive, was short-lived. This did not mean, however, that the political conflicts among Peruvians generated by the war and the occupation did not have a significant impact in the highland department. Indeed, both of the major resistance movements that developed in the region had their origins in intra-elite battles over how best to deal with the Chilean occupation of the country.[17]

By May 1882 an internal coup among Peruvians had transformed the Pierolista subprefect of Chota province, Manuel José Becerra, into a fugitive who was pursued as a rebel through the province of Jaén by government forces. Until his death in 1885 he led a guerrilla movement that repeatedly eluded both occupation and government forces, operating mainly along the commercial routes tying the jungle to the coast, especially in the provinces of Chota and Jaén. Becerra's montonera was instrumental in preventing collaborationist forces, most notably Miguel Iglesias, from establishing full control in the northern highlands. Its popularity in the region was increased by the fact that its leaders were from an intermediate stratum of Chota merchants, small landowners, and village notables, who, while apparently profiting from the prewar boom in Jaén, were never fully incorporated into the local elite.[18]

Even a cursory examination of the montonera's operations on a map emphasizes that its long-term survival depended on the knowledge of trade routes and resources previously amassed by its leaders. There were two main areas of operation. One centered in Bellavista district, in the jungle area of Jaén province, stretching west to Jaén itself and then much farther west to the commercial center of Olmos, on the way down to the coast in the department of Lambayeque. The town of Pimpingos, south of Jaén and en route to the commercial centers of Cutervo and Chota, was also in this first general area. The second base formed a rectangle whose northern, eastern, southern, and western angles were the towns of Querecotillo, Huambos, Llama, and Cachén respectively. Located farther south in the Chota-Cutervo highlands, nearly halfway between Chota and the coastal commercial entrepôts of Ferreñafe, Chiclayo, and Lambayeque, this second guerrilla stronghold was based in the towns from which many of the regulars in Becerra's band originally came. By basing itself in areas familiar to the members of the band, because of previous trade and family connections, Becerra's montonera was able to survive through a combination of stealing and marketing commercial goods, seeking the protection of local village notables whom they knew personally. Local authorities or prominent citizens in the towns and villages through which Becerra passed played a crucial supportive role, providing information, commercializing stolen goods, acquiring arms, and recruiting additional men. Thus, Becerra's montonera operated like a merchant's army based in the small towns and commercial routes of the region.[19]

Although led by merchants and small landowners, the montonera had a much more varied base of support. On one side were the large hacendados, mainly from the western corner of Chota and into the department of Lambayeque, who provided crucial commercial connections to the coast. On the other side were the peasant and Indian populations who provided the fighting men and, particularly in Bellavista, the resources and logistical support for hiding out when government pressure was high. Taken together, this wide variety of contacts and environments was ideal for the survival of a small guerrilla force. Near the coast, influential landowners and others served as a conduit for booty, exchanged for arms and ammunition. In Chota, a base among smallholding peasants and petty merchants provided fighters, occasional refuge, additional commercial connections, and intelligence on troop movements. And in Jaén, Bellavista was the largest producer of cacao in the province, directly on the Marañón River, yet difficult to reach for those traveling overland from west to east. All these characteristics made it an excellent refuge from armies based in the highlands.[20] The question remaining, though, is how Becerra was able to keep such a broad and varied coalition together at all. To answer this question, we must examine the movement's internal sociopolitical dynamics.

The actions of Becerra's band helped construct a common political and symbolic arena in which diverse groups participated according to their own experiences and needs. In Jaén the band's theft of commercial cargoes threatened the expulsion of all large landowners from the province and the destruction of Jaén's Beneficencia. In 1884 Jaén's subprefect submitted a desperate report from his hideout in Cutervo, explaining that Becerra, his father-in-law Manuel Vílchez, and other leaders had made it impossible for merchants from Cutervo or Chota to trade in the province except under threat of violent death. This type of action was clearly attractive to Jaén's petty merchants and smallholders, all of whom had suffered at the hands of state officials and large hacendados before the war. Involved in the attempt to commercialize tropical products but facing competition from more powerful landowners and entrepreneurs, smaller merchants saw in Becerra's band a legitimate way to revenge themselves, even to allow themselves the fantasy that after the war they might take over the more profitable routes. For the Indians and peasants of Jaén, the band's attacks on prominent landowners and its de facto destruction of Jaén's Beneficencia meant a return to the forms of local autonomy they had known before the prewar commercial expansion. In Jaén province, therefore, Becerra was able to unite this variety of sentiments into a powerful movement against the collaborationist Peruvian government and the foreign invader. And one must not forget his sense of theater: in this regard, no image is more telling than that of Becerra riding into one of his local strongholds, appropriating two hundred receipts for the head tax, and tearing them up in the central plaza to general applause.[21]

Becerra's connections with hacendados are certainly more difficult to explain, given his movement's hostility to the prominent landowners in Jaén and Chota. The fact that his landlord connections were outside these two provinces, in or near the coastal departments of Piura and Lambayeque, helps to explain part of the contradiction. So does the fact that separate commercial routes connected Jaén to those coastal areas, in particular through the strategic center of Olmos. Thus, Becerra did not need to go through his Chota strongholds to reach his hacendado allies. But most important, the state also represented an unwelcome interference in the lives of the landowners who supported Becerra. José Mesones, for example, Becerra's strongest hacendado ally, had been involved in a major altercation with local authorities in 1880 when they had attempted to draft men from his hacienda.[22]

Becerra's movement was thus a motley coalition of rebellious hacendados, ambitious merchants, local notables, dispossessed or pauperized peasants, and marginalized frontier producers. What kept them together was a common antistate sentiment. Antistate feelings also united Becerra with his village supporters outside Jaén, for as we shall see in more detail below, many highland villagers had experienced the earlier part of the War of the Pacific as a violent incursion of the Peruvian state, most notably in the form of taxes and conscription. Becerra's opposition to the head tax, and the fact that he fought with a volunteer army, thus made him an attractive ally for villages squeezed by Peruvian or Chilean exactions. People joined him seeking protection from the incursions of the Peruvian state in the form of head taxes, war contributions, conscription, or commercial penetration.

Indeed, the very conditions for the movement's existence were defined by the weakness of the state in the area before the War of the Pacific. During a national emergency state efforts to collect resources and raise an army resulted in violence and aggression against the rural population. Thus, it was the Peruvian state itself that first acted as a foreign invader in the northern highlands. The reaction of the region's population was a multifaceted alliance among a series of groups and classes: antistate landowners and peasants; Indians resisting commercial penetration; and merchants attempting to marginalize larger landowners from the profits of Jaén's commercial boom. Becerra's astute political sense and their common antigovernment position kept them together for the duration. But after Becerra's death in 1885 and Cáceres's triumph over Iglesias, there was no common vision or project to bind them any longer. In the postwar confusion the differences among them would float to the surface.[23]

In contrast to the agrarian radicalism existing in Morelos, Junín, and Puebla, the oppositional political culture constructed in the region of Becerra's influence did not include a project, whether implicit or explicit, for the making of a national politics. In the context of the Chilean invasion, and once the Peruvian state began to collaborate with the Chilean army, Becerra's montonera became a national resistance movement almost by default. Especially once Chilean forces made incursions into the highlands, the Becerrista coalition proved quite effective in resisting them while continuing to strike blows against the Peruvian state. But in the long run such a movement did not present a deep challenge to social control or political consolidation. Without a broader project it would fall apart quite easily once the conditions creating it had ceased to exist.

While sharing some similarities with Becerra's movement, the second major center of resistance against the occupation and the collaborationist Peruvian government was located in a different part of Cajamarca and supported by a different coalition of people. Led by José Mercedes Puga, a prominent hacendado from southern Cajamarca province, this movement began as a response to Miguel Iglesias's political actions in the period between August and December 1882. Iglesias and Puga had confronted each other over issues of local power for years before the war, becoming legendary rivals in the province of Cajamarca and lining up on opposite sides of the emerging national factions. Since Iglesias became a Pierolista and Puga a Civilista during the 1860s and 1870s, it was hardly surprising that Piérola called on Iglesias to organize the northern army during the ill-fated defense of Lima in late 1880. Puga was even further alienated from the political process when Montero named Iglesias his successor in the north. But it seems that the Chilean invasion of Cajamarca in mid-1882, and the forced contributions placed on the local population, began to change Puga's mind. He was perhaps especially influenced by the rather lukewarm defense of the region organized by Iglesias. Thus, when Iglesias issued the Cry of Montán, and even more important when he organized a constituent assembly in Cajamarca to legitimate his role as national leader, Puga decided to act. As of December 1882 he was participating in a growing rebel movement directly to the south of Cajamarca city, in the area between the districts of San Marcos and Ichocán and the city of Cajabamba.[24]

Ichocán and San Marcos, both centers of rebel activity, were villages with a history of resisting taxation and conscription. In July 1880, for example, the governor of Ichocán district was attacked by a group of two hundred women and fifty men, armed with stones and sticks, as he attempted to lead a group of conscripts out of the area. During the following year the authorities encountered major resistance in attempting to tax or draft the local population, often returning from their missions with hands empty. In some cases people simply retired to the hills; in others the local inhabitants—mainly the women—defended prospective conscripts by attacking the officials. San Marcos also resisted violently in October and November 1882, when government representatives tried to charge the contribución personal. The most serious incident occurred on 25 October, when more than five hundred women and men ambushed the governor and his force, firing on them from the surrounding hills.[25]

Local reaction was understandable given the methods used by the government. Forced conscription was quite common. Soldiers entered the villages and broke down doors in the middle of the night, taking people off at gunpoint. The rest of the population usually fled the villages, hiding out on the punas or in caves, fearing a repetition of the attack. It is hard to gauge, on the basis of existing documentation, what proportion of conscripts was taken violently, but correspondence to the prefect's office is full of letters pleading for the freedom of recruits taken by force.

With the Peruvian state perceived as the most direct enemy by many villagers, the stage was set for an alliance with several hacendados in San Marcos and Ichocán districts who had also been dragging their feet on draft or war contribution requests. They had hidden possible recruits and criminals within their properties, ignoring official orders to turn men over to local authorities. Since government representatives apparently needed a special warrant to enter haciendas, protecting individuals within the borders of large estates was quite effective. As of the last months of 1882, landowners in San Marcos and Ichocán districts—most notably José Mercedes Puga, the owner of the hacienda La Pauca—were extending protection within their borders to all peasants resisting state exactions.[26]

This alliance was organized around a common antistate position generated by wartime incursions. As the predominant force in the village resistance, both quantitatively and morally, peasant women were fighting to defend their households and families from outside aggression. But the villagers in general also found the alliance with local hacendados a familiar one, for Puga at least had a long-standing relationship with the inhabitants of Ichocán and San Marcos. As was true in many other parts of Cajamarca, these two villages did not have enough land, especially pasture. Many individuals therefore rented lands from Puga, ostensibly as part of an ongoing patron-client relationship.[27] This preexisting relation, combined with the need to act in a new emergency situation, formed the glue that held the montonera together.

The other important component of Puga's movement was a sizable proportion of the urban Chinese population, particularly from the city of Cajamarca. It is difficult to know why they joined. Perhaps they feared being associated with the coastal Chinese who had rebelled against the hacendados and joined with the Chileans; perhaps their extensive commercial relations in the province had brought them into conflict with members of the anti-Puga faction. Whatever the reasons for their participation, Puga seems to have trusted the Chinese members of his montonera implicitly, perhaps because their position as "outsiders" in local society diminished the possibility of crosscutting loyalties. In addition to acting as his spies in Cajamarca city, the Chinese montoneros formed the main force who escaped with him across the Marañón River when he knew he was being pursued by a superior force in November 1884.[28]

Although this complex alliance of landowners, retainers, village peasants, and urban Chinese was also held together by a common antistate sentiment, the reasons for it were different from the motives behind Becerra's movement. The village peasantry, and especially the women, had risen to defend themselves against the Peruvian state's efforts to raise funds and men for the war. They had been able to count on the aid of a powerful landowner faction that, for reasons of its own, was also opposing state efforts at taxation. The result was a powerful and relatively unified montonera that was quite effective in confronting the collaborationist Peruvians as well as the occupation forces.[29]

Puga's montonera was distinguished by the strength of its connection to landowner politics and hacienda dynamics. In times of trouble the most important hideouts were on Puga's properties. The haciendas were also the storage place for stolen cattle and the most effective battle sites. And Puga's own motivations were highly colored by his ongoing conflict with his fellow hacendado Miguel Iglesias, probably more so than by an abstract sense of or commitment to a broader national project. This was also true of those who fought against him.[30]

Puga's montonera encouraged the intensification of factional and clientelistic battles among the region's hacendados, both during and after the war. Francisco Baldomero Pinillos, for example, an hacendado from Santiago de Chuco who had been involved in border conflicts with Puga before the war, became a rabid Iglesista, leading his own men into battle against Puga's forces and perceiving the entire conflict in local terms. He and his sons Serapio and Juan José received commissions in the national guard. In

October 1885 the Pinillos family demanded the adjudication of the hacienda Uningambal, which bordered their estate Sangual and with which they had been disputing a pasture. As a rationale for their demand, they argued that a commander allied with Puga had invaded their property from a base on Uningambal, damaging their estate in a politically motivated reprisal.[31]

In the end neither Becerra's merchant montonera nor Puga's hacienda-oriented movement generated a regional political culture whose overall vision extended outward, toward the building of a national politics. Both movements were diverse coalitions of people, held together by an antistate sentiment that, in a particular conjuncture, prompted them to fight on the nationalist side. But in neither case did events lead them in the direction of elaborating a national project. Although guerrilla commanders allied with Puga or Becerra continued to fight on the Cacerista side in the civil war of 1884–1885, the situation became increasingly muddy after Puga's and Becerra's deaths in 1885 and the defeat of Iglesias. Into the early 1890s the Cacerista state was unable to come up with an effective strategy for reestablishing control in the region. It would be left to Nicolás de Piérola, and the post-1895 government of national reconstruction, to attempt to restore order in the department of Cajamarca.[32]

In Cajamarca, as in some other areas of the country, Piérola's bid for power was supported by a significant sector of the traditional landowning oligarchy eager to reachieve the prewar status quo. What that support meant in the north, however, was conditioned by the particular nature of the regional political culture that had emerged in previous decades. Although they had rejected state intervention in the years before the War of the Pacific, by 1895 most landowners in Cajamarca were forced to admit that they needed some kind of relationship with a national state. Even if they had not faced an autonomous and militant peasant movement of the kind existing in Morelos, Puebla, or Junín, the disorganization and destruction of the Chilean occupation and subsequent civil strife had badly shaken their economic and political control. In early 1886 Cacerista political officials throughout the north were quick to point out that economic dislocation, continuing political conflict, and the dispersal of weapons and men from the haciendas had sent shock waves through state institutions and the regional economy. After 1890 dislocation increased further because of the increasing demand for labor on the coastal sugar plantations, which threatened to drive a wedge in the local monopoly of labor power. Thus, when Piérola returned to the presidential palace in 1895, he was welcomed warmly by many traditional landowning families in Cajamarca, who viewed him as a savior come to reestablish their position in local society. Yet even as they welcomed the state into their areas, landowners in

Cajamarca negotiated the terms of the relationship in a very different way than did their counterparts in Morelos or Junín.[33]

In Morelos and Junín, as we have seen, emerging national states intervened repeatedly and directly to favor the hacendados in their relatively even conflict with the villages. In northern Peru, by contrast, the Pierolista consolidation tended to underwrite or rebuild a system of private landowner power. This strategy was possible in part because of the relative weakness of independent peasant mobilization in the area. It was also possible because the prewar history of class relations had given the landowners a strong territorial and political base from which to work. The result was an hacendado-state relationship that looked a great deal like traditional *gamonalismo*. In exchange for sanctioning the continued privatization of power in the countryside, the government was assured collaboration from local landlords. And the deal seemed to work to a great extent, at least until the 1920s and 1930s. Although banditry and violence became epidemic in the region, forcing a massive repression in the 1920s by the national state, until the 1960s the police still had trouble penetrating the borders of the great estates in highland Cajamarca.[34]

Conclusion: Haciendas and Communities in the Making of National Politics

By comparing four rural regions that confronted the emergence of a "national question," we have been able to explore a variety of ways in which peasants and other rural people engaged in creative political action, depending on the conditions and traditions they had at their disposal. When villagers were part of a regional political culture that included communal institutions and hegemonic processes, they were more successful in negotiating autonomous spaces and participation within emerging national coalitions. This does not mean, of course, that peasants in areas without such communal traditions were passive or politically naive. Quite to the contrary. In Cajamarca, too, rural people worked creatively and forcefully with the political tools available to them. Nor does it mean that all communities produced the same kind of alternative nationalism, for historical, cultural, and political contingencies yielded a vast array of potential alliances, perceptions, and discourses. But the important general point to be made is that, no matter how original, vigorous, and contingent, peasant political action occurred within the boundaries set by earlier interactions, in the form of communal institutions and regional political cultures. Even in periods of intense change and political "openness," therefore, there were limits on possible transformations and discursive constructions.

In the case of Cajamarca, hacendados dominated the region's political culture because of the historical weakness of communal institutions and the lack of economic alternatives for the area's peasant population. The main lines of contention were between landowner factions, and peasants acted politically by allying with these factions. When a "national question" emerged, therefore, villagers continued their practice of claiming terrain within dominant projects rather than constructing their own. They participated in the making of national politics in a mediated way, through existing multiclass coalitions at the regional level. Thus, they did not formulate their own alternative nationalist discourses.

In Morelos, Junín, and Puebla, by contrast, peasants participated in broader processes of nation-state formation from their foothold in communal institutions and hegemonic processes. Constructing outward from their own political experiences, they sought allies among those merchants, landowners, and politicians who respected their autonomy and agenda for social justice. Peasant leaders mediated between communal politics and broader coalitions, changing both in the process. Yet here it is interesting to note that, despite the negative effect of hacendado dominance on the rise of alternative nationalism in Cajamarca, the presence of conflict with haciendas in other regions actually intensified the autonomy and militancy of peasant nationalisms. Thus, all the strong and politically autonomous alternative nationalisms we have analyzed—Morelos, Puebla's central and eastern sierra, Comas, and the west bank of the Mantaro—emerged in relation to, and conflict with, an expansionary hacendado class. In Jauja, where no major landowner threat existed and patron-client ties worked more successfully, participation in national coalitions was more integrative and quiescent.

These comparisons are, however, meant to be suggestive only. The last thing on my mind is the construction of a rigid model about alternative nationalisms into which we must strain to stuff any and all cases. Variations within these broad boundaries are equally important. Thus, in the case of Puebla we can emphasize the uniqueness and centrality of Xochiapulco. In an area of ethnically distinct and culturally Indian villages, a community carved out of an hacienda helped mediate political discourses and practices into a powerful radical Liberal alliance. Montaña Liberalism would surely have been quite different without the existence of Xochiapulco. In the case of Morelos as well, we can be sure that agrarian Liberalism would have been less sophisticated and complex without forty years of political action alongside Juan Alvarez and other radical federalist caciques of El Sur. And in Peru we can only speculate about what might have happened without Andrés

Cáceres's stubborn commitment to a continued resistance against the Chilean occupying army.

Perhaps the final perception to be gleaned from all this is that, in our ongoing efforts to understand and respect the myriad forms of rural politics, struggle, and discourse that fed into, shaped, and contested nineteenth-century nation-state formation, we must continue to inhabit that narrow and painful edge between rigid generalization and complete dispersion. The more we "name names," the more we get to know specific actors and processes, the harder it is to cram them into predetermined categories and boxes. At the same time, though, we need to reclaim the field of generalization and theory building. While recognizing the need for a more flexible and gentle attitude, we must also realize that refusing to find broader patterns can be as deadly as insisting that all variations fit into one.

3

ALTERNATIVE NATIONAL PROJECTS AND THE CONSOLIDATION OF THE STATE

8 The Intricacies of Coercion

*Popular Political Cultures, Repression,
and the Failure of Hegemony*

A common thread runs through the diverse stories of popular nationalism in nineteenth-century Mexico and Peru. The treacherous old friend or ally, sometimes a former comrade in arms, always a member of the same political coalition, traveled to the village or the region, weapons in hand, to repress his former colleagues. Nicolás de la Portilla in Tepoztlán in 1856; Ignacio Alatorre in the Sierra de Puebla between 1868 and 1874; Andrés Freyre in Comas in 1889—all three moments constitute repression by statemakers, not of their enemies, but of the popular elements in their own coalitions.[1]

In Mexico after the French Intervention (1862–1867) and Peru after the War of the Pacific (1879–1884), presidents Benito Juárez and Andrés Cáceres shared the need to rebuild frayed and decentralized state structures. Whatever their specific histories and motives, they also faced robust, active, and autonomous popular movements that challenged their authority. As they moved to consolidate their own positions and eliminate possible competitors, therefore, they aimed to reconstitute political authority in part through the marginalization of their more radical allies. They rediscovered along the way that authority remade through repression does not carry legitimacy with it.

In Morelos, Junín, and the Sierra de Puebla, the popular nationalisms that emerged from rural social movements before, during, and after foreign intervention became an impediment to the reconstruction of the state. Political leaders interested in the centralization of power opted for domination rather than negotiation. Subduing popular movements without partially incorporating their aspirations and energies, however, prevented the consolidation of a broader national project. Making a hegemonic national state—that is, one that rules through consent as well as coercion—involves some degree of willingness or collaboration on the part of the governed. One needs a "cultural revolution"—the generation of a common social and moral project that includes popular as well as elite notions of political culture.[2] Peruvian and Mexican politicians failed to generate such a project, and their countries entered the twentieth century with state structures built on the violent exclusion of popular constituencies.

Exclusion, however, can take many forms. By tracing the similarities and differences in coercion and repression during the last several decades of the nineteenth century, I will show that the strength, organization, and effect of counterhegemonic movements—even when facing repression and disorganization—was quite distinct in the two countries. The resulting contrast in political legacies, best understood as the ongoing if submerged potentialities of popular political cultures, was indeed great. It helps us understand why, in Mexico, a broad and powerful popular movement was able to transform the succession crisis of 1910 into a major social revolution, whereas in twentieth-century Peru, crisis and popular mobilization have led only to further fragmentation and repression.

Popular Liberalism Versus Liberal Authority:
Indigenous National Guards
and the Consolidation of the State
in Puebla, 1867–1872

On 25 December 1867 Benito Juárez was inaugurated in Mexico City as the reelected constitutional president. By the time he accepted the accolades of his fellow citizens, Juárez was already well on the way to a centralization of power that flew in the face of many stated principles in Mexican Liberalism and that injured regional Liberal sensibilities in many parts of the republic. The consequent alienation of some of his most active and erstwhile supporters would haunt Juárez in the years to come and contribute substantially to frustrating his desire for political stability. Nowhere were the contradictions of this process more evident than in the state of Puebla.[3]

Throughout the Restored Republic (1867–1876), political conflict in Puebla state would be defined by the problematic alliances that Juárez established there between September 1867 and March 1868. His decisions over these months set into motion a series of reactions and modifications in the earlier Liberal coalitions that would continue into the 1870s, ultimately pushing the state's populist Liberals into the arms of Porfirio Díaz. Juárez's decisions followed a simple, linear logic. Local populist leaders, especially Juan Nepomuceno Méndez, had allied closely with Porfirio Díaz during the resistance to the French. Díaz was, as of 1867, Juárez's only remaining potential rival for national power. For Juárez to assure his own hold on power, he had to neutralize Díaz. Ergo, all of Díaz's potential allies also had to be neutralized.

The actions of the Juaristas tied the recognition and legitimacy of popular Liberalism in Puebla state to the identity of the person occupying the governor's chair. Unable to see beyond personalities to the strength of counter-hegemonic coalitions, they formulated a strategy that had no room for factors such as popular support or legitimacy, of which Méndez and his allies had a bountiful supply and the local politicians on whom Juárez relied had much less. As a result, the Juaristas continued fighting the same battle in Puebla for ten years. In the long run, they lost.

Juan N. Méndez sat in the governor's chair in Puebla city when Juárez entered the national capital on 25 July; he had been placed there in an interim capacity by Porfirio Díaz during the siege of Mexico City. Méndez's first confrontation with the returning president would come with the publication, on 14 August, of the Convocatoria, Juárez's call to federal elections for president, members of the supreme court, and representatives to the Fourth National Congress. Tucked among its articles were several projected amendments to the constitution as well as the political rehabilitation of all who had served the empire. As in other parts of the country, the outcry in Puebla was dramatic. Méndez, in his interpretation of his role as state governor, hastened to send representatives to talk to Juárez about the inadvisability of the suggested reforms.[4]

The Convocatoria evoked such strong opposition throughout the country that Juárez issued an explanatory circular on 22 August, attempting to clarify both the content and form of the requested changes. But in Puebla, as elsewhere, many Liberals continued to fear the potential consequences of the document. Méndez, in one of the last letters he wrote to Juárez, gave a particularly impassioned and eloquent explanation for why Liberals could be opposed to the Convocatoria. Many Liberals, he wrote, believed that the Convocatoria was not merely advisory; rather, they feared that government influence would be used to overturn the laws passed by duly elected national representatives. By instituting the executive veto and a senate, and by giving the vote to the clergy and the monarchists, the Convocatoria would set a precedent for reforming the constitution by means outside the legally established channels of national representation. And such a possibility was frightening in a country where the only salvation from constant civil war had been respect for the law.[5]

Méndez's political message to Juárez was that the legislative power served a mediating function between the executive and the popular will. Thus, its autonomy had to be preserved at all costs: only in this way could the rule of law transcend the violence of civil strife. This was, in fact, very similar to the original message and purpose of the 1856–1857 Constituent Congress, where representatives had struggled to place the rule of law above the particularistic interests of different caciques, their regional constituencies, and unbridled executive power. In this sense, the image one usually gets of Méndez as the quintessential sierra cacique, interested only in reproducing his own power, must be modified. At a moment when personalistic interest dictated playing along with Juárez, Méndez risked his position by recalling the original radical vision of the 1855 Revolution, one to which Juárez had originally subscribed. Why was Juárez unable to hear this message? Was it that the president simply could not believe the sincerity of it, coming as it did from someone he considered to be an ally of his opponent Díaz?[6]

From Juárez's perspective, the changing political stakes—especially as the motley Liberal coalition that had defeated the empire began to fall apart in the face of competition and consolidation—made the choice of allies seem more important than the defense of principles. This perception was buttressed by Méndez's actions on 14 September, when he published the Convocatoria with the offending reforms deleted. Three days later Rafael J. García, the Liberal intellectual removed from the governorship by Díaz's appointment of Méndez, wrote a long letter to Juárez. Although Juárez had not answered his previous letters, García began, he was writing again because the situation in Puebla was very difficult. "Worst of all," he continued, "Mr. Mendez is delirious with his desire to govern the state of Puebla, and in order to achieve this he has left no stone unturned, he has in all the Districts, with a few exceptions, political authorities who are his creatures." It would therefore be impossible to have a just election, García argued, even if the Convocatoria had been published in its entirety. And then he reached the core of his message. After an entire page of disclaimers about any personal ambition, he urged Juárez to replace Méndez in the governorship. If this was not done, he concluded, Méndez would succeed in his ambition to become governor, and the results would be catastrophic.

> All the authorities would be according to his desires, and we would have in the midst of a republic a repetition of those famous actas that underwrote the so-called empire. And if today Mr. Méndez's power comes from the constitutional government, and he still becomes a potentate, substituting anarchy for law and raising [his own] flag, imagine what he will do as constitutional governor.[7]

Juárez took up García's invitation, since it coincided with his self-interest. Across the bottom of the letter was written, "Answered on 19 September. Interesting letter from García on the Convocatoria." Even more interesting was the answer García received on 19 September. It was a telegram from

Sebastián Lerdo de Tejada announcing that García had been named governor of Puebla, replacing Méndez.[8]

In a letter to the minister of war three days later, Méndez accepted the situation but protested its legitimacy, claiming the right to be heard based on his previous distinguished service to the nation.

> He who has worked loyally for the homeland, he who has on his body the honorable scars of foreign bullets, considers he has the right to express with respect and clarity his opinions, guided by duty and by the Law that has been and shall continue to be the norm for all his acts.[9]

The contrast between Méndez's stated motivations and those García imputed to him could not have been greater. Where García accused him of personal ambition, Méndez countered with his respect for the law even in the face of personal sacrifice. Where García represented him as a cacique cut from the old cloth, responsible at least symbolically for the chaos leading up to the French Intervention and the empire and potentially condemned to reproduce it, Méndez pointed to the scars he bore from battle with the Interventionists—something to which García had no claim. Able to compare the depth and breadth of the two men's service to the Liberal cause, Juárez could never have doubted that Méndez had the cleaner claim to being heard. And indeed, until Méndez directly challenged presidential authority by publishing an abridged Convocatoria, Juárez had not even answered García's letters. What changed Juárez's mind was the need to maintain and reproduce his authority, and, after pushing all the right buttons in his letter of 19 September, García became the best-placed tool for Juárez's consolidation of power in Puebla state.[10]

What was at issue, after all, was control of the central state apparatus—in the shape of the national election for president. Using an argument analogous to that used against Jesús González Ortega when he had contested Juárez's earlier reelection, Lerdo de Tejada wrote to García that in a state of emergency, different rules applied. Because the governor's power emanated directly from the president, there was simply no justification for any sort of protest from Méndez, who "must obey and come immediately to present himself to the [federal] government, as he has been told, unless he wishes to place himself in the condition of a military man in rebellion, in which case . . . the government will have to dictate the necessary measures." Simply put, it was time to place the principle of authority before any other, no matter how legitimate. This meant Juárez and Juárez's power above all else.[11]

Through September and into October, the crucial issue in Puebla was how to establish political and military control of the electoral districts so that universal male suffrage would successfully reelect Juárez to the presidency. It is in this context that we can best understand the ongoing concerns of Puebla's Juaristas: that Méndez had taken arms with him into the sierra after resigning his post; that supporters of Méndez and Díaz were working in the various districts; and most important, that all the jefes políticos appointed under Méndez were to be replaced by people more sympathetic to García and Juárez. Porfirio Díaz had understood this as well when, on 25 September, he had ordered Méndez not to turn over the governorship under any circumstances.

But Méndez did turn over the governorship on that very same day. And between that moment and the national elections in October, García and his allies struggled town by town to construct political majorities for Juárez and his supporters. At times they forcibly removed Mendista political officials or other supporters from specific villages or electoral districts; when they could not do so, they postponed the elections themselves. Under other circumstances their strategy entailed the use of money to "pay expenses" for those willing to work for Juárez in particular localities. Occasionally Juárez himself established the key political contact, offering help or support for individuals or villages lining up on the correct side. And in this context the primary elections of mid-October served as a key litmus test, designating the electors for the final contest and showing at the local level who was committed to whom.[12]

Dire Juarista predictions to the contrary, there never seems to have been much danger of a hostile outcome in Puebla state. However contested Juárez's publication of the Convocatoria, however unjust his replacement of Méndez seemed to many, in the end people were tired of fighting. We have already seen (in chapter 4) that the construction of a discourse of rebellion in the sierra was complex and difficult during the first half of 1868. Meanwhile, despite Porfirio Díaz's presence in southern Puebla state and Méndez's pledge from Huamantla that he would use force if necessary to prevent Juarista manipulation, the overall contour of alliances at the national level was favorable to Juárez, who had gained victory in the state's electoral college by 20 October.[13]

A Juarista victory in the state government proved more difficult, though not for lack of trying. By the time García published his resignation from the governorship on 26 October, the ground had already been prepared privately for his electoral campaign. Since 30 September, García had been urging Juárez to keep Méndez out of the election for governor, first by refusing to accept the latter's resignation from the army, then by insisting that Méndez go to Mexico City to be tried for his actions concerning the Convocatoria. Over the same period García and Juárez had together worked hard on private negotiations to secure the sierra districts militarily before Méndez's marginalization from state politics became public. As had been true earlier during the federal primary election, the state elections in early November were further litmus tests showing how the factions would vote in the contest for state executive.[14]

In this round, however, things did not turn out quite as Juárez and García would have liked. While Méndez was effectively frozen out of a candidacy for governor, elected congressional deputies did not line up in a clear way. Mendistas gained ground in potential bargaining as the rest of the political spectrum factionalized. García complained to Juárez on 4 November that Ignacio Romero Vargas, another Puebla Liberal, had acted treacherously, manipulating the situation to have his supporters elected to congress against García's wishes. "Had I understood his intentions," García concluded, "I would have separated myself entirely from him."

García was angry because five of the sixteen representatives elected to the state congress were confirmed supporters of Romero, while only three supported García. Four were Mendistas, and the remaining four were undecided. These numbers seemed to assure the governorship for Romero, who sniffed his upcoming victory. Between 11 and 19 November he wrote twice to Juárez, recommending friends and requesting the rehabilitation of one of his supporters to serve in the state congress. In this last case his confidence was so great that he requested that Juárez backdate the rehabilitation to before the election in order to preserve the appearance of legality. Juárez must have agreed, for Romero's friend did indeed serve in the legislature.[15]

Perhaps the most reasoned analysis of Liberal factionalism in the state came from Joaquín Ruiz, who on 16 November wrote a private letter to Juárez urging that he accept Méndez's resignation from the military so that Méndez could legally run for governor. Ruiz assumed, given the results of the primary and congressional contests, that no candidate would be able to win a majority of the popular vote. The decision would then be left to the congress, where furious political head counting was already in progress. What Ruiz feared most, he said, was the election of Romero, an unprincipled, inefficient politician. Given his previous association with Méndez, Juárez probably assumed that Ruiz's letter was a planned Mendista trial balloon and treated it as such, denying any knowledge of Méndez's attempted resignation.[16] Yet in the last analysis, Ruiz was right, no matter what his particular loyalties. Méndez was the only Liberal candidate able to unite a broad consensus for reconstruction in the state.

Ruiz's analysis was proven correct by events in the state congress at the end of November, when representatives nullified the results of the election for governor by a two-thirds majority. In companion letters to Juárez on 29 November, Romero and García each heaped accusations of treachery on the other. The two Liberals had reached a preelection agreement in which each promised to turn over to the other "their" congressional votes should the other come out first in the voting. The original intent of the accord was to marginalize the Mendista representatives, who constituted nearly a third of the votes and were therefore a minority to be reckoned with. According to Romero, however, García had tampered with the electoral results while these were in the governor's office, removing around seven thousand votes from Romero's total. After this maneuver all bets were off, from Romero's perspective. "His" representatives cut a deal with the Mendistas to nullify the results of the election and agree on a provisional governor. This approach, the Mendistas reasoned, would delay the electoral contest long enough that the Ministry of Defense might accept Méndez's resignation from the army, thus making him eligible to run.[17]

The Mendista strategy worked quite well. Not only was Méndez cleared for candidacy by the time of the new election, but the ongoing work of Mendista representatives in the state congress helped fashion an electoral law that left final authority over the process in the hands of the municipal cabeceras. In a direct election where national guard soldiers had the right to vote, political officials at the municipal level were crucial in preparing the ground. They numbered the ballots for all the villages in their municipality. They appointed the people who carried out each local census of voters and distributed the legal identifications that individuals used to gain entry to the polling places. And finally, they oversaw the process of constituting the electoral *mesas*, the personnel who ran the election procedures themselves and helped illiterates mark their ballots.

Under such an electoral law it was precisely those who most strongly supported Mendista populist Liberalism—municipal officials and national guard soldiers—who could most easily organize to influence the outcome. The Juarista faction organized at the district level, with García once again removing jefes políticos loyal to the Montaña party. But with autonomous municipal control, such organization was less effective. Thus, in addition to showing the greater popularity and legitimacy of a Méndez candidacy, the results of the second election for governor demonstrated the greater efficiency of municipal mobilization.[18]

We have already seen what happened to the results of this second election in the congress, where the reunited García and Romero factions in effect brought the state to civil war. What we have not yet considered are the long-term costs of the alliances constructed by and for Juárez, against Méndez, in Puebla. At the broadest level, Juárez chose as state executives two men whose service to their country during the French Intervention was quite limited. García, as we have seen, did not serve in the army at all. Romero was taken prisoner early and lived out the rest of the conflict in exile. Both symbolically and politically, therefore, Juárez gave the most constant fighters, the national guard soldiers of the resistance who had fought under Méndez, a slap in the face. In the sierra as well, Juárez's loyal allies turned out to be men with checkered or dubious resistance records. Unsuccessful at courting Juan Francisco Lucas, Juárez received instead the loyalty of Rafael Cravioto, a self-seeking Liberal general from Huauchinango who had allied with Alatriste in the ill-fated intra-Liberal conflict of 1859–1860, surrendered early to the empire, and attempted to save his own family fortune throughout. In Zacatlán and Tetela, where no self-respecting Liberal would have collaborated with García, the Juaristas were reduced to an alliance with Dimas López, a Liberal of modest prestige whose main motivation was a desire to recover from personal bankruptcy. And in the category of Liberal without portfolio was José María Maldonado, originally a radical and compadre to Juan Francisco Lucas, but in the end tainted by a furious personal vendetta against Méndez and by his desperate attempt to revindicate his personal war record in order to receive a medal and a pension.[19]

But it was in Zacapoaxtla itself, where those opposed to the national guard Liberals from Xochiapulco had always waved a conservative flag, that the cost of these alliances was most achingly clear. In the last, desperate maneuverings before the second governor's election, García wrote to Juárez suggesting a radical change in alliances within that highland district. The *licenciado* Pascual V. Bonilla, he wrote, had asked for rehabilitation.

> He is today the most influential person in that district [Zacapoaxtla], and is entirely in favor of the federal government; he is the author of the letters I sent you in days past and has enough energy to demand obedience. Proof of his influence is the fact that he put himself at the head of the electors from Zacapoaxtla and gave you and Mr. Lerdo their votes, entirely in opposition to and separation from the electors from Tetela and Xochiapulco, [who were] more numerous. If you agree, I think it would be convenient not only to rehabilitate Bonilla but also to give him some consideration and favor, in order to count on him under difficult circumstances and have an ally among the enemy.[20]

With García's suggestion that Juárez rely on Bonilla, the empire's most assiduous collaborator, to neutralize the Liberal national guards in the sierra, the situation had finally come full circle. In an effort to consolidate his personal power in the state, Juárez had isolated himself from his most powerful and legitimate Liberal supporters. Given the factionalism and opportunism of those he chose as his allies, it is perhaps not surprising that the situation continued to degenerate. Refusing to contemplate the candidacy of an independent-minded Liberal fighter, Juárez ended up rehabilitating a man who had served the Austrians in their counterinsurgency campaign. Such was the principle of authority, and it would continue to haunt him and his successors. Between 1868 and the early 1870s, former Conservatives from the 1850s and earlier 1860s would fight the Liberal national guards in the name of the Restored Republic. Small wonder that, when given another chance to overthrow Juarismo in 1876, Mendista Liberals jumped at the chance. Perhaps it is only fitting that the first constitutional governor of Puebla state during the early Porfiriato was Juan Nepomuceno Méndez.[21]

Pierolismo and Peasant Resistance in Junín, 1895–1902

In 1894 the death of Remigio Morales Bermúdez initiated an armed conflict for control of the Peruvian state between the Caceristas and the Democratic party led by Nicolás de Piérola. By March 1895 Piérola had taken Lima and begun the reorganization of the state. The Pierolistas aimed to construct a state that was "relatively autonomous" from the particularistic interests of class or political faction. They reasoned that such a state, constituted above the political fray, could bring true progress to all the country's citizens and establish effective and legitimate authority across the entire national territory.

Establishing effective authority, however, directly contradicted the maintenance of state autonomy. As events in the central highlands and other areas would show, this contradiction was at the center of the process through which the Pierolista state established domination. Beneath a discourse of progress and modernization lay the age-old practices of political favoritism and violent repression. The "modern" Peruvian state, in its initial Pierolista form, was constructed by negotiating a zigzag course between these contradictory markers of progress and cronyism, modernization and repression.[22]

A good example of these contradictions was the Pierolista state's attempt to build a central highway connecting the coast to the jungle and the Amazon River. One of Piérola's pet projects, the highway was meant to facilitate state authority over resources and territory in the Peruvian jungle and to claim the profits from commerce and rubber exploitation in that area. On the international level, the highway was expected to cement state control over national territory by taking rubber profits away from Brazilian entrepreneurs and the infamous Fitzcarrald and preventing the rumored secession of the department of Loreto and its addition to Brazil. Yet at the local level, building the central highway depended on *enganche*: advancing money to peasants who then worked off their debts in road construction. Local merchants and political authorities involved with enganche gleaned high personal profits from the enterprise, and their actions fomented violence and abuses against the village population. Pierolista politicians associated with the project competed among themselves as well, leading to much personal recrimination in their correspondence with the central government. To top it all off, local coffee planters and other landowners complained that the wages and conditions offered by the government were too good and were causing a shortage of labor for the private sector. They demanded, in effect, that the state office of enganche treat workers as poorly as they did.[23]

But the clearest case of sacrificing state autonomy occurred in the central region, in the Mantaro Valley and Ayacucho, between 1894 and 1897. During the civil war Pierolista officials had already gotten their boots veritably encrusted with the mud of political particularisms when they had formed an alliance with the anti-Cáceres hacendados in Huancayo province. These were the landowners who continued to claim lands in the possession of the peasant communities. In addition, Pierolista officials repressed the most enthusiastic Caceristas, such as Bartolomé Guerra. In Jauja city itself they imprisoned and fined Cáceres's supporter and relative, Father José María Dianderas. Once the Pierolista victory was assured, therefore, the representatives of the new government already had debts to particular factions and interests. Reproduction of their authority necessitated, as special envoy Domingo F. Parra was quick to point out, continued vigilance over known and suspected Caceristas as well as quick action to return "usurped lands."[24]

In a nutshell, then, Pierolista policy in the Mantaro Valley combined the repression of known Caceristas in Jauja and on the river's southwestern bank with the rebuilding of an alliance with Huancayo's landowning class. Among the earliest signs of the renewed alliance was the formation, in May 1895, of a Junta de Notables for the province of Huancayo, composed of many of the most well known local hacendados and charged with helping define Pierolista policy vis-à-vis the peasant communities. By June of that same year, moreover, the hacendado Jacinto Cevallos was touring the department of Junín in a semiofficial capacity. He reported to Piérola in a personal letter that his main goal was to mend the divisions created by the recent war. Writing from Tarma, he explained that he would continue his tour at the end of the week to the provinces of Jauja and Huancayo,

> where I shall implant the reforms needed by these important Provinces, and especially in the latter [Huancayo], deserving in so many ways of national gratitude for the contingent of blood that it so generously offered in the last struggle over which you so heroically presided.[25]

The companion piece to this Huancayo-centered policy was the reorganization of local institutions throughout the area to purge real and suspected Caceristas. In May 1896 Domingo F. Parra traveled through the highlands on a special mission to collect Bolivian currency by trading it for Peruvian. He also carried out a general review of political authorities throughout the Mantaro and suggested the revamping of local and provincial political offices to reflect the firm and allegedly disinterested purposes of the new government. In Jauja such revamping included the purging of all officeholders connected to Dianderas, even when it meant removing Parra's own relative and friend from the office of subprefect. "As a general rule," Parra wrote, "people from one locality should not take on the office of subprefect [there]." Yet that general rule did not apply to Huancayo, where the Pierolista appointee Domingo F. Argote made it his personal mission to rail against the Caceristas in his province and, according to the prefect of the department, was

> a person who has large debts here, which clearly limits his independence. In addition, I have been informed that when he was in Huancayo he gave arms belonging to the state to specific people, among them to Mr. Jacinto Zevallos [*sic*], whom I know presently possesses quite a few of them.[26]

The Pierolista alliance with the anti-Cáceres landowners was also reflected in the state's 1896 and 1897 campaigns against the centers of ongoing peasant mobilization in Comas and Huanta. By definition, these campaigns were meant to bring recalcitrant peasant guerrillas under control rather than to negotiate with them or improve conditions in the communities. Whatever the official discourses associated with these efforts, therefore, they directly contradicted Piérola's progressive image as the "protector of the Indian race."[27]

In August and September 1896 the situation around Comas once again became a priority for the government. After expeditions to Llacsapirca and Patalá, haciendas in the general Comas region recently subject to invasion and cattle rustling, Subprefect Domingo Argote wrote that the breakdown of state authority and the return to private violence in the area had made it "normal and necessary for landowners to travel armed with a shotgun attached to their saddles." He concluded with a combined threat and call to action.

> Judging from the behavior of the Indians I saw and from the constant trading they do of a steer for a rifle or shotgun and of a sheep for four or five bullets, with merchants of little conscience, . . . the movement started years ago on the hacienda Punto, spread today to Llacsapirca and Patalá, if not repressed radically, undoubtedly will become more extensive and take on truly alarming proportions.[28]

Prefect Ramón Valle Riestra arrived in Huancayo in September 1896 to sort out the situation. He called a meeting of Huancayo's Junta de Notables to advise him on the best course of action. On 29 September the group of eighteen principal citizens—which included numerous landowners, most notably Jacinto Cevallos himself—made clear that the only permanent solution to the situation would be military. Junta members suggested that, if the central government sent arms and ammunition, they could easily gather a hundred extra men in the city and surrounding villages. Finally, they recommended an attempt at a peaceful solution while the expedition was being organized.[29]

By early October it had become clear that the central government did not have resources to commit to an armed expedition in the area. In response to a petition presented by Cevallos, the Ministry of the Interior ordered the prefect to enforce the 1889 decree that had returned the haciendas Punto and Callanca to their original owner.[30] Under such circumstances an attempted peaceful solution seemed the only alternative, and Prefect Valle Riestra's subsequent policy of negotiation with Comas actually proved quite creative. He wrote to Comas's parish priest, urging him to convince a group of notables from the community to come to Jauja for a conference. At the same time he began separate processes of negotiation with the villages of Andamarca and Comas, hoping to take advantage of any divisions—in his own words, "*rencillas*"—between them. Both strategies worked.

In Comas the parish priest Luis A. González was impressed with the importance of his role as mediator. Although initially unable to convince the villagers to travel to Jauja, he did manage to orchestrate an acta explaining to Valle Riestra that the Comasinos were afraid to travel because of their outstanding problems with Cevallos. They would be very willing to receive the prefect in their village, however; and they hoped that somehow "the Mercy of the Almighty will allow Your Excellency the Prefect to visit these distant places, so that you may feel and note for yourself the many things this forgotten District needs." The acta was accompanied by a separate letter, signed by González and his closest allies Venancio Valdez and José Benito Gil, assuring the prefect that the acta had been signed in public and read to the community as a whole.[31]

A few days later, on 2 November, González wrote to Valle Riestra announcing that he had convinced around a dozen village notables from Comas to make the trip to Jauja. "I await your indication to be ready for the sixteenth or eighteenth [of November]," he wrote. "It pleases me to have convinced these community Indians [*comunales*] with my arguments, I do not want the date they have indicated to pass and afterwards they might change their minds, for in the end they are uneducated Indians."[32] But the priest's allies in the village did not change their minds. They met with Valle Riestra in Jauja on 21 November, and the prefect deemed the long conference highly satisfactory. "I found in these people a natural intelligence," he wrote to the minister of the interior, "and they showed themselves to be docile and accepting of my suggestions." For a total of two hundred soles—distributed fairly evenly between funding a primary school, reorganizing the municipality, and giving new life to public works construction—the village notables signed an acta recognizing the legitimacy of the Pierolista government and specifically denouncing all forms of violent rebellion.[33]

A number of subtexts help explain the apparent ease of these negotiations. The first has to do with internal divisions in Comas village. As had been the case in the 1880s, the Comasinos remained divided over how best to relate to the central government. The coalition that signed the 1896 actas was headed by José Benito Gil and Esteban Paytampoma, both of whom had denounced the Osambela faction in 1888. Baltazar Chávez, Santiago Carrera, and Venancio Martínez—all of whom had struggled for compromise twelve years before—also signed alongside some villagers whose names had not appeared previously on any local political document. Of the three compromise leaders, however, only Carrera and Martínez demonstrated a willingness to go the whole distance, in reality and metaphorically, to the Jauja conference. Chávez limited himself to signing the first document in Comas. And the internal dynamics of this coalition were also represented in the personnel chosen for the new municipal council. With the exception of Carrera and Martínez, the rest were people with no direct political participation in the earlier struggles.[34]

A second subtext to the negotiations in Jauja involved differences among the various villages in the Comas area. Valle Riestra had been aware of these tensions from the beginning of the negotiation process in October 1896 and had proceeded separately in the cases of Andamarca and Comas. The former, an anexo of Comas district, had differences with its district capital that were quite similar to those in other parts of the region. When notables from Andamarca signed their own acta on 17 November, therefore, declaring that they had never participated with the Comasinos in their "nefarious acts," the implicit condition for loyalty to the government was the establishment of a separate district. And although we may never know for sure, the signing of Comas's own acta only four days later may also have been connected, at least in part, to issues of district rivalry.[35]

We find a clue to the final subtext within the very acta the Comas notables signed in Jauja. Along with the usual assurances about respecting constituted authority, the document stated, "We protest against all subversive actions that tend to disrupt public order, as well as against the movement carried out in Huanta last month." The movement in Huanta, ostensibly against a new tax imposed on the purchase of salt, had a strong political undercurrent involving Cacerista and Pierolista factions. The main participants in it, as well as the most direct targets of the repression that followed, were the peasant guerrillas from the Huanta villages who had been Caceristas since the War of the Pacific, allies of the Comasinos and fellow combatants. At the very moment when Valle Riestra was in conference with the notables from Comas—a fact that he surely communicated to his guests—a military expedition under the command of Domingo F. Parra was wiping up the last remnants of resistance in Huanta and La Mar provinces.

In his lightning repression of the region, Parra used dramatic methods of repression. He lined up the population from a number of villages and shot every fifth person (a practice known as *el quintado*); bombed hillsides covered with peasant guerrillas; systematically destroyed village economies and resources; and armed rival ethnic groups as *contraguerrillas*. In his own discourse on the campaign, Parra rendered himself as the hero bringing civilization, for the first time, to a region whose ferocious inhabitants were "comparable to the cannibals of the heart of Africa." But his tactics sent another message to the Comasinos: if resisted, the agents of the Pierolista state would think nothing of planting the flag of progress in ground made soft by the blood of its peasant victims. As played out in Huanta and La Mar, Parra's violent campaign was the necessary counterpoint to Valle Riestra's benign negotiations.[36]

Even in counterpoint with the Huanta campaign, the central sierra peace negotiations confronted a major snag: the peasants expected the government to keep its promises. From the standpoint of the Andamarca villagers, one of the promises involved independent district status. When this status was not forthcoming by 1898, and the Pierolista state began surveying jungle lands for a colonization scheme in nearby Pampa Hermosa and financing the surveyor through a tax levied on peasant properties, some Andamarquinos had had enough. On 3 July, after a state decree on the colonization project was posted in the town, twenty citizens approached the communal building with sticks and stones. They made it known, publicly and emphatically, that they refused to obey the law. In his report to the prefect six days later, Subprefect Dulanto complained that he had tried repeatedly to convince the people that "the decree referred to causes no damage to their interests, but to the contrary tends to improve them." Yet, given the "semisavage state of these villages," it had become clear that only the use of armed force would convince them. Couching his statement in the language of state expansion and effective state authority, the subprefect therefore requested military aid to bring the region into submission.[37]

By September of that year the controversy over colonization had brought to light additional issues concerning commercial penetration and boundaries between the community and the neighboring hacienda Coyllorbamba. On 7 August a second uprising took place in Andamarca. The target of this demonstration was the recently established *comisaría*, or local sheriff's office. The local *comisario*, a merchant with a store in the village square and strong patron-client relations with Ricardo Ribbeck, owner of Coyllorbamba, managed to escape to the hacienda and left his property to be sacked by the crowd. Matters became muddy in the following weeks, when the comisario led a military expedition into Andamarca and supplemented the government's forces with men levied by Coyllorbamba's landowner.[38] In a separate petition a group of Andamarquinos headed by the same people who had led the attack on the comisaría complained of the expedition's abuses, which included several murders, and declared that the root cause of the conflict was land. For quite a long time, they explained, Ribbeck had involved them in a court battle over the boundary between Andamarca and Coyllorbamba, and it had become clear "that he intends to usurp our pasturelands along the boundary, specifying that he wishes to take away a third [of the territory] of our village, even though we have our titles up to date."

Local government officials, however, refused to side with the villagers, for they considered the community a threat to public order and state authority. The petitioners "do not deserve our trust," wrote the jungle surveyor Victor Enzián, "because of their proven hostility toward all forms of existing authority and toward the present regime." Subprefect Dulanto agreed. By 1899–1900, in fact, the Pierolista state had turned from a regional policy of negotiation or reconciliation to one of security and order. Especially in 1902, with Jacinto Cevallos as subprefect of the province of Huancayo, Huanta finally came home to roost in the central highlands.[39]

Between May and July 1902, Cevallos carried out a campaign of violent military repression in the Comas area. In a letter he sent the Comasinos at the end of May, he announced his intent to take back the haciendas Punto and Callanca and thus put into effect the long-standing order from the national government. Finally able to organize the kind of expedition recommended by Huancayo's hacendados since the 1880s, he reached the area in the second half of June, peacefully occupying his hacienda Punto on 22 June. He set up his general headquarters on the hacienda and pursued a two-pronged strategy designed to end, once and for all, any possibility of a renewed movement or rebellion in the region.

One part of his strategy was the severe physical repression of the peasants resident on Punto and Callanca. He beat all prisoners and kept them tied hand and foot. He systematically burned all peasant crops and houses on the estates and removed all peasant livestock from hacienda property. Of course, it is not surprising that Cevallos chose hacienda residents as his most direct target: they had gained the most from the occupation of the haciendas and represented the most direct challenge to hacendado authority. But Cevallos did not stop there. The other part of his strategy involved the villages surrounding his properties and was designed permanently to break the alliance of pueblos that had helped maintain the occupation for so long.[40]

Since the first wave of negotiation and repression in the late 1880s, factions in the villages had struggled for control of the political spaces where communal hegemony was produced and reproduced. Cevallos knew well that the problem had never been the lack of allies within the communities. From the start he and his supporters had found collaborators. The problem was that, over and over again, Cevallos's collaborators had lost prestige and influence in the communal discussions where policy was decided and hegemonic village alliances constructed.

The lesson learned from these earlier experiences was that success came through mixing violent repression and the careful reconstruction of village politics. On the repressive side, Cevallos carried out a psychological and physical war of attrition along the frontiers between the communities and the haciendas, burning houses and crops on both sides of the boundary and taking livestock that belonged to both community and hacienda families. This frontier war had its desired effect not only on those who inhabited the edges of the communities but also on the core population of each village. Gunfire kept people awake at night and, in the words of a petition from Cochas, frightened "the elderly, pregnant women, and children." And on the side of political reconstruction, Cevallos attempted to use negotiation as a way of dividing village notables among themselves, delegitimizing or imprisoning those who would not go along with his wishes.[41]

From the moment Cevallos arrived on Punto, he began inviting the villagers to the hacienda for a conference. His letters mixed promises of leniency with veiled and not so veiled threats of violent reprisal. "What will happen in the future depends on your course of action," he wrote to the gobernador of Comas in his first letter,

> for if you give me the support I am demanding, my conflicts with all the people of that District will have ended, forgetting completely all the damage you have done me, in addition to the immense number of cattle you have robbed from me; if you do not [cooperate] I will proceed differently, and do not doubt that the day will come when I will occupy that town with enough force.[42]

In an exchange of letters with the inhabitants of Canchapalca, Cevallos learned that they were not open to his suggestions. They were the same "thieves and bandits" they had always been, he responded angrily. "And you still have the audacity to call me to the *paraje* [locality] of Pariahuachoco," he continued,

> after having done everything you could on two occasions to assassinate me [there]; remember what you did with Captain Tapia, thinking he was me, when you had called a conference there—remember the ambush you gave me the same day when I was alone at the camp, and I saved myself through my courage, even when one of your bullets grazed my hat, taking down more than thirty of you . . . ,[and you] killed two poor soldiers who accompanied me and whose blood weighs on you and will weigh until your last generation, cursed as you are by God and society in general.[43]

These remarks show how Cevallos's previous experience in the region affected his ability to negotiate. On one side, the shared experiences of enmity and repression, of spilled blood in particular places on particular days, over a period of twenty years, lent a painful intimacy to the struggle between this landowner and the peasants of the area. References to events, surroundings, or individuals—allusions that meant nothing to someone else—resonated deeply for both sides, evoking fear and hatred, making a threat all the more effective because of the multiple references it contained. On the other side, the very emotional depths of the relationship made Cevallos less effective as a negotiator. He did recover from the exchange with Canchapalca, at least sufficiently to send a more official letter four days later that prompted an invitation from Comas to Canchapalca to hammer out a common strategy of negotiation. But in the end the prefect of the department was forced to travel to the area to straighten things out, clean up after Cevallos's abuses, and finalize the formal conciliation with the different villages involved in the confrontation.[44]

Intimate, dirty, bloody threats and repression, when combined with Cevallos's deep knowledge of local factions and problems, were the perfect Huanta-like complement to Prefect Bruno E. Bueno's magnanimous yet distant authority. The campaign worked, and this time for good. What made this success possible, what was accomplished this time that had not been achieved in earlier campaigns, was the final breakdown of the internal hegemonic process generated by the national resistance. Divisions that were there before, from the time of the failed collaboration with Osambela, resurfaced in a new form and finally fractured beyond repair. José Benito Gil and Fabriciano Santa Cruz—the former was a leader of the anti-Osambela group in 1888, and both were involved in the 1896 negotiations sponsored by Father González—answered Cevallos's call from Punto fairly early on, staying on the hacienda throughout the campaign and serving as advisers of sorts. They were joined by Juan Aparicio, the gobernador of Comas district who first attempted to work out a common strategy of negotiation with Canchapalca. From the perspective of the municipal alcalde Baltazar Chávez, leader of the other faction since early on and a former guerrilla leader, it was the treacherous work of these men, "false accusers, shameful ones who have led the way," that finally resulted in his being criminally charged as a leader of the montoneras of Cochas and Canchapalca.[45]

By late July, Prefect Bueno had embarked on his tour of conciliation through the communities. He wrote to the officials of Canchapalca that he was touring

> with the goal of visiting you and learning of your principal necessities and seeing what it will be possible for me to do for the good of your inhabitants to whom I wish to give all sorts of guarantees so that you may dedicate yourself with the greatest tranquility to your work, which constitutes the progress of honest peoples.[46]

As Bueno traveled, people presented him with petitions and requests. These ran the gamut from resolving a family quarrel over inheritance to adjudicating damages to individuals hurt during Cevallos's campaign. As this new morality play about the constitution of state authority was reaching its final act, José Benito Gil was collaborating offstage in the orchestration of the final scene. Santiago Motto, a prominent merchant from Jauja, wrote a letter on 22 July to Pablo Apolinario in Comas. Attaching to it three documents Apolinario had requested, plus two letters sent by Gil, Motto instructed Apolinario on what to do when the prefect arrived in the village.

> When the [military] detachment reaches Comas with the prefect, you will go to the village, and present to the prefect all the papers I am sending you, and explain to him all the things that have happened with those bandits and murderers. . . .
>
> Now is the time for all of you, en masse, to present yourselves to the prefect in Comas and convince him that your lives are in constant danger with all the bandits, and you will present a list of who they are; and that all of them are armed with weapons belonging to the State.
>
> Meet with Sr. Gil so that he can talk for all and explain the just reasons why the authorities should solve this situation, bringing an end to all the evil that has been committed and will continue to be committed if a [military] detachment is not left in Comas.[47]

By 1902, then, the increasingly robust alliance between the Pierolista state and the Huancayo landowners had managed, through a combination of terror and benevolence, finally to break the peasant alliance in the Comas region from the inside. In so doing, they added the finishing touches to an emerging "modern" state deeply rutted by the zigzag path carved between progressive attempts at relative autonomy and ongoing support for the intimate, localized violence of landowner repression. Rather than taking seriously the concerns and demands of peasant movements, state authorities reestablished domination by fragmenting and isolating political constituencies and depriving them of their ability to fight back. They followed the principle of "divide and rule" rather than incorporation; of neocolonial reunification rather than national consolidation.

Thus, the peasant guerrillas in the central region, from Comas to Huanta, Chongos Alto to Canchapalca, were forced back into reconstructed *patrias chicas* that were not of their own making. Some community members helped facilitate the retreat into a style of politics based on abusive and hierarchical patron-client relations—those supposed "triangles without a base." The discourses about savagery and primitiveness that accompanied and legitimated hierarchy were in fact generated by an alliance between ambitious local notables and a supposedly "national" state unable effectively to incorporate the demands and visions of indigenous peasant guerrillas.[48] This same state, in its Pierolista form, climbed into the twentieth century on the backs of a peasantry repressed with blood and fire. As it came, it elaborated the myth of its own benevolent *indigenismo*, a myth parallel to that of an isolated and passive peasantry with no interest in the outside world.

The Making of the State of Morelos, 1869–1876

In contrast to what happened in the Sierra de Puebla between 1867 and 1872, in Morelos it was the large hacendados, the sugar planters, who appropriated the populist discourse of free elections in the postwar period. In 1873 they filed a court case against the state's first governor, the former guerrilla leader Francisco Leyva, protesting his concentration of power, manipulation of the state legislature, and generally authoritarian behavior. The case led to a breakdown in the state's governing capacity at the local level and threatened to become a national crisis as well.

As had been the case in Puebla in 1868, the national government—and especially the president—supported the embattled governor. Yet the supreme court, which ultimately heard the case on appeal from the state government, was divided among Liberal factions. It returned a mixed decision that seemed to challenge the right of states to make their own policy. In the end, therefore, it was more difficult in Morelos than it had been in Puebla to identify the "heroic-popular" position. While the planters seemingly stood for free elections, it was Leyva and his followers who vindicated the autonomy of state governments in the face of federal interference.[49]

A further wrinkle in the Morelos case was the position of the peasantry. During the previous twenty years of struggle, communities had debated and tried out diverse options for political action and alliance. Gone was an easy belief in Liberal promises, broken time and again between 1850 and 1867. Gone also was any hope that the alternative would be better. What remained was a commitment to the reproduction of village politics and regional coalitions, which could then be used to pressure national factions. This much was shared by most peasant villages in the Morelos area, although the possible allies at the national level could be quite distinct in different subregions and at different moments.

Historical differences between eastern and western Morelos also continued to define political options. In the west, specifically the Cuernavaca area, the long-standing alliance with forces from the state of Guerrero—experienced through Francisco Leyva's collaboration with Juan Alvarez—made more difficult the connection to anti-Leyva forces. When the Liberal general Vicente Jiménez launched a rebellion against the domination of the Alvarez clan, for example, and supported the Díaz faction in ongoing Liberal struggles, his success in mobilizing the guerrilla strongholds in western Morelos was sporadic and problematic at best. In eastern Morelos, by contrast, most notably around Jonacatepec and Cuautla, the Díaz faction had support from the very beginning. The spottier record of earlier Liberal guerrillas, when combined with Leyva's general tendency to gravitate toward Cuernavaca, prepared the ground for the opposition. In Jonacatepec, Díaz won the presidential election in 1867, which he failed to do even in the more hotly contested districts of Puebla. Local popular leaders, such as Rosario Aragón, formed enduring connections to Díaz. As in the Puebla highlands, villages in the eastern half of Morelos articulated a discourse that connected the Porfirian faction to land and social justice through the mediation of trusted local notables.[50]

An important part of the story in Morelos was Leyva's transformation from counterhegemonic leader of a guerrilla movement to key organizer of the Juarista faction. The man who suffered house arrest in Veracruz in 1860 for allegedly murdering Spanish citizens, the officer denied permission to form a new guerrilla force in Cuernavaca in 1861—this was not the same man who emerged nine years later as a crucial Juarista politician in Morelos. Part of his transformation was caused by the conflicts inside the Liberal party immediately before and after the defeat of the empire. As the dust cleared in the Morelos area, Benito Juárez recognized Leyva as the most loyal and dependable of all the Liberals interested in claiming that territory as their bailiwick. But part of the transition was also of Leyva's own making, probably the result of lessons he learned in 1860–1861.[51]

These lessons stood Leyva in good stead. He was appointed governor and military commander of the third district of the state of Mexico in 1867 and moved quickly to pacify and reorganize the area. He demobilized the national guards and oversaw the 1867 election for president. He kept in personal touch with Juárez throughout, and in 1867 he bemoaned the results from Jonacatepec that had besmirched an otherwise perfectly unanimous outcome in favor of his ally.[52]

The election also raised a thorny personal problem for Leyva. He was elected federal deputy from Morelos district while still governor of the third military district as a whole. In several consultations with Juárez over the month of November, he asked what to do. Should he remain governor, or should he travel to Mexico City to sit in congress? Such a degree of deference must have been gratifying to Juárez, who wrote back that Leyva should choose the congress, since at least "for now" it was the elective office. This was a clear reference to the plans already being bandied about for the creation of Morelos state and a suggestion that Leyva might run for the elective office of governor in that soon-to-be-created entity.[53]

Leyva ran for governor in 1869 against Porfirio Díaz, who had been invited to run by a coalition of citizens from the southeastern districts and members of the planter class. Although Leyva had changed in the decade between the Liberal Revolution and the Restored Republic, local planters still remembered him as the leader of the guerrilla band that had terrorized and taxed their holdings. Leyva, too, remembered the planters as the group of gachupines who had forced him out of favor with his own government and political party. His victory, contentious because of claims of electoral fraud, served to seal his enmity with Díaz, his former comrade in arms, as well as to deepen the rift with the local landowning class.[54]

Between July 1869, when Leyva became the first governor of Morelos state, and 1876, when the successful rebellion of Tuxtepec tumbled him from power, he was never able to establish a stable governing coalition, primarily because he was ineffective at courting the support of either major social force in the region: the peasant villages or the planters. During the previous fifteen years, as we have seen, the peasants had been strong supporters of the Liberal cause. Almost from the very beginning, however, the strength of popular Liberalism in regional political culture had also galvanized the landowners, who had formed a strong Conservative coalition.

The prosperity and strategic location of the Morelos sugar industry, the importance of the taxes levied on the marketing of Morelos sugar in Mexico City, and the diplomatic connections of the region's numerous Spanish hacendados had given the planter community significant leverage with all governments in power. Throughout the 1850s and early 1860s they had brought Liberal governments to their knees on local political issues. When Leyva forsook his peasant allies in 1867 and 1869, therefore, he was in good company: Comonfort, Alvarez, and Juárez had all done it first. But what Leyva was unable to stomach was the corollary of that decision. If he wanted to build stability in Morelos, he also needed to build an enthusiastic alliance with the planters themselves.[55]

Unable to connect effectively to either of the major forces in regional political culture, Leyva attempted to base his rule on the support of the urban intelligentsia and the federal government. The result was that he lurched from crisis to crisis. First, a regionalist confrontation over the location of the state capital permanently removed most of eastern Morelos state from Leyva's orbit and coalesced popular forces in Cuautla and Jonacatepec around Rosario Aragón, Miguel Negrete, and Porfirio Díaz. Then the sugar planters refused to pay an extraordinary tax that Leyva hoped would help balance the state budget. In 1871 these conflicts led to the arrest of two deputies in the state legislature and to the temporary establishment of two competing congresses, one Leyvista and one anti-Leyva.[56]

In part, the atmosphere of permanent crisis reflected what was going on nationwide, for Juárez, too, was never able to establish an effective governing coalition. The effervescence in eastern Morelos was also connected to uprisings in Puebla state, where neighboring districts rebelled in 1869, 1871–1872, and 1876. But in the final analysis, villagers and landowners in Morelos were in confrontation with each other over who would establish a hegemonic connection to the emerging national state. When Leyva did not facilitate that connection for the villages, they sought out Díaz. And since Leyva also refused to support the planters, they decided to go over his head by means of a *juicio de amparo.*[57]

In December 1873 a group of planters, among whom Leyva's old enemy Pío Bermejillo figured prominently, filed suit in federal district court. They sought an *amparo,* or judicial support, for their claim that an extraordinary tax being levied on their properties was illegal. They based their claim on a series of legal arguments drawn from the Morelos state constitution. First, they argued that Leyva was not the legal governor of Morelos because the state constitution had originally prohibited reelection and had been amended illegally to allow for his election to a second term. Thus, Leyva had no authority to promulgate the new tax passed by the state legislature. In addition, the planters claimed that the tax itself was illegal because it had been passed without a quorum in the legislature. One of the deputies present at the time of the vote, a Leyvista protégé named Vicente Llamas, had been the jefe político of Jonacatepec at the moment when he was elected to congress from the same district. Since this dual officeholding was prohibited by electoral law, Llamas was not a duly elected deputy, and without him a quorum had not existed. After hearing the different arguments, the federal district judge found in favor of the plaintiffs. Leyva then appealed the decision to the supreme court.[58]

Leyva's appeal reached a court deeply divided by issues of political procedure and propriety. As chief justice, José María Iglesias was bent on protecting the people from the abuses of power inherent in political institutions. He insisted that the court could appropriately hear problems related to elections without violating states' rights. Since he would be the presidential candidate of one of the three main Liberal factions in 1876, Iglesias certainly had good personal reasons for standing up against the perceived institutionalization of political machines. But in the specific case of Morelos, Iglesias's leadership resulted in a split decision.

While allowing that the process of state elections was a matter for the state legislature, the court ruled that Leyva's authority was unconstitutional because of the way the state constitution had been amended. Yet the decision, as reached, was difficult to apply. Leyva's unconstitutionality had been decided only for the plaintiffs and only on the specific issue involved in the case. If other individuals had a complaint, or if the same people had further complaints, they would have to present each one separately for judicial review.[59]

While the supreme court's decision evoked national debate over the issues of state's rights and the autonomy of the electoral process, in Morelos it fueled spreading chaos. Suits against Leyva multiplied. Rebellion spread in the eastern part of the state to the extent that the state legislature decided to move the capital to Cuautla as a preventive measure. With Leyva on perpetual leave from the governorship, temporary executives succeeded each other with dizzying frequency. The state government had been brought to a standstill.[60]

Two compromises finally stuck to bring the conflict to a partial resolution. The first involved the judicial branch. As of May 1874 the federal district court began to find against new plaintiffs in the bevy of court cases before it. This trend led to a willingness, on the part of state authorities, to find a middle ground with the federal government on the issue of state's rights. In addition, a reshuffling of supreme court membership began returning decisions favorable to the state government as of August. The second compromise, which took slightly longer to work out, involved a rapprochement between the planters and the state executive. In April 1875 the acting governor reached an agreement with the landowners whereby he would provide state support, in the form of a tax rebate, for each arroba of sugar exported to other countries. At a moment when the Ten Years' War in Cuba had made the international market especially attractive, this was a welcome incentive indeed.[61]

On the eve of the Tuxtepec Revolution, it appeared that the sugar planters had finally inherited Morelos. The juicio de amparo had successfully marginalized Leyva, and the hacendados had reached an attractive settlement with his successor. In regional political culture, where peasants and sugar planters had been locked in conflict since the eighteenth century, the landowners had apparently scored an overwhelming victory. But what of the other side? Just because Leyva had chosen to leave his old allies behind, had the villagers simply dropped off the edge of the political map?

From the standpoint of the peasant communities, Leyva's years in the governorship had not been any better than Maximilian's Second Empire. In an attempt to maintain the government's urban constituency, the few available funds in the state budget had gone to public works and improvements in the cities. At a political level, Leyva seemed a great deal readier to lend support to emerging mutual aid societies for artisans and workers than to provide any assistance to the villages. Thus, the villagers experienced the Restored Republic as a dual offensive: by jefes políticos applying the Liberal land laws to their communal holdings; and by hacendados moving in on their land, water, and forests. Rather than seriously considering the implications of popular Liberalism for the organization of property and politics, Leyva did as Maximilian had done: he spoke out of both sides of his mouth. In his rhetoric he insisted on the equality of all citizens; but his practice made clear that some were more equal than others.[62]

Already in 1874 the villagers in Anenecuilco, Emiliano Zapata's birthplace and an important center of Porfirista sentiment, were writing to Díaz to reiterate their support for his movement. "Those of us who are writing," they said,

> members of your local organization and united to defend our rights, are confident in you and are only waiting, as you told us, for your victory for our lands to be returned to us as you have promised. . . . We will not rest until we have won what belongs to us.

In early 1876 the villagers of nearby Ayala concurred:

> We know that the problem is difficult, but you must understand that we have decided to fight to the finish, joined together with you. And we have all agreed that it is better to destroy the riches of the sugar estates (which can later be repaired) than to continue giving up our land until it has all disappeared. . . . One day we will show that we are the only true owners of this land. . . . We do not want to commit any acts of violence against them; we will wait with patience until you give us the signal to begin our struggle.

By midyear, rebellion had spread throughout the east and south of Morelos state into Tetecala district. Almost everywhere village veterans of the resistance against the French headed the mobilizations. Even in Leyva's original stomping grounds around Cuernavaca and Tepoztlán, there was a quiet lack of enthusiasm for the existing government. Unable to mobilize a resistance, Leyva was at the mercy of national trends. In Morelos, Puebla, and elsewhere, these trends were increasingly against the faction in power.[63]

Indeed, when Díaz came to power in 1876, he stood atop a coalition of popular forces in both Puebla and Morelos. In each case the core of his support was regionally specific: the Sierra de Puebla, the eastern and southern districts of Morelos. The political context was, however, extremely different in the two regions.

In Morelos a popular guerrilla leader had become governor. But given his previous experience with Liberal repression, Leyva had chosen not to throw his political capital behind a populist, peasant-oriented policy. As a result, the political coalitions organized around the rural villages and national guards went for Díaz. In Puebla, by contrast, a popular guerrilla leader had been prevented from assuming the governorship by Juarista manipulation. Méndez remained the focus of counterhegemonic energy and kept the support of the political coalitions organized around the villages and old national guards in the sierra.

The continuity from earlier struggles was therefore more complete in the Porfirista movement in Puebla. But the commonality in both cases was that Díaz, as a prestigious war hero of the French Intervention and an alternative to Juarista machine politics, emerged to inherit the counterhegemonic Liberal coalitions formulated in the villages of central Mexico. What remained to be seen, in 1876 and beyond, was what he would do with this inheritance.

The Legacies of Repression: Regional Political Cultures and State Formation in Mexico and Peru

As Peru and Mexico entered the twentieth century, their states had much in common on the surface. In Peru, Nicolás de Piérola and his successor Eduardo López de Romaña presided over governments interested in order, progress, and economic development. They wished to bring their country into the modern era and supervised the beginning of substantial U.S. investment in production and in the construction of new roads and railroads. In Mexico, Porfirio Díaz oversaw similar, if much more dramatic, trends. In both countries as well, states rested on coalitions whose center was composed of entrepreneurial landowning classes in combination with foreign capital. The reproduction of these states and of the coalitions that supported them necessitated, at various points and in various forms, the violent repression of social movements and popular resistance. But overall the veneer was one of prosperity and order, modernization and progress.[64]

What was not so obvious on the surface was that each of these states had been formed and consolidated in a historically different manner. In Mexico, Díaz came to power as a hero of the popular resistance against the French

Intervention and Second Empire, riding the crest of a coalition composed of multiple regional counterhegemonic movements. Each regional movement had a distinct internal dynamic, based on the particular historical process through which its own regional political culture had been constructed and on the region's experience during the French Intervention, Second Empire, and Restored Republic. But the coalition as a whole gave Díaz a mandate to build national politics on the basis of negotiation and incorporation rather than repression and domination.

To some extent, this seemed to be the practice of the earlier Porfiriato, at least in central Mexico. Governors and other political officials in the state governments were initially veterans of previous Liberal struggles who had earned their constituencies' trust. They were elected through universal manhood suffrage in contests that seemed to reflect regional balances of power. They served as mediators between local populist politics and the national government. Even as power was consolidated, then, regional movements and coalitions continued being heard—if not always listened to. Such was the case during the administrations of Juan Nepomuceno Méndez and Juan Crisóstomo Bonilla in Puebla; such was the case with the governorship of Manuel Alarcón in Morelos. But somewhere along the line the balance of the coalition keeping Díaz in power began to change. Its center came to rest less and less with the popular movements or alliances that had brought Díaz to power and shifted increasingly toward an entrepreneurial class based in Mexico City and its associates among foreign investors. Elections became ritualistic farce.[65]

For the popular movements that spearheaded the 1910 Revolution, this shift in the Porfirian balance of forces was an important precipitating factor. In Puebla, when the octogenarian Juan Francisco Lucas refused to answer the call of his compadre Díaz and instead joined the revolution, he did so with a sense of broken promises. In Morelos, when the formerly Porfirian villages of Anenecuilco and Ayala declared for the revolution, they did so after a nakedly fraudulent election stole the state governorship from Francisco Leyva's son Patricio and installed the first direct representative of the planter class. When the landowner Pablo Escandón campaigned in Cuautla in 1909, the crowd that gathered at the train station met him with the same counterhegemonic slogan that had echoed in 1810 and 1855–1861: "Mueran los gachupines!" Throughout the country people demanded effective suffrage and no reelection.[66]

In Peru, by contrast, Nicolás de Piérola took power from a tarnished Cacerismo unable to stabilize a ruling coalition. Cáceres had been unwilling wholly to identify either with his earlier enemies, the collaborationist landowners, or his former allies, the peasant guerrillas. Piérola rebuilt the state on the corpse of the nineteenth-century popular movement through an open alliance with sectors of the hacendado class in different Peruvian regions. The first Pierolista congress also reaffirmed the 1890 constitutional amendment that made literacy a requirement for the right to vote. As the senate commission explained in October 1895, "The man who does not know how to read or write is not, nor can he be, a citizen in modern society."[67]

While loudly proclaiming its autonomy, Piérola thus encrusted the modern state with the mud of localized and intimate forms of landowner violence. The neocolonial forms of regional fragmentation and clientelism reconstructed in this process helped reproduce state power in the short run. Indeed, the overall Pierolista project might best be summed up in another phrase from the senate commission report on the 1890 constitutional amendment: "It is not in the interest of the Nation that many participate in elections, but rather that those who participate do so well." In other words, in Peru at the beginning of the twentieth century, the nation was composed of a few good men. Yet Peru's subsequent political history suggests that such a base, and the political fragmentation and clientelism necessary to reproduce it, has impeded the consolidation of a truly national state.[68]

9 Whose Bones Are They, Anyway, and Who Gets to Decide?

Local Intellectuals, Hegemony, and Counterhegemony in National Politics

I peered through the wrought-iron gate of a house that occupied a corner lot one block from Xochiapulco's municipal building, and for a moment I thought that the dark eyes staring back at me, eyes set in a stern and suspicious face, belonged to General Juan Francisco Lucas. Although it was the same stare that General Lucas always gave the camera when he was photographed, the eyes belonged instead to Donna Rivera Moreno, a retired schoolteacher and recognized local expert on the history of her village. She later explained that the striking resemblance to Lucas was because her family was related, though out of wedlock, to the famous Liberal general. Her ancestors included, on the Rivera side, her grandfather Francisco, a captain during the French Intervention; her father, Martín; and uncles Juan, Manuel, and Jacinto, all officers in the Constitutionalist army during the 1910 Revolution. At first, however, she refused even to let me into her house. What was I doing there, anyway, and why did I want information from her? Only when I recounted the work I had been doing for the previous eight months, tracking Xochiapulco in the national and regional archives, did her hostility begin to lessen. And when I explained to her that I thought Xochiapulco had been the most important village in the region during the resistance against the French, her eyes filled with tears and she flung open her gate. The next thing I knew I was sitting in her formal living room, stiffly posed photographs staring at me from the walls, and she was rummaging through the piles of papers she kept in her closet.[1]

The most important document Donna Rivera kept in her closet was a manuscript she had written on the history of her pueblo. From the beginning of our relationship, we tussled over my access to it. In the end we agreed that I could keep a copy of it only if I showed her a guarantee—in writing—that the university in Puebla would publish it under her name. Once I had produced this guarantee in 1985, she insisted on traveling with me to Zacapoaxtla, on the back of a truck, in order to photocopy it. She would not let the original out of her sight.

Donna Rivera had good reason to be so cautious. Even with the written guarantee, the university in Puebla shelved her manuscript and the introduction I wrote for it. Only in 1991, as part of the quincentenary, did the state government in Puebla find the money to dust off the work and publish it, with my essay tucked among the various compilations that Rivera had done of others' work on her region. The foreword to the edition, written by officials from the Puebla branch of the Dirección General de Culturas Populares, begins, "History is rushing toward the new millennium, and Indian societies have resolved to investigate their past and present their own assessment."[2]

The meandering six-year history of how Donna Rivera's manuscript became a book represents the complex problems faced by local intellectuals as they attempt to engage their more powerful colleagues at the regional, national, and international levels. From the moment I met her, Rivera saw some of these problems quite clearly. She insisted on keeping control of her work at all times and shared information only on her terms. As a foreign intellectual with broader contacts, both in my country of origin and among intellectuals in Rivera's region, I was forced to mobilize those networks to assure her publication before she would grant me access to the local oral history data I desired. So far so good. Yet in the end neither of us could control the vagaries of economics and politics at the state university. The manuscript languished until, in the shadow of the quincentenary, it could be brought forward as the "Indian version" of Mexican history required by the state government and encouraged by President Salinas de Gortari's new indigenista focus.[3]

The distances and silences between me and Donna Rivera have also accumulated over the years. After concerted attempts by both of us to stay in touch—although I received her letters, she never received mine—we went our own ways. Since that parting I have benefited from my privileged academic situation. I have used her manuscript as a central text in my reconstruction of local history, but I have adopted the more omniscient analytical perspective granted to me by my broader access to archival documentation. Under such circumstances it is nearly impossible for me not to transform her work into folklore, even though I frame the discussion as a dialogue between intellectuals. Here, in this passage, she is correct, I say; but over here, my information demonstrates that she is wrong. I exercise power in my position as an intellectual by not allowing her to answer back.

Although in a different sphere and with distinct results, Donna Rivera has also continued to exercise the power her status as a local intellectual gives her. In the published version of her book she begins the text by narrating her 1989 encounter with an Austrian professor in Xochiapulco, four years after she and I had met. There are many parallels between that encounter and our relationship: Professor Ferdinand Anders sees the bones dug up from the central plaza and the cannon taken from the Austro-Belgian forces; he takes photographs; they talk about the historical events of the time. Rivera invites him to visit the trenches I walked in 1985, but he says he does not have time. Rivera concludes her description by stating that the Interventionists "were unable to find any supposed racial inferiority, because to their surprise they found before them an indigenous people resolved to demonstrate their strength and courage to defend what they rightly considered—and today still consider—their ground."[4]

Donna Rivera's position as a local intellectual is reproduced by the repeated presence of people at her gate, asking her to tell them what happened, asking her to articulate and reproduce local memory and history. Whether the questions are asked by Austrian professors, North American historians, researchers from Puebla city, or local citizens, Rivera chooses the form through which she will exercise the power her knowledge gives her. Repeatedly she has chosen to emphasize the agency, autonomy, strength, and valor of her ancestors, and in so doing she has guarded and reproduced the counterhegemonic content of local discourse. But as we shall see, her choices have also affected the political options open to her community at any given time, weaving webs of counterhegemony and complicity that are often difficult to unravel.

In this chapter I attempt a partial process of unraveling and try hard not to hide the conflicts over meaning and power embedded in my attempt. I begin with a new look at the fate of Xochiapulco's bones, tracking them through the period of consolidation of the postrevolutionary Mexican state in the 1930s and pondering, in critical conversations with Donna Rivera's work, the impact of a successful hegemonic project on local /memory and on the local intellectuals who mold it. Next I consider the contradictory role of intellectuals, both as mediators and enforcers, by examining local examples of the articulation and transformation of discourse in Morelos and Puebla. I then analyze ritual and oral history, not as seamless representations of popular culture, but as arenas of argumentation where local intellectuals play a critical role. Here the examples come from Puebla and Peru's central highlands. Finally I examine the failure of a hegemonic "official story" in Peru's central highlands and show how distinct political trajectories in Mexico and Peru have set different limits within which local intellectuals must operate.

Whose Bones Did They Become?
The Triumph of An Official Story

I first began the search for the identity of the bones dug up in Xochiapulco's plaza in dialogue with Donna Rivera and her work. The official explanation given on the cabinet where they were exhibited, and echoed by the stories told by the inhabitants with whom I talked in 1985, was confirmed by the oral tradition Rivera recorded in one section of her book. The bones belonged to Austrian and French soldiers ambushed in the plaza one night during the Second Empire. Yet in another section she copied the manuscript of the schoolteacher Manuel Pozos, who in 1904 had gathered the oral memories of the era's survivors. Here a different story suggested itself: Pozos told the same story of ambush, but he did not set it during the imperialist period; rather, he described an encounter with a battalion of the federal army in December 1869.[5]

As reproduced by Donna Rivera, Pozos's manuscript takes the form of a recognizable origins myth. Divided into twenty-eight points or numbered paragraphs, it begins with the origins of Xochiapulco in the Liberal Revolution of 1855 and ends with the consolidation of the Porfiriato. If one judges the importance of different events by the space they are granted in the narrative, the Liberal Revolution and ensuing civil war were the most important, occupying over half (seventeen points) of the entire narrative. It is here that the legitimacy of Xochiapulco is defined. The indigenous inhabitants of the region were there long before the Spanish Conquest, and only after independence from Spain did an hacienda claim the land. The dispute with the hacendados led to the foundational alliance with Juan Alvarez, giving Xochiapulco its essential identity as mediator village with the area's indigenous communities, toward whom "the sons of Xochiapulco would be the apostles whose gospel was the Reform Laws." The Intervention and empire occupy less space in the narrative, both quantitatively and qualitatively, serving only to reemphasize the bravery of Xochiapulco's soldiers in defending the Liberal cause. The narrative ends with the conflicts and debates within Liberalism that emerged during the Restored Republic. Analytically, these matters occupy a position equivalent to the Liberal Revolution. They provide the second conceptual bookend that closes the story of the village's Liberal "coming of age" through a narration of the community's resistance to Benito

Juárez's attempts to circumvent the constitution and its support for the rebellions of La Noria and Tuxtepec.[6]

For Pozos and the survivors he interviewed in the early 1900s, the story to be told about the previous fifty years revolved around the triumph of Liberalism and Xochiapulco's role in that victory. It was for this reason that the most important and formative periods were the Revolution of 1855, the subsequent civil war, and the decade before the triumph of Díaz. These were the two most important periods in which Liberalism was defined: the first in conflict against Conservatism; the second in interior conflict among Liberal factions. Xochiapulco's legitimacy as a pueblo, and by implication the legitimacy of Xochiapulquenses as citizens, came from their participation in these two periods as "apostles of the Reform Laws": that is, as individuals responsible for the diffusion and protection of Liberal principles and the constitution of 1857. In such a context the episode of the Intervention and Second Empire, while a dramatic passage in the overall drama, takes on the role of a confirming rather than foundational moment. It reconfirmed the commitment and bravery of the local population, but it did not challenge or reaffirm any basic principle.

In contrast to Pozos's narrative, which occupies a small section of Donna Rivera's book, Rivera's own purpose is to highlight the French Intervention and Second Empire and the Revolution of 1910 as the foundational moments of her village's story. She wishes to revindicate Xochiapulco's central role in the resistance against the French, contrasting it to that of the town of Zacapoaxtla. Although the capital of the district to which Xochiapulco belonged, Zacapoaxtla was a politically Conservative village that allied with the Interventionist and imperialist forces. The bountiful references to the Indians from the Sierra de Puebla who resisted the French as "Zacapoaxtlas," she argues, are thus historically inexact and incorrect. Xochiapulquenses made up the bulk of the sierra forces, burned their own village before allowing it to fall into Austrian hands, and in 1910 buttressed their politically progressive role in the region by making up the bulk of the area's Constitutionalist forces.[7]

On one level, both versions of Xochiapulco's story have a common goal. Based on the compilation of local history and oral memory, they aim to revindicate the village's central role in Mexican history. The schoolteachers Manuel Pozos and Donna Rivera fulfill their obligation as village intellectuals by mediating or articulating local perceptions and political culture to the larger metanarratives of the Mexican nation: the triumph of Liberalism in the nineteenth century, and the 1910 Revolution. But beyond this commonality, there are key differences in emphasis and argument. The context of these differences is the political process of the 1910 Revolution. Most important, it was the consolidation of a postrevolutionary state and political culture in the 1930s, under President Lázaro Cárdenas, that conditioned the modification of the principal moments in Xochiapulco's local history and transformed the bones in the plaza from Mexican to Austrian.

After the violent phase of the 1910 Revolution (1910–1920), during which the sierra's Liberal villages participated enthusiastically on the side of the Constitutionalists, the 1920s and 1930s were a period of political consolidation that attempted to articulate earlier popular struggles to the emerging legacy of 1910. Particularly in the state of Puebla, the battle of the Fifth of May was a central icon in this emerging revolutionary pantheon. More so than in the earlier period of Liberal consolidation under Díaz, the ritual elaborated around the Fifth of May attempted to tie the highlands to a hegemonic political culture at the state and national levels. The role of the Sixth Battalion of the national guard was reconstituted as myth, with the brave Indians of the sierra, remembered as "Zacapoaxtlas," standing at the very center.[8] Here the identification and iconization of the event's survivors became very important.

The first recorded attempt to identify and iconize the survivors of the Fifth of May occurred in May 1924, when Puebla schoolteacher José Gálvez—later secretary of education during the governorship of Maximino Avila Camacho (1937–1941)—traveled to Xochiapulco. In the village's public garden he sat six survivors, whose ages ranged from eighty-six to ninety-nine, in a row and took their picture. As reproduced in a centennial issue of the city newspaper *El Sol de Puebla* on 5 May 1962, the photograph recorded the shy yet baleful stares on their faces, as well as their distinct, seemingly traditional garb. Several of the men sat holding walking sticks. Luis Castro, the author of this centennial article, explained in the caption that the picture had been given to him in 1959 by the engineer Sergio Bonilla, a descendant of Juan Crisóstomo Bonilla.[9]

By 1933, when at the beginning of the Cárdenas years the state government initiated its official participation in the mythification and national integration of the Fifth of May, only one of the six old men was still alive. Enrique Fügueman Adalid, the state secretary of police, was commissioned by the governor, General José Mijares Palencia, to travel to Xochiapulco and bring the survivor down to Puebla city. Fügueman fulfilled his commission, putting the old man in a room of the Embajadores hotel. According to Castro, who interviewed him there, the survivor was don Antonio Carbajal. Ninety-six years old in 1924, he would have been 105 in 1933. Castro described his encounter with Carbajal in the following terms:

"Sir," he [Carbajal] said with trembling voice, "in 1862 they took us by force, and we fought because we are patriots, and now when I'm about to die they bring me by force, too; they say they are going to stand me up like a strange animal in a car, but I can't stand it anymore, I want them to send me home." In effect, they were unable to take him out [to the parade], but sent him home instead.[10]

At least according to Castro, Carbajal remembered being taken by force to fight in the 1862 battle. It is hard to know, from the information available to us, what the use of force might have signified in 1862; certainly not all soldiers in the Sixth Battalion were equally dedicated to the cause. Moreover, Rivera and other local intellectuals, interested as they have been in vindicating the courage and patriotism of the Sixth Battalion, have not even entertained the possibility that some of its soldiers might have been pressed into service. What we do know, however, is that by the late 1930s the institutionalization of the Fifth of May parade in Puebla city involved a relatively high degree of discursive compulsion. While it created spaces in which previous local history could be remembered, it also set the discursive boundaries within which such remembering could take place. For local intellectuals and mediators, the alternatives were clear: either participate on the terms being defined by the Cardenista consolidation, or be marginalized from the discourse altogether.

In March 1943, during the planning stages of that year's Fifth of May parade, the engineer Rodolfo Ricaño G., secretary of Puebla's Mixed Agrarian Commission, wrote to Martín Rivera, a revolutionary officer and Donna Rivera's father. "Dear and distinguished friend," Ricaño began,

> I am writing to you with the purpose of finding out if it is possible that you organize for us there a group of [Indian] natives with their typical costumes, that is with their sandals [*guaraches*], white pantaloons [*calzón blanco*], and dark overshirt [*cotón*], or however it is they dress, so that they can come to Puebla city this Fifth of May to march in the parade,—for the honorable Governor of the State wishes to give the parade a typical folkloric tone with a group from that region, precisely because it celebrates the anniversary of the defeat of the French, in which elements from those places took an active role.
>
> In case it is possible to organize these groups or if they are already organized, I beg you to let us know, for they will need to learn how to march correctly, and if they have the willingness to do so, we can then give you instructions so that you will be acquainted with the way we will be marching here.[11]

As a representative of the state, Ricaño starts by granting the Xochiapul-quenses their history. He informs them that they indeed did participate actively in the battle of the Fifth of May. There is no modifying clause, no "as you are aware" or "as you know"; the Xochiapulquenses are being told. Because of this participation the governor has seen fit to give a folkloric tone to the parade, and the villagers need to dress in "costume." Ricaño tells Rivera what this costume should be, although whatever it is "they" wear will be all right. In a single paragraph, therefore, Ricaño removes all possible historical memory from the Xochiapulquenses, and once they have been constituted as "people without history," he and the governor, as representatives of the state, grant them a history complete with "typical folkloric" costume.

The reconstruction of local history and culture as "folklore" was, in postrevolutionary Mexico, central to the creation of a "revolutionary" culture. Starting in the 1920s, with the founding of Mexican archaeology and anthropology under Manuel Gamio, the twin projects of the state vis-à-vis indigenous communities were to excavate the great ancient civilizations and to provide remedial education and services to the "degenerate" Indians of the present. Only remedial help could reverse the barbarism and superstition produced by centuries of oppression. Through state support for artisanry and folklore, Indians could be taught about their glorious past. At the same time, that past could be reconstructed better to represent the needs of the present. The great mestizo nation of Mexico could emerge in relation to a reorganized and reconstituted Indian past and to the present Indian as "other."[12]

It is in the second paragraph of Ricaño's letter that this process of historical transplantation reaches its ultimate absurdity in the Puebla case. Armed with the new history and "folkloric" costume granted by the state, the Xochiapulquenses will be allowed to march in the Fifth of May parade. To do so, however, they must learn *how* to march! The state writes the script and the music, and then the state teaches the "natives" how to march. Thus were the "Zacapoaxtlas" created. The ultimate message is clear: only those who march to the right music and the right beat can participate. Such is the nature of the hegemonic impulse. But as we have seen throughout, such an impulse is effective only if it engages in a creative dialogue with, and partially incorporates, the counterhegemonic impulse. Once again, this is where Donna Rivera's book comes in.

By now it is easier to understand why Rivera focuses her attention so intensely on the French Intervention, on vindicating Xochiapulco's participation and on separating the Xochiapulquenses from the "Zacapoaxtlas." She is engaging the official discourse that emerged with the institutionalized revolution, yet changing the cast of characters from an undifferentiated, mystified, and dehistoricized group of "Zacapoaxtlas" to a specific, heroic, and deeply politicized group of Xochiapulquenses. In Rivera's version, those marching in Puebla on the Fifth of May are the descendants of the heroes who fought against the French and even burned their own village—as the inhabitants of Moscow had before the advance of Napoleon—rather than let it fall into Austrian hands.[13]

One of the strengths of Rivera's strategy is that, because she engages the official discourse, her story of Xochiapulco forms a part of it, no matter how contentiously and marginally. The cost of her strategy, however, is that important parts of local history, of local memory, must of necessity fall outside the established boundaries of the hegemonic discourse. Only selected parts of counterhegemony will be incorporated. And the unincorporated parts—such as the fact that the bones in Xochiapulco's plaza are Mexican, not Austrian—are increasingly submerged and forgotten.

In this context, let us imagine what happened in Xochiapulco in the mid-1970s, when the municipality was digging to transform the old central plaza into a basketball court. The crew of diggers uncovered a cache of human bones, a shallow mass grave. Someone probably had the idea of asking Donna Rivera about these remains, consulting the local intellectual who could help place the find in village history. When a municipal official appeared at her gate, Rivera most likely consulted her archive of historical documents and recorded oral histories. Among them she found the story of Pascuala Martínez, one of a series of oral traditions she had entitled "From Parents to Children."

> During the French Intervention, Pascuala Martinez was taken to Rosa de Castilla [a region in the mountains surrounding Xochiapulco] by her mother in order to hide her, she is ten years old, unfamiliar with the place she returns following the paths along the mountainside and arrives at the eastern corner of what is today the central plaza, there she sees piles of bodies and large holes for what we today call common graves, the French and Austrians were surprised one night when the inhabitants of Xochiapulco had abandoned their huts and found refuge in Tazcantla [a nearby hacienda inherited by Juan Francisco Lucas after the death of his father-in-law], the invader was sleeping confidently in what we today call the corridor of the former dining room of what used to be the training school for teachers.[14]

The answer seemed clear. The bones were French and Austrian, product of an ambush witnessed by ten-year-old Pascuala Martínez.

Whoever placed the ambush during the French Intervention, thus identifying the ambushed soldiers as French and Austrian, made an error of four years. Refuge in Taxcantla became a common military strategy only during the Restored Republic, for Juan Francisco Lucas did not even marry Asención Pérez, the daughter of the hacienda's owner, until 1867.[15] In combination with the other evidence analyzed in chapter 4 and the Pozos manuscript, this contradiction makes clear that Pascuala Martínez witnessed the scene in the plaza not in 1865 but in 1869.

We do not know exactly how the intense memory of a ten-year-old girl, a memory of the early morning fog lifting as a pile of bodies was being buried in the central plaza, was articulated to a powerful official story. Perhaps Martínez herself, when telling the story to her children or grandchildren, hung the images onto the narratives of the French Intervention. Perhaps her descendants did so when sharing the story with Rivera, or Rivera herself made sense of the images in this way. What we do know is that this hegemonic version, despite internal conflicts and contentiousness, was powerful enough to deny the Mexican identity of the bones any legitimate space in local oral history.

Local intellectuals like Donna Rivera Moreno are thus the archivists of local counterhegemonic discourse. They preserve and reproduce oral history by identifying the bones, talking to the elders, and keeping the papers. Their choices about where to situate themselves in the official parade—whether to march or not to march, and if marching what banner to carry—have important effects on the form taken by local memory and on how their villages can participate in the emerging national polity. Yet even if local intellectuals enjoy substantial power or prestige at the local level, they are "junior partners" in regional or national coalitions. If they choose to articulate local history as counterhegemony to a hegemonic discourse, they can choose neither the form it will ultimately take nor the reciprocal effect this process will have at the local level. By choosing to mediate between their locales and the national political culture, local intellectuals also choose to enforce at least some of its tenets within their villages. In this sense, the more effective they are as mediators, the more they must also take on the role of enforcers.

Mediators and Enforcers: Local Intellectuals in the Construction of Local Discourse

In Morelos and Puebla local intellectuals articulated strikingly similar discourses about death and loss during the 1860s. Using family metaphors to represent the pain suffered during periods of civil war and foreign intervention, they spoke directly to their fellow villagers who had witnessed the destruction and grief brought on by these major conflagrations. At the same time, they articulated these depictions of local conditions to particular regional or national events, taking clear stands on the political issues of the moment. In so doing, they mediated between local debates and broader coalitions, serving the latter by tying their own village alliances to specific political causes, and attempting to extend their influence in their communities by connecting to larger political parties.

In Tepoztlán, Morelos, family metaphors of death and destruction were used to highlight the broken promises of Liberalism and to legitimize a petition to Maximilian. A particular faction of local intellectuals thus made it their project to reconnect the village to a Conservative discourse that granted it a legitimate identity as a corporate Nahua village with access to land reconfirmed in the grants given by the Spanish crown. This discourse was offered as a conscious alternative to earlier articulations of land rights to citizenship and other Liberal rights through support for the Liberal Revolution.

In the Puebla highlands, by contrast, family metaphors of loss and death were used to reaffirm local commitment to the "true" principles of Liberalism. During the period of internal struggle among Liberals that followed the French Intervention, local Liberal intellectuals in the Tetela national guard legitimized their refusal to lay down their weapons by invoking an ongoing responsibility to their fallen comrades and family members, all of whom had died in the struggle to defend Liberal principles against foreign intervention. Justified with references to Tetela de Ocampo's "pure" Liberal pedigree extending back to 1855, this refusal buttressed Liberal consensus in Tetela and pushed a counterhegemonic Liberal critique of the national and state governments during 1868. Local intellectuals thus connected Tetela's Liberalism to the radical Liberal faction represented nationally by Porfirio Díaz, thereby marginalizing Conservatives or lukewarm Liberals who might have been willing to support the repression carried out by Benito Juárez.[16]

It is interesting to note the Janus-faced quality of these intellectuals' interventions. On one side, the concern for local issues—land, the legitimate political identity of the community, and the state's obligation to recognize local demands and experiences—is evident in both cases. On the other side, there is an eagerness to engage in broader regional and national debates and to use this engagement and the power of mediation it bestows as a weapon in local struggles for power. Concern for local issues renders local intellectuals as counterhegemonic heroes championing village interests and demands in broader political arenas. Engagement in broader debates can potentially transform such intellectuals into agents of regional or national power blocs. Most local intellectuals lived this contradiction daily, inhabiting the painful edge between solidarity and surveillance. Nowhere is this duality clearer than in the struggle for local education that took shape in Tetela de Ocampo and Xochiapulco at the end of the 1860s.

Throughout the municipalities of Tetela district—which by the end of the 1860s included Xochiapulco—local officials attempted, between 1867 and 1872, to open public primary schools. At least in part, this effort was in response to a truly popular aspiration that saw education as a form of mass "enabling," as a way of opening doors to achievement, participation, and citizenship. But as it was practiced in this region over these years, the expansion of schooling often became a form more of control than of enablement.

Once again using the metaphor of the parade, education became a way of teaching people how to march: to get to school on time daily, to learn respectfully, to make school a higher priority than the agricultural calendar or the family economy—in essence to be schooled in the ways of "civilization." Instead of remaining a popular aspiration to progress, in forms and with calendars that the people controlled, education became instead a potentially authoritarian and racist discourse about the need to force ignorant or religious villagers, almost without exception Indian, into the enlightened sphere of "science"; this enlightenment was presented as being good for the villagers, even when it contradicted their own judgment. And in the various municipalities of Tetela de Ocampo, it was local intellectuals—schoolteachers, justices of the peace, municipal officers, and officials of the local commissions on public instruction—who stood at the forefront of this battle and helped define the direction it would take.

Even before the end of the Second Empire, as we have already seen (chapter 2), people in the barrio of San Nicolás wrote to the Tetela municipal council about their desire to open a primary school. In their letter, after explaining that they had saved a hundred pesos from a communal agricultural project, they tied the coming of "a stable and lasting peace" to the "prosperity and enlightened progress" they expected a primary school to provide. Several schools opened in Tetela municipality between 1867 and 1870, not only in San Nicolás but also in La Cañada, San José, and Tonalapa; most of these schools enrolled boys, but a few schools for girls were established. Given the number of schools opened, these aspirations were shared fairly widely. That such a large number of schools found the funds to open their doors, when poverty and scarcity were widespread in the aftermath of a decade and a half of civil war and foreign intervention, lends further proof to the depth of the hopes pinned on education. But almost immediately questions of enforcement and surveillance also surfaced, as teachers experienced the frustrations of poor attendance and seeming nonchalance toward learning.[17]

In January 1867, a full month before the barrio of San Nicolás even presented its letter to Tetela's municipal council, this same political body received the resignation of Nicolás García, teacher at La Cañada's school. The reason for his resignation, García explained in his letter, was that various vecinos of the barrio had opposed his presence, while the local justice of the peace had not aided him in looking for truant children. Although other schoolteachers did not take such extreme measures as García, at least not right away, all those whose voices emerge from the municipal documentation shared at least some of his complaints. In June 1867, for example, María Petra González, the teacher of the school Friend of the Girls (Amiga de Niñas), wrote to the mayor of the municipality, complaining about the frequent absences of her girls and asking that the parents be reminded to send them: "I do not believe that this duty is a sacrifice being demanded of them, for if they understand well they know that they must always give their daughters at least a medium-level education, which will be both beneficial and honorable."[18] Although her tone was gentle and relatively respectful, María González had strong and clear opinions. Parents had the duty to provide their children, even their girls, with education, not only for the benefits it would provide them but also for the sake of honor. There is no clue in the letter that González understood either the competing needs of the family economy or the gender hierarchy that assigned women a place in the private sphere. If people "understood well," they would of necessity agree with her. If they did not agree, by implication they lacked understanding.

Many teachers adopted a missionary attitude. They were bringing understanding, knowledge, and civilization to the ignorant. In many cases they were sacrificing themselves, living in poor rural conditions in order to teach. It certainly must have been hard, in such a situation, not to take absences and other obstacles personally.

This was clearly the case with Valentín Sánchez, the teacher of the barrio school in San José, who sent a letter to Tetela's municipal council in October 1871. He had been teaching in San José since April 1870, he explained. Parents and political authorities had shown nothing but indifference, with the result that "the advances of the youths have been few and insignificant." Sánchez admitted to feeling ashamed during the visits of the local Commission on Public Instruction because he was unable to show more advancement. "But what can a teacher do," he asked, "when the boys come only four, six, or eight days during a whole month?" As quickly as they learned, he explained, they also forgot. Of the forty-two boys registered in the school, twenty simply did not show up at all; the rest showed up only occasionally. Although he had written to the local authorities, they had done nothing. If something could not be done, Sánchez concluded, he would be forced to resign. On 21 October, nine days after his original petition, the municipal council asked the local Commission on Public Instruction to "bring the case before the relevant court, so that the children begin attending school or their parents receive the appropriate punishment."[19]

Sometimes the situation could escalate into personal confrontation. Donaciano Arriaga, the new teacher in La Cañada after García resigned the post in 1867, brought a complaint before Tetela municipality in February 1871. His problem was a familiar one. The boys were often absent from school, when they came they were late, and the parents were not cooperating. What was different in this case was that Arriaga accused one father, Antonio Tapia, of organizing opposition to him among the parents, trying to remove Arriaga from his post. The only reason for this opposition, according to the teacher, was that "I constantly reprehend the insubordination to which the children are accustomed, the thefts that are not lacking among them, the pranks and various other things they do incessantly." Arriaga felt a deep responsibility for all the boys and seemed to focus on Tapia and Tapia's son as the root of all his difficulties. He could not discipline Tapia's son, he said, because Tapia would then "state publicly that the children are being mistreated unjustly, and that is why they do not advance with the current teacher." He also used Tapia's son as the example of his deepest frustration: even if the boys were advancing, their parents would not send them to school regularly. "Several of the boys who are writing" were regularly tardy, he explained, "and principally this one [Tapia's son] because of the work his father is making him do, gets to school at eleven in the morning, and at four in the afternoon."

The justice of the peace in La Cañada was called in to investigate and wrote a formal report. He confirmed the absences, tardiness, and insubordination of the children and said that it occurred with the consent of some of the parents. He also reported on a personal meeting with Arriaga and Tapia. At that meeting Tapia admitted that, with two other parents, he had been attempting to establish a private school. But he apologized, saying that whatever things he had done that could be causing problems had been "hot-headed and without reflection" and that he would not do them again. The justice of the peace concluded his report by confirming that several fathers had come to his office demanding a barrio meeting to establish a private school but that he had refused to grant the demand. On 25 March, more than a month after Arriaga's original complaint, the local Commission on Public Instruction asked the local judge to arrange a meeting with the individuals involved in order to determine culpability and relevant punishment.[20]

The case of Donaciano Arriaga and the La Cañada school provides a particularly clear window on issues that were common to most confrontations among local parents, schoolteachers, and municipal officials. One crucial component in most of these cases, but which emerges with particular clarity in the La Cañada case, was the struggle between parents and teachers over the labor time of the children. In the local agricultural economy, parental control over children's labor was a key component of the organization and division of labor more generally and of the system of patriarchal authority (see chapter 3). Interference by outsiders—whether teachers or municipal officials—was both unwelcome and potentially dangerous. Thus, it was not a question of whether education was desirable in the abstract, but rather of who would control the educational process and who would bear the highest cost.

The debates around private schools are particularly telling in this context. They are a clear indictment of the way public schools were being run at the local level. As formulated by schoolteachers, municipalities, and commissions of public instruction, education was not serving the needs of the population, and it was forcing the family economy to bear the highest part of the cost. If that was the case anyway, why not establish private schools? From the standpoint of the parents in La Cañada, a private school would allow those who bore the highest cost to control the process as well.

Local intellectuals who found themselves in the middle of the fray tended to take the conflicts over control very personally. To make sense of the situation, they envisioned themselves as struggling to bring civilization to the ignorant. In Xochiapulco they opposed a superior "science" to the superstitions associated with "religion." In Tuzamapan, a predominantly Totonac municipality in Tetela district, the enlightenment of knowledge was opposed to the allegedly inherent ignorance of the Totonacos as a group. In both cases the ultimate discourse was hierarchical and authoritarian. In Tuzamapan it was also racist.

In early December 1870 ten vecinos from Xochiapulco's barrio of Cuauximaloyan wrote to the jefe político of Tetela district, complaining about the behavior of the municipal officials in their cabecera. Quite a while ago, they wrote, their municipal capital had promised to provide funds from the municipal treasury if the barrio wished to establish a school. What they had done instead, however, was to demand the monthly payment of a one-real tax from each individual in order to support the school in the cabecera. Meanwhile, the people in Cuauximaloyan were very poor, "without seeds, without corn, and without anything else because everything was lost in the past revolution." The purpose of their petition, therefore, was to ask the jefe as a "good father and leader of these pueblos and their unfortunate vecinos" to allow them to keep their money so that they could pay their own teacher.[21]

A week later the juez municipal in Xochiapulco, Juan Francisco Dinorin, responded angrily in his report on the situation. An officer in the Xochiapulco national guard during the previous decade, Dinorin could barely sign his name, yet he had a high respect for education. As he explained the situation, the community had had a meeting on 3 December, during which the vecinos from Cuauximaloyan and Atzalan had agreed that primary education was important enough to warrant a contribution of one real per person. Then, having agreed in a public assembly, the people from Cuauximaloyan presented a petition to the jefe político "using theories that are so well known they should have kept them to themselves. For example: they say they are poor; but who in these parts is not?" People who had suffered more than those from Cuauximaloyan, Dinorin continued, were not refusing to pay the tax. Then Dinorin presented his interpretation of the situation in Cuauximaloyan.

> They are more interested in building a church that they do not need, rather than building the most august of all temples, the one to science. For the first, there has been and is a peso [eight reales] per person, to build the church; but for the second, there isn't even a real per month for the education of their own children; and furthermore: that for education, there are multitudes of elderly, there are many who are ill, poor, or [otherwise] employed; but not so for the church.[22]

The issue of religion was important and contentious in Xochiapulco, a village owing its very existence to the Liberal Revolution of 1855. We have already seen in Pozos's manuscript how local intellectuals played with the image of Xochiapulco as an enlightened village, bringing the "gospel" of the Reform Laws to other indigenous communities in the sierra. We have evidence, moreover, that the issue had come up specifically around the same time as the conflict over education in Cuauximaloyan. On 15 November the acting mayor of Xochiapulco, Juan Martín, had written to Tetela's jefe político requesting permission to organize a communal work party to build a small house or sanctuary for the village saints. Now that the primary school had been completed, he explained, the municipal council had decided that they should invite the same vecinos who had built the school

> to cooperate with their voluntary labor . . . , so that in the same way they can help build a small house in which to keep the saints, that because of the war the then enemies of the interests of the pueblo, took them [the saints] to the barrio of Las Lomas, where they are abandoned, without the veneration of their owners.

The jefe agreed, stipulating only that the work be entirely voluntary.[23]

When Dinorin accused the inhabitants of Cuauximaloyan of preferring religion to education, therefore, he did so in the context of a previously established communal tradition that granted both church and school equivalent public legitimacy, in the sense of requesting communal labor for both. Earlier communal discussions had not privileged one over the other, except in granting first place to the construction of the school; both were considered legitimate. In fact, by denigrating Cuauximaloyan for its commitment to religion, Dinorin was tying into the anticlerical strands present within Liberalism, using them to deflect attention from important underlying issues. The struggle with Cuauximaloyan was not about education versus religion, at least not in any abstract sense, but about local barrio control over the schools and about the equitable use of revenue across all the barrios of the municipality.

The jefe político understood these important underlying issues, and his resolution of the conflict made this clear. Starting on 1 January 1871, he decided, Cuauximaloyan would have its own school. The Xochiapulco municipal council would name a teacher for the school and set the salary, paying it from the municipal treasury. The inhabitants of Cuauximaloyan and Atzalan barrios would continue to contribute to education through the Chicontepec tax, just as the inhabitants of the cabecera would continue to pay. If this tax did not cover the expenses of all the schools, the municipal council would find a way to make up the difference from other funds, distributing them equitably across the whole municipality.[24]

The jefe político in Tetela certainly had his hands full with disputes of this nature. Earlier the same year, in April 1870, he attempted to resolve a very difficult conflict in Tuzamapan, one of the district's municipalities with the highest concentration of Totonac population. On 4 April the jefe received a complaint from the mayor of Tuzamapan, José Galván, about the jefe's handling of a protest by Juan José Galicia, a Totonac Indian from that village. Galván was especially upset that the jefe had not requested a report from him first. According to Galván, Galicia had taken his son out of primary school once he was quite advanced, "reading quite well, writing at a second grade level; in religion he had gotten as far as reciting the Our Father." Galván had punished Galicia, who then went to Tetela to protest, returning after he had managed to get the jefe to write Galván a private letter telling him to leave Galicia alone. At that point, according to Galván, Galicia

> began to tell [everyone] that only here [in Tuzamapan] were people molested, that in Tetela no one said anything and allowed children to leave school; and such disorder has been introduced that [the children] have started getting too many colds, as is proven by the attendance lists and daily absences that I have included, so that you may answer by telling me what I should do, if I should leave them in this state, or if I should obey the law concerning [public] schools.

Throughout the document Galván seemed more interested in asserting his authority than in advancing education, and he consistently justified his actions and his superior knowledge by denigrating the Totonac families. Early on in his letter he explained that the authorities had been forced to punish families for not sending their children to school and that they had succeeded despite grave difficulties. The proof of this success lay in the fact that the children, "despite being dissembling and dull [*cerrados*] Totonacos, they are [actually] too advanced." Later he justified his authoritarian practices by asserting that, in his view, he had the obligation to bring education to the population despite their own poor judgment, "since as Totonac Indians, what is good [for them] appears bad."[25]

In Xochiapulco and Tuzamapan already existing conflicts or tensions were used by local intellectuals to explain why, as they saw it, the local population was resistant to education. Whether the previous conflict was about religion, as in Xochiapulco, or about ethnic negotiations over local power, as in Tuzamapan, in both cases the underlying issue was not education per se but rather the way in which it was being implemented and controlled.[26] The protests of local villagers about their lack of control over the process, their desire to find ways to make access to and organization of education equitable across barrio and ethnic lines—these were transformed discursively into proof of their ignorance, their lack of understanding. This ignorance was then constructed as superstition in Xochiapulco, racial inferiority in Tuzamapan.

In both cases we can perhaps understand the frustration and impatience of local teachers and municipal officials, who, having worked to provide and staff a school, were then faced with parents and children who resisted attendance. Yet from the perspective of the parents themselves, the discourses of superior civilization and enlightenment, the "for their own good" justifications that emerged from the frustration, were anything but liberating. Indeed, these discourses and justifications could easily transform the intellectuals who espoused them into enforcers pure and simple, agents in charge of surveillance whose ties to local forms of communal hegemony and debate seemed quickly to be eroding.

At least implicitly, the use of authoritarian and racist discourses also tied local intellectuals to wider webs of complicity and social control emerging in Mexico after 1867. Both in this book and other works, I have suggested that the struggles surrounding the 1855 Liberal Revolution helped hone a variety of racist discourses on social control that were used broadly, by Conservatives and Liberals, to justify the repression of agrarian social movements. They did so through the "othering" of the rural indigenous population—the identification of Indian peasants with ignorance, superstition, lack of political judgment, and tendencies toward violence and plunder. Conservatives served up these discourses as justifications for corporate and authoritarian politics. Because of the large agrarian Indian population, democracy became equated with bloodshed and carnage. Mexico was not ready for broad participatory politics. Liberals articulated similar discourses in their efforts to control political power. Peasants did not know how to act publicly; they needed strong leadership; if they were left to their own devices, only anarchy could ensue.[27]

Local discourses on education connected especially well to the Liberal variants described above. Indian peasants were seen as unprepared for participation in the public sphere. They put their family interests and religious beliefs before their civic duty to educate their children. Racism became, in the context of debates on education, an element of nested Liberal discourses of control. Local, regional, and national intellectuals of Liberal persuasion had the obligation to educate the masses, regardless of the masses' desires. The Liberals must create the citizen through a process of education and surveillance. Even before the attainment of liberty, the price of citizenship was eternal vigilance.

Arenas of Argumentation: Ritual, Oral History, and Communal Hegemony

In their efforts to mediate between broader political coalitions and their communities, local intellectuals sometimes frayed the edges of their more intimate connections with local political culture. This reminds us that, despite their educational or political privilege, intellectuals participated in arenas of argumentation they could influence and modify but never entirely control. As was quite clear in both Xochiapulco and Tuzamapan, where internal debates over religion and ethnic representation in local politics became articulated to the struggles over village education, building local counterhegemonic consensus was itself a hegemonic process. Local intellectuals might define the boundaries of a particular discourse or even play with the elements to be articulated. But ultimately they controlled neither the conflicts among various perspectives at the village level nor the outcome of the process as a whole.

Ritual and oral history are also examples of these arenas of argumentation. Tracing the various forms of conflict contained within them provides an entry into communal relationships, demonstrating that local memory and ritual are not seamless, unchanging forms of rural or precapitalist culture but dynamic and shifting constructions over and within which people consciously and continuously argue. Analyzing these arguments helps us to see how and why, in the overall process of building hegemonic nation-states, the success or failure of the project must be analyzed from both above and below, focusing not only on dominant ideologies but also on local conflicts and alliances that help define power and meaning.

Let us turn once again to Xochiapulco. In 1888 a funeral service— organized by the municipality's society of teachers—was held in one of the main schools for Miguel Méndez, an important Liberal leader and Juan Nepomuceno Méndez's only son. Four local national guard soldiers stood around the coffin, which was set on a raised platform surrounded by military paraphernalia, Masonic trophies, candles, and floral arrangements. During the previous week or so the local military band (*filarmónica*) had played daily in the evening, and now it provided music for the occasion. Guy P. C. Thomson, on whose article this description is based, gives the following account of the ceremony itself:

> The service was taken by Mr. Byron Hyde, a Methodist minister from the United States. Accompanied by his wife at a piano, Hyde gave renderings (in English) of three Wesleyan hymns. There followed three eulogies of Miguel Méndez, extolling his services to the Liberal cause and on behalf of the "desgraciada nación azteca." These speeches were infused with extreme anticlerical and anti-Conservative sentiments, a martial patriotic liberalism, a reverence for the principles of the French Revolution, an admiration for Garibaldi and Hidalgo (in that order), and an obsession with the importance of education as the only means for emancipating the indigenous population from clerical subjection.

In Thomson's estimation, this event "illustrates the completeness and fervour with which the old order was banished and Liberalism embraced in a single municipality."[28] From the perspective I have been developing here, however, it demonstrates something rather different: "the completeness and fervour" with which local intellectuals, especially teachers, were still engaged in 1888, seventeen years after the initial encounter we have previously recorded, in fighting the good fight between education and superstition. Reorganizing local discourses in the service of a particular liberal coalition, regionally and nationally speaking, was only part of the story. They were also using these discourses in an ongoing internal battle over power and meaning. Seen from this perspective, and in dialogue with what we know about Xochiapulco's previous history, this ritual offers rich potential as an entry into local hegemonic processes.

Most of its elements are, in fact, already familiar. The praise given Méndez for his service to the "unfortunate Aztec nation" ("desgraciada nación azteca") fits well with the image in Pozos's manuscript of Xochiapulco as an evangelical village bringing the true Liberal gospel to the indigenous communities of the Puebla highlands. The obsession with education as the only true alternative to domination by the clergy is another recurring theme: the opposition between superstition and science, church and school. In this particular case as well, the presence of a Methodist minister, who sang in English rather than Spanish or Nahuatl, is striking. Local organizers preferred a foreigner, singing in a foreign language, to the dangerous and invasive presence of a Catholic priest. Taken together, these elements in the ceremony speak to the construction of a particular image of Xochiapulco—its origins and identity—that is quite similar to the one presented in Pozos's manuscript. Born in the cauldron of the nineteenth-century struggle between Liberals and Conservatives, the village of Xochiapulco attained its badge of legitimacy by serving as the bastion of Liberalism and education in a sea of Conservatism and superstition, fighting against Interventionists, Conservatives, and priests with the weapons of national guards and teachers.

Xochiapulco's loyalty to "true" Liberal principles, connected to the national guard tradition and community politics through the village's role in the resistance to the French Intervention, constituted a second set of nested themes at Miguel Méndez's funeral. Not only did national guards keep vigil around the coffin, but the room was decorated with, among other things, weapons—almost certainly those surviving from the Intervention years. These were the same weapons that national guards had refused to turn in during their confrontation with the federal army in 1868 and 1869; the same ones they had taken off the bodies of Austrian soldiers; the same ones that would occupy a prominent place in the municipal museum during the twentieth century. After the establishment of the Fifth of May parade in the 1930s, some of the same weapons would also be taken down to Puebla city to march with the Xochiapulco delegation.[29]

A crucial link between the village and the Méndez funeral ceremony was the local filarmónica. By playing in the central plaza for the previous week or more and then performing at the ceremony, the filarmónica helped articulate village space to the funeral itself, announcing the event and attracting people to it. As Thomson analyzes so well in his article, the filarmónicas played this role of articulation and attraction much more broadly, in terms of who played in the bands, what their local civic role was conceptualized to be, and the types of celebrations in which they were required to perform. Indeed, by taking a closer look at the filarmónicas, we can begin to approximate what was typical or unusual about Xochiapulco and its local intellectuals.

Time and again we have seen that Xochiapulco was an unusual case. As a village born from an hacienda during the 1855 Revolution, its Liberal military tradition usually *was* its community politics. National guard commanders and soldiers served as community leaders. After the dispute with the owners of the former hacienda was finally resolved, people received their land according to rank in the national guard.[30] Yet in its relationship with its anexos, as well as in the transmission of oral history from generation to generation, Xochiapulco was not all that different from other villages. In both of these arenas the legitimacy of the village and its leaders was articulated through remembering Xochiapulco's undying loyalty to the Liberal cause, and to "true" Liberal principles, between 1850 and 1876. Versions of these events were preserved in funeral ritual, local history, and patriotic celebration, almost always articulated by teachers as local intellectuals. They were reproduced, contested, and reconstructed, in communal assembly and filarmónica, throughout the last four decades of the nineteenth century.

Through the overlapping institutions of the national guard, the filarmónicas, and the *juntas patrióticas* that helped organize local celebrations of important regional and national holidays, local Liberal intellectuals encouraged the development of a new counterhegemonic political culture within their villages. Building from established arenas, such as the communal assembly and the municipal council, they pressured for alternative forms of local ritual and community participation. Aside from the national guard itself, which as we have seen (chapter 3) provided a new sociopolitical space for younger and Indian men within village affairs, the filarmónica was the most participatory local institution to come out of the years of Liberal struggle. Formed with the support of community leaders, the local military band connected to the national guard and to evolving forms of popular Liberalism through parades and other ceremonies at which they played. In many cases the band constituted another form of community obligation, for families were often forced to contribute a one-time tax, on a sliding scale, to finance the start-up costs. The musicians, most of whom were humble indigenous or mestizo villagers, many illiterate and without last names, were considered responsible for the brass instruments and obligated to play at the various functions to which the band was invited. In exchange, they were exempted from taxation and military service.[31]

As Thomson points out, the filarmónicas were often conceptualized as an alternative form of local ceremonial, in a situation where the public ceremonial space of the Catholic church had been radically circumscribed by the Liberal Reform Laws.[32] Indeed, as we have already seen (chapter 4), it was on the issue of ritual that the Liberals had found it hardest to connect to village constituencies. Through the military bands, therefore, the municipal councils and the intellectuals and political officials who composed them might oversee and help reproduce ritual spaces that were independent from the church but that nevertheless proved satisfactory to the village population. Yet predictably enough, given the complexity of local hegemonic processes, such reorganizations of ritual did not go uncontested.

Conflicts occurred within the filarmónicas themselves. Thomson records several incidents in Zapotitlán, a heavily indigenous municipality within Tetela district, over the 1870s. In 1872 and 1876, for example, two members of the local band were disciplined by the alcalde for not living up to their obligations. In one case the mayor had twice imprisoned the clarinet player for not showing up at band practice, which the musician had begun to do after losing his instrument. In another the municipal official imprisoned the mother of a band member who had moved to another village, insisting that he would release the woman only when her son returned the instrument and sheet music he had taken with him. Yet at the same time, despite sometimes hierarchical or authoritarian methods of enforcement, the filarmónicas could constitute sources of local community or ethnic pride. In a third incident involving the same mayor of Zapotitlán, when the local tax collector complained about having to contribute money to support such a poor quality band, the alcalde imprisoned the tax collector and forced him to listen to a concert by the band he had insulted![33]

Another local arena of ceremonial contention involved the local juntas patrióticas and their organization of village celebrations for important regional or national holidays. Thomson describes a particularly lavish celebration of the Fifth of May in Tetela de Ocampo in 1879:

> [It] began on 3 May with a prize-giving ceremony for all the secular public schools of the district. The prize-giving committee, accompanied by the *cuerpo filarmónico*, proceeded first to the boys' then to the girls' school, where prizewinners from outlying municipalities were boarding. . . . The procession advanced to the main square, there to be greeted by a rendition of the national anthem, seven broadsides of artillery, bell ringing and the release of pyrotechnic rockets. The prize-giving was followed by a circus, an acrobatic display and the release of aerostatic balloons. In the evening, public and private buildings were illuminated while the orchestra played serenades. At 4 p.m. on 4 May, the National Guard of the district carried out manoeuvres and staged a mock battle under the supervision of General Juan Francisco Lucas. This was followed by more serenades and fireworks. At day-break on 5 May, the national flag was hoisted and military bands paraded through all the streets of the town, accompanied by bell-ringing and fireworks. A packed programme of ceremonies, patriotic speeches, concerts, plays, mock battles, cannonades, firework displays and walkabouts continued through 5 May until midday on the 6th when, satiated with patriotism (and deafened), the district's prizewinning children, public employees and national guardsmen returned to their villages and barrios.[34]

The length, drama, and extravagance of such a celebration rivaled any major religious festival organized at the village level; indeed, these celebrations were clearly intended to serve as an alternative, bringing together people from outlying barrios in symbolic patriotic unity. That this type of event was part of a contentious process of debate and local conflict might not be obvious from descriptions of its structure and content; but it becomes abundantly so when we examine other events and struggles around it.

In Tetela in 1869, for example, the parish priest refused to lend the town some rugs and other objects of adornment. Although usually kept in the church, they were often used to give pomp and circumstance to important municipal occasions. He then went on physically to prevent municipal officials from entering the church to ring the bells for the Fifth of May celebration. On both counts the municipal representatives who had suffered insults at the hand of the priest reported back to the town council, requesting that the cleric be disciplined for breaking the law.

Tetela's jefe político also heard disputes about the competition between secular and religious symbolism in public spaces throughout the 1860s and

1870s. A series of the barrios and municipalities of Tetela district petitioned the jefe about which local religious ceremonies might be performed and when and if it was appropriate to march the saints in procession outside the walls of the church. Indeed, each program for a municipal or village celebration needed the jefe's approval, serving as a form of surveillance or of encouragement in the direction of more secular events. And in cases where saints were brought out of the church or other violations of secular public space occurred—particularly after they had been prohibited—district officials brought the organizers to trial.[35]

By the 1870s and 1880s, then, the actions of Liberal intellectuals within village contexts had helped articulate new arenas of argumentation in a reorganized public space. The combination of national guard, local schoolteacher, military band, and junta patriótica consciously provided an alternative to the church, parish priest, and local pantheon of saints. As is always the case with hegemonic processes, success was measured not in the total displacement of the latter by the former but rather in the reconfiguration of the boundaries of what was possible, legitimate, and desirable in the public arenas of village life. The cases of conflict that survive, those that find their way into the documentation, are precisely the ones that involve redrawing those boundaries: the disciplining of wayward or truant musicians, the establishment of the overall format for holiday celebrations, the prosecuting of villagers who insisted on parading their saints through the streets to collect alms—even after the jefe político had said no. And it is in these dynamic local celebrations and confrontations that we can best see the dual role of the local intellectual, not only as the creator and articulator of new possibilities but also as the enforcer of the new discursive boundaries they entail.

From this new vantage, it might be particularly informative to reconsider the changes brought about by the 1910 Revolution, and in particular the attempts to make official, at the state level, the celebrations of the Fifth of May. For even as the postrevolutionary state constructed its own parade, even as its representatives pretended to give history back to the Indians and peasants who supposedly did not possess it, they painted the larger, more official canvas of the Puebla city celebration with the scenes, colors, and brushes elaborated at the local level, during the previous fifty years, in village-level arenas of argumentation delineated and enforced by local intellectuals.

In this context as well, we can begin to speculate on some additional reasons why local intellectuals might decide to march in the official parade. Given the ongoing contingency and contestation of all local discourse, the potential connection to a related and more official version could be quite attractive. Local intellectuals might feel supported in their efforts and, confident of their ability to negotiate within its boundaries, participate enthusiastically in state efforts to teach the people how to march.

We have seen that the price they paid, even as they received some state support for their efforts, was quite high. In addition to the transformation of the bones, people in Xochiapulco also ended up accepting the state's terms on another issue of local importance: whether or not the village national guard had ever surrendered to the French. The Papantla accords of January 1866, accepted by communal assembly in Xochiapulco a month later, have been expunged from the local historical record. The ensuing six-month hiatus in the fighting, during which the Xochiapulco national guard submitted itself to the terms set by the imperial government, has disappeared from local memory. The reason for this collective amnesia lies precisely in the fact that, in order to differentiate Xochiapulco from the mythified "Zacapoaxtlas," local intellectuals constructed the image of the Xochiapulquenses as the tireless defenders of the nation, the only ones who never surrendered. To replace this image with one that takes account of the six-month period in 1866 would simply not have the same discursive punch.

Yet ironically, the implication of this denial of surrender is that the Xochiapulquenses are held to a higher standard of admission to citizenship than any other group. Despite the fact that they waged a two-year guerrilla struggle, armed mainly with the weapons taken from enemy soldiers; that they sustained multiple invasions and burned their own village to the ground to avoid its being taken by the enemy; that they overcame exhaustion, death, and misery over a period of twenty-five years in their struggle to support the Liberal cause—despite all this, they must also prove that they never surrendered; only then will they be given their badge of national belonging. If other groups were held to the same standard, Mexico would have few citizens.[36]

As local forms of ritual that were constructed through complex and contested processes of communal hegemony, *Los Avelinos* and *Los Mactas*—dances from the central highlands of Peru that represent the resistance to the Chileans during the War of the Pacific—share much with the various forms of ritual celebration elaborated in the Sierra de Puebla during and after the French Intervention. The difference is that in Peru no successful "official story" emerged to which local intellectuals could contribute or with which they could articulate. An analysis of a local arena of argumentation that remains floating, unencumbered and unanchored by connections to broader hegemonic discourses, might actually help clarify what is gained and lost in the process of creating a relatively inclusive and enduring nation-state.

The dance of Los Avelinos originated in the Mantaro Valley town of San Gerónimo at the beginning of the twentieth century. The characters that give the dance its name dress in rags, with masks and tattered hats, and carry weapons. From the beginning, even though most ceremonial dancing in the village already occurred in Spanish, the performers of Los Avelinos (themselves called *los avelinos*) took Quechua nicknames to hide their identities and spoke only in the indigenous language. By taking Andrés Avelino Cáceres's middle name, moreover, they became symbolic representations of soldiers from the War of the Pacific, both of the poor villager who had suffered privations and returned to his community in rags and of the *chuto*, or vagabond, a disguise used by many Cacerista spies.[37]

The dance did not begin as a transparent commemoration of the 1880s resistance. According to Zoila Mendoza, who has studied it in detail, it originated in a struggle for power between two ayllus of the community of San Gerónimo: Huando, the poor one; and Tuna, the wealthy and influential one. Although Tuna predictably won the political battle, it was Huando that created the dance of Los Avelinos as symbolic retribution for their defeat. In a clear discursive opposition between poverty and wealth, powerlessness and power, some inhabitants of Huando ayllu danced on the feast day of San Roque, the saint of the poor, in counterpoint to the celebration of San Gerónimo, the patron saint of the community. From the beginning, los avelinos were the band of dancers who represented the poor. Not only did they dress in rags and speak Quechua, but they danced to music performed on traditional peasant wind instruments rather than the fancier customary band of the region, which included violin, harp, and clarinet. The message of Los Avelinos, of the peasant guerrillas vis-à-vis the Peruvian state, of the inhabitants of Huando vis-à-vis Tuna, was that under a poor and ragged exterior is hidden the pride and power to fight back.[38]

Through the first four decades of the twentieth century, and especially in the 1920s, the dance underwent a process of evolution and diffusion. As people from the central highland villages began to migrate to the mines and to Lima in search of work, mutual aid societies formed by migrants from the same communities danced the dance in new settings. One result was that Los Avelinos was adopted by people from other central highland communities, who then took it back to their villages in new forms. Another result was that other sectors of San Gerónimo itself began to appropriate the dance and, especially after more prosperous migrants to Lima formed a new mutual aid society in honor of San Roque, Los Avelinos began to be danced in Tuna; in addition, it was performed on the day of San Gerónimo rather than that of the original saint.[39]

By the 1930s and 1940s, then, a dance that had originated in a specific context of conflict and with a particular message of resistance had been transformed in a variety of ways. In Acolla, north of Jauja, a version was adopted by migrants to the mines and to the construction of the road from Huancayo to Huancavelica. Danced originally by migrants during Holy Week, it became known as *La Mactada*, the dance of the young. The dancers wore elegant clothes rather than rags, perhaps to denote the new prosperity they had acquired through migration. They attempted symbolically to conquer public space and prestige within the community on their return. Back in San Gerónimo La Mactada was ultimately danced by the descendants of the very families against whom it had evolved in the first place. And throughout the Mantaro Valley, versions of Los Avelinos as patriotic celebration, folklore, or carnivalesque farce also began to proliferate.[40]

In the absence of a "national parade," no single official version has emerged. The avelinos have not been forced to learn how to march. Yet as we have seen, this does not mean that a more seamless, transparent, "autochthonous" version or memory has been preserved. Instead, local intellectuals and powerholders have played their dual role of mediators and enforcers within a physically smaller arena of argumentation. The rituals are still argued over and transformed, but they continue to be specific constructions of particular villages or regions rather than general symbols of the nation. The avelinos who have danced in Lima have not been invited, as an official delegation, by the central state. Instead, they have danced at the initiative of highland migrants who, turning the tables on an unsuccessful hegemonic process, have begun to colonize the ceremonial spaces of the capital city.

Local Intellectuals and Official Stories: The Costs of Success and the Consequences of Failure

There is a story about Juan Francisco Lucas, told by his granddaughter Aurora, although it is probably apocryphal. During the Porfiriato two officers of the federal army were given a commission by Díaz to visit Lucas and assess the local situation. When they arrived at the general's house on Xochiapulco's central plaza, they passed the reins of their horses to an Indian standing at the corner, then entered the building. No one was more shocked than they to learn, once inside, that the Indian to whom they had entrusted their horses was the very man they had come to see![41]

This is a story about a successful local intellectual, someone who is an effective mediator yet remains true to his village. Although sought out by the president of the republic, with whom he cultivated a relationship of *compadrazgo,* Lucas remained a humble man, living in his community, taking care not to distinguish himself too dramatically from those on whose support he depended. We can recall as well, in this context, the image of him given by Donna Rivera. He was the brave military leader, always on the front lines with his men, torching his own house first when it became necessary to burn Xochiapulco rather than letting it fall into the hands of the Austrians. We can also remember the image that emerged in the military documents of the Restored Republic, when despite the threats of the federal army and his former comrade in arms Ignacio Alatorre, Lucas insisted that the decision to fight or lay down weapons was not his alone but belonged to all the national guard soldiers in the towns under his command. Finally, we can also see the general as the "good patriarch," using his newly acquired hacienda Taxcantla as a refuge for his soldiers, a source of funds to equip them and to buy Xochiapulco's land from its recalcitrant former owners, while always being very careful to keep good relations with the peasants living at its borders. This is indeed the story of a successful local intellectual.[42]

What Lucas shares with his great-granddaughter Donna Rivera, also a successful local intellectual, is the presence of many different kinds of people at his gate. From local peasants to national dignitaries, all sought out Lucas and Rivera as the people who knew and who kept the archive. The successful articulation of local discourses to national projects is represented, with all its limitations and costs, by the presence of national or even international powerholders at their gates.

The situation of Major Eduardo Mendoza Meléndez, a local intellectual in the central highlands of Peru, provides a striking contrast. Originally from Concepción, Mendoza has, since 1952, been collecting oral histories from the La Breña campaign. In December 1981 he received a national prize, given by the Centro de Estudios Histórico-Militares (Center for the Study of Military History), for the first edition of his book on the central highlands resistance. It was also Mendoza who donated the memoirs of Ambrosio Salazar y Márquez, Cáceres's military commander in Comas, to the national military archive. Yet in Mendoza's case, no parade of dignitaries has made it to his gate in search of knowledge, archival or otherwise. Instead, Mendoza has been forced to wander in search of the connections that would validate and reproduce his authority.[43]

Earlier in this chapter I examined the costs incurred by local intellectuals in Mexico when they successfully articulated local discourses to an emerging national story. In this concluding section I will consider the consequences of a failed attempt at articulation in Peru's central highlands.

Although the case of Eduardo Mendoza serves as the most appropriate entry point into the discussion, I hope to show that other central sierra intellectuals share many of his difficulties and frustrations. Finally, I will suggest that, while successful mediation has substantial costs at the local level, the failure of mediation has severe consequences not only for local and regional intellectuals but for political society more generally.

In 1982, for the centennial of the resistance to the Chilean invasion, the Permanent Historical Commission of the Peruvian Army set out to create an official story. As the commission's official historian, Eduardo Mendoza supervised the tour of the central highlands, visiting all the major villages that had participated in the La Breña campaign. He and the other members of the commission inaugurated monuments to the resistance, celebrated anniversaries with bands and parades, took down the oral histories preserved by local intellectuals, and had pictures taken with local political officials in every town on their crowded itinerary.

This was a pilgrimage, a journey of symbolic articulation. Every village was marked in the chain with a photograph, an oral history, and some kind of monument or celebration. And the journey itself was given national importance, not only by the fact that the commission carrying it out was the *permanent* historical commission of the Peruvian Army but also by its publication of a multivolume collection on the War of the Pacific, two volumes of which were dedicated to reconstructing the La Breña campaign. These books, especially the one that logs the journey and centennial commemorations in the various villages, constitute one of my most important primary sources for narrating the failure of this official story.[44]

Comas plays a foundational role in these pages. Already in the first, more analytical section that considers the campaign from a military standpoint, a large insert reproduces a painting by a local artist that gives us a fictionalized rendition of how the Sierra Lumi ambush must have happened. Then, after a few explanatory pages, the case of Comas opens the section on oral history. "This is the historic town of Comas," writes Mendoza in his introduction. The discussion of Comas ends with a local *huayno*, or folk song, entitled "Sierralumi," some of which goes as follows:

> We are all Comasinos, members of a warlike race.
> Our fathers who have died wrote a history.
> Here is Sierralumi, when in eighty-two . . .
> Some second of March you'll be worthy of a monument.

And the implication is, of course, that it will no longer be "some second of March" but 2 March 1982, when the Permanent Commission commemorated the centennial of Sierra Lumi and painted, at the base of the mountain, a Peruvian flag with the dates 1882–1982 under it.[45]

On 2 March 1982 the centennial celebration was inaugurated in Comas's central plaza by raising the Peruvian flag, singing the national anthem, and holding a military mass. Two speakers, one representing the army and the other the district's centennial commission, extolled the virtues and courage of the original guerrillas. Then the local Sierra Lumi Cultural Center sang a hymn composed for the occasion. These presentations were followed by a parade, in which marched schoolchildren, delegations in typical costume or La Breña military gear representing the various communities of the district, and a platoon from the army. "It is important to emphasize that this was the first time that a unit from the army was present in a [local] parade," wrote the Permanent Commission, "and for this reason it received much applause." Finally, after the parade was over, flowers were deposited at the bottom of Sierra Lumi, right under the flag and dates painted on the stone.[46]

This ceremony shares much with what we have described for Puebla. An intricate ceremonial ritual combined parade with schoolchildren and military paraphernalia, "folkloric" costume with historical participation. What is different is that, in contrast to Mexico, this parade did not represent or help reproduce an enduring sense of nationhood and of belonging within a bounded official discourse. Five years after the celebration Sendero Luminoso had established de facto control in the Comas region. Two years after Sendero moved into the area, peasants from Comas, Cochas, and Andamarca carried out several new ambushes, hacking to death or decapitating numerous guerrillas. They sent the severed heads in a plastic bag to the army commander in Concepción, along with the weapons and leaflets they had confiscated, as symbols of the state's inability to live up to its side of a potential national pact.[47] Why did this happen in Peru and not in Mexico? Why did the parade "work" in the latter but not in the former?

A first answer can be found in the failure to integrate and unify different local discourses within a more official "master" version. This failure was caused not by a lack of dynamism in the local discourses but rather by an inability to articulate them to a broader narrative. On the official side the basic message throughout the Permanent Commission's volumes can be discerned through a comparison of two distinct texts: Mendoza's introduction to the second edition of his prize-winning *Historia de la Campaña de la Breña*; and a short essay that concludes the first volume of the Permanent Historical Commission's history of the La Breña campaign.

Both texts are concerned with the lessons the guerrilla war can teach Peruvians who live a century later. For Mendoza the lessons are moral exempla about the superiority of Peru's ancestors and the need of present-day Peruvians to live up to their example. The way he delivers the message, moreover, is highly gendered:

> And now, it is at the doors of the nation's morality that we knock, with the primordial goal of definitely revindicating, against any other kind of statement, [the nation's] honor and dignity. Our heroes did their best; now it is up to the entire nation to do the same. . . .
> Before our soldiers and schoolchildren, the past demands from the present a more masculine and virile strategy.

In the work of the Permanent Historical Commission, as stated at the end of the first volume on the resistance, the purpose of the 1982 pilgrimage was to excavate and publicize the heroes of Peru's past, not only to build a more "masculine" and "virile" future but also to find the core of Peruvian nationality. In a sense, the pilgrimage was an attempt to return to the primeval origins of the Peruvian nation. "The territory on which the la Breña campaign occurred has been, from time immemorial, the spinal column of Peru as an Andean nation, and its primeval [*telúrico*] influence on the biological constitution and behavior of man [*sic*] has been evident at all times." But more important, conditions for the highland population had not changed or improved substantially in the century since the La Breña campaign. This stagnation was to be interpreted, soberly, as a challenge for the future. Under a photograph of a poor Indian family, reproduced intentionally to confuse the reader between nineteenth and twentieth centuries, the caption reads: "When we see the same human reality today, this suggests that we need to carry out substantive tasks to achieve national integration."[48]

This is a very different type of project or parade than that carried out in Mexico. In the latter a self-confident revolutionary state set out to grant space to local historical characters in a parade it had constructed, teaching them how to march and what to wear. In the former a hesitant national state set out to find local parades, march in them for the first time, and—so it hoped—learn to keep time. Small wonder, then, that at the local level Peruvian intellectuals and political officials were not entirely convinced.

Yes, they applauded the army for marching in their parade. But they were also very clear on what they thought they might get in return. Perhaps a bit of stone, a refurbished plaza, a new flag; maybe their faces on television. They did not expect to participate in a unified, just nation-state. As Teogonio Ordaya, a local historian from Chupaca, told the Permanent Commission:

> We wish that all this could be recorded in Military History, for the good of our generations, because otherwise they will say we have kept quiet, that we have not known how to raise our voices; and we want the central government [*supremo gobierno*] to pay us back for the blood of our grandfathers, no matter how modest or humble they have been, the 600 Peruvians who sacrificed themselves on the altar of love for their homeland [*amor patrio*], at least by fixing the village's park which is so run down. I was telling the mayor some days ago, why don't you petition, why don't you do this, in Concepción they're fixing their main road and their park, and we have nothing. Yes, Mr. Ordaya, they have promised to make us into a new province, and I don't think this is only a congressional promise, which doesn't get any further than the words, with which they have been silencing us.[49]

Ordaya's words make clear that village intellectuals and political officials had little faith in the state's capacity to deliver. Given such an evident lack of political and material resources, local intellectuals must have perceived that they had little to gain, in terms of improving their local position of power, by joining a broader national coalition.

What was at stake went far beyond the role of local intellectuals in the articulation of village discourses and the degree to which it was possible to mediate regionally or nationally. Constructing a successful national parade also concerned the hegemonic consolidation of power, the kind of "cultural revolution," the mix of coercion and consent, discussed in chapter 8. A cultural revolution of this sort is successful when it is a nested process, going on at all levels, incorporating local hegemonic and counterhegemonic processes into the walls of its "great arch."[50] Yet the great arch itself must also exist: there must be something to incorporate into or mediate with. That is precisely what was generated in Mexico between 1855 and 1920 but was missing in Peru.

In Peru the only systematic attempt to provide a structure of mediation between local constituencies and a national political system occurred with the military revolution of 1968. Until 1975 the populist regime of Juan Velasco Alvarado created a series of mass organizations designed to connect popular movements to the state; but much of this work was reversed in the post-1975 "second phase" of military rule.[51] It is interesting to note, in this context, that the political rhetoric of the Permanent Historical Commission represents Velasquista "first-phase" populism.

Eduardo Mendoza was, in this sense, an heir of Velasco Alvarado. As late as 1982 he had no parade to march in, no eager group of dignitaries or intellectuals with whom to share his abundant knowledge and archive. Had anyone appeared at his gate, it would not have been a historian of national or international repute. The knock would likely have come from a Senderista guerrilla, charged with punishing those considered complicit with an illegitimate and repressive national state.

10 Popular Nationalism and Statemaking in Mexico and Peru

The Deconstruction of Community and Popular Culture

The 1980s were a decade of crisis in Mexico and Peru. In Peru the intensifying civil war waged by Sendero Luminoso ate away at the state and at the legitimacy and authority of elected officials. In Mexico a deepening economic and political crisis led, in 1988, to the first major electoral challenge the PRI had faced in a half-century of rule. And in both countries the crises and the responses to them paralleled the distinct historical constructions of the state I have been narrating for the 1850–1900 period.

The 1988 opposition candidate in the Mexican presidential elections was Cuauhtémoc Cárdenas, the leader of the Corriente Democrática that had recently broken off from the PRI's own left wing. The son of Lázaro Cárdenas, who in the 1930s built the hegemonic postrevolutionary state, Cuauhtémoc represented the "true" revolutionary legacy against the technocratic reformism of the PRI candidate, Carlos Salinas de Gortari. When Salinas won anyway, according to many observers through massive fraud, protests were held in the villages and neighborhoods throughout central Mexico. And by November 1991, when the Salinas government initiated attempts to reform article 27 of the 1917 constitution—the article pertaining to agrarian reform—coalitions of farmers and peasants formed to defend the revolutionary legacy. Once again they called on the symbolism of Zapata and the 1910 Revolution, turning their attention to Anenecuilco, that historic village in Morelos.[1]

During the first half of 1987 guerrillas from Sendero Luminoso began a concerted offensive in the central highlands of Peru. In addition to establishing de facto liberated zones along the uplands of the Mantaro's western bank—precisely in the regions where nineteenth-century guerrillas had also fought—they terrorized village authorities, merchants, and rural entrepreneurs throughout the region, murdering mayors and demanding an end to all commercial agricultural investment. As a political party, Sendero emerged from the ruins of the 1968 military revolution, Peru's most concerted attempt to build a hegemonic political order. From the beginning Sendero's political discourse consistently emphasized the total bankruptcy of the Peruvian state; any tactics that would help bring it down were considered legitimate. But in the wake of violent confrontation, the villagers of the central sierra organized self-defense units, or *rondas campesinas*, to push Sendero out of their communities. The discourse of *rondero* leaders from Comas eerily paralleled that of the nineteenth-century guerrillas: a collaboration with the army in defense of the nation would lead to the recognition of the Comasinos as citizens. And thus Senderistas and ronderos faced each other in the same upland regions and reproduced, even in their conflict, the figure of the eternally vigilant guerrilla, always on the margins of a nonexistent nation.[2]

These contrasting images serve to clinch the distinctions I have been making throughout this book: between a Mexican state that emerged as hegemonic because it incorporated a part of the popular agenda and a Peruvian state that never stabilized precisely because it repeatedly repressed and marginalized popular political cultures. These different trajectories were not sealed by events in the nineteenth century. But certainly the distinct options fashioned between 1850 and 1910—one completely submerging the popular discourses that emerged during periods of national resistance and political conflict, the other providing limited spaces within which they could survive and be reproduced—conditioned what has been possible since then.

Through an examination of popular political cultures, regional struggles, and the construction of alternative national discourses, this book offers a new, multilayered explanation for this distinction. Building such an explanation has meant embarking on a methodological and theoretical journey. I have explored the challenge of postmodernism within a perspective informed by Third World concerns and by a commitment to the historical analysis of power relations. The resulting narrative began with my intention to deconstruct the democratic revolution, to explore the multiple popular struggles and discourses buried within it. My initial assumption was that liberalism, nationalism, and democracy all had multiple meanings, both emancipatory and exclusionary. Bringing these ideals or ideologies to fruition involved specific historical struggles among various visions or projects regarding how they might be put into practice. Through these struggles some visions were repressed or submerged by others. The resulting "official story" was only a partial rendition of what had come before.

My narrative has rested on the combined analysis of discourse and political struggle. I have shown how neither can exist without the other. Concrete historical actors struggle over power, but they articulate the meaning of their struggles through discourses about citizenship, legitimacy, justice, and community. Discourses are not political or historical actors but the products of alliance and confrontation among human beings as they attempt to construct and own the meanings of their actions.

I have found explanations for the success or failure of hegemonic outcomes in the careful, long-term analysis of specific empirical regions and political movements and in the weaving together of communal, regional, and national levels of analysis. In applying this perspective to specific instances of nineteenth-century state formation in Latin America, I began with the case of the Mexican Sierra de Puebla. During the period of the Liberal Revolution of 1855, popular Liberalism was constructed as an alternative ideology in two contingent political alliances: the first between the Liberal leader Juan Alvarez and the peons of the haciendas Xochiapulco and La Manzanilla; and the second among the populist sierra Liberal Juan N. Méndez, the villagers of Xochiapulco, and the Totonac communities of the region's northeastern lowlands. In both cases the alliance was negotiated through specific interpretations of Liberal principles concerning land rights and political autonomy and through modifications of Liberal discourse to include concepts of social and ethnic justice. The Liberal leaders Alvarez and Méndez were willing to accept a more populist interpretation of Liberal principles because they needed popular political and military support in their efforts to claim space in emerging regional and national coalitions. Nahua and Totonac peasants in the sierra's villages promised military and political support in exchange for reestablishing control over their communal lands and municipal institutions through the medium of Liberal democratization. Yet despite its historical contingency, the alliance that yielded populist serrano Liberalism turned out to be the most effective, militarily speaking, throughout the civil war (1858–1861), the French Intervention (1861–1867), and the Restored Republic (1867–1876). It would also provide one of the most enduring nuclei of support for Porfirio Díaz's antistate movements in the 1870s and bring Montaña Liberalism to power in Puebla state during the early Porfiriato.

The indigenous peasant communities that underwrote this powerful counterhegemonic political and military coalition were not seamless or undifferentiated. Quite to the contrary. The villages were themselves political creations whose solidarity and unity were precariously articulated through processes of communal hegemony. Power differences along gender, generational, and ethnic and spatial lines were negotiated in the public spaces of the community—the civil-religious hierarchies, municipal governments, and communal assemblies—to yield a local "official version" of the community. This "official version" then served as the focus of articulation to, and negotiation with, emerging regional and national alliances and political cultures. Through articulation, communal, regional, and national political cultures mutually transformed each other, creating varied spaces of negotiation and conflict for the historical actors involved at each level.

In the Sierra de Puebla during the 1850s and 1860s, the national guard served as the main space of articulation between communal and regional political cultures. The younger Indian men who served in the national guard used their new status, and their influence with Liberal statemakers, to reconstruct the balance of power within their villages. They worked out a compromise with the elder pasados that I have called "democratic patriarchy." While continuing to marginalize women, this compromise distributed the fruits of citizenship and participation more evenly among men. At the regional and national levels the national guards used their access to communal hegemonic politics to bargain for further influence in the emerging Liberal coalitions during the 1855 Revolution and the French Intervention.

These multiple, shifting coalitions and conflicts were represented and worked out, at the discursive level, through the construction of what I have called alternative nationalist discourses. Taking the perspective of the village and region, I have demonstrated that evolving Liberal land policy—most notably the difference between the June 1856 law and the clarificatory circulars of October 1856—can best be explained by examining communal challenges to Liberal definitions of property. Moreover, beginning with the 1858–1861 civil war and continuing through the French Intervention, peasant guerrillas resisting the French and Austrian armies in the Sierra de Puebla worked out discourses on citizenship, and on entitlement to the fruits of national consolidation, that located rights in bravery rather than social status. The result was an alternative vision of nationalism in which property rights were tempered by a commitment to solidarity and social justice, while the status of citizen was tied to honorable actions rather than to birth, social class, or education.

In the second part of the book I have used the perspectives elaborated for the Sierra de Puebla to examine events in Morelos and in the Peruvian regions of the Mantaro Valley and Cajamarca. Specifically for Morelos, I have emphasized the creative engagement of rural peoples with both Liberal and Conservative discourses. This engagement occurred in the context of changing opportunities for political alliance at the regional and national levels, which in turn modified the terms of political debate within the villages. As was the case in Puebla, federalist leaders needed to take village issues in Morelos seriously in order to build broader coalitions. Doing so created spaces where communal political cultures could articulate within an emerging radical federalism, leading ultimately to the victory of Juan Alvarez in the 1855 Revolution.

In this context villagers, artisans, townspeople, and national guards in the districts of Cuernavaca and Cuautla Morelos elaborated increasingly radical and militant popular Liberal discourses. They connected access to land and citizenship to questions of workers' rights and social contract, prompting moderate Liberals as well as Conservatives to hone their own response in the racist articulation of indigenous democracy with barbarism. Yet in the end, as was also true in Puebla, Liberals faced a quandary. Their militarily most effective allies were also the ones who elaborated a radical discourse on citizenship and entitlement. The Liberal leaders of the 1855 Revolution, and of the Restored Republic of the late 1860s and early 1870s, would repeatedly stumble on this political contradiction. Their inability to resolve it would make hegemonic rule elusive.

In the Peruvian central highlands the Cacerista resistance to the Chilean occupation created, through the organization of montoneras, an intermediate space between communal institutions and regional or national coalitions that was roughly analogous to the Mexican national guard. In contrast to Mexico, however, where national guardsmen were an institutionally recognized part of the military sector, the very informality of the montoneras made their leaders less effective as mediators. Moreover, even though Cáceres relied heavily on montonero military support in his resistance campaign, he was not forced to depend on the montoneras at the political level. A politically marginal institution, the montonera was headed by mestizo or wari officers loyal to Cáceres. The goal of these officers, such as Ambrosio Salazar y Márquez or Bartolomé Guerra, was to use their control of the montoneras to ensure their upward mobility in the Cacerista coalition. Salazar in particular, but also other Cacerista officers such as Guerra or Esponda, struggled to claim the stories of resistance and victory that belonged to the villages, for they considered these narratives to be their strongest political stock in the struggle for advancement.

Given these tendencies, the more radical forms of local communal discourse in central Peru remained more isolated than those in Mexico and potentially less available for connection to alternative national coalitions. Rather than involving themselves in the construction of broadly popular nationalist discourses, villagers in the various subregions of the Mantaro fought to control their own narratives of heroism and resistance. Even during the Comas Alliance (1884–1902), the broader project for a federal state remained mainly within Comas district, and it was in any case constantly challenged by internal debates and divisions. Thus, despite the radicalism and sophistication of local politics, between 1885 and 1902 both the Cacerrista and Pierolista states successfully submerged alternative discourses through violent repression as well as various forms of racist "othering."

It should hardly surprise us, then, that the Peruvian state, consolidated through the repression and fragmentation of popular political cultures, had no capacity for inclusion or hegemony. Starting with the Cacerista years and gaining strength under Nicolás de Piérola, official political discourse conceptualized a limited national polity defined by quality rather than quantity. Only the civilized and educated—which by definition excluded communal peasants and illiterate Indians—could participate in modern political society. Thus structured around neocolonial principles of ethnic and spatial fragmentation, the first "modern" Peruvian state of the Aristocratic Republic would throw its long shadow of authoritarianism and exclusion across the entire twentieth century.

Despite the many differences among the cases of Puebla, Morelos, and Junín, they also shared a very important similarity. In all three areas strong and relatively autonomous communities nurtured local politics and spaces for communal hegemony and made more feasible the construction of alternative nationalist discourses. With Cajamarca as the limiting case, a comparison of the three regions makes clear that the existence and reproduction of communal political cultures and spaces was probably the most important single precondition for the development of alternative nationalisms. Yet even if communal hegemonic processes were necessary for the development of alternative nationalisms, we have also seen that they were not sufficient in and of themselves. Nor did they define the actual content or fate of the alternative nationalisms that did develop. Here, in fact, the differences among the regions of Morelos, Puebla, and Junín prove analytically central.

The contrasts among these three regions demonstrate that national politics were constructed through a three-tiered, nested process of struggle and interaction among communal hegemonic processes, regional political cultures, and emerging "national" arenas. Within the villages hegemonic popular political cultures were produced and reproduced through conflict and negotiation along gender, ethnic, generational, economic, and ecological and spatial lines. At the regional level various factions confronted or allied with each other in struggles over power and meaning, constructing and redefining regional political cultures. And at the emerging "national" level political and economic elites vied for hegemony among themselves, attempting to construct supraregional coalitions that could conquer and rebuild state power.

It is only through an analysis of all three levels, as well as their mutual interactions and articulations, that we can fully understand any one of the three. Differences among the cases existed within each tier as well as in the processes connecting each to the rest. An important distinction emerges, for example, in the way communal hegemonic processes combined village issues with regional struggles in Morelos and in Puebla. In the former, the stronger presence of radical federalism at the regional level throughout the first half of the nineteenth century made the maintenance of internal communal unity both easier and more desirable. In Puebla, by contrast, a more conflictual and fragmented regional political culture gave greater importance to internal conflict within communal spaces. Central Peru was more like Puebla in this regard. The lack of a viable popular political culture at the regional level yielded a wide range of communal and subregional political struggles and conditioned what was possible during the resistance to the Chileans. Finally, although the presence of the hacienda was a negative precondition to the development of alternative nationalism in Cajamarca, where communities were weak, it turned out to be a radicalizing force in regions with dynamic communal processes.

Differences also existed at the "national" level. In Mexico throughout the 1850–1876 period, Liberal politicians were more combative and Liberal discourses more responsive and open to popular participation. Deep sociopolitical cleavages among Mexico's elites, as well as repeated and long-lasting foreign intervention, provide a partial explanation for this openness and combativeness. So does the historical construction, across the first half of the nineteenth century, of regional political cultures where the practice of citizenship and popular federalism became a reality. Taken together, these conditions helped nurture popular nationalisms by articulating them to regional and national coalitions.

In Peru, though, the paths of political and discursive articulation, from communal to regional as well as regional to national, were more consistently and effectively blocked. Beginning with the repression of Túpac Amaru and ending with the fragmentation and "othering" that followed the War of the Pacific, power was accumulated through bloody exclusion rather than coalition or co-optation. This process led to the more complete fragmentation of potential popular nationalisms, both through repression and internal dissension. Despite the oppositional voice of the anarchist intellectual Manuel González Prada, the alternative popular discourses that had begun to emerge during the resistance to the Chilean occupation were effectively and fairly completely resubmerged.[3] As a result, rural popular discourses had no recognizable effect on emerging national agendas or on the form taken by the consolidating state.

In Mexico, by contrast, the popular agrarian movements and ideologies of the 1855–1876 period accomplished two major things. First, they established a presence in the emerging national discourses on political organization and land policy. Even if these were increasingly honored only in the breach, they ultimately set the context for the 1910 Revolution. Second, given their more successful articulations at the communal, regional, and national levels, alternative nationalist discourses in Mexico helped formulate and preserve an ever more coherent popular political agenda. When it reemerged in the post-1910 revolutionary context, this agenda put an enduring mark on the twentieth-century Mexican state.

The last link in my argument is the role of local intellectuals both in articulating local counterhegemonic discourses and in mediating among communal, regional, and national political arenas. In attempting to understand the diverse possibilities open to local intellectuals in Mexico and Peru, I began by placing the group as a whole in the difficult terrain between articulation and surveillance, arguing that all local intellectuals must make hard choices between two roles. One is the local counterhegemonic hero, who organizes local discourses and represents them to the outside. The other is the enforcer of more dominant forms of political culture who brings these more "official" discourses back into village politics.

In Mexico, where regional or national political coalitions were most responsive to local issues, needs, and perspectives, local intellectuals could mediate more effectively. Yet at the same time, the powerful hegemonic discourses of the postrevolutionary Mexican state limited the autonomy of local intellectuals, forcing them to choose between alienation and marching in the official parade. The latter choice, while giving the village intelligentsia a limited say in how official revolutionary culture was constructed and reproduced, also forced self-censorship around the more radical elements in local oral memory and political culture.

In Peru, the very lack of effective connection between community politics and regional or national coalitions gave local intellectuals few opportunities to serve as mediators. In contrast to the Mexico of the 1930s and beyond, Peruvian statemakers were unable to provide spaces where official versions of popular culture could emerge. The potentially positive side of this was, of course, that local and village intellectuals of necessity remained autonomous, unless they chose, like Eduardo Mendoza, to venture out in search of broader influence or authority. The negative result, however, was an inability to mediate or articulate local discourse to an emerging national polity. In Peru today, this lack of mediation and articulation continues to block the emergence of effective, accountable, national-level political coalitions. Civil war, and the erosion of effective state institutions, has been the long-term result of these failures.

My comparative, bottom-up approach to politics, discourse, and state formation in Mexico and Peru suggests some important revisionist directions for our understanding of nineteenth- and twentieth-century history. In Mexico the very success of the postrevolutionary hegemonic project has given priority to the study of high politics in attempts to unlock the workings of the state. While an equally thick tradition has existed in the analysis of social movements, rarely have the two been blended together successfully. Often this dichotomy has led scholars to "choose" between bottom-up approaches strong on socioeconomic analysis and top-down perspectives rich on political detail. Recently even John Womack, for so long associated with a bottom-up approach to the 1910 Revolution, announced his change of heart. "The subject is therefore no longer so much social revolution as political management," he wrote in defense of an analysis "short on social movements" and "long on the politics that created the new state." Yet for Womack as for others, the politics creating the new state remains overwhelmingly high, imbued with management and business metaphors.[4]

A different perspective is suggested by the complex political alliances and contestations I have unearthed for Morelos and Puebla, both at the communal and regional levels, and their various articulations within the emerging "national" political arena between 1850 and 1872. Only when these discourses and coalitions are taken seriously will it be possible to move beyond the dualistic divisions still present in so many of the analyses of social movements and political management in modern Mexico. And this is true not only in the analyses of social movements that privilege the socioeconomic but even in those that, more recently, have begun to explore political issues and alliances within the popular classes.

One such literature deals with peasant responses to the Liberal Revolution and the Reform Laws. Recent work on Sonora, Nayarit, Mexico City, and Oaxaca has confirmed, in a variety of settings, Jean Meyer's original revisionist insight about the destructive effects of Liberal policy on Indian communities and the consequent attraction of Conservatism for many indigenous movements. Yet the tendency has been, following Meyer, to create a new dualistic opposition between, on the one hand, a Conservatism more friendly to indigenous corporatism and more willing to ally with communal peasant movements and, on the other, a Liberalism always bent on the destruction of collectivism and the repression and containment of protest. But once we reach the early twentieth century and agrarian movements become allied with radical and revolutionary factions, it is hard to reconcile the supposedly enduring and conservative corporatism of peasant communities with radical *agrarista* politics. Is this simply *caciquista* manipulation? Extreme land hunger (once again the economic predominates)? Or, as John Tutino recently suggested, is it contradictory only for "elites and ideologues" since, from the standpoint of the peasantry, there was an enduring loyalty to corporatist goals that could be furthered through either Conservative or radical allies?[5]

If we take seriously the internal complexity and political sophistication of peasant and communal politics, we need not recreate dualisms between Conservatism and Liberalism, "high" politics and popular culture. As I have shown for Puebla and Morelos, choices between Liberal and Conservative allies were made through multifaceted and historically contingent struggles over power and meaning. Peasants were not wedded to an undifferentiated corporatism; Conservatives and Liberals were also internally divided, with some factions more open to alliances from below. And it was within the villages, in discursive and political conflicts organized around gender, class, and ethnic issues, that coalitions were forged between particular community factions and regional or national political allies. These ongoing struggles, with a long nineteenth-century genealogy, provide a much more satisfying backdrop to peasant radicalism at the turn of the century than does the concept of an unchanging commitment to corporatism.

Such a perspective also provides a welcome corrective to François-Xavier Guerra's recent study of the Porfiriato. Guerra contends that this "ancien régime" was the institutional expression of a "holistic" society untouched by "modern" politics.[6] In my analysis the Porfiriato emerges, quite to the contrary, as a problematic attempt to articulate the various regional political alliances, discourses, and agendas formed during the conflicts of the 1850–1876 period. This attempt became increasingly problematic in the 1890s and beyond, as Díaz moved away from his earlier base in regional populist coalitions and toward a base of positivist Liberals, *científicos*, and foreign and capital centered in Mexico City. The resuscitation of nineteenth-century popular agendas after 1910, by actors analogous (if not identical) to those who had participated in the earlier conflicts, thus did not constitute the reactivation of atavistic peasant communities but rather the reorganization of already sophisticated political alliances and discourses in a new context.

Finally, by examining the conflicts of the post-1910 period with an eye for the discursive continuities with earlier radical popular movements, I hope to establish a dialogue between my findings and Alan Knight's now classic attempt to resuscitate the 1910 conflict as a popular, agrarian revolution. A thorough treatment of his encyclopedic, complex, two-volume book is, of course, beyond the confines of my argument here. But one theme emerges in the book that merits particular attention: the relationship between what Knight calls *agrarista* and *serrano* rebellions.

Knight locates his distinction between agrarista and serrano rebellions both politically and spatially. He sees the former as occurring in lowland areas, where the dominance of the hacienda was more common. *Agrarismo* was thus a distinctly class-based, agrarian movement against the large hacendados, dominated by the demand for land. Serrano movements, by contrast, tended to occur in the upland regions where smaller properties survived more easily and where the village population, even if internally quite differentiated economically, was ready to form part of a cross-class alliance against the centralization of state power and in favor of regionalism or local autonomy. Serranos, then, according to Knight, participated in movements more diffuse in terms of social content, where lines of conflict were vertical (around differences in political power) rather than horizontal (along class lines). Thus, for Knight the two core demands of the popular revolution—land and political autonomy—can be mapped differently across national territory, following lines of ecology as well as politics. In a certain sense, the agrarista/serrano opposition relocates the division of social movements versus politics to a place inside the popular revolution.[7]

My work suggests, to the contrary, that the two core demands of the popular revolution after 1910 had emerged in constant historical interaction throughout the political, social, and discursive conflicts of the nineteenth century. Questions of land and political autonomy were the discursive cores around which political programs were debated. Communities, regional alliances, and coalitions vying for national power all hammered out their terms of unity around both issues. For most people, in fact, land and political autonomy could not be separated. The two questions interlocked and reverberated constantly in the ongoing struggles over power and meaning that formed communal and regional political cultures. The situations in Morelos and Puebla make this clear.

Even in a quintessentially agrarista area like Morelos, the more serrano regions of eastern Cuautla district, northeastern Guerrero, and the western sierra of Huitzilac were intimately related to the emerging popular movements in the *tierra caliente* near Cuernavaca. Land and political autonomy were debated and connected constantly in the villages and towns, where coalitions among peasants, landless laborers, petty merchants, and national guards formed as early as 1850. And the interconnection of both is clear in the Plan de Ayala as well.

In a quintessentially serrano region like the Sierra de Puebla, the alliance that underwrote Montaña Liberalism—during the Liberal-Conservative civil war; in the French Intervention and Second Empire; and throughout the federalist, Porfirista conflicts of the 1870s—was built through the political and discursive articulation of access to land and to political autonomy. This articulation occurred not only between the mestizo dwellers of Tetela de Ocampo and the Nahua former peons of the defunct haciendas Xochiapulco and La Manzanilla but also among the Totonac lowland villagers of Tenampulco and Tuzamapan, whose ejidos were being challenged by white entrepreneurs from Teziutlán. This alliance, both serrano and agrarista, was the military center of the resistance against the French. It would reemerge not only in the 1870s—when Porfirio Díaz established one of his La Noria general headquarters in Xochiapulco—but again during the 1910 Revolution, when Xochiapulco's old Nahua leader, Juan Francisco Lucas, led the region's peasants into battle for the Constitutionalists.

In addition to addressing issues of politics and social movements, my analysis of Mexico can be considered an intellectual history from below. As such, it establishes a dialogue with Charles Hale's two books on Mexican Liberalism, which together cover most of the nineteenth century. Since the core of my project as intellectual history is the placing of ideas and discourses in the context of sociopolitical conflict and shifting power alliances, in some ways the contours of my analysis fit better with Hale's first book, where he covers the period leading up to the Liberal Revolution of 1855. In this first volume he explores the ways in which, despite deep disagreements over the path to follow in the political and economic development of Mexico, both Conservative and Liberal intellectuals ended up agreeing on the saliency of the "social question" and on their common fear of uprising or caste war. In part because of this common fear, Hale suggests, Liberals especially were unable to formulate a more creative approach to social policies and to the political and economic inclusion of the masses in an evolving Mexican nation. Ultimately, therefore, the limits on Liberalism's social creativity in the 1855 Revolution must be sought at least in part in the overriding imperative of social control that emerged, for all members of Mexico's elite groups, during the first half of the nineteenth century. As I have shown here, this imperative was reconstructed and justified over and over in the 1855–

1867 period as both Conservative and moderate Liberal intellectuals and politicians elaborated racist discourses of exclusion in confrontation with radical agrarian movements.[8]

My findings on Mexican Liberalism between 1855 and 1867 also speak directly to the issues Hale treats in his second book on the rise of positivist Liberalism in late-nineteenth-century Mexico. Focusing on the Porfiriato, Hale examines the rise of positivism, or scientific politics, from within the Liberal camp in a period when Liberalism as such, having militarily and ideologically defeated the Conservative option, emerged as clearly dominant. Given the dominance of Liberalism, Hale argues, an understanding of positivism must emerge from an internal analysis of the tensions and contradictions in the various manifestations of Liberal thought in the Mexico of the Restored Republic and beyond. This line of argument fits quite well with my conceptualization of communitarian Liberalism and its demise after 1867. It was during a period of attack from without, whether during the Liberal-Conservative civil war or the French Intervention and the Second Empire, that the boundaries of antagonism around Liberalism could be much more flexible and the differences among its variants could be more fully submerged. Only after Liberalism had triumphed over its enemies, attaining dominance in the fields of politics and ideas, did internal differences take center stage. But it is in the kinds of internal differences we treat, and the priority we give to social conflict in the construction of these differences, that Hale and I part company.

Hale focuses his analysis on the internal tensions within the thought of prominent elite Liberals and on various debates among prominent intellectuals and policymakers about the proper way to promulgate the principles of the 1857 constitution. He does so consciously, as a historian of ideas who finds too mechanistic those analyses that treat ideas as reflections of economic and class interests. I agree. But I also hope that I have shown how it is possible, through an analysis of discourse and the construction of political coalitions, to decenter intellectual and political history to the point where the actions, language, and ideas of peasants, local intellectuals, and regional political coalitions become germane to our understanding of national politics and ideological debates. In this context the internal differences within Liberalism that I find most relevant to an understanding of positivism's rise in Mexico are precisely those that existed between locally and regionally constructed popular Liberalisms and the more centralizing, moderate Liberalisms that grew in opposition to them. These differences, however, must not be considered inherent in the class or regional identity of the people who had them; instead, they were the contingent result of specific processes of conflict over power and meaning. In this sense political, ideological, and social antagonisms within Liberalism were the result of the conflicts of the 1855–1867 period—interestingly enough, the only years in the nineteenth century not covered by Hale's two books. With the rise of scientific politics, positivism provided centralizing and more moderate Liberals with the new discursive weapons they needed to continue marginalizing the radical, federalist Liberalisms of the 1855–1867 period. Constructed through the struggles of that earlier period, radical Liberalism would again emerge to inspire the renewed struggles of 1910 and beyond.[9]

What unites my various dialogues with diverse works on nineteenth-century Mexico and the 1910 Revolution is an ongoing insistence that a careful analysis of local forms of politics—discourse and struggle, communal conflict and regional coalition, the actions and position of local intellectuals—must necessarily change the way we view the broad political, intellectual, and military events that so often form the core of our method in political history. This is an answer, in the Mexican context, to the ongoing challenge to reintegrate social history into politics. But it is an answer that does not transform the union into one of its component parts. Instead, I hope that I have demonstrated throughout the book that intellectual, political, and military history can and must be done "from below," and that done this way they transform our understanding of what is "above." Only in this way can we make political analysis into more than a one-way conversation, more than the sound of one hand clapping.[10]

The attempt to redefine politics through careful attention to popular culture and discourse has found increasing numbers of adherents in recent years. For Mexico it has emerged most strongly in the study of the 1910 Revolution, especially in the work by María Teresa Koreck, Daniel Nugent, and Ana María Alonso on various aspects of the Villista revolution in Chihuahua. Combining local ethnographic work with historical analysis, these scholars have used their examinations of local discourse to challenge unified analyses of "revolutionary" ideology. They have demonstrated, for the villages that formed the core of Villismo, how complex, contradictory, and violent has been the construction of the "official revolution" and how discourses of "reason," "legitimacy," and political inclusion have been contested throughout the twentieth century.[11]

Generally, however, these works have continued to draw the lines of conflict and contestation between "the popular" and more dominant forms of politics and discourse. What is still missing is a more complete appreciation of the internal complexity, hierarchy, and dynamism of popular political culture. And here lies, I hope, the deepest challenge of my work: in the commitment to, and partial carrying out of, an analytical agenda that places struggle and argument, conflict and coalition, solidarity and surveillance, at the center of our understandings of popular politics and popular culture. Even as the limitations of sources keep us from equal access to all voices within communities, even as we hear the voices murmured along the edges of the crowd mainly through hypothesis and imagination, we must resist the temptation to assume seamless unity or simplicity at any level of politics or discourse.[12]

By applying the concept of communal hegemony to our understanding of village politics, and by combining perspectives on gender, ethnicity, and class in my understanding of power relations, I have attempted to problematize the concept of community. Although my thickest description has been, of necessity, at the intersection between communal politics and regional coalitions, I have not assumed that local intellectuals or mediators represented a transparent consensus. Instead, I have worked from the assumption that, in any society organized around power relations, "the popular" is simultaneously oppositional and hegemonic. Our challenge, therefore, is to be sensitive to exclusion and repression not only in the relationship between dominant and popular discourses but within popular culture as well.

Yet in the end such a sensitivity must also make room for the very real cases where, despite internal hierarchy, exclusion, and domination, communal consensus is achieved, however partially or momentarily. At such moments local intellectuals truly do represent their communities, not because division and exploitation has ceased but because it has been put aside in the achievement of a historically specific political coalition. In my view much agrarian history can be summarized as the search for, and the occasional attainment and often very rapid loss of, such moments of consensus and unity. Despite its precious and ephemeral nature, however, I hope that I have shown that solidarity and consensus in popular political culture has a powerful transformative effect on political history more generally.

How do these musings apply to the case of Peru? In contrast to Mexico, the Peruvian project for national integration has remained on the drafting table. Dualistic political and cultural constructions of coast versus highlands, so important to colonial and neocolonial forms of rule and social control, have also affected intellectual production. Until the late 1960s and early 1970s few scholars were involved in work that would attempt to integrate an analysis of the highlands to the political history of the coast. Instead, the coast seemed to belong to historians, while the sierra (with the partial exception of Cuzco) was inhabited by anthropologists and political scientists. Only with the development of ethnohistory and the "new" social history has there been an attempt to historicize the highlands and connect them to the coastal centers of power.[13]

Since then the proliferation of studies has begun to define new arenas of debate, yet the dualism of earlier approaches has proved more stubborn than many would have predicted. Although we now know much more about regions, commercial routes, communities, and political movements than we ever did before, in many ways the challenge continues to be to find a methodology that effectively integrates highland and coast into an analysis of Peruvian politics. For some, such as Alberto Flores Galindo, the problem has been a lack of full attention to Andean political visions and practices. For others, such as Nelson Manrique, the problem has been too narrow a class approach to politics. And for some, such as Paul Gootenberg, the problem continues to be that analyses of coastal politics have been too superficial and broad fully to explain the nature of political debate or policy formation. My comparative and bottom-up approach to nineteenth-century political history provides, I think, some important revisionist clues that establish a dialogue with all three approaches.

In his recent book on Liberal economic policy, Gootenberg uses "thick description" and close processual analysis of coastal trade policy debates to trace the problematic evolution of Liberalism in nineteenth-century Peru. On one level I share Gootenberg's interest in demonstrating the complex ways in which political outcomes occur. Earlier in this book I analyzed numerous layers of conflict and discourse to probe the authoritarian underpinnings of Peru's "modern" state. At the same time, however, by establishing a political and discursive arena that connects highland and coast as well as different parts of the highlands, my analysis demonstrates the dangers of substituting a history of Lima—or of the coast more generally—for a history of Peru. While we can certainly benefit from the kind of more complex and nuanced study of the coast provided by Gootenberg, his tendency to claim "national" value for his analysis and to dismiss the relevance of the highlands reconstructs earlier dualisms rather than moving us beyond them.[14]

More promising, in this regard, is Nelson Manrique's recent and adventurous attempt to compare Cuzco and the central highlands between 1879 and 1910. In Peru, Manrique suggests, the War of the Pacific came to interrupt the project of a coastal bourgeoisie in formation. The resulting struggles and fragmentation, during a decade dominated by war, civil war, and foreign occupation, strengthened the traditional landowning class and forced the coastal elite to come to terms. Because of this, Peru entered the twentieth century with a state dominated by an alliance of coastal entrepreneurs and highland landowners, increasingly circumscribed by foreign capital. The implications were felt throughout the twentieth century, until the Velasquista revolution of the 1960s and 1970s attempted to undo what this alliance had wrought.

Especially in the central highlands, Manrique suggests, the nationalist indigenous peasantry, in coalition with a few "patriotic" elements of the landowning class, constituted a possible alternative alliance that might have provided the base for the incipient coastal bourgeoisie to pursue a more radical national project in the postwar period. Yet this alternative seemed doomed from the start because of the very isolation of such potential—which did not emerge at all in Cuzco, nor apparently in other parts of the country—and the ethnic and racial divisions that gnawed at the heart of the central sierra patriotic alliance itself. And, Manrique concludes, the peasants themselves did not have an advanced enough consciousness to pursue the obvious further alternative, which would have been a socialist project beyond the nationalism of Peru's elites.[15]

My analysis of the central highlands movement highlights two crucial aspects not considered by Manrique: the multilayered nature of peasant politics and peasant consciousness; and the importance of rural movements in the articulation of Peru's authoritarian option in the post-1895 period. In terms of peasant politics, my analysis of the internal conflicts and attempted processes of communal hegemony, not only within villages but also in distinct subregions, makes clear that the failure to unite around a more radical alternative was not the result of "undeveloped" consciousness. Quite to the contrary. Debates were intense in situations where mediation with broader coalitions was problematic at best. Villagers elaborated alternatives in creative and politically nuanced ways, working with the materials and options available to them.

On the nature of Peru's post-1895 authoritarianism, my approach makes clear that ethnicity was as crucial a variable as Manrique suggests. It divided the village population as much as it did campesinos and hacendados, however; and gender also established lines of internal fragmentation and of communal unity. Conflicts within communities, therefore, were as politically relevant as those between communities and landowners. When social control became the central imperative in the construction of the postwar state, authoritarianism emerged as much from the failure of mediation by village intellectuals and other intermediate elites as it did from a renewed alliance with the landowners.

My dialogue with Manrique makes it clear that measuring political outcomes along a linear, class-based yardstick—even when that approach is tempered by attention to ethnic factors—does not allow for a sufficiently profound look at Andean popular discourses and political cultures. This is indeed the starting point of Alberto Flores Galindo's work on the Andean utopia. On the basis of a long-term historical vision that spanned the period from the Spanish Conquest to the Sendero wars of the 1980s, Flores maintained that the core of a Peruvian political future must be found in the utopian indigenous traditions of the Andes. Along with his collaborator, Manuel Burga, Flores spent years tracing the origins and character of these utopian visions. From their beginnings among colonial indigenous intellectuals in the seventeenth century, through their articulation to movements as diverse as the Great Andean Civil War of the 1780s and the land reclamation movements of the 1920s, these visions consistently opposed a view of the more just and humane society and polity ruled by the Incas, to the creole- or coastal-dominated societies in existence at various points in Peruvian history.

In what was perhaps his most creative and radical statement, Flores suggested that all forms of creative oppositional politics in twentieth century Peru—from indigenismo to the populist APRA party to the socialism of José Carlos Mariátegui—were dynamic and creative precisely because they were indebted to the Andean utopia.[16] Such a perspective provides both inspiration and support for my attempts to argue for a political history from below. It connects as well, although I think unconsciously so, to Ernesto Laclau's earlier attempts to theorize, through a redefinition of populism, an approach to politics that does not involve reductionist views of class. Popular politics, according to Laclau, are the traditions formed in the context of struggles between "the people" and those in power. Such traditions are not necessarily tied to specific classes and can be articulated to a variety of different political movements. This is why, Laclau concludes, it is possible to think of populism in such a broad way—as leftist or rightist, fascist or socialist.[17] This is also why in the Andes, according to Flores Galindo, movements as diverse as indigenismo, APRA, socialism, and, more recently, Sendero Luminoso have all attempted to articulate to themselves the discourses of the Andean utopia.

But clearly, and as I have been arguing all along, the very articulation of popular politics to an emerging political coalition fundamentally changes the dynamics and meaning not only of the coalition in question but also of the popular discourses and practices themselves. In the case of the Andean utopia, for example, we must ask ourselves why there is no strong tradition of utopian movements in the nineteenth century and what effect this lack has had on their reemergence in the twentieth.[18] We must also ask what effect the emergence of a new republican order had on the alternatives open to popular discourse and practice, and whether this transition might have modified utopian visions and their potential articulation to broader movements.[19]

During the "long nineteenth century," when Latin American peoples faced the potentials and problems contained in the twin processes of capitalist transition and nation-state formation, Túpac Amaru represented the most widespread and sophisticated attempt to build a national project from the perspective of Andean political culture. According to the Bolivian social theorist René Zavaleta Mercado, the repression of Túpac Amaru was as deep as it was precisely because the alternative the movement presented was so subversive. Thus, it was especially important to close it off as violently and completely as possible.[20] After the 1780s the next conjuncture when Andean peasants were once again presented with the possibility of participating in an emerging multiethnic, multiclass nationalist coalition was during the War of the Pacific. In this case, however, the dominant internal discourse seemed to be a republican rather than an Andean one. Villagers claimed space within its boundaries through their memories of participation in defense of the nation. In the long run, of course, this claim also proved unacceptable because it radically called into question the existing balance of power. And so, from 1895 on, a new system of neocolonial domination was built, once again on the principles of an ethnic and spatial policy of divide and rule.

In the twentieth century, then, the revived importance of Andean utopian ideology must be assessed in the context of a double failure, across the "long nineteenth century," in the construction of an inclusive national project. First the Andean option failed with the repression of Túpac Amaru; then the republican option was eliminated by a "modern" neocolonial and authoritarian state built on the ruins of a peasant-inspired national resistance.[21] When the Andean utopia resurfaced in the twentieth century, therefore, its potential as counterhegemonic force was a great deal more peripheral, no longer the center of a populist national agenda but a marginal discourse murmured by voices along the edges of the nation. Because the potentially more inclusive forms of nineteenth-century republican state-making foundered on the realities of social conflict and social control, twentieth-century attempts to articulate popular discourses, whether by indigenous villagers or counterhegemonic intellectuals, would fall more readily between the reopened cracks of ethnic and spatial fragmentation.

Both nineteenth- and twentieth-century processes would also make clear, from a village perspective, that neither option, republican or Andean, was necessarily superior. To this day villagers and oppositional intellectuals continue to debate the consequences of these occurrences.

In Peru and Mexico, then, we have seen how multiple struggles over power—between and among popular and elite factions; between and among regional political cultures; within and between rural communities, villages, and towns; between young and old, women and men, rich and poor, and different ethnic groups—helped to make the kind of nation-states that Mexico and Peru brought into the contemporary period. We have also seen that the forms taken by these nation-states have reverberated back into the histories written about them, making certain questions inevitable and others unthinkable, placing limits on what intellectuals might allow themselves to imagine. Here, too, the challenge is to excavate: to clear out the accumulated dust and rock of earlier hegemonies and attempted hegemonies, thus unearthing the buried treasures of popular imaginings. In both Peru and Mexico these treasures are abundant and priceless. While in the latter country some of them were dug up and placed on display (even if usually mislabeled) in the museum of the 1910 Revolution, in the former they have been pushed even farther underground. These different histories, too, must affect the possible ways in which we rewrite the past today.

Rewriting the past, in ongoing and dialectical relation to our reinterpretations of the present, is the most important challenge I face as a historian. In an effort to continue meeting it, I wish to reiterate that, by decentering my approach to politics, I have rightfully placed popular political cultures at the core of all change, conflict, and creativity that accompanied nineteenth-century nation-state formation in Mexico and Peru. However, excavating the multiple, rich layers of rural intellectual and political life not only facilitates our understanding of the large historical processes but also prevents the romanticization and simplification of popular politics and rural communities. Neither task can be performed successfully in the absence of the other.

I am convinced that any process of burying or expunging local voices, even if it is done for the larger good of participation and solidarity, bears too high a cost. Simplifying local political and discursive practices denies the dignity, agency, and complexity of rural peoples and facilitates the kinds of racist and dualistic "otherings" to which they are still subject. When we pretend that oral history, ritual, and communal politics are not arenas of argumentation where power gets consolidated and contested, we submerge dissenting voices and help reproduce a false image of rural Eden (or idiocy) that has been repeatedly invoked, on the right and the left, to explain why urban politicians and intellectuals know what is best for innocent, ignorant, or naive rural folk. By omission or commission, many of us who write rural history, along with many local intellectuals, have been part of this ongoing conspiracy of silence.

Yet if we renounce a conspiracy of silence that simplifies popular culture, expunging its internal hierarchies, complexities, or disagreements, we must also break the silences that help us reproduce the simplicity of politics more generally. Politics is not, except in an official version, about the triumph of one class, idea, great man, nation, world region, or socioeconomic system. As a struggle over power, politics has always been about coalition and conflict along many lines of hierarchy; it has always involved the transformative power of discourse and confrontation.

Politics is also about hegemony, as process and outcome. In the making of nation-states, the discursive, intellectual, military, and political struggles of Latin American peoples, rural and otherwise, were central to defining both success and failure. Only by excavating the archaeological layers of these struggles, embedded in successful and unsuccessful hegemonic outcomes, can we understand present-day institutions and conflicts.

As was the case with Xochiapulco's bones, excavation is always a two-part process. First you dig, and then you struggle to identify what you found. We will never all agree on what the bones are, or why their identity matters. But historians can and must continue to dig and to place what we find in relation to present-day concerns, issues, and debates. In so doing, our labor in articulating past and present remakes both, endlessly.

Notes

ACDN	Archivo de Cancelados de la Defensa Nacional, Mexico City
ACEP	Archivo del Congreso del Estado de Puebla, Puebla City
ADC	Archivo Departamental de Cajamarca, Cajamarca, Peru
AGNEP	Archivo General de Notarías del Estado de Puebla, Puebla City
AGNM	Archivo General de la Nación, Mexico, Mexico City
AHDN	Archivo Histórico de la Defensa Nacional, Mexico City
AHM	Archivo Histórico Militar, Lima, Peru
AHMTO	Archivo Histórico Municipal de Tetela de Ocampo, Tetela, Puebla
AHMZ	Archivo Histórico Municipal de Zacapoaxtla, Zacapoaxtla, Puebla
AL	Archivo Leyva, Archivo General de la Nación, Mexico
APJ	Archivo Prefectural de Junín, Huancayo, Peru
BN-AJ	Biblioteca Nacional–Archivo Juárez, Mexico City
BN-LAF	Biblioteca Nacional–Colección Lafragua, Mexico City
BNP	Biblioteca Nacional del Perú, Sala de Investigaciones, Lima
CEHM-C	Centro de Estudios para la Historia de México, Condumex
CPHEP	Comisión Permanente de Historia del Ejército Peruano, Lima
Doc.	Documento
Exp.	Expediente
INAH	Instituto Nacional de Antropología e Historia, Archivo, Mexico City
Leg.	Legajo
Paq.	Paquete
Prot.	Protocolo
SAHOP-BN	Bienes Nacionalizados, Archivo General de la Nación, Mexico City
SRE	Secretaría de Relaciones Exteriores, Archivo, Mexico City
TP	Tranquilidad Pública, Archivo General de la Nación, Mexico City

PREFACE

1. The relationship between structure and agency is especially well developed in the work of Anthony Giddens; see *A Contemporary Critique of Historical Materialism*, 2 vols. (Berkeley: University of California Press, 1981, 1987), and *Central Problems in Social Theory* (London: Hutchinson, 1977).

CHAPTER 1. POLITICAL HISTORY FROM BELOW

1. Nelson Manrique, Ludy Ugarte, and I worked in the prefect's archive in Huancayo between the second half of 1977 and the first months of 1978. We gained admission to the collection through our affiliation with the Instituto de Estudios Andinos, a Huancayo research institute.

2. For the most developed form of this argument, see Heraclio Bonilla, "The War of the Pacific and the National and Colonial Problem in Peru," *Past and Present*, Nov. 1978, 92–118. See also Bonilla, "The Indian Peasantry and 'Peru' During the War with Chile," in Steve J. Stern, ed., *Resistance, Rebellion, and Consciousness in the Andean Peasant World, Eighteenth to Twentieth Centuries* (Madison: University of Wisconsin Press, 1987), 219–31.

3. See Florencia E. Mallon, *The Defense of Community in Peru's Central Highlands: Peasant Struggle and Capitalist Transition, 1860–1940* (Princeton: Princeton University Press, 1983), especially chapter 3; and Nelson Manrique, *Campesinado y nación: Las guerrillas indígenas en la guerra con Chile* (Lima: Ital Perú–C.I.C., 1981).

4. For an example of Manrique's later work, which helped refine, in a comparative context, some of his earlier formulations, see *Yawar mayu: Sociedades andinas terratenientes serranas, 1879–1910* (Lima: Instituto Francés de Estudios Andinos/DESCO, 1988). An advance on my comparative work within Peru is "Nationalist and Antistate Coalitions in the War of the Pacific: Junín and Cajamarca, 1879–1902," in Stern, *Resistance, Rebellion, and Consciousness*, 232–79. On Mexico, see Mallon, "Peasants and State Formation in Nineteenth-Century Mexico: Morelos, 1848–1858," *Political Power and Social Theory* 7 (1988): 1–54.

5. See, for example, Hans Kohn, *The Idea of Nationalism* (New York: Macmillan, 1944); Kohn, *The Age of Nationalism* (New York: Harper, 1962); Ernest Gellner, *Nations and Nationalism* (Oxford: Basil Blackwell, 1983); Carleton J. H. Hayes, *Essays on Nationalism* (New York: Russell and Russell, 1966); Charles Tilly, ed., *The Formation of National States in Western Europe* (Princeton: Princeton University Press, 1975); Eugen Weber, *Peasants into Frenchmen: The Modernization of Rural France* (London: Chatto and Windus, 1977); Elie Kedourie, *Nationalism* (London: Hutchinson, 1960); Hugh Seton-Watson, *Nations and States: An Enquiry into the*

Origins of Nations and the Politics of Nationalism (London: Methuen, 1977); and E. J. Hobsbawm, *Nations and Nationalism since 1780: Programme, Myth, Reality* (Cambridge and New York: Cambridge University Press, 1990).

6. The concept of an Indian-based socialism was developed most creatively by José Carlos Mariátegui, *Siete ensayos de interpretación de la realidad peruana* (Lima: Biblioteca Amauta, 1957). Indigenistas who partially shared his vision included Luis Valcárcel, *Tempestad en los Andes* (Lima: Editorial Universo, 1972), and the bibliography compiled in Valcárcel, *Memorias*, ed. José Matos Mar, José Deustua, and José Luis Rénique (Lima: Instituto de Estudios Peruanos, 1980); and Hildebrando Castro Pozo, *Nuestra comunidad indígena*, 2d ed. (Lima: Perugraph Editores, 1979). On the conservative side, notable examples include José de la Riva Agüero, *Afirmación del Perú* (Lima: Pontífica Universidad Católica del Peru, 1960); and, most recently, Mario Vargas Llosa, "Questions of Conquest," *Harper's*, December 1990, 45–53. For an analysis of the limitations and complexities of indigenista thinking, see Marisol de la Cadena, "'Indianness' and Interethnic Struggle: Popular and Elite Intellectuals in Cuzco, Peru, 1910–1990," Ph.D. diss., University of Wisconsin, in progress.

7. For a more extensive discussion of the implications of these debates and a complete bibliography of the discussion, see Mallon, "Peasants and State Formation," and Guy P. C. Thomson, "Popular Aspects of Liberalism in Mexico, 1848–1888," *Bulletin of Latin American Research* 10, no. 3 (1991): 265–92.

8. Benedict Anderson, *Imagined Communities: Reflections on the Origin and Spread of Nationalism* (London: Verso Books, 1983).

9. My definition of discourse owes most to Ernesto Laclau and Chantal Mouffe, *Hegemony and Socialist Strategy: Toward a Radical Democratic Politics* (London and New York: Verso Books, 1985), esp. ch. 3.

10. For the original definition of hegemony as the combination of coercion and consent, see Antonio Gramsci, *Selections from the Prison Notebooks*, ed. and trans. Quintin Hoare and Geoffrey Nowell Smith (New York: International Publishers, 1971). I developed the distinction between hegemonic process and hegemonic outcome for my presentation at the conference Everyday Forms of State Formation, Center for U.S.-Mexican Studies, San Diego, California, February 1991, in dialogue especially with the work of James Scott. See Scott, *Weapons of the Weak: Everyday Forms of Peasant Resistance* (New Haven: Yale University Press, 1985). Other works that influenced my formulation include Raymond Williams, *Marxism and Literature* (New York: Oxford University Press, 1977), esp. 108–14; Laclau and Mouffe, *Hegemony and Socialist Strategy*; Alastair Davidson, "Gramsci, the Peasantry and Popular Culture," *Journal of Peasant Studies* 11, no. 4 (July 1984): 139–53; Ranajit Guha, "Preface," *Subaltern Studies: Writings*

on South Asian History and Society, vol. 1 (Delhi: Oxford University Press, 1982), vii–viii; David Arnold, "Gramsci and Peasant Subalternity in India," *Journal of Peasant Studies* 11, no. 4 (July 1984): pp. 155–77; and Ernesto Laclau, *Politics and Ideology in Marxist Theory* (London: Verso Books, 1979), esp. 81–198.

11. For the consolidation of the state as a process of cultural revolution, see Philip Corrigan and Derek Sayer, *The Great Arch: English State Formation As Cultural Revolution* (Cambridge, Mass.: Basil Blackwell, 1985).

12. In addition to the sources cited in note 5, see also Horace B. Davis, *Nationalism and Socialism* (New York: Monthly Review Press, 1967); Davis, *Toward a Marxist Theory of Nationalism* (New York: Monthly Review Press, 1978); V. I. Lenin, *National Liberation, Socialism, and Imperialism* (New York: International Publishers, 1968); Rosa Luxemburg, *The National Question: Selected Writings*, ed. Horace B. Davis (New York: Monthly Review Press, 1976); Joseph Stalin, *Marxism and the National Question. Selected Writings* (New York: International Publishers, 1942); Anthony Giddens, *A Contemporary Critique of Historical Materialism*, 2 vols. (Berkeley: University of California Press, 1981, 1987); Tom Nairn, "The Modern Janus," *New Left Review*, no. 94 (1975): 3–29; and E. J. Hobsbawm, "Some Reflections on 'The Break-Up of Britain,'" *New Left Review*, no. 105 (1977): 3–23.

13. Janet L. Abu-Lughod, *Before European Hegemony: The World System A.D. 1250–1350* (New York: Oxford University Press, 1989). See also James M. Blaut, *The National Question: Decolonising the Theory of Nationalism* (London and New Jersey: Zed Press, 1987), and "Where Was Capitalism Born?" *Antipode: A Radical Journal of Geography* 8, no. 2 (1976): 1–11.

14. Among the authors who have begun to explore this relationship, and on whose work I have relied though not always agreeing with them, are Homi K. Bhabha, ed., *Nation and Narration* (London and New York: Routledge, 1990), especially the essays by Bhabha, 1–7 and 291–322, and Timothy Brennan, 44–70; Immanuel Wallerstein, *Capitalist Agriculture and the Origins of the European World-Economy in the Sixteenth Century* (New York: Academic Press, 1974), and *Mercantilism and the Consolidation of the European World-Economy, 1600–1750* (New York: Academic Press, 1980); Giddens, *Contemporary Critique*; Orlando Patterson, *Slavery and Social Death: A Comparative Study* (Cambridge: Harvard University Press, 1982); Anderson, *Imagined Communities*; Eugene Genovese, *From Rebellion to Revolution: Afro-American Slave Revolts in the Making of the Modern World* (Baton Rouge: Louisiana State University Press, 1979); and C. L. R James, *The Black Jacobins: Toussaint L'Ouverture and the San Domingo Revolution* (New York: Vintage Books, 1963).

15. Edward Said, *Orientalism* (New York: Vintage Books, 1978). For suggestions on the way in which orientalism was used to construct European exceptionalism, see esp. 111–97.

16. Partha Chatterjee, *Nationalist Thought and the Colonial World—A Derivative Discourse?* (Tokyo: Zed Books for the United Nations University, 1986), esp. 36–53. On some of the additional hierarchical forms taken by national-democratic thought, see Jean Bethke Elshtain, *Women and War* (New York: Basic Books, 1987); Catharine MacKinnon, *Toward a Feminist Theory of the State* (Cambridge: Harvard University Press, 1989); Partha Chatterjee, "The Nationalist Resolution of the Women's Question," in Kumkum Sangari and Sudesh Vaid, eds., *Recasting Women: Essays in Indian Colonial History* (New Brunswick: Rutgers University Press, 1990), 233–53; Ferenc Feher, *The Frozen Revolution: An Essay on Jacobinism* (Cambridge and New York: Cambridge University Press, 1987); and Jürgen Habermas, *The Structural Transformation of the Public Sphere: An Inquiry into a Category of Bourgeois Society*, trans. Thomas Burger with the assistance of Frederick Lawrence (Cambridge: MIT Press, 1989).

17. The struggles over the practice and meaning of national-democratic discourse occurred everywhere, not just in Europe. For some examples in the Americas, see James, *Black Jacobins*; René Zavaleta Mercado, *Lo nacional-popular en Bolivia* (Mexico City: Siglo XXI Editores, 1986); Genovese, *From Rebellion to Revolution*; and Steven Rosswurm, *Arms, Country, and Class: The Philadelphia Militia and "Lower Sort" During the American Revolution, 1775–1783* (New Brunswick: Rutgers University Press, 1988).

18. Nicos Poulantzas, *State, Power, Socialism* (London: New Left Books, 1978). For efforts to place this book within his general intellectual development, see Martin Carnoy, *The State and Political Theory* (Princeton: Princeton University Press, 1984), 151–71; and Bob Jessop, *Nicos Poulantzas: Marxist Theory and Political Strategy* (New York: St. Martin's Press, 1985).

19. The classic on the cultural and historical construction of class relations remains E. P. Thompson, *The Making of the English Working Class* (London: V. Gollancz, 1963). On gender, see Joan Scott, *Gender and the Politics of History* (New York: Columbia University Press, 1989). On ethnicity, I have relied especially on Paul Brass, "Ethnic Groups and the State," in Brass, ed., *Ethnic Groups and the State* (London: Croom Helm, 1985), 1–56; John Lonsdale, "When Did the Gusii (Or Any Other Group) Become a 'Tribe'?" *Kenya Historical Review* 5 (1977): 123–33; and Ronald Cohen, "Ethnicity: Problem and Focus in Anthropology," *Annual Review of Anthropology* 7 (1978): 379–403.

20. The concept of "pact of domination" comes from Poulantzas, *State, Power, Socialism*. Some of the works that have helped me conceptualize the interaction between gender hierarchies and other forms of power are

Elshtain, *Women and War*; MacKinnon, *Feminist Theory of the State*; Nancy Fraser, *Unruly Practices: Power, Discourse, and Gender in Contemporary Social Theory* (Minneapolis: University of Minnesota Press, 1989); Gerda Lerner, *The Creation of Patriarchy* (New York: Oxford University Press, 1986); R. W. Connell, *Gender and Power* (Stanford: Stanford University Press, 1987); Scott, *Gender and the Politics of History*; Chatterjee, "Nationalist Resolution"; and Ranajit Guha, "Chandra's Death," *Subaltern Studies*, vol. 5 (Delhi: Oxford University Press, 1986), 135–65. On the interactions between ethnicity and other forms of power, see, in addition to the sources cited in note 19, Partha Chatterjee, "Caste and Subaltern Consciousness," *Subaltern Studies*, vol. 6 (Delhi: Oxford University Press, 1987), 169–209.

21. Eric Van Young pointed to the economistic tendency in the literature on Mexican peasants in his essay "To See Someone Not Seeing: Historical Studies of Peasants and Politics in Mexico," *Mexican Studies / Estudios Mexicanos* 6, no. 1 (Winter 1990): 133–59. Breaking down the division between analysts and subjects is one of the central projects in Steven Feierman, *Peasant Intellectuals: Anthropology and History in Tanzania* (Madison: University of Wisconsin Press, 1990), from which I have derived much inspiration. For the quotation, see William Roseberry, *Anthropologies and Histories: Essays in Culture, History, and Political Economy* (New Brunswick: Rutgers University Press, 1989), 14. See also William Roseberry, "Beyond the Agrarian Question in Latin America," and Florencia E. Mallon, "Dialogues among the Fragments: Retrospect and Prospect," in Frederick Cooper, Allen Isaacman, Florencia Mallon, William Roseberry, and Steve J. Stern, *Confronting Historical Paradigms: Peasants, Labor and the Capitalist World-System in Africa and Latin America* (Madison: University of Wisconsin Press, 1992), 318–68 and 371–401, respectively.

22. For statements on the simplicity of politics inside the rural community, see Laclau and Mouffe, *Hegemony and Socialist Strategy*, 136–38; Partha Chatterjee, "More on Modes of Power and the Peasantry," in *Subaltern Studies*, vol. 2 (Delhi: Oxford University Press, 1983), 311–49; and Giddens, *Contemporary Critique*, 2:93–94, 150–54, 159–62. For a more detailed discussion of the implications of Laclau and Mouffe's perspective, see Mallon, "Dialogues among the Fragments." A longer discussion of these issues, and of the sources dealing with them, appears in chapter 3.

23. In addition to the sources on ethnicity and gender already cited, see Gayatri Chakravorty Spivak, "Subaltern Studies: Deconstructing Historiography," in Spivak, ed., *In Other Worlds: Essays in Cultural Politics* (New York and London: Routledge, 1988), 197–221. See also Michael E. Meeker, *The Pastoral Son and the Spirit of Patriarchy: Religion, Society, and Person among East African Stock Keepers* (Madison: University of Wisconsin Press, 1989).

24. On local intellectuals, see Feierman, *Peasant Intellectuals*.

25. On the question of transition and cultural openness, I have found the work of Mikhail Bakhtin especially helpful. See Mikhail Bakhtin, *Rabelais and His World*, trans. Hélène Iswolsky (Bloomington: Indiana University Press, 1984); Bakhtin, "Discourse in the Novel," in *The Dialogic Imagination: Four Essays*, ed. Michael Holquist, trans. Caryl Emerson and Michael Holquist (Austin: University of Texas Press, 1981), 259–422; Robert Stam, "Mikhail Bakhtin and Left Cultural Critique," in E. Ann Kaplan, ed., *Postmodernism and Its Discontents: Theories, Practices* (London and New York: Verso Books, 1988), 116–45; Ken Hirschkop, "A Response to the Forum on Mikhail Bakhtin," in Gary Saul Morson, ed., *Bakhtin: Essays and Dialogues on His Work* (Chicago: University of Chicago Press, 1981), 73–79; and Hirschkop, "Bakhtin, Discourse, and Democracy," *New Left Review*, no. 160 (1986): 92–114.

26. On the "moment of departure," see Chatterjee, *Nationalist Thought*, 50, 54–81.

27. On the "moment of manoevre," see ibid., 51, 85–125; quotation on p. 51. The following sources were also helpful for thinking about the innovation in popular culture: Bakhtin, *Rabelais and His World*, esp. 101, 121; Hirschkop, "Response to the Forum" and "Bakhtin, Discourse, and Democracy."

28. On the "moment of arrival," see Chatterjee, *Nationalist Thought*, 51, 131–62; quotation on p. 51.

29. Giddens, *Contemporary Critique*, develops the dynamic interaction between structure and agency. The quotation is from Chatterjee, *Nationalist Thought*, 52.

30. Florencia E. Mallon, "Editor's Introduction," *Latin American Perspectives* 13, no. 1 (Winter 1986): 3–17 (special issue, Latin America's Nineteenth-Century History); and "Peasants and the 'National Problem' During the 'Middle Period' of Latin American History: Alternative National Projects in Mexico and Peru, 1850–1910," paper presented at the American Historical Association Conference, Washington, D.C., December 1987.

31. The literature on the Mexican Revolution is far too vast to cite here. For an introduction to the issues, see Roger Bartra, *La jaula de la melancolía: Identidad y metamorfosis del mexicano* (Mexico City: Grijalbo, 1987); Alan Knight, *The Mexican Revolution*, 2 vols. (Cambridge and New York: Cambridge University Press, 1986); David Brading, ed., *Caudillo and Peasant in the Mexican Revolution* (Cambridge and New York: Cambridge University Press, 1980); Arnaldo Córdova, *La política de masas del cardenismo* (Mexico: Ediciones Era, 1974); Nora Hamilton, *The Limits of State Autonomy* (Princeton: Princeton University Press, 1982); Jean Meyer, *La Cristiada*, 3 vols. (Mexico: Siglo XXI Editores, 1974); Alan Knight, "Revolutionary Project, Recalcitrant People: Mexico, 1910–1940," in Jaime

E. Rodríguez O., *The Revolutionary Process in Mexico: Essays on Political and Social Change, 1880–1940* (UCLA: Latin American Center Publications, University of California–Los Angeles, 1990), 227–64; and John Womack, Jr., "The Mexican Revolution, 1910–1920," in Leslie Bethell, ed., *The Cambridge History of Latin America*, vol. 5 (Cambridge and New York: Cambridge University Press, 1986), 79–153.

32. Some works that have helped me understand the first decades of the twentieth century in Peru are Alberto Flores Galindo, *La agonía de Mariátegui: La polémica con la Komintern* (Lima: DESCO, 1980); Manuel Burga and Alberto Flores Galindo, *Apogeo y crisis de la república aristocrática*, 2d ed. (Lima: Rikchay Peru, 1981); Peter Klarén, *La formación de las haciendas azucareras y los orígenes del APRA*, 2d ed. (Lima: Instituto de Estudios Peruanos, 1976); Baltazar Caravedo Molinari, *Clases, lucha política y gobierno en el Perú (1919–1933)* (Lima: Retama Editorial, 1977); Manuel Burga, "Los profetas de la rebelión, 1920–23," and Alberto Flores Galindo, "El horizonte utópico," in Jean Paul Deler and Yves Saint-Geours, comps., *Estados y naciones en los Andes: Hacia una historia comparativa: Bolivia, Colombia, Ecuador, Perú*, vol. 2 (Lima: Instituto de Estudios Peruanos / Instituto Francés de Estudios Andinos), 465–517, 519–69, respectively; and Steve Stein, *Populism in Peru: The Emergence of the Masses and the Politics of Social Control* (Madison: University of Wisconsin Press, 1980).

33. I give this comparison more extensive treatment in Florencia E. Mallon, "Indian Communities, Political Cultures, and the State in Latin America, 1780–1990," *Journal of Latin American Studies* 24, suppl. (fall 1992): 35–53.

34. On independence in Mexico, see John Lynch, *The Spanish American Revolutions, 1808–1826* (New York: Norton, 1973), 294–334; Brian Hamnett, *Roots of Insurgency: Mexican Regions, 1750–1824* (Cambridge: Cambridge University Press, 1986); "Royalist Counterinsurgency and the Continuity of Rebellion: Guanajuato and Michoacán, 1813–20," *Hispanic American Historical Review* 62, no. 1 (Feb. 1982): 19–48; William B. Taylor, "Banditry and Insurrection: Rural Unrest in Central Jalisco, 1790–1816," in Friedrich Katz, ed., *Riot, Rebellion, and Revolution: Rural Social Conflict in Mexico* (Princeton: Princeton University Press, 1988), 205–46; and Eric Van Young, "Moving Toward Revolt: Agrarian Origins of the Hidalgo Rebellion in the Guadalajara Region," in Katz, *Riot, Rebellion, and Revolution*, 176–204. On connections and survivals in the 1821–1855 period, see Peter Guardino, "Peasants, Politics, and State Formation in Nineteenth-Century Mexico: Guerrero, 1800–1857," Ph.D. diss., University of Chicago, 1992; and Leticia Reina, *Las rebeliones campesinas en México (1821–1906)* (Mexico City: Siglo XXI Editores, 1980).

35. On Túpac Amaru, see, in Stern, *Resistance, Rebellion, and Consciousness*, the essays by Stern (29–93), Magnus Möerner and Efraín Trelles (94–

109), Leon Campbell (110–39), and Jan Szeminski (166–92); see also Alberto Flores Galindo, ed., *Túpac Amaru II—1780: Sociedad colonial y sublevaciones populares* (Lima: Ediciones Retablo de Papel, 1976). On independence, see Mallon, *Defense of Community*, 42–52; Lynch, *Spanish American Revolutions*, 266–93; Heraclio Bonilla and Karen Spalding, eds., *La independencia en el Perú* (Lima: Instituto de Estudios Peruanos, 1972); and Raúl Rivera Serna, *Los guerrilleros del centro en la emancipación peruana* (Lima: Edición Talleres Gráficos Villanueva, 1958). On the nineteenth century up to the War of the Pacific, see Mallon, *Defense of Community*, 42–79; Mallon, "Minería y agricultura en la sierra central: Formación y trayectoria de una clase dirigente regional," in *Lanas y capitalismo en los andes centrales*, Taller de Estudios Andinos, Universidad Nacional Agraria La Molina, Serie Andes Centrales, no. 2, part 2: Estudios, pp. 1–12 (mimeo); Nelson Manrique, *Mercado interno y región: La sierra central, 1820–1930* (Lima: DESCO, 1987); Nils Jacobsen, "Landtenure and Society in the Peruvian Altiplano: Azángaro Province, 1770–1920," Ph.D. diss., University of California, Berkeley, 1982; and Paul Gootenberg, *Between Silver and Guano: Protectionist Elites to a Liberal State in Peru, 1820–1850* (Princeton: Princeton University Press, 1990).

36. On debates about Indian citizenship in Mexico, see especially Jean Meyer, *Problemas campesinos y revueltas agrarias (1821–1910)* (Mexico City: Secretaría de Educación Pública, 1973), and Francisco Pimentel, *Memoria sobre las causas que han originado la situación actual de la raza indígena de México y medios de remediarla* (Mexico City: Imprenta de Andrade y Escalante, 1864). On Peru, see Víctor Andrés Belaúnde, *La crisis presente, 1914–1939* (Lima: Ediciones "Mercurio Peruano," n.d.), 32–79. I am grateful to Marisol de la Cadena for bringing this source to my attention. See also Mark Thurner, "From Two Nations to One Divided: The Contradictions of Nation-Building in Andean Peru: The Case of Huaylas," Ph.D. diss., University of Wisconsin–Madison, 1993; and Tristan Platt, "Simón Bolívar, the Sun of Justice and the Amerindian Virgin: Andean Conceptions of the *Patria* in Nineteenth-Century Potosí," *Journal of Latin American Studies* 25, no. 1 (Feb. 1993): 159–85.

37. In my conceptualizations of the national guard as a crucial political space, I was greatly aided by my ongoing discussions with colleague and fellow Puebla enthusiast Guy Thomson. See especially his article "Bulwarks of Patriotic Liberalism: The National Guard, Philharmonic Corps and Patriotic Juntas in Mexico, 1847–88," *Journal of Latin American Studies* 22, no. 1 (Feb. 1990): 31–68.

38. See the sources cited in note 31.

39. See the sources cited in note 32. For my use of the term "divide and rule" and its origins in colonial forms of domination, I am indebted to the work of Cynthia Enloe, especially *Ethnic Soldiers: State Security in Divided*

Societies (Athens: University of Georgia Press, 1980) and *Police, Military and Ethnicity: Foundations of State Power* (New Brunswick, N.J.: Transaction Books, 1980).

40. The questions I raise here are and have been the subject of intense debate. See, for example, James Clifford, "On Ethnographic Authority," and "Power and Dialogue in Ethnography," in Clifford, *The Predicament of Culture: Twentieth-Century Ethnography, Literature, and Art* (Cambridge: Harvard University Press, 1988), 21–54, 55–91. See also the response of Nicole Polier and William Roseberry to some of the issues raised more generally by postmodern anthropologists: "Tristes Tropes: Postmodern Anthropologists Encounter the Other and Discover Themselves," *Economy and Society* 18, no. 2 (May 1989): 245–64. I have drawn inspiration, in a variety of ways, from the following sources: Paul Friedrich, *The Princes of Naranja: An Essay in Anthrohistorical Method* (Austin: University of Texas Press, 1986); Jeffrey Gould, *To Lead As Equals: Rural Protest and Political Consciousness in Chinandega, Nicaragua, 1912–1979* (Chapel Hill: University of North Carolina Press, 1990); June Nash, *We Eat the Mines and the Mines Eat Us: Dependency and Exploitation in Bolivian Tin Mines* (New York: Columbia University Press, 1979); and Gerald M. Sider, *Culture and Class in Anthropology and History: A Newfoundland Illustration* (New York: Cambridge University Press, 1986).

41. Williams, *Marxism and Literature*, 112, 116.

CHAPTER 2. CONTESTED CITIZENSHIP (1)

1. The picture presented in this paragraph is a composite of the following sources: AGNM, Gobernación: Leg. 1161 (2), Exp. 18, "Oficio del Prefecto de Tulancingo al Ministerio de Gobernación," 19 Mar. 1865; "Oficio del Prefecto de Tulancingo al Ministerio de Gobernación," 23 Mar. 1865; AHDN, D/481.4/9519, ff. 50–51: "Sobre el ofrecimiento de sumisión de D. Simon Cravioto," Oct.–Nov. 1864; AHDN, XI/481.4/9109, ff. 249–50: "Oficio del Comandante Militar de Tulancingo al Ministerio de Guerra," 30 Oct. 1863; and BN-AJ, Doc. 2592: "Rafael Cravioto a Benito Juárez," Huauchinango, 29 July 1867.

2. Xochiapulco's resistance to the French Intervention is analyzed in further detail below. Xochiapulco's surrender to the empire is reproduced in *Diario del Imperio*, 9 Mar. 1866, p. 264. Evidence of renewed liberal resistance in the area appears in AHMTO, Gobierno, Caja s/n 1866: Exps. 35, 41, and 71.

3. Despite extensive writings on nineteenth-century Mexican Liberal politics, few authors have treated systematically the immense differences and conflicts within Liberalism. One creative start in this direction is Alan Knight, "El liberalismo mexicano desde la Reforma hasta la Revolución (una interpretación)," *Historia Mexicana* 35, no. 1 (July–Sept. 1985): 59–91. See

also Guy P. C. Thomson, "Popular Aspects of Liberalism in Mexico, 1848–1888," *Bulletin of Latin American Research* 10, no. 2 (1991): 265–92. A recent overview of the development of creole elite liberalism is D. A. Brading, *The First America: The Spanish Monarchy, Creole Patriots, and the Liberal State, 1492–1867* (Cambridge: Cambridge University Press, 1991). For the differences within the liberal coalition that would emerge after the defeat of the empire, see Laurens B. Perry, *Juárez and Díaz: Machine Politics in Mexico* (De Kalb: Northern Illinois University Press, 1978), 3–56. For differences within Liberalism during the Porfiriato, see Charles A. Hale, *The Transformation of Liberalism in Late Nineteenth-Century Mexico* (Princeton: Princeton University Press, 1989).

4. On the active commercial relations with Veracruz that existed in the Zacapoaxtla area during the 1840s, see AGNEP, Zacapoaxtla, Caja 6, 1841–1848: Año 1842, ff. 2v–3v, 3v–4v, 4v–6, 78–79; Año 1843, ff. 22–23, 67v–69v, 99v–100v; Año 1844, ff. 4–5v; Año 1847, ff. 20v–22; and Caja 7, 1849–1869: Libro 1852–1853, ff. 12–12v. On attempts from Zacapoaxtla to control commerce in other centers in the area, as well as on uses of debt originating in commerce to tie laborers to properties, see AGNEP, Zacapoaxtla, Caja 6, 1841–1848: Prot. 1841, José Antonio Ochorena, ff. 65–66v; Año 1842, ff. 31–32; Caja 7, 1849–1869: Libro 1852–1853, ff. 55v, 57–57v; Libro 1855, ff. 7–7v, 9. On the changing management of the haciendas Xochiapulco and La Manzanilla during the 1840s, including the planting of sugar cane, see AGNEP, Zacapoaxtla, Caja 6, 1841–1848: Año 1843, ff. 51–54, 71–78v, and 78v–83v. On the larger economic and entrepreneurial activities of the Salgados, see also AGNEP, Zacapoaxtla, Caja 6, 1841–1848: Año 1848, ff. 56v–58; Caja 7, 1849–1869: Libro 1852–1853, 14v–16v. Beyond the evidence provided in the above documents on the new use of the resident labor force, as well as the issue of grazing rights, disputes over livestock grazing are also remembered as a cause for the original confrontation in Xochiapulco's own oral history. See Donna Rivera Moreno, *Xochiapulco: Una gloria olvidada* (Puebla: Dirección General de Culturas Populares, 1991), 49–50, based on the oral accounts originally gathered by Manuel Pozos, a schoolteacher in Xochiapulco at the turn of the century. See also Secretaría de Educación Pública, Dirección General de Internados de Enseñanza Primaria, Internado Núm. 19 "Pedro Molina Corona," "Homenaje al Heroe Nacional Gral. Juan Francisco Lucas, Patriarca de la Sierra, en Ocasión de Inaugurarse el Monumento Erigido a su Memoria en el Lugar de Su Nacimiento," Comaltepec, Zacapoaxtla, 12 Oct. 1956, p. 13.

5. On Manuel Lucas's sojourn in Veracruz and on his activities as a wool merchant, see Rivera Moreno, *Xochiapulco*, 44, and Secretaría de Educación Pública, "Homenaje al Heroe Nacional Gral. Juan Francisco Lucas." On the differentiation between indigenous and white commerce, see Bernardo García Martínez, *Los pueblos de la sierra: El poder y el espacio entre los indios*

del norte de Puebla hasta 1700 (Mexico City: El Colegio de México, 1987), and Lourdes Arizpe S., *Parentesco y economía en una sociedad Nahua: Nican Pehua Zacatipan* (Mexico City: Instituto Nacional Indigenista / Secretaría de Educación Pública, 1973), esp. 30, 34. On the interpenetration of ethnic domination and commercial relations, especially by Zacapoaxtla against its barrios and sujetos, see AGNEP, Zacapoaxtla, Caja 6, 1841–1848: Año 1842, ff. 31–32, 64–66v; Prot. 1841, José Antonio Ochorena, ff. 65–66v; Caja 7, 1849–1869: Libro 1852–1853, ff. 55v, 57–57v; Libro 1855, ff. 7–7v, 9.

6. On the military role of Xochiapulco between 1850 and 1858 and the persecution of Juan Francisco Lucas as liberal leader, see Rivera Moreno, *Xochiapulco*, 44–51; and AHDN, XI/481.3/5435, f.1: "Parte telegráfico del Com. Gral. del Edo. de Veracruz," 29 Aug. 1856; XI/481.3/5307: "Parte del Gral. Tomás Moreno al Ministerio de Guerra y Marina," 6 Nov. 1856, esp. f. 23; "Oficio del Comandante Militar de Teziutlán," 8 Nov. 1856; "Parte de Rafael Junguito al Ministerio de Guerra y Marina," Cuartel General en Zacapoaxtla, 22 Dec. 1856, esp. f. 293; XI/481.3/5321: "Parte de Agustín Roldán al Gral. de las fuerzas de Chignahuapan," Zacapoaxtla, 14 Nov. 1856, esp. f. 18v; "Parte de Manuel F. Soto al Ministerio de Guerra y Marina," 29 Nov. 1856.

7. *Trapiches* were local crushing and milling operations for sugar; *aguardiente* is a rough liquor made from sugar cane. On the history of Tetela, see García, *Los pueblos de la sierra*, 117, 134, 144, 148–49, 159, 214, 232–33, 233n; Guy P. C. Thomson, "*Montaña* and *Llanura* in the Politics of Central Mexico: The Case of Puebla, 1820–1920," in Wil Pansters and Arij Ouweneel, eds., *Region, State, and Capitalism in Mexico: Nineteenth and Twentieth Centuries* (Amsterdam: CEDLA, 1989), esp. 60–67; CEHM-C, Colección Puebla, *Corona Fúnebre Dedicada al Señor General de División Juan N. Méndez por Algunos Ciudadanos de Tetela de Ocampo, Amigos y Admiradores del Ilustre Soldado del Progreso y la Democracia* (Mexico City: Imprenta de Daniel Cabrera, 1895); and *Corona Fúnebre que la Gratitud Pública Coloca sobre la Tumba del General Juan Crisóstomo Bonilla* (Mexico City: Imprenta de Francisco Díaz de León, 1884). For some of the commercial relationships and the issues that started to come up with mining and aguardiente production in the nineteenth century, see AGNEP, Zacatlán, Caja 12, 1847–1879: Libro 1847–1849, Prot. 1847, ff. 1–1v, 53v–59, 59–60; and AHMTO, Gobierno, Caja 8: Exp. 11, "Lista de todos los Señores que tienen giros mercantiles y establecimientos industriales," 2 May 1856. On agriculture, both its relative egalitarianism and the potential changes during the first half of the nineteenth century, see also AHMTO, Gobierno, Caja 5: Exp. 7, "Informe municipal sobre la administración y agricultura locales," 27 July 1841; Caja 6: Exp. 2, "Copia de la Escritura de arrendamiento del Rancho de Taxcantla de los propios y arbitrios del Ayunta-

miento, la que se ha otorgado en favor del C. Francisco Perez," 3 Nov. 1852; Exp. 6, "Inventario de los útiles que pertenecen á la Municipalidad de Tetela del Oro . . . ," 16 Aug. 1855; Caja 8: Exp. 11, "Lista de los Señores que en esta municipalidad benefician Fincas Rusticas de labor . . . ," 5 May 1856.

8. Around Tetela, the villages of Olintla, Huehuetla, San Gerónimo, Huitzilan, and Atlequizayan (Hueytlalpan) all sought legal representation in matters referring to boundaries. See AGNEP, Zacapoaxtla, Caja 6, 1841–1848, Año 1847: ff. 2v–4; Caja 7, 1849–1869: ff. 132–35v; and Zacatlán, Caja 12, 1847–1879, Prot. 1848: ff. 44–44v. On the conflicts between, on the one hand, Teziutlán and Atempan and, on the other, Ecatlán and Tenampulco— the last two sujetos of Xonotla (or Jonotla) municipality in the *partido* of Tetela—see AGNEP, Zacapoaxtla, Caja 6, 1841–1848: Año 1842, ff. 28v–29v; Año 1846, ff. 2v–6.

9. Around Huauchinango and Zacatlán, the pueblos of Ahuacatlán, Xaltepec, Cuaxicala, Coyay, Xuxupango, Cuatoloi, San Cristobal, San Marcos, and Analco all engaged in legal action about boundaries among villages. See AGNEP, Huauchinango, Caja 1, 1851–1860: Libro 1853, 12 May 1853; and Zacatlán, Caja 12, 1847–1879: Libro 1847–49, Prot. 1847, ff. 49–50; Prot. 1849, ff. 36v–38, 38–39, 39–40v, 43v–44v. On the colonial history of Huauchinango and Zacatlán, see García, *Los pueblos de la sierra,* esp. 139, 148–49, 232–33, 234–35, 237, 253–54. On the development of an aguardiente industry after independence, the increment of commerce and commercial production, and the development of the mining economy in Tetela, see Thomson, "*Montaña* and *Llanura,*" 60–67; Jacinto Anduiza, *Rasgos biográficos del señor General Rafael Cravioto* (Mexico City: Imp. "La Europea" R. Arquero y Comp., 1892); and AGNEP, Zacatlán, Caja 12, 1847–1879: Libro 1847–49, Prot. 1847, ff. 1–1v, 59–60; Prot. 1849, ff. 24–25; Huauchinango, Caja 1, 1851–1860: Libro 1851, 2 Jan., 7 Mar., 9 Dec.; Libro 1853, 2 Apr., 12 July; Libro 1854, 3 Aug.; Libro 1855, 20 and 31 Mar. On the struggles of Chignahuapan and Aquixtla with Zacatlán and Tetela, see García, *Los pueblos de la sierra,* 160n, 232–33, 233n, 300–301; on Huauchinango and the struggles over labor drafts to Tulancingo, see 253–54. On the new political divisions after independence, see Aurea Commons de la Rosa, *Geohistoria de las divisiones territoriales del Estado de Puebla (1519–1970)* (Mexico City: UNAM, 1971), and map appendix "Anexos cartográficos."

10. The various and complex alliances that villages along the western sierra established with Liberals, Conservatives, and Interventionists can be traced most completely in the AHDN. See XI/481.3/5562: "Copia del Plan formulado en Zacapoaxtla, el 19 de diciembre de 1855, . . . y adhesiones del Gral. Manuel Andrade y Prefectura de Tulancingo"; XI/481.3/5321: "Partes de Manuel F. Soto, Comandante Militar en Zacatlán, al Ministerio de Guerra y Marina," 9 and 20 Nov. 1856; "Parte de M. O'Horan al Ministerio de Guerra y Marina," 24 Nov. 1856; "Oficios de Manuel F. Soto al Ministerio

de Guerra y Marina [2]," 24 Nov. 1856; "Diario de D. Fernando López, jefe conservador en Zacapoaxtla," 10 Oct.–8 Nov. 1856. See also BNM, LAF 839: "Ejército de operaciones sobre Puebla: Parte general," 23 Mar. 1856.

11. The Catholic church gained popular support in this region by supporting Zacapoaxtla in its struggles with Tlatlauquitepec. See García, *Los pueblos de la sierra*, 217–20, 218n. On the 1849 action by the alcaldes of Zongozotla, Nanacatlán, and Tuxtla, see AGNEP, Zacapoaxtla, Caja 7, 1849–1869: Libro 1849–1851, ff. 6–9. Suggestions of possible conflict among the barrios in western Zacapoaxtla over the lands of Xochiapulco appear in Ramón Sánchez Flores, *Zacapoaxtla: Relación histórica*, 2d ed. (Puebla: Edición del XIV Distrito Local Electoral de Zacapoaxtla, Puebla, 1984), 132–33. On the Plan de Zacapoaxtla, see BNM, LAF 394: Antonio de Haro y Tamariz, "Manifiesto acompañando el plan político proclamado en Zacapoaxtla [*sic*] el 19 de diciembre de 1855," Puebla, 23 Jan. 1856; CEHM-C, Fondo XXVIII-1, Carpeta 1–7, Doc. 46: "Plan de Zacapoaxtla," Dec. 1855; and Jan Bazant, *Antonio Haro y Tamariz y sus aventuras políticas, 1811–1869* (Mexico City: El Colegio de México, 1985). For Haro y Tamariz's commercial and patron-client ties in the sierra, around Nauzontla and Xochitlán, see AGNEP, Zacapoaxtla, Caja 6, 1841–1848: Año 1842, ff. 64–66v.

12. On the conference with Juan Alvarez and the agreements reached, see Rivera Moreno, *Xochiapulco*, 50–51; AHDN, XI/481.3/6829 (Administración Zuloaga): "Partes de los Comandantes Generales de Tlaxcala y Puebla, sobre movimientos de fuerzas liberales entre Puebla, Guerrero y Veracruz," 1858, ff. 4–4v; and AGNM, Gobernación, TP: "Puebla, Prefecturas: Informe sobre la situación en Zacapoaxtla, Marzo-Abril, 1865," esp. ff. 1–1v. For general narratives of political and military events between 1855 and 1861, see Ralph Roeder, *Juárez and His Mexico*, 2d ed. (New York: Greenwood Press, 1968); Jan Bazant, *A Concise History of Mexico: From Hidalgo to Cárdenas, 1805–1940* (New York: Cambridge University Press, 1977), 62–94; Ivie E. Cadenhead, Jr., *Benito Juárez y su época* (Mexico City: El Colegio de México, 1975), 49–90; and Walter V. Scholes, *Política mexicana durante el régimen de Juárez, 1855–1872* (Mexico City: Fondo de Cultura Económica, 1972), 19–85.

13. This paragraph constitutes a quick summary of events detailed below in this chapter.

14. On the general outlines of Liberal policy at the national level, see Jan Bazant, *The Alienation of Church Wealth: Social and Economic Aspects of the Liberal Revolution, 1856–1875* (Cambridge: Cambridge University Press, 1971); Richard Sinkin, "The Mexican Constitutional Congress, 1856–1857: A Statistical Analysis," *Hispanic American Historical Review* 53, no. 1 (Feb. 1973): 1–26; and Sinkin, *The Mexican Reform, 1855–1876: A Study in Nation-Building* (Austin: Institute of Latin American Studies, University of Texas Press, 1979).

15. In addition to the information provided in AHDN, cited throughout this chapter, the expedientes of individual military officers located in the ACDN were particularly helpful in identifying local liberal leaders. See especially ACDN, D/111/2/425: Exp. de Juan Francisco Lucas; D/111/2/442: Exp. de Ramón Márquez Galindo; XI/111/3–248: Exp. de Juan Crisóstomo Bonilla; and XI/111/1–131: Exp. de Juan Nepomuceno Méndez. See also *Corona Fúnebre . . . al Gral. Juan N. Méndez; Corona Fúnebre . . . del Gral. Juan Crisóstomo Bonilla*; and Secretaría de Educación Pública, "Homenaje al Heroe Nacional Gral. Juan Francisco Lucas."

16. On the common background of Méndez, Bonilla, and Lucas as school-teachers, and their training in Veracruz, see Secretaría de Educación Pública, "Homenaje al . . . Gral. Juan Francisco Lucas."

17. For the Conservative declarations and the political and military be-havior of Aquixtla and Chignahuapan, see AHDN, XI/481.3/6814: "Partes del Corl. Antonio Daza y Argüelles," f. 4; and XI/481.3/6392: "Comandante Principal de Tulancingo a Guerra y Marina," 23 Mar. 1858. For other exam-ples, see *Diario Oficial*, no. 33, 24 Feb. 1858, p. 3; no. 35, 26 Feb. 1858, p. 4.

For the ins and outs of district competition, see AHDN, XI/481.3/6392: "Contestación de Guerra al Comandante Principal de Tulancingo," 27 Mar. 1858; "Comandante Principal del Departamento de Puebla a Guerra y Ma-rina," 3 Apr. 1858; "Comandante Militar de Tulancingo a Guerra y Marina," 4 Apr. 1858; "Comandante Principal de Tulancingo a Guerra y Marina," 11 Apr. 1858; "Oficio del Comandante del Departamento de Puebla a Guerra y Marina," 12 Apr. 1858.

18. On the role of Zacatlán as refuge for the Craviotos, see AHDN, XI/481.3/5783: "Parte de la Comandancia Principal de Tulancingo," 22 Aug. 1858, and AGN (M), Gobernación: Leg. 1173, Exp. 1, "Parte de Manuel María Escobar al Ministro," 7 Sept. 1858. On cooperation between Zacatlán and Tetela, see AHDN, XI/481.3/6807: "Carta de Vicente Márquez a su madre," Tetela de Ocampo, 29 Aug. 1858. For pressure from Xochiapulco on Zacapoaxtla, see XI/481.3/5876: "Parte del Gral. Manuel Noriega a Guerra y Marina," 21 July 1858, ff. 1–1v. For evidence of Xochiapulco's collabora-tion with Tetela, see XI/481.3/5882: "El Prefecto de Puebla Noriega, sobre acciones militares contra Xochiapulco," 26–27 Aug. 1858; XI/481.3/5794: "Oficio del Comandante General del Departamento de Puebla a Guerra y Marina," 11 Sept. 1858; and XI/481.3/6829, ff. 4–4v: "Parte del Comandante Militar de Zacapoaxtla al Comandante General de Puebla," 30 July 1858, where it is claimed that the Xochiapulquenses had been getting arms and ammunition from Tetela for two years. For liberal pressure on Teziutlán and Alatriste's role in it, see XI/481.3/6439: "Oficio del subprefecto de Tla-tlauqui," 14 May 1858; *Diario Oficial*, 23 July 1858, p. 1; and AGNM, Gobernación: Leg. 1173, Exp. 1, "Oficio del Gobernador de Puebla a Guerra y Marina," 9 Aug. 1858.

19. On the encirclement of Zacapoaxtla, see AHDN, XI/481.3/5794: "Parte del Gral. Manuel Noriega," 17 Sept. 1858; XI/481.3/5818: "Parte de la Comandancia Principal de Zacapoaxtla, relativo a la defensa de dicha plaza," 5 Nov. 1858; XI/481.3/7111: "Oficio de Francisco Pérez, Comandante Militar de Puebla," 10 Feb. 1859, ff. 1–1v. For Roldán's correspondence with Negrete, see XI/481.3/7111: "Oficio del Comandante Militar de Zacapoaxtla, transcrito por el Gral. Miguel Negrete," 8 Feb. 1859, ff. 7–8.

20. My narrative of the events is based on AGNM, Gobernación: Leg. 1389(1), "Parte del General Miguel Cástulo de Alatriste al Ministro de Gobernación," Teziutlán, 16 Feb. 1859. Alatriste's final report, which includes Juan N. Méndez's report, is from AHDN, XI/481.3/6443: "Parte del General Miguel Cástulo de Alatriste al Ministro de Guerra y Marina," Teziutlán, 18 Feb. 1859, ff. 1–4v. The quote by Méndez is on f. 3v. For the creation of the new Zacapoaxtla municipal council, see AGNM, Gobernación: Leg. 1389(1): "Acta de Instalación del nuevo ayuntamiento de Zacapoaxtla," 13 Mar. 1859. On the Nahua names, I am assuming that the officials who signed without last names were indigenous. The Lucas listed was apparently the brother of José Manuel Lucas. Rivera Moreno, *Xochiapulco*, 51.

21. For Alatriste's personal background, see CEHM-C, Colección Puebla, "Biografía Parte-Apolojetica y Parte-Critica del Gral. Alatriste," Puebla, 1862. For his two reports on the battle in Zacapoaxtla, see the previous note. On Alatriste's plans for Teziutlán, see AHDN, XI/481.3/7433: "Oficio de la Prefectura de Teziutlán al Ministro de Guerra y Marina," Teziutlán, 15 Apr. 1859.

22. For Conservative pressure on Zacapoaxtla, see AHDN, XI/481.3/7116: "Parte del Gral. Francisco Pérez al Ministerio de Guerra," 22 Feb. 1859. For Méndez's background, see *Corona Fúnebre al . . . Gral. Juan N. Méndez*. For his independent connections to the Juárez government, see AGNM, Gobernación: Leg. 1389(1), Exp. 1, "Oficio de Juan N. Méndez al Presidente Benito Juárez," 8 Apr. 1859; and AHDN, XI/481.3/7433: "Oficio del Secretario de Guerra y Marina al Coronel Juan N. Méndez," Veracruz, 28 Apr. 1859, ff. 14–14v. For the success of his efforts in Veracruz, see XI/481.3/7433: "Oficio del Secretario de Guerra al General Alatriste," Veracruz, 5 May 1859, ff. 2–3; "Oficio de Juan N. Méndez al Ministro de Guerra y Marina," Zacapoaxtla, 14 May 1859, ff. 13–13v; and "Oficio de Juan N. Méndez al Secretario de Guerra," Zacapoaxtla, 23 May 1859, ff. 11–11v.

23. On Conservative pressure near Zacatlán, see AGNM, Gobernación: Leg. 1389(1), Exp. 1, "Oficios del General en Gefe de la Brigada Gutiérrez (2)," 1 July 1859. For Méndez's activities in the Zacatlán and Huauchinango region, "Oficio de Miguel Cástulo de Alatriste, Gobernador de Puebla, al Ministro de Gobernación," originally 7 July 1859, transcribed 14 July; "Oficio de Miguel Cástulo de Alatriste al Ministro de Gobernación," original

8 July 1859, transcribed 14 July. The decree and the proclamation are both in AGNM, Gobernación: Leg. 1389(2), Exp. 2, "El C. L. Miguel Castulo de Alatriste, Gobernador Constitucional y Gefe de la Guardia Nacional del Estado de Puebla, a sus habitantes," Zacapoaxtla, 1 June 1859; and "El Ciudadano Licenciado Miguel C. de Alatriste, Gobernador Constitucional del Estado Libre y Soberano de Puebla, a los habitantes del partido de Zacapoastla [*sic*]," Zacapoaxtla, 5 June 1859.

24. AGNM, Gobernación: Leg. 1389(2), Exp. 2, "El C. L. Miguel C. de Alatriste," 5 June 1859, for the quotation. On the pervasiveness of racial thinking in nineteenth-century Mexico, see Florencia E. Mallon, "Peasants and State Formation in Nineteenth Century Mexico: Morelos, 1848–1858," *Political Power and Social Theory* 7 (1988): 1–54. Charles Hale is also clear on the issue of race as a stumbling block for liberals in *Mexican Liberalism in the Age of Mora, 1821–1853* (New Haven: Yale University Press, 1968), esp. 215–47.

25. For the secret conservative agreement, see AHDN, XI/481.3/6964, ff. 18–20, 7 June 1859.

26. Rivera's letter can be found in AHDN, XI/481.3/7433: "Oficio del Comandante Militar de Tetela a Juan N. Méndez," Tetela, 29 Aug. 1859, ff. 48–48v. My account is based on a comparison of Liberal and Conservative versions of the events, found in the following documents: 481.3/6964: "Oficio del General Alatriste al Ministro de Guerra y Marina," Zacapoaxtla, 30 Aug. 1859, ff. 2–3; "Parte del General Alatriste al Ministro de Guerra, Zacapoaxtla, 30 Aug. 1859, ff. 4–5; "Oficio del General Manuel Robles Pezuela al Ministro de Guerra y Marina," Mexico City, 7 Sept. 1859, ff. 7–8; and XI/481.3/7433: "Oficio del Gobernador del Estado de Veracruz," original 3 Sept. 1859, transcribed 7 Sept., ff. 12–12v.

27. For Alatriste's earlier report to Veracruz, see AHDN, XI/481.3/7433: "Oficio del General Alatriste al Secretario de Guerra y Marina," Zacapoaxtla, 5 Aug. 1859, ff. 57–58v. For liberal suspicions and recriminations about Alatriste's presence in Xochitlán at the time of the Conservative takeover, see XI/481.3/7433: "Oficio del Comandante Militar de Zacatlán al Ministro de Guerra," 31 Aug. 1859, ff. 9–10; XI/481.3/7024: "Acta levantada en Zacatlán contra Alatriste," 21 Sept. 1859, ff. 31–34; "Acta levantada en Tetela del Oro contra Alatriste," 29 Sept. 1859, ff. 22–23v.

28. This analysis is based on the documents listed in note 26.

29. See note 26.

30. For Méndez's behavior during the Zacapoaxtla incident, see AHDN, XI/481.3/7433: "Oficio del Comandante Militar de Zacatlán al Ministro de Guerra," 31 Aug. 1859, ff. 9–10. For his attempts to explain himself to Veracruz, see XI/481.3/7024: "Contestación de J. N. Méndez a Ocampo sobre la rebelión en contra de Alatriste," Zacatlán, 12 Oct. 1859. The quotation appears on f. 19v.

31. For Méndez's renewed independent communications with Veracruz, see AHDN, XI/481.3/6958: "Parte del Coronel Juan N. Méndez," Zacatlán, 30 July 1858. For the declarations against Alatriste, see XI/481.3/7024: "Acta levantada en Zacatlán contra Alatriste," 21 Sept. 1859, ff. 31–34; and "Acta levantada en Tetela del Oro contra Alatriste," 29 Sept. 1859, f. 22v.

32. "Acta levantada en Zacatlán."

33. "Acta levantada en Tetela"; the quotation is on f. 22v.

34. AHDN, XI/481.3/7024: "Oficio del secretario del gobierno del estado de Puebla al prefecto de Zacatlán," Zacapoaxtla, 14 Sept. 1859, ff. 1–2; "Copia del acta levantada en San Juan de los Llanos," 16 Sept. 1859.

35. On the presence of Alatriste's secretary Joaquín Martínez in Veracruz, see AHDN, XI/481.3/7024: "Carta de acusación escrita por Joaquín Martínez en representación de Alatriste al Ministro de Guerra y de Gobernación," Veracruz, 6 Nov. 1859, ff. 35–40v; and "Oficio de Joaquín Martínez protestando la resolución del gobierno sobre que Alatriste se separe del mando de Puebla," Veracruz, 6 Nov. 1859, ff. 41–44v. For the Veracruz decree, see "Copia hecha por Antonio Carvajal de la copia trascrita por Méndez de la Orden que Alatriste se presente en Veracruz," ff. 14–14v. For Alatriste's evacuation of Zacapoaxtla, see "Lista de los pertrechos de guerra que dejó Alatriste al separarse de la plaza de Zacapoaxtla, hecha por Ramón Márquez Galindo," Zacapoaxtla, copied 27 Nov. 1859, f. 3.

36. For Alatriste's decree and Méndez's trip to Veracruz, see AHDN, XI/481.3/7748: "Oficio de Ramón Márquez Galindo al Teniente Coronel Rafael Cravioto," Zacapoaxtla, 30 Dec. 1859, ff. 1–2. Later on, while trying to clear his name, Alatriste would admit he printed the decree, although he claimed never to have signed or sealed it. See CEHM-C, "Bando del Gobernador Miguel Cástulo de Alatriste a los habitantes del Estado," Puebla, 22 Apr. 1862. For the various other political machinations and military movements through November, see XI/481.3/7024: "Carta de Antonio Carvajal a J. N. Méndez reconociendo su nombramiento," Hacienda de Acocotla, 7 Nov. 1859, f. 7; "Carta de Antonio Carvajal al Ministerio de Guerra," Tlaxcala, 8 Nov. 1859; "Proclama de Alatriste a los ciudadanos de Zacatlán," copied in Zacapoaxtla, 27 Nov. 1859; "Circular de Alatriste al jefe político y militar de Zacapoaxtla," copied in Zacapoaxtla, 27 Nov. 1859, f. 5; "Circular de Juan N. Méndez a los habitantes del estado sobre su nombramiento como jefe interino," Zacapoaxtla, 22 Nov. 1859, f. 6; "Carta de Juan N. Méndez al Ministro de Guerra y Marina," Zacapoaxtla, 27 Nov. 1859, ff. 8–11.

37. For the relationship of Juan N. Flandes to Alatriste and his allies, see AGNM, SAHOP-BN, Puebla, 79/103: Exp. 9068, 24 Aug. 1860; 13 Sept. 1860; 2 Nov. 1860; 1 July 1864; and, especially for the existence of the dispute with Tlatlauqui, 4 July 1864. For claims on municipal and ecclesiastical properties, see AHDN, XI/481.3/8057: ff. 154–56, 9 July 1859; ff. 161–63, 25 Oct. 1859; and ff. 143–51v, 25 Sept. 1859. For disputes between

Teziutecos and Indians from Tenampulco, one of the indigenous communities in Teziutlán district, see ACDN, D/111/2/442: Exp. Ramón Márquez Galindo, ff. 60–60v; and "Carta[s] de Rafael Avila a Alatriste," Teziutlán, 12 and 15 Mar. 1860, ff. 61–63. See also note 8 for sources on conflicts between Teziutlán and Atempan and Ecatlán and Tenampulco dating back to the 1840s.

38. For the events in Teziutlán in the early months of 1860, see ACDN, D/111/2/442: Exp. Ramón Márquez Galindo, ff. 60–60v, 61–63. The quotation is on f. 62v.

39. For Carvajal's behavior in Tlatlauqui, see AHDN, XI/481.3/8025: f. 22v–24, 24–26: "ficio[s] del subprefecto y comandante militar de Tlatlauqui al Comandante General del Estado de Puebla," 5 and 10 Apr. 1860. For the vision of the Teziutecos, see the sources in note 38.

40. For conflicts between ethnic and market definitions of property, as well as the difficulties in establishing territoriality in a context where physical boundaries between groups and the centralization of population had both been diffuse in prehispanic times, see García, *Los pueblos de la sierra.*

41. The best example of the Alatriste group's ideology can be found in AGNM, Gobernación: Leg. 1389(2), Exp. 2, "El Ciudadano Licenciado Miguel C. de Alatriste, Gobernador Constitucional del Estado Libre y Soberano de Puebla, a los habitantes del partido de Zacapoastla [*sic*]," Zacapoaxtla, 5 June 1859. The best example of the Méndez emphasis can be found in AHDN, XI/481.3/7024: "Contestación de J. N. Méndez a Ocampo sobre la rebelión en contra de Alatriste," Zacatlán, 12 Oct. 1859. See also XI/481.3/8025: "Oficio de Ramón Márquez Galindo al General Carvajal," 12 Apr. 1860; "Oficio de Ramón Márquez Galindo al Ministro de Guerra y Marina," Zacapoaxtla, 15 Apr. 1860.

42. My summary here is based on the following additional sources through the end of 1860: AHDN, XI/481.3/7663: ff. 2 and 3; XI/481.3/7747: 19 Jan. 1860; XI/481.3/7749: 19 and 24 Jan. 1860; XI/481.3/7024, ff. 35–40v, 41–44v; XI/481.3/8025: 21 Apr., 2 May, 1 July, and 15 Oct. 1860.

43. On lack of support for Alatriste in Puebla, see BN-AJ, Docs. 90–95: "Varias cartas de Ildefonso Jáuregui y Esparza a Benito Juárez y otros," Oct.–Dec. 1860. On the prevention of Alatriste's entry into Puebla city, see CEHM-C, Colección Puebla, "Biografía Parte-Apolojetica y Parte-Critica del Gral. Alatriste," Puebla, 1862. On the interim administrations and his apparent reestablishment of legitimacy, see CEHM-C, Colección Puebla: "Proclama de Fernando M. Ortega, Gobernador Interino, a sus conciudadanos al entregar el mando del Estado," Puebla, 4 Jan. 1861; and "Felipe N. Chacón, General en Gefe de las Tropas Constitucionales de Puebla, a sus habitantes," Puebla, 4 Jan. 1861. On his renewed role as governor, see AHDN, D/481.4/8505: "Decreto de Miguel Cástulo de Alatriste, Gober-

nador del Estado de Puebla, sobre la formación de la Guardia Nacional," Puebla, 15 Mar. 1861.

For the decree on Tetela, see CEHM-C, Colección Puebla: "Licenciado Miguel Cástulo de Alatriste, Gobernador del Estado, publica decreto dado por el Congreso del Estado en 23 de julio de 1861," Puebla, 26 July 1861. For Alatriste's resignation, see "El C. Lic. José Antonio Marin, Presidente del Tribunal Superior de Justicia y encargado del Gobierno del Estado, a sus habitantes," Puebla, 30 July 1861; and CEHM-C, Fondo XXVIII–1: Doc. 341, "Congreso del Estado de Puebla acepta la renuncia del Gobernador Miguel Cástulo de Alatriste, 2 Sept. 1861, y manda que se publique," published in Puebla, 3 Sept. 1861.

44. On the naming of Ibarra as interim governor, see CEHM-C, Fondo XXVIII–1: Doc. 342, "Congreso del Estado de Puebla nombra gobernador interino del Estado a Francisco Ibarra y Ramos, 4 Sept. 1861," Puebla, 5 Sept. 1861; and Colección Puebla, "El C. Francisco Ibarra, Gobernador Interino, a sus habitantes," Puebla, 11 Sept. 1861. The call to elections can be found in Fondo XXVIII–1: Doc. 354, "Francisco Ibarra, Gobernador Interino del Estado de Puebla, publica la Convocatoria a elecciones," Puebla, 2 Oct. 1861. On Méndez's job in Ibarra's administration, see Doc. 358, "Decreto del Ministerio de Gobernación publicado en Puebla," 25 Oct. 1861. On the elections, see BN-AJ, 145–46; 3227–3228: "Correspondencia entre Benito Juárez y Francisco Ibarra, Gobernador Interino de Puebla," Sept. and Nov. 1861; AGNM, AL: Leg. XLIV, "Memoria del General José María Maldonado . . . , 1862 y 1863" [Copia], pp. 8–10; and CEHM-C, Colección Puebla: "Lista Nominal de los CC que resultaron electos Gefes Políticos de los Distritos del Estado," Puebla, 27 Dec. 1861. On the invasion and the declaration of the state of siege, see Fondo XXVIII–1: Doc. 362, "Convocatoria de Francisco Ibarra, Gobernador Interino, a los ciudadanos del Estado de Puebla para defender la independencia de la Republica frente al invasor extranjero"; and Maldonado, "Memoria . . . 1862 y 1863," 1–2.

45. For the most authoritative account of the incident, based on access to the largest number of official records and sources, see Antonio Carrión, *Historia de la Ciudad de Puebla de los Angeles (Puebla de Zaragoza)*, 2 vols. (Puebla: Vda. de Dávalos é Hijos, 1897; rpt. Puebla: Editorial José M. Cajica Jr., S.A., 1970), 2:409–17.

46. I encountered multiple examples of this oral tradition in my frequent visits to the highlands during the first half of 1985: a mural of the battle painted on the wall of the Zacapoaxtla library; municipal exhibits of ammunition, weaponry, and other memorabilia in Tetela de Ocampo and Xochiapulco; and the participation of contingents from the highlands in the annual Fifth of May parade in Puebla city. For written examples of this tradition, see especially Rivera Moreno, *Xochiapulco*, and Sánchez Flores, *Zacapoaxtla*.

47. For the list of officers and soldiers in the Sixth Battalion, see AHDN, D/481.4/8853: "Lista de soldados y oficiales de la División Negrete: Batallón 6° GN de Puebla," Puebla, 28 Apr. and 5 May, 1862, ff. 127–28v. For a description of the actions the Battalion took, see Maldonado, "Memoria . . . 1862 y 1863," 10–11. See also *Archivo del General Porfirio Díaz*, vol. 1, *Memorias*, 152–53. It is interesting to note that no one addresses the issue of why an indigenous battalion—in which, according to the lists of soldiers, approximately half had no last name—would fight so enthusiastically and well—indeed, more bravely than the regular troops. Maldonado offers a clearly racist explanation, saying that the indigenous guerrillas fought because Méndez "offered the leaders musical instruments for their villages and other things that pleased those Indians" (9).

48. For some of the early conflicts between Liberals and Interventionists, see AHDN, XI.481.4/8944: ff. 33–35v; XI/481.4/8881: 12 Sept. 1862; XI/481.4/8930: 14 Oct. 1862; XI/481.4/8757: f. 13; XI/481.4/8947: ff. 14, 62–62v; XI/481.4/8758, f. 27; XI/481.4/9034, ff. 14–14v; Genaro García, ed., *Documentos inéditos ó muy raros para la historia de México, vol. 4, Correspondencia secreta de los principales Intervencionistas Mexicanos* (Mexico City: Librería de la Vda. de Ch. Bourey, 1906), part 2: "Carta de José María Yáñez," Pacho, 25 Oct. 1862, pp. 196–200; BN-AJ, Doc. 279: "Carta de Jesús González Ortega a Benito Juárez," Zaragoza, 26 Dec. 1862. On the contradictions faced by local Liberals, see AHMTO, Gobierno, Caja 8: Exp. 8, "Dos cartas del general Miguel Negrete al Jefe Político de Tetela," Palmar, 5 Sept. 1862; "Oficio de la Junta Proveedora de víveres del distrito de Zapotitlán, al Jefe Político de Tetela," 6 Oct. 1862; Exp. 7, "Proceso a José Antonio Cruz, por homicidio y reaccionario," began 30 Aug. 1862; AHMZ, Paq. 1862: "Circular del Gobernador de Puebla, Fernando María Ortega, sobre víveres y forrajes," Zacapoaxtla, 29 Sept. 1862; Paq. 1863–64–65: "Oficio del Juez Constitucional de Xochiapulco, al Jefe Político de Zacapoaxtla, sobre la aprehensión de solteros y vagos para el servicio militar," Xochiapulco, 25 Oct. 1862; "Circular de Jesús González Ortega al Jefe Político de Zacapoaxtla, pidiendo 100 re-emplazos," Puebla, 6 Nov. 1862; Leg. 35, "Varios documentos de las autoridades de Xochitlán, Nauzontla y Huahuaxtla, sobre remisión de víveres para el ejército," Jan. 1863; "Manifiesto de Juan Francisco Lucas al pueblo de Zacapoaxtla," 1 Oct. 1862; Paq. 1862: Leg. 74, "Acta de Xochiapulco renovando los cargos municipales," 24 Oct. 1862; "Decreto del Comandante Militar de Zacapoaxtla, José María Maldonado, declarando la plaza en riguroso estado de sitio," Jan. 1863. On French and Conservative propaganda, see AHDN, XI/481.4/8759, ff. 9–9v; XI/481.4/8761, ff. 15–16.

49. On the Mexican defeat in Puebla, see Gen. Jesús de León Toral, *Historia Documental Militar de la Intervención francesa en México y el denominado Segundo Imperio. Recopilación, notas y comentarios* (Mexico City: Secretaría de la Defensa Nacional: Departamento de Archivo, Corres-

pondencia e Historia. Comisión de Historia Militar, 1967), 131–86; *La defensa de la Plaza de Puebla de Zaragoza en 1863. Parte general que dió al Supremo Gobierno de la Nación el C. General Jesús González Ortega,* 2d ed. (Mexico City: Tipografía del Departamento de Estado Mayor, 1904). For Negrete's appointment, see AHDN, D/481.4/9706: "Exp. sobre nombramientos," 28 May 1863, ff. 5–6. For his instructions to all military commanders, see D/481.4/9038: "Instrucciones del General Negrete a los Comandantes Militares de los distritos de Puebla y Tlaxcala," 5 June 1863; and *Archivo de Porfirio Díaz,* 3:257–5.

50. For complaints about abuses in the draft and requisitions, resistance to exactions, and other issues, see *Archivo de Porfirio Díaz,* 3:269–70, 272–73, 273–74, 278–80, 280–82; AHMZ, Paq. 1863–65–64: Leg. 3, "Proclama del Comandante de Zacapoaxtla, José María Maldonado, al pueblo," Zacapoaxtla, 10 July 1863; and BN-AJ, Doc. 3: "El Comandante Militar de Veracruz al Presidente Juárez," Veracruz, 24 June 1863. For the heaviness of exactions and village protests, see AHMTO, Gobierno, Caja 8: Exp. 8, "Oficio de la Junta proveedora de Víveres al Jefe Político de Tetela," Zapotitlán, 6 Oct. 1862; AHMZ, Paq. 1863–65–64: Exp. 214, "Oficio del Juez Municipal y Comandante Militar de Cuetzalan," 5 Jan. 1863; "Oficio del Jefe Político de Tlatlauqui al Jefe Político de Zacapoaxtla," 18 Jan. 1863; "Vecinos de Nauzontla al Comandante Militar de Zacapoaxtla," 22 Jan. 1863; "Jefe Político de Tlatlauqui al Comandante Militar de Zacapoaxtla," 19 Jan. 1863; "Oficio del Juez Municipal de Cuetzalan al Jefe Político y Comandante Militar de Zacapoaxtla," 22 Jan. 1863; Exp. 245, "41 Boletas de víveres para la Guardia Nacional de Xochiapulco," Zacapoaxtla, April 1863; Leg. 26, "51 Recibos de víveres para el Batallón Guardia Nacional de Xochiapulco," May 1863. On the eruption of simmering political and land conflicts, see AHMTO, Gobierno, Caja 8: Exp. 8, "Oficio del Juez de Nanacatlán al Jefe Político de Tetela," 18 July 1862; AHMZ, Paq. 1863–65–64: Exp. 222, "Oficio del Juez de Paz de Taitic al Comandante Militar de Zacapoaxtla," 8 Feb. 1863; Leg. 36, "Solicitud de Marcial Antonio, natural y jornalero de Nauzontla, al Jefe Político de Zacapoaxtla," 21 Feb. 1863; Exp. 214, "Acta del Ayuntamiento de Xochiapulco, sobre diferencias con algunos vecinos de Yantetelco," Xochiapulco, 30 Jan. 1863; Leg. 37, "Dos solicitudes del pueblo y los pasados de Cuetzalan a Juan Francisco Lucas," 23 Mar. 1863; "Acta de los vecinos de Xochitlán pidiendo una nueva elección de comandante militar," 25 July 1863; and "Memoria del General José María Maldonado . . . , 1862 y 1863." Unfortunately, given Maldonado's later battles with Méndez and his desperate desire to vindicate his own actions in order to receive a larger military pension, it is difficult to determine from the evidence of his memoirs the exact causes of those conflicts. On Negrete's focus on the western sierra and his preference for the Craviotos, see AHDN, D/481.4/9038: ff. 74–82, 71–73v, 97–98, 107–10v. For the attitudes and ac-

tions of commanders from outside the area area brought in by Negrete, see *Archivo de Porfirio Díaz*, 3:269–70, 273–74, 265–67, 278–80, 280–82, 4:279.

51. On the Regencia's decree, see AGNM, II Imperio, Caja 80: "Decreto de la Regencia del Imperio, en 19 de Agosto 1863, prohibiendo la leva para reclutar al ejército." For the Interventionist offensive against Negrete, see AHDN, XI/481.4/9109. For Cravioto's report, see BN-AJ, Doc. 461: "Carta de Rafael Cravioto al presidente Benito Juárez," Huauchinango, 5 Oct. 1863.

52. On the rebellion in Chiconcautla, see AHDN, XI/481.4/9099: "Parte de Rafael Cravioto acerca del motín de Chiconcautla," 24–28 Sept. 1863. For his letter to his brother, see AGNM, Archivo Leyva: Leg. 45, pp. 8–9: "Carta de Rafael Cravioto a su hermano Agustín," Huauchinango, 9 Oct. 1863.

53. My assessment of the Craviotos' behavior in the towns and villages is based on AHDN, XI/481.4/9099 and 9109. They appear as legal representatives for indigenous villages in AGNEP, Huauchinango, Caja 1, 1851–1860: Libro 1857, 5 Nov. 1857; Caja 2, 1861–1870: Libro 1861, ff. 10–11v, 23–24v; Libro 1862, ff. 46–52; Libro 1864, 17 Dec. 1864. The suggestion that all forced contributions should be abolished—with the concomitant problem of where to get support for the Liberal forces—is discussed in AHDN, XI/481.4/9099: 24–28 Sept. 1863, and BN-AJ, Doc. 461: "Carta de Rafael Cravioto al presidente Benito Juárez," Huauchinango, 5 Oct. 1863. The need to find a bugle for the allied village of Tuto is discussed in AGNM, Archivo Leyva: Leg. 45, pp. 8–9: "Carta de Rafael Cravioto a su hermano Agustín," Huauchinango, 9 Oct. 1863. It is important to note here that, as Guy Thomson points out ("Bulwarks of Patriotic Liberalism: The National Guard, Philharmonic Corps and Patriotic Juntas in Mexico, 1847–1888," *Journal of Latin American Studies* 22, no. 1 [Feb. 1990]: 31–68), the formation of village orchestras and the purchase of European-style brass instruments played an important cultural and ritualistic role in binding together indigenous, mestizo, and even white Liberals in other parts of the sierra. The problem with Cravioto's using it here is that it was isolated from the rest of his political practice. On the Craviotos' revenge campaign, see AHDN, XI/481.4/9109: "Oficio de varios vecinos del pueblo de Tepeixco, jurisdicción de Huauchinango, al Prefecto y Comandante Militar de Tulancingo," 22 Oct. 1863. On the increase of popular support for the Intervention in the Huauchinango and Zacatlán areas, see the same expediente, ff. 214–15, 232–33, 255–55v, 249–50; and AGNM, Archivo Leyva: Leg. 45, pp. 4–6, "Carta de Agustín Cravioto a José María Maldonado, explicando porqué no puede ir a auxiliarle."

54. On the relationship of the situation in the sierra to the arrival of Maximilian and Carlota, see AGNM, Gobernación: Leg. 1126, Exp. 2, "Oficio del Prefecto de Puebla, transcribiendo oficio del Prefecto Municipal de los Llanos," Puebla, 8 June 1864; and II Imperio, Caja 81: "Oficio de

Francisco Pavón, Prefecto del Departamento de Tulancingo, felicitando al monarca," 12 June 1864. On Interventionist campaigns along the Huauchinango/Zacatlán/Chignahuapan axis, the important role played by the Chignahuapan forces, and the alliance of the Huauchinango Liberals with the plateados, see Gobernación: Leg. 1126, Exp. 1, "Oficio del Prefecto Político de Tulancingo al Subsecretario de Gobernación," 9 June 1864; "Oficio del Prefecto Político de Tulancingo sobre actividades de disidentes en la sierra y Huasteca," 26 June 1864, with attached liberal proclamation to the French soldiers; "Oficio del Prefecto de Tulancingo informando de la retirada de los franceses y escuadrón Chignahuapan de Zacatlán," 5 July 1864; Exp. 3, "Solicitud de D. José de la Luz Alvares, pidiendo protección de S. M. contra los disidentes," México, 12 Aug. 1864; Leg. 1339(1), Exp. 3, "Oficio del Prefecto Superior de Tulancingo al Ministerio de Gobierno," 13 Jan. 1865; Leg. 1161(2), Exp. 18, "Oficio del Prefecto Político de Tulancingo, transcribiendo oficio del Prefecto Político de Zacatlán," 16 Feb. 1865; "Oficio del Prefecto de Tulancingo, transcribiendo oficio de Fernando Vergara, conservador de Huauchinango," 19 Feb. 1865; II Imperio, Caja 69: "Oficio del Prefecto de Tulancingo, sobre ocupación y desocupación de la plaza de Huauchinango por fuerzas francesas," 19 July 1864; "El Subprefecto de Chignahuapan, sobre ocupación de Zacatlán por los rebeldes," Chignahuapan, 25 Aug. 1864; Caja 65: "Dn. Manuel Andrade, vecino de Huauchinango, se queja del saqueo de su tienda por tropas francesas," Mexico, 14 Sept.–14 Oct. 1864; AHDN, C/481.4/9519: esp. 15 Aug., 25 Aug., 9 Oct., 16 Oct., 8 Nov., 19 Nov. 1864; El Pájaro Verde, 25 Nov. 1864, p. 3; 21 Jan. 1865, p. 3. For the combination of repression and proffered pardons, see AGNM, Gobernación: Leg. 1126, Exp. 1, "Oficio de la Prefectura Superior de Tulancingo, sobre la rendición e indulto del capitan Diodoro Zagua, de Huauchinango," 15 Dec. 1864; and Leg. 1161(2), Exp. 18, "Oficio del Ministro de Guerra y Marina al Prefecto de Tulancingo," 2 Jan. 1865. On the negotiations and final surrender of the Craviotos, see AHDN, D/481.4/9519: "D. Simón Cravioto, disidente del Distrito de Huauchinango, ofreciendo someterse al Gob^no Imperial bajo condiciones, y contestación del Ministro de Guerra y Marina," Oct.– Nov. 1864, ff. 50–51; AGNM, Gobernación: Leg. 1161(2), Exp. 18, "Dos oficios del Prefecto Político de Tulancingo, sobre la rendición de Rafael Cravioto," 19 and 23 Mar., 1865; and Diario del Imperio, 274–76, 279–80.

55. For the combined French and Conservative takeover of Zacapoaxtla, see Sánchez Flores, Zacapoaxtla 193–97, citing Carrión, Historia de la Ciudad de Puebla, 2:499–505. For liberal victories in Cuetzalan and Zacapoaxtla, see Carrión, 506–16; Sánchez, Zacapoaxtla, 198–204; AHDN, XI/481.4/9032: "Oficios del Gobernador Rafael Cravioto, remitiendo partes de Juan Francisco Lucas y José María Maldonado," 4–9 Oct. 1863; AGNM, Archivo Leyva: Leg. 45, pp. 7–8, 8–9, 11, 11–12, 13.

56. For evidence of Conservative activity and receptivity to it around Tlatlauqui, Zacapoaxtla, and Cuetzalan, see AHMZ, Paq. 1863–65–64: Leg. 35, "Oficio del Comandante Militar de Zacapoaxtla al General en Jefe del Ejército de Oriente," 25 Jan. 1863; Exp. 204, "Oficio al General en Jefe de la Segunda División del Ejército de Oriente," Zacapoaxtla, 9 Nov. 1863, ff. 2–2v; "Oficio al General en Jefe de la Segunda División del Ejército de Oriente," 11 Nov. 1863, ff. 2v–3; "Circular a las autoridades del Distrito," 2 Dec. 1863, ff. 3v–4; "Oficio al Comandante Militar de Cuetzalan," 2 Dec. 1863, f. 3v; "Oficio al Comandante Militar de Papantla," 11 Dec. 1863, ff. 4–4v; *Archivo de Porfirio Díaz*, 3:286–87. For Maldonado's pardon, see AHMZ, Paq. 1863–65–64: "Manifiesto de José María Maldonado a los ciudadanos de Zacapoaxtla," 6 Dec. 1863. For the Interventionist victory in Teziutlán, see Exp. 204, "José María Maldonado al Gobernador de Puebla," Zacapoaxtla, 12 Jan. 1864, ff. 6v–8. For the Conservative report on Teziutlán, which emphasizes the role played by Conservative civil guards from Zacapoaxtla, Tlatlauqui, and San Juan de los Llanos, see *Periódico Oficial del Imperio Mexicano*, 14 Jan. 1864, p. 2. On the negotiations between Liberal commander Cuéllar and the village of Tlatlauqui, see AHMZ, Paq. 1863–65–64: Exp. 204, "José María Maldonado al Comandante Militar de Tlatlauqui," Zacapoaxtla, 1 Mar. 1864, ff. 9–10; and Exp. 257, "Convenio entre el representante de Tlatlauqui y el Coronel Ignacio Cuéllar, presidido por José María Maldonado," 7 Mar. 1864.

In all fairness, Maldonado was not always as sensitive to the needs of the villages as his handling of the land laws and the Tlatlauqui-Cuéllar affair seems to suggest. In March 1863, when the municipal judge of Xochitlán wrote to him requesting permission to hold the customary processions during Holy Week, Maldonado flatly turned him down. Yet this refusal does not seem to have affected the support of Xochitlán for the Liberal cause. For the petition and answer, see AHMZ, Paq. 1863–65–64: Exp. 219, "Oficio del Juez Municipal y Comandante Militar de Xochitlán, M. Castañeda, al Comandante Militar de Zacapoaxtla," Xochitlán, 9 Mar. 1863, and answer on 10 Mar. 1863.

57. AHMZ, Paq. 1863–65–64: Exp. 204, "Circular a los comandantes militares de Xochitlán, Nauzontla y Cuetzalan sobre las leyes de Reforma," Zacapoaxtla, 18 Mar. 1863, ff. 10–11v. The first quotation is on f. 10v; the second on 11v. We know for sure that the circular began to be applied in Xochitlán and Nauzontla between May and August of 1864 and that most of the beneficiaries of the adjudicaciones were people who did not know how to sign their names. See Exp. 252, "Adjudicaciones de terrenos en Xochitlán y Nauzontla."

58. Sánchez Flores, *Zacapoaxtla*, 194–99, citing Carrión, *Historia de la Ciudad de Puebla*, 2:498–506. The specific incident and slogans are found in Sánchez, 198, and Carrión, 505–6. It is interesting to note as well the possi-

ble symbolic importance of the banquet prepared by Juan Francisco Lucas. For the twentieth century, Lourdes Arizpe comments that in Zacatipan, a Nahua community near Cuetzalan, "when the celebration reaches a certain magnitude, pigs are slaughtered. It is common to raise [pigs] but only among wealthier families, since their feeding is expensive" (*Parentesco y economía*, 82).

59. For Chilapa's petition and its rapid acceptance, see AHMZ, Paq. 1863–65–64: "Solicitud de los vecinos de Chilapa, pertenecientes a la municipalidad de Zautla, sobre pertenecer al municipio de Xochiapulco," Chilapa, 18 Dec. 1863; Exp. 204, "Oficio al Comandante Militar de San Miguel, avisando que se accede a la solicitud de los vecinos de Chilapa," Zacapoaxtla, 24 Dec. 1863. For the petitions from Cuetzalan to Lucas, see Leg. 37, "Solicitud de los pasados, regidores, y todas las familias del pueblo a D. Juan Francisco Lucas, sobre los abusos del cura Castrillo," Cuetzalan, 23 Mar. 1863; "Solicitud de Francisco Cortez a Don Juan de politico [*sic*]," Cuetzalan, 23 Mar. 1863. For the rebellion in Tetela, see Exp. 204, "Oficio de José María Maldonado al gobernador del estado, sobre el motín en Tetela," Zacapoaxtla, 9 Oct. 1864, ff. 24–25. For Lucas's operations in Cuetzalan and his warning to Maldonado, see AGNM, AL: Leg. 45, "Carta de Juan Francisco Lucas a José María Maldonado desde Quezala [*sic*]," 20 Oct. 1863, p. 11.

60. On the incident with the plateados in Acaxochitlán, see AHDN, D/481.4/9519: "Oficio del Comandante Superior de Tulancingo al Ministro de Guerra y Marina," 26 Nov. 1864, ff. 81–81v. That this incident is part of a general military offensive being carried out by the plateados becomes clear on ff. 83–83v. On the actions of the Cuatecomacos, see AGNM, Gobernación: Leg. 1126, Exp. 3, "Oficio del Prefecto de Puebla, transcribiendo oficio del Prefecto Municipal de San Juan de los Llanos," 31 Oct. 1864.

61. On the French-Mexican campaign in the eastern sierra, see AHDN, XI/481.4/9594: "Oficio del Mariscal Bazaine al Secretario de Guerra," 13 June 1864; AGNM, Gobernación: Leg. 1126, Exp. 1, "Parte del Prefecto de Puebla sobre movimientos de tropa," 27 June 1864; Exp. 2, "Parte del Prefecto de Puebla de 27 Junio, y transcripción de un parte del Subprefecto de San Juan de los Llanos de 23 de Junio," 1864; "Comunicaciones del Prefecto de Puebla sobre la organización de una guardia civil pro-Imperio," 22 June–22 July 1864; "Oficio del Prefecto de los Llanos, sobre operaciones," 10 June 1864; "Oficio del Prefecto Político del Departamento de Puebla al Subsecretario de Gobernación," 10 June 1864; "Oficio del Coronel Rodríguez al Ministro de Gobernación," San Juan de los Llanos, 22 June 1864. On the Austro-Belgian Legion and operations after its arrival, see *Diario del Imperio*, 5 Jan. 1865, p. 16; 19 Jan. 1865, p. 59; 17 Feb. 1865, p. 162; 20 Feb. 1865; 15 Mar. 1865, p. 246; 1 Mar. 1865, p. 197; 6 Mar. 1865, p. 214; *El Pájaro Verde*, 1 Mar. 1865, p. 3; *Periódico Oficial de Puebla*, 9 Mar. 1865, p. 2; and AGNM, Gobernación: Leg. 1161(3), Exp. 13, "Oficio del Prefecto de Jalapa,"

6–11 Feb. 1865. For reports in the Mexico City press about Zacapoaxtla, see *El Pájaro Verde*, 13 Apr. 1864, p. 3; 18 Aug. 1864, p. 3; 27 Jan. 1865, p. 3.

62. On continued Liberal pressure around Zacapoaxtla after its occupation by Austrian and Mexican troops, see *El Pájaro Verde*, 28 Mar. 1865, p. 3; and 20 Apr. 1865, p. 376.

63. For Esteva's report, and the granting of his request to negotiate politically, see AGNM, Gobernación, TP: "Puebla, Prefecturas. Informe sobre la situación en Zacapoaxtla, Marzo–Abril 1865"; "Oficio del Prefecto Superior de Puebla, José María Esteva, al Ministro de Gobernación," Puebla, 29 Mar. 1865, 2ff. The quotation is on f. 1v.

64. On the emergence of a more coherent, liberally oriented imperial policy, see Roeder, *Juárez and His Mexico*, 571–90; Luis González y González, "El indigenismo de Maximiliano," in Arturo Arnaiz y Freg and Claude Bataillon, eds., *La intervención francesa y el Imperio de Maximiliano cien años después, 1862–1962* (Mexico City: Asociación Mexicana de Historiadores / Instituto Francés de América Latina, 1965), 103–10; T. G. Powell, *El liberalismo y el campesinado en el centro de México (1850 a 1876)*, trans. Roberto Gómez Ciria (Mexico City: Secretaría de Educación Pública, 1974), 102–20; CEHM-C, Fondo XXXVI: Doc. 60, "Circular reservada del Ministro de Gobierno Esteva . . . "; Doc. 80, "Circular del Ministro de Gobierno Esteva a los prefectos de los Deptos. del Centro del país . . . "; Doc. 84, "Circular del Ministro de Gobierno Esteva, sobre la colonización de terrenos baldíos. . . . " It was also at this time that Maximilian confronted the church on the issue of the Liberal reform laws and gave qualified support to the reform. See Roeder, *Juárez and His Mexico*, 590, and Egon Caesar Conde Corti, *Maximiliano y Carlota* (Mexico City: Fondo de Cultura Económica, 1944), 303–13. Finally, the Junta Protectora de las Clases Menesterosas, envisioned as a judicial body to which rural and urban popular classes could have recourse when faced with abuses, also began to function around this time. A committee headed by Francisco Villanueva (later the first imperial negotiator in the Sierra de Puebla) presented a report on the condition of indigenous peoples in March 1865. This report led to the creation, in April of the same year and with much of the same personnel, of the junta. See González y González, "El indigenismo de Maximiliano," 104; Powell, *El liberalismo y el campesinado*, 113; and AGNM, Junta Protectora de las Clases Menesterosas, Libros 1–5. For Maximilian's initial tour of the countryside, Bazaine's policies, the disagreements between Maximilian and Bazaine, and the initial removal of French troops, see Roeder, *Juárez and His Mexico*, 543–44, 571, 581.

65. AGNM, Gobernación, TP: "Informe sobre la situación en Zacapoaxtla," "Oficio de Pascual V. Bonilla al Secretario de Gobierno José María Fernández," Zacapoaxtla, 9 Apr. 1865, 3ff.; the quotation appears on ff. 1–1v. My summary of Bonilla's conflicts with other Conservatives, most notably

Agustín Roldán, is based on "Oficios de Pascual V. Bonilla al Prefecto Superior de Puebla," Zacapoaxtla, 1 and 9 Apr., 1865, 2 and 3 ff., respectively. The first quotation is from the first letter, f. 1v; the second quotation is from the second letter, f. 1v. My assessment of Roldán's long history in Conservative politics is based on his presence, since 1856, as commander of the Conservative forces in Zacapoaxtla. See AHDN, XI/481.3/5321: "Copia de las comunicaciones encontradas á D. Fernando Lopez," ff. 18–20v., copies taken in Zacatlán, 19 Nov. 1856.

66. AGNM, Gobernación, TP: "Oficio de Pascual Bonilla al Secretario de Gobierno en Puebla," Zacapoaxtla, 19 Apr. 1865, 2 ff.

67. AGNM, II Imperio, Caja 44: Letter from General Thun to the Emperor (in German), Zacapoaxtla, 3 April 1865. Translation thanks to Gerda Lerner.

68. For military actions near Xochiapulco in April, see Carrión, *Historia de la Ciudad de Puebla*, 2:542; AGNM, II Imperio, Caja 44: "Carta del Mayor Polak al Jefe del Gabinete Militar de SM," Puebla, 16 Apr. 1865 (in French); *Diario del Imperio*, 20 Apr. 1865, p. 376. On negotiations and the conditions of the armistice, see Carrión, *Historia de la Ciudad de Puebla*, 543–44, and AHMZ, Paq. 1863–65–64: "Proclama de Juan Francisco Lucas a los habitantes de Zacapoaxtla," Xochiapulco, 10 July 1865. On the failure of the armistice and the return to combat, see *El Pájaro Verde*, 1 July 1865, p. 3; for the Liberal interpretation, see AHMZ, "Proclama de Juan Francisco Lucas."

69. For the various battles going on in July and August, see *El Pájaro Verde*, 22 July 1865, p. 3; *Diario del Imperio*, 7 Aug. 1865, pp. 131–32; 29 Aug. 1865, p. 206; AGNM, II Imperio, Caja 24: "Corps Expeditionnaire du Méxique: Etat-Major-Général, N° 48—Ordre Général," Mexico, 15 Oct. 1865; "Partes de varios encuentros con los disidentes," Zacatlán, Ahuacatlán, Tetela del Oro, 19 July 1865; Caja 39: Various reports from General Thun to Marshall Bazaine (in French), 20 July–24 Aug. 1865; Caja 69: "Oficio del Prefecto de Tulancingo," July 1865; Caja 73: "Pedidos de condecoraciones para soldados austríacos y mexicanos," July 1865; Caja 89: "Parte del General Thun al Mariscal Bazaine sobre acciones en Teziutlán," Zacapoaxtla, 11 Aug. 1865; Gobernación, TP: "Oficio del Prefecto del Depto. de Tulancingo al Ministro de Gobernación," 18 July 1865; "Oficio del Prefecto Superior del Depto. de Tulancingo, al Ministerio de Gobernación," 26 July 1865.

70. AGNM, II Imperio, Caja 78: General Thun to Marshall Bazaine, Las Lomas, 5 Aug. 1865 (French translation).

71. Donna Rivera Moreno, "Los héroes anónimos: Xochiapulco ante la historia," unpublished manuscript, Puebla, 1985. This is an excerpt Rivera takes from Valeria Carroll, *La vida fascinante de Juan Crisóstomo Bonilla*, which does not appear in the later published version of Rivera Moreno, *Xochiapulco*. All quotations appear on p. 55 of the manuscript.

72. For Thun's optimism about resolving the situation in the highlands, see AGNM, II Imperio, Caja 78: "Oficio del General Thun al Mariscal Bazaine," Zacapoaxtla, 10 Aug. 1865; Caja 89: "Oficio del General Thun al Mariscal Bazaine," Zacapoaxtla, 11 Aug. 1865. The quotation is in the first document. For additional evidence of conflict in the sierra, see *Diario del Imperio*, 4 Aug. 1865, p. 122; 29 Dec. 1865, p. 732; *El Pájaro Verde*, 11 Aug. 1865, p. 3; 8 Nov. 1865, p. 3; *Periódico Oficial de Puebla*, 13 Aug. 1865, p. 3; AGNM, II Imperio, Caja 6: "Sumario del Ministerio de Guerra al Gabinete Militar Imperial," Mexico City, 11 Nov. 1865; Caja 44: "Carta del Gral. Thun al Emperador," Puebla, 17 Oct. 1865. For Thun's move into southern Puebla and Veracruz, see *El Pájaro Verde*, 9 Sept. 1865, p. 3; and AGNM, II Imperio, Caja 25: "Resolución del Consejo Departamental de Veracruz, sobre la necesidad de expedicionar en Tierra Caliente para asegurar la tranquilidad pública," Veracruz, 27 Sept. 1865. For Thun's circulars as commander of the Second Territorial Division, see AGNM, II Imperio, Caja 23: "Serie de circulares del Comandante Superior de la IIª Division Territorial del Imperio," Puebla, 19 Sept. 1865.

73. For the intensifying threat of troop withdrawals following the victory of the Union in the U.S. Civil War, see Roeder, *Juárez and His Mexico*, 602. Maximilian's decree on the death penalty appears in CEHM-C, Fondo XXVIII–1: Doc. 468, "Decreto de Maximiliano estableciendo la pena de muerte para los liberales atrapados con las armas en la mano," Mexico City, 3 Oct. 1865. See also AGNM, II Imperio, Caja 77: "Decreto de Maximiliano sobre que las bandas o reuniones armadas, serán juzgados por cortes marciales," Mexico City, 3 Oct. 1865; and Roeder, *Juárez and His Mexico*, 606. For the various strategies tried in the Puebla highlands between late 1865 and early 1866, see AGNM, II Imperio, Caja 46: Letter from General Thun to the Emperor Maximilian (in German), 9 July 1865 (translation by Gerda Lerner); JPCM, III: Exp. 3, ff. 20–27; INAH (Archivo): "Puebla, Estado. Actas del Ayuntamiento de Zacapoaxtla, 1865–1867," esp. ff. 6–7, 17–17v, 21–21v, 32.

74. For concerns about armistice with Liberal troops, see INAH (Archivo): "Actas del Ayuntamiento de Zacapoaxtla," f. 32. For the correspondence concerning the charitable organization in Zacapoaxtla, see AGNM, II Imperio, Caja 2: "Oficio de María Antonia Navarro de Suárez al General en Jefe de la 2ª División Territorial," Zacapoaxtla, 27 July 1865; Caja 66: Letter from General Thun to the Emperor (in German with French translation), Zacapoaxtla, 29 July 1865; and Caja 65: "Carta del Jefe del Gabinete Militar a la Sra. Dª Antonia Suarez de Navarro," Mexico City, 3 Aug. 1865. For the complaints about the abuses of the draft, see II Imperio, Caja 23: "Carta del Prefecto Interino de Puebla al Ministro de Gobernación," Puebla, 10 Nov. 1865.

75. On the Papantla agreements, see Ignacio R. Alatorre, *Reseña de los acontecimientos ocurridos en las líneas del Norte y Centro del Estado de Veracruz en los años de 1863 a 1867* (Veracruz, 1887); AGNM, II Imperio, Caja 80: "Oficio del Gabinete Militar al Emperador: Reportaje del Visitador Imperial Dn. José María Galicia," Mexico City, 10 Feb. 1866; Gobernación, TP: "Telegrama del prefecto político de Puebla al Ministerio de Gobernación," 19 Jan. 1866; "Oficio del Visitador Imperial Galicia y Azostegui al Ministerio de Gobernación," Zacapoaxtla, 21 Feb. 1866; "Oficio del Ministro de Gobierno al Secretario del Gabinete Civil de S.M.," Mexico City, 13 Feb. 1866; Exp. 8, "Oficio de J. M. Galicia al Ministro de Gobierno," Zacapoaxtla, 21 Feb. 1866, f. 3; "Oficio sobre una carta del visitador imperial en la sierra de Puebla, que incluye un acta de adhesión de los de Xochiapulco al Emperador, y otros documentos," Mexico City, 26 Feb. 1866; "Carta del Visitador de la Sierra al Ministro José María Esteva," Zacapoaxtla, 21 Feb. 1866; Gobernación: Leg. 1742(3), Exp. 13, "Memorandum del Ministerio de Estado al Emperador," Mexico City, 20 Feb. 1866; *Diario del Imperio*, 22 Jan. 1866, p. 104. For the decree naming Galicia, see AGNM, II Imperio, Caja 45: "Decreto del Emperador Maximiliano nombrando a José María Galicia y Azostegui Visitador Imperial en el departamento de Tuxpan, distritos de Jalapa y Jalacingo en Veracruz; Teziutlán, Zacapoaxtla y San Juan de los Llanos en Puebla; Zacatlán en Tlaxcala, y demas de la Sierra de Puebla," Mexico City, 25 Dec. 1865. For the agreement celebrated with Xochiapulco, see *Diario del Imperio*, 9 Mar. 1866, and ACDN, C-64, D/111/2/425: "Exp. de Juan Francisco Lucas," ff. 47, 66–67.

76. AGNM, II Imperio, Caja 80: "Oficio del Gabinete Militar al Emperador, acerca del parte del Visitador Imperial," Mexico City, 10 Feb. 1866; Gobernación, TP: "Oficio del Visitador Imperial Galicia y Azostegui al Ministro de Gobernación," Zacapoaxtla, 21 Feb. 1866; Exp. 8, "Oficio de José María Galicia al Ministro de Gobernación," Zacapoaxtla, 21 Feb. 1866, f. 3. In this last document Galicia promises to use his own personal fortune to help Méndez go into voluntary exile. On Galicia's distinctions among the conditions acceptable to different liberal leaders, as well as his attempts to reorganize the municipal governments or political districts in dissident areas, see "Carta del Visitador de la Sierra al Ministro José María Esteva," Zacapoaxtla, 21 Feb. 1866; and II Imperio, Caja 80: "Oficio del Gabinete Militar al Emperador, acerca del parte del Visitador Imperial," Mexico City, 10 Feb. 1866. For an example of the broad variety of petitions Galicia was willing to hear, see Caja 42: "Solicitud de un grupo de extranjeros arrendatarios a don José María Galicia," Jicaltepec, 25 Feb. 1866.

77. The claims under 100 pesos are as follows: AGNM, II Imperio, Caja 42: "Reclamo de María Joaquina Tunesto," Zacapoaxtla, 31 Jan. 1866; "Reclamo de Cayetana Vasquez," Zacapoaxtla, Jan. 1866; "Reclamo de María

Juana," Zacapoaxtla, 1 Feb. 1866; "Reclamo de Manuel Antonio," Zacapoax-tla, 1 Feb. 1866; "Reclamo de Vicente Soto," Zacapoaxtla, 31 Jan. 1866; "Reclamo de Manuel Antonio Pérez," Zacapoaxtla, 1 Feb. 1866; "Reclamo de José Manuel Salgado," Zacapoaxtla, 30 Jan. 1866; "Reclamo de José Soto," Zacapoaxtla, 30 Jan. 1866; "Reclamo de José Juan Soto," Zacapoaxtla, 30 Jan. 1866; "Reclamo de José Miguel Valentín," Zacapoaxtla, 30 Jan. 1866; "Re-clamo de José Antonio Soto," 31 Jan. 1866; "Reclamo de María Asención," Zacapoaxtla, 1 Feb. 1866; "Reclamo de María Francisca," Zacapoaxtla, 1 Feb. 1866; "Reclamo de María Gertrudis del Carmen," Zacapoaxtla, 1 Feb. 1866; "Reclamo de Jose Juan Francisco," Zacapoaxtla, 31 Jan. 1866; Caja 43: "Re-clamo de José Luciano," Zacapoaxtla, 20 Feb. 1866; Caja 41: "Reclamo de José Antonio Soto," Zacapoaxtla, 30 Jan. 1866. The claims between 100 and 200 pesos are as follows: Caja 41: "Reclamo de Miguel Soto," Zacapoaxtla, 30 Jan. 1866; Caja 43: "Reclamo de Pedro Soto," Zacapoaxtla, 30 Jan. 1866; Caja 42: "Reclamo de Apolinario Soto," Zacapoaxtla, 5 Mar. 1866; "Reclamo de José Tomás," Zacapoaxtla, 20 Feb. 1866; "Reclamo de la testamentaría del rancho Apulco," Zacapoaxtla, 30 Jan. 1866. The claims over 200 pesos are as follows: Caja 20 and 41: "Reclamos de la testamentaría de Miguel Guevara en el Mesón de la Aurora," Zacapoaxtla, 17 Feb. and 25 Jan. 1866; Caja 20: "Reclamo de Marcelino Limón," Zacapoaxtla, 21 Feb. 1866. By contrast, only one claim each is recorded for Teziutlán, Tlatlauqui, Misantla / Tlapa-coya, and El Espinal / Papantla, each for a comparatively more sizeable amount. See Caja 20: "Reclamo de Josefa y Luz Ruiz," Teziutlán, 16 Jan. 1866; "Reclamo de José Antonio Luna," Tlatlauqui, 16 Feb. 1866; "Liqui-dación de créditos reconocidos por Pérez y Anticochea," Misantla / Tlapa-coyan, 1866; "Reclamo de Nicolás Arteaga," Espinal / Papantla, 11 Feb. 1866.

78. The document analyzed can be found in *Diario del Imperio*, 9 Mar. 1866, p. 264. For other documents that recognize the legitimacy of the emperor and imperial institutions, see those immediately following on the same page, as well as *Diario del Imperio*, 23–24 Mar. 1865, pp. 274–76; AHDN, D/481.4/9717, Jan.–Mar. 1864: "Declaraciones de varios pueblos de la región de Antigua Veracruz a favor del Imperio"; and D/481.4/9718, Jan. 1865: "Declaración de los vecinos de Antigua Veracruz a favor de las auto-ridades del Imperio."

79. AGNM, II Imperio, Caja 67: "Varios oficios del Visitador Imperial José María Galicia al Ministro de Gobernación, sobre la rebelión en Papan-tla," 24 June–8 July 1866. On the contradictory effects of Maximilian's attempts to attract moderates and other Liberals, see BN-AJ, MS. J 11–1621: "Carta de E. S. Herrera a Pedro Santacilia," Veracruz, 19 June 1866; AGNM, II Imperio, Caja 90: "Queja de Diego Gallegos y Vicente Monroy al Empera-dor," Mexico City, 17 June 1865; "Informe sobre el ocurso de Gallegos y Monroy," 13 July 1865; Caja 45: "Carta de los comisionados de los pueblos

del distrito de San Pedrito de la Sierra," Mexico City, 22 Aug. 1865; INAH (Archivo): "Actas del Ayuntamiento de Zacapoaxtla," f. 32.

80. On abuses by the foreign countersinsurgency forces, see Emile de Keratry, *La contraguerrilla francesa en México. 1864*, trans. Daniel Molina A. (Mexico City: Fondo de Cultura Económica, 1981); AGNM, Gobernación: Leg. 1738, Exp. 2, "Oficio de José María Esteva al Ministerio de Guerra," Puebla, 15 Oct. 1866; and the sources cited in note 82. On Maximilian's increasing dependence on diminishing and counterproductive foreign armies, see Roeder, *Juárez and His Mexico*, 333–524, 591–658.

81. This summary of events during 1866 is based on Conde Corti, *Maximiliano y Carlota*, 409–540.

82. On the renewed resistance of different Liberal forces, see BN-AJ, MS. J 11–1621: "Carta de E. S. Herrera a Pedro Santacilia," Veracruz, 19 June 1866; AHMTO, Gobierno, Caja s/n 1866: Exp. 35, "Desconocimiento del Imperio en Tetela," 12 Aug. 1866; Exp. 41, "Proclama de Juan Francisco Lucas a sus fuerzas en Teziutlán," 21 Aug. 1866; "Oficio de Juan Francisco Lucas al jefe político de Tetela," Zacapoaxtla, 24 Aug. 1866; Exp. 71, "Proclama de Juan Francisco Lucas a los ciudadanos de Teziutlán," 22 Aug. 1866; "Proclama de Juan Crisóstomo Bonilla a las fuerzas de Zacapoaxtla," Zacapoaxtla, 23 Aug. 1866; "Actas de adhesión al desconocimiento del Imperio firmado en Tetela, por los pueblos de Tuzamapan, Jonotla, y Zapotitlán," 25 Aug. 1866; BN-AJ, Doc. 1383: "Carta de I. R. Alatorre al Presidente Benito Juárez," Teziutlán, 23 Sept. 1866. On the defection of Chignahuapan, see AHMTO, Caja s/n 1866: Exp. 71, "Declaración de adhesión a la república por los jefes y oficiales del escuadrón Chignahuapan," Zacatlán, 9 Sept. 1866. On the difficulties with paying the Austrian forces, see Conde Corti, *Maximiliano y Carlota*, 446. On Austrian abuses see AGNM, Gobierno: Leg. 1738, Exp. 2, "Oficio de Antonio Rodríguez Bocardo al Comisario Imperial de la 2ª División," Los Llanos, 20 Sept. 1866; "Oficio del Comisario José María Esteva al Ministerio de Gobernación," Puebla, 27 Sept. 1866; "Oficio del Comisario José María Esteva al Ministerio de Gobernación," Puebla, 28 Sept. 1866; and "Oficio del Comisario José María Esteva al Ministro de Gobernación," Puebla, 5 Oct. 1866. For the sense of impotence in official documents, see AGNM, Gobierno: Leg. 1738, Exp. 2, "Oficio del Ministro de Guerra al Ministro de Gobernación, sobre los abusos de la fuerza austríaca en Los Llanos," Mexico City, 5 Oct. 1866; II Imperio, Caja 13: "Oficio de los vecinos de Acaxochitlán al Emperador," 24 Sept. 1866; "Respuesta del Secretario Militar del Emperador a los vecinos de Acaxochitlán," Mexico City, 4 Oct. 1866; Caja 14: "Solicitud de D. Asencio Hernández, vecino de Xicotepec, sobre la situación de los vecinos leales al Imperio," Mexico City, 9 Oct. 1866; "Respuesta del Ministerio de Guerra," Mexico City, 18 Oct. 1866.

83. For the reestablishment of broader liberal authority in the Sierra de Puebla, see AHMTO, Gobierno, Caja s/n 1866: Exp. 41, "Oficio de Juan N.

Méndez al jefe político de Tetela, informándole que el General Porfirio Díaz lo ha nombrado jefe político y militar de la línea de Teziutlán," Zacapoaxtla, 5 Sept. 1866; "Instrucciones del Cuartel General de Oriente a Juan N. Méndez como jefe de la línea de Teziutlán," 25 Aug. 1866; "Carta de Juan N. Méndez al jefe político de Tetela, informándole que Porfirio Díaz ha nombrado a Rafael J. García Gobernador Interino del Estado de Puebla," Zacapoaxtla, 5 Sept. 1866; *Archivo del General Porfirio Díaz*, 4:39–40, 42–43. For the measures taken by local liberal authorities, see AHMTO, Gobierno, Caja s/n 1866: "Decreto de José Daniel Posadas, jefe político de Tetela, a los ciudadanos del distrito," 28 Oct. 1866; Exp. 41, "Oficio de Juan N. Méndez al jefe político de Tetela de Ocampo," 29 Oct. 1866; "Oficio de Juan N. Méndez al jefe político de Tetela," Huamantla, 8 Dec. 1866; "Oficio de Ramón Márquez Galindo al jefe político de Tetela," Zacatlán, 11 Dec. 1866. For additional information on the push that occurred in the early months of 1867, see AHMTO, Gobierno, Caja 9: Exp. 9, no. 47; Exp. 7, no. 267; and Exp. 9.

84. The emphasis on unity can be seen in all the Liberal proclamations and correspondence during the second half of 1866 and the early months of 1867. See, for example, AHMTO, Gobierno, Caja s/n 1866: Exp. 35, "Acta de desconocimiento del Imperio," Tetela de Ocampo, 12 Aug. 1866; Exp. 71, "Proclama de Juan Francisco Lucas a los ciudadanos de Teziutlán," 22 Aug. 1866; "Actas de Tuzamapan, Jonotla y Zapotitlán, reiterando su adhesión al desconocimiento del Imperio suscrito en la cabecera de Tetela de Ocampo," 25 Aug. 1866; "Proclama de Juan Crisóstomo Bonilla a las fuerzas de Zacapoaxtla," Zacapoaxtla, 23 Aug. 1866; Exp. 41, "Proclama de Juan Francisco Lucas a sus fuerzas en Teziutlán," Teziutlán, 21 Aug. 1866; "Oficio de Juan Francisco Lucas al jefe político de Tetela," Zacapoaxtla, 24 Aug. 1866; Caja 9: Exp. 7, no. 267, "José Daniel Posadas al alcalde constitucional," Tetela de Ocampo, 5 Feb. 1867. The term *second independence* was used already at the time to refer to the victory of Mexican forces over Interventionist and imperial troops.

85. On the acceptance of people like Pascual Bonilla, see AHMTO, Gobierno, Caja s/n 1866: "Parte sobre dos combates de Rodríguez Bocardo con las fuerzas austríacas cerca del pueblo del Carmen," 2 Oct. 1866; Exp. 71, "Proclama de Juan Crisóstomo Bonilla a las fuerzas de Zacapoaxtla," 23 Aug. 1866; "Oficio de Rafael J. García a Juan Francisco Lucas," Zacapoaxtla, 28 Sept. 1866. On the Liberal acceptance of the surrender of the forces in Chignahuapan and the guarantees given to Conservative citizens, see "Declaración de adhesión a la república por los jefes y oficiales del escuadrón Chignahuapan," Zacatlán, 9 Sept. 1866. On the caution exhibited by Rafael J. García upon being named provisional governor, see Exp. 41, "Carta de Rafael J. García a Juan N. Méndez," 3 Sept. 1866; and BN-AJ, Doc. 1562: "Carta del Gobernador Interino del Estado de Puebla, Rafael J. García, a Benito Juárez," Zacapoaxtla, 3 Oct. 1866. On the acceptance García received

from Liberal leaders in the sierra and his initial policies, see also AHMTO, Caja s/n 1866: Exp. 41, "Carta de Juan N. Méndez al jefe político de Tetela," 5 Sept. 1866; Exp. 34, "Carta del Gobernador interino del Estado, al Jefe Político de Tetela," Zacapoaxtla, 7 Sept. 1866; CEHM-C, Fondo XXVIII–1: Doc. 481, "Proclama de Rafael J. García a sus conciudadanos al ser nombrado Gobernador del Estado," Zacapoaxtla, 23 Sept. 1866; Doc. 483, "Proclama del Gobernador Rafael J. García a los habitantes del Estado de Puebla," Zacapoaxtla, 29 Sept. 1866. García was a journalist in the city of Puebla during the Empire; his claim to fame was an article he published in his newspaper *La Idea Liberal*, entitled "La situación," in which he suggested that people be allowed to vote on whether or not the emperor should remain. See *El Pájaro Verde*, 13 July 1865, 19 Aug. 1865.

86. The letter from the barrio of San Nicolás is in AHMTO, Gobierno, Caja 9: Exp. 3, "Oficio de los vecinos del barrio de San Nicolás al ayuntamiento de Tetela de Ocampo," 16 Feb. 1867. Other examples of the early desire for education, as well as the difficulties involved, are "Oficio del preceptor de la escuela de la Cañada, Tiburcio García, al ayuntamiento de Tetela," 16 Jan. 1867; and Exp. 6, no. 52, "Oficio del Ayuntamiento de Aquixtla al Jefe Político de Tetela, sobre educación," Aquixtla, 22 July 1867.

87. The documents on land adjudications can be found in AHMTO, Caja s/n 1866: Exp. 71, "Actas de varios pueblos en las municipalidades de Jonotla y Tuzamapan, y acta de Tenampulco, considerando la circular sobre la desamortización de tierras," 9–16 Mar. 1867.

88. The importance and endurance of this counterhegemonic alliance can be seen in a variety of contexts during the rest of the nineteenth century, starting with the strength of the Montaña party in resisting Juarista centralization, to its dominance of Puebla state politics during the early Porfiriato, to its resuscitation during the Mexican Revolution of 1910, when Juan Francisco Lucas led the Sierra in supporting the Constitutionalists. Aside from subsequent chapters of this book, some interesting treatments of these events are Thomson, "Bulwarks of Patriotic Liberalism"; Thomson, "*Montaña* and *Llanura*"; Guy P. C. Thomson, "Movilización conservadora, insurrección liberal y rebeliones indígenas, 1854–76," in Antonio Annino, Marcello Carmagnani, et al., eds., *America latina: Dallo stato coloniale allo stato nazione*, vol. 2 (Turin: Franco Angeli, 1988), 592–614; and David LaFrance and Guy P. C. Thomson, "Juan Francisco Lucas: Patriarch of the Sierra Norte de Puebla," in William H. Beezley and Judith Ewell, eds., *The Human Tradition in Latin America: The Twentieth Century* (Wilmington, Del.: Scholarly Resources, 1987), 1–13.

89. The unusual quality of Xochiapulco is also very clear in Thomson, "Bulwarks of Patriotic Liberalism," where he describes the funeral held for Juan N. Méndez's son Miguel in 1888, during which a North American Methodist minister and his wife sang hymns in English and all the speeches

subscribed to the radical Liberalism of the French Revolution, Garibaldi, and Hidalgo (1). See also chapter 9 of this book. The point was further emphasized for me in my visits in April and May of 1985. Even then Xochiapulco's central square did not sport a Catholic church; and Donna Rivera Moreno, descendant of Juan Francisco Lucas and my most valuable informant, confided to me that her village's tradition of rabid anticlericalism had led to a counterproductive level of general antireligiosity.

CHAPTER 3. THE CONFLICTUAL CONSTRUCTION
OF COMMUNITY

1. My first visit to Xochiapulco occurred on 17 April 1985, with a follow-up stay of two days a month later. The summary of the guerrilla movement contained in the previous two paragraphs relies on a variety of documents that I located in 1984–1985 and cite throughout this book. The most important archives for understanding the movement were ACEP, AGNM, AGNEP, AHDN, AHMTO, AHMZ, BN-AJ, and SRE.

2. The problems involved with occupying Xochiapulco are clear from a variety of documents, both from the Intervention (1862–1867) and the subsequent civil wars (1868–1872), located in the AGNM and AHDN and in the newspapers of the day. See especially AGNM, II Imperio, Caja 78: "Report by Austrian Commander Thun to the French Mariscal Bazaine," Las Lomas, 5 Aug. 1865; Caja 89: "Report by Thun to Bazaine from Zacapoaxtla," 11 Aug. 1865; and "Extracto del Parte Oficial sobre el Combate del 2 y 3 de diciembre entre el 60. Batallón de Cazadores y los de Xochiapulco," *El Monitor Republicano*, 17 Dec. 1869.

3. The local political process underlying guerrilla warfare emerges in AHMTO, Gobierno, Caja s/n 1866: Exp. 71, "Acta levantada en el pueblo de S. Martin Tuzamapan, desconociendo al Gobierno Imperial," 25 Aug. 1866; "Acta de la Guardia Nacional en Tetela de Ocampo, rechazando las condiciones impuestas por Ignacio R. Alatorre," 22 July 1868; Exp. 90, "Carta de Juan Francisco Lucas al Jefe Político de Tetela, acusando recibo de las actas desconociendo a Rafael J. García," Xochiapulco, 21 June 1868; Caja s/n 1868: Exp. 65, "Oficio del Juez/Alcalde de Jonotla, Francisco Rodríguez, sobre el acta levantada en Tetela," 6 June 1868; Exp. 64, "Oficio del Alcalde de Huitzilan al Jefe Político de Tetela," 8 June 1868; "Oficio del Juez de Huitzilan al Jefe Político de Tetela," 26 July 1868; and AHMZ, Paq. 1869: Exp. 118, "Elección de oficiales por la Guardia Nacional de Xochiapulco," 14–15 June, 1869. For Alatorre's plan, see ACEP, Expedientes, vol. 15: "Oficio del Gobernador de Puebla, Ignacio Romero Vargas, al Ministro de Guerra y Marina, describiendo el proceso de pacificación en la sierra," 4 June 1870.

4. Among the works that were most influential in the development of this perspective were James C. Scott, *The Moral Economy of the Peasant*

(New Haven: Yale University Press, 1976); Eric Wolf, *Peasant Wars of the Twentieth Century* (New York: Harper and Row, 1969); Eric Hobsbawm, *Primitive Rebels* (New York: Norton, 1959); E. P. Thompson, *The Making of the English Working Class* (New York: Vintage, 1963); and Thompson, "The Moral Economy of the English Crowd in the Eighteenth Century," *Past and Present*, Feb. 1971, 76–136. The phrase "backward toward revolution" comes from Edward Friedman, *Backward Toward Revolution: The Chinese Revolutionary Party* (Berkeley: University of California Press, 1974).

5. Perhaps it is important to emphasize here that I am addressing *political* definitions of rural communities. On the economic front, there has been a great deal more variation and investigation of internal communal relations. For an example of such an analysis, as well as some limited bibliography, see Florencia E. Mallon, *The Defense of Community in Peru's Central Highlands: Peasant Struggle and Capitalist Transition, 1860–1940* (Princeton: Princeton University Press, 1983). See also William Roseberry, "Beyond the Agrarian Question in Latin America," in Frederick Cooper, Allen Isaacman, Florencia Mallon, William Roseberry, and Steve Stern, *Confronting Historical Paradigms: Peasants, Labor, and the World-System in Africa and Latin America* (Madison: University of Wisconsin Press, 1992), 318–68, and Carmen Diana Deere, *Household and Class Relations: Peasants and Landlords in Northern Peru* (Berkeley: University of California Press, 1990). For an early gender-based critique of the "seamless community" approach, see Judith Stacey, *Patriarchy and Socialist Revolution in China* (Berkeley: University of California Press, 1983). For a recent critique of the concept of community as used in E. P. Thompson's and Natalie Davis's works, see Suzanne Desan, "Crowds, Community, and Ritual in the Work of E. P. Thompson and Natalie Davis," in Lynn Hunt, ed., *The New Cultural History* (Berkeley: University of California Press, 1989), 47–71. For a particularly pessimistic view of whether the concept of community has any relevance whatsoever, see Gayatri Chakravorty Spivak, "Subaltern Studies: Deconstructing Historiography," in Spivak, ed., *In Other Worlds: Essays in Cultural Politics* (New York: Routledge, 1988), 197–221. For examples of the "rational choice" approach to the peasant community and peasant politics, see Samuel L. Popkin, *The Rational Peasant: The Political Economy of Rural Society in Vietnam* (Berkeley: University of California Press, 1979); Michael Taylor, ed., *Rationality and Revolution* (Cambridge: Cambridge University Press, 1988); and Taylor, "Structure, Culture, and Action in the Explanation of Social Change," *Politics and Society* 17, no. 2 (1989): 115–62. Since his earlier work on moral economy, James C. Scott has also moved on to examine community politics from the inside; see *Weapons of the Weak: Everyday Forms of Peasant Resistance* (New Haven: Yale University Press, 1985) and *Domination and the Arts of Resistance: Hidden Transcripts* (New Haven: Yale University Press, 1990). His position differs from mine in that

he postulates the existence of a hidden culture of resistance separate from official or hegemonic culture and thus somehow still autonomous and internally coherent, untouched by the dirt of official politics.

6. I also discuss the concept of communal hegemony in chapter 1. Despite the obvious debt I owe to Ernesto Laclau and Chantal Mouffe in the elaboration of this concept (*Hegemony and Socialist Strategy: Towards a Radical Democratic Politics* [London: Verso Books, 1985]), my use of their concept of hegemony to analyze communal politics runs counter to their method because they see noncapitalist politics as transparent and therefore not in need of hegemonizing.

7. This metaphor, which has been attributed to Mao Zedong, was quite popular during the Vietnam War. The close and reciprocal relation it signifies between guerrillas and the peasant community, in contrast to the more superficial and contingent relation conceptualized in the guerrilla *foco* theory, was also central to the interpretation and application of the Guerra Popular Prolongada (prolonged people's war) strategy in Central America during the 1970s and early 1980s.

8. This paragraph summary is based on my reading of a variety of sources on the Sierra de Puebla and on colonial institutions more generally: Bernardo García, *Los pueblos de la sierra: El poder y el espacio entre los indios del norte de Puebla hasta 1700* (Mexico City: El Colegio de México, 1987); Hugo G. Nutini and Betty Bell, *Ritual Kinship: The Structure and Historical Development of the Compadrazgo System in Rural Tlaxcala*, vol. 1 (Princeton: Princeton University Press, 1980); Hugo G. Nutini, *Todos Santos in Rural Tlaxcala: A Syncretic, Expressive, and Symbolic Analysis of the Cult of the Dead* (Princeton: Princeton University Press, 1988); Marcello Carmagnani, *El regreso de los dioses: El proceso de reconstitución de la identidad étnica en Oaxaca* (Mexico City: Fondo de Cultura Económica, 1988); John K. Chance and William B. Taylor, "Cofradías and Cargos: An Historical Perspective on the Mesoamerican Civil-Religious Hierarchy," *American Ethnologist* 12, no. 1 (Feb. 1985): 1–26; Jan Rus and Robert Wasserstrom, "Civil-Religious Hierarchies in Central Chiapas: A Critical Perspective," *American Ethnologist* 7, no. 3 (Aug. 1980): 466–78; Charles Gibson, *The Aztecs under Spanish Rule: A History of the Indians of the Valley of Mexico, 1519–1810* (Stanford: Stanford University Press, 1964); Marcello Carmagnani, "Local Governments and Ethnic Government in Oaxaca," in Karen Spalding, ed., *Essays in the Political, Economic and Social History of Colonial Latin America* (Newark, Del.: Latin American Studies Program, 1982), 107–24; Luisa Paré, "Inter-ethnic and Class Relations (Sierra Norte Region, State of Puebla)," in *Race and Class in Post-Colonial Society: A Study of Ethnic Group Relations in the English-Speaking Caribbean, Bolivia, Chile, and Mexico* (Paris: UNESCO, 1977), 377–420; Gregory G. Reck, *In the Shadow of Tlatloc: Life in a Mexican Village* (New York: Penguin,

1978); Lourdes Arizpe, *Parentesco y economía en una sociedad Nahua: Nican Pehua Zacatipan* (Mexico City: Instituto Nacional Indigenista / Secretaría de Educación Pública, 1973); and James M. Taggart, *Estructura de los grupos domésticos de una comunidad Nahuat de Puebla* (Mexico City: Instituto Nacional Indigenista/Secretaría de Educación Pública, 1975).

9. In addition to all the sources listed above, I am basing my argument on Peter Guardino, "Peasants, Politics, and State Formation in Nineteenth-Century Mexico: Guerrero, 1800–1857," Ph.D. diss., University of Chicago, 1992. Guardino argues that the transition from *gobiernos de república* to municipalities was quite conflictual and opened up potential new spaces for mestizos and outsiders in village society. In such a context it is particularly useful to see the system of pasados as an emerging compromise, worked out in dialogue with the new municipal institutions, among different groups and factions within the community. On the dynamism of the transition to municipalidad in other regions of nineteenth-century Mexico, see Rodolfo Pastor, *Campesinos y reformas: La mixteca, 1700–1856* (Mexico City: El Colegio de México, 1987), and Alicia Hernández Chávez, *Anenecuilco: Memoria y vida de un pueblo* (Mexico City: El Colegio de México, 1991).

10. The information on patrilocality contained in this paragraph is a composite of the descriptions given in several ethnographies of the region, most notably Arizpe, *Parentezco y economía*; James W. Dow, *Santos y supervivencias: Funciones de la religión en una comunidad Otomí, Mexico* (Mexico City: Instituto Nacional Indigenista / Secretaría de Educación Pública, 1974); and Taggart, *Estructura*. Of course, using twentieth-century ethnographies in order to describe a nineteenth-century reality is always risky. Some clues, however, make it slightly less risky than it would otherwise be. One of these is that Lourdes Arizpe identifies her informants by age and gender. Based on the memories of her oldest informants, married between fifty and sixty years, she identifies patrilocality as the norm, with the authority of the father paramount, according to her male informant. Her female informant describes the process of how the family of her husband ("mi señor") asked for her hand; she then went to live in her husband's family's house and did the work she was given (62–63). Since Arizpe's data were collected between 1969 and 1970, the information given was for the first decade of the twentieth century. I am therefore assuming that patrilocality, and the general relations associated with it, were the norm in the second half of the nineteenth century as well.

11. The information in this paragraph is a composite of that provided in regional ethnographies, most notably Arizpe, *Parentezco y economía*; Dow, *Santos y supervivencias*; Taggart, *Estructura*; and Hugo G. Nutini and Barry L. Isaac, *Los pueblos de habla Náhuatl de la región de Tlaxcala y Puebla* (Mexico City: Instituto Nacional Indigenista / Secretaría de Educación Pública, 1974). A comparison of the different villages and cases presented by

Nutini and Isaac suggests that the increasing cultivation of coffee, the short-ages of land, and the increasing use of wage labor all tended to loosen the bonds of patriarchal control by providing younger males with independent sources of income, lessening the resources patriarchs could promise and increasing women and children's participation in agricultural labor. This reading confirms the impression one gets from Arizpe that patrilocality and patriarchal control over land and labor power were more potent before commercialization and land hunger became intense.

12. A particularly helpful description of local religious ritual and the use of oratorio rituals to buttress or organize financial and labor exchanges can be found in Dow, *Santos y supervivencias*, esp. 121–31, 181, 218, 226–27, 243–44. See also Nancy M. Farriss, *Maya Society under Colonial Rule: The Collective Enterprise of Survival* (Princeton: Princeton University Press, 1984), esp. 320–54, for a comparative example from a very different Mexi-can region.

13. Especially clear descriptions of mayordomías are to be found in Arizpe, *Parentezco y economía* (the quotation appears on p. 205); and Dow, *Santos y supervivencias*, 145–47, 176–211. See also Taggart, *Estructura*, 177–78.

14. On the definition of local leadership and prestige through the holding of religious and political posts and on the relationship of these to kinship and community, see, for Puebla and Tlaxcala, Hugo G. Nutini, Pedro Carras-co, and James M. Taggart, eds., *Essays on Mexican Kinship* (Pittsburgh: University of Pittsburgh Press, 1975); Arizpe, *Parentesco y economía*; Nu-tini and Isaac, *Los pueblos de habla Náhuatl*; Nutini and Bell, *Ritual Kin-ship*; Nutini, *Ritual Kinship*, vol. 2 (Princeton: Princeton University Press, 1984); and Nutini, *Todos Santos*. On the complex formal and informal roles played by pasados in village politics, see especially Dow, *Santos y su-pervivencias*, 145–47, 153–57, 171–73, 178, 180, 226.

15. In addition to the sources cited in the previous note, see also María Teresa Sierra Camacho, *El ejercicio discursivo de la autoridad en asambleas comunales (metodología y análisis del discurso oral)* (Mexico City: Cua-dernos de la Casa Chata, 1987), 8, 11–12, 14–18, 25, 109. On ethnic negotia-tions over positions of power at the local level, see also AHMTO, Gobierno, Caja s/n 1866: Exp. 71, "Acta del pueblo de S. Martin Tuzamapan descono-ciendo al gobierno imperial," 25 Aug. 1866; "Acta del pueblo de Jonotla desconociendo al gobierno imperial," 24 Aug. 1866; "Acta del pueblo de Zapotitlan desconociendo al gobierno imperial," 3 Sept. 1866; Caja s/n 1868: Exp. 66, "Oficio de Antonio Sánchez, juez de Tuzamapan, al jefe político de Tetela, sobre las elecciones municipales en Tenampulco," 24 Sept. 1868; "Oficio del nuevo juez de Tuzamapan, Nicolás Galicia, al jefe político de Tetela, sobre el arreglo en Tenampulco," 20 Oct. 1868; and AGNEP, Huauchinango, Caja 2, 1861–1870: Libro 1863, "Arrendamiento de algunos

solares comunales por Manuel Antonio, alcalde de Michiuca, suplente José Francisco Telles, y algunos pasados," 23 Nov. 1863.

16. For the quotation, see Nutini and Isaac, *Los pueblos de habla Náhuatl*, 156. For further data on the possible variations within the general theme of patrilocality and possible widespread conflicts or disputes, see also ibid., 151–247; Dow, *Santos y supervivencias*, 74–78; and Taggart, *Estructura*.

17. The information in this paragraph is a composite of the following sources: Nutini and Isaac, *Ritual Kinship*; Arizpe, *Parentezco y economía*; Taggart, *Estructura*; and Dow, *Santos y supervivencias*.

18. For the song, see Arizpe, *Parentezco y economía*, 213–14. The rest of the information in the paragraph comes from the sources cited in the previous note, along with Sergio López Alonso, coord., *Las condiciones de vida en una comunidad totonaca: Caxhuacan, Puebla*, Departamento de Antropología Física, Colección Científica no. 124 (Mexico City: Instituto Nacional de Antropología e Historia, 1982), 13, 16.

19. For the way women calculated their age, see Arizpe, *Parentezco y economía*, 56. Taggart, *Estructura*, 176–77, also emphasizes the relationship between age and prestige for women.

20. The analysis in this paragraph was inspired by Carmagnani, "Local Governments and Ethnic Government," and by conversations with Steve J. Stern. Dow, *Estructura*, 147–56, also suggests that the cargo system becomes increasingly selective at the top; only around half of the men, he calculates, are able to earn the status of elder. See also Arizpe, *Parentezco y economía*, 121–24.

21. See especially Sierra Camacho, *El ejercicio discursivo*, for an analysis of the contingent and dynamic ways in which communal assemblies could be used for the accumulation or reproduction of local power. On the complexity of popular politics and popular culture, see also Mikhail Bakhtin, *Rabelais and His World*, trans. Hélène Iswolsky (Bloomington: Indiana University Press, 1984).

22. For the use of familial language when referring to the community, see especially AHMZ, Paq. 1863–65–64: Exp. 222, "Oficio del Juez de Paz de Taitic al Comandante Militar y Jefe Político de Zacapoaxtla," 2 Aug. 1863; Leg. 37, "Carta de Francisco Cortes al Capitán D. Juan Francisco Lucas," Cuetzalan, 23 Mar. 1863; and AHMTO, Gobierno, Caja s/n 1866: Exp. 71, "Acta de la Guardia Nacional de Tetela de Ocampo rechazando las condiciones impuestas por Ignacio R. Alatorre." For the political role of los pasados, see Exp. 7, "Acta del pueblo de San Francisco Zoquiapan sobre adjudicaciones de terrenos," 11 Mar. 1867, and "Acta del pueblo de Tenampulco sobre adjudicaciones de terrenos," 16 Mar. 1867; AHMZ, Paq. 1869: Exp. 111: "Relativo a la ley de desamortización en el pueblo de Yancuitlalpan: Copia del acta de los vecinos de Santiago Yancuitlalpan sobre escoger un terreno para ejido," 17 Jan. 1869.

23. In a personal communication, Steve J. Stern has confirmed a similar role of community authorities as checks against abusive patriarchs for Oaxaca in the late colonial and early national periods.

24. The description of Mora's abuse of his companion occurs in AHMTO, Gobierno, Caja s/n 1868: Exp. 68, "Oficio del Juez Constitucional de los Reyes al Alcalde Municipal de Tuzamapan," 20 May 1868. See also Exp. 66, "Informe del Juzgado Constitucional de San Miguel Tzinacapan, sobre la conducta de Gavino Mora," 20 May 1860; and "Oficio del Alcalde de los Reyes al Juez de Tuzamapan," 1 June 1860.

25. AHMTO, Gobierno, Caja 11: "Solicitud de Juan Francisco Lucas al P. Ayuntamiento de Tetela de Ocampo," 1 Dec. 1868. For the general importance of Lucas in the sierra during the last decades of the nineteenth century, see David LaFrance and Guy P. C. Thomson, "Juan Francisco Lucas: Patriarch of the Sierra Norte de Puebla," in William H. Beezley and Judith Ewell, eds., *The Human Tradition in Latin America: The Twentieth Century* (Wilmington, Del.: Scholarly Resources, 1987), 1–13, esp. 4–9.

26. Arizpe, *Parentezco y economía*, 123; Sierra Camacho, *El ejercicio discursivo*. In some documents from the nineteenth century, moreover, it becomes clear that the various offices of local government were negotiated ethnically, often with the more indigenous leader occupying the alcalde or juez position and the mestizo or ladino occupying the *suplente* or *secretario* role. See, for example, AHMTO, Gobierno, Caja s/n 1866: Exp. 71, "Acta del pueblo de S. Martin Tuzamapan desconociendo al gobierno imperial," 25 Aug. 1866; "Acta del pueblo de Jonotla desconociendo al gobierno imperial," 24 Aug. 1866; "Acta del pueblo de Zapotitlan desconociendo al gobierno imperial," 3 Sept. 1866; Caja s/n 1868: Exp. 66, "Oficio de Antonio Sánchez, juez de Tuzamapan, al jefe político de Tetela, sobre las elecciones municipales en Tenampulco," 24 Sept. 1868; "Oficio del nuevo juez de Tuzamapan, Nicolás Galicia, al jefe político de Tetela, sobre el arreglo en Tenampulco," 20 Oct. 1868; and AGNEP, Huauchinango, Caja 2, 1861–1870: Libro 1863, "Arrendamiento de algunos solares comunales por Manuel Antonio, alcalde de Michiuca, suplente José Francisco Telles, y algunos pasados," 23 Nov. 1863.

27. For a more extensive discussion of the commercial trends in the 1840s and beyond, and how this might lead to intensified conflict between villages or municipalities, see chapter 2. My speculations about how such changes might open up new spaces for younger men are based on what did happen in the twentieth century with additional commercial, wage labor, and migration opportunities. For examples, see Arizpe, *Parentezco y economía*; Dow, *Santos y supervivencia*; Taggart, *Estructura*; and Nutini and Isaac, *Ritual Kinship*.

28. For other elaborations of the concept of nation as constructed by peasants in the Sierra de Puebla and elsewhere, see chapters 2 and 4–8.

29. Stacey, *Patriarchy and Revolution*, 116–17, 155–57.

30. The definition of women as outside combat becomes clear from even a cursory examination of the battle reports available throughout the AHDN. It is also clear in the oral traditions that have survived in Xochiapulco, and in particular the accounts of what women actually did, which was to witness battles or hide out in caves, giving birth or surviving on water until "rescued" by male soldiers. See Donna Rivera Moreno, *Xochiapulco: Una gloria olvidada* (Puebla: Dirección General de Culturas Populares, 1991), 102. Cynthia Enloe, *Does Khaki Become You? The Militarization of Women's Lives* (London: Pluto Press, 1983), esp. 4–7, 15, 23–24, 211–12, treats the issue of women's marginalization from combat. In her chapter on guerrilla warfare, Enloe also describes the special confusion that occurs between homefront and battlefront with the development of irregular or informal, community-based combat units.

31. On assigning tortilla rations and on their composition, see especially AHMZ, Paq. 1869: Exp. 42, "Productos suministrados a la fuerza en Apulco," 9–11 July 1868. See also AHMTO, Gobierno, Caja s/n 1868: Exp. 64, "El juez de paz de Huitzilan al jefe político de Tetela," 26 July 1868; and Exp. 65: "Oficio del Juez de Jonotla al jefe político de Tetela," 27 July 1868. On the tasks involved in making tortillas, and on modern calculations, see Oscar Lewis, *Five Families: Mexican Case Studies in the Culture of Poverty* (New York: Basic Books, 1959), 25.

32. AHMTO, Gobierno, Caja 8: Exp. 9; Caja 9: Exps. 3, 6, 10.

33. Personal communication, Donna Rivera Moreno, Xochiapulco, May 1985; LaFrance and Thomson, "Juan Francisco Lucas," esp. 6.

34. AHMZ, Paq. 1869, Exp. 115: "Oficio del juez constitucional de Tzicuilan, Juan Bautista, al jefe político de Zacapoaxtla, sobre desacato a su autoridad," 23 June 1868.

35. In Mexico, elections after the Liberal Revolution of 1855—all the way through the Restored Republic (1867–1876) and the Porfiriato (1976–1910)—were held, on principle, according to the election law of 12 February 1857, which instituted universal male suffrage. See Laurens Ballard Perry, *Juárez and Díaz: Machine Politics in Mexico* (De Kalb: Northern Illinois University Press, 1978).

36. Nancy Huston, "Tales of War and Tears of Women," *Women's Studies International Forum* 5, nos. 3–4 (1982): 271–82. The quotation appears on p. 275; emphasis in the original. Interestingly, the oral traditions that have survived in Xochiapulco, and in particular the accounts of what women actually did, parallel exactly some of Huston's points, especially about women as witnesses and outsiders to the war experience. In addition to those already cited in note 30, Pascuala Martínez, a ten-year-old girl, returns from the cave where she has been hiding to encounter piles of enemy corpses as the remains of an ambush by the guerrillas of Xochiapulco. Rivera Moreno, *Xochiapulco*, 101.

37. AHDN, Exp. XI/481.3/8025: "Oficio del Subprefecto y Comandante Militar de Tlatlauqui al Comandante General del Estado de Puebla," 5 Apr. 1860; "Oficio del Subprefecto y Comandante Militar de Tlatlauqui al Comandante General del Estado de Puebla," 10 Apr. 1860. In another document contained in the same expediente, the commander of the federal army in the state of Puebla explained to the minister of defense that similar abuses were being committed by the same troops in other local Indian villages and that sections of the local national guard had refused to participate, returning to their own communities. "Oficio de Ramón Márquez Galindo, Comandante del Ejército Federal en el estado de Puebla, al Ministro de Guerra y Marina," Zacapoaxtla, 13 Apr. 1860.

38. On the ubiquity of requisitions, and how much this meant in goods and men, see AHMZ, Paq. 1862: "Circular del Gobernador de Puebla, Fernando María Ortega, sobre la necesidad de reunir víveres y forrajes," Zacapoaxtla, 29 Sept. 1862; Paq. 1863–64–65: "Oficio del Juez Constitucional de Xochiapulco al Jefe Político de Zacapoaxtla," 25 Oct. 1862; "Circular de José González Ortega al Jefe Político de Zacapoaxtla," Puebla, 6 Nov. 1862; Exp. 245, "41 Boletas de víveres para la Guardia Nacional de Xochiapulco," Zacapoaxtla, Apr. 1863; Leg. 26, "51 Recibos de víveres para el Batallón G.N. Xochiapulco, en Zacapoaxtla," May 1863; Leg. 35, "Varios documentos de las autoridades de Xochitlán, Nauzontla y Huahuaxtla, sobre remisión de víveres para el ejército," Xochitlán, 5 Jan. 1863; Exp. 214, Comunicaciones oficiales, "Oficio del juez municipal y comandante militar de Cuetzalan al jefe político y comandante militar de Zacapoaxtla," 5 Jan. 1863; "Oficio del jefe político de Tlatlauqui al comandante militar de Zacapoaxtla," 18 Jan. 1863; "Oficio del jefe político de Tlatlauqui al comandante militar de Zacapoaxtla," 19 Jan. 1863; "Oficio del Juez municipal de Cuetzalan al Jefe Político y Comandante Militar de Zacapoaxtla," 22 Jan. 1863; Paq. 1869: Exp. 42, "Relativo a los artículos de miniestra que dieron las municipalidades para el sosten de la guardia nacional que permaneció en la cumbre de Apulco," July–Nov. 1868; AHMTO, Gobierno, Caja s/n 1868: Exp. 66, "Antonio Sánchez, juez de Tuzamapa, informa a Tetela que se recogieron en Tenampulco 16 armas de los milicianos," 28 Feb. 1868; and Exp. 65, "Francisco Rodríguez, Juez de Jonotla, al Jefe Político de Tetela de Ocampo," 27 July 1868. The apology from Juan Francisco Lucas appears in Exp. 64, "Juez de Huitzilan al Jefe Político de Tetela de Ocampo, transcribiendo oficio de Juan Francisco Lucas," 26 July 1868.

39. For the arguments from Cuetzalan, see AHMZ, Paq. 1863–64–65: Exp. 214, Comunicaciones oficiales, "Oficio del juez municipal de Cuetzalan la jefe político y comandante militar de Zacapoaxtla," Cuetzalan, 5 Jan. 1863; and "Oficio del Juez Municipal de Cuetzalan, Ignacio Arrieta, al Jefe Político y Comandante Militar de Zacapoaxtla," Cuetzalan, 22 Jan. 1863. For an additional case where mestizo officials sought goods from indigenous popu-

lations, see Leg. 35, "Varios documentos de las autoridades de Xochitlán, Nauzontla y Huahuaxtla, sobre remisión de víveres para el ejército," Xochitlán, 5 Jan. 1863. For other cases in which ethnic arguments are used to buttress a plea of poverty, see also Exp. 214, "Oficio del jefe político de Tlatlauqui al comandante militar de Zacapoaxtla," Tlatlauqui, 18 Jan. 1863; and AHMTO, Gobierno, Caja 8: Exp. 11, "Nota del Juez de Jonotla al jefe político de Tetela," 29 Aug. 1864, where the pasados met to legitimize the plea of poverty.

40. AHMZ, Paq. 1862: Leg. 74, "Acta de Xochiapulco renovando sus cargos municipales," Xochiapulco, 24 Oct. 1862; Paq. 1863–64–65: Exp. 214, "Acta levantada en Xochiapulco por los miembros del ayuntamiento sobre la rebelion de varios vecinos de Yautetelco," Xochiapulco, 30 Jan. 1863; and Exp. 222, "Oficio del Comandante Militar de Xochiapulco, Juan José Español, al Comandante Militar de Zacapoaxtla," Xochiapulco, 18 Feb. 1863.

41. For Castañeda's role in requisitions, see AHMZ, Paq. 1863–64–65: Leg. 35, "Varios documentos de las autoridades de Xochitlán, Nauzontla y Huahuaxtla, sobre remisión de víveres para el ejército," Xochitlán, 5 Jan. 1863. On the communal assembly and the petition by Xochitlán's alcalde, see Paq. 1863–64–65: "Acta de los vecinos de Xochitlán eligiendo un comandante militar," Xochitlán, 25 July 1863; and "Oficio del Alcalde de Xochitlán al Comandante Militar de Zacapoaxtla," 1 June 1864.

42. AHMZ, Paq. 1862: Leg. 74, "Acta de Xochiapulco renovando sus cargos municipales," Xochiapulco, 24 Oct. 1862; Paq. 1863–64–65: Exp. 214, "Acta levantada en Xochiapulco por los miembros del ayuntamiento sobre la rebelion de varios vecinos de Yautetelco," Xochiapulco, 30 Jan. 1863; and Exp. 222, "Oficio del Comandante Militar de Xochiapulco, Juan José Español, al Comandante Militar de Zacapoaxtla," Xochiapulco, 18 Feb. 1863.

43. AHMTO, Gobierno, Caja 8: Exp. 8, "Nota del juez de Nanacatlán al jefe político de Tetela," Nanacatlán, 18 July 1862.

44. AHMTO, Gobierno, Caja s/n 1868: Exp. 67, "Oficio de Francisco Domínguez, juez de Aquixtla, al jefe político de Tetela," 6 Aug. 1868; and for the quotation, "Oficio de Francisco Domínguez, Juez de Aquixtla, al Jefe Político de Tetela," 31 July 1868.

45. AHMTO, Gobierno, Caja s/n 1866: Exp. 66, "Desconocimiento al Gobierno del Imperio," Tetela de Ocampo, 12 Aug. 1866.

46. AHMTO, Gobierno, Caja s/n 1866: Exp. 66. "Acta de los vecinos de Tuzamapan secundando el desconocimiento del imperio hecho en Tetela," Tuzamapan, 19 Aug. 1866.

47. AHMTO, Gobierno, Caja s/n 1866: Exp. 38, "Oficio del alcalde de Jonotla al jefe político de Tetela secundando la declaracion del doce de agosto," Jonotla, 20 Aug. 1866. For the more "legitimate" declarations, see Exp. 71, "Acta del pueblo de Sn. Martin Tuzamapan adhiriéndose al acta levantada en Tetela de Ocampo," Tuzamapan, 25 Aug. 1866; and "Acta del

pueblo de Jonotla adhiriéndose al acta levantada en Tetela de Ocampo," Jonotla, 25 Aug. 1866. For other cases in which patriotic declarations were seconded, in a relatively submissive way, by sujetos, see "Acta del pueblo de Zapotitlán, aceptando el acta de Tetela de Ocampo," 5 June 1868; "Acta levantada en la municipalidad de Huizila [sic] secundando el acta de Tetela de Ocampo," 7 June 1868; Caja s/n 1868: Exp. 64, "Oficio del Juez/Alcalde de Huitzilan, Miguel Cipriano, al jefe político de Tetela," 8 June 1868; Exp. 65, "Oficio del Juez/Alcalde de Jonotla, Francisco Rodríguez, sobre el acta levantada en Tetela," 6 June 1868; "Oficio de Antonio Sánchez, Juez de Tuzamapa, al jefe político de Tetela," 7 June 1868.

48. For the case of Jonotla, see AHMTO, Gobierno, Caja 8: Exp. 11, "Nota del juez de Jonotla al jefe político de Tetela," 29 Aug. 1864. For the case of Tuzamapan, see Caja s/n 1868: Exp. 66, "Nicolás Galicia, juez de Tuzamapan, al jefe político de Tetela," 25 Oct. 1868.

49. For the case of Chilapa, see AHMZ, Paq. 1863–64–65: "Solicitud de los vecinos de Chilapa, perteneciente a la municipalidad de Zautla, para pertenecer a la de Xochiapulco," Chilapa, 18 Dic. 1863. For Nauzontla (including the quotation), see Exp. 214, "Oficio de los vecinos de Nauzontla al comandante militar de Zacapoaxtla, pidiendo que se les de cuota de miniestras directamente y no atraves de Xochitlán," 22 Jan. 1863.

50. AHMZ, Paq.1863–64–65: Leg. 214, "Oficio del jefe político de Tlatlauqui al comandante militar de Zacapoaxtla," Tlatlauqui, 19 Jan. 1863.

51. A list of soldiers and officers with and without last names appears in AHMZ, Paq. 1869: Exp. 118, "Elección de oficiales por la Guardia Nacional de Xochiapulco," 14–15 June 1869, for the case of the Xochiapulco national guard.

52. For a particularly passionate explanation for the decision to decline Alatorre's terms, see AHMTO, Gobierno, Caja s/n 1866: Exp. 70, "Carta del General Juan Francisco Lucas, en jefe de la línea del norte del Estado de Puebla, informando de su respuesta al General Alatorre," Xochiapulco, 25 July 1868.

53. AHMTO, Gobierno, Caja s/n 1866: Exp. 71: "Acta de la Guardia Nacional en Tetela de Ocampo, rechazando las condiciones impuestas por el General Ignacio R. Alatorre," 22 July 1868.

54. On the struggles over disentailment and the importance of communal ideologies and solidarity, see chapter 4.

55. AHDN, Exp. XI/481.4/9893: "Correspondencia entre el Comandante Militar de Veracruz y el Ministerio de Guerra y Marina, sobre los prisioneros de guerra de Zacapoaxtla," 19 Sept.–1 Oct. 1868, ff. 211–14v; "Oficio de Rafael J. García al Ministerio de Guerra y Marina, adjuntando copia de la lista de presos de Zacapoaxtla," 12 Oct. 1868, ff. 218–19.

56. For the process of inheritance related to the will of Francisco Pérez and the fundo Taxcantla, see AGNEP, Tetela de Ocampo, Caja 1, 1869–1880:

Libro 1869, "Hijuelas de la testamentería de Francisco Pérez," 18 Oct. 1869, ff. 7v–9v. For the use of Taxcantla as the base for the Xochiapulquenses in the 1869–1872 period, and even Porfirio Díaz retiring there to recover from a wound during the rebellion of La Noria, see *El Siglo XIX*, 22 Dec. 1869, p. 3; 9 Jan. 1870, p. 3; 14 Dec. 1871; *Diario Oficial*, 9 Jan. 1870, p. 1; 10 Jan. 1870, p. 3; 16 Jan. 1870, p. 3; 5 Mar. 1872, p. 3 (reference to Porfirio Díaz); and *Publicación Oficial de Puebla*, 11 Jan. 1870, p. 4. For the two references to Lucas from Cuetzalan, see AHMZ, Paquete 1863–64–65: Leg. 37, "Dos oficios de las autoridades de Cuetzalan a Juan Francisco Lucas," 23 Mar. 1863. For Lucas's baptismal and marriage records, see (Lic.) Francisco Landero Alamo, *Zacapoaxtla*, available in the municipal library in Zacapoaxtla, pp. 8–9.

CHAPTER 4. ALTERNATIVE NATIONALISMS
AND HEGEMONIC DISCOURSES

1. I had access to the images and memories contained in these two paragraphs during two short visits to Xochiapulco in April and May of 1985. My discussions about the bones occurred in the municipal building during my first visit.

2. For some examples of the interrelation between land disputes and political boundaries, see AGNEP, Huauchinango, Caja 2, 1861–1870: Libro 1867, ff. 4–5, 5v–7; Libro 1868, 11 Feb. 1868; Libro 1869 (II), 26 July 1869, 13 Aug. 1869, 24 Nov. 1869; Libro 1870, ff. 25–30v; and AHMTO, Gobierno, Caja 9: Exp. 6, "Deslinde entre Escatlan, Jonotla, Yancuitlalpan y Tuzamapan," 21 Dec. 1868; Exp. 8, "Oficio del Gobernador del Estado al Jefe Político de Tetela, sobre el conflicto de tierras entre Teziutlán y Tenampulco," Puebla, 25 June 1867; Caja s/n 1868: Exp. 61, "Oficios del Gobernador del Estado al jefe político de Tetela, sobre las diferencias entre Jonotla, Tuzamapan y Jalacingo (Ver.) sobre terrenos," Puebla, 25 Nov. 1868; Exp. 63, "Oficio del Juez de Zapotitlán al Jefe político de Tetela, sobre terrenos en disputa con Hueytlapan," 13 Jan. 1868.

3. On elections during the colonial period, see Bernardo García, *Los pueblos de la sierra: El poder y el espacio entre los indios del norte de Puebla hasta 1700* (Mexico City: El Colegio de México, 1987); and Marcelo Carmagnani, "Local Governments and Ethnic Government in Oaxaca," in Karen Spalding, ed., *Essays in the Political, Economic, and Social History of Colonial Latin America* (Newark, Del.: Latin American Studies Program, 1982), 107–24. On local elections in the 1850s and 1860s, see *El Estandarte Nacional*, 8 Aug. 1857, p. 4; AHMTO, Gobierno, Caja 9: Exp. 6, "Ocurso de varios vecinos de Jonotla al jefe político de Tetela, protestando irregularidades en las elecciones," 13 Sept. 1868; Exp. 52, "Escrutinio de la elección de Gobernador del Estado," Aquixtla, 30 Oct. 1867; Caja s/n 1866: Exp. 71,

"Expediente de elección en la municipalidad de Huizila en el distrito de Tetela de Ocampo," 30 Oct. 1867; Exp. 67, "Francisco Domínguez, Juez de Aquixtla, al jefe político de Tetela, sobre las elecciones," 16 Jan. 1868; Exp. 66, "Oficio del Juez de Tuzamapan al jefe político de Tetela, sobre la elección de electores que deben elegir magistrados para la Suprema Corte," 20 June 1868; SRE, Exp. 6–16–116: "Solicitud de varios vecinos de Santa María Coronanco, sobre que no se les dejó votar por Ignacio Romero Vargas en la elección de gobernador," 24 Jan. 1868.

4. CEHM-C, Fondo XXVIII–1: Doc. 49, "Manifiesto del Gral. Luis Osollo, al tomar posesión de Puebla al mando del Ejército Restaurador de la Libertad y el Orden," Puebla, 23 Jan. 1856, p. 1; BN-LAF 394: "Manifiesto de Antonio Haro y Tamariz, acompañando el Plan de Zacapoaxtla," Puebla, 23 Jan. 1856.

5. On priestly involvement in Conservative politics, see AGNM, Gobernación: Leg. 1091, Exp. 1, "Oficio del Gobernador de Puebla al Ministro de Gobierno," 17 Dec. 1855; AHDN, XI/481.3/5321: "Diario de D. Fernando López, jefe conservador en Zacapoaxtla," 20 Oct.–8 Nov. 1856; "Copia de un extracto de conversación entre Ramón Argüelles y Fernando López," 19 Nov. 1856; "Oficio del Gral. Manuel F. Soto al Ministro de Guerra y Marina," 24 Nov. 1856; AGNEP, Zacapoaxtla, Caja 7, 1849–1869: Libro 1860, ff. 16–18v. On the consciousness of political officials about priestly involvement, see AHDN, XI/481.3/5321: "Manuel F. Soto al Ministerio de Guerra y Marina," Zacatlán, 24 Nov. 1856; XI/481.3/6921: "Parte del Gral. Pedro de Ampudia al Ministerio de Guerra y Marina," Alpatlahua, 1 Apr. 1859; XI/481.3/8111: "Oficio del Comandante General del Territorio de Tlaxcala al Ministerio de Guerra," Apam, 7 July 1857, ff. 81–81v.

6. For the case of the baby, see *El Estandarte Nacional*, 29 Aug. 1857, p. 3. López's will appears in AGNEP, Zacapoaxtla, Caja 7, 1849–1869: Libro 1866, ff. 63–65. Other examples of priestly abuses were found in AHMZ, Paq. 1863–65–64: Leg. 37, "Cartas de Francisco Cortes al Capitán Juan Francisco Lucas, sobre los procedimientos del cura Castrillo," Cuetzalan, 23 Mar. 1863.

7. AHDN, XI/481.3/4253, ff. 39–39v: "Oficio del Prefecto de Tulancingo, Manuel F. Soto, al Ministerio de guerra," 2 Apr. 1857.

8. See, for example, AHMZ, Paq. 1863–65–64: Exp. 219, "Oficio del Juez Mpal y CM de Xochitlán, M. Castañeda, al CM de Zacapoaxtla," Xochitlán, 9 Mar. 1863.

9. CEHM-C, Fondo XXVII: Doc. 43, "Carta de C. Arellano a Rafael J. García, desde la Hacienda de Santa Anna," 15 Nov. 1865. The quotation is on ff. 1v–2.

10. AGNM, Gobernación: Leg. 1091, Exp. 1, "Oficio del Gobernador de Puebla al Ministro de Gobierno," 17 Dec. 1855. The document includes copies of the actas written up at assemblies in Zacapoaxtla and Zapotitlán, 12–16 Dec. The quotation appears on the bottom of the acta from Zapotitlán.

11. For an earlier analysis of Liberal-Conservative lines, see chapter 2. For the case of Chignahuapan's priest, who donated a piece of land with 40 pesos of annual rent to the community in order to support the annual fiesta for the patron saint, see AHMTO, Gobierno, Caja 9: Exp. 6, "Oficio del Alcalde Municipal de Aquixtla al Jefe Político de Tetela," 5 Feb. 1867.

12. AGNM, Gobernación: Leg. 1091, Exp. 1, "Oficio de Francisco Ibarra al Ministro de Gobernación, transcribiendo oficio del Prefecto de Huamantla," Puebla, 15 Jan. 1856.

13. I also treat national guard participation in the liberal campaign in Puebla in chapter 5. See as well BN-LAF 839: "Ejército de Operaciones sobre Puebla: Parte General," Puebla, 23 Mar. 1856.

14. There are some clear similarities between the argument I am making here and those presented by Jean Meyer, *Problemas campesinos y revueltas agrarias (1821–1910)* (Mexico City: Secretaría de Educación Pública, 1973), as well as T. G. Powell, "Priests and Peasants in Central Mexico: Social Conflict During 'La Reforma,'" *Hispanic American Historical Review* 57, no. 2 (May 1977): 296–313. As I proceed, however, I trust that the differences will also become clear.

15. Jean Meyer, in *Problemas campesinos* and *Esperando a Lozada* (Zamora: El Colegio de Michoacán, 1984), makes one of the strongest and most convincing cases for the illusory connection between Liberalism and communal or peasant rights.

16. México, Secretaría de Hacienda y Crédito Público, *Documentos relativos a la espedicion de títulos de propiedad de los terrenos llamados de comun repartimiento, a los indijenas que los poseen* (Puebla: Imprenta del Gobierno del Hospicio, 1869), 3–4: "Circular de Miguel Lerdo de Tejada, Secretario de Hacienda y Crédito Público, a los gobernadores de los estados," Mexico City, 9 Oct. 1856. Both quotations appear on p. 3.

17. Ibid., 5–7. The quotation appears on p. 7.

18. Overlapping claims on municipal lands were made even more confusing by the ongoing conflicts over boundaries between municipalities and districts, both between Zacapoaxtla and Teziutlán (Tenampulco ending up in the former's subdivision and Tlatlauqui in the latter's), as well as between Teziutlán and Tlatlauqui or Atempan. See, for example, AHDN, XI/481.3/883: "Parte del Comandante General del Estado de Puebla, dando cuenta de la rivalidad existente entre los pueblos de Zacapoaxtla y Teziutlán," Puebla, 29 June 1832; XI/481.3/8166: "Acta levantada en la villa de Zacapoaxtla el día veintinueve de marzo de mil ochocientos cincuenta y seis"; XI/481.3/5307: "Expediente sobre operaciones militares en Puebla y Veracruz con motivo de la rebelión de Marcelino Cobos," esp. 18 Dec. 1856–6 Jan. 1857; *Diario Oficial*, 13 June 1858, pp. 1–2, in which the Conservative government separates Zacapoaxtla off from Teziutlán to form an independent prefectura; and ACEP, Libro 1: Sesión pública y ordinaria, 21 Dec.

1867, "Definición de distritos," ff. 37–37v. Much of this conflict, which continued through the 1860s, can also be seen in the documents on disentailment from the 1867–1868 period, treated in more detail below. Particularly telling in the case of the conflicts between Teziutlán and Tenampulco is AHMTO, Gobierno, Caja 9: Exp. 8, "Oficio del Gobernador del Estado al Jefe Político de Tetela, comunicando el acuerdo del Gobierno sobre el conflicto de tierras entre Teziutlán y Tenampulco," Puebla, 25 June 1867.

19. ACDN, Exp. de Ramón Márquez Galindo, ff. 60–60v: "Carta de Rafael Avila a Alatriste, quejándose de los procedimientos de Márquez," Teziutlán, 12 Mar. 1860 (quotations appear on f. 60); ff. 61–63: "Carta de Rafael Avila a Alatriste describiendo el ataque de las fuerzas de Márquez Galindo," Teziutlán, 15 Mar. 1860.

20. See above, chapter 2.

21. AHMZ, Paq. 1863–65–64: Exp. 204, "Circular a los comandantes militares de Xochitlán, Nauzontla y Cuetzalan sobre las leyes de Reforma," Zacapoaxtla, 18 Mar. 1864, ff. 10–11v; quotations appear on ff. 10v and 11, respectively.

22. Ibid.; quotation on f. 11v.

23. "Decreto de Fernando María Ortega, General de Brigada, Gobernador y Comandante Militar del Estado de Puebla, a sus habitantes," Zacapoaxtla, 5 Dec. 1864; reproduced in Donna Rivera Moreno, *Xochiapulco: Una gloria olvidada* (Puebla: Dirección General de Culturas Populares, 1991), 220–22. Also summarized in Ana María Dolores Huerta Jaramillo, *Insurrecciones rurales en el estado de Puebla, 1868–1870*, Cuadernos de la Casa Presno 4 (Puebla: Universidad Autónoma de Puebla, 1985), 122–23.

24. For the correspondence between Tetela de Ocampo and the state government, see AHMTO, Gobierno, Caja 9: Exp. 7, "Jefe Político y Militar de Tetela de Ocampo al Alcalde," 25 Feb. 1867; Exp. 8, "Oficio del Gobierno del Estado de Puebla al Jefe Político de Tetela," 2 July 1867; "Oficio del Gobierno del Estado de Puebla al Jefe Político de Tetela de Ocampo," 17 July 1867. On the creation of medals honoring those who fought, see AHDN, XI/481.4/8621: "Copia del decreto del presidente Benito Juárez creando las condecoraciones Cruz de 1ª y 2ª clase por la Guerra de la Intervención," Mexico City, 5 Aug. 1867, and "Expediente sobre las Condecoraciones de Cruz de 1ª y 2ª clase por la Guerra de la Intervención, según el decreto de 5 de Agosto de 1867," ff. 18–77.

25. For the document from San Nicolás, see AHMTO, Gobierno, Caja 9: Exp. 3, "Oficio de los vecinos de San Nicolás al ayuntamiento de Tetela de Ocampo," 16 Feb. 1867. On Aquixtla, see Exp. 6, "Oficio del Ayuntamiento de Aquixtla al Jefe Político de Tetela," 22 July 1867. Other teachers leaving their posts in these early months appear in Exp. 3, "Oficio de Tiburcio García, preceptor de la escuela de La Cañada, al ayuntamiento de Tetela," 16 Jan. 1867; and Exp. 7, "Oficio de la preceptora de la escuela

'Amiga de las Niñas' al Alcalde Constitucional de Tetela," 22 June 1867. For requests for funds from the state government, see ACEP, Libro 2: "Sesión pública y ordinaria," 21 Jan. 1868, ff. 111v–15v, and Libro 2: "Sesión pública y ordinaria," 5 Mar. 1868, s/n/f, both of which consider a petition by Zautla to use money from the national guard tax (*rebajados*) to finance a primary school. For a communal assembly to finance education, see AHMTO, Gobierno, Caja s/n 1866: Exp. 71, "Sesión municipal de Jonotla," 13 Apr. 1868.

26. AHMTO, Gobierno, Caja s/n 1866: Exp. 71, "Sesión municipal de Jonotla," 13 Apr. 1868. For the 1864 discussion of who gets access to communal lands, see AHMZ, Paq. 1863–65–64: Exp. 204, "Oficio al Comandante Militar de Cuetzalan," Zacapoaxtla, 9 Feb. 1864; the quotation appears on f. 9. For the communal assemblies in Jonotla, Tuzamapan, and Tenampulco, see AHMTO, Caja s/n 1866: Exp. 71, "Actas de varios pueblos en las municipalidades de Jonotla, Tuzamapan y Tenampulco," 9–16 Mar. 1867.

27. On the decree from the Eastern Army, see AHMTO, Gobierno, Caja 9: Exp. 8, "Oficio del Gobierno del Estado de Puebla al Jefe Político de Tetela, transcribiendo oficio del General en Jefe del Ejército de Oriente," Puebla, 8 June 1867. On the disagreements caused by the *Convocatoria* in Puebla, see BN-AJ, Doc. 2960: "Rafael J. García a Benito Juárez, sobre la Convocatoria," Puebla, 24 Aug. 1867.

28. For the congressional decree, see CEHM-C, Gobierno del Edo. Libre y Soberano de Puebla: "Decreto Nº 12 del Congreso, sobre preferir en empleos públicos a los que lucharon contra el Imperio, y prohibir la ocupación de cargos públicos por los que recibieron sueldo del Imperio," Puebla, 25 Jan. 1868. For the debates, see ACEP, Libro 1: "Sesión pública ordinaria," 24 Feb. 1868, ff. 149v–52; Libro 2: "Sesión pública ordinaria," ff. 42v–46v, 9 May 1868.

29. For other cases of rehabilitation, see ACEP, Libro 1: "Sesión pública ordinaria," 20 Jan. 1868, ff. 90–92v; and BN-AJ, MS. J. 3920: "Ignacio Romero Vargas al presidente Benito Juárez," Puebla, 11 Nov. 1867. For the military records of García and Méndez, see ACDN, "Expediente del General Juan N. Méndez" and "Expediente del General Rafael García." For García's being condemned to prison, see *El Pájaro Verde*, 19 Aug. 1865, p. 2. For other evidence of persecution, such as his mail being opened or confiscated, see CEHM-C, Fondo XXXVII: Doc. 29, "Carta de Francisco O. Arce a Rafael J. García," Durango, 19 Oct. 1865, 2ff.; Doc. 31, "Carta de F. Ibarra a Rafael J. García," New York, 21 Oct. 1865; Doc. 113, "Carta de Francisco Zarco a Rafael J. García," New York, 10 Mar. 1866; Doc. 171, "Orden de José M. Esteva al Gral. José J. Landero," Puebla, 15 June 1866; Doc. 183, "Carta de Regino Aguirre a Rafael J. García," Veracruz, 21 June 1866; Doc. 184, "Carta de Juan Sánchez a Rafael J. García," Veracruz, 23 June 1866.

30. For the work done by supporters of Méndez and Díaz in different districts, see BN-AJ, Doc. 4212: "Pablo María Zamacona a Benito Juárez desde Puebla," 2 Oct. 1867; Doc. 2974: "Rafael J. García a Benito Juárez," 13 Oct. 1867; Doc. 3393: "José María Maldonado a Benito Juárez," 13 Oct. 1867; Doc. 2976: "Rafael J. García a Benito Juárez," 14 Oct. 1867; and Doc. 2977: "Rafael J. García a Benito Juárez," 15 Oct. 1867. For the removal of political authorities loyal to Méndez and the importance of this to the result of the elections, see BN-AJ, Doc. 2965: "Informe reservado de Rafael J. García a Benito Juárez," 3 Oct. 1867; Doc. 2968: "Rafael J. García a Benito Juárez," 8 Oct. 1867; Doc. 2969: "Rafael J. García a Benito Juárez," 10 Oct. 1867; Doc. 2971: "Rafael J. García a Benito Juárez," 11 Oct. 1867; and Doc. 2976: "Rafael J. García a Benito Juárez," 14 Oct. 1867. On the rapidity with which a rivalry developed between Juárez and Díaz in the postwar period, see also Laurens Ballard Perry, *Juárez and Díaz: Machine Politics in Mexico* (De Kalb: Northern Illinois University Press, 1978).

31. ACEP, Libro 1: "Sesión pública ordinaria," 15 Feb. 1868, ff. 132–33v.

32. Ibid., ff. 135v–36.

33. Ibid., ff. 137–38; the quotation appears on f. 138.

34. Ibid., f. 138v.

35. BN-AJ, Doc. 20/150: "Carta de Juan Francisco Lucas al Presidente Benito Juárez," Xochiapulco, 10 Oct. 1867. The image of the sierra rebels referred to at the beginning of this paragraph is especially stark in the editorials of S. Nieto in the *Periódico Oficial de Puebla*, 27 Mar. 1868, 30 Mar. 1868, and 4 Apr. 1868, all pp. 1–2; and 9 and 11 June, also pp. 1–2.

36. The letter from the deputies appeared in *El Monitor Republicano*, 21 Feb. 1868, p. 3. For the account of the assembly in Zacatlán, see AHDN, D/481.4/9892, ff. 26–27v: "Rafael J. García al Ministro de Guerra y Marina, transcribiendo oficio de Rafael Cravioto," Puebla, 26 Mar. 1868. Specifically on the actas sent to the state congress, see BN-AJ, MS. J. 5298: "Rafael J. García al Presidente Benito Juárez, anunciando la rebelión en Zacapoaxtla y adjuntándole carta de Juan Francisco Lucas; Respuesta de Benito Juárez a Rafael J. García," 24 Mar. 1868; MS. J. 5300: "Rafael J. García al Presidente Benito Juárez, sobre las peticiones de los pueblos de la sierra," 27 Apr. 1868; MS. J. 5302: "José María Velázquez a Rafael J. García, sobre las peticiones de los pueblos," 27 Apr. 1868; AHMTO, Gobierno, Caja s/n 1868: Exp. 61, "Oficio del Gobierno del Estado a Daniel Posadas, jefe político de Tetela de Ocampo," 28 May 1868; "Oficio del Secretario del Gobierno del Estado, Joaquín Martínez, al jefe político de Tetela de Ocampo," 1 June 1868; S. Nieto, "Algo sobre las actas de los distritos rebelados" (editorial), *Periódico Oficial de Puebla*, 30 May 1868, pp. 1–2; and *Diario Oficial*, 11 July 1868, p. 3.

37. The acta from Zacatlán, 25 Feb. 1868, including the quote from Pablo M. Urrutia, appears in *El Monitor Republicano*, 5 Mar. 1868, p. 1. The acta from Tetela was found in AHMTO, Gobierno, Caja s/n 1866: Exp. 71, "Acta

del Ayuntamiento de la Villa de Tetela de Ocampo, a la H. Legislatura del Estado," 26 Feb. 1868; the quotation appears on ff. 1v–2.

38. ACEP, Libro 7: "Sesión secreta ordinaria," 7 May 1868, ff. 20v–27v.

39. The analysis and narrative in the previous two paragraphs is based on the following documents: BN-AJ, MS. J. 5300: "Oficio de Rafael J. García al Presidente Benito Juárez," Puebla, 27 Apr. 1868; MS. J. 5302: "José María Velázquez a Rafael J. García," 27 Apr. 1868; MS. J. 5305: "Rafael J. García al Presidente Benito Juárez," 1 May 1868; MS. J. 5308: "Rafael J. García al Presidente Benito Juárez," 5 May 1868; ACEP, Libro 7: "Sesión secreta ordinaria," 7 May 1868, ff. 20v–27v; Libro 3: "Sesión pública ordinaria," 8 May 1868, f. 40v.

40. ACEP, vol. 4: Exp. 215, "Formado con una comunicación del gobierno consultando se tomen en consideración las actas levantadas en las municipalidades que han desconocido al actual Jefe del Estado," 6 ff. (García's quote appears on f. 1); ACEP, Libro 3: "Sesión sobre un oficio de Rafael J. García," 23 May 1868, ff. 72v–73; *Periódico Oficial de Puebla*, 30 May 1868, pp. 2–3. For a particularly good example of how the circuitous official discourse was used, see S. Nieto, "Algo sobre las actas de los distritos rebelados," *Periódico Oficial de Puebla*, 30 May 1868, pp. 1–2.

41. AHMTO, Gobierno, Caja s/n 1866: Exp. 71, "Acta levantada en la municipalidad de Huizila, distrito de Tetela de Ocampo," 7 June 1868; "Actas levantadas en los pueblos de Escatlan y San Francisco Zoquiapan," 6 June 1868; "Acta del pueblo de Zapotitlán, aceptando el acta de Tetela de Ocampo de 1° de junio, desconociendo a Rafael J. García y nombrando a Juan Francisco Lucas Jefe de la Línea del Norte," 5 June 1868; "Carta de Juan Francisco Lucas al jefe político de Tetela, anunciando que acepta su nombramiento como jefe de la línea del norte," Xochiapulco, 6 June 1868; "Carta de Juan Francisco Lucas al jefe político de Tetela, remitiendo copia del manifiesto que mandó al gobierno del Estado," Xochiapulco, 6 June 1868; "Oficio de Juan Francisco Lucas al jefe político de Tetela, estableciendo bases para el gobierno durante el período de la rebelión," 10 June 1868; Caja s/n 1868: Exp. 66, "Oficio del Alcalde de Jonotla, Francisco Rodríguez, sobre el acta levantada en Tetela desconociendo a Rafael J. García," 6 June 1868; Exp. 64, "Oficio del Alcalde de Huitzilan, Miguel Cipriano, al jefe político de Tetela, remitiendo copias de las actas secundando el acta de Tetela," 8 June 1868.

42. For the role of Alatorre in the repression, see AHDN, XI/481.4/9892, 9893, and 9894, passim. For his participation in the resistance against the French, see chapter 2, and Ignacio R. Alatorre, *Reseña de los acontecimientos ocurridos en las líneas del Norte y Centro del Estado de Veracruz en los años de 1863 a 1867* (Veracruz, 1887).

43. The first quotation is from AHMTO, Caja s/n 1866: "Juan Francisco Lucas convocando a diferentes jefes de los distritos del norte, para decidir qué hacer frente al ejército federal," Xochiapulco, 21 June 1868. For the way

in which different districts made choices, as well as the confusion this sometimes caused, see BN-AJ, MS. J. 5321: "Oficio de Rafael J. García a Benito Juárez, acompañando cartas desde Zacapoaxtla," Puebla, 27 June 1868; AHDN, XI/481.4/9893: "Acta en Tlatlauqui reconociendo al Supremo Gobierno y las autoridades legítimas," 8 July 1868, f. 42; "Acta en Zacapoaxtla sometiéndose al gobierno federal," 7 July 1868; and "Oficio de Juan Francisco Lucas a Ignacio R. Alatorre," Xochiapulco, 10 July 1868, f. 47. This last document includes the long quotation.

44. For Alatorre's version of the agreement with Lucas, see AHDN, XI/481.4/9893, f. 50: "Parte de Ignacio R. Alatorre al Ministro de Guerra Ignacio Mejía, sobre su conferencia con Juan Francisco Lucas," Zacapoaxtla, 17 July 1868. For Lucas's answer, see ff. 64–64v: "Oficio de Ignacio R. Alatorre al Ministro de Guerra Ignacio Mejía, transcribiendo oficio de Juan Francisco Lucas," Zacapoaxtla, 26 July 1868, which includes the quotation.

45. AHMTO, Gobierno, Caja s/n 1866: Exp. 71, "Acta de la Guardia Nacional de Tetela de Ocampo, sobre las condiciones impuestas por Ignacio R. Alatorre," 22 July 1868; and "Parte del Comandante de la Guardia Nacional de Tetela de Ocampo, sobre el encuentro en Apulco," 25 July 1868.

46. AHMTO, Gobierno, Caja s/n 1866: Exp. 71, "Acta de la Guardia Nacional de Tetela de Ocampo."

47. Ibid.; here the word *ciudadano (citizen)* is consistently capitalized.

48. For the cabecera-anexo dynamic between Zacatlán and Chignahuapan in the original petitions to the congress, see *El Monitor Republicano*, 5 Mar. 1868, pp. 1–2. For a similar dynamic in Tetela district around the declaration of rebellion in June, see AHMTO, Gobierno, Caja s/n 1866: Exp. 71, "Acta levantada en la municipalidad de Huizila, distrito de Tetela de Ocampo," 7 June 1868; "Actas levantadas en los pueblos de Escatlan y San Francisco Zoquiapan," 6 June 1868; "Acta del pueblo de Zapotitlán, aceptando el acta de Tetela de Ocampo," 5 June 1868; Caja s/n 1868: Exp. 66, "Oficio del Alcalde de Jonotla, Francisco Rodríguez, sobre el acta levantada en Tetela desconociendo a Rafael J. García," 6 June 1868; Exp. 64, "Oficio del Alcalde de Huitzilan, Miguel Cipriano, al jefe político de Tetela, remitiendo copias de las actas secundando el acta de Tetela," 8 June 1868. On the counterdiscourses around the edges of the crowd, see chapter 3, and María Teresa Sierra Camacho, *El ejercicio discursivo de la autoridad en asambleas comunales (metodología y análisis del discurso oral)* (Mexico City: Cuadernos de la Casa Chata, 1987). For some of the requirements for rations, and the fact that Juan Francisco Lucas even felt moved at times to apologize for them, see AHMTO, Gobierno, Caja s/n 1868: Exp. 64, "Oficio del juez de Huitzilan al jefe político de Tetela, transcribiendo oficio de Juan Francisco Lucas," 26 July 1868; Exp. 65, "Oficio del Juez de Jonotla, Francisco Rodríguez, al jefe político de Tetela de Ocampo," 27 July 1868; AHMZ, Paq. 1869: Exp. 42, "Relativo a los artículos de miniestra que dieron las municipalidades para el

sosten de la guardia nacional que permanecio en la cumbre de Apulco,"
July–Nov. 1868.

49. AHMTO, Gobierno, Caja s/n 1866: Exp. 71, "Acta de la Guardia
Nacional de Tetela de Ocampo."

50. The only systematic analysis of the 1868–1870 rebellions in
Cuetzalan is Guy P. C. Thomson, "Agrarian Conflict in the Municipality of
Cuetzalán (Sierra de Puebla): The Rise and Fall of 'Pala' Agustín Dieguillo,
1861–1894," *Hispanic American Historical Review* 71, no. 2 (May 1991):
205–58. Thomson's and my interpretations of the meaning of the Cuetzalan
case within the sierra rebellions, however, are quite different.

51. Thomson, "Agrarian Conflict," 220–21; the quotation appears on
p. 220.

52. Thomson, "Agrarian Conflict," 222–26. An extensive quotation from
Francisco Agustín's letter to Arrieta appears on p. 222; Thomson's statement
appears on p. 223.

53. Thomson, "Agrarian Conflict," 224–26. For the report by the adjudication commission, see AHMZ, Paq. 1869: Exp. 115, "Informe de la comisión
de adjudicaciones al jefe político de Zacapoaxtla, sobre la situación en
Tzicuilan," Cuetzalan, 23 April 1868.

54. On direct action in Tzicuilan, see Thomson, "Agrarian Conflict," 224,
228. On the alliance with the serrano rebels, see ibid., 229–30, and AHMTO,
Gobierno, Caja s/n 1866: Exp. 90, "Parte de Pilar Rivera, comandante de la
guardia nacional de Tetela de Ocampo, sobre el encuentro en Apulco,"
25 July 1868 (which includes the quotation), and "Orden de Juan Francisco
Lucas a Pilar Rivera," Xochiapulco, 25 July 1868.

55. The quotation appears in AHDN, XI/481.4/9893: "Oficio de Rafael
J. García al Ministro de Guerra y Marina, remitiendo solicitudes de los
indígenas de Cuetzalan," Puebla, 29 Dec. 1868, ff. 255–55v. I have also
traced the fortunes of the prisoners from Cuetzalan in the following documents: AHMTO, Caja s/n 1866: Exp. 90: "Parte de Pilar Rivera, comandante de la guardia nacional de Tetela de Ocampo, sobre el encuentro en
Apulco," 25 July 1868; AHMZ, Paq. 1869: Exp. 29, "Oficio de Ignacio R.
Alatorre al Comandante Militar de Zacapoaxtla, sobre la rebelión de
soldados en Tzicuilan," 31 July 1868; "Informe del juez municipal de
Cuetzalan, Ignacio Arrieta, sobre la rebelión de soldados en Tzicuilan,"
18 Aug. 1869; AHDN, SI/481.4/9893: "Relación nominal de los prisioneros hechos al enemigo en distintas acciones de guerra, sin incluir a Zacatlán," 23 Aug. 1868, f. 163; "Oficio de Ignacio R. Alatorre al Ministerio
de Guerra y Marina," Zacapoaxtla, 26 Aug. 1868, f. 189; "Oficio de Ignacio
R. Alatorre al Ministerio de Guerra y Marina, transcribiendo oficio del jefe
político de Zacapoaxtla," Zacapoaxtla, 6 Sept. 1868, f. 204; "Correspondencia entre el Comandante Militar de Veracruz y el Ministerio de Guerra y
Marina, sobre los prisioneros de guerra de Zacapoaxtla," 19 Sept.–1 Oct.

1868, ff. 211–14v; "Oficio de Rafael J. García al Ministerio de Guerra y Marina, adjuntando copia de la lista de presos de Zacapoaxtla," Puebla, 12 Oct. 1868, ff. 218–19; "Solicitud de varios indígenas de Cuetzalan al presidente Benito Juárez, pidiendo la libertad de sus deudos en Yucatán," Jalapa, 29 Oct. 1868, ff. 233–34v; "Solicitud de Francisco Santiago, Pedro Antonio, Juan Nicolás, Pedro Francisco, y Francisco Jiménez, todos indígenas de Cuetzalan, pidiendo regresar al seno de nuestras familias," Puebla, 7 Dec. 1868, ff. 249–50.

56. AHDN, XI/481.4/9893: "Solicitud de unos indígenas de Cuetzalan al presidente Benito Juárez, pidiendo libertad para sus deudos en Yucatán," Jalapa, 29 Oct. 1868, ff. 233–34v. The first quotation appears on f. 234; the other two appear on ff. 234–34v.

57. For subsequent petitions, see AHDN, XI/481.4/9893: "Solicitud de Francisco Santiago, Pedro Antonio, Juan Nicolás, Pedro Francisco, Francisco Jiménez, todos indígenas de Cuetzalan, sobre regresar al seno de sus familias," Puebla, 7 Dec. 1868, ff. 249–50; "Otra solicitud de los indígenas de Cuetzalan sobre su prisión injusta," Puebla, n.d., ff. 251–51v; and "Otra solicitud de los indígenas de Cuetzalan pidiendo su libertad," Puebla, 2 Jan. 1869, ff. 258–59.

58. The classic study on the process of disentailment during the war years is Jan Bazant, *The Alienation of Church Wealth in Mexico: Social and Economic Aspects of the Liberal Revolution, 1858–1875* (Cambridge: Cambridge University Press, 1971). For cases in the state of Puebla, see AGNM, SAHOP-BN, Puebla.

59. AHMTO, Gobierno, Caja s/n 1868: Exp. 66, "Oficio del Juez de Tuzamapan al jefe político de Tetela," 6 May 1868; "Oficio del Juez Municipal de Tuzamapan al jefe político de Tetela, sobre el litigio de terrenos con Jonotla," 18 May 1868; "Oficio del Juez de Tuzamapan a Luis Cavañes, informándole que debe quitar su ganado de La Junta según órdenes de Tetela," 19 May 1868; "Contestación de Luis Cavañes al Juez de Tuzamapan," 20 May 1868; Exp. 65, "Oficio del Juez de Jonotla al jefe político de Tetela," 19 May 1868; Caja s/n 1870/73–1874/78: Exp. 112, "Oficio del Juez Constitucional de Tenampulco, Antonio Arroyo, al jefe político de Tetela," 28 Sept. 1870; "Oficio de Tiburcio Reyes, Juez de Tuzamapan, al jefe político de Tetela, sobre un intento de adjudicación por Vicente García," 30 Sept. 1870; "Oficio del Jefe Político de Tetela de Ocampo al alcalde de Tuzamapan, sobre la adjudicación de Pascual Sanchez," 10 Dec. 1870; AHMZ, Paq. 1869: Exp. 74, "Informe de Luis Ortega, comisionado para ver el deslinde de tierras entre Xocoyolo y Jonotla," 4 Feb. 1869.

60. For Tuzamapan, see AHMTO, Gobierno, Caja s/n 1868: Exp. 66, "Oficio del Juez Municipal de Tuzamapan al jefe político de Tetela," 18 May 1868. For Jonotla, see Exp. 65, "Oficio de Francisco Rodríguez, Juez de Jonotla, al jefe político de Tetela," 19 May 1868.

61. For the decree, see CEHM-C, Gobierno del Estado Libre y Soberano de Puebla: "Decreto N° 122 del 2° Congreso Constitucional, sobre litigios pendientes entre los pueblos del Estado y nombramiento de arbitradores amigables componedores," Puebla, 22 May 1869; and AHMTO, Paq. 1869: Exp. 33, "Decreto #122 del Congreso de Puebla, sobre resolver litigios de tierras con arbitros amigables componedores," Puebla, 22 May 1869. Some of the attempts to put the decree into effect are to be found in AHMZ, Paq. 1869: Exp. 33, "De la ley de 22 de mayo del corriente año sobre terminar los litigios pendientes por causa de terrenos, por medio de árbitros amigables componedores," Zacapoaxtla, June–Oct. 1868; Exp. 74, "Oficio del Alcalde de Jonotla, Vicente García, al jefe político de Zacapoaxtla," 27 Sept. 1870; "Oficio del juez de Cuetzalan al jefe político de Zacapoaxtla, sobre nombramiento de arbitro por Xocoyolo," 10 Oct. 1870; "Oficio del alcalde de Jonotla, Vicente García, al jefe político de Zacapoaxtla, informándole de la necesidad de escoger nuevo arbitro," 24 Oct. 1870.

62. For Nauzontla, see AHMZ, Paq. 1869: Exp. 109, "Reclamo de los vecinos de Nauzontla acerca de la adjudicación de terrenos de Xiliapa por Rafael Bonilla," 6 Feb. 1868. For Escatlan and Jonotla, see AHMTO, Gobierno, Caja 9: Exp. 6, "Ocurso de las autoridades de Escatlan y Jonotla al jefe político de Tetela, sobre denuncios de tierras," 10 Dec. 1868, which includes the quotation, and Caja s/n 1868: Exp. 61, "Oficio del gobierno del Estado al jefe político de Tetela, sobre el fraccionamiento de los terrenos comunales de Jonotla y Tuzamapan," Puebla de Zaragoza, 21 Dec. 1868. On Tuzamapan and the Mora brothers, see Caja s/n 1870/73–1874/78: Exp. 112, "Oficio del alcalde municipal de Tuzamapan al jefe político de Tetela," 9 Aug. 1870. It is also interesting to remember that Gavino Mora was earlier involved in another dispute with the authorities of Los Reyes, in which his refusal to obey village officials became connected to his mistreatment of his partner, a local indigenous woman. See above, chapter 3.

63. For the case of Luis Cabañez, see AHMTO, Gobierno, Caja s/n 1866: Exp. 66, "Ocurso de Luis Cabañez, vecino y propietario de Papantla, al jefe político de Tetela," Tetela, 25 Sept. 1868. On Octaviano Pérez, see Thomson, "Agrarian Conflict," 220–21, and AGNEP, Zacapoaxtla, Caja 7, 1849–1869: Libro 1869, ff. 82v–96. On Juan Rosas, see AHMTO, Gobierno, Caja s/n 1866: Exp. 71, "Solicitud de Juan Rosas al jefe político de Tetela, sobre su separación de Jonotla," 27 June 1868. For other cases of rentals and adjudications, see AGNEP, Huauchinango, Caja 2, 1861–1870: Libro 1869 (II), 15 Dec. 1869; Libro 1870, ff. 21–22, 32–32v; and AHMTO, Gobierno, Caja s/n 1870/73–1874/78: Exp. 112, "Solicitud de Pascual Sánchez, vecino del barrio del Chacal, al jefe político de Tetela," 27 Sept. 1870.

64. AHMTO, Gobierno, Caja s/n 1870/73–1874/78: Exp. 112, "Oficio del Juez Constitucional de Tenampulco al jefe político de Tetela," 28 Sept. 1870; "Oficio del Juez de Tuzamapan al jefe político de Tetela," 30 Sept. 1870;

"Oficio del Juzgado Constitucional de Tenampulco al jefe político de Tetela," 22 Nov. 1870. For the attempted negotiation with Sánchez, which includes the quotation, see "Oficio de Antonio Arroyo, Juez Constitucional de Tenampulco, al alcalde de Tuzamapan," 13 Jan. 1871.

65. Some other cases of adjudicaciones can be found in AHMZ, Paq. 1869: Exp. 123, "Relativo a la ley de desamortización en el pueblo de Huahuaxtla," Mar.–Aug. 1869; Exp. 113, "Relativo a la ley de desamortización en el pueblo de Xocoyolo," 1869; Exp. 115, "Relativo a la ley de desamortización en el pueblo de Tzicuilan," 1869; AHMTO, Gobierno, Caja s/n 1870/73–1874/78: Exp. 112, "Oficio del Juez Constitucional de Tenampulco al jefe político de Tetela," 28 Oct. 1870; "Oficio de Pascual Sánchez al jefe político de Tetela, sobre adjudicación de terreno en El Chacal," 28 Nov. 1870; Caja s/n 1868: Exp. 66, "Juez de Tuzamapan, Nicolás Galicia, al jefe político de Tetela," 27 Nov. 1868. See also AGNEP, Zacapoaxtla, Caja 7, 1849–1869: Libro 1869, ff. 78v–82v; Tetela de Ocampo, Caja 1, 1868–1880: Libro 1870, ff. 29v–30v, 43v–46; Libro 1871, ff. 31–32v, 33–34v, 44v–46, 51–53.

66. On the exemption of ejidos from disentailment, see article 8 of the June 1856 Law, reproduced in Jean Meyer, *Problemas campesinos*, 68–70; the quotation appears on p. 69.

67. AHMZ, Paq. 1869: Exp. 116, "Relativo á la ley de desamortización en el pueblo de Xochitlán"; Exp. 117, "Relativo a la ley de desamortización en el pueblo de Nauzontla" and "Copia del acta de la Junta Municipal de Nauzontla, escogiendo ejidos para su pueblo en cumplimiento con la ley de 25 de junio de 1856," 14 Jan. 1869; Exp. 113, "Juez Constitucional de Xocoyolo, Francisco Mora, al jefe político de Zacapoaxtla, sobre la necesidad de un ejido en el bosque," 17 Nov. 1868; Exp. 111, "Nicolás Francisco, alcalde 1º de Yancuitlalpan, al jefe político de Zacapoaxtla," 4 Dec. 1868; "Acta de los vecinos de Santiago Yancuitlalpan, municipalidad de Cuetzalan, respondiendo al oficio del jefe político de Zacapoaxtla sobre ejidos," 17 Jan. 1869; Exp. 115, "Acta levantada por la junta municipal de Tzicuilan sobre ejidos," 5 Apr. 1869; AHMTO, Gobierno, Caja s/n 1870/73–1874/78: Exp. 130, "Oficio de los vecinos y autoridades de Jonotla al jefe político de Tetela, sobre adjudicaciones de terrenos y el fundo legal del pueblo," 10 Aug. 1870; Exp. 112, "Oficio del Alcalde Municipal José Galván al jefe político de Tetela, sobre adjudicaciones," Tuzamapan, 7 Sept. 1870; "Oficio del Juez de Tuzamapan al jefe político de Tetela, transcribiendo oficio del alcalde de Tenampulco," 28 Sept. 1870; "Oficio del Juez Municipal de Tuzamapan al jefe político de Tetela, sobre ejido para el pueblo y otros asuntos," 9 Nov. 1870; "Acta del P. Ayuntamiento de Tuzamapan, sobre la necesidad de ejidos para el pueblo," 14 Nov. 1870; "Oficio del jefe político de Tetela al alcalde de Tuzamapan, acusando recibo del oficio declarando ejidos para el pueblo," 17 Nov. 1870; "Informe de Tiburcio Reyes, Juez Municipal de Tuzamapan," al jefe político de Tetela, sobre las quejas de

algunos vecinos que tienen derechos en las tierras que Tuzamapan escogió para su ejido," 23 Nov. 1870.

68. AHMZ, Paq. 1869: Exp. 113, "Oficio de Francisco Mora, juez constitucional de Xocoyolo, al jefe político de Zacapoaxtla," 17 Nov. 1868; Exp. 111, "Nicolás Francisco, alcalde 1° de la junta municipal de Yancuitlalpan, al jefe político de Zacapoaxtla," 4 Dec. 1868; "Acta de los vecinos de Santiago Yancuitlalpan, municipalidad de Cuetzalan, respondiendo a un oficio del jefe político de Zacapoaxtla," 17 Jan. 1869; Exp. 115, "Acta levantada por la junta municipal de Tzicuilan sobre ejidos," 5 Apr. 1869; AHMTO, Gobierno, Caja s/n 1870/73–1874/78: Exp. 130, "Oficio de los vecinos y autoridades de Jonotla al jefe político de Tetela, sobre las adjudicaciones de terrenos," 10 Aug. 1870; Exp. 112, "Acta del P. Ayuntamiento de Tuzamapan, sobre la necesidad de ejidos para el pueblo," 14 Nov. 1870; "Informe de Tiburcio Reyes, juez municipal de Tuzamapan, al jefe político de Tetela," 23 Nov. 1870.

69. AHMZ, Paq. 1869: Exp. 111, "Acta de los vecinos de Santiago Yancuitlalpan, municipalidad de Cuetzalan, respondiendo a un oficio del jefe político de Zacapoaxtla," 17 Jan. 1869; AHMTO, Caja s/n 1870/73–1874/78: Exp. 130, "Oficio de los vecinos y autoridades de Jonotla al jefe político de Tetela, sobre adjudicaciones de terrenos," 10 Aug. 1870; Exp. 112, "Acta del P. Ayuntamiento de Tuzamapan, sobre la necesidad de ejidos para el pueblo," 14 Nov. 1870.

70. For Arriaga's declaration of rebellion, see "Oficio del Juez Municipal de Atlequizayan al jefe político de Zacatlán, transcribiendo oficio de Francisco J. Arriaga desde la cumbre de Apulco," reproduced in *Diario Oficial*, 1 Dec. 1869, p. 3, and in *El Siglo XIX*, 3 Dec. 1869, p. 3. On Molina's manipulations during the 1868 rebellion, see AHMTO, Caja s/n 1866: Exp. 90, "Parte de Pilar Rivera, comandante de la guardia nacional de Tetela de Ocampo, sobre el encuentro en Apulco," 25 July 1868, and "Orden de Juan Francisco Lucas a Pilar Rivera," Xochiapulco, 25 July 1868; BN-AJ, MS. J 5321: "Oficio de Rafael J. García a Benito Juárez, acompañando cartas de Zacapoaxtla," Puebla, 27 July 1868; AHDN, XI/481.4/9893: "Acta en Zacapoaxtla sometiéndose al gobierno federal, suscrita por el personal del ayuntamiento," Zacapoaxtla, 7 July 1868, f. 41; "Oficio de Ignacio R. Alatorre al Ministro de Guerra y Marina, transcribiendo oficio de Juan Francisco Molina desde la cumbre de Apulco," 26 July 1868, ff. 66–66v; "Oficio de Rafael J. García al Ministerio de Guerra y Marina, transcribiendo nota del comandante militar de Zacapoaxtla del 27 de julio," Puebla, 3 Aug. 1868, ff. 87–87v; "Oficio de Rafael J. García al Ministerio de guerra y Marina, transcribiendo oficio del comandante militar de Zacapoaxtla, Juan Francisco Molina, del 31 de julio," Puebla, 4 Aug. 1868, ff. 95–96; "Oficio de Ignacio R. Alatorre al Ministerio de Guerra y Marina, transcribiendo oficio del jefe político de Zacapoaxtla, Juan Francisco Molina Alcántara, del 2 de septiem-

bre," 6 Sept. 1868, f. 204. On Arriaga's later ambitions, see *Expediente Geográfico-Estadístico, por el Ciudadano Francisco Javier Arriaga, Diputado al 6° Congreso General por el Distrito de Zacapoaxtla, en el Estado de Puebla* (Mexico City: Imprenta del Gobierno en Palacio, 1873), and Thomson, "Agrarian Conflict," 239–42, where there is also a detailed description of Arriaga's alliance with the Cuetzalan national guard.

71. On Xochiapulco's initial hesitation to get involved in Arriaga's rebellion, see "Carta de un particular anónimo de Zacapoaxtla a *La Tribuna* de Puebla," reproduced in *El Siglo XIX*, 22 Dec. 1869, p. 3. In addition, Ignacio R. Alatorre's early reports of encounters with the rebels do not mention Xochiapulco: "Telegrama de Ignacio R. Alatorre al Ministerio de Guerra y Marina, sobre encuentro con los amotinados de Zacapoaxtla," Teziutlán, 1 Dec. 1869, reproduced in *El Siglo XIX*, 3 Dec. 1869, p. 3. The campaign against Xochiapulco did not begin officially until 28 December, more than a month after the initial declaration in Apulco. See *Diario Oficial*, 10 Jan. 1870, p. 3. See also Huerta, *Insurrecciones rurales*, 54–56.

72. "Parte telegráfico del General Ignacio R. Alatorre al Ministro de Guerra y Marina," Zacapoaxtla, 3 Dec. 1868, in *Diario Oficial*, 5 Dec. 1868, p. 2; "Parte del Teniente Coronel José María Vásquez, comandante del Sexto Batallón de Cazadores, sobre el combate en Xochiapulco," 7 Dec. 1869, in *Diario Oficial*, 14 Dec. 1869, p. 2.

73. The first quotation, as well as the report on fighting in the plaza, comes from "Parte del capitán Florencio Villedas, que tomó el mando del 6° en la plaza de Xochiapulco," 5 Dec. 1869, in *Diario Oficial*, 14 Dec. 1869, p. 2. The rest of the information, including the last quotation, comes from "Parte del Coronel Francisco de P. Castañeda, en jefe de la 2ª Brigada mandada a proteger la retirada del 6° batallón de Xochiapulco," 6 Dec. 1869, in *Diario Oficial*, 14 Dec. 1869, p. 2.

74. In addition to "Telegrama urgente de Ignacio R. Alatorre al Ministro de Guerra y Marina Ignacio Mejía, sobre haber puesto en estado de sitio al distrito de Zacapoaxtla," Cuartel General en Zacapoaxtla, 3 Dec. 1869, in *Diario Oficial*, 5 Dec. 1869, p. 2, which has the quotation, evidence for my analysis of Alatorre's motives can also be found in *Diario Oficial*, 5 Dec. 1869, p. 2; 14 Dec. 1869, p. 2; and 6 Dec. 1869, p. 4.

75. "Carta de un particular anónimo de Zacapoaxtla a *La Tribuna* de Puebla," 7 Dec. 1869, in *El Siglo XIX*, 22 Dec. 1869, p. 3. On the burning of Xochiapulco, see *El Siglo XIX*, 29 Dec. 1869, p. 3; 8 Jan. 1870, p. 3; and, finally, confirmation in AHMZ, Paq. 1869: Exp. 36, "Lista de municipalidades y pueblos que componen el distrito de Zacapoaxtla," 14 Feb. 1870.

76. On the pacification process and what it revealed about underlying grievances, see ACEP, Expedientes, vol. 20: "Contestación de Juan Francisco Lucas a Pablo M. Urrutia, sobre las condiciones de la capitulación," 3 June 1870; vol. 15: "Oficio del Gobernador de Puebla, Ignacio Romero Vargas, al

Ministro de Guerra y Marina, describiendo el proceso de pacificación en la sierra," 4 June 1870; and vol. 20: "Informe rendido por Ignacio Romero Vargas, gobernador del Estado de Puebla, al Congreso del Estado, sobre su visita a la sierra norte," 31 Oct. 1871. See also AHMTO, Gobierno, Caja s/n 1870/73–1874/78: Exp. 124, "Solicitud para el repartimiento de terrenos hecha por la autoridad de Xochiapulco," 19 Sept. 1870; "Oficio del jefe político de Tetela de Ocampo al alcalde de Xochiapulco," 23 Sept. 1870; "Oficio del alcalde de Xochiapulco, Juan Francisco Dinorin, al jefe político de Tetela de Ocampo, pidiendo resolución sobre el repartimiento de los terre-nos de Xochiapulco y La Manzanilla," 23 Dec. 1870; "Nota del jefe político de Tetela a Juan Francisco Dinorin," 24 Dec. 1870; Exp. 113, "Oficio del Alcalde de Xochiapulco, Juan Francisco Dinorin, al jefe político de Tetela," Xochiapulco, 22 Sept. 1870; "Juan Martín, Alcalde Municipal de Xo-chiapulco, al jefe político de Tetela," 15 Nov. 1870; "Oficio del jefe político de Tetela de Ocampo al alcalde municipal de Xochiapulco," 19 Nov. 1870; "Oficio del alcalde municipal de Xochiapulco, Juan Martín, al jefe político de Tetela," 19 Nov. 1870; "Oficio del Alcalde Municipal de Xochiapulco al jefe político de Tetela, informando que se ha suspendido el reparto de las tierras de Xochiapulco y La Manzanilla por falta de recursos," 1 Feb. 1871; Caja s/n 1871: Exp. 11, "Informe de la Comisión Especial del patriótico ayuntamiento, sobre los terrenos de Zitlacuautla," 21 Jan. 1871. On the political conflicts between villages or municipalities, their connection to issues of land and resources, and the leadership role played by Xochiapulco in a populist alliance of villages, see AHMZ, Paq. 1869: Exp. 111, "Oficio del juez municipal de Yancuitlalpan, Andrés Antonio, al jefe político de Za-capoaxtla," 20 Mar. 1868; CEHM-C, Colección Puebla: "Representación de los vecinos de Chilapa para ser agregados a la municipalidad de Xochiapulco y aprobación del Congreso," Puebla, 29 June 1869; AHMTO, Gobierno, Caja s/n 1870/73–1874/78: Exp. 113, "Luis A. Díaz, alcalde de Xochiapulco, al jefe político de Tetela," 7 June 1870; "Juan Francisco Dinorin, alcalde municipal de Xochiapulco, al jefe político de Tetela," 5 Oct. 1870; "Oficio de Juan Francisco Dinorin, alcalde de Xochiapulco, al jefe político de Tetela," 10 Oct. 1870; "Oficio del jefe político de Tetela al alcalde municipal de Xochiapulco," 11 Oct. 1870; "Oficio del alcalde municipal de Xochiapulco al jefe político de Tetela," 18 Oct. 1870; "Oficio del alcalde municipal de Xochiapulco al jefe político de Tetela," 26 Oct. 1870; "Oficio del jefe político de Tetela al jefe político de Zacapoaxtla, sobre los abusos de los vecinos de Las Lomas," 31 Oct. 1870; "Oficio del jefe político de Zacapoaxtla al jefe político de Tetela," 3 Nov. 1870; ACEP, Expedientes, vol. 20: "Aprobación por Ignacio Romero Vargas del decreto de Fernando María Ortega, sobre los terrenos de Xochiapulco y La Manzanilla," Puebla, 29 June 1870; vol. 19: "Correspondencia intercambiada entre los jefes políticos de Tetela y Zacapoaxtla, sobre dónde está la línea divisoria para la municipalidad de Xochiapulco," Jan.–Feb. 1871;

vol. 18, Apr.–May 1874: "Aprobación de los límites entre Xochiapulco y Zacapoaxtla," 27–29 May 1874; SRE, Exp. 6-16-107: "Carta del gobernador del estado, Ignacio Romero Vargas, a la Asamblea General del Congreso del Estado, sobre los límites entre Zacapoaxtla y Xochiapulco," 19 May 1874.

77. ACEP, Expedientes, vol. 15: "Oficio del Gobernador de Puebla, Ignacio Romero Vargas, al Ministro de Guerra y Marina, describiendo el proceso de pacificación en la sierra," 4 June 1870.

78. For evidence of resistance in allied villages, see AHMTO, Gobierno, Caja s/n 1870/73–1874/78: Exp. 112, "Oficio del alcalde municipal de Tuzamapan al jefe político de Tetela," 12 Apr. 1870; "Oficio del alcalde municipal de Tuzamapan al jefe político de Tetela," 14 Apr. 1870; AHMZ, Paq. 1869: Exp. 17, "Informe del jefe político de Zacapoaxtla sobre la alteración de la tranquilidad pública en Cuetzalan," 30 Apr. 1870; and Exp. 74, "Oficio del juez municipal de Cuetzalan al jefe político de Zacapoaxtla, sobre movimientos de tropas," 20 May 1870. For the quotation, see ACEP, Expedientes, vol. 20: "Informe rendido por Ignacio Romero Vargas, gobernador del Estado de Puebla, al Congreso del Estado, sobre su visita a la sierra norte," 31 Oct. 1871. For the surrender, and the quotation taken from it, see "Copia certificada del acta de sumisión de Juan Francisco Lucas y sus fuerzas, sacada en Tetela de Ocampo, 4 de junio de 1870," in *El Siglo XIX*, 10 June 1870, p. 2.

79. ACEP, Expedientes, vol. 20: "Informe rendido por Ignacio Romero Vargas, gobernador del Estado de Puebla, al Congreso del Estado, sobre su visita a la sierra norte," 31 Oct. 1871.

80. On the Sierra de Puebla during the revolt of La Noria, see AHDN, XI/481.4/9787: ff. 91–91v, 93–93v, 94–94v, 95–98, 99, 100, 102, 103–3v, 104, 105, 106, 107–9, 110, 111, 113–17, 118, 124, 126; "Sobre el nombramiento de Juan N. Méndez como gobernador del estado de Puebla," *El Siglo XIX*, 27 Nov. 1871; "Proclama del General Juan N. Méndez a los ciudadanos de la Línea Norte del Estado de Puebla, Xochiapulco, 1 Dec. 1871," *El Monitor Republicano*, 20 Dec. 1871, p. 3; "Carta de un vecino de Teziutlán de 7 Dic. 1871," *Periódico Oficial de Puebla*, 19 Dec. 1871, p. 4; "Correspondencia de Ixtamaxtitlán, del 7 Dic. 1871," *El Siglo XIX*, 14 Dec. 1871, p. 3; "Oficio del gobernador Ignacio Romero Vargas, transcribiendo parte del General Rafael Cravioto, desde Zacapoaxtla," *Diario Oficial*, 24 Dec. 1871, p. 3; *Diario Oficial*, 5 Mar. 1872, p. 3, about Porfirio Díaz arriving in the Sierra de Puebla; "Parte de un encuentro con las tropas juaristas, en 23 de marzo de 1872, desde Taxcantla," *El Siglo XIX*, 1 Apr. 1872, p. 3; "Informe sobre Don Juan Bonilla, jefe de los sublevados de la sierra, y su acogimiento a la amnistía," *El Siglo XIX*, 27 Aug. 1872, p. 3.

81. On Juárez's manipulation of the election of 1871, see Perry, *Juárez and Díaz*, 163–65, 373–74, 376–77; on Tuxtepec, ibid., 203, 211–19, 221–22, 230, 233, 236–41, 253–54, 257, 261–84, 335–37, 429–31. On the strength of

the revolt of La Noria and the importance of Juárez's death in stopping it, see also Charles A. Weeks, *The Juárez Myth in Mexico* (Tuscaloosa: University of Alabama Press, 1987), 23–25; AHDN, XI/481.4/9787, Cuaderno 2: ff. 162–64, 174–75; and Cuaderno 3: ff. 269–70, 272–74, 342. On Lerdo's able use of amnesty, see XI/481.4/9204: "Operaciones militares contra rebeldes, diferentes partes del país, 1872 y 1874"; XI/481.4/9205: "Amnistía General de 1872: Lista de Oficiales y Jefes Amnistiados," including f. 7: "Decreto de Amnistía General," 27 July 1872; "Manifiesto de Porfirio Díaz a Lerdo de Tejada, proponiendo condiciones de pacificación, 1 agosto de 1872," *Periódico Oficial de Puebla*, 6 Sept. 1872, pp. 3–4; "Se notifica que Juan N. Méndez ha mandado cartas al presidente interino, diciendo que quiere acogerse a la ley de amnistía," *El Siglo XIX*, 29 Aug. 1872, p. 3; "Se reproduce intercambio de oficios entre Porfirio Díaz y el Ministro de Guerra Mejía, sobre el sometimiento de Díaz al gobierno," *Diario Oficial*, 30 Sept. 1872, p. 3.

82. This comparison is based on the oral tradition collected in Xochiapulco in April 1985 and on the following documents that describe the encounter of 1869: "Parte del Teniente Coronel José María Vásquez, comandante del Sexto Batallón de Cazadores, sobre el combate en Xochiapulco," 7 Dec. 1869, in *Diario Oficial*, 14 Dec. 1869, p. 2; "Parte del capitán Florencio Villedas, que tomó el mando del 6° en la plaza de Xochiapulco," 5 Dec. 1869, in *Diario Oficial*, 14 Dec. 1869, p. 2; and "Parte del Coronel Francisco de P. Castañeda, en jefe de la 2ª Brigada mandada a proteger la retirada del 6° batallón de Xochiapulco," 6 Dec. 1869, in *Diario Oficial*, 14 Dec. 1869, p. 2.

83. The burial is described in "Parte del Coronel Francisco de P. Castañeda, en jefe de la 2ª Brigada mandada a proteger la retirada del 6° batallón de Xochiapulco," 6 Dec. 1869, in *Diario Oficial*, 14 Dec. 1869, p. 2.

84. Daniel Cosío Villegas, *Historia moderna de México: La República Restaurada. La vida política*, 2d ed. (Mexico City: Editorial Hermes, 1959), 604. The analysis of the plan goes on through p. 621. Much the same analysis was published, a few years earlier, by Cosío Villegas under a different title: *Porfirio Díaz en la revuelta de la Noria* (Mexico City: Editorial Hermes, 1953), with the specific project of finding the roots of Porfirian authoritarianism in his behavior during the Restored Republic.

85. This quotation, as well as subsequent ones from the plan, come from "El Plan de la Noria, suscrito por el general Porfirio Díaz," version published in *El Siglo XIX*, 14 Nov. 1871, p. 3.

86. Ibid. In *Historia moderna*, Cosío's critique of the economic arguments of the plan appears on pp. 611–12.

87. The quotations are from the version of the plan in *El Siglo XIX*.

88. Again, the quotations are from the version in *El Siglo XIX*. On Cosío's use of the word *constituent* (*constituyente*), see *Historia moderna*, 601. The version of the plan in *El Siglo XIX* talks about "constitutional reconstruc-

tion" (*reconstrucción constitucional*), which is vague enough to mean either a reconstruction of the constitution or a reconstruction done by the Constitutionalist party, i.e., the Porfiristas. On this use of "Constitucionalista," see *El Siglo XIX*, 27 Nov. 1871, p. 3.

89. For the reformed version of the Plan de la Noria, see "Modificación del Plan de la Noria dado por Porfirio Díaz en Ameca, 3 de abril de 1872," *El Siglo XIX*, 28 May 1872, p. 3. On the debates between centralist and federalist tendencies in Mexican Liberalism, see Richard Sinkin, "The Mexican Constitutionalist Congress, 1856–1857: A Statistical Analysis," *Hispanic American Historical Review* 53, no. 1 (1973): 1–26; Sinkin, *The Mexican Reform, 1855–1876: A Study in Nation-Building* (Austin: University of Texas Press, 1979); Charles A. Hale, *Mexican Liberalism in the Age of Mora, 1821–1853* (New Haven: Yale University Press, 1968); Hale, *The Transformation of Liberalism in Late Nineteenth-Century Mexico* (Princeton: Princeton University Press, 1989); Friedrich Katz, "Mexico: Restored Republic and Porfiriato, 1867–1910," in Leslie Bethell, ed., *The Cambridge History of Latin America*, vol. 5 (Cambridge and New York: Cambridge University Press, 1986), 3–78; and Florencia E. Mallon, "Peasants and State Formation in Nineteenth-Century Mexico: Morelos, 1848–1858," *Political Power and Social Theory* 7 (1988): 1–54.

CHAPTER 5. CONTESTED CITIZENSHIP (2)

1. My analysis here is based on AGNM, Gobernación: Leg. 1144(1), Exp. 1, "Petición de cinco vecinos y notables de Tepoztlán al Emperador," Mexico City, 28 Aug. 1865. All quotations are drawn from the same document.

2. On the Liberal tradition of Tepoztlán, see below, this chapter. On Tepoztlán as a center of Zapatista organizing, see John Womack, Jr., *Zapata and the Mexican Revolution* (New York: Knopf, 1968); Oscar Lewis, *Pedro Martínez: A Mexican Peasant and his Family* (New York: Random House, 1964), 73–110; and Lewis, *Life in a Mexican Village: Tepoztlán Restudied* (Urbana: University of Illinois Press, 1963), 231–36.

3. On Anenecuilco, see, in addition to Womack, *Zapata*, Jesús Sotelo Inclán, *Razón y vida de Zapata*, 2d ed. (Mexico City: Comisión Federal de Electricidad, 1970); the petition from Anenecuilco to Maximilian appears on p. 321. See also Alicia Hernández Chávez, *Anenecuilco: Memoria y vida de un pueblo* (Mexico City: El Colegio de México, 1991), esp. 67–69, where she discusses the situation during the Empire. Hernández, however, allows less room for internal division and contradiction around the question of Liberalism in Anenecuilco, arguing instead that the petition to Maximilian was a conscious stratagem to cause problems for the imperial authorities. This line of argument makes it a great deal more difficult to account for later political differences, however.

4. AGNM, "Petición de cinco vecinos y notables de Tepoztlán."

5. For Morelos's siege of Cuautla, see Brian R. Hamnett, *Roots of Insurgency: Mexican Regions, 1750–1824* (Cambridge: Cambridge University Press, 1986), esp. 157–64; for a pessimistic overview of Morelos's social impact in the region, see John Tutino, *From Insurrection to Revolution in Mexico: Social Bases of Agrarian Violence, 1750–1940* (Princeton: Princeton University Press, 1986), 188–93. For the rebellions in 1850 and 1854, see Florencia E. Mallon, "Peasants and State Formation in Nineteenth-Century Mexico: Morelos, 1848–1858," *Political Power and Social Theory* 7 (1988): 1–54, and below, this chapter.

6. The social context attached to the term *gachupín* emerges, for example, in the fact that protests against the planter governor of Morelos, Pablo Escandón, included as late as 1909 the shout "Mueran los gachupines!" See Womack, *Zapata*, 33. Pedro Martínez uses the term in the same way in his life history when referring to Pablo Escandón, even though the Escandón family had well-established roots in Mexico. See Lewis, *Pedro Martínez*, 73. For an example from the years immediately following the wars of independence, see Arturo Warman, *. . . y venimos a contradecir: Los campesinos de Morelos y el estado nacional* (Mexico City: Centro de Investigaciones Superiores del INAH, Ediciones de la Casa Chata, 1976), 90. On the historical etymology of the word, see John Lynch, *The Spanish American Revolutions, 1808–1826* (New York: Norton, 1973). For an overview of the early republican conflicts around the presence of Spaniards in Mexico, see Harold Dana Sims, *The Expulsion of Mexico's Spaniards, 1821–1836* (Pittsburgh: University of Pittsburgh Press, 1990).

7. On the interpenetration of social issues and anti-Spanish feeling, see, in addition to the sources in the previous footnote, Mallon, "Peasants and State Formation," esp. 10–12; Romeo Flores Caballero, *La contrarevolución en la independencia: Los españoles en la vida política y económica de México (1804–1838)* (Mexico City: El Colegio de México, 1969); and Harold D. Sims, *La expulsión de los españoles de México (1821–1828)* (Mexico City: Fondo de Cultura Económica, 1974). On the various kinds of social issues emerging in Morelos between the late colonial period and the mid–nineteenth century, see especially Cheryl English Martin, "Haciendas and Villages in Late Colonial Morelos," *Hispanic American Historical Review* 62, no. 3 (1982): 407–27, and Warman, *. . . y venimos a contradecir*, 60–77, 89–93.

8. Hamnett, *Roots of Insurgency*, 71–72 (on Tlaltizapán), 163–64 (on Yautepec and Francisco Ayala). On the oral tradition, as well as additional insurgent action to the east, see Warman, *. . . y venimos a contradecir*, 89–90.

9. On Cuautla in 1850, see AHDN, XI/481.3/3119: "Oficio del Subprefecto de Morelos al Prefecto del Distrito," Morelos, 17 Oct. 1850, ff. 24–25; and Leticia Reina, *Las rebeliones campesinas en México (1891–1906)*

(Mexico City: Siglo XXI Editores, 1980), 162–63. On the connections between Cuautla and other areas of Morelos and El Sur in 1854, see AHDN, XI/481.3/5051: "Oficio de Manuel Céspedes al Ministerio de Guerra," Cuernavaca, 31 Dec. 1854, ff. 19–19v; "Parte de Manuel Céspedes al Ministerio de Guerra," Xochitepec, 1 Jan. 1855, ff. 21–21v; "Parte de Manuel Céspedes al Ministerio de Guerra," Cuernavaca, 2 Jan. 1855, ff. 23–24; "Miguel Franco al Comandante en Jefe de la línea del sur," Jonacatepec, 31 Mar. 1854, ff. 126–28; and XI/481.3/5052: "Parte del Encargado de la Comandancia Principal de Cuernavaca al Ministerio de Guerra," 15 Dec. 1854, ff. 1–2; "Parte de Manuel Céspedes al Ministerio de Guerra y Marina sobre la rebelión en Cuautla, Morelos," Hacienda San Gabriel, 16 Dec. 1854, ff. 8–8v; and "Oficio del encargado de la Comandancia Principal de Cuernavaca al Ministerio de Guerra y Marina," 23 Dec. 1854, ff. 80–81v.

10. On the definition of a region of protest between independence and the 1850s, see Reina, *Las rebeliones campesinas*, 85–120, 157–77; and John M. Hart, "The 1840s Southwestern Mexico Peasants' War: Conflict in a Transitional Society," in Friedrich Katz, ed., *Riot, Rebellion and Revolution: Rural Social Conflict in Mexico* (Princeton: Princeton University Press, 1988), 249–68. On the mobilization of regional movements through negotiated convergences among leaders and constituencies, see also Hamnett, *Roots of Insurgency*, 142–47, 209–10; and Fernando Díaz y Díaz, *Caudillos y caciques* (Mexico City: El Colegio de México, 1972).

11. This paragraph is based on Peter Guardino, "Peasants, Politics, and State Formation in Nineteenth-Century Mexico: Guerrero, 1800–1857," Ph.D. diss., University of Chicago, 1992.

12. Guardino, "Peasants, Politics, and State Formation," especially chaps. 3, 4, and 5. *Oficiales de república* were the political authorities in charge of administering the older institutions of *cabildo* government set up during the colonial period, in many cases "domesticated" by local ethnic hierarchies to represent Indian communal interests. The municipalities organized after independence in some cases came to compete with these older forms, providing mestizos or outsiders with a possible avenue to local influence or power.

13. Horacio Crespo, coord., *Morelos: Cinco siglos de historia regional* (Mexico City and Cuernavaca: Centro de Estudios Históricos del Agrarismo en México and Universidad Autónoma del Estado de Morelos, 1985); Martin, "Haciendas and Villages"; and Martin, *Rural Society in Colonial Morelos* (Albuquerque: University of New Mexico Press, 1985).

14. Guardino, "Peasants, Politics, and State Formation"; Mallon, "Peasants and State Formation."

15. Mallon, "Peasants and State Formation"; Cecilia Noriega Elío, *El Constituyente de 1842* (Mexico City: Universidad Nacional Autónoma,

1986); Charles Hale, *Mexican Liberalism in the Age of Mora* (New Haven: Yale University Press, 1968). On the potential use of El Sur by Bravo and Alvarez, see Reina, *Las rebeliones campesinas*, 85–116; Hart, "Southwestern Mexico Peasants' War," 254–61; and Mallon, "Peasants and State Formation," esp. 31–39.

16. For the legislation on the national guard battalions, see Alicia Hernández Chávez, "Origen y ocaso del ejército porfiriano," *Historia Mexicana* 39, no. 1 (1989): esp. 265–70. On the formation of the battalions in Morelos, Alvarez's relationship to them, and the participation of guard commanders in social movements in the area, see Mallon, "Peasants and State Formation." On the identification of specific national guard commanders in Morelos, see AHDN, XI/481.3/5051: "Parte del Gral. Francisco Güitián al Ministerio de Guerra y Marina," Jojutla, 10 Jan. 1855, ff. 68–69; "Oficio del Comandante Militar de Jonacatepec al jefe de la línea del sur," 31 Mar. 1854, ff. 124–25; AHDN, XI/481.3/3119: "Informe de Nicolás de la Portilla al Ministro de Guerra," Cuernavaca, 7 May 1856, ff. 17–18v; and D/481.4/9541: "Proclama del teniente coronel Amado Popoca a los habitantes del canton de Tetecala," Campo de Nespa, Dec. 1863, ff. 130–31.

17. Alejandro Villaseñor, *Memoria política y estadística de la prefectura de Cuernavaca presentada al Superior Gobierno del Estado Libre y Soberano de México* (Mexico City: Imprenta de Cumplido, 1850), 7.

18. The law creating an hacienda-based rural police was passed in October 1849, probably directly related to the mobilizations then going on. See Villaseñor, *Memoria política*, Doc. 8, pp. 7, 18; Reina, *Las rebeliones campesinas*, 157–60.

19. For the incident with Arellano, see Reina, *Las rebeliones campesinas*, 157–61.

20. I have borrowed the concept of "radical federalism" from Peter Guardino, "Peasants, Politics, and State Formation," esp. chap. 4. Guardino argues quite convincingly, at various points in his dissertation, that it was radical federalism rather than Liberalism that propelled Juan Alvarez into the presidential chair in 1855.

21. The references to caste war are numerous in the documents over these years and will be discussed in more detail below. For the general climate of unrest, see also Mallon, "Peasants and State Formation," 14–21; Reina, *Las rebeliones campesinas*; Díaz y Díaz, *Caudillos y caciques*.

22. On the progress of the rebellion in Cuautla Morelos, see AHDN, XI/481.3/3119; the quotation appears on f. 24. This incident, and the documentation available on it in AHDN, are also discussed by Reina, *Las rebeliones campesinas*, 162–64, and Mallon, "Peasants and State Formation," 17.

23. On the repression of the movement, see the sources cited in the previous note.

24. On anarchist machinations, see AHDN, XI/481.3/3119: "Informe del coronel José de la Piedra," Hacienda de Buena Vista, 23 Oct. 1850, ff. 32–32v. On the problems the minister of defense had with de la Piedra's strategy of repression, see 31–31v, 33–34v, 56–57v.

25. AHDN, XI/481.3/3119: "Copia del oficio del subprefecto de Morelos al prefecto del distrito," 17 Oct. 1850, ff. 24–24v; "Copia del informe del Coronel José de la Piedra sobre su entrada a Morelos," Hacienda Buena Vista, 23 Oct. 1850, ff. 32–32v; "Oficio del Ministerio de Guerra y Marina al coronel José de la Piedra," Mexico, 24 Oct. 1850, ff. 31–31v; "Oficio del Comandante General del estado de México al Ministerio de Guerra y Marina," Morelos, 25 Oct. 1850, ff. 33–34.

26. On the repression in Cuautla, see AHDN, XI/481.3/3119: "Oficio del Comandante General del Estado de México al Ministro de Guerra y Marina," Mexico, 7 Nov. 1850, 103v–4. On the other events mentioned for the general region, see AHDN, XI/481.3/3268: "Oficio del Comandante General de México al Ministro de Guerra y Marina," Mexico, 12 July 1852, ff. 5–6 (the quote from Parres appears on f. 5v); XI/481.3/5051: "Miguel Franco al comandante en jefe de la línea del sur," Jonacatepec, 31 Mar. 1854, ff. 126–28; "Oficio del Comandante Militar de Jonacatepec al jefe de la línea del sur," 31 Mar. 1854, ff. 124–25; and Reina, *Las rebeliones campesinas*, 165–66.

27. CEHM-C, Fondo XXVIII–1: Doc. 11. All quotations appear in this document.

28. On the attempt to arrest those who had voted for Alvarez in the popular juntas, see AGNM, Gobernación: "Circular reservada del Ministerio de Gobernación," 11 Dec. 1854. For the conspiracy in Cuautla, see AHDN, XI/481.3/5052: "Parte del encargado de la comandancia militar de Cuernavaca al Ministerio de Guerra," 15 Dec. 1854, ff. 1–2; the quotation appears on f. 1v.

29. On the outbreak and initial process of the Cuautla rebellion, see AHDN, XI/481.3/5052: "Parte de Manuel Céspedes al Ministro de Guerra y Marina," Hacienda San Gabriel, 16 Dec. 1854, ff. 8–8v; "Parte de Francisco Saldivar al Ministro de Guerra y Marina," Tenextepango, 17 Dec. 1854, ff. 20–21v (the quotation appears on f. 21).

30. For the report from Puente de Ixtla, see AHDN, XI/481.3/5052: "Parte del Comandante Militar de Cuernavaca al Ministro de Guerra y Marina," 18 Dec. 1854, ff. 42–42v. For Céspedes's report on Cuautla, see "Parte de Manuel de Céspedes al Ministro de Guerra y Marina," Hacienda San Carlos, 18 Dec. 1854, ff. 35–36. For the minister's crotchety answer, see "Comunicación del Ministro de Guerra y Marina al Gral. Manuel Céspedes," Mexico City, 19 Dec. 1854, ff. 37–38. The quotations appear on ff. 37–37v and f. 37v, respectively.

31. On the routing of the Cuautla rebels, see AHDN, XI/481.3/5052: "Oficio del prefecto del distrito de Texcoco al Ministerio de Guerra y Ma-

rina," Chalco, 19 Dec. 1854, ff. 48–48v. For evidence of ongoing mobilization in the Tlaquiltenango area, see "Parte del Gral. Manuel Céspedes al Ministro de Guerra y Marina," Tlaquiltenango, 24 Dec. 1854, ff. 87–88. The Cuernavaca commander's report appears on ff. 80–81v; the quotation appears on f. 80v. For early examples of the continuing problems after the first of the year, see XI/481.3/5051: "Oficio de A. F. Galárraga al comandante militar de Tetecala," Hacienda Cocoyotla, 6 Jan. 1855, ff. 173; XI/481.3/5052: "Parte del Gral. Francisco Güitián al Ministro de Guerra y Marina," Hacienda San Nicolás, 7 Jan. 1855, ff. 109–109v.

32. AHDN, XI/481.3/5051: "Parte del Gral. Francisco Güitián," ff. 109–109v; "Oficio del Comandante Militar Manuel Céspedes al Ministro de Guerra y Marina," Cuernavaca, 9 Jan. 1855, ff. 62–63; "Oficio de A. F. Galárraga al comandante militar de Tetecala," Hacienda Cocoyotla, 6 Jan. 1855, f. 173; "Parte del Gral. Francisco Güitián al Ministerio de Guerra y Marina," Jojutla, 10 Jan. 1855, ff. 71–72; "Parte del Gral. Francisco Güitián al Ministro de Guerra y Marina," Jojutla, 13 Jan. 1855, ff. 87–87v.

33. AHDN, XI/481.3/5051: "Parte del Gral. Francisco Güitián al Ministerio de Guerra y Marina," Hacienda San Nicolás, 7 Jan. 1855, ff. 109–109v; "Oficio del Comandante Militar Manuel Céspedes al Ministerio de Guerra y Marina," Cuernavaca, 9 Jan. 1855, ff. 62–63. For Güitián's report detailing escape and hideout strategies, see "Parte del Gral. Francisco Güitián al Ministro de Guerra y Marina," Jojutla, 10 Jan. 1855, ff. 68–69.

34. AHDN, XI/481.3/5051: "Parte del Gral. Nicolás de la Portilla al Ministro de Guerra y Marina," Morelos, 15 Jan. 1855, ff. 100–101v; the quotations appear on ff. 100 and 101, respectively.

35. For the combination of banditry and political leaflets, see AHDN, XI/481.3/5054: "Parte de Nicolás de la Portilla al Ministerio de Guerra y Marina," Morelos, 19 Feb. 1855, ff. 6v–7. For the quotation, see XI/481.3/5051: "Parte de Nicolás de la Portilla al Ministro de Guerra y Marina," Morelos, 21 Jan. 1855, f. 129. For an excellent example of the racist connotations of *pinto suriano* and the "darkening" of Alvarez's forces, and of Alvarez himself, by Conservatives, see "Parte No Oficial," *Diario Oficial* (Mexico City), 19 May 1855, pp. 2–3.

36. AHDN, XI/481.3/5051: "Oficio del Gral. Güitián al Ministerio de Guerra y Marina," Jojutla, 11 Jan. 1855, ff. 73–73v; "Parte del Gral. Nicolás de la Portilla," Morelos, 15 Jan. 1855, ff. 100–101v.

37. For the position of Lucas Alamán, see his *Historia de Méjico desde los primeros movimientos que prepararon su independencia en el año de 1808, hasta la epoca presente*, 4 vols. (Mexico City: Imprenta de J. M. Lara, 1849–1852). For some of the implications and workings out of this ideology during and after the Liberal Revolution, see Mallon, "Peasants and State Formation." The editorial cited is "Parte No Oficial." Another example linking Alvarez to caste war and racial violence is José María Bermúdez, *Verda-*

dera causa de la revolucion del sur... (Toluca: Imp. del Gobierno del Estado, 1831).

38. For a case in which Alvarez and Morelos were linked in a popular battle cry, see AHDN, SI/481.3/5052: "Parte de Manuel Céspedes al Ministerio de Guerra y Marina," Hacienda San Gabriel, 16 Dec. 1854, ff. 8–8v. Alvarez's manifesto itself makes the connection to Guerrero: CEHM-C, Fondo XXVIII–1, Doc. 11. The identification with Guerrero also pops up in Lewis, *Pedro Martínez*, 5. For the overall sense of an oppositional political culture, see Mallon, "Peasants and State Formation," 14–21, and Guardino, "Peasants, Politics, and State Formation."

39. For the identification of Manuel Casales, see AHDN, XI/481.3/5051: "Parte del Gral. Francisco Güitián al Ministerio de Guerra y Marina," Jojutla, 10 Jan. 1855, ff. 68–69. For the identification of Popoca, see "Oficio del Comandante Militar de Jonacatepec al jefe de la línea del sur," 31 Mar. 1854, ff. 124–25, and D/481.4/9541: "Proclama del teniente coronel Amado Popoca a los habitantes del canton de Tetecala," Campo de Nespa, Dec. 1863, ff. 130–31. For the identification of Trejo, Carrillo, Arellano, and Rubio, see XI/481.3/3119: "Informe de Nicolás de la Portilla al Ministro de Guerra sobre ocurrencias en la zona de su mando," Cuernavaca, 7 May 1856, ff. 17–18v.

40. On the Conservative revolution of Zacapoaxtla and the siege of Puebla, see BN-LAF 839: "Ejército de operaciones sobre Puebla: Parte general," 23 Mar. 1856; LAF 394: Antonio de Haro y Tamariz, "Manifiesto acompañando el plan político proclamado en Zacapoaztla [*sic*] el 19 de diciembre de 1855," Puebla, 23 Jan. 1856; AHDN, XI/481.3/5562: "Copia del Plan formulado en Zacapoaxtla," 1856; CEHM-C, Fondo XXVIII-1: Doc. 46, "Plan de Zacapoaxtla," Dec. 1855; Doc. 49: "Manifiesto del Gral. Luis Osollo," Puebla, 23 Jan. 1856, p. 1; AGNM, Gobernación: Leg. 1091, Exp. 1, "Oficio del Gobernador de Puebla Francisco Ibarra al Ministro de Gobierno," Puebla, 17 Dec. 1855; and Jan Bazant, *Antonio Haro y Tamariz y sus aventuras políticas, 1811–1869* (Mexico City: El Colegio de México, 1985).

41. AHDN, XI/481.3/5602: "Representacion de los hacendados de los distritos de Morelos, Cuautla y Cuernavaca al Presidente de la República," Mexico, 24 Mar. 1856, 1–2v. The quotations, in order of appearance in the text, appear on f. 1v, f. 2, and f. 2v.

42. AHDN, XI/481.3/5577: "Oficio del prefecto de Morelos dirigido al presidente de la República," 17 Apr. 1856, ff. 1–2; and "Informe del General de la Portilla al Ministerio de Guerra," Cuernavaca, 23 Apr. 1856, ff. 7–9v.

43. For a more systematic overview of the 1856 movements and their repression, see Mallon, "Peasants and State Formation." Specifically on the land invasions and land cultivation by peasants with guns on their backs, see also AHDN, XI/481.3/5577: "Informe del General de la Portilla al Ministe-

rio de Guerra," Cuernavaca, 23 Apr. 1856, f. 9. On the reference to socialism, see "Carta de A. de Radepont al Ministro Plenipotenciario de Francia en México," Atlihuayan, 1 May 1856, ff. 15–16; the quotation appears on f. 15v.

44. Mallon, "Peasants and State Formation," 21–24, 28, 37–39.

45. On the quick response of Comonfort's government, see AHDN, XI/481.3/5577: "Informe del General de la Portilla," f. 1. Portilla's force arrived in Morelos around mid-April; see AHDN, XI/481.3/5577: "Informe de Nicolás de la Portilla al Ministro de Guerra y Marina," Cuernavaca, 23 Apr. 1856, ff. 7–9v. For a more detailed analysis of events in Tepoztlán, see Mallon, "Peasants and State Formation," esp. 21–28. Evidence for the directness of Portilla's alliance with the haciendas and the hacienda police can be found in his immediate response to the news that the hacienda Atlihuayan was being burned; he himself says "abandoning everything I had to do I ran to help them." AHDN, XI/481.3/3119: "Oficio del General de la Portilla al Ministro de Guerra," Cuernavaca, 27 May 1856, ff. 24–25v; the quotation appears on f. 25. Also, according to the report of Pascual Rojas, Tepoztlán's alcalde, when Portilla's troops took a prisoner in their raid on Tepoztlán, they carried him off to the hacienda Atlihuayan; XI/481.3/5577: "Carta del Alcalde de Tepoztlán, al Gral. Juan Alvarez," Tepoztlán, 7 July 1856, esp. f. 87. A final piece of evidence is that, even though Portilla received orders to disarm the haciendas as well as nearby villages (XI/481.3/5577: "Orden de Guerra al Com. Gral. Nicolás de la Portilla," Mexico City, 10 June 1856, f. 34), he proceeded only against the pueblos. Luckily for him, perhaps, the order was rescinded on 4 July ("Orden reservada al Gral. de la Portilla," Mexico City, 4 July 1856, f. 44); but the damage in the villages had already been done.

46. For Portilla's reference to warlike Indians, see AHDN, XI/481.3/5577: "Copia de una carta de Nicolás de la Portilla al General Angel Frías," copied in Cuernavaca, 30 June 1856, ff. 42–43. For his association of village soldiers with bandits and thieves, see "Informe del General de la Portilla al Ministerio de Guerra," Cuernavaca, 23 Apr. 1856, ff. 7–9v; see also his reference to Arellano in the quotation. Portilla's ambivalent attempt to separate the peasant soldiers in Morelos and Cuernavaca from his concept of the "real" national guard can be found in XI/481.3/3119: "Informe de Nicolás de la Portilla al Ministro de Guerra," Cuernavaca, 7 May 1856, ff. 17–18v.

47. For a detailed description of the 1856 incident, see Mallon, "Peasants and State Formation." A particularly cogent exposition of the Spanish point of view can be found in Tomás Ríos, *Los hechos y los datos oficiales contra el Memorandum del Sr. D. Jose M. Lafragua, y algunas noticias mas sobre la cuestion de Mejico* (Madrid: Estab. Tipográfico de D. A. Vicente, 1858).

48. The eight incidents are to be found in *Diario Oficial*, 3:213, 1 Mar. 1855, p. 3; 3:315, 11 June 1855, p. 3; ACDN, Expediente de Miguel Negrete: "Oficio de Miguel Negrete al Ministerio de Guerra y Marina," Iguala,

30 June 1857, ff. 28–30v; AHDN, XI/481.3/6267: "Representación del Enviado Extraordinario de Francia," Jan. 1858; XI/481.3/6268: "Representación del Vizconde de Gabriac, Enviado Extraordinario de Francia," Aug.–Dec. 1858; and XI/481.3/6388: "Investigación practicada ... en el pueblo de Zacualpan Amilpas," 1858; AGNM, Gobernación: Exp. 48, "Oficio de Angel Perez Palacios al Ministro de Gobernación," Cuernavaca, 24 May 1858, ff. 6–7v; Leg. 1173, Exp. 2, "Oficio de Angel Perez Palacios al Ministro de Gobernación, sobre el ataque a la tienda del español don Benito Alvarez, en la hacienda de San Vicente," Cuernavaca, 2 July 1858.

49. For the declaration by the three Spanish merchants, which includes the quotation, see AHDN, XI/481.3/6268: "Representación al Supremo Gobierno hecha por Manuel Maria Rubin, Manuel Abascal y José Ros y Prats," Mexico City, 31 Aug. 1858, ff. 12–14; the quotation appears on f. 13.

50. AHDN, XI/481.3/6268: "Testimonio del subprefecto de Yautepec en la averiguación sumaria de los hechos del 22 de agosto," 13 Sept. 1858, ff. 17–21v; "Interrogatorio y respuestas del General Angel Perez Palacios en el mismo caso," Cuernavaca and Mexico City, 11 and 15 Sept. 1858, ff. 36–37, 38–42v; "Declaración de don Alejandro Oliveros en el mismo caso," 14 Sept. 1858, ff. 22–24v; "Declaración de don Francisco Perez Palacios en el mismo caso," 15 Sept. 1858, ff. 25–28v.

51. AHDN, XI/481.3/6268: "Carta del Secretario de Relaciones Exteriores al Ministro de Guerra," Mexico City, 18 Dec. 1858, ff. 1–2v.

52. On Liberal activity, see AHDN, XI/481.3/6268: "Interrogatorio y respuestas del General Angel Perez Palacios en el mismo caso," Cuernavaca and Mexico City, 11 and 15 Sept., ff. 41–41v; "Declaración de don Francisco Perez Palacios en el mismo caso," 15 Sept. 1858, f. 26v. Pío Bermejillo's letter is in XI/481.3/6781: "Carta de Pio Bermejillo a Don Telesforo Escalante," Mexico City, 11 Oct. 1858, ff. 4–5. The quotations appear on ff. 4v and 5, respectively.

53. For the incident with the *Mexican Extraordinary*, see *Diario Oficial*, 20 Apr. 1858, p. 2. For the case involving Ruiz, see ACDN, Expediente de Miguel Negrete: "Oficio de Miguel Negrete al Ministro de Guerra y Marina," Iguala, 30 June 1857, ff. 28–30v. It is also clear from the other sources in the previous note that Spaniards engaged in a great deal of grandstanding and imperious behavior that fed into the situations.

54. ACDN, Expediente de Francisco Leyva: "Parte de Francisco Leyva al Ministro de Guerra y Marina," Cuartel General en Tepoztlán, 6 May 1860, ff. 33v–35v; "Oficio de Francisco Leyva al administrador de la hacienda de Chiconcuac," Tecalita, 29 Apr. 1860, f. 43v; "Testimonio del sargento José María Rebollar," Ameca, 10 May 1860, ff. 36–36v; "Declaración de dn. Silviano Betanzos," Zacualpan, 31 Aug. 1860, ff. 93–95; "Declaración de Francisco Orozco," Cuernavaca, 31 Aug. 1860, ff. 95–98; "Declaración de Joaquín Rivas," Cuernavaca, 1 Sept. 1860, ff. 98–99v; "Segunda declaración de dn.

Silviano Betanzos," Cuernavaca, 1 Sept. 1860, ff. 100v–102; "Declaración de Tomás Medina," Cuernavaca, 2 Sept. 1860, ff. 102–103v. In his later declaration at his trial in Veracruz, Leyva insisted that he had carried out an investigation of Guadalupe Sánchez, the soldier who had shot the prisoners: "Testimonio de Francisco Leyva," Veracruz, 17 Dec. 1860, ff. 68–72.

55. For Spanish pressure and Mexican government reactions, see ACDN, Expediente de Francisco Leyva: "Oficio del Ministro de Guerra y Marina al Ministro de Relaciones Exteriores," Mexico City, 11 May 1860, ff. 196–97; "Oficio del Ministro de Gobernación al de Guerra y Marina," H. Veracruz, 15 May 1860, f. 42; "Oficio del General en Jefe del Ejército Federal al Ministro de Guerra y Marina," San Luis Potosí, 6 June 1860, f. 44. The justification along issues of credit and colonization appears in "Oficio del Ministro de Relaciones Exteriores al Ministro de Guerra," H. Veracruz, 29 June 1860, ff. 44v–45v.

56. ACDN, Expediente de Francisco Leyva: "Oficio del Comandante Principal de Cuernavaca y Morelos al Ministro de Guerra y Marina," Morelos, 4 Aug. 1860, ff. 53–53v; "Respuesta del Gral. Felipe Berriozabal al Gral. Juan Alvarez," Querétaro, 5 Sept. 1860, ff. 54v–55; "Oficio de Francisco Leyva al Ministro de Guerra y Marina," H. Veracruz, 3 Dec. 1860, f. 62; "Oficio de Francisco Leyva al jefe de las fuerzas constitucionales del estado de Veracruz," H. Veracruz, 25 Jan. 1860, ff. 152–53; "Oficio de Francisco Leyva al Ministerio de Guerra y Marina," Mexico City, 29 June 1860, ff. 210–210v; "Oficio de Ignacio de la Peña al Ministro de Guerra y Marina," Tepoztlán, 9 Sept. 1860, ff. 55–56; "Oficio de I. de la Peña al Ministro de Guerra y Marina," Tepoztlán, 9 Sept. 1860, ff. 56v–58; "Oficio de I. de la Peña al Ministro de Guerra y Marina," Tepoztlán, 9 Sept. 1860, ff. 58–59; "Oficio de I. de la Peña al Ministro de Guerra y Marina," Tepoztlán, 9 Sept. 1860, ff. 59–60; "Oficio de I. de la Peña al Gral. José Fandiño," Tepoztlán, 11 Sept. 1860, f. 61.

57. On Tepoztlán's participation in conspiracies against the Conservative government, and on the attempt to smuggle arms, see AHDN, XI/481.3/6032: "Parte del Gral. Angel Perez Palacios dando cuenta de una conspiración en Tepoztlán," 12 July 1858; and AGNM, Guerra y Marina, Archivo de Guerra, vol. 126: Exp. 1458, "Proceso contra Gregorio Benítez, comerciante de Yautepec," begun 17 Dec. 1859, ff. 1–65. On Oñate, see ACDN, Expediente de Miguel Negrete: "Oficio de Miguel Negrete al Ministro de Guerra y Marina," Iguala, 30 June 1857, ff. 28–30v; and Expediente de Francisco Leyva: "Declaración del capitán Ramón Oñate de la brigada Leyva," Mexico City, 11 June 1861, ff. 187–91. In the same expediente (ff. 95–98, 98–99v), Francisco Orozco and Joaquín Rivas, both employees on the hacienda San Gaspar, single Oñate out in their testimony as particularly anti-Spanish. In his testimony (f. 190v) Oñate also says that Tepoztlán was always the headquarters of the brigada Leyva. On the hopes and promises

nurtured by Tepoztlán from the Ayutla Revolution, as well as the custom of addressing Alvarez as "el tata Juan," see Mallon, "Peasants and State Formation."

58. Leyva's two communications to the minister of defense, as well as the responses, are in ACDN, Expediente de Francisco Leyva: "Francisco Leyva al Ministerio de Guerra y Marina," Mexico City, 29 June 1861, and answer on 2 July, ff. 210–210v; and "Francisco Leyva al Ministerio de Guerra y Marina," Mexico City, 18 Dec. 1861, and "Acuerdo del Presidente," communicated to Leyva on 26 Jan. 1862, ff. 219–20, 222.

59. On Teloloapam in particular, and the western side of the Morelos-Guerrero region more generally, see AGNM, Gobernación: Leg. 1126 (2), "Autoridades del distrito de Bravos, zona de Teloloapam, al Gobernador de Cuernavaca," 14 Aug. 1864; Exp. 18, "Oficio de los vecinos de Acapetlahuaya, distrito de Teloloapam, desde México," Aug. 1864; "Informe de la autoridad política de Cuernavaca," 3 Jan. 1865; Leg. 1162(2), Exp. 18, "Información del Prefecto Político de Iturbide sobre la Tranquilidad Pública," Cuernavaca, 20 Jan.–20 Mar. 1865; II Imperio, Caja 14: "Oficio de Abraham Ortiz de la Peña, transcribiendo oficio del Crel. Carranza sobre la situación en la zona del Mescala," 2 Oct. 1866; TP, "Correspondencia del Prefecto Político del Departamento de Iturbide al Ministro de Gobernación," Feb.–Oct. 1866; "Expediente sobre la comisión especial de D. Abraham Ortiz de la Peña en Teloloapam," begun 2 Apr. 1866; "Correspondencia del Prefecto Político del Departamento de Iturbide con el Ministro de Gobernación," Cuernavaca, Jan.–Apr. 1866; "Oficio del Prefecto de Iturbide al Ministerio de Gobernación," Cuernavaca, 5 June 1865; "Oficio del Prefecto Político de Iturbide al Ministerio de Gobernación," Cuernavaca, 24 July 1865; AHDN, XI/481.4/9450: ff. 211–13; D/481.4/9536, 9526, 9532, 9449, and 9451: ff. 30–32, 162–62v. On Alvarez's general headquarters on the hacienda La Providencia, see AGNM, Gobernación: Leg. 1423, Exp. 4, "Prefecto Político de Iturbide al Ministerio de Gobernación," 6 Nov. 1866. For the Sierra de Huitzilac, see *Periódico Oficial del Imperio Mexicano* 2, no. 13 (30 Jan. 1864), p. 1; *El Pájaro Verde*, 9 Feb. 1864, p. 2; AHDN, D/481.4/8864: "En el pueblo de Huitzilac . . . ," 2 Oct. 1862, D/481.4/9541: ff. 91, 92–93, 125–25v, 164–64v; D/481.4/9540: f. 65; AGNM, Gobernación: Leg. 1161(2), Exp. 18, "Oficio del Ministro de Guerra al Ministro de Gobernación," Mexico City, 29 Jan. 1865; "Oficio del Prefecto de Iturbide al Ministerio de Gobernación," Cuernavaca, 20 Feb. 1865; Leg. 500(3), Exp. 1, "Oficios varios del Jefe político del territorio de Iturbide," Cuernavaca, Jan.–June 1860; and TP: "Oficio del Prefecto Político de Iturbide al Ministerio de Gobernación," Cuernavaca, 24 July 1865. For the rest of the district of Cuernavaca, see AHDN, D/481.4/9541: ff. 89–90; 94–95v; 75–76v; 77–78; 130–31; 132–32v; D/481.4/9526: ff. 2–2v; 52–53v; *El Pájaro Verde*, 16 Jan. 1864, p. 2; 16 Jan. 1865, p. 3; 24 Feb. 1865, p. 3; AGNM, Gobernación: Leg. 1144(1), Exp. 2, "Queja de vecinos del barrio de Nexpa,"

29 Apr. 1865–17 Jan. 1866; Leg. 1423, Exp. 4, "Oficio del Visitador Imperial de Iturbide al Subsecretario de Gobernación," Cuernavaca, 17 Dec. 1866; Leg. 1161(2), Exp. 18, "Oficio del Prefecto Político de Iturbide al Ministerio de Gobernación," Cuernavaca, 13 Jan. 1865; "Varios oficios del Prefecto Político de Iturbide a Gobernación," Cuernavaca, 25–26 Feb. 1865; TP, "Expediente formado sobre un desorden en Coatlán, Morelos," Cuernavaca, 25 Aug. 1865; and II Imperio, Caja 74: "Resumen de hechos para S. M. el Emperador, N° 1216," 7–12 Aug. 1865.

60. AHDN, D/481.4/9541: ff. 75–76v, 77–78, 79–79v. On the organization of repression by the haciendas, see Villaseñor, *Memoria política y estadística de la prefectura de Cuernavaca*, Anexo N° 8; and AHDN, D/481.4/9541: "R. Hernández, administrador de la hacienda San Nicolás, al subprefecto de Tetecala," 25 Oct. 1865, ff. 79–79v. On government attempts to tax the haciendas to finance the government, including its activities of social control, see AGNM, Leg. 500, Exp. 2: "Quejas de los hacendados del 3ᵉʳ Distrito del Estado de México al Gobernador del Distrito y al Presidente de la República," Aug.–Sept. 1862. On the general issues of the hacendados' role in repression, see also Mallon, "Peasants and State Formation."

61. For the incident with the Liberal forces, see AHDN, D/481.4/8927: "Oficio del Coronel Rafael Cuéllar al Ministerio de Guerra y Marina," 16 July 1862, ff. 5–5v; "Oficio del Comandante Militar del 3ᵉʳ distrito del estado de México al Ministro de Guerra y Marina," 20 July 1862, ff. 8–12; and "Informe de Comandante Militar del 3ᵉʳ distrito del estado de México al Ministro de Guerra y Marina," Yautepec, 5 Aug. 1862, ff. 19–19v, 21–21v. More generally on the activities of the plateados, see *El Pájaro Verde*, 29 Jan. 1864, p. 2; 9 Feb. 1864, p. 3; 7 Apr. 1864, p. 3; 25 Apr. 1864, p. 3; AHDN, XI/481.4/8879, ff. 13–13v: "Oficio del Comandante Principal de Morelos al Ministerio de Guerra y Marina," 25 Mar. 1862; D/481.4/8860: ff. 1–3, 8–10; D/481.4/8755: ff. 1–1v; D/481.4/8860: "Comandante Principal de Cuernavaca al Ministro de Guerra," 20 Oct. 1862; D/481.4/9541: ff. 64–64v; D/481.4/9449; AGNM, II Imperio, Caja 59: "Oficio del Gobernador y Comandante Militar del 3ᵉʳ distrito del estado de México al Ministro de Relaciones Exteriores y Gobernación," Cuernavaca, 23 May 1863; Caja 81: "Oficio del Cura Tomás Luis G. Falco pidiendo indulto para un grupo de plateados del distrito de Morelos," and "Oficio del Arzobispo de México sobre el párroco D. Luis F. Falco," 24 Sept. 1865; Gobernación: Leg. 1161(1), Exp. 10, "Correspondencia del Subprefecto de Cuautla Morelos con el Ministerio de Gobierno"; Leg. 1126, Exp. 3, "Expediente sobre dar armas a los vecinos de Jantetelco," 31 Aug. 1864; "Oficio de los hacendados del distrito de Cuautla al Emperador," 1 Oct. 1864; TP, "Oficio del Prefecto Político de Iturbide al Ministro de Gobernación," Cuernavaca, 29 July 1865.

62. On plateados' use of liberty and the Liberal cause, see *El Pájaro Verde*, 15 Nov. 1864, p. 2. On the case of Mapazlán and the hacienda

Tenextepango, see AHDN, D/481.4/9541: "Oficio del Comandante Militar de Cuernavaca," 7 Dec. 1863, ff. 101–2, and "Oficio del comandante militar de Cuernavaca," 30 Dec. 1863, ff. 107–107v; the quotation appears on f. 107.

63. Sotelo Inclán, *Razón y vida de Zapata*, 309–10. Hernández, *Anenecuilco*, 67–68, provides further evidence of the lack of support for the Conservative cause when she discusses Anenecuilco's refusal to pay taxes in 1865–1866. But she does not see the ambivalence toward the Liberals that emerges so clearly in Sánchez's behavior.

64. On the backgrounds of men from the Xochitepec national guard, see Mallon, "Peasants and State Formation," 31. On Pascual Rojas's level of education and his political status, see AHDN, XI/481.3/5577: "Carta del alcalde de Tepoztlán Pascual Rojas, al Gral. Juan Alvarez," Tepoztlán, 7 July 1856, ff. 87–89. On Trejo, see XI/481.3/5577: "Carta de Agustín Trejo a Juan Alvarez," Tepecoamilco, 11 July 1856, f. 86. On Amado Popoca, see D/481.4/9541: "Proclama del teniente coronel Amado Popoca a los habitantes del canton de Tetecala," Campo de Nespa, Dec. 1863, ff. 130–31.

65. On the Conservative leaders in Tepoztlán, see AGNM, Gobernación: Leg. 1144(1), Exp. 1, "Petición de cinco vecinos y notables de Tepoztlán," Mexico City, 28 Aug. 1865.

66. Sotelo Inclán, *Razón y vida de Zapata*, 320–22, 337–38, 360–61, 366–69.

67. Ibid., 321.

68. For Maximilian's decree answering Tepoztlán, see AGNM, Gobernación: Leg. 1144(1), Exp. 1, "Decreto del Emperador Maximiliano sobre la petición de Tepoztlán," Palacio de México, 2 May 1865. On the alternative interpretation of the liberal land laws, see chapter 4. Sotelo Inclán, *Razón y vida de Zapata*, 319–20, also makes the point that this particular policy was dissatisfying to the Conservatives as well as the villages.

69. For the lawyer's opinion and Tepoztlán's alcalde's letter, see AGNM, Gobernación: Leg. 1144(1), Exp. 1, "Oficio del Prefecto Político del Departamento de Iturbide al Ministro de Gobernación," Cuernavaca, 15 Jan. 1866; and "Extracto de la opinión del abogado nombrado en el caso de Tepoztlán." The alcalde's letter is dated 27 October 1865, suggesting it sat on the prefect's desk for two months without receiving any attention.

70. AGNM, Gobernación: Leg. 1144(1), Exp. 1, "Respuesta de J. M. Marrana al Prefecto de Cuernavaca," Hacienda de Oacalco, 15 Aug. 1866.

71. AGNM, Gobernación: Leg. 1144(1), Exp. 1, "Oficio de Maximino Centeno al Emperador," Mexico City, 29 Aug. 1866; and attached "Resolución Imperial en el caso de Tepoztlán," 3 Sept. 1866.

72. Sotelo Inclán, *Razón y vida de Zapata*, 322–30.

73. AGNM, JPCM, IV: Exp. 20, "Decretos y leyes imperiales sobre tierras comunales y las clases menesterosas," 1864–66, ff. 196–202.

74. AGNM, JPCM, vols. 1–4. The decrees and laws cited are, respectively, AGNM, JPCM, IV: Exp. 20, "Decreto del Emperador creando la Junta Protectora de las Clases Menesterosas," Chapultepec, 10 Apr. 1865; "Decreto del Emperador reglamentando el trato de los trabajadores del campo," Palacio Nacional de México, 1 Nov. 1865; "Ley para dirimir las diferencias sobre tierras y aguas entre los pueblos," Palacio Nacional de México, 1 Nov. 1865; and "Ley sobre terrenos de comunidad y de repartimiento," Mexico, 26 June 1866.

75. For additional imperial decrees fitting the populist mold, see AGNM, JPCM: Exp. 20, "Decreto del Emperador autorizando a la Junta Protectora a formar juntas auxiliares en todos los municipios del Imperio," 19 July 1865, f. 197; "Circular del Ministro de Gobernación sobre las tierras de colonización," 14 Sept. 1865, ff. 197–197v; "Decreto del Emperador sobre daños y perjuicios de animales en pastos y sembrados," 25 June 1866, f. 200. For cases in which pueblos attempted to use imperial laws in their favor, see II Imperio, Caja 83: "Alcalde auxiliar de Temoaca y vecinos de la municipalidad de Zacualpan," 18 Oct. 1866; "Oficio del Juez de Paz de Cuernavaca al Director del Archivo General del Imperio," 23 Aug. 1866; Caja 43: "Solicitud de Audiencia con el Emperador, de la Comisión del Estado de Guerrero," Mexico City, 28 May 1866; JPCM, I: Exp. 9, ff. 236–50; IV: Exp. 20, ff. 193, 190–92v; Gobernación: Leg. 1786(2), Exp. 6, "Solicitud de los vecinos del barrio de Amilcingo al Emperador," 22 Dec. 1865. On the limits of cooperation by local authorities and the dependence of the Junta Protectora on them, see JPCM, IV: Exp. 15, ff. 142–43, 140–41v, 154–55; Exp. 20, ff. 194–94v; II Imperio, Caja 95: "Solicitud de los alcaldes auxiliares de algunos pueblos de la zona de Cuernavaca," 16 June 1866.

76. AGNM, JPCM, IV: Exp. 15, ff. 146–46v, 142–43, 147–48v, 140–41v, 144–45v, 154–55; II Imperio, Caja 95: "Solicitud de los alcaldes auxiliares de algunos pueblos de la zona de Cuernavaca," 16 June 1866. See also Sotelo Inclán, *Razón y vida de Zapata*, 326–30.

77. AGNM, JPCM, V: Exp. 26, ff. 215–18v; Exp. 37, ff. 268–71; Gobernación: Leg. 1786(2), Exp. 6, "Expediente formado en ocasión de la prisión de Juan Cataño y José María Portela," 13 Sept.–29 Oct. 1866.

78. Guardino, "Peasants, Politics, and State Formation," makes a similar argument for Guerrero in the 1810–1855 period as well as for the Liberal Revolution.

CHAPTER 6. FROM CITIZEN TO OTHER

1. For the Comas area during the Juan Santos rebellion, see Steve J. Stern, "The Age of Andean Insurrection, 1742–1782," in Stern, ed., *Resistance, Rebellion, and Consciousness in the Andean Peasant World, Eighteenth to Twentieth Centuries* (Madison: University of Wisconsin Press, 1987), 51–53. On the 1968 guerrilla foco, see Richard Gott, *Guerrilla Movements in*

Latin America (Garden City, N.Y.: Doubleday, 1972), 351–65, and Michael F. Brown and Eduardo Fernández, *War of Shadows: The Struggle for Utopia in the Peruvian Amazon* (Berkeley: University of California Press, 1991). On Sendero Luminoso, see NACLA (North American Congress on Latin America), *Report on the Americas* 24, no. 4 (Dec. 1990–Jan. 1991); Alberto Flores Galindo, *Tiempo de plagas* (Lima: El Caballo Rojo, 1988); Carlos Iván Degregori, *Sendero Luminoso: I. Los hondos y mortales desencuentros. II. Lucha armada y utopía autoritaria* (Lima: Instituto de Estudios Peruanos, 1986); Nelson Manrique, "La década de la violencia," *Márgenes*, nos. 5–6 (1989): 137–82; Robin Kirk, *The Decade of Chaqwa: Peru's Internal Refugees* (Washington, D.C.: U.S. Committee for Refugees, 1991); and Deborah Poole and Gerardo Rénique, "The Chroniclers of Peru: U.S. Scholars and Their 'Shining Path' of Peasant Rebellion," unpublished manuscript, n.d. Attention was first drawn to the importance of Comas in the 1880s in books by Nelson Manrique, *Campesinado y nación: Las guerrillas indígenas en la guerra con Chile* (Lima: Ital Perú–C.I.C., 1981), and Florencia E. Mallon, *The Defense of Community in Peru's Central Highlands: Peasant Struggle and Capitalist Transition, 1860–1940* (Princeton: Princeton University Press, 1983), chap. 3.

2. For the quotation, see Eduardo Mendoza Meléndez, *Historia de la Campaña de la Breña*, 2d ed. (Lima: Ital Perú, 1983), 189. Both of these incidents are considered in more detail below.

3. I have identified the people who participated most actively in the events of 1882 through AHM, "Memorias sobre la resistencia de la Breña del Tte. Crel. Ambrosio Salazar y Marquez (escrita por su hermano Juan P. Salazar)," Huancayo, 1918, p. 9. I identified the participants in 1888 in APJ, "Oficio de las autoridades de Comas a las autoridades y notables de la Comunidad de Uchubamba," Comas, 25 Jan. 1888; "Oficio de Estevan Paytampoma, Jose R. Paytampoma y otros al Subprefecto de la Provincia," Comas, 1 Feb. 1888; and "Oficio de las autoridades del Distrito de Comas al Subprefecto de la Provincia," Comas, 1 Feb. 1888.

4. This overview is based on Mallon, *Defense of Community*, 15–41; Carlos Samaniego, "Location, Social Differentiation, and Peasant Movements in the Central Sierra of Peru," Ph.D. diss., University of Manchester, 1974; and Gavin Smith, *Livelihood and Resistance: Peasants and the Politics of Land in Peru* (Berkeley: University of California Press, 1989), 38–57. The original insight on the Huancas' alliance with the Spaniards belongs to Waldemar Espinoza Soriano.

5. Samaniego, "Location," esp. 79, 95–96; Mallon, *Defense of Community*, 15–47.

6. Samaniego, "Location," 72–78, 88–99. For an interesting general analysis of the wari-llacuaz conflict, see Pierre Duviols, "Huari y llacuaz. Agricultores y pastores. Un dualismo prehispánico de oposición y comple-

mentación," *Revista del Museo Nacional* (Lima) 39 (1973): 153:91. It is important to emphasize here, however, that my usage of the terms *wari* and *llacuaz* is more symbolic and heuristic than historically representative. People in the nineteenth century did not refer to themselves in those terms, even though the dynamics between uplands and lowlands were quite analogous to the wari-llacuaz dichotomy.

7. Samaniego, "Location," 96–99. On the conflicts of the 1780s, see also Stern, "Age of Andean Insurrection," 64–66.

8. Samaniego, "Location," 72–73; Smith, *Livelihood and Resistance*, 26–28.

9. On the independence struggle in the central highlands, see Mallon, *Defense of Community*, 42–52; and Raúl Rivera Serna, *Los guerrilleros del centro en la emancipación peruana* (Lima: Talleres Gráficos Villanueva, 1958). On the reemergence of a historical memory of independence, see below, this chapter.

10. Mallon, *Defense of Community*, 42–79; Nelson Manrique, *Mercado interno y región: La Sierra central, 1820–1930* (Lima: DESCO, 1987), 15–166; Carlos Contreras, *Mineros y campesinos en los Andes* (Lima: IEP, 1988).

11. On cabecera-anexo conflicts, see Florencia E. Mallon, "Nationalist and Anti-State Coalitions in the War of the Pacific: Junín and Cajamarca, 1879–1902," in Stern, ed., *Resistance, Rebellion, and Consciousness*, 240; Samaniego, "Location," 121–22; and Richard N. Adams, *A Community in the Andes: Problems and Progress in Muquiyauyo* (Seattle: University of Washington Press, 1959), 29–31. On the changing conditions for suffrage and what they meant, see Cámara de Diputados, *Constituciones Políticas del Perú, 1821–1919* (Lima: Imprenta Torres Aguirre, 1922), 258–59, 286, 318–19; and Víctor Andrés Belaúnde, *La crisis presente* (Lima: Ediciones Mercurio Peruano, n.d.), 32–79. I am grateful to Marisol de la Cadena for bringing this last work to my attention and opening up the question of suffrage in nineteenth-century Peru.

12. Mallon, *Defense of Community*, 52–79.

13. Perhaps it bears repeating that the success of patron-client networks did not mean an absence of conflict but rather their generally more peaceful resolution. Even within the folds of these relationships there were daily battles and forms of resistance. My discussion of Acolla and Muquiyauyo's petitions is based on conversations with Don Moisés Ortega, Acolla, throughout 1977; SINAMOS, cc205 (Marco): "Expediente sobre la reivindicación del molino de propiedad comunal," 1939, ff. 134–364; and Adams, *Community in the Andes*, 30.

14. Mendoza, *La Campaña de la Breña*, 233; Waldemar Espinoza Soriano, *Enciclopedia departamental de Junín*, vol. 1 (Huancayo: Editorial San Fernando, 1974), 330–36.

15. This discussion of the conflicts surrounding the creation of the district of San Juan is based on Carlos Samaniego, "Peasant Movements at the Turn of the Century and the Rise of the Independent Farmer," in Norman Long and Bryan R. Roberts, eds., *Peasant Cooperation and Capitalist Expansion in Central Peru* (Austin: University of Texas Press, 1978), 45–71, and Samaniego, "Location," 88–94, 136–46.

16. Samaniego, "Location," 88–94, 95–99, 104–12, 125–27, 157–65, 178–79, 181–86.

17. Ibid., 178–79, 186; Smith, *Livelihood and Resistance*, 64–65; Samaniego, "Peasant Movements." On Ibarra's presence in the congress, and the changes following the creation of Huancayo province, see *Constituciones políticas*, 308–9, 337–39.

18. On the development of the hacienda economy in the decades after 1850, starting from the destruction caused by independence, see Florencia E. Mallon, "Minería y agricultura en la sierra central: Formación y trayectoria de una clase dirigente regional," *Lanas y capitalismo en los andes centrales*, Taller de Estudios Andinos, Universidad Nacional Agraria La Molina, Serie: Andes Centrales, no. 2 (1977), part 2: Estudios, pp. 1–12 (mimeograph); and Manrique, *Mercado interno y región*, 65–150. On competition between waris and hacendados, see Samaniego, "Location," 178–87; and Smith, *Livelihood and Resistance*, 64–67. On the murkiness of boundaries, see Samaniego, "Location," 89–92, 183–84.

19. Mallon, "Nationalist and Anti-State Coalitions," 266; Mallon, *Defense of Community*, 83–84; Manrique, *Campesinado y nación*, 58–83; Nelson Manrique, *Yawar mayu: Sociedades terratenientes serranas, 1879–1910* (Lima: DESCO, 1988), 25–29; Luis Milón Duarte, *Exposición que dirije el Coronel Luis Milón Duarte a los Hombres de Bien*, ed. José Dammert Bellido (Cajamarca: privately published, 1983), 3–4; BNP, Archivo Piérola, s/n 1895–1897: Correspondencia Oficial y Particular, "Instrucciones del Comandante General de la 1ª Division del 2° Ejército del Centro, Luis Milón Duarte, al teniente D. Bernardo Vera," Huancayo, 31 May 1880; interview with Hernán Valladares, Huancayo, 3 June 1977; Mendoza, *La Campaña de la Breña*, 23–68; Adolfo Bravo Guzmán, *La segunda enseñanza en Jauja*, 2d ed. (Jauja, 1979), 654–58; AHM, "Memorias sobre la resistencia."

20. For a more detailed analysis of the organization of the resistance, see Andrés A. Cáceres, *La guerra del 79: Sus campañas. Memorias*, ed. Julio C. Guerrero (Lima: Editoria Milla Batres, 1973), 95–196 (*"idóneos"* appears on p. 99); Manrique, *Campesinado y nación*, 85–180; Mallon, "Nationalist and Anti-State Coalitions," 241–46; Mallon, *Defense of Community*, 82–95. On the possible inspiration Cáceres might have received from the Mexican experience, see Duarte, *Exposición . . . a los Hombres de Bien*, 11–12.

21. On the relatively successful and "seamless" nature of alliances in the area around Jauja, see Mallon, *Defense of Community*, 87–88, 94; Mendoza,

La Campaña de la Breña, 146–49; Manrique, *Campesinado y nación*, 159–62.

22. AHM, "Memorias sobre la resistencia," 5–8. The picture of Salazar presented here is a composite of the information provided in Bravo Guzmán, *La segunda enseñanza*, 291n, and Mendoza, *La Campaña de la Breña*, 233–34; I also benefited from the reproduction of a photograph of Salazar, in Mendoza, 193. For reproductions of the letters exchanged between the alcalde of Comas and Salazar, furnished by Salazar himself, see ibid., 383–84.

23. Salazar's version is found in AHM, "Memorias sobre la resistencia," 5–8; and Mendoza, *La Campaña de la Breña*, 137–40. The official communiqués about the battle are also reproduced by Mendoza, 386–90. The second of these reports, supposedly by the officials of Comas, is written in language that smacks of reworking and "packaging"—though by whom it is hard to say.

24. Duarte, *Exposición . . . a los Hombres de Bien*, 30–33. The first long quotation appears on p. 30; the discussion of the virgins and the second long quotation on p. 31. The construction of a racist discourse in order to justify his collaboration with the Chileans—particularly around the apathy, barbarism, and politically primitive nature of the Indian masses—is apparent at various points in the memoirs. See esp. pp. 4, 33–37, 38, 47, 50–51, 52, 56–59.

25. Rafael Concha Posadas, *Nuestras gestas guerrilleras indígenas*, Comas, distrito ochentenario de Jauja, en la Defensa Nacional de la Campaña de la Breña, prologue by Dr. M. Leopoldo García, notes by Nelson Manrique (Lima: Taller de Lontipia, 1937), 14–21; CPHEP, *La Guerra del Pacífico, 1879–1883: La resistencia de la Breña*, tomo 2, *La contraofensiva de 1882: 23 Feb. 1882–5 Mayo 1883* (Lima: Ministerio de Guerra, 1982), 152–55.

26. CPHEP, *La resistencia de la Breña*. The quote from Duarte appears on p. 34.

27. Concha Posadas, *Nuestras gestas guerrilleras indígenas*, 20–38; CPHEP, *La resistencia de la Breña*, 2:152–56.

28. Mendoza (*La Campaña de la Breña*) reproduces the following documents that help demonstrate the form taken by Salazar's personal ambitions and his translation of Comas's participation into personal gain: "Parte oficial del combate de Sierralumi elevado al General Cáceres por el Comandante Salazar," 3 Mar. 1882 (386–88); "El General Cáceres nombra a Ambrosio Salazar Comandante Militar de la Plaza de Comas," 30 Mar. 1882 (391–92); "Contestación del General Cáceres a Ambrosio Salazar," 30 May 1882 (390–91); "Parte del Combate de Concepción elevado por el Comandante Ambrosio Salazar, Jefe de las Guerrillas de Comas, al Coronel Juan Gastó," 10 July 1882 (397–401); "Expediente Militar del

Teniente Coronel Ambrosio Salazar y Márquez" (442–44). See also AHM, "Memorias sobre la resistencia," especially the introduction, p. 5. The comparison to Bernal Díaz del Castillo is based on his *The Conquest of New Spain*, trans. J. M. Cohen (Baltimore: Penguin Books, 1963). I am grateful to Steve J. Stern for a conversation that suggested the parallel between Salazar's memoirs and the colonial *documentos de probanza*.

29. CPHEP, *La resistencia de la Breña*, 2:151–56.

30. Mendoza, *La Campaña de la Breña*, 388–90, reproduces the official *parte* sent to Cáceres by the political authorities of Comas. For hints of the conflict, see p. 389. I have doubts about the authenticity of this document, given its language, date, and source; but it is difficult to know one way or the other, since village documents were often written down by local intellectuals, such as teachers or priests. In any case, it is clearly an elaborated and "constructed" narrative. Also, what would have constituted a total victory under the circumstances? The total lack of survivors? For other hints of divisions within the community, see Concha Posadas, *Nuestra gestas guerrilleras indígenas*, 20–32.

31. It is easy to build a case for Salazar's hearing of the ambush while in Marancocha, then rushing to the community to appropriate the "official narrative." The differences between his version and those in Comas, as well as his total silence on the issues of the virgins and of women's participation, lend credence to suspicions concerning his absence, as does the fact that he did not compose the letter to Cáceres until the next day, quite unusual after such an important victory. All the versions of the Comas action except Salazar's are in agreement on the demand for virgins. All the versions for Chupaca are also in agreement on this point. See below, this chapter. On gender as a central element in the elaboration of war narratives, see also Nancy Huston, "Tales of War and Tears of Women," *Women's Studies International Forum* 5, nos. 3–4 (1982): 271–82.

32. Manrique, *Campesinado y nación*, 144–48, 155–61; Mendoza, *La Campaña de la Breña*, 142–78; Mallon, *Defense of Community*, 87–88; Cáceres, *La guerra del 79*, 174–75.

33. Aquilino Castro Vásquez, *Los guerrilleros de Chupaca y la guerra con Chile* (Lima: Editorial Universo, 1982), 50–52. Other versions of what happened in Chupaca can be found in CPHEP, *La resistencia de la Breña*, 2:157–61, and Mendoza, *La Campaña de la Breña*, 144–45.

34. Castro Vásquez, *Los guerrilleros de Chupaca*, 60–61; CPHEP, *La resistencia de la Breña*, 2:157–61.

35. Castro Vásquez, *Los guerrilleros de Chupaca*, 60–62. The quotations are from pp. 61 and 62, respectively.

36. CPHEP, *La resistencia de la Breña*, 2:155–61. The quotation on errors appears on p. 155, as does the reference to *emponchados*. The long quotation appears on p. 161.

37. We owe this insight to Waldemar Espinoza Soriano. See especially his *Enciclopedia Departamental de Junín*, vol. 1 (Huancayo: Editor Enrique Chipoco Tovar, 1974).

38. APJ, "Acta de los hijos del pueblo de Cincos," Sincos, 11 Apr. 1882.

39. On the use of the violation of female chastity as a symbolic "marker" in the case of Huaripampa, see CPHEP, *La resistencia de la Breña*, 2:172. For the oral memory from Acolla, see 2:180–82; for Huaripampa and Muqui-yauyo, see 2:172–77. For the maintenance of unity during the years of national reconstruction, see Mallon, *Defense of Community*, 105–7.

40. The letter was found in APJ, "Oficio de los guerrilleros de Acobamba al Sor. Civilista Don Jacinto Cevallos," 16 Apr. 1882. It has been previously analyzed in the following places: Mallon, *Defense of Community*, 89–92; Mallon, "Nationalist and Anti-State Coalitions," 243–45; Manrique, *Campesinado y nación*, 167; and Manrique, *Yawar mayu*, 54–55.

41. Despite his decidedly pro-Salazar position and his tendency to mini-mize the autonomous importance of the montoneras, Mendoza provides the data for my counterinterpretation. See *La Campaña de la Breña*, 187–90. For Mendoza's opinions about the montoneras, see pp. 71, 86, 141. For his position on Salazar, see pp. 233–36. For Salazar's version of the battle of Concepción, see AHM, "Memorias sobre la resistencia," 105. For another discussion of the same battle that takes issue with some of Salazar's pro-nouncements, see Manrique, *Campesinado y nación*, 188–94.

42. Duarte, *Exposición . . . a los Hombres de Bien*, 50–51; the long quo-tation appears on p. 50. On dating the invasion of Punto, Manrique cites a document from the Huancayo notary M. F. Peña in which Benjamina Ibarra, Jacinto Cevallos's wife and owner of the hacienda Punto, already considered the property invaded in June 1882 (*Yawar mayu*, 54n).

43. On this period of activity for the llacuaz guerrillas, see especially Manrique, *Campesinado y nación*, 263–77, and Smith, *Livelihood and Re-sistance*, 67–74. On the changing contours of Iglesias's alliance with the Chileans, see below, this chapter.

44. The evidence on this point is indirect. It is interesting to note, for example, that in the known battles in the Mantaro Valley during 1883, against the Urriola expedition, Comas did not participate substantially (CPHEP, *La Guerra del Pacífico, 1879–1883: La resistencia de la Breña*, tomo 3, vol. 2, *Huamachuco en el alma nacional: 1882–1884* [Lima: Minis-terio de Guerra, 1983], 1129–44). By 1886 Cáceres had sent an expedition to the central sierra to collect the firearms in the hands of private citizens, especially peasant guerrillas (APJ, "Oficio del Ministerio de Gobierno al Prefecto del Departamento de Junín," Lima, 18 Jan. 1886); and we have specific information that by 1888 firearms were fairly widespread among Comasinos (Manrique, *Yawar mayu*, 70–75). Finally, in a document from 1887 cited by Nelson Manrique (ibid., 65n) the gobernador de Concepción

reported that a woman from Comas had been buying gunpowder in the market and asking if lead was available.

45. On the changing priorities of alliance for Cáceres, see Nelson Manrique, "La ocupación y la resistencia," in Jorge Basadre et al., eds., *Reflecciones en torno a la Guerra de 1879* (Lima: Francisco Campodónico–Centro de Investigación y Capacitación, 1979), 304–5; *Campesinado y nación*, 331–73; Mallon, *Defense of Community*, 99–101; and Mallon, "Nationalist and Anti-State Coalitions," 247–48.

46. AHM, Paq. 0.1884.2: "Oficio del General Remigio Morales Bermúdez al Ministro de Guerra y Marina," Lima, 24 Dec. 1884; "Oficio del Comandante General de la Quinta Division al Jefe del Estado Mayor General del Ejército," Huancayo, 15 Dec. 1884; "Oficio del Comandante General de la Quinta Division al Jefe del Estado Mayor del Ejército," Huancayo, 31 Dec. 1884; Paq. s/n 1885: "Oficio del Prefecto y Comandante General del departamento de Junín al Ministro de Guerra y Marina," Cerro de Pasco, 2 Feb. 1885; Paq. 0.1884.6, Prefecturas: "Oficio del Prefecto de Junín al Ministro de Guerra," Chongos Alto, 7 Dec. 1884; "Parte del Prefecto de Junín al Ministro de Guerra y Marina," Huancayo, 10 Dec. 1884; "Oficio del Prefecto al Ministro de Guerra y Marina," Tarma, 23 Dec. 1884; and "Oficio de Andrés Recharte al Ministro de Guerra," Tarma, 26 Nov. 1884.

47. APJ, "Oficio de los guerrilleros de Acobamba al Sor. Civilista Don Jacinto Cevallos," 16 Apr. 1882.

48. The translation of the Laimes quotation is taken from Smith, *Livelihood and Resistance*, 75; the quotation from Smith appears on p. 74.

49. For Esponda's version of the Laimes incident, see the section of his memoirs reproduced in CPHEP, *La resistencia de la Breña*, 2:301–2. For other accounts of the execution of Laimes, see Manrique, *Campesinado y nación*, 358–64; Mallon, *Defense of Community*, 100; and Smith, *Livelihood and Resistance*, 75–76. The versions that deal most directly with the accusations against Laimes, as presented in the version of the trial reproduced in the Lima newspaper *El Comercio*, are Manrique and Smith.

50. My summary of the "official versions" of the Laimes story relies heavily on Manrique, *Campesinado y nación*, 358–64, which reproduces the Prialé quotation on p. 363 and quotes extensively from *El Comercio* on pp. 358–59; and on Smith, *Livelihood and Resistance*, 74–76, with citations of Prialé and *El Comercio* on pp. 76 and 75, respectively.

51. Smith, *Livelihood and Resistance*, 76.

52. Smith (ibid., 244 n. 14) discusses the Hobsbawm assertion. Manrique discusses these issues in *Campesinado y nación*, 361, 364.

53. On the consolidation of the Capitán, see Manuel Burga, *Nacimiento de una utopía: Muerte y resurrección de los Incas* (Lima: Instituto de Apoyo Agrario, 1988). A more general discussion of conquest dances can be found in Nathan Wachtel, *The Vision of the Vanquished: The Spanish Conquest of*

Peru Through Indian Eyes, 1530–1550, trans. Ben and Sian Reynolds (New York: Barnes and Noble, 1977). The specific descriptions of the Capitán in Burga appear on pp. 36–39 and 41–51. The quotations appear on pp. 43 and 51, respectively.

54. On the prohibitions on dances in the southwestern Mantaro during the early 1880s, which included the Capitán, and the short permission granted in 1882, see Manrique, *Yawar mayu,* 44–46. Samaniego's description of the dance occurs in "Location," 324.

55. My reasoning on the Capitán dance for the central highlands, and the possible changes it underwent, is based on Samaniego, "Location," 324–37, and Burga, *Nacimiento de una utopía,* 36–51. The evidence on resonance with Juan Santos and Túpac Amaru comes from Stern, "Age of Andean Insurrection," 51–53, 64–66. Evidence of "borrowing" with regard to another dance in the central highlands, Los Avelinos or La Mactada, which represents the guerrilla war of the 1880s and was reintroduced to Acolla from Huancavelica, comes from Zoila S. Mendoza, "La danza de 'Los Avelinos,' sus orígenes y sus múltiples significados," *Revista Andina* 7, no. 2 (Dec. 1989): 501–21; and from oral testimony in Acolla by don Moisés Ortega, CPHEP, *La resistencia de la Breña,* 2:182–84.

56. In the debates about the "Andean utopia," I do not think that my analysis of Inca symbolism in this new context would contradict the spirit of Alberto Flores Galindo's work (*Buscando un Inca: Identidad y utopía en los Andes* [Havana: Casa de las Américas, 1986]), although I would have more trouble tying it into Burga's work in *Nacimiento de una utopía.*

57. The conflict over the livestock taken from the haciendas in Comas district can be traced in the following documents: APJ, "Solicitud de Juan E. Valladares, Fernando Valladares, Petronila Ruiz V. de Ibarra, José Maria Lora, Antonio Galarza y Jacinto Cevallos, al Prefecto del Departamento de Junín," Huancayo, 10 Aug. 1886; "Solicitud de Juan E. Valladares al Ministro de Gobierno," Lima, 4 June 1886, and attached resolution; "Copia de la resolución de Andrés Cáceres sobre el expediente seguido por Manuel Fernando Valladares," Huancayo, 18 June 1884; "Nueva resolución sobre la misma materia," Jauja, 23 July 1885; and "Oficio del Ministerio de Gobierno al Prefecto del Departamento de Junín, sobre la situación en Comas y Pariahuanca," Lima, 3 Aug. 1886. For the letter from Guillermo Ferreyros to the Comasinos, see APJ, "Copia de la Nota del Sr. Prefecto al Governador de Comas con insercion del decreto espedido por el Presidente Provisorio V.S.S. D. Andres A. Caseres [*sic*] en la causa criminal que sigue D. Manuel Fernando Balladares [*sic*]," Huancayo, 31 July 1884.

58. For the meeting in Santa Rosa de Ocopa, see APJ, "Copia del compromiso preliminar de las autoridades y vecinos notables del pueblo de Comas, con el Señor Manuel Fernando Valladares, firmado en el pueblo de Santa Rosa de Ocopa, 22 de febrero de 1886," copy taken in Concepción,

27 July 1886. The 1887 letter, including the quotation, was found in APJ, "Solicitud de tres vecinos y naturales de Parco del Distrito de Comas, al Prefecto del Departamento," Jauja, 9 Sept. 1887.

59. Mallon, *Defense of Community*, 105–7.

60. For an overview of the political events of this period, see Jorge Basadre, *Historia de la república del Perú, 1822–1933*, 6th ed., 17 vols. (Lima: Editorial Universitaria, 1968), 8:448–55, 9:7–23.

61. Ibid., 9:24–32; AHM, Paq. 0.1884.2: "Parte de Remigio Morales Bermúdez, poniendo sus fuerzas a disposición del Ministerio de Guerra y Marina," Lima, 24 Dec. 1885.

62. AHM, Paq. 0.1884.2: "Oficios de Pedro Más, Comandante General de la 1ª División del Ejército, 'Pacificadora del Centro,'" Acobamba, 21 Nov. 1884; Ayacucho, 28 Nov. 1884. For the actas from the municipal assemblies held in November 1884, see BNP, D4355: "Oficio dirigido por el Prefecto del departamento de Junín al Director de Gobierno," Pachachaca, 7 Nov. 1885. For sources on the skirmishes with montoneras, see the next three notes.

63. On Acobamba, see AHM, Paq. 0.1884.2: "Parte de Luis R. Irigoyen sobre el combate de 16 de noviembre," 17 Nov. 1884; "Oficios de Pedro Más, Comandante General de la 1ª División del Ejército, 'Pacificadora del Centro,'" Acobamba, 21 Nov. 1884, and Ayacucho, 28 Nov. 1884, the second of which contains the quotation; and Paq. 0.1884.6, Prefecturas: "Oficio del Gobernador del distrito de Acobamba al Subprefecto de la provincia," Acobamba, 30 Nov. 1884. On Huancavelica, see AHM, Paq. s/n 1885: "Parte del Prefecto y Comandante General de Huancavelica al Ministro General de Estado," Acoria, 24 Nov. 1884; Paq. 0.1884.2: "Oficio de Pedro Más al Ministro de Guerra y Marina," Ayacucho, 30 Nov. 1884; and BNP, D4257: "Oficio dirigido por el Prefecto de Huancavelica sobre el ataque de los montoneros," Huancavelica, 1 Dec. 1884. On Huanta, see AHM, Paq. 0.1884.2: "Oficio de Remigio Morales Bermúdez al Ministro General del Estado," Andahuaylas, 5 Dec. 1884; "Oficio de Pedro Más al Ministro de Guerra y Marina," Ayacucho, 17 Dec. 1884; and Paq. 0.1885.2: "Oficio de Remigio Morales Bermúdez al Ministro General de Estado," 3 Jan. 1885. For further comments on the important activities of the guerrillas along this axis between November 1884 and February 1885, see also AHM, Paq. 0.1884.2: "Oficios de Remigio Morales Bermúdez al Ministro General del Estado," Ayacucho, 17 and 20 Nov. 1884; and "Oficios de Pedro Más al Ministro de Guerra y Marina," Ayacucho, 4 and 12 Dec. 1884.

64. For Recharte's letter to the War Ministry, see AHM, Paq. 0.1884.6, Prefecturas: "Oficio del Prefecto de Junín al Ministro de Guerra," Chongos Alto, 7 Dec. 1884, which includes the quoted matter.

65. The rest of Recharte's report can be found in AHM, Paq. 0.1884.6, Prefecturas: "Parte del Prefecto del Departamento de Junín al Ministro de Guerra y Marina," Huancayo, 10 Dec. 1884. For Godinez's commentary, see

Paq. 0.1884.2: "Oficios de José Godinez al Coronel Jefe del Estado Mayor General del Ejército," Huancayo, 15 and 31 Dec. 1884, the latter one containing the word "imprudence." For further evidence of the montoneros' autonomy in this area, see AHM, 0.1885.2: "Parte de Eduardo Jessup a Pedro Más," Huancayo, 12 May 1885; "Parte de Pedro Más al Ministerio de Guerra," Huancayo, 22 May 1885; Paq. s/n 1885: "Oficio del Prefecto de Junín al Ministerio de Guerra y Marina," Cerro de Pasco, 2 Feb. 1885; "Oficio del Prefecto de Junín al Ministerio de Guerra y Marina," Cerro de Pasco, 17 Feb. 1885; and "Oficio del Prefecto al Ministerio de Guerra y Marina," Jauja, 20 Apr. 1885.

66. For events around Huaripampa, see Basadre, *Historia de la República del Perú*, 9:27–29; BNP, D4355: "Oficio del Prefecto del departamento de Junín al Director de Gobierno," Pachachaca, 7 Nov. 1885; and AHM, Paq. 0.1884.2: "Parte final de Remigio Morales Bermúdez, Comandante en Jefe del Ejército Constitucional," Lima, 24 Dec. 1885. See also the rest of Morales Bermúdez's report.

67. AHM, Paq. 0.1884.2: "Parte final de Remigio Morales Bermúdez," Lima, 24 Dec. 1885.

68. On Guerra's commission, see APJ, "Oficio del Ministerio de Gobierno al Prefecto del Departamento de Junín," Lima, 18 Jan. 1886. For Rizo Patrón's assessment, see AHM, Paq. s/n 1886: "Oficio del Prefecto de Junín al Ministerio de Guerra," Cerro de Pasco, 16 Feb. 1886, which also includes the quotation. On Guerra's position in Chupaca and his earlier relationship with the llacuaces, see above, this chapter.

69. I discuss the failure of Guerra's mission in Mallon, *Defense of Community*, 101–3. See also Manrique, *Yawar mayu*, 59–61. The importance of the region's peasant guerrillas to overall stability had already been proven in the civil war, when small armies of between two and five thousand regular soldiers could be most effectively harassed by a contingent of two thousand guerrillas, favored by their knowledge of the geography and by the use of hit-and-run tactics. In such a situation the Cacerista officials—having used these guerrillas to overturn Iglesias—were particularly eager to not have it happen to them.

70. On the place occupied by Cáceres's Jauja strategy in his overall attempt to pacify the central region, see Mallon, "Nationalist and Anti-State Coalitions," 247–48. On the process in the Jauja area itself, see also Mallon, *Defense of Community*, 105–7; BNP, D6954: "Nuevo Personal de los Concejos Distritales, Junín," June 1888; Adams, *Community in the Andes*, 29–32; Bravo Guzmán, *La segunda enseñanza*, 302; William B. Hutchinson, "Sociocultural Change in the Mantaro Valley Region of Peru: Acolla, a Case Study," Ph.D. diss., Indiana University, 1973, 29–30; and APJ, "Informe de la Subprefectura de Huancayo al Prefecto del Departamento," Huancayo, 17 Feb. 1897.

71. On the role of riverbank notables, such as Bartolomé Guerra, in the earlier conflicts, and the execution of the region's independent commanders in 1884, see above, this chapter. On the organization of the Comisión Especial, see APJ, "Oficio del Ministerio de Gobierno al Prefecto del Departamento de Junín," Lima, 12 Nov. 1888.

72. For some examples of the pressure put on the state by the central sierra hacendados and their allies in congress, see APJ, "Oficio de Juan E. Valladares al Ministro de Gobierno," Huancayo, 7 June 1886; "Oficio de Juan E. Valladares y otros al Prefecto del Departamento de Junín," Huancayo, 10 Aug. 1886; and the follow-ups by congressional representatives in BNP, D11941: "Expediente seguido para la devolución a sus legítimos dueños de las haciendas ocupadas por los indios de Jauja y Huancayo, a raíz de la última contienda civil," Lima, 3 Sept. 1886; "Oficio de los Diputados por la provincia de Huancayo, Arturo Morales Toledo y Juan Quintana, al Ministro de Gobierno," Lima, 3 Sept. 1886; "Oficio de los Diputados Teodomiro A. Gadea y Daniel de los Heros, al Ministro de Estado en el Despacho de Gobierno," Lima, 24 Aug. 1888.

73. BNP, D8207: "Copia certificada de los decretos expedidos por la Comisión Especial del Supremo Gobierno en el departamento de Junín sobre las cuestiones agrarias promovidas por las comunidades de Putaca y Chongos Alto con la Hacienda Antapongo," Huancayo, 26 Apr. 1889. The document includes other cases not directly mentioned in the title. The quotation on "social order" is from one of these, "Decreto de la Comisión Especial sobre el pedido de las Sras. Josefa y María Jesús Cárdenas," Huancayo, 6 May 1889.

74. For sources on the pattern of conflict during the 1884–85 civil war, and the generally low profile of Comas, see above, notes 44, 46, 62, 65, and 66. For the assassination of the political authority from Apata, see AHM, Paq. 0.1885.2: "Parte de Pedro Más sobre el asesinato del teniente gobernador de Apata," Huancayo, 19 May 1885. For the one reference I have found to Comasino participation in the civil war, see APJ, "Solicitud de varios vecinos de Comas al Prefecto del Departamento," Jauja, 9 Sept. 1887.

75. On the occupation of Punto and Callanca by guerrillas from the Comas area, see Manrique, *Yawar mayu*, 54–55. On the issue of livestock in the same region, see ibid., 63–66. On the initial demand by Cacerista officials that the villages return the livestock, see APJ, "Oficio del Prefecto del Departamento de Junín al Gobernador del Distrito de Comas," Huancayo, 31 July 1884. For the letter from representatives of Comas to the prefect, see APJ, "Solicitud de varios vecinos de Comas al Prefecto del Departamento," Jauja, 9 Sept. 1887, which also includes the quotation.

76. APJ, "Copia de un oficio de las autoridades de Comas a las autoridades y notables de la comunidad de Uchubamba, hecha por Manuel Oré," Comas, 25 Jan. 1888.

77. I have analyzed the letter from the Comas authorities to Uchubamba in Mallon, *Defense of Community*, 111–13, and "Nationalist and Anti-state Coalitions," 249–50. Manrique analyzes it in *Yawar mayu*, 72–79.

78. Manrique discusses the possible socialist pedigree of Osambela and the letter, as well as the peasantry's lack of "advanced" consciousness, in *Yawar mayu*, 76–79. For the possible relationship to Mexican discourses on rights, see above, chapter 5.

79. For the letter signed by Esteban Paytanpoma and others, see APJ, "Oficio de varios vecinos de Comas al Subprefecto de la Provincia," Comas, 1 Feb. 1888; it includes the quotation. For the rejoinder by the authorities, see "Oficio de las autoridades del distrito de Comas al Subprefecto de la provincia," Comas, 1 Feb. 1888. For the other documents mentioning Osambela, see "Oficio del Gobernador de Concepción al Subprefecto de la provincia de Jauja," Concepción, 2 Feb. 1888; and "Oficio del Subprefecto de Jauja al Prefecto del Departamento de Junín," Jauja, 14 Feb. 1888.

80. On the renewed pressure by congressional authorities, see BNP, D11941: "Oficio de los Diputados Teodomiro A. Gadea y Daniel de los Heros, al Ministro de Estado en el Despacho de Gobierno," Lima, 24 Aug. 1888. On the preparation of the military expedition, see BNP, D11466: "Parte Oficial sobre la expedición a 'Punto,'" Huancayo, 15 Jan. 1889.

81. BNP, D11466: "Parte Oficial sobre la expedición a 'Punto,'" Huancayo, 15 Jan. 1889; this document includes the quotation.

82. Ibid.

83. For the actions of Carvallo in the area, see BNP, D12845: "Expediente sobre la reclamación de propiedad de la Hacienda Punto, formulada por los vecinos de ella," Huancayo, 8 May 1889. For the attempt to inventory Callanca, see APJ, "Oficio de Estevan Paytanpoma, Bacilio Espinoza y Bruno Solís, al Prefecto del Departamento," Comas, 24 June 1889. For attempts to communicate and enforce Carvallo's decision, see APJ, "Oficio del Subprefecto de Huancayo, Andrés Freyre, al Prefecto del Departamento," Huancayo, 25 June 1889; and "Oficio del Subprefecto de Jauja al Prefecto Accidental del Departamento," Jauja, 25 Mar. 1890.

84. On Valladares's complaint, see APJ, "Denuncia de Manuel Fernando Valladares al Prefecto del Departamento," Concepción, 10 Mar. 1892; "Denuncia de Manuel Fernando Valladares al Subprefecto de Jauja," Jauja, 11 Mar. 1892; "Queja de Andrés A. Reyes, del Distrito de Comas, al subprefecto de Jauja," Comas, 11 June 1892; "Parte de los comisionados Ames, Carpio y Bullón sobre su investigación en Comas," Comas, 23 July 1892; "Resolución en el caso de Manuel F. Valladares contra el Gobernador del distrito de Comas y otros," 27 Aug. 1892. For the subprefect's report on the continuing elusiveness of state authority in Comas, see APJ, "Memoria Administrativa del Subprefecto Andrés Freyre al Prefecto del Departamento," Jauja, 3 June 1893. The issue of the contribución, moreover, is

quite complex. In July 1886 the Cacerista government had decreed that those who had fought in the Cacerista army should be exempted from its payment through 1888 (APJ, "Copia de la Suprema Resolución de 3 de julio de 1886, sobre la contribución personal," Lima, 8 July 1886). It was specified in that decree, however, that only those soldiers fighting in the civil war with Iglesias, and only those with an official discharge, would receive the exemption. Many of the Comasinos, as members of autonomous irregular forces, did not have any papers and were therefore liable for payment. In keeping with the spirit of the decree as they understood it, however, as well as their own earlier understanding of their rights, they did not pay.

85. BNP, Doc. D12842: "Proyecto de ley sobre repartición de las tierras de comunidad," Tarma, 11 July 1889. Quotations appear, in order of appearance in the paragraph, on ff. 8, 9, 11, 12. I am grateful to Mark Thurner for bringing this document to my attention.

86. Ibid., ff. 13–15.

87. Peru, Congreso Ordinario de 1892, *Diario de los Debates de la H. Cámara de Senadores* (Lima: Imprenta de "El Comercio," 1892), 437, 719–33; the quotation appears on p. 719. See also Congreso Ordinario de 1895, *Diario de los Debates de la H. Cámara de Senadores* (Lima: Imprenta de "El País," 1895), 442.

88. Peru, Congreso Ordinario de 1891, *Diario de los Debates de la H. Cámara de Senadores* (Lima: Imprenta de "El Comercio," 1891), 675.

CHAPTER 7. COMMUNAL HEGEMONY
AND ALTERNATIVE NATIONALISMS

1. Some of the texts reproducing the heroic narrative of the Mexican Revolution, and the role of Zapatismo in it, are Jesús Sotelo Inclán, *Razón y vida de Zapata*, 2d ed. (Mexico City: Comisión Federal de Electricidad, 1970); John Womack, Jr., *Zapata and the Mexican Revolution* (New York: Knopf, 1968); Arturo Warman, . . . *y venimos a contradecir: Los campesinos de Morelos y el estado nacional* (Mexico City: Centro de Investigaciones Superiores del INAH, Ediciones de la Casa Chata, 1976); Gastón García Cantú, *Utopías mexicanas*, 2d ed. (Mexico City: Fondo de Cultura Económica, 1986), 165–89, esp. 180–89; and Alan Knight, *The Mexican Revolution*, 2 vols. (Cambridge and New York: Cambridge University Press, 1986).

2. For a more complete analysis of the literature on the Peruvian central highlands, see chapter 6. For a broad comparative view of the history of the two countries, see Florencia E. Mallon, "Indian Communities, Political Cultures, and the State in Latin America, 1780–1990," *Journal of Latin American Studies* 24, suppl. (fall 1992): 35–53.

3. Sotelo Inclán, *Razón y vida de Zapata*, 420–21; quotation from p. 421.

4. Ibid., 501.

5. Oscar Lewis, *Pedro Martínez: A Mexican Peasant and His Family* (New York: Vintage Books, 1964), 102.

6. Ibid., 265.

7. Oscar Lewis, *Life in a Mexican Village: Tepoztlán Restudied* (Urbana: University of Illinois Press, 1963), 53.

8. Lewis, *Pedro Martínez*, 88.

9. Sotelo Inclán, *Razón y vida de Zapata*, and Womack, *Zapata and the Mexican Revolution*. On the Sierra de Puebla, see Luisa Paré, "Inter-ethnic and Class Relations (Sierra Norte Region, State of Puebla)," in *Race and Class in Post-Colonial Society: A Study of Ethnic Group Relations in the English-Speaking Caribbean, Bolivia, Chile, and Mexico* (Paris: UNESCO, 1977), 377–420. A recent ethnohistory of an upland community in Peru's central highlands is Gavin Smith, *Livelihood and Resistance: Peasants and the Politics of Land in Peru* (Berkeley: University of California Press, 1989). An original and stimulating discussion of "othering" as central to colonial discourse is Edward Said, *Orientalism* (New York: Vintage Books, 1979). See also Kumkum Sangari and Sudesh Vaid, eds., *Recasting Women: Essays in Indian Colonial History* (New Brunswick: Rutgers University Press, 1990).

10. The quotations compared here are from AGNM, Gobernación: Leg. 1144(1), "Petición de cinco vecinos y notables de Tepoztlán al Emperador," Mexico City, 28 Aug. 1865, and AHMTO, Gobierno, Caja s/n 1866: Exp. 71, "Acta de la Guardia Nacional de Tetela de Ocampo, sobre las condiciones impuestas por Ignacio R. Alatorre," 22 July 1868.

11. Carmen Diana Deere, "Changing Relations of Production and Peruvian Peasant Women's Work," *Latin American Perspectives* 4, nos. 1–2 (winter–spring 1977): 48–69; Deere, "The Development of Capitalism in Agriculture and the Division of Labor by Sex: A Study of the Northern Peruvian Sierra," Ph.D. diss., University of California, Berkeley, 1978; Deere, *Household and Class Relations: Peasants and Landlords in Northern Peru* (Berkeley: University of California Press, 1990), part 1; and Lewis Taylor, "Main Trends in Agrarian Capitalist Development: Cajamarca, Peru, 1880–1976," Ph.D. thesis, University of Liverpool, 1979.

12. Taylor, "Main Trends," 17–23.

13. Ibid., 27–32; Lewis Taylor, "Los orígenes del bandolerismo en Hualgayoc, 1870–1900," in Carlos Aguirre and Charles Walker, eds., *Bandoleros, abigeos y montoneros: Criminalidad y violencia en el Perú, siglos XVIII–XX* (Lima: Instituto de Apoyo Agrario, 1990), 213–47; ADC, Particulares, 1880–1889: "Carta del hacendado Daniel Silva Santisteban al Subprefecto de la provincia," Hacienda Chonta, 21 Apr. 1881; Gobernadores del Distrito de San Marcos, 1854–1899: "Oficio del Gobernador José Castañaduy al Subprefecto," n.d.; "Oficio del Gobernador José Castañaduy al Subprefecto," 13 Dec. 1881; Prefectura, 1880–1885: "Circular del Prefecto P. J. Carrión al Subprefecto del Cercado," 1 Sept. 1881; Particulares, 1880–89: "Oficio de

Manuel María Arana, hacendado de La Laguna, al Subprefecto," Cajamarca, 1 Jan. 1881; Prefectura, 1880–1885: "Resolución del Jefe Superior del Norte, comunicado por el Prefecto Tadeo Terry al Subprefecto del Cercado," 19 Oct. 1881; "Decreto del Prefecto Tadeo Terry sobre la solicitud de Dn. Carlos Montoya Bernal, apoderado de María Arana," 15 Oct. 1881; Subprefectura de Cajamarca, 1880–1885: "Oficio del Subprefecto Manuel B. Castro a las autoridades de su dependencia," 22 Sept. 1881; and Particulares, 1880–1889: "Oficio de la Abadesa del Convento de Religiosas Descalzas Concebidas de Cajamarca, al Prefecto," 28 Oct. 1884.

14. Taylor, "Main Trends," 13–14, 16, 19; ADC, Subprefectura de Jaén, 1880–1889: "Marjesí de las Rentas de la extinguida Beneficencia de la Provincia de Jaén presentada por el Subprefecto Baltazar Contreras," 15 Mar. 1885; Particulares: "Solicitud de Manuel Collazos al presidente de la República Miguel Iglesias," Lima, 3 Nov. 1885; Subprefectura de Jaén, 1880–1889: "Informe del Subprefecto Arróspide sobre la provincia de Jaén," 2 May 1887.

15. ADC, Subprefectura de Jaén, 1880–1889: "Oficio del Gobernador de San Felipe al Subprefecto de Jaén," 29 Apr. 1880; "Oficio del Subprefecto de Jaén al Prefecto," Pucará, 10 Dec. 1882; Subprefectura de Chota, 1880–1889: "Oficio del Subprefecto de Chota al Prefecto del Departamento," 12 May 1884; "Oficio del Subprefecto de Chota al Prefecto del Departamento, transcribiendo oficio del gobernador del distrito de Llama," May 1884; Subprefectura de Jaén, 1880–1889: "Oficio del Subprefecto de Jaén al Prefecto," Cutervo, 15 Oct. 1884; "Marjesí de las Rentas de la extinguida Beneficencia de la Provincia de Jaén presentada por el Subprefecto Baltazar Contreras," 15 Mar. 1885.

16. Taylor, "Los orígenes del bandolerismo"; ADC, Gobernadores del Distrito de San Marcos, 1854–1899: "Oficio del Gobernador Manuel María Lazo al Prefecto," 8 Apr. 1880; "Oficio del Gobernador José Castañaduy al Subprefecto," n.d.; "Oficio del Gobernador José Castañaduy al Subprefecto," 13 Dec. 1881; Prefecturas, 1880–1885: "Oficio del Prefecto Leonardo Cavero al Subprefecto del Cercado," 13 May 1881; and "Oficio del Gobernador Manuel Rubio al Subprefecto," 15 May 1882.

17. Jorge Basadre, *Historia de la república del Perú, 1822–1933*, 6th ed., 17 vols. (Lima: Editorial Universitaria, 1968), 6:272–80, 406–11; Patricio Lynch, *Segunda memoria que el Vice-Almirante D. Patricio Lynch presenta al supremo Gobierno de Chile*, 2 vols. (Lima: Imp. de la Merced, 1883–1884), 2:94–100; and Nelson Manrique, "La ocupación y la resistencia," in Jorge Basadre et al., eds., *Reflecciones en torno a la guerra de 1879* (Lima: Francisco Campodónico–Centro de Investigación y Capacitación, 1979), 277–78.

18. On Becerra's being named subprefect of Chota and on his support for continued resistance, see ADC, Subprefectura de Chota, 1880–1889: "Oficio del Subprefecto Manuel J. Becerra al Prefecto, acusando recibo de la copia del

oficio de Montero," 22 May 1881; ADC, Subprefectura de Chota, 1880–1889: "Oficio del Subprefecto Eulogio Osores al Prefecto," 25 May 1880; "Terna para gobernador del distrito de Cuervo, presentada por Manuel A. Negrón," Chota, 28 Mar. 1881; Subprefectura de Jaén, 1880–1889: "Oficio del Subprefecto J. de la R. Salgado al Prefecto," 20 May 1882; "Oficio del Subprefecto de Jaén Baltazar Contreras al Prefecto," 10 Sept. 1885; BNP, D3712: "Oficio N° 3: Prefecto de Cajamarca Miguel Pajares, al Director de Gobierno," Cajamarca, 1883.

19. ADC, Subprefectura de Jaén, 1880–1889: "Oficio del Subprefecto J. de la R. Salgado al Prefecto," Pucará, 1 Apr. 1883; Subprefectura de Chota, 1880–1889: "Oficio del Subprefecto de Chota al Prefecto del departamento," 12 May 1884; "Oficio del Subprefecto de Chota al Prefecto del departamento, transcribiendo oficio del gobernador del distrito de Llama," May 1884; Subprefectura de Jaén, 1880–1889: "Oficio del Subprefecto de Jaén al Prefecto," Cuervo, 7 Sept. 1884; "Oficio del Subprefecto de Jaén al Prefecto," Cuervo, 15 Oct. 1884; Subprefectura de Chota, 1880–1889: "Oficio del Subprefecto de Chota Timoteo Tirado al Prefecto," 6 Feb. 1884; Subprefectura de Jaén, 1880–1889: "Oficio del Subprefecto de Jaén al Prefecto del Departamento," Cuervo, n.d.; Subprefectura de Chota, 1880–1889: "Oficio del Subprefecto de Chota Timoteo Tirado al Prefecto," Bambamarca, 26 May 1884; "Oficio del Subprefecto de Chota al Prefecto del Departamento," 18 Dec. 1884; Subprefectura de Jaén, 1880–1889: "Oficio del Subprefecto de Jaén al Prefecto," Cuervo, 6 Feb. 1885; "Oficio del Subprefecto de Jaén al Prefecto," Cuervo, 14 Feb. 1885; Subprefectura de Chota, 1880–1889: "Oficio del Subprefecto de Chota al Prefecto," 27 Mar. 1885; Subprefectura de Jaén, 1880–1889: "Oficio del Subprefecto de Jaén al Prefecto," Cuervo, 13 May 1885; "Oficio del Subprefecto de Jaén Baltazar Contreras al Prefecto," 10 Sept. 1885; Particulares, 1880–1889: "Oficio de Baltazar Contreras al Alcalde Pedro Ceballos," Cuervo, 25 May 1885.

20. ADC, Subprefectura de Jaén, 1880–1889: "Oficio del Subprefecto J. de la R. Salgado al Prefecto," Pucará, 1 Apr. 1883; Subprefectura de Chota, 1880–1889: "Oficio del Subprefecto de Chota al Prefecto," 12 May 1884; "Oficio del Subprefecto de Chota al Prefecto del Departamento, transcribiendo oficio del gobernador del distrito de Llama," May 1884; "Oficio del Subprefecto de Chota Timoteo Tirado al Prefecto," Bambamarca, 26 May 1884; "Oficio del Subprefecto de Chota al Prefecto," 18 Dec. 1884; Subprefectura de Jaén, 1880–1889: "Oficio del Subprefecto de Jaén Baltazar Contreras al Prefecto," 10 Sept. 1885; "Oficio del Subprefecto de Jaén al Prefecto," Cuervo, 14 Feb. 1885; "Oficio del Subprefecto de Jaén al Prefecto," Cuervo, 13 May 1885; Particulares, 1880–1889: "Oficio de Baltazar Contreras al Alcalde Pedro Ceballos," Cuervo, 25 May 1885; "Oficio de Nicolás Tellos, Hacienda Llaucan, al Prefecto del Departamento," 18 Nov. 1885; Subprefectura de Jaén, 1880–1889: "Informe del Subprefecto Miguel

Arróspide sobre la provincia de Jaén," 2 May 1887; "Informe del Subprefecto Miguel Arróspide sobre el Presupuesto para 1889," 16 Apr. 1888.

21. The desperate report from Jaén's prefect is found in ADC, Subprefectura de Jaén, 1880–1889: "Oficio del Subprefecto de Jaén al Prefecto," Cutervo, 15 Oct. 1884. The description of Becerra tearing up receipts for the head tax is found in "Oficio del Subprefecto de Jaén al Prefecto," Cutervo, 7 Sept. 1884. See also "Oficio del Subprefecto de Jaén al Prefecto," Cutervo, n.d.; "Oficio del Subprefecto de Jaén al Prefecto," Cutervo, 3 Nov. 1884; Particulares: "Solicitud de Manuel Collazos al presidente de la República Miguel Iglesias," Lima, 3 Nov. 1885; Subprefectura de Jaén, 1880–1889: "Oficio del Subprefecto de Jaén Baltazar Contreras al Prefecto," 10 Sept. 1885; "Oficio del Subprefecto de Jaén al Prefecto," Cutervo, 6 Feb. 1885; "Oficio del Subprefecto de Jaén al Prefecto," Cutervo, 13 May 1885.

22. ADC, Subprefectura de Chota, 1880–1889: "Oficio del Subprefecto Eulogio Osores al Prefecto," 25 May 1880; Subprefectura de Jaén, 1880–1889: "Oficio del Subprefecto de Jaén al Prefecto," Cutervo, 13 May 1885.

23. ADC, Subprefectura de Jaén, 1880–1889: "Informe del Subprefecto Arróspide sobre la provincia de Jaén," 2 May 1887.

24. Taylor, "Main Trends," 81–82; Nelson Manrique, *Campesinado y nación: Las guerrillas indígenas en la guerra con Chile* (Lima: Ital Perú–C.I.C., 1981), 218–22; Basadre, *Historia de la república del Perú*, 8:408–12; AHM, Colección Vargas Ugarte: Leg. 54, "Organización del Ejército del Norte dicatada por el General Miguel Iglesias," Lima, 3 Jan. 1880; ADC, Subprefectura de Cajamarca, 1880–1885: "Oficio del Subprefecto Serna al Prefecto," 19 Feb. 1882; Gobernadores del Distrito de San Marcos, 1854–1899: "Oficio del Gobernador Manuel Rubio al Subprefecto de Cajamarca," 28 Dec. 1882; "Oficio del Gobernador Manuel Rubio al Subprefecto," 25 Jan. 1883.

25. ADC, Gobernadores del Distrito de Ichocán, 1856–1899: "Oficio del Gobernador Santos G. Cobán al Prefecto," Distrito de Ichocán, 18 July 1880; "Oficio del Gobernador Santos G. Cobán al Subprefecto," 18 Sept. 1881; "Oficio del Gobernador Santos G. Cobán al Subprefecto," 12 Dec. 1881; Gobernadores del Distrito de San Marcos, 1854–1899: "Oficio del gobernador Manuel Rubio al Subprefecto," 25 Oct. 1882; "Oficio del gobernador Manuel Rubio al Subprefecto de la provincia," 12 Oct. 1882; "Oficio del gobernador Manuel Rubio al Subprefecto de la provincia," 20 Sept. 1882; "Oficio del gobernador Manuel Rubio al Subprefecto de Cajamarca," 27 Oct. 1882; "Oficio del gobernador Manuel Rubio al Subprefecto de Cajamarca," 31 Oct. 1882.

26. ADC, Gobernadores del Distrito de San Marcos, 1854–1899: "Oficio del Gobernador Manuel María Lazo al Prefecto," 8 Apr. 1880; "Oficio del Gobernador José Castañaduy al Subprefecto," n.d., 1881; "Oficio del Gobernador José Castañaduy al Subprefecto," 13 Dec. 1881; "Oficio del Gober-

nador Lizardo Zevallos al Subprefecto," 26 June 1881; "Oficio del Gobernador Manuel Rubio al Subprefecto," 15 May 1882; Subprefectura de Cajamarca, 1880–1885: "Oficio del Subprefecto Manuel Castro al Prefecto," 28 Oct. 1881; "Oficio del Subprefecto Serna al Prefecto," 19 Feb. 1882.

27. ADC, Gobernadores del Distrito de San Marcos, 1854–1899: "Oficio del Gobernador Manuel Rubio al Subprefecto," 15 May 1882; Alcaldías de los distritos de Cajamarca, 1855–1899: "Oficio del Alcalde Pedro W. Zevallos al Prefecto," Ichocán, 31 July 1883. It is interesting, in this context, to note the presence of two women in auxiliary combat roles in Puga's montonera in 1884: AHM, Paq. 0.1884.6, Prefecturas: "Oficio de Gregorio Relayze, Comandante General de la División de Operaciones en el Norte, al Ministro de Estado en el Despacho de Guerra y Marina," Cajabamba, 27 May 1884.

28. On conflicts between members of the Chinese community and "Peruvians" in Cajamarca, see ADC, Corte Superior de Justicia, Causas ordinarias: Leg. 58, "El asiático Wing-Walon con Don Justiniano Guerrero sobre cumplimiento de un contrato," Cajamarca, 15 Oct. 1881; Leg. 62, "D. Manuel Rubio con el asiático Colorado sobre pago de cantidad de soles," Cajamarca, 11 Jan. 1882; Leg. 54, "Dn. Juan Chavarria con Dn. Luis Maradiegue, sobre entrega de dos caballos," Cajamarca, 19 May 1880. On the participation of Chinese men in Puga's montonera, see ADC, Alcaldías de los distritos de Cajamarca, 1855–1899: "Oficio del Alcalde Pedro W. Zevallos al Prefecto," Ichocán, 31 July 1883; Particulares, 1880–1889: "Solicitud de Francisco Deza, asiático, al Prefecto del Departamento," Cajamarca, 7 Dec. 1883; and AHM, Correspondencia General, Paq. 0.1883.1: "Oficio del Comandante en Jefe de las fuerzas del Norte al Ministro de Estado en el Despacho de Guerra y Marina," Cajamarca, 6 Jan. 1884.

29. For a very different kind of involvement by women during a period of war, see Florencia E. Mallon, *Constructing Third World Feminisms: Lessons from Nineteenth-Century Mexico (1850–1874)*, Women's History Working Papers Series, no. 2 (Madison: University of Wisconsin, 1990), and chapter 3 of this book.

30. AHM, Correspondencia General, Paq. 0.1883.1: "Oficio del Comandante en Jefe de las fuerzas del Norte al Ministro de Estado en el Despacho de Guerra y Marina," San Marcos, December 1883; "Oficio del Comandante en Jefe de las fuerzas del Norte al Ministro de Estado en el Despacho de Guerra y Marina," Cajamarca, 9 Dec. 1883; Colección Recavarren, Manuscritos, Cuaderno 10: "Oficio de José Mercedes Puga a Recavarren," Hacienda Huagal, 18 July 1883, pp. 72–73; Ordenes Generales y Correspondencia, Paq. 0.1883.2: "Oficio del Jefe de las fuerzas expedicionarias al distrito de la Asunción," Cajamarca, 6 May 1883; BNP, D3710: "Nota dirigida por el Prefecto y Comandante General del Departamento de la Libertad D. Z. Relayze adjuntando documentos relativos a la invasion de la provincia de Huamachuco por el caudillo Dr. José Mercedes Puga," Trujillo, 29 Mar. 1885.

31. BNP, D3710: "Nota dirigida por el Prefecto y Comandante General del Departamento de la Libertad D. Z. Relayze adjuntando documentos relativos a la invasion de la provincia de Huamachuco por el caudillo Dr. José Mercedes Puga," Trujillo, 29 Mar. 1885; AHM, Paq. s/n 1885: "Oficio de la Prefectura y Comandancia General del departamento de La Libertad, firmado por Juan N. Vargas, al Oficial Mayor del Ministerio de Guerra y Marina," Trujillo, 7 Nov. 1885; BNP, D7974: "Expediente sobre la petición hecha por Josefa Hoyle vda. de Pinillos y Ana Hoyle de Loyer para que se declare sin lugar la solicitud de los Sres. Pinillos sobre la confiscación de la Hda. 'Uningambal,'" Trujillo, 3 Oct. 1885; Archivo Piérola, Caja (Antigua), no. 53, Correspondencia Oficial y Particular: "Carta de M. Serapio Pinillos a Nicolás de Piérola," Santiago de Chuco, 16 Apr. 1896.

32. For Puga's and Becerra's deaths, see ADC, Particulares: "Solicitud de Manuel Collazos al presidente de la República Miguel Iglesias," Lima, 3 Nov. 1885; and BNP, D3710: "Nota dirigida por el Prefecto y Comandante General del Departamento de la Libertad D. Z. Relayze adjuntando documentos relativos a la invasion de la provincia de Huamachuco por el caudillo Dr. José Mercedes Puga," Trujillo, 29 Mar. 1885. On the lack of Cacerista control in the area, see BNP, D3980: "Memoria que presenta el Prefecto de Lambayeque, Crel. Federico Ríos, al Ministro de Gobierno, Policía y Obras Públicas sobre el estado del Departamento de su mando," Chiclayo, 26 Apr. 1886; D11375: "Expediente sobre el oficio dirigido por el Prefecto del departamento de Cajamarca, Jacinto A. Bedoya, al Director de Gobierno, pidiéndole el aumento de la fuerza pública en esa plaza," Cajamarca, 21 Oct. 1889; D5156: "Memoria del Subprefecto de Cajamarca, Tomás Ballón, al Prefecto del Departamento," Cajamarca, 3 June 1892; and D7611: "Notas sobre el envio de una expedición a Gorgor con el fin de capturar a Román Egües García y Cia," Cajatambo, 7 Dec. 1895. On the Cacerista commanders fighting during the civil war, see BNP, D3704: "Inventario de los daños causados en la casa prefectural de la ciudad de Cajamarca por las montoneras comandadas por el Dr. José Mercedes Puga," Cajamarca, 11 Jan. 1884; D3995: "Memorial elevado al Ministro de Gobierno por los vecinos de la villa de Supe . . . ," Supe (Provincia de Chancay), 13 Feb. 1884; D3797: "Oficio dirigido por el Prefecto del departamento de la Libertad a la Dirección de Gobierno, adjuntando documentos relativos a las correrías de la montonera capitaneada por Romero," Trujillo, 9 May 1885; AHM, Paq. 0.1884.2: "Carta del gobernador del distrito de Huánuco, Pedro P. Reina, al prefecto y comandante general del departamento," 17 Mar. 1884; Paq. 0.1884.6, Prefecturas: "Oficio del Prefecto y Comandante General del Departamento de Lambayeque al oficial mayor del Ministerio de Guerra y Marina," Chiclayo, 9 July 1884; Paq. 0.1884.1: "Oficio de Fernando Seminario al coronel jefe de la expedición," Pariamonga, 30 Nov. 1884; Paq. s/n 1885: "Oficio de M. Mondoñedo,

designado jefe superior político y militar de los departamentos de Piura, Lambayeque y Cajamarca, por don Andrés A. Cáceres, al alcalde del distrito de Chongoyape," 1 May 1885.

33. On support for Piérola in the Cajamarca area, see BNP, Archivo Piérola, Copiador no. 16, 1889–1890, Correspondencia Oficial y Particular, Norte: "Oficio de Piérola al Presidente del Comité Departamental de Trujillo, José María de la Puente," 3 July 1889; Caja (Antigua) no. 41, 1892–1895: "Cartas de Nicolás Rebaza y Santiago Rebaza Demóstenes, de Trujillo, felicitando a Piérola y comunicándole ser partidarios fervorosos de él . . . ," 28 Mar. 1895; "Carta de Vicente González y Orbegoso a Piérola," Hacienda Motil, 12 Apr. 1895; "Carta de Rafael Villanueva a Piérola," Cajamarca, 13 Apr. 1895; Caja (Antigua) no. 45, 1895: "Carta de José María de la Puente a Piérola," Trujillo, 13 July 1895; "Carta de Isidro Burga a Piérola," Cajamarca, 17 June 1895; "Oficio de Isidro Burga a Cruz Toribio Cruz," 29 May 1895; and s/n Correspondencia Oficial y Particular: "Carta de Miguel Iglesias a Nicolás de Piérola," Hacienda Udima, 18 July 1895. On the difficulties of control after the war, see Taylor, "Main Trends," 86–87, 103–15, 177–79; AHM, Paq. 0.1885.2: "Oficio de J. Borgoño al Ministro de Guerra y Marina," Trujillo, 3 Jan. 1886; and "Oficio del Prefecto del Departamento de Piura al señor oficial mayor del Ministerio de Guerra," 15 June 1886.

34. In Peru, the term *gamonalismo* has generally been used to designate the system of regionalization of power in which local powerholders, most often hacendados, delivered the loyalty of "their" areas in return for support from the central state in maintaining their personal control in their regions. On the pandemic nature of violence in the area, see BNP, Archivo Piérola, Caja (Antigua) no. 50, 1895–1899: "Carta de Rafael Villanueva a Piérola," Cajamarca, 27 June 1897; "Carta del Prefecto de Cajamarca, Belisario Ravinez, a Piérola," Cajamarca, 21 June 1897; "Carta del Prefecto de Cajamarca, Belisario Ravinez, a Piérola," Cajamarca, 20 June 1897; "Carta del Prefecto de Cajamarca, Belisario Ravinez, a Piérola," Cajamarca, 24 May 1897; "Carta de Rafael Villanueva a Piérola," Cajamarca, 1 Feb. 1897; "Carta del Prefecto de Cajamarca, Belisario Ravinez, a Piérola," Cajamarca, 11 Jan. 1897; "Carta del Prefecto de Cajamarca, Belisario Ravinez, a Piérola," Cajamarca, 28 Dec. 1896. On banditry, see John Gitlitz, "Conflictos políticos en la Sierra Norte del Perú: La montonera Benel contra Leguía, 1924," *Estudios Andinos* 9, no. 16 (1980): 127–38; Taylor, "Main Trends," 106–15; Lewis Taylor, *Bandits and Politics in Peru: Landlord and Peasant Violence in Hualgayoc, 1900–1930* (Cambridge: Centre of Latin American Studies, 1987); and especially Taylor, "Los orígenes del bandolerismo." Rodrigo Montoya commented to me in personal conversation, Lima 1981, about the difficulties the police had encountered entering the boundaries of Cajamarca's haciendas as late as the 1960s.

CHAPTER 8. THE INTRICACIES OF COERCION

1. On the case of Nicolás de la Portilla, see above, chapter 5, and Florencia E. Mallon, "Peasants and State Formation in Nineteenth-Century Mexico: Morelos, 1848–1858," *Political Power and Social Theory* 7 (1988): esp. 25–28. On Ignacio Alatorre, see chapters 2 and 4 of this book. On Andrés Freyre, see chapter 6.

2. Philip Corrigan and Derek Sayer, *The Great Arch: English State Formation as Cultural Revolution* (Cambridge, Mass.: Basil Blackwell, 1985). For an application of Gramsci and theories of hegemony to "Third World" processes of state formation, see Partha Chatterjee, *Nationalist Thought and the Colonial World—A Derivative Discourse?* (Tokyo: Zed Books for the United Nations University, 1986).

3. A recent and well-reasoned consideration of how Juárez moved toward the centralization of power, often over the bodies of principled liberal allies, is Laurens Ballard Perry, *Juárez and Díaz: Machine Politics in Mexico* (De Kalb: Northern Illinois University Press, 1978).

4. For Díaz's appointment of Méndez, see Perry, *Juárez and Díaz*, 55, and CEHM-C, Fondo XXVIII-1: Doc. 495, "Carta del General Porfirio Díaz a Rafael J. García," Guadalupe Hidalgo, 25 Apr. 1867. For the Convocatoria, see CEHM-C, Fondo XXVIII-1:, Doc. 513, "Convocatoria a elecciones dada por el Presidente Benito Juárez," Mexico City, 14 Aug. 1867. For reactions in Puebla and elsewhere, see BN-AJ, Doc. 3494: "Juan N. Méndez a Benito Juárez," 22 Aug. 1867; Doc. 2960: "Rafael J. García a Benito Juárez," 24 Aug. 1867; Doc. 3360: "Clemente López a Benito Juárez," 26 Aug. 1867; and Perry, *Juárez and Díaz*, 38–44, 55–56. On Méndez's sending representatives to discuss the issues more fully with Juárez, see BN-AJ, 3494: "Juan N. Méndez a Benito Juárez," 22 Aug. 1867.

5. On Juárez's clarification, see Perry, *Juárez and Díaz*, 40–41. For Méndez's particularly impassioned letter, see BN-AJ, Doc. 3499: "Juan N. Méndez a Benito Juárez," 30 Aug. 1867. For additional correspondence between Juárez and Méndez about the Convocatoria, see BN-AJ, Doc. 3497: "Juan N. Méndez a Benito Juárez," 26 Aug. 1867; and Doc. 3498: "Juan N. Méndez a Benito Juárez," 26 Aug. 1867. For additional opposition and Juárez's response, see BN-AJ, Doc. 3360: "Clemente López a Benito Juárez," 26 Aug. 1867, and attached answer, 30 Aug. 1867.

6. For an analysis of the contradictions involved in instituting the rule of law in distinction both to the executive power and to regional constituencies, see Mallon, "Peasants and State Formation"; Richard Sinkin, "The Mexican Constitutional Congress, 1856–1857: A Statistical Analysis," *Hispanic American Historical Review* 53, no. 1 (Feb. 1973); and Sinkin, *The Mexican Reform, 1855–1876: A Study in Nation-Building* (Austin: Institute of Latin American Studies, University of Texas Press, 1979). For the view of Méndez as a cacique, see Perry, *Juárez and Díaz*, 32, 56, 83; and François-Xavier

Guerra, *México: Del antiguo régimen a la revolución*, trans. Sergio Fernández Bravo, 2 vols. (Mexico City: Fondo de Cultura Económica, 1988), 1:78, 96, 98, 101.

7. For the publication of the dismembered Convocatoria, see CEHM-C, Fondo XXVIII-1: Doc. 523, "Juan N. Méndez, Gobernador Civil y Militar del Estado de Puebla, publica la Convocatoria," Puebla, 14 Sept. 1867. For García's letter, which contains both quotations, see BN-AJ, Doc. 2961: "Rafael J. García a Benito Juárez," 17 Sept. 1867.

8. For the words written across the bottom of the letter, see BN-AJ, 2961: "Rafael J. García a Benito Juárez," 17 Sept. 1867. For the telegram from Lerdo, see AHDN, XI/481.4/9786, f. 44.

9. AHDN, XI/481.4/9786: "Oficio de Juan N. Méndez al Ministro de Guerra," Puebla, 22 Sept. 1867, ff. 48–49v; the quotation appears on f. 49.

10. I engage in a more detailed comparison of Méndez's and García's military records in chapter 4. The original information is in ACDN, "Expediente del General Juan N. Méndez" and "Expediente del General Rafael García."

11. On the earlier case with González Ortega, see Perry, *Juárez and Díaz*, 36–39. For Lerdo's communication to García, see AHDN, XI/481.4/9786: "Telegrama del Ministerio de Guerra a Rafael J. García, con copia a Juan N. Méndez," ff. 50–51; the quotation appears on f. 50v.

12. For concerns about Méndez's cache of arms, see BN-AJ, Doc. 2964: "Rafael J. García a Benito Juárez," 30 Sept. 1867; Doc. 2389: "Carta de Antonio Carvajal a Benito Juárez," 1 Oct. 1867; Doc. 4211: "Pablo María Zamacona a Benito Juárez," 1 Oct. 1867; Doc. 2390: "Antonio Carvajal a Benito Juárez," 3 Oct. 1867; and AHDN, XI/481.4/9786: "General Luis P. Figueroa al Ministerio de Guerra," 25 Sept. 1867, f. 67. For the work done by supporters of Méndez and Díaz in different districts, see BN-AJ, Doc. 4212: "Pablo María Zamacona a Benito Juárez," 2 Oct. 1867; Doc. 2974: "Rafael J. García a Benito Juárez," 13 Oct. 1867; Doc. 3393: "José María Maldonado a Benito Juárez," 13 Oct. 1867; Doc. 2976: "Rafael J. García a Benito Juárez," 14 Oct. 1867; and Doc. 2977: "Rafael J. García a Benito Juárez," 15 Oct. 1867. For the removal of political authorities loyal to Méndez and the importance of this to the result of the elections, see BN-AJ, Doc. 2965: "Informe reservado de Rafael J. García a Benito Juárez," 3 Oct. 1867; Doc. 2968: "Rafael J. García a Benito Juárez," 8 Oct. 1867; Doc. 2969: "Rafael J. García a Benito Juárez," 10 Oct. 1867; Doc. 2971: "Rafael J. García a Benito Juárez," 11 Oct. 1867; and Doc. 2976: "Rafael J. García a Benito Juárez," 14 Oct. 1867. For the instructions from Díaz to Méndez, see BN-AJ, Doc. 3503: "José de Jesús Islas a Juan N. Méndez," 25 Sept. 1867. Méndez's resignation can be found in AHDN, XI/481.4/9786: "Oficio de Juan N. Méndez al Ministerio de Guerra y Marina," 25 Sept. 1867, f. 63. The process of reconstructing Juarista majorities began with the publication of the "real"

Convocatoria by García on September 28. See CEHM-C, Colección Puebla: "Rafael José García, Gobernador Civil y Militar del Estado de Puebla, a sus habitantes," Puebla de Zaragoza, 28 Sept. 1867. For the removal of Mendista political officials or postponement of elections, see BN-AJ, Doc. 2965: "Informe reservado de Rafael J. García a Benito Juárez," 3 Oct. 1867; Doc. 2968: "Rafael J. García a Benito Juárez," 8 Oct. 1867; Doc. 2969: "Rafael J. García a Benito Juárez," 10 Oct. 1867; Doc. 2971: "Rafael J. García a Benito Juárez," 11 Oct. 1867; Doc. 2972: "Rafael J. García a Benito Juárez," 12 Oct. 1867; Doc. 2976: "Rafael J. García a Benito Juárez," 14 Oct. 1867; Doc. 2977: "Rafael J. García a Benito Juárez," 15 Oct. 1867; and Doc. 2978: "Rafael J. García a Benito Juárez," 16 Oct. 1867. On the use of money to support those working for Juárez, as well as on the general work done by Juaristas in the different political districts, see BN-AJ, Doc. 3111: "Julio H. González a Benito Juárez," 11 Oct. 1867; Doc. 2319: "Jose Antonio Rodríguez Bocardo a Benito Juárez," 11 Oct. 1867; Doc. 2973: "Rafael J. García a Benito Juárez," 12 Oct. 1867; Doc. 3393: "José María Maldonado a Benito Juárez," 13 Oct. 1867; Doc. 4202: "Antonio Zamacona a Benito Juárez," 17 Oct. 1867. On Juárez's direct intervention, see BN-AJ, Doc. 3378: "Juan Francisco Lucas a Benito Juárez," 10 Oct. 1867; Doc. 3393: "José María Maldonado a Benito Juárez," 13 Oct. 1867; Doc. 3394: "José María Maldonado a Benito Juárez," 18 Oct. 1867; and Doc. 3395: "José María Maldonado a Benito Juárez," 20 Oct. 1867. On the primary elections as litmus test, as well as the general process and results of the elections, see BN-AJ, Doc. 3393: "José María Maldonado a Benito Juárez," 13 Oct. 1867; Doc. 3394: "José María Maldonado a Benito Juárez," 18 Oct. 1867; Doc. 3395: "José María Maldonado a Benito Juárez," 20 Oct. 1867; Doc. 2974: "Rafael J. García a Benito Juárez," 13 Oct. 1867; Doc. 2594: "Rafael Cravioto a Benito Juárez," 21 Oct. 1867; Doc. 3324: "Miguel Lira y Ortega a Benito Juárez," 21 Oct. 1867; and Doc. 3112: "Julio H. González a Benito Juárez," 22 Oct. 1867.

13. On the construction of a discourse of rebellion in 1868, see above, chapter 4. On Porfirio Díaz's presence in Puebla, Méndez's work from Tlaxcala, and a general overview of the 1867 electoral process in the state, see Perry, *Juárez and Díaz*, 75–88.

14. For the correspondence around García's resignation, see BN-AJ, Doc. 2982: "Rafael J. García a Benito Juárez," 22 Oct. 1867; AHDN, XI/481.4/9786: "Renuncia formal de Rafael J. García," 22 Oct. 1867, f. 71. For the publication of his formal resignation, see *Periódico Oficial de Puebla*, 31 Oct. 1867, p. 1. For the various maneuvers to keep Méndez from being able to present a legal candidacy for governor, see BN-AJ, Doc. 2964: "Rafael J. García a Benito Juárez," 30 Sept. 1867; Doc. 2968: "Rafael J. García a Benito Juárez," 8 Oct. 1867; Doc. 2972: "Rafael J. García a Benito Juárez," 12 Oct. 1867; Doc. 2980: "Rafael J. García a Benito Juárez," 17 Oct. 1867; and Doc. 2985: "Rafael J. García a Benito Juárez," 25 Oct. 1867. For the private

negotiations with Rafael Cravioto, resulting in the Cravioto family's being able to cover some of their war debts from the customs receipts at Tuxpan, see BN-AJ, Doc. 2594: "Rafael Cravioto a Benito Juárez," 21 Oct. 1867; Doc. 3112: "Julio H. González a Benito Juárez," 22 Oct. 1867; Doc. 2596: "Rafael Cravioto a Benito Juárez," 28 and 29 Oct. 1867; and AGNEP, Huauchinango, Caja 2, 1861–1870, Libro 1867, s/n/f 7 Nov. 1867: "Poder que otorga Luz Moreno, viuda de Simón Cravioto, a Don Domingo Calzada." On the negotiations with Juan Francisco Lucas, which resulted in a payment of an indemnity of 2,400 pesos to Xochiapulco, see BN-AJ, Doc. 3377: "Juan Francisco Lucas a Benito Juárez," 23 Oct. 1867; Doc. 3378: "Juan Francisco Lucas a Benito Juárez," 31 Oct. 1867; Doc. 2991: "Rafael J. García a Benito Juárez," 6 Nov. 1867; Doc. 3397: "José María Maldonado a Benito Juárez," 6 Nov. 1867; Doc. 3379: "Benito Juárez a Juan Francisco Lucas," 14 Nov. 1867; Doc. 3398: "José María Maldonado a Benito Juárez," 16 Nov. 1867. On the elections for state congress as litmus test for political factions, see BN-AJ, Doc. 2990: "Rafael J. García a Benito Juárez," 4 Nov. 1867; Doc. 3397: "José María Maldonado a Benito Juárez," 6 Nov. 1867; and Doc. 2321: "José Antonio Rodríguez Bocardo a Benito Juárez," 7 Nov. 1867.

15. BN-AJ, Doc. 2990: "Rafael J. García a Benito Juárez," 4 Nov. 1867, including the quotation; BN-AJ, Doc. 3398: "José María Maldonado a Benito Juárez," 16 Nov. 1867; and BN-AJ, Doc. 3921 and 3920: "Ignacio Romero Vargas a Benito Juárez," 19 and 11 Nov. 1867, respectively. Romero's rehabilitated friend was Gutiérrez Delgado, whose name appears in the sessions of ACEP, Book 1, 1868.

16. BN-AJ, Doc. 3969: "Carta reservada de Joaquín Ruiz a Benito Juárez," 16 Nov. 1867.

17. The analysis in this paragraph is based on the following documents: BN-AJ, Doc. 2997: "Rafael J. García a Benito Juárez," Puebla, 29 Nov. 1867; Doc. 3924: "Ignacio Romero Vargas a Benito Juárez," Puebla, 29 Nov. 1867; and Doc. 3399: "José María Maldonado a Benito Juárez," Puebla, 2 Dec. 1867.

18. On the process and outcome of debates over the electoral law, its ultimate content, and García's attempts to influence outcomes at the district level, see ACEP, Libro 1: Sesión ordinaria, 13 Dec. 1867, f. 16; Sesión pública ordinaria, 14 Dec. 1867, f. 18; Sesión extraordinaria, 16 Dec. 1867, ff. 21–25; Sesión pública extraordinaria, 17 Dec. 1867; Sesión pública extraordinaria, 20 Dec. 1867, ff. 35–37v; Sesión pública y ordinaria, 21 Dec. 1867, ff. 37–37v.

19. For an analysis of the second gubernatorial election and congressional debate, see above, chapter 4. On García's military record, see ACDN, "Expediente del General Rafael García." On Romero's record, see "Expediente del General Ignacio Romero Vargas." On Rafael Cravioto, see above, chapter 2, and BN-AJ, Doc. 2592: "Rafael Cravioto a Benito Juárez," 29 July 1867; Doc. 2593: "Rafael Cravioto a Benito Juárez," Distrito Federal, 24 August 1867.

Cravioto was one of those chameleon-like Liberal politicians who survived extremely well throughout the Porfiriato. See Guerra, *México*, 1:98. For a late Porfirian attempt to discredit Cravioto on the basis of his record, though clearly not from an entirely disinterested point of view, see Miguel Galindo y Galindo, *La gran década nacional, o relación histórica de la guerra de reforma, intervención extranjera y gobierno del Archiduque Maximiliano. 1857–1867*, 3 vols. (Mexico City: Imprenta y Fototipía de la Secretaría de Fomento, 1906), 3:174–83. On Dimas López, see BN-AJ, Doc. 3004: "Rafael J. García a Benito Juárez," Puebla, 20 Dec. 1867, and Doc. 2599: "Rafael Cravioto a Benito Juárez," Huauchinango, 25 Dec. 1867. On José María Maldonado, see AGN(M), Archivo Leyva, Leg. XLIV: "Memoria del General José María Maldonado, sobre los sucesos en la sierra de Puebla en 1862 y 1863"; Ramón Sánchez Flores, *Zacapoaxtla: Relación histórica*, 2d ed. (Puebla: Edición del XIV Distrito Local Electoral de Zacapoaxtla, Puebla, 1984), 139–214. On Maldonado's frantic search for a pension and vendetta with Méndez, see, in addition to his letters to Juárez widely cited above, ACDN, "Expediente del General José María Maldonado." I also discuss Maldonado's radicalism in chapters 2 and 4.

20. BN-AJ, Doc. 2993: "Rafael J. García a Benito Juárez," 19 Nov. 1867.

21. On Bonilla's role during the empire, see above, chapter 2. On García's recommendation for another rehabilitation of an important Conservative leader in Zacapoaxtla, see BN-AJ, Doc. 3001: "Rafael J. García a Benito Juárez," Puebla, 8 Dec. 1867. On the participation of former Conservatives on the side of the federal government during the 1868 rebellion, see Doc. 5321: "Rafael J. García a Benito Juárez," 27 June 1868, and AHDN, XI/481.4/9786: "Oficio de J. A. Rodríguez Bocardo al Ministerio de Guerra," Tulancingo, 8 July 1868. On the collaboration of former Conservatives with the federal and state governments in the early 1870s, see XI/481.4/9787, Cuaderno II, passim; AHMTO, Gobierno, Caja s/n 1870/73–1874/78: "José María Bonilla, teniente coronel de la guardia nacional de Aquixtla, al General Rafael Cravioto," Aquixtla, 4 Apr. 1870; AHMZ, Paq. 1869: Exp. 74, "Oficio de Cenobio Cantero, comandante de batallón, al coronel del batallón en Zacapoaxtla," 5 Apr. 1870; "Oficio del gobierno de Puebla al jefe político de Zacapoaxtla," 4 May 1870; and ACEP, Expedientes, vol. 25, Apr.–Sept. 1870: "Aprobación de una resolución concediendo pensión a la viuda de Cenobio Cantero," Apr.–May 1873. On Méndez serving as the first Porfirian governor, see CEHM-C, Colección Puebla, *Corona Fúnebre Dedicada al Señor General de División Juan N. Méndez por Algunos Ciudadanos de Tetela de Ocampo, Amigos y Admiradores del Ilustre soldado del Progreso y la Democracia* (Mexico City: Imprenta de Daniel Cabrera, 1895).

22. On Morales Bermúdez's death and the subsequent civil war, see Jorge Basadre, *Historia de la república del Perú*, 6th ed., 17 vols. (Lima: Editorial

Universitaria, 1968), 10:93–128. The desire for a "disinterested" state comes out most clearly in the letters of Domingo F. Parra to Piérola. As special envoy, general troubleshooter, and personal friend to Piérola, Parra often wrote directly and sincerely of the overall concept and ambitions of the regime. See especially BNP, Archivo Piérola, Caja (Antigua), no. 53, 1895–1897, Correspondencia Oficial y Particular: "Carta de Domingo F. Parra a Nicolás de Piérola," Huancayo, 14 May 1896, and "Carta de Domingo F. Parra a Nicolás de Piérola," Huancayo, 18 May 1896; Archivo Piérola, 1895–1897, Correspondencia Oficial y Particular: "Carta Reservada de Domingo F. Parra a Nicolás de Piérola," Ayacucho, 29 Apr. 1897. For the appearance of similar discourses in the writings of others, see also BNP, D4505: "Memoria del Prefecto de Huancavelica," 1895; Archivo Piérola, Caja (Antigua), no. 53, 1895–97, Correspondencia Oficial y Particular: "Carta de F. Urbieta a Nicolás de Piérola," Jauja, 5 Apr. 1897; "Carta de E. Zapata a Nicolás de Piérola," Tarma, 19 Feb. 1897; and "Carta de E. Zapata a Nicolás de Piérola," Tarma, 19 Mar. 1897. Some sources on the "relative autonomy" of the state are: Nicos Poulantzas, *Political Power and Social Classes*, trans. Timothy O'Hagan (London: New Left Books, 1973); Poulantzas, "The Problem of the Capitalist State," *New Left Review*, no. 58 (Nov.–Dec. 1969): 67–78; Ralph Miliband, "The Capitalist State: Reply to Nicos Poulantzas," *New Left Review*, no. 59 (1970): 53–60; Miliband, "Poulantzas and the Capitalist State," *New Left Review*, no. 82 (1973): 83–92; Ernesto Laclau, "The Specificity of the Political: Around the Poulantzas-Miliband Debate," *Economy and Society* 4, no. 1 (Feb. 1975): 87–110; Nicos Poulantzas, "The Capitalist State: A Reply to Miliband and Laclau," *New Left Review*, no. 95 (Jan.–Feb. 1976): 63–83; Martin Carnoy, *The State and Political Theory* (Princeton: Princeton University Press, 1984); Nora Hamilton, *The Limits of State Autonomy: Post-Revolutionary Mexico* (Princeton: Princeton University Press, 1983); and Peter Evans, Theda Skocpol, et al., *Bringing the State Back In* (Cambridge and New York: Cambridge University Press, 1985).

23. On the idealized image of what the jungle highway could accomplish, see especially BNP, Archivo Piérola, 1895–1897, Correspondencia Oficial y Particular: "Carta Reservada de Domingo F. Parra a Nicolás de Piérola," Ayacucho, 29 Apr. 1897; and Caja (Antigua) no. 53, 1895–1897, Correspondencia Oficial y Particular: "Carta de F. Urbieta a Nicolás de Piérola," Jauja, 5 Apr. 1897. For an earlier analysis of this same issue, see Florencia E. Mallon, *The Defense of Community in Peru's Central Highlands: Peasant Struggle and Capitalist Transition, 1860–1940* (Princeton: Princeton University Press, 1983), 140–44. On conflicts among officials and accusations of corruption, see BNP, Archivo Piérola, Caja (Antigua) no. 53, 1895–1897, Correspondencia Oficial y Particular: "Carta de Francisco F. Urbieta a Nicolás de Piérola," Tarma, 27 Oct. 1896; "Carta de E. Zapata a Nicolás de Piérola," Tarma, 19 Mar. 1897; "Carta de E. Zapata a Nicolás de Piérola,"

Tarma, 25 Mar. 1897; and "Carta de F. Urbieta a Nicolás de Piérola," Jauja, 5 Apr. 1897. A complaint by a local hacendado about government competition on enganche can be found in BNP, Archivo Piérola, Caja (Antigua) no. 53, 1895–1897, Correspondencia Oficial y Particular: "Carta de V. Monier al Señor Nicolás de Piérola," Hacienda Naranjal, Chanchamayo, 7 Oct. 1896.

24. On the Piérola years in the central highlands, see Mallon, *Defense of Community*, 125–67. On the imprisonment and taxation of Dianderas, see BNP, Archivo Piérola, Caja (Antigua) no. 38, July–Dec. 1894, Correspondencia Oficial y Particular: "Carta de José María Dianderas a Nicolás de Piérola," Jauja, 30 Dec. 1894. On the repression of other enthusiastic Caceristas, and its importance for the reproduction of Pierolista authority in the area, see BNP, Archivo Piérola, Caja (Antigua) no. 53, 1895–1897, Correspondencia Oficial y Particular: "Carta de Domingo F. Argote a Nicolás de Piérola," Huancayo, 25 Nov. 1895; "Carta de Antonio Aliaga a Nicolás de Piérola," Chupaca, 23 Feb. 1896; "Carta de Domingo F. Parra a Nicolás de Piérola," Jauja, 11 May 1896; "Carta de Domingo F. Parra a Nicolás de Piérola," Huancayo, 14 May 1896; and "Carta de Domingo F. Parra a Nicolás de Piérola," Huancayo, 18 May 1896. The quotation appears in the last letter.

25. On the formation of the Junta de Notables in Huancayo, see APJ, "Oficio del Alcalde Provincial de Huancayo al Prefecto del Departamento," 18 May 1895. Viterbo Hostas, the new provincial mayor, had also served as representative for the owners of the hacienda Antapongo in earlier conflicts with Chongos Alto. See BNP, D12844: "Expediente sobre la cuestión surgida entre Chongos Alto y la hacienda Antapongo," Huancayo, 13 May 1889. On the advisory role the junta played in the formulation of Piérola's policy vis-à-vis Comas, see below, this chapter, and BNP, D5044: "Oficio dirigido por el Prefecto del departamento de Junín al Director de Gobierno," Huancayo, 29 Sept. 1896. On Jacinto Cevallos's tour, and the quotation, see BNP, Archivo Piérola, Caja (Antigua) no. 45, 1895: "Carta personal de Jacinto Cevallos a Nicolás de Piérola," Tarma, 18 June 1895. For other examples of Pierolista support for the landowner class, see also APJ, "Oficio del Subprefecto de Jauja al Prefecto del Departamento de Junín," Jauja, 7 Feb. 1898, and "Acta de formación de la Guardia Urbana de la ciudad de Concepción," Concepción, 10 Sept. 1898.

26. Domingo Parra's letter from Jauja, which includes the quotation about the subprefect, is in BNP, Archivo Piérola, Caja (Antigua) no. 53, 1895–1897, Correspondencia Oficial y Particular: "Carta de Domingo F. Parra a Nicolás de Piérola," Jauja, 11 May 1896. The other letters he wrote while on the same mission are "Carta de Domingo F. Parra a Nicolás de Piérola," Huancayo, 14 May 1896, and "Carta de Domingo F. Parra a Nicolás de Piérola," Huancayo, 18 May 1896. Argote's letter railing against Cacerristas is "Carta de Domingo F. Argote a Nicolás de Piérola," Huancayo, 25 Nov. 1895. For the quotation tying Argote to Cevallos, see ANP, Archivo

Piérola, Caja (Antigua) no. 53, 1895–1897, Correspondencia Sobre Varios Asuntos: "Carta de E. Zapata a Nicolás de Piérola," Tarma, 19 Feb. 1897.

27. For an earlier analysis of Piérola's self-identification as "protector of the Indian race," see Mallon, *Defense of Community*, 116, 133–34. For the contradictions in such a representation, see below, this chapter.

28. BNP, D5041: "Sucesos en la Hacienda Llacsapirca," Aug.–Sept. 1896.

29. BNP, D5044: "Oficio dirigido por el Prefecto del departamento de Junín al Director de Gobierno," Huancayo, 29 Sept. 1896, and accompanying "Acta de los notables de Huancayo," 29 Sept. 1896.

30. APJ, "Copia de la resolución del Gobierno sobre la solicitud de D^n Jacinto Cevallos," Lima, 6 Oct. 1896. Part of the reason for the government's refusal to commit arms to Comas in October 1896 could very well have been the recent resolution of a separatist rebellion in the jungle department of Loreto. See Basadre, *Historia de la república del Perú*, 10:175–80.

31. For the prefect's use of the word *rencillas*, see BNP, D5051: "Pacificación de Comas, y Acta de Adhesión por sus vecinos al Supremo Gobierno," Tarma-Jauja, 21–23 Nov. 1896, 5ff., especially "Carta del Prefecto C. Ramón Valle Riestra al Director de Gobierno," Tarma, 23 Nov. 1896. For some of the correspondence between González and Valle Riestra, and the first acta signed in Comas, see BNP, D5048: "Oficio del Prefecto del departamento de Junín al Director de Gobierno," Tarma, 6 Nov. 1896.

32. BNP, D5048: "Oficio de Luis A. González, cura-párroco de Comas, al Prefecto del Departamento," Comas, 2 Nov. 1896.

33. For the acta, as well as Valle Riestra's report on the conference, see BNP, D5051: "Oficio dirigido por el Prefecto del departamento de Junín al Director de Gobierno," Tarma, 23 Nov. 1896.

34. The analysis presented in this paragraph is the product of a comparison of the following documents: APJ, "Copia de un oficio de las autoridades de Comas a las autoridades y notables de la comunidad de Uchubamba," Comas, 25 Jan. 1888; "Oficio de varios vecinos de Comas al Subprefecto de la Provincia," Comas, 1 Feb. 1888; "Oficio de las autoridades del distrito de Comas al Subprefecto de la provincia," Comas, 1 Feb. 1888; BNP, D5048: "Acta de los vecinos de Comas, en cabildo abierto," Comas, 25 Oct. 1896; and D5051: "Acta de las autoridades y notables de Comas," Jauja, 21 Nov. 1896.

35. For other cases of district rivalry, and its importance to local politics over these years, see above, chapters 2, 4, 5, and 6. See also Mallon, *Defense of Community*, 65, 105–7, 291–93; and Florencia E. Mallon, "Alianzas multiétnicas y problema nacional: Los campesinos y el estado en Perú y México durante el siglo XIX," in Heraclio Bonilla, comp., *Los Andes en la encrucijada: Indios, comunidades y estado en el siglo XIX* (Quito, Ecuador: Ediciones Libri Mundi/FLASCO, 1991), 457–95.

36. The reference to Huanta by the Comasinos occurs in BNP, D5051: "Acta de las autoridades y notables de Comas," Jauja, 21 Nov. 1896. Basadre,

Historia de la república del Perú, 10:182–84, presents a schematic overview of the rebellion and the repression that followed. Patrick Husson provides a more in-depth vision of the movement based on primary sources: "Los campesinos contra el cambio social? El caso de dos sublevaciones en la provincia de Huanta (Perú) en el siglo XIX," in J. P. Deler and Y. Saint-Geours, comps., *Estados y naciones en los Andes: Hacia una historia comparativa*, 2 vols. (Lima: Instituto de Estudios Peruanos / Instituto Francés de Estudios Andinos, 1986), 1:154–68, esp. 161–65; see 1:163 for the reference to "el quintado." For bombings, ethnic contraguerrillas, and Parra's general discourse on the campaign, see AHM, Colección Vargas Ugarte: Leg. 69, "Memorandum de la Pacificación de las Provincias de Huanta y La Mar," by Domingo F. Parra, dated in Huanta, 20 Apr. 1897. The reference to African cannibals occurs on p. 4, insert on the back.

37. APJ, Subprefecturas: "Oficio del Subprefecto de Jauja al Prefecto del Departamento," Jauja, 9 July 1898; this document includes the quotation. On the issue of military force to reestablish order in Andamarca, see also APJ, "Oficio del Subprefecto Dulanto al Prefecto," Jauja, 14 July 1898; "Oficio del Subprefecto Dulanto al Prefecto," Jauja, 25 July 1898; and "Oficio del Subprefecto Dulanto al Prefecto," Jauja, 4 Aug. 1898.

38. On the attack on the comisaría, see APJ, "Oficio del Subprefecto Dulanto al Prefecto del Departamento," Jauja, 11 Aug. 1898; and "Solicitud de Vicente A. Pando y Brigido Bocanegra al Prefecto del Departamento," Concepción, 12 Sept. 1898, which also has an additional account of the attack from the perspective of the comisario himself, Vicente A. Pando. This second document also discusses the follow-up military expedition.

39. The petition by the Andamarquinos, including the quotation, can be found in APJ, "Solicitud de varios vecinos del pueblo de Andamarca al Prefecto del Departamento," 24 Nov. 1898. The opinions of surveyor Enzián and Subprefect Dulanto are attached to Enzián's report on the petition. Other examples of the renewed emphasis on security and repression can be found in the formation of an urban guard in Concepción, financed and supported by landowners and government officials, and the subsequent request for a military garrison in that same city, formulated by the same alliance of hacendados and state officials. See APJ, "Acta de formación de la guardia urbana de la ciudad de Concepción," Concepción, 10 Sept. 1898; and "Solicitud de Manuel F. Valladares, Gobernador de Concepción, y otros sobre la creación de una guarnición en la ciudad," Concepción, February 1903.

40. For Cevallos's May 26 letter to the Comasinos, see APJ, "Copia de la carta escrita por Jacinto Cevallos al Gobernador de Comas." In addition to the government troops he commanded, Cevallos also took with him some local soldiers recruited in Chupaca. See APJ, "Solicitud de algunos vecinos de Comas al Prefecto del Departamento," Tarma, 8 July 1902; and "Oficio de Baltazar Chavez, alcalde del distrito de Comas, al Prefecto del depar-

tamento," Comas, 8 July 1902. On his peaceful occupation of Punto, see APJ, "Oficio de Jacinto Cevallos, subprefecto de Huancayo, al Gobernador de Comas," Hacienda Punto, 23 June 1902. On the physical repression of the hacienda residents, see APJ, "Oficio de las autoridades y notables del anexo de Canchapalca al Subprefecto de la provincia de Jauja," Canchapalca, 28 June 1902; "Oficio de Baltazar Chavez, alcalde del distrito de Comas, al Prefecto del departamento," Comas, 8 July 1902; "Oficio de Aurelio Ponce al Prefecto del departamento," Comas, 19 July 1902; and "Oficio de Jacinto Cevallos a los vecinos de Canchapalca," Hacienda Punto, 28 July 1902.

41. APJ, "Oficio de las autoridades y notables del anexo de Canchapalca al Subprefecto de la provincia de Jauja," Canchapalca, 28 June 1902; "Oficio de algunos vecinos de Comas al Prefecto del departamento," Tarma, 8 July 1902, which includes the quotation about pregnant women; "Oficio de Baltazar Chavez, alcalde del distrito de Comas, al Prefecto del departamento," Comas, 8 July 1902; "Oficio de Jacinto Cevallos al Prefecto del departamento," Punto, 14 July 1902; and "Oficio de varios ciudadanos y autoridades del anexo de Canchapalca al Sub Prefecto [sic] del de Partamiento [sic] de Junin," Canchapalca, 18 July 1902.

42. APJ, "Oficio de Jacinto Cevallos, Subprefecto de la provincia de Huancayo, al Gobernador de Comas," Hacienda Punto, 23 June 1902.

43. For the letter quoted, see APJ, "Oficio de Jacinto Cevallos a los vecinos de Canchapalca," Hacienda Punto, 26 June 1902. Other letters that refer to the earlier exchange of correspondence are: "Oficio de Jacinto Cevallos a las autoridades y personas notables del pueblo de Canchapalca," Hacienda Punto, 25 June 1902, and "Oficio del Subprefecto Jacinto Cevallos a las autoridades y notables de Canchapalca," Hacienda Punto, 25 June 1902.

44. For the reaction elicited by Cevallos's letter in Canchapalca, see APJ, "Oficio de las autoridades y notables del anexo de Canchapalca al Subprefecto de la provincia de Jauja," Canchapalca, 28 June 1902. On the more official exchange four days later, see APJ, "Oficio de Jacinto Cevallos, Subprefecto de Huancayo, al pueblo de Comas," Hacienda Punto, 30 June 1902, and accompanying "Oficio de Juan C. Aparicio, Baltazar Chavez y Pedro N. Cárdenas, autoridades de Comas, a los señores de Canchapalca." The prefect's cleanup campaign began, in effect, with his arrival in Jauja on July 6, although he did not make it to the communities until later in the month. See APJ, "Oficio de Pedro N. Cárdenas, subprefecto de Jauja, al gobernador de Comas," 6 July 1902.

45. On the presence of Gil, Santa Cruz, and Aparicio on the hacienda Punto, see APJ, "Oficio de un ayuntamiento popular en Comas al Prefecto del Departamento," Comas, 7 July 1902. On Aparicio's presence in the earlier attempt to formulate a common negotiation strategy, see "Oficio de Jacinto Cevallos al pueblo de Comas," Hacienda Punto, 30 June 1902, and the accompanying "Oficio de Juan C. Aparicio, Baltazar Chavez y Pedro N.

Cárdenas, autoridades de Comas, a los señores de Canchapalca." For Baltazar Chávez's perspective, see "Oficio de Baltazar Chavez a las autoridades y notables de Comas," Comas, 15 July 1902. It is interesting to note, in this context, that on Chávez's earlier petition to the prefect about Cevallos's abuses, in which he identified himself as alcalde, there is written across the bottom: "For alcalde—Fabriciano Santa Cruz." See APJ, "Oficio de Baltazar Chavez, alcalde del distrito de Comas, al Prefecto del departamento," Comas, 8 July 1902.

46. APJ, "Oficio del Prefecto Bruno E. Bueno al Teniente Gobernador del pueblo de Canchapalca," Hacienda Punto, 18 July 1902. While still in Jauja the week before, Bueno had already published a decree in which he made clear that his role would be conciliatory. See APJ, "Decreto de Bruno Bueno, Prefecto del Departamento de Junín," Jauja, 12 July 1902.

47. On the variety of petitions and forms of reception encountered by Bueno in the communities, see APJ, "Oficio del Gobernador de Comas al Prefecto del Departamento," Comas, 16 July 1902; "Solicitud de José F., Manuel E. y Anselmo V. Martínez al Prefecto del departamento," Macon, 18 July 1902; "Solicitud de los ciudadanos y autoridades del anexo de Canchapalca al Sub Prefecto [*sic*] del de Partamiento [*sic*] de Junin," Canchapalca, 18 July 1902; "Oficio de Aurelio Ponce al Prefecto del departamento," Comas, 19 July 1902; "Solicitud de Castulo Muñoz al Prefecto del Departmento," Comas, 20 July 1902; "Solicitud de Gregorio de la O, Mariano de la O y Rafael Caja al Prefecto del Departamento," Canchapalca, 20 July 1902; and "Solicitud de Justo Sanchez al Prefecto del Departamento," Comas, 21 July 1902. For the letter sent by Santiago Motto, see APJ, "Carta de Santiago Motto al Sr. Pablo Apolinario en Comas," Jauja, 22 July 1902.

48. This interpretation of the relationship between hierarchical relations of clientelism and the development of the state is the exact opposite of that initially developed by Julio Cotler in his work on traditional systems of domination and the triangle without a base. Cotler argues that these forms of clientelism, traditional and basically unchanging, stood in the way of the consolidation of a modern national state. By contrast, I argue that they were the by-products of the first formation of a modern state. See Julio Cotler, "La mecánica de la dominación interna y del cambio social en la sociedad rural," in José Matos Mar et al., *Perú problema: 5 ensayos* (Lima: F. Moncloa Editores, 1968), 153–97; and Cotler, "Haciendas y comunidades tradicionales en un contexto de movilización política," in José Matos Mar, comp., *Hacienda, comunidad y campesinado en el Perú*, 2d ed. (Lima: Instituto de Estudios Peruanos, 1976), 311–42.

49. The best overall analysis of this period in Morelos is Dewitt Kennieth Pittman, "Planters, Peasants, and Politicians: Agrarian Classes and the Installation of the Oligarchic State in Mexico, 1869–1876," Ph.D. diss., Yale University, 1983.

50. On previous political events in Morelos between 1850 and 1867, see above, chapters 5 and 7, and Mallon, "Peasants and State Formation." On Jiménez's rebellion, see Perry, *Juárez and Díaz*, 90–96, 144–46. On its general lack of support in western Morelos, see BN-AJ, Doc. 4450: "Carta del jefe político de Tetecala al Coronel Jesus Alcaraz," 16 Jan. 1868; Docs. 4451, 4453–4455, 4457–4460, 4462, 4463: "Cartas del jefe político de Tetecala al presidente Benito Juárez," Jan.–Nov. 1868. On eastern Morelos, see Pittman, "Planters, Peasants, and Politicians," 40–46, 55. On the election results, see BN-AJ, Doc. 3307: "Carta de Francisco Leyva al presidente Benito Juárez," Jonacatepec, 9 Oct. 1867. Alicia Hernández Chávez, in *Anenecuilco: Memoria y vida de un pueblo* (Mexico City: El Colegio de México, 1991), 69–72, does not examine Leyva's contradictions in any great depth but sees a straight line from his earlier Liberal heroism to the magic of the Leyva name in 1909–1910. She also sees Porfirio Díaz through an undifferentiated late-nineteenth-century lens and thus fails to explore the ambivalences villagers felt toward the conflict between two former allies, Díaz and Leyva. See also Hernández, 83.

51. On the 1860–1861 incident, see above, chapter 5. On the internal conflict and jockeying for position that ultimately yielded Leyva as the best Juarista candidate in the area, see BN-AJ, Doc. 1387: "Carta de Ignacio Altamirano al presidente Benito Juárez," Cuautla de Morelos, 22 Dec. 1866; Doc. 2096: "Carta de Ignacio Altamirano al presidente Benito Juárez," Morelos, 15 Jan. 1867; Doc. 3824: "Carta de Vicente Riva Palacio al presidente Benito Juárez," Toluca, 7 Feb. 1867; Doc. 3300: "Carta de Francisco Leyva al presidente Benito Juárez," Cuernavaca, 23 Feb. 1867; and Doc. 21/271: "Carta del General Nicolás de Régules al presidente Benito Juárez," Morelia, 25 Feb. 1867.

52. On the close contact Leyva maintained with Juárez after being appointed governor of the Third Military District of the state of Mexico, see BN-AJ, Doc. 3301: "Carta de Francisco Leyva al presidente Benito Juárez," Cuernavaca, 2 Aug. 1867; Doc. 3303: "Carta de Francisco Leyva al presidente Benito Juárez," Cuernavaca, 12 Aug. 1867, in which he discusses the demobilization of the national guards; Doc. 3304: "Carta de Francisco Leyva al presidente Benito Juárez," Cuernavaca, 16 Aug. 1867, in which he presents his plan of government; Doc. 3305: "Carta de Francisco Leyva al presidente Benito Juárez," Cuernavaca, 21 Aug. 1867. On the election, see Doc. 3307: "Carta de Francisco Leyva al presidente Benito Juárez," Jonacatepec, 9 Oct. 1867.

53. Leyva's communications with Juárez concerning his quandary over choosing between the governorship and the congress are BN-AJ, Doc. 3312: "Carta de Francisco Leyva al presidente Benito Juárez," Cuernavaca, 13 Nov. 1867; Doc. 3314: "Carta de Francisco Leyva al presidente Benito Juárez," Cuernavaca, 14 Nov. 1867; and Doc. 3316: "Carta de Francisco Leyva al

presidente Benito Juárez," Cuernavaca, 22 Nov. 1867. Juárez's answer, which includes the language suggestive of a future gubernatorial candidacy for Morelos state, is Doc. 3317: "Borrador de una carta del presidente Benito Juárez al General Francisco Leyva," México, 25 Nov. 1867.

54. On the 1869 election in Morelos, see Pittman, "Planters, Peasants, and Politicians," 33–38. On Leyva's continued identification of the planters as Spaniards, see also CEHM-C, Julian e Isidro Montiel y Duarte, *Alegato presentado al Juzgado de Distrito del Estado de Morelos en el Juicio de Amparo que ante él promovieron algunos propietarios del mismo estado por la violación del Art. 16 de la Constitución de 1857* (Mexico City: Imprenta de Díaz de Leon y White, 1874), 3, 4.

55. Leyva's inability to decide between the peasants and the landowners in his attempt to govern Morelos is one of the strongest themes in Pittman, "Planters, Peasants, and Politicians." On the constitution of previous political alliances in the area, see above, chapter 5. See also Mallon, "Peasants and State Formation," which in addition treats in detail the diplomatic crisis of 1858 and the repression of the national guards in 1856.

56. Pittman discusses Leyva's narrow basis of support in "Planters, Peasants, and Politicians," 65–66, 151–52. On the confrontation over the location of the state capital, see pp. 39–47. Struggles with the planters over taxation are discussed on pp. 48–51. On the 1871 conflict and arrest of the two deputies, see Pittman, p. 52, and AGN(M), Gobernación: "Expediente sobre las divisiones en la legislatura de Morelos," Apr. 1871.

57. On the earlier rebellions in Puebla state, see Ana María Dolores Huerta Jaramillo, *Insurrecciones rurales en el estado de Puebla, 1868–1870,* Cuadernos de la Casa Presno 4 (Puebla: Universidad Autónoma de Puebla, 1985). On Tuxtepec, see Perry, *Juárez and Díaz,* 244–46.

58. My account is based on Pittman's excellent summary, "Planters, Peasants, and Politicians," 121–23. On the amparo, see also BN-LAF 94: *Sentencia pronunciada por el Juez interino de distrito del Estado de Morelos, en el juicio de amparo promovido por los Sres. D. Ramón Portillo y Gómez y socios contra el decreto promulgado en 7 de mayo de 1874* (H. Cuautla de Morelos: Imprenta del Gobierno en la calle de Galeana, 1874); *El ciudadano Manuel Gómez Parada refuta una representación que varios propietarios del Estado de Morelos dirigen á los Ciudadanos Diputados al Congreso de la Union* (H. Cuautla, Imprenta del Gobierno, 1874); CEHM-C, Emilio Velasco, *El Amparo de Morelos. Colección de Artículos publicados en "El Porvenir"* (Mexico City: Imprenta de Díaz de Leon y White, 1874); Montiel y Duarte, *Alegato presentado;* and *Exposición dirigida a la Suprema Corte de Justicia de la Nación por los cc. Hilarión Frías y Soto y Joaquín M. Alcalde, Representantes de la H. Legislatura del Edo. de Morelos, con motivo del juicio de amparo promovido por los señores Portillo y Gomez y Socios contra la Ley de Hacienda de 12 de*

Octubre de 1873 (Mexico City: Imprenta del Comercio, de N. Chávez, 1874).

59. On the divisions in the supreme court, see Perry, *Juárez and Díaz*, 285–89. On the decision reached for Morelos, see Pittman, "Planters, Peasants, and Politicians," 130–32.

60. On the national debate evoked by the Morelos decision, see Perry, *Juárez and Díaz*, 286; and BN-AJ, Suppl. 71: "Carta de Ignacio F. Chávez al Coronel Dn. Bernardo del Castillo," Aguascalientes, 13 May 1874. On the growing chaos in Morelos, see Pittman, "Planters, Peasants, and Politicians," 132–52.

61. On the first compromise, see Pittman, "Planters, Peasants, and Politicians," 136, 141. On the second compromise, see ibid., 160–70.

62. On Leyva's policy toward the villagers, as well as his discourse more generally, see ibid., 82–89, 100, 127. On his overall "progressive" plan of government, see BN-AJ, Doc. 3304: "Carta de Francisco Leyva al presidente Benito Juárez," Cuernavaca, 16 Aug. 1867. The governor's urban constituency is discussed in Pittman, "Planters, Peasants, and Politicians," 65–66, 151–52. On Maximilian's Janus-faced policy in Morelos, see above, chapter 5.

63. The quotations from Ayala and Anenecuilco are taken from Jesús Sotelo Inclán, *Raíz y razón de Zapata*, 2d ed. (Mexico: Comisión Federal de Electricidad, 1970), and translated in Pittman, "Planters, Peasants, and Politicians," 137–38 and 185–86, respectively. On the nature and spread of the Tuxtepec rebellion in Morelos, see Pittman, 186–91.

64. On Piérola and Romaña, see Mallon, *Defense of Community*, 125–68. The literature on the Porfiriato is much too voluminous to cite here. The best introduction to the subject is still Daniel Cosío Villegas, *Historia moderna de México: El Porfiriato* (Mexico City: Editorial Hermes, 1956). See also Guerra, *México*.

65. On Méndez and Bonilla in Puebla, see Guerra, *México*, 1:78, 79, 98, 101, 2:22. On Alarcón in Morelos, see John Womack, Jr., *Zapata and the Mexican Revolution* (New York: Random House, 1968), 13–15, and Hernández, *Anenecuilco*, 95–107. On the shift in the Porfirian balance of forces, see Walter Goldfrank, "Theories of Revolution and Revolution Without Theory: The Case of Mexico," *Theory and Society* 7 (1979): 135–65, esp. 151–53.

66. On Juan Francisco Lucas joining the revolution, see David LaFrance and Guy P. C. Thomson, "Juan Francisco Lucas: Patriarch of the Sierra Norte de Puebla," in William H. Beezley and Judith Ewell, eds., *The Human Tradition in Latin America: The Twentieth Century* (Wilmington, Del.: Scholarly Resources, 1987), 1–13; David LaFrance, "Puebla: Breakdown of the Old Order," in Thomas Benjamin and William McNellie, eds., *Other Mexicos: Essays on Regional Mexican History* (Albuquerque: University of New

Mexico Press, 1984), 88; and "Breves datos biográficos del señor General don Juan Francisco Lucas, Proporcionados por el ex-Teniente Coronel Martín Rivera Torres," Donna Rivera Moreno, personal archive, Xochiapulco. On the process in Morelos, see Womack, *Zapata and the Mexican Revolution,* 10–36; the quotation appears on p. 33.

67. Peru, Congreso Ordinario de 1895, *Diario de los Debates de la H. Cámara de Senadores* (Lima: Imprenta de "El Pais," 1895), 443.

68. Ibid.

CHAPTER 9. WHOSE BONES ARE THEY, ANYWAY,
AND WHO GETS TO DECIDE?

1. My first visit to Xochiapulco, during which I had the initial encounter with Donna Rivera described in this paragraph, occurred on 17 April 1985. A month later I returned for a second visit, during which I stayed with Maestra Donna for two days. During this second visit I acquired the rest of the information about her background and negotiated access to her manuscript.

2. Donna Rivera Moreno, *Xochiapulco: Una gloria olvidada* (Puebla: Dirección General de Culturas Populares, 1991); the quotation appears on p. 5.

3. Ociel Mora López, of the regional division of the Dirección de Culturas Populares, was in touch with my colleague and fellow Puebla enthusiast Guy Thomson. It was through Thomson that I discovered the new attempt to publish Rivera's manuscript and sent a new copy of the introduction I had written for the previous edition. In the context of the quincentenary, and of Salinas's interest in presenting an indigenista image, Mora finally got the opportunity to publish the manuscript.

4. Rivera's description of her encounter with Anders is given in *Xochiapulco,* 11–12; the quotation appears on p. 12.

5. I heard the stories about the bones on my first visit to the municipal building on 17 April 1985, when I examined the small museum that included a cabinet with human bones marked as Austrian. See also chapter 4. The oral history recorded by Rivera appears in a section of her book, *Xochiapulco,* entitled "De la tradición hecha de padres a hijos." The identity of the bones is discussed on p. 101. The Pozos manuscript, entitled "Historia suscinta de la población," is reproduced in ibid., 47–53, 131–34. The discussion of the 1869 ambush appears on p. 133 (paragraph 26).

6. Pozos, "Historia suscinta," in Rivera, *Xochiapulco,* 47–53, 131–34. The quotation about the "apostles of the Reform Laws" appears on p. 51.

7. Rivera, *Xochiapulco,* esp. 9–17, 93–106, 157–303.

8. Examples of the iconization and mystification of the indigenous role in the battle of the Fifth of May can be found in local histories, such as Ramón Sánchez Flores, *Zacapoaxtla: Relación histórica,* 2d ed. (Zacapoaxtla:

Edición del XIV Distrito Local Electoral de Zacapoaxtla, Puebla, 1984), and in the Puebla city military museum and annual parade, both of which I observed in 1985. Interestingly, this type of iconization did occur during the Porfiriato, at the national level, with regard to Benito Juárez (see Charles A. Weeks, *The Juárez Myth in Mexico* [Tuscaloosa: University of Alabama Press, 1987]). But the celebrations of the Fifth of May were not similarly integrated until the 1930s. For examples of earlier, more localized Fifth of May celebrations, see AHMZ, Paq. 1863–65–64, Leg. 3: "Proclama del jefe político y comandante militar de Zacapoaxtla sobre la celebración del cinco de mayo," Zacapoaxtla, 4 May 1863, and *Reseña de las festividades que han tenido lugar en Puebla de Zaragoza en el aniversario del glorioso 5 de mayo de 1862, con inserción del discurso pronunciado en la Alameda de esta ciudad por el orador oficial C. Eduardo E. Zarate, y de la composición leída en el mismo lugar por el C. Manuel Carreto* (Puebla: Imprenta del Hospicio, 1870). See also below, this chapter.

9. The article by Luis Castro that appeared in *El Sol de Puebla* on 5 May 1962, written in collaboration with Donna Rivera, is reproduced in *Xochiapulco*, 83–91. Although the manuscript included two original photographs, one of the survivors and another of Juan Francisco Lucas's house on Xochiapulco's central plaza, only the former is reproduced in the book (91).

10. Rivera, *Xochiapulco*, 85–86; the quotation appears on p. 86.

11. "Carta del Ing. Rodolfo Ricaño G., Secretario de la Comisión Agraria Mixta, al Señor Martín Rivera," Puebla, 22 Mar. 1943, in Donna Rivera, personal archive, Xochiapulco. This letter was not reproduced in the book.

12. Sources on "folklorization" and on the construction of Indian as "other" in postrevolutionary Mexico include Marjorie R. Becker, *Setting the Virgin on Fire: Lázaro Cárdenas, Michoacán Peasants, and the Redemption of the Mexican Revolution* (Berkeley: University of California Press, forthcoming), esp. chaps. 4–6; Alan Knight, "Racism, Revolution, and *Indigenismo*: Mexico, 1910–1940," in Richard Graham, ed., *The Idea of Race in Latin America, 1870–1940* (Austin: University of Texas Press, 1990), 71–113; and Florencia E. Mallon, "Indian Communities, Political Cultures, and the State in Latin America, 1780–1990," *Journal of Latin American Studies* 24, suppl. (fall 1992): 35–53. For an interesting comparative treatment of these issues for the case of Bolivia, see Thomas Abercrombie, "To Be Indian, to Be Bolivian: 'Ethnic' and 'National' Discourses of Identity," in Greg Urban and Joel Sherzer, eds., *Nation-States and Indians in Latin America* (Austin: University of Texas Press, 1991), 95–130.

13. It is Pozos who makes the comparison between Xochiapulco and Moscow; see Rivera, *Xochiapulco*, 52 (paragraph 20).

14. Pascuala Martínez's story is reproduced in ibid., 101.

15. For Juan Francisco Lucas's baptismal and marriage records, see Licenciado Francisco Landero Alamo, *Zacapoaxtla*, available in the munici-

pal library in Zacapoaxtla, pp. 8–9. For the process of inheritance related to the will of Francisco Pérez and Fundo Taxcantla, see AGNEP, Tetela de Ocampo, Caja 1, 1869–1880: Libro 1869, "Hijuelas de la testamentaría de Francisco Pérez," 18 Oct. 1869, ff. 7v–9v. For the use of Taxcantla as the base for the Xochiapulquenses in the 1869–1872 period, and even Porfirio Díaz retiring there to recover from a wound during the rebellion of La Noria, see *El Siglo XIX*, 22 Dec. 1869, p. 3; 9 Jan. 1870, p. 3; 14 Dec. 1871, p. 3; *Diario Oficial*, 9 Jan. 1870, p. 1; 10 Jan. 1870, p. 3; 16 Jan. 1870, p. 3; 5 Mar. 1872, p. 3 [reference to Porfirio Díaz]; and *Publicación Oficial de Puebla*, 11 Jan. 1870, p. 4.

16. For the case of Tepoztlán, see above, chapter 5. For the complexities of the Liberal alliances in Puebla over these years and the form taken by the sierra Liberals in the Montaña party, see above, chapters 2 and 8, and Guy P. C. Thomson, "*Montaña* and *Llanura* in the Politics of Central Mexico: The Case of Puebla, 1820–1920," in Wil Pansters and Arij Ouweneel, eds., *Region, State and Capitalism in Mexico: Nineteenth and Twentieth Centuries*, CEDLA Latin American Studies no. 54 (Amsterdam: Center for Latin American Research, 1989), 59–78.

17. For the letter from the barrio of San Nicolás, see AHMTO, Gobierno, Caja 9: Exp. 3, "Oficio de los vecinos del barrio de San Nicolás al ayuntamiento de Tetela de Ocampo," 16 Feb. 1867. For the other cases mentioned in the paragraph, see AHMTO, Gobierno, Caja 9: Exp. 3, "Oficio del preceptor de la escuela de La Cañada al ayuntamiento de Tetela," 16 Jan. 1867; Caja 9: Exp. 7, no. 267, Notas oficiales, "Oficio de la preceptora de la escuela 'Amiga de Niñas' al alcalde constitucional de Tetela," Tetela de Ocampo, 22 June 1867; Caja s/n 1871: "Expediente promovido por el preceptor de la escuela del barrio de La Cañada," Tetela de Ocampo, 11 Feb.–25 Mar. 1871; Caja s/n 1871: Exp. 5, "Oficio del preceptor de la escuela del barrio de San José al Ayuntamiento de Tetela," 12 Oct. 1871; Caja s/n 1871: Exp. 10, "Sobre la renuncia del preceptor de la escuela de Tonalapa," 10–21 Apr. 1871.

18. AHMTO, Gobierno, Caja 9: Exp. 7, no. 267, Notas oficiales: "Oficio de la preceptora de la escuela 'Amiga de Niñas,'" Tetela de Ocampo, 22 June 1867; quotation included. For the resignation of García, see Exp. 3, "Oficio del preceptor de la escuela de La Cañada," 16 Jan. 1867.

19. AHMTO, Gobierno, Caja s/n 1871: Exp. 5, "Oficio del preceptor de la escuela del barrio de San José al Ayuntamiento de Tetela," 12 Oct. 1871.

20. On the case of Arriaga, see AHMTO, Gobierno, Caja s/n 1871: "Expediente promovido por el preceptor de la escuela del barrio de La Cañada," Tetela de Ocampo, 11 Feb.–25 Mar. 1871. All the quotations are included.

21. AHMTO, Gobierno, Caja s/n 1870/73–1874/78: Exp. 113, "Ocurso de 10 vecinos del barrio de Cuauximaloyan al jefe político de Tetela de Ocampo," 6 Dec. 1870.

22. AHMTO, Gobierno, Caja s/n 1870/73–1874/78: Exp. 113, "Informe del Juez Municipal de Xochiapulco, Juan Francisco Dinorin, al jefe político de Tetela," 14 Dec. 1870. On the earlier identification of Dinorin with the Xochiapulco national guard, see AHMZ, Paq. 1869: Exp. 118, "Relativo a la organización de la guardia nacional con el nombramiento y propuesta de jefes y oficiales de ella," Xochiapulco, June–Oct. 1869.

23. AHMTO, Gobierno, Caja s/n 1870/73–1874/78: Exp. 113, "Oficio del alcalde municipal interino de Xochiapulco al jefe político de Tetela," 15 Nov. 1870.

24. AHMTO, Gobierno, Caja s/n 1870/73–1874/78: Exp. 113, "Resolución del jefe político de Tetela de Ocampo sobre el problema de la escuela en Cuauximaloyan," 15 Dec. 1870.

25. AHMTO, Gobierno, Caja s/n 1870/73–1874/78: Exp. 112, "Oficio del alcalde municipal de Tuzamapan al jefe político de Tetela," 4 Apr. 1870; all quotations appear in this document.

26. On the conflict over religion in Xochiapulco, see the documents in notes 21–23, above. On the problem of ethnic power sharing in Tuzamapan, see also AHMTO, Gobierno, Caja s/n 1868: Exp. 66, "Oficio del juez de Tuzamapan al jefe político de Tetela," 24 Sept. 1866; and "Oficio del nuevo juez de Tuzamapan al jefe político de Tetela," 20 Oct. 1868.

27. I analyze the articulation of racist discourses by Liberals and Conservatives in Mexico throughout this book, especially in chapters 2, 4, 5, 7, and 8. See also Florencia E. Mallon, "Peasants and State Formation in Nineteenth-Century Mexico: Morelos, 1848–1858," *Political Power and Social Theory* 7 (1988): 1–54. For a subtle and particularly interesting use of racism to "prove" that the people cannot govern themselves and need a centralized state and effective leadership to be part of political society, see S. Nieto, "Legitimidad de la Administración Actual del Estado," parts 1–3, *Periódico Oficial del Estado libre y soberano de Puebla* 1, nos. 64, 65, 67 (27 Mar., 30 Mar., 4 Apr. 1868): pp. 1–2 in all three numbers.

28. Guy P. C. Thomson, "Bulwarks of Patriotic Liberalism: The National Guard, Philharmonic Corps, and Patriotic Juntas in Mexico, 1847–1888," *Journal of Latin American Studies* 22, no. 1 (Feb. 1990): 31–68. The long quotation appears on pp. 31–32 and is reproduced with permission; the short one on p. 32.

29. On my trips to Xochiapulco in April and May 1985, I had occasion to view the various weapons taken from the Austrians that decorated monuments and the museum in the municipality and to see the exhibition of weapons by the Xochiapulco delegation marching in the Fifth of May parade. Donna Rivera also reproduces, in the manuscript version of her book, p. 70, photographs of Xochiapulquenses marching in Puebla city with an Austrian cannon. These photographs were not reproduced in the published version.

30. Personal communication, Donna Rivera, Xochiapulco, May 1985; David LaFrance and Guy P. C. Thomson, "Juan Francisco Lucas: Patriarch of the Sierra Norte de Puebla," in William H. Beezley and Judith Ewell, eds., *The Human Tradition in Latin America: The Twentieth Century* (Wilmington, Del.: Scholarly Resources, 1987), esp. 6.

31. Thomson, "Bulwarks of Patriotic Liberalism," 51–61. See also AH-MTO, Gobierno, Caja s/n 1866: Exp. 71, "Acta para formalizar la creación de una orquesta filarmónica," Tetela, 2 July 1867.

32. Thomson, "Bulwarks of Patriotic Liberalism," esp. 53–58.

33. Ibid., 56–61.

34. Ibid., 62. For other examples of these patriotic ceremonies and the processes by which they were organized, see AHMTO, Gobierno, Caja s/n 1870/73–1874/78: Exp. 118, "Programa aprobado por la Junta Patriótica de Tetela de Ocampo para celebrar la Independencia," Tetela, 15–17 Sept. 1870; and BN-LAF, *Promulgación de las reformas y adiciones a la Constitución de 1857, en la villa de Tetela de Ocampo* (Mexico City: Imprenta y Litografía del Colegio de Artes y Oficios, 1873).

35. Thomson, "Bulwarks of Patriotic Liberalism," 63–67.

36. I have made a similar argument in Florencia E. Mallon, "Los héroes anónimos: Xochiapulco ante la historia," in Rivera, *Xochiapulco*, 116–17. The documentation for the six-month surrender, beginning with the "Bases de Papantla," is found in Ignacio R. Alatorre, *Reseña de los acontecimientos ocurridos en las líneas del Norte y Centro del Estado de Veracruz en los años de 1863 a 1867* (Veracruz, 1887), 50–54; ACDN, Exp. C-64, D/111/2/425: General Juan Francisco Lucas, ff. 66–67; and *Diario del Imperio*, 9 Mar. 1866, p. 264.

37. I am basing my account of the origins of the dance on the revisionist account presented by Zoila S. Mendoza, "La danza de 'Los Avelinos': Sus orígenes y sus múltiples significados," *Revista Andina* 7, no. 2 (Dec. 1989): 501–21; the discussion of origins appears on pp. 504–8. Another, more folkloric version of the dance's origins is reproduced in CPHEP, *La Guerra del Pacífico, 1879–1883: La resistencia de la Breña*, tomo 2, *La contraofensiva de 1882: 23 Feb. 1882–5 Mayo 1883* (Lima: Ministerio de Guerra, 1982), 186–89.

38. Z. Mendoza, "La danza de 'Los Avelinos,'" 504–8.

39. Ibid., 508.

40. For the case of Acolla, two competing versions of the origins and process of La Mactada appear within the pages of CPHEP, *La resistencia de la breña*, vol. 2: the one given by Acolla's most prominent local intellectual, Moisés Ortega Rojas (2:182–83); and the one given in an article by Pablo Macera, "El arte popular y la Guerra con Chile" (2:421–26, esp. 424, 425). I am relying on Ortega's account because it is more historical. Macera tends to view the dance as a folkloric object which, though rich in texture, repre-

sents the war directly. On the further evolution of Los Avelinos in San Jerónimo, and its diffusion in "folkloric" form throughout the Mantaro region, see Z. Mendoza, "La danza de 'Los Avelinos,'" 509–11.

41. LaFrance and Thomson, "Juan Francisco Lucas," 8.

42. On Rivera's image of him, see Rivera, *Xochiapulco*, and above, chapter 2. On the image emerging during the Restored Republic, see above, chapter 8. On his image as the "good patriarch," see above, chapter 3.

43. My description of Mendoza's personal intellectual trajectory is based on Eduardo Mendoza Meléndez's prize-winning book, *Historia de la Campaña de la Breña*, 2d ed. (Lima: Ital Perú, 1983). The diploma certifying the prize is reproduced at the beginning, before the title page. Mendoza discusses his own history of researching the La Breña campaign on pp. 16–17. Mendoza's donation of Ambrosio Salazar y Márquez's memoirs is duly recorded on the copy in the AHM: Teniente Coronel Ambrosio Salazar y Márquez, "Memorias sobre la Resistencia de la Breña (Escrita por su hermano Juan P. Salazar)," typescript donated by Eduardo Mendoza Meléndez, Magdalena del Mar, 8 Oct. 1974.

44. The entire series put out by CPHEP comprised one introductory volume, entitled *Reflexiones sobre la resistencia de la Breña: Significado y proyección históricos* (Lima: Ministerio de Guerra, 1982), and the multivolume *La Guerra del Pacífico, 1879–1883: La resistencia de la Breña*, tomos 1–3 (Lima: Ministerio de Guerra, 1982), of which tomo 2 provides the most material about the central highlands.

45. CPHEP, *La resistencia de la Breña*, tomo 2; the artist's rendition of Sierra Lumi, by Josué Sánchez, is inserted between pp. 54 and 55. The quotation from Mendoza appears on p. 147, and the huayno is on p. 156. The description of the commemoration on 2 March 1982, which includes a photograph of the flag and dates, can be found on pp. 430–31.

46. CPHEP, *La resistencia de la Breña*, 2:430–31; the quotation appears on p. 431.

47. Between December 1989 and February 1990, villagers from the Comas area killed a total of twenty-five Senderista guerrillas, of whom thirteen were decapitated; *New York Times*, 15 February 1990, p. A15, and 4 March 1990, p. 13.

48. E. Mendoza, *La Campaña de la Breña*, 17–18 (the quotation appears on both pages); CPHEP, *La resistencia de la Breña*, 1:251–53; the first quotation appears on p. 252, the photograph and caption on p. 253.

49. CPHEP, *La resistencia de la Breña*, 2:159–160.

50. Philip Corrigan and Derek Sayer, *The Great Arch: English State Formation as Cultural Revolution* (Cambridge, Mass.: Basil Blackwell, 1985).

51. On the military regime that took power in 1968, a good place to start is with Alfred Stepan, *The State and Society: Peru in Comparative Perspective* (Princeton: Princeton University Press, 1978); Abraham F. Lowenthal,

ed., *The Peruvian Experiment* (Princeton: Princeton University Press, 1975); and Abraham F. Lowenthal and Cynthia McClintock, eds., *The Peruvian Experiment Reconsidered* (Princeton: Princeton University Press, 1983). On the difficulties of the regime with popular mobilization, see especially Rodrigo Sánchez E., *Toma de tierras y conciencia política campesina* (Lima: Instituto de Estudios Peruanos, 1981).

CHAPTER 10. POPULAR NATIONALISM AND
STATEMAKING IN MEXICO AND PERU

1. For an excellent discussion of contemporary Mexican politics, see *Latin America Weekly Report* (London: Latin American Newletters), 1988–. On reactions by peasants to the modifications of the agrarian reform laws by the Salinas government, the ongoing importance of the hegemonic revolutionary legacy, and the enduring symbolic role of Anenecuilco, see *Washington Post*, 7 July 1988, p. A30; and *San José Mercury News*, 18 Nov. 1991, p. 2A, where there is also a reference to protests among peasants who claim they understand better than Salinas what Zapata's revolutionary legacy means; *Phoenix Gazette*, 29 Nov. 1991, p. D4; and "Ejido-reform Opposition Takes Form," sipro carnet.mexnews, 2 Dec. 1991, where there is a reference to a "Plan de Anenecuilco." Of course, even more recently the guerrilla uprising in Chiapas points to the existence of multiple interpretations of Zapata's legacy.

2. On the rise of Sendero Luminoso, some good introductions are NACLA (North American Congress on Latin America), *Report on the Americas* 24, no. 4 (Dec.–Jan 1990–91); Alberto Flores Galindo, *Tiempo de plagas* (Lima: El Caballo Rojo, 1988); Carlos Iván Degregori, *Sendero Luminoso*: vol. 1, *Los hondos y mortales desencuentros*; vol. 2, *Lucha armada y utopía autoritaria* (Lima: Instituto de Estudios Peruanos, 1986); Nelson Manrique, "La década de la violencia," *Márgenes*, nos. 5–6 (1989): 137–82; Robin Kirk, *The Decade of Chaqwa: Peru's Internal Refugees* (Washington, D.C.: U.S. Committee for Refugees, 1991); Deborah Poole and Gerardo Rénique, "The New Chroniclers of Peru: U.S. Scholars and Their 'Shining Path' of Peasant Rebellion," *Bulletin of Latin American Research* 10, no. 2 (1991): 133–91; and David Scott Palmer, ed., *Shining Path of Peru* (New York: St. Martin's, 1992). For the discourse of the ronderos, I have relied on transcriptions from the IEP Conference on the rondas campesinas, December 1991, courtesy of Orin Starn. See also Orin Starn, "Sendero, soldados y ronderos en el Mantaro," *Quehacer*, no. 74 (Nov.–Dec. 1991): 60–68.

3. I am referring here to Manuel González Prada's famous 1888 quote, "The nation is made up of the Indian multitudes spread along the eastern slopes of the mountains"; quoted in *Páginas Libres* (Madrid: Biblioteca Andrés Bello, 1915), 78. I reproduce the quote, and discuss it in the context of the War of the Pacific, in Florencia E. Mallon, "Nationalist and Anti-State

Coalitions in the War of the Pacific: Junín and Cajamarca, 1879–1902," in Steve J. Stern, ed., *Resistance, Rebellion, and Consciousness in the Andean Peasant World, Eighteenth to Twentieth Centuries* (Madison: University of Wisconsin Press, 1987), 232–79.

4. John Womack, Jr., "The Mexican Revolution, 1910–1920," in Leslie Bethell, ed., *The Cambridge History of Latin America* (Cambridge and New York: Cambridge University Press, 1986), 5:79–153; the quotation appears on p. 82.

5. The original insight was in Jean Meyer, *Problemas campesinos y revueltas agrarias, 1821–1910* (Mexico City: Secretaría de Educación Pública, 1972). The works confirming it are Evelyn Hu-DeHart, *Yaqui Resistance and Survival: The Struggle for Land and Autonomy* (Madison: University of Wisconsin Press, 1984); Jean Meyer, *Esperando a Lozada* (Zamora: El Colegio de Michoacán, 1984); Andrés Lira, *Comunidades indígenas frente a la ciudad de México: Tenochtitlán y Tlatelolco, sus pueblos y sus barrios, 1812–1919* (Zamora: El Colegio de Michoacán, 1983); and Rodolfo Pastor, *Campesinos y reformas: La mixteca, 1700–1856* (Mexico City: El Colegio de México, 1987). The quotation comes from John Tutino, "Peasants and Politics in Nineteenth-Century Mexico," *Latin American Research Review* 22, no. 3 (1987): 237–44; the quotation appears on p. 243. In this review essay, Tutino considers three of the four books cited.

6. François-Xavier Guerra, *México: Del antiguo régimen a la revolución*, trans. Sergio Fernández Bravo, 2 vols. (Mexico City: Fondo de Cultura Económica, 1988).

7. Alan Knight, *The Mexican Revolution*, 2 vols. (Cambridge and New York: Cambridge University Press, 1985), 1:78–127, 150–70.

8. Charles A. Hale, *Mexican Liberalism in the Age of Mora, 1821–1853* (New Haven: Yale University Press, 1968).

9. Charles A. Hale, *The Transformation of Liberalism in Late Nineteenth-Century Mexico* (Princeton: Princeton University Press, 1989).

10. Some other very promising moves in this direction are, for Mexican history, Gilbert Joseph and Daniel Nugent, eds., *Everyday Forms of State Formation: The Negotiation of Rule in Modern Mexico* (Durham: Duke University Press, forthcoming); Marjorie R. Becker, *Setting the Virgin on Fire: Lázaro Cárdenas, Michoacán Peasants, and the Redemption of the Mexican Revolution* (Berkeley: University of California Press, forthcoming); and Guy P. C. Thomson, "Popular Aspects of Liberalism in Mexico, 1848–1888," *Bulletin of Latin American Research* 10, no. 3 (1991): 265–92. I made a similar call in "Peasants and State Formation in Nineteenth-Century Mexico: Morelos, 1848–1858," *Political Power and Social Theory* 7 (1988): 1–54.

11. Ana María Alonso, "The Effects of Truth: Re-presentations of the Past and the Imagining of Community," *Journal of Historical Sociology* 1, no. 1

(1988): 33–57; Alonso, "'Progress' as Disorder and Dishonor: Discourses of *Serrano* Resistance," *Critique of Anthropology* 8, no. 1 (1988): 13–33; María Teresa Koreck, "Space and Revolution in Northeastern Chihuahua," in Daniel Nugent, ed., *Rural Revolt in Mexico and U.S. Intervention*, Center for U.S.-Mexican Studies, University of California, San Diego, Monograph Series, no. 27 (1988), 127–48; and Daniel Nugent, "'Are We Not (Civilized) Men?': The Formation and Devolution of Community in Northern Mexico," *Journal of Historical Sociology* 2, no. 3 (1989): 206–39.

12. In my view, a strong inspiration for recent work on popular culture and the transformation of politics and state structures can be found in the work of Michel Foucault. The decentering of power relations, and the understanding of Liberal and Enlightenment discourses as forms of control and surveillance, was much more difficult before he wrote. Yet even in Foucault the richness and complexity of power relations and discursive meanings is developed best in the relation between official and popular discourses and practices rather than within "the popular." See especially Foucault, *Power/Knowledge: Selected Interviews and Other Writings, 1972–1977*, ed. Colin Gordon (New York: Pantheon, 1980); and *Discipline and Punish: The Birth of the Prison* (New York: Vintage Books, 1979).

13. These attempts are best represented in the following: Heraclio Bonilla, *Guano y burguesía en el Perú* (Lima: Instituto de Estudios Peruanos, 1974); Bonilla and Karen Spalding, eds., *La independencia en el Perú* (Lima: Instituto de Estudios Peruanos/Campodónico, 1972); Alberto Flores Galindo, *La agonía de Mariátegui: La polémica con la Komintern* (Lima: DESCO, 1980); *Arequipa y el sur andino: Ensayo de historia regional (siglos XVII–XX)* (Lima: Editorial Horizonte, 1977); Flores Galindo, *Aristocracia y plebe, Lima 1760–1830: Estructura de clases y sociedad colonial* (Lima: Mosca Azul Editores, 1984); Flores Galindo, *Buscando un Inca: Identidad y utopía en los Andes* (Havana: Casa de las Américas, 1986); Flores Galindo, ed., *Túpac Amaru II—1780: Sociedad colonial y sublevaciones populares* (Lima: Ediciones Retablo de Papel, 1976); Brooke Larson, *Colonialism and Agrarian Transformation in Bolivia: Cochabamba, 1550–1900* (Princeton: Princeton University Press, 1988); Florencia E. Mallon, *The Defense of Community in Peru's Central Highlands: Peasant Struggle and Capitalist Transition, 1860–1930* (Princeton: Princeton University Press, 1983); Mallon, "Nationalist and Anti-State Coalitions"; Mallon, "Patriarchy and the Transition to Capitalism in Central Peru, 1830–1950," *Feminist Studies* 13, no. 2 (summer 1987): 379–407; Nelson Manrique, *Colonialismo y pobreza campesina: Caylloma y el valle del Colca, siglos XVI–XX* (Lima: DESCO, 1985); Manrique, *Campesinado y nación: Las guerrillas indígenas en la guerra con Chile* (Lima: Ital-Perú–C.I.C., 1981); *Yawar mayu: Sociedades terratenientes serranas, 1879–1910* (Lima: Instituto Francés de Estudios Andinos/DESCO, 1988); Karen Spalding, *De indio a campesino:*

Cambios en la estructura social del Perú colonial (Lima: Instituto de Estudios Peruanos, 1974); *Huarochirí: An Andean Society under Inca and Spanish Rule* (Stanford: Stanford University Press, 1984); Steve J. Stern, *Peru's Indian Peoples and the Challenge of Spanish Conquest: Huamanga to 1640* (Madison: University of Wisconsin Press, 1982); and Stern, ed., *Resistance, Rebellion, and Consciousness.*

14. Paul E. Gootenberg, *Between Silver and Guano: Commercial Policy and the State in Postindependence Peru* (Princeton: Princeton University Press, 1989).

15. Manrique, *Yawar mayu.*

16. Alberto Flores Galindo, "El horizonte utópico," in his *Buscando un Inca*, 241–316. See also Manuel Burga, *Nacimiento de una utopía: Muerte y resurrección de los Incas* (Lima: Instituto de Apoyo Agrario, 1988); and Burga, "Los profetas de la Rebelión (1919–1923)," in Jean-Paul Deler and Yves Saint-Geours, eds., *Estados y naciones en los Andes: Hacia una historia comparativa* (Lima: Instituto de Estudios Peruanos / Instituto Francés de Estudios Andinos, 1986), 2:463–517.

17. Ernesto Laclau, *Politics and Ideology in Marxist Theory* (London: Verso Books, 1979), 81–198.

18. In all of Flores's and Burga's work on the Andean utopia, the nineteenth century is conspicuously missing. No one has offered a satisfactory explanation for this lapse.

19. Two recent dissertations address this issue for very different parts of Peru. See Sarah Chambers, "The Many Shades of the White City: Urban Society and Culture in Arequipa, Peru, 1780–1854," Ph.D. diss., University of Wisconsin–Madison, 1992; and Mark Thurner, "From Two Nations to One Divided: State and Peasantry in Colonial and Republican Peru (Huaylas, ca. 1550–1900)," Ph.D. diss., University of Wisconsin–Madison, 1992.

20. René Zavaleta Mercado, *Lo nacional-popular en Bolivia* (Mexico City: Siglo XXI Editores, 1986).

21. For a recent analysis of Bolivia that confirms, broadly speaking, this perspective on the double failure of the republican or national promise for indigenous Andean peoples, see Tristan Platt, "Simón Bolívar, the Sun of Justice, and the Amerindian Virgin: Andean Conceptions of the *Patria* in Nineteenth-Century Potosí," *Journal of Latin American Studies* 25, no. 1 (Feb. 1993): 159–85.

Index

451